Psychological Perspectives on Lesbian and
Gay Male Experiences

BETWEEN MEN ≈ BETWEEN WOMEN

Lesbian and Gay Studies

Lillian Faderman and Larry Gross, Editors

BETWEEN MEN ≈ BETWEEN WOMEN

Lesbian and Gay Studies

Lillian Faderman and Larry Gross, Editors

Psychological Perspectives on Lesbian and Gay Male Experiences

Edited by
Linda D. Garnets and
Douglas C. Kimmel

Columbia University Press
New York

Columbia University Press
New York   Chichester, West Sussex
Copyright (c) 1993 Columbia University Press
All rights reserved

Library of Congress Cataloging-in-Publication Data

Psychological perspectives on lesbian and gay male experiences /
    edited by Linda D. Garnets and Douglas C. Kimmel.
        p.   cm.—(Between men—between women)
    Includes bibliographical references and index.
    ISBN 0–231–07884–6.—ISBN 0–231–07885–4 (pbk.)
    1. Homosexuality—United States. 2. Lesbians—United States—Psychology.
3. Gays—United States—Psychology. I. Garnets, Linda. II. Kimmel, Douglas C.
III. Series.
HQ76.3.U5P78   1993
305.9′0664—dc20   93–35562
                                                                         CIP

⊗

Casebound editions of Columbia University Press books are printed on
permanent and durable acid-free paper.

Printed in the United States of America
c 10 9 8 7 6 5 4 3 2 1
p 10 9 8 7 6 5 4 3 2

Contents

Preface

Interest in lesbian and gay studies is growing rapidly. It is important that psychological perspectives be represented in this emerging field. This anthology reflects the best thinking in social science about psychological issues affecting lesbians and gay men. While most of the articles are psychological in focus, anthropology, history, law, neuroendocrinology, and sociology are included as well.

Although the book is designed for upper-level undergraduate students with some experience in social science courses, it is also intended to be used in graduate courses in psychology that focus on human diversity. Graduate students in clinical and counseling psychology, nursing, psychiatry, and social work in particular will find this book to be a useful introduction to issues relevant to professional practice.

General readers will find this book of interest because critical issues reflecting the contemporary relevance of each section are discussed. These are, in turn, outing, the debate regarding choice versus no choice of sexual orientation, the effects of historical differences between older and younger generations of lesbians and gay men, homophobia and antilesbian/antigay violence, racism in the gay and lesbian community, legal recognition of relationships, the impact of HIV/AIDS on adolescents and the aging process, and the health effects of coping with social oppression.

The origin of this book was an invited lecture at the American Psychological Association meetings in 1990 by the two co-editors. That lecture is reprinted here as an introduction to the various readings. Having developed this broad overview, we felt the articles most central to the field should be collected together and made available in one source. The articles range from classic works that helped define the field to some recent publications reflecting contemporary research and practice. We have written a brief introduction to each of the eight sections to provide background and perspective for each topic.

Part 1, "The Meaning of Sexual Orientation," reviews three levels of analysis of the meaning of sexual orientation: 1) sociocultural—sexual orientation has a particular meaning because one's social environment imposes that meaning; 2) individual psychological—the complexity of conceptualizing an individual's sexual orientation; and 3) interactive perspective—the connection between a stigmatized identity and minority status within a culture. The contemporary issue discussed is "outing"—revealing someone else's homosexuality to public view.

Part 2, "Origins of Sexual Orientation," examines three perspectives to explain the nature and origins of sexual orientation: 1) essentialist—that one's sexuality is a relatively fixed and essential characteristic of one's identity; 2) social constructionist—that the meaning of sexuality is created by social processes within a given culture; and 3) interactionist—although prenatal or early experience may predispose individuals to particular sexual interests, much of adult sexuality reflects scripts that are defined by one's culture. Bisexuality is also discussed here as an important example of the complexity of understanding sexual orientation. The contemporary issue addressed is the debate regarding the degree of choice versus no choice of sexual orientation.

Part 3, "Identity Development and Stigma Management," explores the process of individual development of a positive gay male or lesbian identity in the social context of stigma about homosexuality; it includes strategies used to manage this stigma and to traverse the boundaries between the gay and straight worlds. How people balance the costs and benefits of communicating their sexual orientation to others and disclosure to family, to a spouse in a heterosexual marriage, and at work is also discussed. The contemporary issue focuses on the effects of historical differences between older and younger generations of lesbians and gay men with regard to identity and coming out.

Part 4, "Gender Differences in Roles and Behavior," discusses three themes for understanding gender differences as they apply to gay men and lesbians: 1) how social conceptions of gender and sexual orientation are interrelated and differ across cultures; 2) the impact of gender roles on lesbians and gay men; and 3) the relationship between gender role norms and antigay attitudes. The contemporary issue addresses the relationship between homophobia and antilesbian and antigay violence.

Part 5, "Cultural Diversity Among Lesbians and Gay Men," builds on the general process of identity development to explore differences among gay men and lesbians based on racial and ethnic background, including the dimensions of religion, gender roles, and family structure and values. The focus is the interface between ethnic minority status and sexual orientation. Perspectives include those from African-American, Asian-American, Latino, and Native American cultures. The contemporary issue is the significance of racism within the gay and lesbian community.

Part 6, "Relationships and Parenthood," summarizes research on characteristics of sexual and romantic relationships within lesbian and gay male couples. Comparisons with heterosexual couples highlight the relative impact of sexual orientation and gender on factors that characterize intimate relationships. This part also reviews research that refutes many of the myths and stereotypes about gay men and lesbians who are parents. The contemporary issue focuses on the legal recognition of same-gender relationships.

Part 7, "Adolescence, Midlife, and Aging," provides a lifespan perspective on lesbian and gay male development. It addresses a wide range of issues that adolescents face in coping with the knowledge of their being gay or lesbian, summarizes a recent study of lesbians in midlife, and discusses central themes in adult development and aging. The contemporary issue examines the impact of HIV/AIDS on adolescents and aging people.

Part 8, "Health," focuses on four major health-related topics within the gay and lesbian community: 1) lesbian health care, with particular attention to the association with minority group status as women and as lesbians; 2) HIV/AIDS; 3) substance abuse; and 4) the impact of antigay and antilesbian violence. The contemporary issue considered is the health effects of coping with social oppression on gay men and lesbians.

A brief conclusion calls attention to implications of the gay affirmative paradigm in psychology for research, practice, and public policy. It also considers the broad impact of lesbians and gay men on society and the importance of continuing the dialogue and research on lesbian, gay, and bisexual political, legal, emotional, sexual, and relational issues.

This book was made possible through the generosity of authors and publishers who allowed articles to be reprinted without charge: John D'Emilio, Barbara Sang, the American Association for Counseling and Development, the American Psychological Association, Elsevier Science Publishing Company, Haworth Press, Sage Publications, the Socialist Review, and the Society for the Psychological Study of Social Issues. Royalties from the sale of the book go to support the Alan Malyon and Adrienne Smith Memorial Fund of the Society for the Psychological Study of Lesbian and Gay Issues, a division of the American Psychological Association. The articles reprinted here have been edited for style by Columbia University Press. The original sources should be consulted for any extended quotations.

We are indebted to Connie Chan, Tony D'Augelli, Jacqueline Goodchilds, Greg Herek, Barrie Levy, Steve Morin, and Anne Peplau for advice and reviews of the manuscript. Johanna Pundyk, Ron Schwizer, and Elizabeth Sheldon provided extensive technical assistance. Gioia Stevens and Jonathan Director of Columbia University Press made this book possible and Ann Miller made it part of the *Between Men ≈ Between Women* series. The support of our partners, Barrie and Ron, who understood how important it has been for us to work together on this project is deeply appreciated.

Sadly, there are friends and colleagues, whose contributions are cited here, who did not live to see it published.

Introduction: Lesbian and Gay Male Dimensions in the Psychological Study of Human Diversity

Linda D. Garnets and Douglas C. Kimmel

Sexual orientation has become an aspect of the psychological study of human diversity during the last few years. We survey this emerging field from the perspective of four main themes: 1) the meaning of sexual orientation and why it is relevant to the psychological understanding of people; 2) the development of gay and lesbian identity within a multicultural society; 3) differences between lesbians and gay men; and 4) the impact of sexual orientation on two central themes of human development (relationships and parenting). Our basic assumption is that an understanding of sexual orientation will enhance psychological research and practice by reducing heterosexist bias, will increase the perception of similarity and appreciation of difference among those who differ in sexual orientation, and will support efforts to remove the stigma and discrimination against lesbians and gay men.

> Imagine, for example, a hypothetical society that attached a great deal of importance to the question of whether its citizens were dog lovers or cat lovers. Imagine that scientists constructed complicated psychological questionnaires to determine whether someone was a "feliphile" or a "caniphile,"

scored people on scales of "petual orientation," and received or were denied tenure on the basis of whether they could prove the existence of "bipetuality." (Weinrich and Williams 1991:47)

OVERVIEW

Until the 1970s most psychological research on homosexuality focused on its presumed pathological aspects. Morin (1977) documented the bias that dominated the field up to that time as "heterosexist bias," which he defined as "a belief system that values heterosexuality as superior to and/ or more 'natural' than homosexuality" (p. 631). Only a few pioneers (such as Kinsey, Pomeroy, and Martin 1948; Kinsey et al. 1953; Ford and Beach 1951; Hooker 1957) stood out as questioning the dominant model of homosexuality as a sign of mental illness. A significant change occurred as a result of a concerted effort by gay-affirmative mental health professionals who called attention to the empirical data that led the American Psychiatric Association in 1973 to remove homosexuality per se from its list of mental disorders (Bayer 1981). The American Psychological Association (APA) supported this change and further urged mental health professionals to take the lead in removing the stigma that previously had been associated with homosexuality (Conger 1975; Kooden et al. 1979). Subsequent psychological research on homosexuality has shifted from a preoccupation with the causes and pathology of homosexuality to a much greater focus on the characteristics and psychosocial concerns of lesbians and gay men, including social attitudes about homosexuals (Watters 1986).

In recent years there has been much positive change, but the effects have been limited. On the one hand, a gay-affirmative perspective has emerged within American psychology. From this perspective homosexuality is viewed as a natural variant in the expression of erotic attractions and relationships, the adoption of a gay male or lesbian identity is considered to be a viable and healthy option, and many of the problems of living associated with being lesbian or gay are thought to result from negative social attitudes about homosexuality. On the other hand, a recent survey of a large and diverse sample of psychologists by the APA Committee on Lesbian and Gay Concerns Task Force (1990) showed that a wide range of negative biases and misinformation about homosexuality persisted that could affect therapy practice with lesbians and gay men.

Likewise, in recent years, social attitudes have been affected by the increased visibility and political power of lesbians and gay men. Few aspects of human behavior, however, evoke the intensity of opposition that homosexuality arouses in some circles. For example, in 1990, the United States Congress passed a bill to collect statistics on hate crimes, significantly including those based on sexual orientation, and the president signed it at a ceremony that included openly lesbian and gay male community leaders. Moreover, empirical research has documented the persistence of institutional and personal hostility toward gay men and lesbians and the mental health consequences of hate crimes, victimization, and verbal abuse (Garnets, Herek, and Levy 1990; Herek 1991).

The emergence of acquired immune deficiency syndrome (AIDS) has focused considerable attention on gay male life-styles and has brought renewed stigma to and discrimination against lesbians and gay men (Herek 1990b). Psychology, to its credit, has played a leading role in the fight against the epidemic and the related discrimination against those people affected by the disease (cf. Backer et al. 1988). It has been a tragic episode and the end is not yet in sight. Certainly it has affected sexual behavior, intimate relationships, and the development experiences of bereaved survivors, but it is too soon to know the extent of the impact or the long-term consequences of this historical event.

Within this contradictory social-historical context, we seek to describe the complex phenomenon of sexual orientation from a psychological perspective in the 1990s. Time does not allow us to discuss AIDS or other important issues, such as the extraordinary process of building a community that has taken place over the last two decades. We focus, instead, on the nature of sexual orientation, gay male and lesbian identity, gender differences, and some relevant life-span development issues.

DEFINITIONS

At the outset, it is useful to define the terminology that we use (see appendix A). We have selected these definitions for the purposes of this introduction; they are not engraved in stone. They are based on, but modified from, those developed by Money (1988:191–216). We have adopted some of his terms, such as *homophilia* and *heterophilia*, because they emphasize love (*philia*) instead of only sexual behavior and because they focus on affectional and erotic desire instead of viewing homosexuals as "certain kinds of people" (Risman and Schwartz 1988).

These definitions make subtle distinctions that are important. First, an individual may be *homophilic* without being *lesbian* or *gay* because the latter terms implies a life-style with some degree of self-awareness and identification with the larger lesbian and gay male community. Second, *homosexuality* may involve sexual acts without a gay life-style or self-identification. Third, homophilia, similar to heterophilia, does not imply that an individual acts on the erotic feelings; for example, one may be celibate or may use heterophilic fantasy to facilitate a homosexual encounter, or vice versa. Fourth, *sexual orientation* generally reflects the affectional-erotic attraction to same gender, other gender, or to both women and men. We consider it to be the relative balance between an individual's homophilia and heterophilia—not a bipolar dichotomy but two parallel dimensions (cf. Shively and DeCecco 1977). That is, homosexuality and heterosexuality reflect correspondingly high and low degrees of homophilia and heterophilia. A bisexual status reflects relatively high homophilia and heterophilia (androgynophilia), whereas an asexual status reflects relatively low levels of both homophilia and heterophilia.

Clearly, sexual orientation is more complex than either *homosexual* or *heterosexual.* It is similar to the continuum of colors in a rainbow. For example, Coleman (1987) pointed out the multiple dimensions involved in sexual orientation: self-identification, behavior, fantasies, emotional attachments, and current relationship status. Klein, Sepekoff, and Wolf (1986) proposed a similar model but also included a temporal dimension (past, present) and one's self-defined "ideal." In addition, Masters and Johnson's (1979) study of ambisexuals provided a fascinating example of the interaction of gender with sexual orientation and behavior: the same ambisexual men moved more quickly toward orgasm with female partners than with male partners; the same ambisexual women engaged in mutual "my turn, your turn" sexual interaction with their female partners but let their male partners "set the pace throughout the entire sexual interaction" (p. 169). Moreover, it should be noted that there is not a necessary relationship between biological gender, gender identity or role, and sexual orientation; they represent separate components of sexual identity (Larsen 1981; Ross 1987; Shively and DeCecco 1977).

LIMITATIONS AND CAVEATS REGARDING RESEARCH

Because representative sampling of the population is problematic insofar as many people will not disclose their sexual orientation, differing levels of confidence in research with regard to sexual orientation must be noted.

First, research that focuses on refuting universal stereotypes about lesbians and gay men does not require representative samples to be compelling because it focuses on disproving these generalizations. For example, Hooker's (1957) study showed that homosexual men cannot be distinguished from heterosexual controls on the basis of psychological tests, and Masters and Johnson's (1979) laboratory study showed that homosexual men and homosexual women showed the same physiological sexual response as did heterosexual men and heterosexual women, respectively. In neither study was a representative sample used, yet both were convincing. Likewise, studies of patterns of aging among gay men (Kimmel 1978) can lead one to conclude that, contrary to stereotypes, there is considerable diversity—probably even more than was found among the limited sample—without claiming the findings are representative of all gay men.

Second, limited generalizations can be made from nonrepresentative samples if proper caution is taken. Because most research has focused on White gay male samples, we can be relatively comfortable describing this population, noting that the volunteer samples tend to be better educated and more affluent than their age group as a whole. Obvious biases, such as samples of men from gay bars or from gay community organizations, are typically noted. It is clear, however, that such samples cannot be generalized to gay men of color or to women; urban samples also cannot be generalized to rural gay men, youthful samples to older adults, and so on.

Third, we cannot claim certainty regarding the proportion of respondents manifesting various characteristics. For example, we do not know how many gay men have children or how many lesbians are living in committed relationships with another woman. We do not know how many parents accept their child's homosexuality or whether gay male or lesbian life expectancy is different from that of heterosexual men and women. Recently, however, survey researchers have developed techniques for sampling this population, (e.g., telephone surveys that inquire about sexual orientation and related themes). Although problems exist, if limitations are specified, it may now become possible to describe some characteristics of the lesbian and gay male population (cf. Herek 1990a, 1991).

Moreover, it is important that research be replicated before it is accepted with confidence. A study by Kolodny et al. (1971) showed that testosterone levels were lower in gay men than in heterosexual controls; this was not found in a careful replication study (Sanders, Bain, and Langevin 1985). Similarly, research by Gladue, Green, and Hellman (1984) that showed different gonadotropic hormone response in homosexual and heterosexual men was not replicated in a later study (Hendricks, Graber, and Rodriguez-Sierra 1989).

An additional problem is that research studies often include people with some heterosexual experience in the "homosexual" sample and rarely distinguish bisexuals as a distinct group. In that sense, as MacDonald (1983) and others have noted, "a little bit of lavender"—that is, a little same-gender sexual experience — can make an individual homosexual for research purposes. Thus, depending on how much other gender interest is required, and the particular dimension measured, some people might more accurately be classified as bisexual instead of homosexual.

We must be cautious, therefore, about placing either too little or too much confidence in the research on which we rely. In this introduction, except where specifically noted, it may be assumed that the sample was predominately White with a higher than average level of education than that of the general population. Many findings have been replicated to a large extent in other studies and appear to be robust. Many topics would benefit, however, from additional research with different samples.

SEXUAL ORIENTATION IS AN IMPORTANT PSYCHOLOGICAL VARIABLE

Sexual orientation, similar to gender, age, race, and ethnicity, is an important psychological variable. The determinants of sexual orientation reflect a complex interaction of biology, culture, history, and psychosocial influences. The mix is unlikely to be identical for different individuals (Richardson 1987). The result is a mosaic of diversity in life-style, behavior, and adaptation. Gender, economic and class differences, chronological age, ethnic and racial variation, and whether one is a parent are among other relevant dimensions of diversity in gay and lesbian lives.

There are several characteristics that stand out for lesbian and gay people within the context of Western society. These include the following:

1. Gay men and lesbians discover their sexual orientation at a relatively late point in the process of identity development, often at the time sexual desire begins to be recognized. It is not recognized or acknowledged from birth but is an *achieved* instead of an *ascribed* status (cf. Weinberg and Williams 1974:288). Often there is a time lag between the discovery and owning of one's identity.
2. Lesbians and gay men learn negative attitudes about homosexuality, gay men, and lesbians from others (both significant others and conventional society); do not imagine that such negative attitudes could apply to them; and then learn that they do indeed apply.
3. Because families of lesbians and gay men typically are heterosexual, they do not provide useful role models for normal transitions and developmental periods of gay and lesbian lives.

4. Family disruption often results when a gay or lesbian sexual orientation is revealed. Moreover, it may be revealed in different ways: by conscious decision, by positive transition (new relationship, birth of grandchild), or by some negative circumstance (e.g., arrest, divorce, illness).

5. Because lesbians and gay men are diverse and the majority are not easily identifiable, most move in and out of gay and straight identities, and many hide their sexual orientation from public view. In addition, they may be assumed to be gay or not gay as roles shift during the day or week, and often they are treated as if they were heterosexual.

6. Even when gay men and lesbians are open about their sexual orientation, they do not automatically invalidate stereotypes about them because each individual can be discounted as an exception to the general pattern.

7. The lesbian and gay male community encompasses diversity in terms of gender, race, ethnicity, age, socioeconomic status, relationship status, parenthood, health, disabilities, politics, and sexual behavior. For many lesbians and gay men, this community may introduce them to greater social diversity than they had experienced before coming out as gay or lesbian.

8. Gay and lesbian people have had little awareness of any community history until relatively recently. Although the gay and lesbian community has a history, it is not passed on through family traditions. There are few road maps; each person tends to be an individual creation. This may lead to greater potential for "normative creativity" (Brown 1989).

9. Gay men and lesbians are often encouraged or permitted by their deviance from accepted norms to explore androgynous gender role behavior, independence, self-reliance, and educational and occupational options.

10. Lesbians and gay men raise issues that some members of the public may find potentially threatening, such as a) anyone can be gay (stereotypes are inaccurate predictors); b) same-sex sexual fantasies can be explored (everyone is not 100 percent heterosexual all the time); and c) relationships and sexual relations need not be based on gender role constraints. Moreover, gay men and lesbians without children may benefit economically from not having a family; two gay men in a relationship without children or alimony payments may be particularly advantaged

because male income typically exceeds female income levels. Also, lesbians may be perceived as having greater power than heterosexual women because they live independently of men and do not depend on men for sexual, emotional, or financial support.

We might even think that gay men and lesbians are perceived as a threat to the traditional power structure because sexual orientation is nearly always excluded from the list of protected minorities in civil rights legislation except in a few cities and one or two states; conversely, same-gender sexual relations are illegal in nearly half the states in the United States.

It should also be noted that people who are neither exclusively homosexual nor heterosexual tend to be viewed with suspicion by both groups. On the one hand, they may be seen as trying to avoid the stigma of being homosexual; on the other hand, they may be viewed as being less normal than a heterosexual. Although research data are limited, there is some evidence of a different process of development for bisexuals. Many report no same-gender sexual experience until adulthood. Moreover, many bisexuals reported moving from a same-gender sexual relationship to an other-gender sexual relationship and then back again, or vice versa (Blumstein and Schwartz 1977; cf. Bell, Weinberg, and Hammersmith 1981).

In summary, gay male and lesbian sexual orientations are important characteristics within the context of American culture at the present time. They represent complex psychosocial factors that affect heterosexuals, as well as lesbians and gay men. We have pointed out the multidimensional nature of sexual orientation, suggested the extent of recent social change regarding the psychological understanding of sexual orientation, and outlined some of the issues related to contemporary research on sexual orientation. In the next section, we discuss the determinants of sexual orientation as an aspect of an individual's unique pattern of sexuality.

SEXUAL ORIENTATION AND AN INDIVIDUAL'S LOVEMAP

My mother made me a homosexual.
If I give her the yarn will she make me one too?
            —graffiti on a wall, circa 1970

Present research suggests that the origins of sexual orientation are not well understood. One perplexing issue concerns the stability of sexual orientation over the life span. On the one hand, retrospective reports indicate that gay male and lesbian sexual orientation appears to be established by the time one reaches adolescence, often before sexual activity begins, and is frequently preceded by an awareness of same-gender sexual attraction (Bell, Weinberg, and Hammersmith 1981). Also, cases of change from an exclusively homosexual sexual orientation as a result of psychotherapy have not been convincingly documented (Money 1988:87; Zuger 1988). These data suggest that for some people sexual orientation develops relatively early in life and does not undergo major changes in adulthood. On the other hand, some individuals appear to have flexibility in their sexual orientation or adopt one orientation after considerable experience with the other orientation in adulthood (Dixon 1984, 1985; Golden 1987; Kimmel 1978; LaTorre and Wedenberg 1983; Lowenstein 1985). Money (1988) termed this phenomenon *sequential bisexuality.* These data suggest that there may be different origins of sexual orientation for different individuals.

A second controversial issue concerns the possible biological-physiological origins of sexual orientation. One site of presumed difference has been located in the sexual dimorphic nucleus of the hypothalamus, but no difference in number of cells in this nucleus was found in an autopsy study between homosexual and heterosexual men despite a marked difference between men and women (Swaab and Hofman 1988). Moreover, the data regarding endocrine factors and sexual orientation are inconsistent and contradictory (Gladue 1987; Sanders, Bain, and Langevin 1985).

Money (1987, 1988) proposed a process by which sexual orientation develops in stages beginning in prenatal development and results from an interaction among prenatal cultural, experiential, and socialization influences, with the mix depending on the individual situation. We find this model useful because sexual orientation (e.g., heterophilia and homophilia) can be conceptualized as aspects of an individual's unique "lovemap." The lovemap reflects the wide range of sexual interests and attractive characteristics in one's idealized lover (Money 1988, chap. 4). This concept implies the developmental interaction of mind and brain, hormones and experience, and prenatal and postnatal influences that lead to a personalized template of erotic and sexual feelings, fantasy, and activity that is as unique as one's fingerprint or voiceprint.

Moreover, the concept of a unique lovemap sheds light on the debate between the social constructionist and essentialist perspectives on homosexuality (Hart and Richardson 1981; Kitzinger 1987; Plummer 1981; Weeks 1981). The former view is that sexual orientation is a creation of

Western culture that can be traced back to the nineteenth century, when the terminology and supportive ideology of homosexuality as a pathology emerged. The latter view is that sexual orientation reflects an essential characteristic of people that is based in deep-seated biological or psychological influences.

> The debate currently raging between "essentialist" scholars, who propound a biological base for gender and sexuality, versus "social constructionists," who emphasize cultural origins, is perhaps more accurately viewed from the perspective that human lives are shaped by the interaction of both of these factors. (Williams 1987:137)

These differing perspectives may be integrated if the unique varieties of lovemaps are seen as reflections of some essential characteristics of persons that have been constructed by social convention into concepts such as a bipolar sexual orientation. In this sense, the lovemap may resemble a "script" defined by social convention, as well as by an idiosyncratic "fingerprint" (cf. Tiefer 1987). It should also be noted that the lovemap can evolve over time; it may be constructed and reconstructed by the individual and need not be the same at age forty-five or seventy as it was at age fifteen or twenty-five.

In summary, homophilia and heterophilia are aspects of an individual's unique pattern of sexual responsiveness. To reduce this complex lovemap to a bipolar dichotomy of homosexuality versus heterosexuality is not only a gross oversimplification, but also a reflection of Western religious beliefs and "either/or" logic. This simplistic perspective has led to a denial of similarity between and diversity within these supposedly dichotomous sexual orientations. It may also be observed that whereas our culture has emphasized the importance of this dimension of human sexuality, other cultures and historical eras have structured the meaning of homosexual behaviors and heterosexual behaviors differently (cf. Blackwood 1985; Greenberg 1988; Weinrich and Williams 1991).

LESBIAN AND GAY MALE IDENTITY

Since the nineteenth century, the meaning of homosexuality has evolved from a purely sexual act to a personal identity (Foucault 1979; Hart and Richardson 1981; Weeks 1977, Weinberg 1983). Thus, in American culture, as Herek has stated, "What a person *does* sexually defines who the person *is*" (Herek 1986:568). The social forces that have transformed the awareness and conditions of gay and lesbian life, in part through the homophile rights movement, to produce a greater recognition of group identity have been documented by social historians (Adam 1987; Altman 1981; D'Emilio 1983). In addition, the feminist movement changed women's ideas about sexuality in general, raised questions about traditional gender roles, and reduced stigma surrounding lesbianism; this led to visible communities based on lesbian-feminist ideology (Faderman 1984; Krieger 1982; Lockard 1985). To a surprising extent, lesbian and gay male identity has been transformed in recent history from abnormal to *normatively different* (Brown 1989).

> Back in 1948 to 1950 . . . there wasn't as yet in the minds of my fellow Queers, let alone the American society at large, even the beginnings of such a concept as that of a GAY IDENTITY. Everywhere we were constantly being told . . . that we were heteros who occasionally performed nasty acts. . . . The tremendous leap forward in consciousness that was the Stonewall Rebellion changed the pronoun in Gay identity from "I" to "WE." (Hay 1990:5)

As a result of these social changes, in Western societies today individuals have the opportunity to construct gay male and lesbian identities in ways that did not exist earlier (Herdt 1989; Herek 1985). For example, as a member of an oppressed minority (D'Emilio 1983; Herdt 1989; Herek 1991), as a publicly acknowledged member of a community (Herek 1991; Paul 1982), as "women-identified-women" (Radicalesbians 1973), or as part of a "lesbian continuum" (Rich 1980). Like racial and ethnic minority identity, the contemporary view is that gay male and lesbian identity formation represents an emergent, continuous life process that does not have any necessary static endpoint (Boxer and Cohler 1989; Golden 1987; Lowenstein 1985; Peplau 1991; Troiden 1988).

Gay and Lesbian Identity as a Minority Status

Lesbians and gay men share some elements in common with other minority groups (Bierly 1985; Bradford and Ryan 1987). For example, society defines gay men and lesbians largely in terms of characteristics that relegate them to unequal status and set them apart from the dominant group (Adam 1978; de Monteflores 1986; Herek 1991). Similarly, on the basis of group stereotypes, gay men and lesbians are still denied full social participation and civil rights (cf. Herek 1990a). Gay men and lesbians, therefore, represent a minority as a consequence of conditions imposed by majority reaction and treatment (Paul 1982; Yearwood and Weinberg

1979). As a result, lesbians and gay men have developed strategies to manage their differences from the mainstream and to respond to overt and covert oppression (Barrett 1990; de Monteflores 1986). Lesbians and gay men show great resilience in the face of social oppression. As individuals, they typically manage to form a positive sense of self and do not suffer from low self-esteem. As members of groups, gay men and lesbians have worked together to form support networks and communities to facilitate a positive individual and group identity (Harry and Duvall 1978; Kurdek 1988; Weinberg and Williams 1974).

> The political minority status of gay people was recognized by the California Supreme Court in 1979 (*Gay Law Students Association v. Pacific Telephone and Telegraph*). Noting that the civil rights struggle of the gay community "must be recognized as political activity" (p. 32) and that publicly acknowledging one's own homosexual orientation is an important aspect of this struggle, the Court ruled that discrimination against openly gay individuals constitutes illegal discrimination on the basis of political activity. (Herek 1991)

THE PROCESS OF LESBIAN AND GAY IDENTITY DEVELOPMENT

Gay male and lesbian identity development, or coming out, includes realization of one's own homosexuality, as well as disclosure of this realization to others. Coming out has been conceptualized as a rite of passage during which one constructs one's own sense of self as gay or lesbian within the context of contemporary society (Herdt 1989; Kleinberg 1986). Self-labeling as gay, accepting this label, self-disclosing, and feeling accepted by others have been found to be strongly related to psychological adjustment (Bell and Weinberg 1978; McDonald 1982; Miranda and Storms 1989). Similarly, a more positive gay male or lesbian identity has been found to be correlated with significantly fewer symptoms of neurotic or social anxiety, higher ego strength, less depression, and higher self-esteem (Hammersmith and Weinberg 1973; Savin-Williams 1989; Schmitt and Kurdek 1987).

Zimmerman (1984) discussed the power of shared storytelling of lesbians through telling their coming out experiences: "The personal narrative, particularly the coming out story, forms our 'tribal lore,' our myth of origins" (p. 674). Whenever gay men and lesbians meet, sooner or later they get around to practicing this ritual of telling their coming out stories.

Today one can also speak about *coming in:* the realization of having entered into a community and the process of identifying with a larger group of gay and lesbian people (Petrow 1990). The presence of a gay male and lesbian support system has been found to be associated with adaptive coping strategies and lower levels of stress (Gillow and Davis 1987), positive well-being (Weinberg and Williams 1974), psychological adjustment (Kurdek 1988), and more emotional intimacy in relationships (Harry 1984). For lesbians, feminist values and involvement in feminist activities may also provide sources of validation, self-esteem, self-acceptance, and social support that facilitates development of lesbian identity (Leavy and Adams 1986; Peplau and Cochran 1981; Sophie 1985/1986). For gay men, the gay community can function as a kind of club that provides social support, professional contacts, and entree into social networks when traveling or relocating.

Considerable research has been devoted to the topic of lesbian and gay identity development. We can summarize three major themes here: developmental tasks in the acquisition of a positive identity, cultural diversity in identity development, and the time lag in achieving a positive lesbian or gay identity.

Developmental Tasks in Acquisition of Identity. Empirical studies of gay male and lesbian identity development have focused on how individuals identify, label, and construct their sense of identity as lesbians and gay men and on understanding the developmental tasks necessary to form and to maintain a positive gay male or lesbian identity. Numerous stage-sequential models have been developed to organize and interpret the data on lesbian and gay identity development; some have been empirically tested (Cass 1984; Chapman and Brannock 1987; Coleman 1981/1982; Hanley-Hackenbruck 1988; Hencken and O'Dowd 1977; Lee 1977; Lewis 1984; Minton and McDonald 1983/1984; Weinberg 1983; Sophie 1985/1986). Five central points may be drawn from these studies:

1. Initial awareness of same-gender sexual desires initiates a developmental transition in which individuals report feeling different and being off course (Boxer and Cohler 1989; Schaefer 1977; Troiden 1979). During the period from first awareness to self-labeling, many gay men and lesbians experience a period of identity confusion characterized by feeling in limbo between questioning a heterosexual identity and recognizing a potential gay male or lesbian one (Cass 1979; Troiden 1988). Cass (1984) described the in-limbo phase of identity confusion in the following way: "You feel that you *probably* are a homosexual, although you're not definitely sure. . . . You feel distant or cut off from

other people. . . . You are beginning to think that it might help to meet other homosexuals but you're not sure whether you really want to or not. . . . You prefer to put on a front of being completely heterosexual" (Cass 1984:156).

2. Gay male and lesbian identity development requires individuals to reconcile their own uniqueness with society's template, with only partial success. In order to form a positive lesbian or gay male identity one must assess, confront, and reject the negative identity provided by society and transform that identity into a positive and viable self-concept (Espín 1987; Fein and Nuehring 1981; Malyon 1982; Ponse 1984). This process is accomplished by transforming the cognitive category *gay* or *lesbian* from negative stereotypes to positive labels (Dank 1971). This is followed by increased acceptance and commitment of the label as applied to oneself. Cass (1979) described the growth of self-acceptance in the following terms: "I might be gay, I'm different"; then "I probably am gay"; then "I'm proud I'm gay"; then "I am gay and being gay is one aspect of who I am."

3. Throughout the identity-formation process, gay men and lesbians use a variety of strategies to evade the stigma associated with homosexuality, to manage the boundary between the heterosexual and the gay worlds, and to manage discrepancies between their same-gender sexual feelings or behaviors and their self-definition as gay or lesbian (de Monteflores 1986; Hencken 1984).

4. An important aspect of identity development involves exploration of the lesbian and gay subcultures and socialization into their norms (Plummer 1975). Contact with these subcultures is available today in most cities, by newspaper subscriptions, and by toll-free information services. This contact helps to foster group identity, provides role models, reveals the diversity among homosexuals, diminishes feelings of isolation or alienation, and facilitates learning the folkways, behavior, language, and structure of the lesbian and gay male community (Harry 1984; Kurdek 1988).

5. Over time, gay men and lesbians experience an increased desire to disclose their identity to an expanding group of others that may include other lesbians and gay men, heterosexual friends, family, coworkers, acquaintances, and the public at large (Troiden 1988).

Although generally a stage-sequential linear progression is assumed in lesbian and gay male identity development, the data indicate that the process might be better conceptualized as a repeating spiral pattern (Ponse 1978; Troiden 1988). In common with other aspects of adult development, one may traverse the same psychological territory again and again, albeit at different "elevations" (cf. Shneidman 1989). Moreover, some events do not happen to everyone and, if they do occur, they happen in different ways (McDonald 1982; Sophie 1985/1986; Troiden and Goode 1980).

> A great variety exists in the order and timing of events. . . . Self-definition may precede contact with other lesbians . . . or it my follow such contact; disclosure to others, homosexual or heterosexual, may occur at any time, and probably occurs throughout the process; and one may enter a relationship with another woman before, at the same time, or after identifying oneself as a lesbian. (Sophie 1985/1986:49–50)

Cultural Diversity in Identity Formation. Acquiring a gay male or lesbian identity takes place against a background of family and cultural tradition, values, and social networks. Furthermore, racial and ethnic groups in the United States experience prejudice and discrimination on the basis of minority group status, which places additional constraints on life options, relationships, and identity (Cazenave 1979, 1984; Ericksen 1980; Mays 1985). Frequently, the dilemma for racial or ethnic minority lesbians and gay men becomes one of managing conflicting allegiances among different communities (Loiacano 1989; Morales 1989). They must participate in divergent social worlds, balancing demands and crossing boundaries of the different groups, including the gay male and lesbian community, one's ethnic culture, the majority culture, and, for women, the women's or feminist community. Individuals with double and triple minority status may experience discrimination and prejudice as outsiders in each community (Kanuha 1990; Mays and Cochran 1986). Although the goal may be to identify with, or be part of, both the ethnic or racial and lesbian or gay male communities, typically the result is greater comfort in the gay male and lesbian community but a stronger identity with the ethnic or racial group (Chan 1989; Espín 1987; Icard 1985/1986; Wooden, Kawasaki, and Mayeda 1983).

> I would be extremely unhappy if all my Latin culture were taken out of my lesbian life. . . . I identify myself as a lesbian more intensely than as a

Cuban/Latin. But it is a very painful question because I feel that I am both, and I don't want to have to choose. (Espín 1987:47)

In research with small samples, race and skin color more frequently contribute to childhood harassment than cross-gender behavior (Sears 1989). Similarly, as adults, samples of Asian-American, Latina, and African-American lesbians reported that discrimination was more frequent because of their race; gender was second and their sexual orientation was third (Chan 1989; Espín 1987; Mays and Cochran 1986). Chan (1989) found, however, that Asian-American gay men reported more frequent discrimination by the majority culture because they were gay.

Cooperation, interdependence, and strong commitment to one's extended family and ethnic community as a primary reference group are highly valued in many cultures. Thus, gay men and lesbians may be perceived as challenging or violating social expectations not only for their personal life-style but also because they are placing personal desires above the needs of their family or the community (Amaro 1978; Kanuha 1990). Moreover, some misperceive homosexuality as a "White Western" phenomenon that is alien to their own ethnic group: "Even though there are a lot of black homosexuals, a lot of blacks do not want to accept that fact. A homosexual thing is a white thing" (Sears 1989:428). Thus, lesbians and gay men often feel like outcasts within their ethnic or racial community, may remain closeted there, and avoid disclosure to their families (Espín 1987; Loiacano 1989; Tremble, Schneider, and Appathurai 1989).

Within the gay male and lesbian community, ethnic and racial discrimination can lead to being unacknowledged, unaccepted, or perceived as exotic (Chan 1989). Often, gender or sexual stereotypes become linked with racial stereotypes (Icard 1985/1986; Wooden, Kawasaki, and Mayeda 1983). As a result, it is often difficult to find a niche because of discrimination (Klein 1986; Morales 1989; Tremble, Schneider, and Appathurai 1989) and because prevailing Anglo norms may conflict with norms from their own ethnic communities (de Monteflores 1981; Zimmerman 1984): "Lionel was in love with black people but not in love with black individuals. He had an image that because I was black, I was a stud, and if I didn't continually portray that image, that would upset him" (Silverstein 1981:164).

In recent years, lesbians and gay men of color have formed groups and organizations specifically created to provide support and a kind of extended family (Hidalgo 1984; Icard 1985/1986). For example, Mays and Cochran (1986) found that the main source of social support for their sample of African-American lesbians was other African-American lesbians.

Despite some similarities of experience, considerable diversity exists among ethnic and racial groups on the basis of ancestral heritage, national origin, generation, language, and socioeconomic status. In the United States several different traditions can be identified. For example, many African-Americans view homosexuality as a threat to the family and group survival in the face of racism. Although sexuality is viewed as a natural and positive part of life that leads to childbearing and continues the race despite forces that threaten its members (Wilson 1986) and there is some flexibility in gender roles within the family (Cazenave 1979, 1984; Ericksen 1980; Greene 1986); nonetheless, homosexuality and interracial marriage are perceived by some as racial genocide. As a result, lesbians and gay men are perceived as guilty for failing to promote group survival through propagation of the race and for not supporting the racial struggle against oppression (Greene 1986; Icard 1985/1986). Although many Black churches are intolerant of homosexuality, there is a movement toward the development of Black gay churches (Tinney 1986:73, 76).

> If Black lesbians and gay men are willing to check their sexuality at the door of the church, and come bearing gifts of talent, there are relatively few problems. . . . The development of Black gay churches will make it possible for Black gay Christians, for the first time, to hear the gospel in their own "language of the Spirit," respond to the gospel in their own ways, and reinterpret the gospel in their own cultural context—taking into account both race and sexual orientation at every step in this process.

For some Latino men, it is not infrequent for sexual contacts to include same-gender behavior, beginning in adolescence (Carballo-Dieguez 1989; Espín 1984). Sexual behavior is defined by the "masculinity" of the act: men who insert their penises are regarded as masculine; those who receive them are viewed as feminine and degraded (Paz 1961). Thus, same-gender sexual contact is tolerated if it is seen as masculine, but gay men are perceived as feminine and are subjected to stigma, shame, and prejudice (Carrier 1976, 1980, 1985). Latino communities are less aware of the existence of lesbians than of gay men within their culture. Generally, only the openly butch types (i.e., those violating gender roles) are recognized as lesbians (Espín 1984; Tremble, Schneider, and Appathurai 1989). Vasquez (1979) found that lesbians who were more acculturated into "American ways" were less likely to be involved in playing the husband-wife roles in their relationships. Furthermore, Latina lesbians challenge the well-defined role of women in these cultures. They are perceived as being too independent from the family and not sufficiently feminine. They violate the cultural norms of submissiveness, virtuousness, respectfulness toward elders, deference to men, interdependence, and the expectation to reside within their family until marriage. Therefore, many Latina lesbians hide their sexual orientation to avoid stigmatization within their own ethnic communities (Amaro 1978; Espín 1987; Hildalgo 1984): "Being a lesbian is by definition an act of treason against our cultural values. . . . To be a lesbian we have to leave the fold of our family, and seek support within the mainstream white lesbian community" (Romo-Carmona 1987:xxvi).

Asian-Americans often regard sex as a taboo topic that is not to be discussed and see homosexuality as a potential threat to marriage and carrying on the family line. Within Confucian tradition, men are the carriers of the family name, kinship linkage, and family heritage (Lee and Saul 1987). To fail to produce offspring is a serious matter, especially because sexuality cannot be discussed openly. Being gay may represent one's first serious violation of parental norms (Abramson 1986; Aoki 1983). Therefore, gay men must manage the loss of face for not carrying on the family name and for making an individual choice rather than giving unquestioning respect to their elders (Bradshaw 1990; Gock 1986; Wooden, Kawasaki, and Mayeda 1983). Asian communities in the United States still emphasize sharply delineated gender roles and negate or deny the possibility of lesbian existence (Lin 1978). If acknowledged, lesbians are perceived as tarnishing the family honor by not being dutiful daughters, by rejecting the role of wife and mother, and by rejecting passive reliance on and deference to men and the submersion of identity within the family structure (Chan 1987; Pamela 1989; Shon and Ja 1982). In addition, there is strong community pressure to remain closeted and not to be open about being gay or lesbian (Chan 1989).

> My family holds Western culture somehow responsible for off-beat youth. They think my being lesbian is my being young, and confused, and rebellious. They feel it has something to do with trying to fit into White culture. It's one aspect among many that they don't like abut me. . . . And they're waiting for me to stop rebelling and to be heterosexual, go out on dates, and come home early. (Tremble, Schneider, and Appathurai 1989:260)

Native American cultures have strong historical traditions of acceptance of homosexuality for both men and women, but Anglo values and reservation life have modified those values to some extent. Traditional values of many Native American tribes did not link physical anatomy to gender roles. Anthropological evidence documents that socially recognized cross-gender roles and third gender roles were widespread, including *berdache* for men and *women warriors* for women (Blackwood 1984; Whitehead 1981; Williams 1985). Anglo culture eventually altered and suppressed this traditional view. As a result, contemporary Native Americans report greater stigmatization and great difficulty in being open about their homosexuality (Owlfeather 1988). In addition, many migrated to cities where they had to manage racism and were cut off from traditional values (Williams 1986).

> In the old days, during life on the plains, the people respected each other's vision. Berdaches had an integral place in the rigors and lifestyle of the tribe. The way they were viewed was not the same as the contemporary Indian gay lifestyle and consciousness that we have now—they were not fighting for a place in society and to be accepted by that society. They already had a place, a very special and sacred place. (Owlfeather 1988:100)

It would be expected that lesbians and gay men of color and those from ethnic or religious backgrounds with especially negative attitudes about homosexuality would find it difficult to come out and to develop a positive gay male or lesbian identity.

Time Lag in Sexual Identity Development. Heterosexual adolescents probably do not question their sexual orientation because other-gender sexual feelings, life-style, and identity are not inconsistent with social expectations (cf. Stein and Cohen 1986). Gay men and lesbians, however, appear to require several years to move from their initial awareness of same-gender sexual feelings to self-identification and then to acceptance of and commitment to a positive gay male or lesbian identity (McDonald 1982; Riddle and Morin 1977; Vance and Green 1984). The modal pattern is shown in Table 1. On the average, gay men are aware of same-

TABLE I

Modal Ages for Milestones of Lesbian and Gay Male Identity Development

Identity Development	Age (in years)	
	Lesbians	Gay Men
Initial awareness of same-gender affectional-erotic feelings	14–16	12–13
Initial same-gender sexual experience	20–22	14–15
Self-identification as lesbian or gay	21–23	19–21
Initial same-gender sexual relationship	20–24	21–24
Positive gay or lesbian identity	24–29	22–26

NOTE: These data represent a summary of the following studies: Bell and Weinberg (1978), Jay and Young (1979), and Riddle and Morin (1977). Data from lesbians only: Chapman and Brannock (1987), Granick (1984), Schaefer (1976), and Vance and Green (1984). Data from gay men only: Dank (1971), Harry and Duvall (1978), Lynch (1987), McDonald (1982), Remafedi (1987), Roesler and Deisher (1972), and T. S. Weinberg (1978).

gender sexual feelings and act on this awareness during early to midado-lescence. Lesbians are aware of these feelings during mid- to late adolescence but do not act on them until early adulthood, on the average.

Several factors may contribute to the delay, or time lag, for lesbian and gay adolescents. First, gay men and lesbians learn about homosexuality before they know that they are part of that group (Fein and Nuehring 1981); their identity process is thereby delayed because they feel they share little in common with homosexuals as a group as they are defined by conventional society (Troiden 1979). Second, societal attitudes toward homosexuality, such as degree of openness and tolerance, availability of accurate information, significant others who share a positive view of les-bians and gay men, and legal protections to buffer discrimination and prejudice, have been found to be inversely related to the length of time it takes individuals to form a gay male or lesbian identity (Carrier 1980; Harry and Duvall 1978; McDonald 1982; Troiden and Goode 1980). For example, in a study of four cultures by Ross (1989), the more sexually restrictive and negative the attitudes were regarding homosexuality in the culture, the greater the suppression of the respondents' gay identity and the later the ages that the gay men discovered their homosexuality. Third, social assumptions about universal development of heterosexuality com-plicate and delay gay male and lesbian identity development (Herdt 1989; Herek 1986; Stein and Cohen 1986). That is, the absence of social affir-mation of homosexuality and lack of explicit roles means that lesbians and gay men must invent their own personal framework for identity and for maintenance of self-esteem (Brown 1989). Fourth, because of heterosexist assumptions and social pressure, the vast majority of gay men and lesbians report both same-gender and other-gender sexual arousal and behavior during adolescence and early adulthood (Bell and Weinberg 1978; Bell, Weinberg, and Hammersmith 1981; Jay and Young 1979; Remafedi 1987). Engaging in other-gender sexual experiences (including marriage) may delay self-discovery as gay (Bozett 1989; Gramick 1984; Troiden and Goode 1980). Thus, lesbians and gay men may misclassify themselves, their behavior, or experiences as heterosexual, which would interfere with the labeling process of homosexual identity development (Hencken 1984).

This delay in sexual identity development appears to be more pro-nounced for women than for men, especially because sexual maturation occurs earlier in girls than in boys. There are several plausible reasons for this difference. Lesbians are more likely to be involved in other-gender sexual activity than gay men, less likely to have same-gender sexual contact, more likely to continue other-gender sexual activity after questioning their sexual identity and after having sexual contact with another woman, and more likely to get married than gay men (Bell and Weinberg 1978; Chapman and Brannock 1987). It may be that lesbians continue other-gender sexual activities because they are conforming to social norms that emphasize heterosexual dating (Gramick 1984; Schaefer 1976). One woman in Troiden's (1989) study stated a common theme: "I thought my attraction to women was a passing phase and would go away once I started having intercourse with my boyfriend" (p. 57). In contrast, during adolescence gay men are more likely than lesbians to engage in same-gender sexual behavior, fantasize about same-gender sex, and be sexually attracted to members of the same gender (Bell and Weinberg 1978; Sears 1989).

Other factors, such as geographic setting, may facilitate or hinder gay male and lesbian identity development. For example, gay men who live in proximity to urban centers arrive at a gay identity sooner than those living in outlying areas (D'Augelli 1989; Troiden and Goode 1980). In contrast, gay men living in suburban areas tend to be more circumspect in revealing their identity, have fewer same-gender sexual relationships, have less social involvement with other gay men and more social involvement with heterosexuals than do those living in urban areas (Lynch 1987; Weinberg and Williams 1974). Likewise, gay men and lesbians living in rural areas experience greater isolation and find it more difficult to make enduring friendships and relationships; rural social networks tend to be more inaccessible and exclusionary than in urban areas (D'Augelli, Collins, and Hart 1987; Hollander 1989; Moses and Buckner 1980).

Recent social change regarding greater visibility of the gay male and lesbian community, as noted earlier, may have reduced the extent of this lag time in development. Moreover, it may have increased the willingness of lesbians and gay men to disclose their identity to others.

IDENTITY DISCLOSURE TO FAMILY, FRIENDS, AND COWORKERS

Data strongly suggest that a prerequisite for the emergence of a positive gay male or lesbian identity is the communication of one's sexual orientation to others (Bell and Weinberg 1978; Bradford and Ryan 1987; Hammersmith and Weinberg 1973; Miranda and Storms 1989). Moreover, studies have demonstrated these psychological benefits of coming out to others: enhancement of personal integrity (Rand, Graham, and Rawlings 1982); increased self-affirmation (Wells and Kline 1987); identity integration (Murphy 1989); increased intimacy in relationships (Cramer and Roach 1988; Wells and Kline 1987); greater freedom from concealing, anticipating, and defending against rejection (Cramer and Roach 1988;

Weinberg and Williams 1974); decreased feelings of isolation (Murphy 1989); increased sense of public affirmation of sexual identity (Schneider 1986); and greater acceptance from others (Olsen 1987).

In deciding whether or not to tell, lesbians and gay men must weigh problems presented by their marginal status that reflect the social realities and risks of their environment (Bradford and Ryan 1987). Gay men and lesbians expect and report experiences of negative reactions, discrimination, and prejudice on the basis of disclosures of their sexual identity in a variety of areas of life, including child custody (Actenberg 1988; Falk 1989), antigay hate crimes (Garnets, Herek, and Levy 1990; Herek 1989), and discrimination or fear of discrimination in employment (Hall 1989; Levine 1979; Levine and Leonard 1984).

Balancing the costs and benefits of identity disclosure is a multifaceted, lifelong process of decision making. The principle of *rational outness* is usually the pragmatic solution: "to be as open as possible, because it feels healthy to be honest, and as closed as necessary to protect against discrimination" (Bradford and Ryan 1987:77). Generally, gay men and lesbians disclose to close heterosexual friends and to siblings more often than to parents, coworkers, or employers.

Moreover, data have indicated that the recipient of the coming out message either is more positive to begin with or also benefits. That is, people who know someone who is lesbian or gay (even those from groups with generally antigay attitudes) tend to have more positive attitudes about gay men and lesbians compared with other members of their group (Herek 1991).

Disclosure to parents and other significant relatives often precipitates a period of turmoil for the family, frequently involving three initial reactions. First, parents feel guilt and personal responsibility for their child's homosexuality and experience a sense of failure as parents (Griffin, Wirth, and Wirth 1986; Robinson, Walters, and Skeen 1989). Second, parents may ignore their child's individuality and personal experience by applying negative values and misconceptions about homosexuality to their son or daughter; likewise, they may fear others will similarly apply stereotypes to them, leading to isolation and ostracism from their social network. Third, the "new" identity may create feelings of alienation, and family members might react as if the person were unfamiliar and estranged; as a result, family roles and relationships can be disrupted (Devine 1984; Strommen 1989). Often, parents' reactions are based on early psychological theories that attributed the cause of homosexuality to the parent-child relationship; these theories, which were based on studies with biased samples such as psychotherapy patients, have not been supported by more recent empirical research (e.g., Bell, Weinberg, and Hammersmith 1981). A typical reaction is the following:

> Every book that I had seen said homosexuality was caused by a disturbance in the family. They said that there was usually an absent or rejecting father and a domineering, seductive, or binding kind of mother. I thought about how much Jack worked when the kids were small and the fact that I was the one who stayed home and took care of them. I twisted it all around and said "Yes, maybe we are like that. Maybe there was something really wrong with us." (Griffin, Wirth, and Wirth 1986:7)

Resolution of the family issues that result from disclosure by a son or daughter is often a complex and lengthy process, sometimes aided by a peer support group known as Parents and Friends of Lesbians and Gays (Collins and Zimmerman 1983; Griffin, Wirth, and Wirth 1986; Kleinberg 1986; Robinson, Walters, and Skeen 1989).

There are few data about coming out to other relatives, such as siblings or to grandparents. Often, disclosure may be made to relatives who are expected to be the most supportive, and sometimes the family protects the secret from members who are thought to be most unwilling to react positively.

Several studies have focused on married bisexual, gay, or lesbian individuals coming out to their heterosexual spouses. Disclosure of the wife's bisexuality or lesbianism seems almost always to lead to divorce; thus, most research has focused on bisexual or gay men who remain married (Coleman 1985a). Disclosure of the husband's gay or bisexual orientation also often results in separation or divorce (Bozett 1982; Miller 1978, 1979). Sometimes, however, disclosure ends barriers to intimacy in marriage and helps to integrate homosexuality or bisexuality into restructured marital relationships, such as open or semiopen marriages or asexual friendships (Brownfain 1985; Coleman 1985b; Gochros 1989; Latham and White 1978; Wolfe 1985). In general, bisexual-identified men report greater contentment in marriages, more sexual activity with wives, and longer marriages than men who are gay identified (Brownfain 1985). The most salient factors for the stabilization of mixed-orientation marriages appear to be that the bisexual orientation is disclosed by husbands early and acknowledged by spouses as a fact of the marriage and that the husbands show an ongoing ability to face their same-gender sexual desires realistically without losing empathy and concern for their wives' needs and rights (Gochros 1989; Matteson 1985, 1987). Wives have been found to react both to the homosexuality and to issues of isolation, lack of support, stigma, and loss (Auerback and Moser 1987; Gochros 1985; Hays and

Samuels 1989). Support groups for wives of gay and bisexual men have been found to be helpful in negotiating and adapting to the disclosure (Auerback and Moser 1987; Gochros 1989).

Researchers have noted that it is rare to find women who remain married or in sexually open relationships among bisexual samples (Coleman 1985a); in one study 97 percent of the lesbian wives were divorced, compared with 78 percent of gay husbands (Wyers 1987). The primary reasons lesbian and bisexual women give for ending their marriages relatively quickly are lack of sexual desire for the spouse, low tolerance for open marriages or for secretive extramarital relationships, and their husband's lack of tolerance of their bisexual life-style (Coleman 1985a; Matteson 1987).

> As in female homosexual relationships, bisexual women seem to be less able than bisexual males to tolerate multiple relationships. So in their marital relationships they might feel a greater need to end the relationship because of the basic incompatibility they perceive between their homosexual feelings and activities and their marriage. In addition, their husbands might not be able to tolerate their wives' homosexual activity, although, with the roles reversed, such a double standard allows the males to tolerate their own outside homosexual interests and activities without much difficulty. (Coleman 1985a:97)

It should be noted that these differences in the marital adaptations of bisexual and homosexual men and women may reflect gender differences between women and men.

Coming out at work typically causes lesbians and gay men a great deal of anxiety about both formal and informal employment discrimination (Levine and Leonard 1984). For example, more than two-thirds of gay men and lesbians reported, in surveys conducted across a variety of occupational and work settings (Levine and Leonard 1984; Winkelpleck and Westfield 1982), that their disclosure would be a problem at work. Reports of actual discrimination and related problems at work ranged from 20 percent to 35 percent (Blumstein and Schwartz 1983; Bradford and Ryan 1987; Taylor 1986). Lesbians appear to experience double jeopardy in the work setting both as women and as lesbians (Hall 1989; Schneider 1986). Gay men and lesbians in higher-status occupations are less likely to disclose their sexual identity at work than those in lower-status occupations (Bradford and Ryan 1987; Harry and Duvall 1978; Schneider 1986). The most common coping strategy reported is that gay men and lesbians tend to lead a somewhat double life at work, putting a significant amount of energy into monitoring a heterosexual facade through the use of managed information, avoidance of leisure with coworkers, and separation of work and home life (Hall 1989; Shachar and Gilbert 1983). Usually they come out to coworkers more frequently than to employers and use a strategy of partial and highly selective disclosure (Bell and Weinberg 1978; Olsen 1987; Weinberg and Williams 1974). Often, lesbians and gay men experience at work the greatest discrepancy between the extent to which they would like to be out and the degree to which they actually are open (cf. Kooden et al. 1979). Other solutions adopted include self-employment and forming support groups at work sites or within one's profession or career (Bell and Weinberg 1978; Levine and Leonard 1984; Russo 1982).

SOME DIFFERENCES BETWEEN GAY MEN AND LESBIANS

Gender is a powerful organizer of sexual behavior, identity, and relationship patterns. In general, gay men are more similar to heterosexual men, and lesbian women more similar to heterosexual women, than to each other. For example, in an undergraduate course on the psychology of the lesbian experience taught by Linda Garnets, the gay men and lesbians initially are closely aligned. As the class progresses, however, the alliances switch: the lesbian and heterosexual women feel they share more in common, and the gay and heterosexual men experience greater similarities. On the one hand, lesbians and gay men experience the same social pressure to conform to gender expectations as is the case for others. Moreover, they share many gender-typed experiences and predispositions with others of the same gender. On the other hand, they create patterns of behavior, identity, and relationships that neither mirror nor duplicate heterosexual patterns.

GENDER DIFFERENCES IN ROLES AND BEHAVIOR

In the United States, what it means not to be heterosexual is different in many respects for lesbians and gay men. In particular, lesbians share with women the institutional oppression of sexism (which includes access to fewer material resources) and with gay men the denial of civil rights and the social stigma of homosexuality (Eldridge 1987; Zimmerman 1984). Moreover, women and men are unequally constrained from same-gender intimacy and from gender nonconformity (Blumstein and Schwartz 1989; Henderson 1984). In short, lesbians are not identical to gay men.

Heterosexual masculinity is an identity defined in terms both of what it is and what it is not: the absence of any trace of femininity or any interest in men that could be interpreted as potentially homosexual (Herek 1986; Thompson and Pleck 1986). Endorsement of traditional masculine roles is related to fear of femininity and homophobia (Herek 1988; O'Neill, Helms, and Gable 1986). In addition, men are socialized to be sexually active and initiating and to strive for immediate gratification. They receive greater social support than women do for sexual experimentation, for separating sex and love, and for enjoying casual sex for its own sake without emotional involvement (Fracher and Kimmel 1987; Gagnon and Simon 1973).

Heterosexual femininity involves assuming social roles, specifically those of wife and mother. This is achieved by learning to attract a man and to define oneself in terms of psychological, emotional, and physical dependence on men. Part of the ideology of heterosexual femininity is experiencing male approval and love as central to self-esteem (Faraday 1981). Women learn to be sexual in the context of social relationships, to place constraints on exploration of their sexuality, to emphasize feelings, to minimize the importance of immediate sexual activity, to experience emotional involvement and commitment toward another person before sexual activity is initiated, and to be reactive to male sexual needs. As a result, female gender socialization may limit sexual expression for both heterosexual and lesbian women and inhibit discovery on one's unique sexuality (Blackwood 1985; Faraday 1981; Palladino and Stephenson 1990).

Gay men tend to be sexually active with male partners before labeling themselves as gay and generally seek experiences in settings where they gather for sexual purposes to help define themselves as gay (Dank 1971; Herdt 1989; Larsen 1982; Weinberg 1978). For example, Paroski (1987), in a study of gay male and lesbian adolescents, found that 95 percent of males compared to 16 percent of females learned about homosexuality through sexual encounters; similarly, he reported that 81 percent of males and 31 percent of females visited locations thought or known to be gay or lesbian (many of these places, such as public rest rooms, are used only by men for sexual purposes). Moreover, gay men are likely to have sexual experiences with a variety of partners before they focus on one special person (Bell and Weinberg 1978; Sears 1989; Weinberg and Williams 1974). Sexual and erotic compatibility (e.g., physical appearance) appears to be more salient for gay men than for lesbians in selecting partners (Blumstein and Schwartz 1983; Sergio and Cody 1985). Gay men tend to develop affectional relationships out of sexual ones (Harry 1983). These patterns parallel data on heterosexual men (Green 1985; Hunt 1974; Phillis and Gramko 1985; Wilson 1987).

Lesbians tend to experience sexual feelings in situations of romantic love and emotional attachment (Blumstein and Schwartz 1989; Vetere 1983). Several studies have shown that lesbians experience emotional attraction to another female several years before experiencing physical attraction—mean ages were 14.5 and 17.4 years, respectively (Gramick 1984; Vance and Green 1984; cf. Schaefer 1977). Unlike gay men, lesbians are more likely to have sexual experiences in the context of emotional relationships with one woman or a series of "special women" (Hedblom 1973; Ponse 1978; Sears 1989). Many lesbians have their first same-gender sexual experience with a peer or in a friendship context (Schaefer 1977; Vetere 1983). Moreover, women who identify as lesbian tend to do so primarily on the basis of a lesbian relationship and only secondarily on the basis of sexual contact. These findings parallel data on heterosexual women (Blumstein and Schwartz 1989; Wilson 1987).

In summary, gay men are similar to heterosexual men and lesbians are similar to heterosexual women. Gay men and lesbians, however, do not adhere rigidly to traditional gender roles (Kurdek 1987; Kurdek and Schmitt 1986a; Macklin 1983). Frequently, gay men and lesbians adopt a nontraditional identity that includes nontraditional gender role norms. Thus, the experience of gay men and lesbians provides a unique opportunity to see the impact on identity, behavior, and relationships when the traditional patterns based on gender are reduced or removed.

Differences in Meaning of Sexual Feelings and Experiences

Gay men have been noted to emphasize erotic and genital meanings of their sexual relationships (Riddle and Morin 1977; Sears 1989). Moreover, gay men tend to believe that sexual orientation is discovered and to define gay in terms of sexual arousal and sexual behavior (Hencken 1984). Lesbians are more likely than are gay men to define their sexual identity in terms of affectional preferences (emotional quality and love between partners), political choices (affirmation of solidarity with all women or breaking with certain traditional standards of behavior for women), and the idea that sexual orientation is chosen (Hunnisett 1986; Peplau and Cochran 1981; Ponse 1984; Vetere 1983). Moreover, lesbians are more likely than gay men to define themselves in terms of their total identity and not only by their sexual behavior (Faderman 1984; Ponse 1984). It has been suggested by Blumstein and Schwartz (1989) that if the Kinsey scale were to assess sexuality in women more accurately, it would have evaluated the "intensity and frequency of love relationships, some of which might have only incidental, overt erotic components" (p. 23). For example, a lesbian in Sears's (1989) study defined a homosexual as a person who "has intimate love for a person of the same sex." A gay man in this study defined a homosexual as "someone who has sex with the same sex."

Likewise, gay men and lesbians use different stigma-management strategies in order to avoid labeling themselves as gay or lesbian (de Monteflores and Schultz 1978; Groves and Ventura 1983; Hencken 1984). Consistent with male role expectations, gay men tend to use strategies that deny affective involvement in order to minimize the importance of sexual experiences with men. For example, Hencken (1984) noted that gay men may neutralize emotions by emphasizing sexual gratification as a goal of sexuality ("It's just physical," "I was just horny") or by denying responsibilities for feelings or actions ("I was drunk"). Lesbians are more likely to avoid identifying as lesbian by emphasizing their feelings and minimizing the saliency of sexuality than are gay men. For example, lesbians more often report using the "special case" strategy to avoid identifying as gay; they romanticize sexual events and explain them in terms of intense love and feeling for a particular woman (de Monteflores and Schultz 1978; Hencken 1984): "I never thought of my feelings and our lovemaking as lesbian. The whole experience was too beautiful for it to be something so ugly. I didn't think I could ever have those feelings for another woman" (Troiden 1988:49).

SANCTIONS FOR VIOLATING MALE AND FEMALE GENDER ROLES

In order to assume a gay male or lesbian identity, individuals must diverge from traditional gender norms regarding sexual behavior. As children both lesbians and gay men report a similar incidence of cross-gender behavior (60 percent in one study), but girls are much less likely to experience harassment for it (Sears 1989). As a consequence, gay men may become sensitized sooner in childhood to being "different" (Bell and Weinberg 1978; Bell, Weinberg, and Hammersmith 1981; Troiden 1988). These data are consistent with those found for heterosexual boys and girls. That is, girls who act like boys receive fewer negative sanctions than boys who act like girls. Both mothers and fathers view cross-gender activities as being more strongly associated with homosexuality for boys than for girls (Block 1983; Bolton and MacEachron 1988). Similarly, same-gender intimacy and affection are permitted in Anglo-European families for girls and women but are highly suspect for boys and men (Henderson 1984; Lewis 1978). Likewise, homophobic attitudes are more prevalent among men than among women, at least in heterosexual samples (Herek 1988; Kite 1984).

> Proving one's manhood/womanhood is in the popular imagination bound up with the rejection of any fag or dyke characteristics. If this seems more obvious in the case of men, it is because women have traditionally been defined as inferior, and whereas there is some grudging respect accorded women with masculine qualities, none is given to "womanly" men. Even among children "tomboys" are more acceptable than "sissies." (Altman 1971:69–70)

Fear of being labeled homosexual is an especially important socialization influence in American society. It is the most frequently selected as the "worst thing" a man can call another man (Preston and Stanley 1987). Both women and men who manifest characteristics inconsistent with those prescribed by the culture are more likely to be labeled homosexual (Deaux and Lewis 1984; Herek 1984; Storms et al. 1981). One significant function of this social stigma is to define limits of acceptable behavior for men and for women (Herek 1986). Thus, gender roles are enforced through the stigma of homosexuality. Moreover, the content of antigay stereotypes is tied to gender nonconformity (Herek 1991).

> Homophobia begins in elementary school when "girl," sissy," "queer," "virgin," and "fag" are the worst put-downs boys can hear. . . . Then homophobia begins to play itself out in locker-room talk where "the guys" boast of "scoring." To be "cool," and to avoid being called "gay," boys forcibly push for intercourse with girls. . . . Even masturbation is affected by homophobia and misogyny. In the hallways, and in sexuality education classes, boys often say, "only fags masturbate" or "why masturbate, you can always find an ugly girl willing to have sex." Homophobia thus encourages boys to label people based on stereotypes; to compete with and distance themselves from other boys; and to objectify, and even rape, girls. (Friedman 1989:8)

It therefore may be suggested that homophobia is harmful to heterosexuals as well as to lesbians and gay men because it keeps everyone in their place by raising fears that deviation from traditional gender roles will lead to one being seen as a "fag" or "lezzie."

GAY AND LESBIAN RELATIONSHIPS

Same-gender sexual relationships develop within a social context of societal disapproval with an absence of social legitimization and support; families and other social institutions often stigmatize such relationships and there are no prescribed roles and behaviors to structure such relationships (Dailey 1979; Kurdek and Schmitt 1987a; Risman and Schwartz 1988). In part because of the absence of prescribed patterns, lesbian and gay male relationships are diverse and do not conform to heterosexist role stereotypes (Peplau 1991). In contrast, they tend to rely on innovative processes of creating idiosyncratic rules, expectations, and division of labor within the relationship (Peplau and Cochran 1990). Moreover, same-gender sexual relationships tend to be as loving, committed, stable, and satisfying as heterosexual marriages (Kurdek and Schmitt 1986c; Peplau and Gordon 1983): "Same-sex relationships seem to be a naturally occurring experiment in role-free relationships" (Harry 1984:3).

Researchers have investigated the experiences of gay men and lesbians and made comparisons across married, cohabiting heterosexual, gay male, and lesbian couples. The same-gender and cross-gender comparisons have provided an opportunity to assess varying influences of gender and sexual orientation on intimate relationships, the unique characteristics of gay male and lesbian relationships, and factors that characterize intimate relationships regardless of sexual orientation. Some of the major findings are the following:

1. Many similarities are found between heterosexual and homosexual couples, indicating commonality in dynamics within the relationship and a similar range of diversity among relationships (Dailey 1979; Eldridge and Gilbert 1990; Jones and DeCecco 1982; Kurdek and Schmitt 1987a). For example, homosexual and heterosexual couples matched on age, education, and length of relationship reported similar relationship values and level of relationship satisfaction (related to duration of the relationship), perceived the relationship as loving and satisfying, and sought similar characteristics in their partners (Cardell, Finn, and Marecek 1981; Kurdek and Schmitt 1986c; Harry 1983; Peplau and Cochran 1981; Peplau, Cochran, and Mays 1986).

2. Gender roles appear to be more powerful than sexual orientation in influencing behaviors in intimate relationships. In general, gender roles exert stronger effects than biological sex; for example, relationships in which both partners were androgynous or feminine showed higher relationship quality than for masculine or undifferentiated partners (Kurdek 1987). Psychological femininity has been associated with stability, security, and support for continuation of both heterosexual and homosexual relationships (Schullo and Alperson 1984), intimacy among gay men (Harry

1984), and constructive responses to dissatisfaction in close relationships (Rusbult, Zembrodt, and Iwaniszek 1986).

3. Gay men and lesbians bring to love relationships many of the same expectations, values, and interests as heterosexuals of the same gender. That is, lesbians are more likely than gay men to live with their primary partner and be in a steady relationship (Bell and Weinberg 1978; Duffy and Rusbult 1986; Peplau and Amaro 1982; Schaefer 1977); prefer having sex only with partners they care about, view sexuality and love as closely linked, and desire sexual exclusivity (Bell and Weinberg 1978; Cotton 1974; Peplau and Amaro 1982; Schaefer 1977); place greater importance on emotional intimacy (Blumstein and Schwartz 1983; Kurdek and Schmitt 1986a; Lewis, Kozac, and Grosnick 1981; Vetere 1983); value and have equality of involvement and equality in power (Blumstein and Schwartz 1983; Caldwell and Peplau 1984; Lynch and Reilly 1986); and find variations in dyadic attachment and personal autonomy values to be more relevant and important to lesbian relationship experiences (Eldridge and Gilbert 1990; Peplau and Cochran 1981; Peplau et al. 1978). Gay men are more likely than lesbians to report an interest in sex, sexual variety, and for sexual openness to be the most frequent relationship pattern (Bell and Weinberg 1978; Blasband and Peplau 1985; Blumstein and Schwartz 1983; Peplau and Cochran 1981). A typical pattern is a progression from sexual exclusivity during the initial phase of the relationship toward greater sexual openness; gay male couples experiment with and modify sexually exclusive arrangements (Blasband and Peplau 1985). Researchers who have compared gay men in open and closed relationships have found no significant differences in psychological adjustment (Blasband and Peplau 1985; Harry 1984; Kurdek and Schmitt 1986b).

4. A gender-based division of labor is not necessary for relationships to function well. Traditional gender roles are less common in lesbian and gay couples than in heterosexual couples (Cardell, Finn, and Marecek 1981; Howard, Blumstein, and Schwartz 1986; Kurdek 1987; Marecek, Finn, and Cardell 1982). Partners in gay male and lesbian relationships show greater equality, reciprocity, and role flexibility than partners in heterosexual relationships (Blumstein and Schwartz 1983; Kurdek and Schmitt 1986c; Lynch and Reilly 1986). Most gay male and lesbian couples value power equality and shared decision making as a goal

for their relationships (Blumstein and Schwartz 1983; Kurdek and Schmitt 1986a; Peplau 1983). In general, lesbian and gay male couples frequently adopt a peer-friendship model of intimate relationships; few incorporate elements of husband-wife roles into their relationship (Bell and Weinberg 1978; Blumstein and Schwartz 1983; Caldwell and Peplau 1984; Harry 1983).

5. Lesbians and gay men and heterosexuals receive similar amounts of emotional and social support, but from different sources; nonetheless, they report similar levels of satisfaction (Kurdek 1988; Kurdek and Schmitt 1986c, 1987b; Peplau 1991). In general, married heterosexuals perceive greater levels of support from family of origin than do lesbians and gay men, whereas gay men and lesbians perceive greater support from friends and partners than do their heterosexual counterparts (Blumstein and Schwartz 1983; Kurdek 1988; Kurdek and Schmitt 1987b; McWhirter and Mattison 1984).

LESBIAN AND GAY PARENTING

Gay men and lesbians become parents in several ways: by heterosexual contact, often during a marriage; by alternative (artificial) insemination, in which the donor may or may not be known; by mutual agreement to rear a child communally, perhaps between a gay male couple and a lesbian couple (parenthood may be known or may be randomly selected); and by foster parenthood, where allowed, or by adoption—in which case, race or cultural background may be discordant from the parents and other siblings. Each of these types of parenthood presents unique issues, potential problems, and opportunities for creative innovation: "My younger son picked up a girl in a bar in Virginia Beach one summer who was grieving over her mother having come out to her. 'My Mom is a Lesbian, too,' he told her, and took her home to look through his photograph album at our pictures, our happy family" (MacPike 1989:37).

Considerable research attention has focused on lesbian and gay male parents, primarily because of custody and adoption issues. The findings have supported the conclusion that lesbian mothers are likely to be good parents and to have no ill effects on their children because of their sexual orientation (Falk 1989; Green et al. 1986; Hill 1987). Likewise, Green et al. (1986) reported no differences between children from heterosexual and lesbian families in peer group relationships, popularity, or social adjustment. Moreover, there is considerable evidence that the sexual orientation of mothers has no detrimental effect on the child's gender role development and is not associated with the child's sexual orientation (Falk 1989; Gibbs 1989; Green 1982; Green et al. 1986; Hoeffer 1981). Because women-headed households tend to be economically disadvantaged, whether they are lesbian or heterosexual, socioeconomic factors are likely to override sexual orientation in terms of effects on children of lesbian mothers. "They think . . . that instead of getting up / in the middle of the night / for a 2 A.M. and 6 A.M. feeding / we rise up and chant / *you're gonna be a dyke / you're gonna be a dyke*" (Parker 1987:208).

Although research on the effects of gay fathers is scarce, it suggests that gay fathers are likely to be good parents, that the children can cope with this family arrangement satisfactorily, and that the father's openness about his sexual orientation is beneficial (Bozett 1987, 1988, 1989; Miller 1979, 1987).

Some research has examined the effects of the social stigma of having a gay or lesbian parent on the child. In general, although such stigma exists, its effects have tended to be no greater than for children from divorcing families and may be offset by the parents' efforts to prevent or counteract it (Bozett 1987; Falk 1989). Likewise, parental disclosures of their sexual orientation appears to have a positive effect on the parent-child relationship by strengthening the relationship between gay male and lesbian parents and their children and by reducing the psychological distance between the parents and their children (Auerback and Mosher 1987; Bell and Weinberg 1978; Miller 1979). Moreover, parents often perceive benefits of disclosure for their children, such as learning to have empathy for others and an opportunity to be exposed to different viewpoints (Cramer 1986; Harris and Turner 1985).

> Rather than posing a menace to children, gays may actually facilitate important developmental learning. To offset the pressures of a heterosexual society toward adopting traditional sex-role behavior, gays often demonstrate a variety of alternative adaptations. . . . Presumably, an increased comfort with diversity could result in a greater ability to make personal choices independent of societal pressures to conform. Comfort with diversity appears crucial to effecting a reversal of present attitudes towards homosexuality. (Riddle 1978:53)

Additional research is clearly needed on the uniqueness of lesbian and gay parenting, especially focusing on the growing number of lesbians and gay men who are choosing to parent and the complex issues of the effects of coparenting.

Similarly, greater research attention needs to be given to the uniqueness of lesbian and gay male experiences of other life span issues such as adolescence and aging.

> Lesbians who are middle-aged today are a unique population. We constitute the "Bridge Generation." We were young and most of us "came out" before the women's movement or the gay liberation movement. Our midlife changes are occurring in a world which is substantially different from the world in which we learned "how to be a lesbian." (Sang, Warshow, and Smith 1991)

CONCLUSIONS

The psychological study of lesbian and gay issues is an emerging field that has only begun to explore the ramifications of the social significance attributed to sexual orientation. Although homosexuality is no longer considered to be a form of mental illness, considerable attention has been given to a wide range of factors thought to predispose individuals to homosexuality. Nonetheless, today no more is known about the specific origins of sexual orientation than is known about the origins of other characteristics such as expertise in ballet, chess, or the violin. The best conclusion is that a complex set of factors interact, varying from individual to individual, to produce lesbian and gay adults. Likewise, the gay male and lesbian community is diverse and multiethnic and differs by gender, socioeconomic status, and few generalizations apply across cultural borders.

We have discussed the relevance of sexual orientation to the psychological understanding of people, the development of gay male and lesbian identity within a multicultural society, some differences between lesbians and gay men, and lesbian and gay male relationships and parenting. Throughout, we have noted the broader context of gender roles, social change, and the interrelation of these issues to the political arena. In concluding, we call attention to the salient issues for psychology in terms of practice and research.

Two waves of gay and lesbian affirmative practice have been noted (Gonsiorek 1988). The first wave assisted gay men and lesbians in understanding and accepting their sexual orientation as a natural part of themselves, helped them develop strategies for coping and forming a positive sense of identity, and taught them the effect of social attitudes, prejudice, discrimination, and heterosexism on psychological functioning. A second wave has now emerged, and four themes are evident: 1) using education, training, ethical and professional guidelines, and research to reduce bias in theories and practice; for example, a recent issue of *American Psychologist* focused on the theme of removing the stigma—fifteen years later; 2) integrating gay affirmative concepts into current personality theories and therapeutic approaches; 3) promoting empirical testing of gay affirmative modes and theories; and 4) examining ways in which gay and lesbian paradigms help inform and reconceptualize issues of sexuality, gender roles, identity, intimacy, family relationships, and life-span development.

> By defining norms and terms from within lesbian and gay realities, psychologists ask themselves how these new paradigms might broaden the understanding of heterosexual realities as well. (Brown 1989:454–55)

Similarly, psychological research has shifted from removing the stigma of pathology from lesbians and gay men to examining issues of implicit concern to them. Five major themes have emerged: 1) research on mental health has documented that as individuals, couples, and a social community, gay men and lesbians do not show lower levels of adjustment. Moreover, research has focused on the nature and impact of negative social attitudes toward lesbians and gay men and has documented the pervasive effects of heterosexist bias and homophobia within American society; 2) research has shifted from viewing homosexuals as a group with definite characteristics to a recognition of the diversity that exists among lesbians and gay men. This view has led to an increased awareness of the similarity between heterosexuals and homosexuals, on the one hand, while on the other, it has called attention to the effects of gender, ethnicity, race, age, socioeconomic status, geographic locale, and life-style on salient characteristics of gay men and lesbians; 3) theoretical perspectives on homosexuality have shifted from attention to an illness model that emphasized origins and treatment to an affirmative model that examines how gay men and lesbians form and maintain their identity and manage ordinary problems of life span development; 4) the view that sexual orientation is an inherent characteristic of an individual has been broadened to include the role of social and historical influences in shaping the meaning and expression of homosexuality; 5) the relationship between gender roles and sexual orientation has received greater attention. Research has indicated that gender is a central organizing factor for heterosexuals, lesbians, and gay men in personal experiences, values, and relationship styles.

Finally, the importance of understanding sexual orientation for heterosexuals has become apparent. Social policy, legislative deliberations, and judicial decisions have increasingly recognized the legitimacy of gay male and lesbian issues, often encouraged by psychological research and perspectives. Moreover, all people can benefit from acknowledging the restrictive constraint of heterosexist bias that limits behavior to rigid gender roles, requires 100 percent heterosexuality, and defines one's value as a man or woman by one's rejection of homosexuality. In particular, lesbians and gay men can make a contribution to greater appreciation of human diversity and the benefits that result from examining predetermined constraints that limit fulfillment of one's unique potential.

ACKNOWLEDGMENTS

We are grateful to several colleagues who read and commented on earlier drafts of this article: Connie Chan, Jacqueline Goodchilds, Greg Herek, Barrie Levy, Steve Morin, and Anne Peplau. We also thank Ron Schwizer for his technical assistance in preparing the manuscript and the slides for the lecture, and Elizabeth Sheldon for library research. The APA Continuing Education Committee was also very helpful in providing support for two lecturers to cover this topic.

REFERENCES

Abramson, P. R. 1986. The cultural context of Japanese sexuality: An American perspective. *Psychologia* 29:1–9.

Actenberg, R. 1988. Preserving and protecting the families of lesbians and gay men. In M. Shernoff and W. A. Scott, eds., *The Sourcebook on Lesbian/Gay Health Care*, pp. 237–45. Washington, D.C.: National Lesbian and Gay Health Foundation.

Adam, B. D. 1978. Inferiorization and self-esteem. *Social Psychology* 41:47–57.

Adam, B. 1987. *The Rise of a Gay and Lesbian Movement.* Boston: Twayne.

Altman, D. 1971. *Homosexual Oppression and Liberation.* New York: Outerbridge and Dienstfrey.

Altman, D. 1981. *Coming Out in the Seventies.* Boston: Alyson.

Amaro, H. 1978. "Coming out" conflicts for Hispanic lesbians. Paper presented at the National Coalition of Hispanic Mental Health and Human Service Organizations (COSSMHO), Austin, Tex., October 2.

Aoki, B. 1983. Gay Asian Americans: Adapting within the family context. Paper presented at the 91st Annual Convention of the American Psychological Association, Anaheim, Calif., August.

Auerback, S., and Moser, C. 1987. Groups for the wives of gay and bisexual men. *Social Work* 32:321–25.

Backer, T. E., W. F. Batchelor, J. M. Jones, and V. M. Mays. 1988. Introduction to the special issue: Psychology and AIDS. *American Psychologist* 43:835–36.

Barrett, S. E. 1990. Paths toward diversity: An intrapsychic perspective. *Women and Therapy* 9(1/2):41–52.

Bayer, R. 1981. *Homosexuality and American Psychiatry: The Politics of Diagnosis.* New York: Basic Books.

Bell, A. P., and M. S. Weinberg. 1978. *Homosexualities: A Study of Diversity among Men and Women.* New York: Simon and Schuster.

Bell, A. P., M. S. Weinberg, and S. K. Hammersmith. 1981. *Sexual Preference: Its Development in Men and Women.* Bloomington: Indiana University Press.

Bierly, M. M. 1985. Prejudice toward contemporary outgroups as a generalized attitude. *Journal of Applied Social Psychology* 15:189–99.

Blackwood, E. 1984. Sexuality and gender in certain Native American tribes: The case of cross-gender females. *Signs* 10:27–42.

Blackwood, E. 1985. Breaking the mirror: The construction of lesbianism and the anthropological discourse on homosexuality. *Journal of Homosexuality* 11(3–4):1–17.

Blasband, D., and L. A. Peplau. 1985. Sexual exclusivity versus openness in gay male couples. *Archives of Sexual Behavior* 14:395–412.

Block, J. H. 1983. Differential premises arising from differential socialization of the sexes: Some conjectures. *Child Development* 54:1335–54.

Blumstein, P., and P. Schwartz. 1977. Bisexuality: Some social psychological issues. *Journal of Social Issues* 33(2):30–45.

Blumstein, P., and P. Schwartz. 1983. *American Couples: Money, Work, Sex.* New York: Morrow.

Blumstein, P., and P. Schwartz. 1989. Intimate relationships and the creation of sexuality. In B. Risman and P. Schwartz, eds., *Gender in Intimate Relationships: A Microstructural Approach*, pp. 120–29. Belmont, Calif.: Wadsworth.

Bolton, F. G., and A. MacEachron. 1988. Adolescent male sexuality: A developmental perspective. *Journal of Adolescent Research* 3:259–73.

Boxer, A., and B. Cohler. 1989. The life course of gay and lesbian youth: An immodest proposal for the study of lives. *Journal of Homosexuality* 17(2–3–4):317–55.

Bozett, F. W. 1982. Heterogeneous couples in heterosexual marriages: Gay men and straight women. *Journal of Marital and Sexual Therapy* 8:81–89.

Bozett, F. W. 1987. Children of gay fathers. In F. W. Bozett, ed., *Gay and Lesbian Parents*, pp. 39–57. New York: Praeger.

Bozett, F. W. 1988. Social control of identity by children of gay fathers. *Western Journal of Nursing Research* 10:550–65.

Bozett, F. W. 1989. Gay fathers: A review of the literature. *Journal of Homosexuality* 18(1–2):137–62.

Bradford, J., and C. Ryan. 1987. *National Lesbian Health Care Survey. Mental Health Implications.* Washington, D.C.: National Lesbian and Gay Health Foundation.

Bradshaw, C. K. 1990. A Japanese view of dependency: What can Amae psychology contribute to feminist theory and therapy? *Women and Therapy* 9(1–2):67–86.

Brown, L. S. 1989. New voices, new visions: Toward a lesbian/gay paradigm for psychology. *Psychology of Women* 13:445–58.

Brownfain, J. J. 1985. A study of the married bisexual male: Paradox and resolution. *Journal of Homosexuality* 11(1–2):173–88.

Caldwell, M. A., and L. A. Peplau. 1984. The balance of power in lesbian relationships. *Sex Roles* 10:587–600.

Carballo-Dieguez, A. 1989. Hispanic culture, gay male culture, and AIDS: Counseling implications. *Journal of Counseling and Development* 68:26–30.

Cardell, M., S. Finn, and J. Marecek. 1981. Sex-role identity, sex-role behavior, and satisfaction in heterosexual, lesbian, and gay male couples. *Psychology of Women Quarterly* 5:488–94.

Carrier, J. M. 1976. Cultural factors affecting urban Mexican male homosexual behavior. *Archives of Sexual Behavior* 5:103–24.

Carrier, J. M. 1980. Homosexual behavior in cross-cultural perspective. In J. Marmor, ed., *Homosexual Behavior: A Modern Reappraisal*, pp. 100–22. New York: Basic Books.

Carrier, J. M. 1985. Mexican male bisexuality. *Journal of Homosexuality* 11(1–2):75–85.

Cass, V. C. 1979. Homosexual identity formation: A theoretical model. *Journal of Homosexuality* 4(3):219–35.

Cass, V. C. 1984. Homosexual identity formation: Testing a theoretical model. *Journal of Sex Research* 20:143–67.

Cazenave, N. A. 1979. Social structure and personal choice. Effects on intimacy, marriage and the family alternative lifestyle research. *Alternative Lifestyles* 2:331–58.

Cazenave, N. A. 1984. Race, socioeconomic status, and age: The social context of American masculinity. *Sex Roles* 11:639–56.

Chan, C. S. 1987. Asian lesbians: Psychological issues in the "coming out" process. *Asian American Psychological Association Journal* 12(1):16–18.

Chan, C. S. 1989. Issues of identity development among Asian American lesbians and gay men. *Journal of Counseling and Development* 68:16–20.

Chapman, B. E., and J. C. Brannock. 1987. A proposed model of lesbian identity development: An empirical investigation. *Journal of Homosexuality* 14(3–4):69–80.

Coleman E. 1981/1982. Developmental stages of the coming-out process. *Journal of Homosexuality* 7:31–43.

Coleman, E. 1985a. Bisexual women in marriages. *Journal of Homosexuality* 11(1–2):87–99.

Coleman, E. 1985b. Integration of male bisexuality and marriage. *Journal of Homosexuality* 11(1–2):189–207.

Coleman, E. 1987. Assessment of sexual orientation. *Journal of Homosexuality* 14(1–2):9–24.

Collins, L., and N. Zimmerman. 1983. Homosexual and bisexual issues. In J. C. Hansen, J. D. Woody, and R. H. Woody, eds., *Sexual Issues in Family Therapy*, pp. 82–100. Rockville, Md.: Aspen.

Committee on Lesbian and Gay Concerns. 1990. *Final Report of the Task Force on Bias in Psychotherapy With Lesbians and Gay Men*. Washington, D.C.: American Psychological Association.

Conger, J. J. 1975. Proceedings of the American Psychological Association, Incorporated, for the year 1974: Minutes of the annual meeting of the Council of Representatives. *American Psychologist* 30:620–51.

Cotton, W. L. 1974. Social and sexual relationships of lesbians. *Journal of Sex Research* 11:139–48.

Cramer, D. 1986. Gay parents and their children: A review of research and practical implications. *Journal of Counseling and Development* 64:504–7.

Cramer, D. W., and A. S. Roach. 1988. Coming out to mom and dad: A study of gay males and their relationships with their parents. *Journal of Homosexuality* 15(3–4):79–91.

Dailey, D. M. 1979. Adjustment of heterosexual and homosexual couples in pairing relationships: An exploratory study. *Journal of Sex Research* 15:143–57.

Dank, B. M. 1971. Coming out in the gay world. *Psychiatry* 34:180–97.

Deaux, K., and L. L. Lewis. 1984. Structure of gender stereotypes: Interrelationships among components and gender label. *Journal of Personality and Social Psychology* 46:991–1004.

D'Augelli, A. R. 1989. The development of a helping community for lesbians and gay men: A case study in community psychology. *Journal of Community Psychology* 17:18–29.

D'Augelli, A. R., C. Collins, and M. Hart. 1987. Social support patterns of lesbian women in a rural helping network. *Journal of Rural Community Psychology* 8:12–22.

D'Emilio, J. 1983. *Sexual Politics, Sexual Communities: The Making of a Homosexual Minority in the United States, 1940–1970.* Chicago: University of Chicago Press.

de Monteflores, C. 1981. Conflicting allegiances: Therapy issues with Hispanic lesbians. *Catalyst* 12:31–36.

de Monteflores, C. 1986. Notes on the management of difference. In T. Stein and C. Cohen, eds., *Contemporary Perspectives on Psychotherapy with Lesbians and Gay Men*, pp. 73–101. New York: Plenum Press.

de Monteflores, C., and S. Schultz. 1978. Coming out: Similarities and differences for lesbians and gay men. *Journal of Social Issues* 34(3):59–72.

Devine, J. L. 1984. A systematic inspection of affectional preference orientation and the family of origin. *Journal of Social Work and Human Sexuality* 2(2–3):9–17.

Dixon, J. K. 1984. The commencement of bisexual activity in swinging married women over age thirty. *Journal of Sex Research* 20:71–90.

Dixon, J. K. 1985. Sexuality and relationship changes in married females following the commencement of bisexual activity. *Journal of Homosexuality* 11(1–2):115–33.

Duffy, S. M., and C. E. Rusbult. 1986. Satisfaction and commitment in homosexual and heterosexual relationships. *Journal of Homosexuality* 12(2):1–24.

Eldridge, N. S. 1987. Gender issues in counseling same-sex couples. *Professional Psychology: Research and Practice* 18:567–72.

Eldridge, N. S., and L. A. Gilbert. 1990. Correlates of relationship satisfaction in lesbian couples. *Psychology of Women Quarterly* 14:43–62.

Ericksen, J. A. 1980. Race, sex, and alternative lifestyle choices. *Alternative Lifestyles* 3:405–24.

Espín, 0. M. 1984. Cultural and historical influences on sexuality in Hispanic/Latin women: Implications for psychotherapy. In C. Vance, ed., *Pleasure and Danger. Exploring Female Sexuality*, pp. 149–63. London: Routledge and Kegan Paul.

Espín, 0. M. 1987. Issues of identity in the psychology of Latina lesbians. In Boston

Lesbian Psychologies Collective, eds., *Lesbian Psychologies: Explorations and Challenges*, pp. 35–51. Urbana: University of Illinois Press.

Faderman, L. 1984. The "new gay" lesbian. *Journal of Homosexuality* 10(3–4):85–95.

Falk, P. J. 1989. Lesbian mothers: Psychosocial assumptions in family law. *American Psychologist* 44:941–47.

Faraday, A. 1981. Liberating lesbian research. In K. Plummer, ed., *The Making of the Modern Homosexual*, pp. 112–29. London: Hutchinson.

Fein, S. B., and E. M. Nuehring. 1981. Intrapsychic effects of stigma: A process of breakdown and reconstruction of social reality. *Journal of Homosexuality* 7(1):3–13.

Ford, C. S., and F. Beach. 1951. *Patterns of Sexual Behavior*. New York: Harper.

Foucault, M. 1979. *The History of Sexuality*. London: Allen Lane.

Fracher, J. C., and M. S. Kimmel. 1987. Hard issues and soft spots: Counseling men about sexuality. In M. Scher, M. Stevens, G. Good, and G. A. Eichenfield, eds., *Handbook of Counseling and Psychotherapy with Men*, pp. 83–96. Newbury Park, Calif.: Sage.

Friedman, J. 1989. The impact of homophobia on male sexual development. *Siecus Report* 17(5):8–9.

Gagnon, J. H., and W. Simon. 1973. *Sexual Conduct: The Social Sources of Human Sexuality*. Chicago: Aldine.

Garnets, L., G. M. Herek, and B. Levy. 1990. Violence and victimization of lesbians and gay men: Mental health consequences. *Journal of Interpersonal Violence* 5:366–83.

Gibbs, E. D. 1989. Psychological development of children raised by lesbian mothers: A review of research. *Women and Therapy* 8(1–2):65–75.

Gillow, K. E., and L. L. Davis. 1987. Lesbian stress and coping methods. *Journal of Psychosocial Nursing* 25(9):28–32.

Gladue, B. A. 1987. Psychobiological contributions. In L. Diamant, ed., *Male and Female Homosexuality: Psychological Approaches*, pp. 129–53. Washington, D.C.: Hemisphere.

Gladue, B. A., R. Green, and R. E. Hellman. 1984. Neuroendocrine response to estrogen and sexual orientation. *Science* 225:1496–99.

Gochros, J. S. 1985. Wives' reactions to learning that their husbands are bisexual. *Journal of Homosexuality* 11(1–2):101–13.

Gochros, J. S. 1989. *When Husbands Come Out of the Closet*. New York: Haworth.

Gock, T. 1986. Issues in gay affirmative psychotherapy with ethnically/culturally diverse populations. Paper presented at the 94th Annual Convention of the American Psychological Association, Washington, D.C., August.

Golden, C. 1987. Diversity and variability in women's sexual identities. In Boston Lesbian Psychologies Collective, eds., *Lesbian Psychologies: Explorations and Challenges*, pp. 19–34. Urbana: University of Illinois Press.

Gonsiorek, J. C. 1988. Current and future directions in gay/lesbian affirmative mental health practice. In M. Shernoff and W. A. Scott, eds., *The Sourcebook on Lesbian/Gay Health Care*, pp. 107–13. Washington, D.C.: National Lesbian and Gay Health Foundation.

Gramick, J. 1984. Developing a lesbian identity. In T. Darty and S. Potter, eds., *Women-Identified Women*, pp. 31–44. Palo Alto, Calif.: Mayfield.

Green, R. 1982. The best interests of the child with a lesbian mother. *American Academy of Psychiatry and the Law Bulletin* 10:7–15.

Green, R., J. B. Mandel, M. E. Hotvedt, J. Gray, and L. Smith. 1986. Lesbian mothers and their children: A comparison with solo parent heterosexual mothers and their children. *Archives of Sexual Behavior* 15:167–84.

Green, V. 1985. Experimental factors in childhood and adolescent sexual behavior: Family interactions and previous sexual experiences. *Journal of Sex Research* 21:157–82.

Greenberg, D. F. 1988. *The Construction of Homosexuality.* Chicago: University of Chicago Press.

Greene, B. 1986. When the therapist is white and the patient is black: Considerations for psychotherapy in the feminist heterosexual and lesbian communities. In D. Howard, ed., *The Dynamics of Feminist Therapy*, pp. 41–65. New York: Haworth.

Griffin, C., M. Wirth, and A. Wirth. 1986. *Beyond Acceptance: Parents of Lesbians and Gays Talk about Their Experiences.* Englewood Cliffs, N.J.: Prentice-Hall.

Groves, P., and L. Ventura. 1983. The lesbian coming out process: Therapeutic considerations. *Personnel and Guidance Journal* 61:146–49.

Hall, M. 1989. Private experiences in the public domain: Lesbians in organizations. In J. Hearn, D. L. Sheppard, P. Tancred-Sheriff, and G. Burrell, eds., *The Sexuality of Organization*, pp. 125–38. Newbury Park, Calif.: Sage.

Hammersmith, S. K., and M. S. Weinberg. 1973. Homosexual identity: Commitment, adjustments, and significant others. *Sociometry* 36(1):56–78.

Hanley-Hackenbruck, P. 1988. Psychotherapy and the "coming out" process. *Journal of Gay and Lesbian Psychotherapy* 1(1):21–39.

Harris, M. B., and P. H. Turner. 1985. Gay and lesbian parents. *Journal of Homosexuality* 12(2):101–13.

Harry, J. 1983. Gay male and lesbian relationships. In E. Macklin and R. Rubin, eds., *Contemporary Families and Alternative Lifestyles: Handbook on Research and Theory*, pp. 216–34. Beverly Hills, Calif.: Sage.

Harry, J. 1984. *Gay Couples.* New York: Praeger.

Harry, J., and W. B. Duvall. 1978. *The Social Organization of Gay Males.* New York: Praeger.

Hart, J., and D. Richardson, eds. 1981. *The Theory and Practice of Homosexuality.* London: Routledge and Kegan Paul.

Hay, H. 1990. Identifying as gay there's the key. *Gay Community News* (April 22–28):5.

Hays, D., and A. Samuels. 1989. Heterosexual women's perceptions of their marriage to bisexual or homosexual men. *Journal of Homosexuality* 18(1–2):81–100.

Hedblom, J. H. 1973. Dimensions of lesbian sexual experience. *Archives of Sexual Behavior* 2:329–41.

Hencken, J. 1984. Conceptualizations of homosexual behavior which preclude homosexual self-labeling. *Journal of Homosexuality* 9(4):53–63.

Hencken, J., and W. O'Dowd. 1977. Coming out as an aspect of identity formation. *Gai Saber* 1(1):18–22.

Henderson, A. I. 1984. Homosexuality in the college years: Developmental differences between men and women. *Journal of American College Health* 32:216–19.

Hendricks, S. E., B. Graber, and J. F. Rodriguez-Sierra. 1989. Neuroendocrine responses to exogenous estrogen: No differences between heterosexual and homosexual men. *Psychoneuroendocrinology* 14:177–85.

Herdt, G. 1989. Gay and lesbian youth, emergent identities, and cultural scenes at home and abroad. *Journal of Homosexuality* 17(1–4):1–42.

Herek, G. M. 1984. Attitudes toward lesbians and gay men: A factor-analytic study. *Journal of Homosexuality* 10(1–2):39–52.

Herek, G. M. 1985. On doing, being, and not being: Prejudice and the social construction of sexuality. *Journal of Homosexuality* 12(1):135–51.

Herek, G. M. 1986. On heterosexual masculinity: Some psychical consequences of the social construction of gender and sexuality. *American Behavioral Scientist* 29:563–77.

Herek, G. M. 1988. Heterosexuals' attitudes toward lesbians and gay men: Correlates and gender differences. *Journal of Sex Research* 25:451–77.

Herek, G. M. 1989. Hate crimes against lesbians and gay men: Issues for research and policy. *American Psychologist* 44:948–55.

Herek, G. M. 1990a. Gay people and government security clearances: A social science perspective. *American Psychologist* 45:1035–42.

Herek, G. M. 1990b. Illness, stigma, and AIDS. In G. R. VandenBos and P. T. Costa, eds., *Psychological Aspects of Serious Illness*, pp. 107–50. Washington, D.C.: American Psychological Association.

Herek, G. M. 1991. Stigma, prejudice, and violence against lesbians and gay men. In J. C. Gonsiorek and J. D. Weinrich, eds., *Homosexuality: Research Findings for Public Policy*, pp. 60–80. Newbury Park, Calif.: Sage.

Hidalgo, H. A. 1984. The Puerto Rican lesbian in the United States. In T. Darty and S. Potter, eds., *Women-Identified Women*, pp. 105–15. Palo Alto, Calif.: Mayfield.

Hill, M. 1987. Child-rearing attitudes of Black lesbian mothers. In Boston Lesbian Psychologies Collective, ed., *Lesbian Psychologies: Explorations and Challenges*, pp. 215–26. Urbana: University of Illinois Press.

Hoeffer, B. 1981. Children's acquisition of sex-role behavior in lesbian-mother families. *American Journal of Orthopsychiatry* 51:536–44.

Hollander, J. P. 1989. Restructuring lesbian social networks: Evaluation of an intervention. *Journal of Gay and Lesbian Psychotherapy* 1:63–71.

Hooker, E. 1957. The adjustment of the male overt homosexual. *Journal of Projective Techniques* 21:18–31.

Howard, J. A., Blumstein, P., and P. Schwartz. 1986. Sex, power, and influence tactics in intimate relationships. *Journal of Personality and Social Psychology* 51:102–9.

Hunnisett, R. 1986. Developing phenomenological method for researching lesbian existence. *Canadian Journal of Counseling* 20:255–86.

Hunt, M. 1974. *Sexual Behavior in the 1970s*. Chicago: Playboy Press.

Icard, L. 1985/1986. Black gay men and conflicting social identities: Sexual orientation versus racial identity. *Journal of Social Work and Human Sexuality* 4:83–92.

Jay, K., and A. Young. 1979. *The Gay Report.* New York: Summit.

Jones, R. W., and J. P. DeCecco. 1982. The femininity and masculinity of partners in heterosexual and homosexual relationships. *Journal of Homosexuality* 8(2):37–44.

Kanuha, V. 1990. Compounding the triple jeopardy: Battering in lesbian of color relationships. *Women and Therapy* 9:169–84.

Kimmel, D. C. 1978. Adult development and aging: A gay perspective. *Journal of Social Issues* 34:113–30.

Kinsey, A. C., W. B. Pomeroy., and C. E. Martin. 1948. *Sexual Behavior in the Human Male.* Philadelphia: W. B. Saunders.

Kinsey, A. C., W. B. Pomeroy, C. E. Martin, and P. H. Gebhard. 1953. *Sexual Behavior in the Human Female.* Philadelphia: W. B. Saunders.

Kite, M. E. 1984. Sex differences in attitudes towards homosexuals: A meta-analytic review. *Journal of Homosexuality* 10(1–2):69–81.

Kitzinger, C. 1987. *The Social Construction of Lesbianism.* London: Sage.

Klein, C. 1986. *Counseling Our Own.* Seattle: Consultant Services Northwest.

Klein, F., B. Sepekoff, and T. J. Wolf. 1986. Sexual orientation: A multi-variable dynamic process. *Journal of Homosexuality* 11(1–2):35–49.

Kleinberg, L. 1986. *Coming Home to Self, Going Home to Parents: Lesbian Identity Disclosure.* Stone Center Work in Progress Series, no. 24. Wellesley, Mass.: Wellesley College.

Kolodny, R. C., W. H. Masters, J. Hendryx, and G. Toro. 1971. Plasma testosterone and semen analysis in male homosexuals. *New England Journal of Medicine* 285:1170–74.

Kooden, H. D., S. F. Morin, D. I. Riddle, M. Rogers, B. E. Sang, and F. Strassburger. 1979. *Removing the Stigma: Final Report of the Board of Social and Ethical Responsibility for Psychology's Task Force on the Status of Lesbian and Gay Male Psychologists.* Washington, D.C.: American Psychological Association.

Krieger, S. 1982. Lesbian identity and community: Recent social science literature. *Signs* 8:91–108.

Kurdek, L. A. 1987. Sex role self-schema and psychological adjustment in coupled homosexual and heterosexual men and women. *Sex Roles* 17:549–62.

Kurdek, L. A. 1988. Perceived social support in gays and lesbians in cohabiting relationships. *Journal of Personality and Social Psychology* 54:504–9.

Kurdek, L. A., and J. P. Schmitt. 1986a. Interaction of sex role self concept with relationship quality and relationship beliefs in married, heterosexual cohabiting, gay and lesbian relationships. *Journal of Personality and Social Psychology* 51:365–70.

Kurdek, L. A., and J. P. Schmitt. 1986b. Relationship quality of gay men in closed or open relationships. *Journal of Homosexuality* 12(2):85–99.

Kurdek, L. A., and J. P. Schmitt. 1986c. Relationship quality of partners in heterosexual married, heterosexual cohabiting, and gay and lesbian relationships. *Journal of Personality and Social Psychology* 51:711–20.

Kurdek, L. A., and J. P. Schmitt. 1987a. Partner homogamy in married, heterosexual cohabiting, gay, and lesbian couples. *Journal of Sex Research* 23:212–32.

Kurdek, L. A., and J. P. Schmitt. 1987b. Perceived emotional support from family and friends in members of gay, lesbian, and heterosexual cohabiting couples. *Journal of Homosexuality* 14(3–4):57–68.

Larsen, P. C. 1981. Sexual identity and self-concept. *Journal of Homosexuality* 7(1):15–32.

Larsen, P. C. 1982. Gay male relationships. In W. Paul, J. D. Weinrich, J. C. Gonsiorek, and M. E. Hotvedt, eds., *Homosexuality: Social, Psychological, and Biological Issues*, pp. 219–32. Beverly Hills, Calif.: Sage.

Latham, J. D., and G. D. White. 1978. Coping with homosexual expression within heterosexual marriages: Five case studies. *Journal of Sex and Marital Therapy* 4:198–212.

LaTorre, R. A., and K. Wedenberg. 1983. Psychological characteristics of bisexual, heterosexual, and homosexual women. *Journal of Homosexuality* 91:87–97.

Leavy, R., and E. Adams. 1986. Feminism as a correlate of self-esteem, self-acceptance, and social support among lesbians. *Psychology of Women Quarterly* 10:321–26.

Lee, J. A. 1977. Going public: A study in the sociology of homosexual liberation. *Journal of Homosexuality* 31:49–78.

Lee, D. B., and T. T. Saul. 1987. Counseling Asian men. In M. Scher, M. Stevens, G. Good, and G. A. Eichenfield, eds., *Handbook of Counseling and Psychotherapy with Men*, pp. 180–91. Newbury Park, Calif.: Sage.

Levine, M. P. 1979. Employment discrimination against gay men. *International Review of Modern Sociology* 9(5–7):151–63.

Levine, M. P., and Leonard, R. 1984. Discrimination against lesbians in the workforce. *Signs* 9:700–10.

Lewis, L. A. 1984. The coming out process for lesbians: Integrating a stable identity. *Social Work* 29:464–69.

Lewis, R. 1978. Emotional intimacy among men. *Journal of Social Issues* 34(1):108–21.

Lewis, R. A., E. B. Kozac, and W. A. Grosnick. 1981. Commitment in same-sex love relationships. *Alternative Lifestyles* 4:22–42.

Lin, Y. 1978. The spectrum of lesbian experience: Personal testimony. In G. Vida, ed., *Our Right to Love: A Lesbian Resource Book*, pp. 227–29. Englewood Cliffs, N.J.: Prentice-Hall.

Lockard, D. 1985. The lesbian community: An anthropological approach. *Journal of Homosexuality* 11(3–4):83–95.

Loiacano, D. K. 1989. Gay identity issues among black Americans: Racism, homophobia, and the need for validation. *Journal of Counseling and Development* 68:21–25.

Lowenstein, S. F. 1985. On the diversity of love object orientations among women. *Journal of Social Work and Human Sexuality* 3(2/3):7–24.

Lynch, F. R. 1987. Non-ghetto gays: A sociological study of suburban homosexuals. *Journal of Homosexuality* 13(4):13–42.

Lynch, J. M., and M. E. Reilly. 1986. Role relationships: Lesbian perspectives. *Journal of Homosexuality* 12(2):53–69.

MacDonald, A. P., Jr. 1983. A little bit of lavender goes a long way: A critique of research on sexual orientation. *Journal of Sex Research* 19:94–100.

McDonald, G. J. 1982. Individual differences in the coming out process of gay men: Implications for theoretical models. *Journal of Homosexuality* 8(1):47–60.

Macklin, E. D. 1983. Effect of changing sex roles on the intimate relationships of men and women. *Marriage and Family Review* 6(3–4):97–113.

MacPike, L., ed. 1989. *There's Something I've Been Meaning to Tell You.* Tallahassee, Fla.: Naiad Press.

McWhirter, D. P., and A. M. Mattison. 1984. *The Male Couple.* Englewood Cliffs, N.J.: Prentice-Hall.

Malyon, A. K. 1982. Psychotherapeutic implications of internalized homophobia in gay men. *Journal of Homosexuality* 7(2–3):59–69.

Marecek, J., S. E. Finn, and M. Cardell. 1982. Gender roles in the relationships of lesbians and gay men. *Journal of Homosexuality* 8(2):45–49.

Masters, W. H., and V. E. Johnson. 1979. *Homosexuality in Perspective.* Boston: Little, Brown.

Matteson, D. R. 1985. Bisexual men in marriage: Is a positive homosexual identity and stable marriage possible? *Journal of Homosexuality* 11(1–2):149–73.

Matteson, D. R. 1987. The heterosexually married gay and lesbian parent. In F. W. Bozett, ed., *Gay and Lesbian Parents,* pp. 138–61. New York: Praeger.

Mays, V. M. 1985. Black women working together: Diversity in same sex relationships. *Women's Studies International Forum* 8:67–71.

Mays, V. M., and S. D. Cochran. 1986. The Black Lesbian Relationship Project. Relationship experiences and the perception of discrimination. Paper presented at the 94th Annual Convention of the American Psychological Association, Washington, D.C., August.

Miller, B. 1978. Adult sexual resocialization: Adjustments towards a stigmatized identity. *Alternative Lifestyles* 1:207–34.

Miller, B. 1979. Gay fathers and their children. *Family Coordinator* 28:544–52.

Miller, B. 1987. Counseling gay husbands and fathers. In F. W. Bozett, ed., *Gay and Lesbian Parents,* pp. 175–87. New York: Praeger.

Minton, H. L., and G. J. McDonald. 1983/1984. Homosexual identity formation as a developmental process. *Journal of Homosexuality* 9(2–3):91–104.

Miranda, J., and M. Storms. 1989. Psychological adjustment of lesbians and gay men. *Journal of Counseling and Development* 68:41–45.

Money, J. 1987. Sin, sickness, or status? Homosexual gender identity and psychoneuroendocrinology. *American Psychologist* 42:384–99.

Money, J. 1988. *Gay, Straight, and In-Between: The Sexology of Erotic Orientation.* New York: Oxford University Press.

Morales, E. S. 1989. Ethnic minority families and minority gays and lesbians. *Marriage and Family Review* 14:217–39.

Morin, S. 1977. Heterosexual bias in psychological research on lesbianism and male homosexuality. *American Psychologist* 32:629–37.

Moses, A. E., and J. A. Buckner. 1980. The special problems of rural gay clients. In A. E. Moses and R. 0. Hawkins, Jr., eds., *Counseling Lesbian Women and Men: A Life Issues Approach,* pp. 173–80. St. Louis: C. V. Mosby.

Murphy, B. 1989. Lesbian couples and their parents: The effects of perceived parental attitudes on the couple. *Journal of Counseling and Development* 68:46–51.

Olsen, M. R. 1987. A study of gay and lesbian teachers. *Journal of Homosexuality* 13(4):73–81.

O'Neill, J. M., B. J. Helms, and R. K. Gable. 1986. Gender-Role Conflict Scale: College men's fear of femininity. *Sex Roles* 14:335–50.

Owlfeather, M. 1988. Children of grandmother moon. In W. Roscoe, ed., *Living the Spirit. A Gay American Indian Anthology*, pp. 97–105. New York: St. Martin's.

Palladino, D., and Y. Stephenson. 1990. Perceptions of the sexual self: Their impact on relationships between lesbian and heterosexual women. *Women and Therapy* 9:231–53.

Pamela, H. 1989. Asian American lesbians: An emerging voice in the Asian American community. In Asian Women United of California, eds., *Making Waves: An Anthology of Writings by and about Asian American Women*, pp. 282–90. Boston: Beacon Press.

Paroski, P. 1987. Healthcare delivery and the concerns of gay and lesbian adolescents. *Journal of Adolescent Health Care* 8:188–92.

Parker, P. 1987. Legacy. In S. Pollack and J. Vaughn, eds., *Politics of the Heart: A Lesbian Parenting Anthology*, pp. 208–12. Ithaca, N.Y.: Firebrand Books.

Paul, W. 1982. Minority status for gay people: Majority reactions and social context. In W. Paul, J. D. Weinrich, J. C. Gonsiorek, and M. E. Hotvedt, eds., *Homosexuality: Social, Psychological, and Biological Issues*, pp. 351–69. Beverly Hills, Calif.: Sage.

Paz, 0. 1961. *The Labyrinth of Solitude: Life and Thought in Mexico*. New York: Grove.

Peplau, L. A. 1983. Roles and gender. In H. H. Kelley, E. Berscheid, A. Christensen, J. H. Harvey, T. L. Huston, G. Levinger, E. McClintock, L. A. Peplau, and D. R. Peterson, eds., *Close Relationships*, pp. 220–64. San Francisco: Freeman.

Peplau, L. A. 1991. Lesbian and gay relationships. In J. C. Gonsiorek and J. D. Weinrich, eds., *Homosexuality: Research Findings for Public Policy*, pp. 177–96. Newbury Park, Calif.: Sage.

Peplau, L. A., and H. Amaro. 1982. Understanding lesbian relationships. In W. Paul, J. D. Weinrich, J. C. Gonsiorek, and M. E. Hotvedt, eds., *Homosexuality: Social, Psychological, and Biological Issues*, pp. 233–48. Beverly Hills, Calif.: Sage.

Peplau, L. A., and S. D. Cochran. 1981. Value orientations in the intimate relationships of gay men. *Journal of Homosexuality* 6(3):1–19.

Peplau, L. A., and S. D. Cochran. 1990. A relationship perspective on homosexuality. In D. P. McWhirter, S. A. Sanders, and J. M. Reinisch, eds., *Homosexuality/Heterosexuality: The Kinsey Scale and Current Research*, pp. 321–49. New York: Oxford University Press.

Peplau, L. A., S. D. Cochran, and V. M. Mays. 1986. Satisfaction in the intimate relationships of black lesbians. Paper presented at the 94th Annual Convention of the American Psychological Association, Washington, D.C., August.

Peplau, L. A., S. D. Cochran, K. Rook, and C. Padesky. 1978. Women in love: Attachment and autonomy in lesbian relationships. *Journal of Social Issues* 34(3):7–27.

Peplau, L. A., and S. L. Gordon. 1983. The intimate relationships of lesbians and gay men. In E. R. Allgeier and N. B. McCormick, eds., *The Changing Boundaries: Gender Roles and Sexual Behavior*, pp. 226–44. Palo Alto, Calif.: Mayfield.

Petrow, S. 1990. Together wherever we go. *The Advocate* (May):42–44.

Phillis, D. E., and M. H. Gramko. 1985. Sex differences in sexual activity: Reality or illusion. *Journal of Sex Research* 21:437–48.

Plummer, K. 1975. *Sexual Stigma: An Interactionist Account*. London: Routledge and Kegan Paul.

Plummer, K. 1981. Going gay: Identities, life cycles, and lifestyles in the male gay world. In J. Hart and D. Richardson, eds., *The Theory and Practice of Homosexuality*, pp. 93–110. London: Routledge and Kegan Paul.

Ponse, B. 1978. *Identities in the Lesbian World: The Social Construction of Self*. Westport, Conn.: Greenwood Press.

Ponse, B. 1984. The problematic meanings of "lesbian." In J. D. Douglas, ed., *The Sociology of Deviance*, pp. 25–33. Boston: Allyn and Bacon.

Preston, K., and K. Stanley. 1987. "What's the worst thing . . . ?" Gender-directed insults. *Sex Roles* 17:209–19.

Radicalesbians. 1973. Women-identified women. In A. Koedt, E. Levine, and A. Rapone, eds., *Radical Feminism*, pp. 240–45. New York: Quadrangle Books.

Rand, C., D. L. Graham, and E. Rawlings. 1982. Psychological health and factors the court seeks to control in lesbian mother custody trials. *Journal of Homosexuality* 8(1):27–39.

Remafedi, G. 1987. Male homosexuality: The adolescent's perspective. *Pediatrics* 79:326–30.

Rich, A. 1980. Compulsory heterosexuality and lesbian existence. *Signs* 5:631–60.

Richardson, D. 1987. Recent challenges to traditional assumptions about homosexuality: Some implications for practice. *Journal of Homosexuality* 13(4):1–12.

Riddle, D. I. 1978. Relating to children: Gays as role models. *Journal of Social Issues* 34:38–58.

Riddle, D. I., and S. F. Morin. 1977. Removing the stigma. Data from individuals. *APA Monitor* (November):16, 28.

Risman, B., and P. Schwartz. 1988. Sociological research on male and female homosexuality. *Annual Review of Sociology* 14:125–47.

Robinson, B. E., L. H. Walters, and P. Skeen. 1989. Response of parents to learning that their child is homosexual and concern over AIDS: A national study. *Journal of Homosexuality* 18(1–2):59–80.

Roesler, J., and R. W. Deisher. 1972. Youthful male homosexuality. *Journal of the American Medical Association* 219:1018–23.

Romo-Carmona, M. 1987. Introduction. In J. Ramos, ed., *Compañeras: Latina Lesbians*, pp. xx–xxix. New York: Latina Lesbian History Project.

Ross, M. W. 1987. A theory of normal homosexuality. In L. Diamant, ed., *Male and Female Homosexuality: Psychological Approaches*, pp. 237–59. Washington, D.C.: Hemisphere.

Ross, M. W. 1989. Gay youth in four cultures: A comparative study. *Journal of Homosexuality* 17(1–4):299–314.

Rusbult, C. E., I. M. Zembrodt, and J. Iwaniszek. 1986. The impact of gender and sex-role orientation on responses to dissatisfaction in close relationships. *Sex Roles* 15:1–20.

Russo, A. J. 1982. Power and influence in the homosexual community: A study of three California cities. *Dissertation Abstracts International* 43:561B (University Microfilms No. DA8215211).

Sanders, R. M., J. Bain, and R. Langevin. 1985. Peripheral sex hormones, homosexuality, and gender identity. In R. Langevin, ed., *Erotic Preference, Gender Identity, and Aggression in Men: New Research Studies*, pp. 227–47. Hillsdale, N.J.: Erlbaum.

Sang, B., J. Warshow, and A. Smith, eds. 1991. *Lesbians at Midlife: The Creative Transition.* San Francisco: Spinsters.

Savin-Williams, R. C. 1989. Coming out to parents and self-esteem among gay and lesbian youth. *Journal of Homosexuality* 18(1–2):1–35.

Schaefer, S. 1976. Sexual and social problems of lesbians. *Journal of Sex Research* 12:50–69.

Schaefer, S. 1977. Sociosexual behavior in male and female homosexuals. *Archives of Sexual Behavior* 6:355–64.

Schmitt, J. P., and L. A. Kurdek. 1987. Personality correlates of positive identity and relationship involvement in gay men. *Journal of Homosexuality* 13(4):101–9.

Schneider, B. 1986. Coming out at work: Bridging the private/public gap. *Work and Occupations* 13:463–87.

Schullo, S. A., and B. L. Alperson. 1984. Interpersonal phenomenology as a function of sexual orientation, sex, sentiment, and trait categories in long-term dyadic relationships. *Journal of Personality and Social Psychology* 47:983–1002.

Sears, J. T. 1989. The impact of gender and race on growing up lesbian and gay in the South. *National Women's Studies Association Journal* 1:422–57.

Sergio, P. A., and J. Cody. 1985. Physical attractiveness and social assertiveness skills in male homosexual dating behavior and partner selection. *Journal of Social Psychology* 125:505–14.

Shachar, S. A., and L. A. Gilbert. 1983. Working lesbians: Role conflicts and coping strategies. *Psychology of Women Quarterly* 7:244–56.

Shon, S. P., and D. Y. Ja. 1982. Asian families. In M. McGoldrick, J. K. Pearce, and J. Giordano, eds., *Ethnicity and Family Therapy*, pp. 208–29. New York: Guilford Press.

Shively, M. G., and J. P. DeCecco. 1977. Components of sexual identity. *Journal of Homosexuality* 3:41–48.

Shneidman, E. 1989. The Indian summer of life: A preliminary study of septuagenarians. *American Psychologist* 44:684–94.

Silverstein, C. 1981. *Man to Man: Gay Couples in America.* New York: William Morrow.

Sophie, J. 1985/1986. A critical examination of stage theories of lesbian identity development. *Journal of Homosexuality* 12(2):39–51.

Stein, T. S., and C. J. Cohen, eds. 1986. *Psychotherapy with Lesbians and Gay Men.* New York: Plenum.

Storms, M. D., M. L. Stivers, S. M. Lambers, and C. A. Hill. 1981. Sexual scripts for women. *Sex Roles* 3:257–63.

Strommen, E. F. 1989. "You're a what?": Family members' reactions to the disclosure of homosexuality. *Journal of Homosexuality* 18(1–2):37–58.

Swaab, D. F., and M. A. Hofman. 1988. Sexual differentiation of the human hypothalamus: Ontogeny of the sexually dimorphic nucleus of the preoptic area. *Developmental Brain Research* 44:314–18.

Taylor, N., ed. 1986. *All in a Day's Work: A Report on Anti-Lesbian Discrimination in Employment and Unemployment in London.* London: Lesbian Employment Rights.

Thompson, E. H., and J. H. Pleck. 1986. The structure of male role norms. *American Behavioral Scientists* 29:531–43.

Tiefer, L. 1987. Social constructionism and the study of human sexuality. In P. Shaver and C. Hendrick, eds., *Review of Social and Personality Psychology*, pp. 70–94. Beverly Hills, Calif.: Sage.

Tinney, J. S. 1986. Why a black gay church? In J. Beam, ed., *In the Life: A Black Gay Anthology*, pp. 70–86. Boston: Alyson.

Tremble, B., M. Schneider, and C. Appathurai. 1989. Growing up gay or lesbian in a multicultural context. *Journal of Homosexuality* 17(1–4):253–67.

Troiden, R. R. 1979. Becoming homosexual: A model of gay identity acquisition. *Psychiatry* 42:362–73.

Troiden, R. R. 1988. *Gay and Lesbian Identity: A Sociological Analysis.* New York: General Hall.

Troiden, R. R. 1989. The formation of homosexual identities. *Journal of Homosexuality* 17(1–4):43–73.

Troiden, R. R., and E. Goode. 1980. Variables related to the acquisition of a gay identity. *Journal of Homosexuality* 5(4):383–92.

Vance, B. K., and V. Green. 1984. Lesbian identities: An examination of sexual behavior and sex role acquisition as related to age of initial same-sex encounter. *Psychology of Women Quarterly* 8:293–307.

Vasquez, E. 1979. Homosexuality in the context of the Mexican-American culture. In D. Kuhnel, ed., *Sexual Issues in Social Work: Emerging Concerns in Education and Practice*, pp. 131–47. Honolulu: University of Hawaii School of Social Work.

Vetere, V. A. 1983. The role of friendship in the development and maintenance of lesbian love relationships. *Journal of Homosexuality* 8(2):51–65.

Watters, A. T. 1986. Heterosexual bias in psychological research on lesbianism and male homosexuality (1979–1983), utilizing the bibliographic and taxonomic system of Morin 1977. *Journal of Homosexuality* 13(1):35–58.

Weeks, J. 1977. *Coming Out: Homosexual Politics in Britain from the Nineteenth Century to the Present.* London: Quartet.

Weeks, J. 1981. Discourse, desire and sexual deviance: Some problems in a history of homosexuality. In K. Plummer, ed., *The Making of the Modern Homosexual*, pp. 76–111. London: Hutchinson.

Weinberg, M. S., and C. Williams. 1974. *Male Homosexuals: Their Problems and Adaptations.* New York: Oxford University Press.

Weinberg, T. S. 1978. On "doing" and "being" gay: Sexual behavior and homosexual male self-identity. *Journal of Homosexuality* 4(2):143–56.

Weinberg, T. S. 1983. *Gay Men, Gay Selves: The Social Construction of Homosexual Identities.* New York: Irvington.

Weinrich, J., and W. L. Williams. 1991. Strange customs, familiar lives: Homosexualities in other cultures. In J. C. Gonsiorek and J. D. Weinrich, eds., *Homosexuality: Research Findings for Public Policy*, pp. 44–59. Newbury Park, Calif.: Sage.

Wells, J. W., and W. B. Kline. 1987. Self-disclosure of homosexual orientation. *Journal of Social Psychology* 127:191–97.

Whitehead, H. 1981. The bow and the burden strap: A new look at institutionalized homosexuality in native North America. In S. B. Ortner, and H. Whitehead, eds., *Sexual Meanings: The Culture Construction of Gender and Sexuality*, pp. 80–115. New York: Cambridge University Press.

Williams, W. L. 1985. Persistence and change in the Berdache tradition among contemporary Lakota Indians. *Journal of Homosexuality* 11(3–4):191–200.

Williams W. L. 1986. *The Spirit and the Flesh: Sexual Diversity in American Indian Culture.* Boston: Beacon Press.

Williams, W. L. 1987. Women, men, and others. Beyond ethnocentrism in gender theory. *American Behavioral Scientist* 31:135–41.

Wilson, G. D. 1987. Male-female differences in sexual activity, enjoyment and fantasies. *Personality and Individual Differences* 8:125–27.

Wilson, P. M. 1986. Black culture and sexuality. *Journal of Social Work and Human Sexuality* 4(3):29–46.

Winkelpleck, J. M., and J. S. Westfeld. 1982. Counseling considerations with gay couples. *Personnel and Guidance Journal* 60:294–96.

Wolf, T. J. 1985. Marriages of bisexual men. *Journal of Homosexuality* 11(1–2):135–48.

Wooden, W. S., H. Kawasaki, and R. Mayeda. 1983. Lifestyles and identity maintenance among gay Japanese-American males. *Alternative Lifestyles* 5:236–43.

Wyers, N. L. 1987. Homosexuality in the family: Lesbian and gay spouses. *Social Work* 32:143–48.

Yearwood, L., and T. Weinberg. 1979. Black organizations, gay organizations: Sociological parallels. In M. Levine, ed., *Gay Men: The Sociology of Male Homosexuality*, pp. 301–16. New York: Harper and Row.

Zimmerman, B. 1984. The politics of transliteration: Lesbian personal narratives. *Signs* 9:663–82.

Zuger, B. 1988. Is early effeminate behavior in boys early homosexuality? *Comprehensive Psychiatry* 29:509–19.

Appendix A

Definitions of Key Terms

Several of these definitions are based on those proposed by Money (1988).

Androgynophilia: Emotional attraction and sexual desire in which love and lust are attached to both a man and a woman serially or simultaneously by a person of either gender (from Greek *andros* (man) + *gyne* (woman) + *philia* (love).

Bisexual: Sexual contacts with people of the same gender and people of the other gender, either concurrently or sequentially; it may involve either genital acts or a long-term affectional-erotic status. It is also a term for people whose affectional-erotic status or life-style reflects androgynophilia; sometimes termed *ambisexual.*

Coming out: The sequence of events through which individuals recognize their same-gender sexual orientation and disclose it to others.

Gay: Term for a person whose affectional-erotic status and life-style reflect homophilia; it often refers to men but may include both women and men.

Heterophilia: A type of emotional attraction and sexual desire in which love and lust are attached to people of the other gender (from Greek *hetero* (other) + *philia* (love).

Heterosexual: Sexual contacts with people of the other gender; it may involve either genital acts or a long-term affectional-erotic status.

Heterosexism: The belief that heterophilia and heterosexual affectional-erotic status are better or more natural than homophilia or homosexual affectional-erotic status.

Homophilia: A type of emotional attraction and sexual desire in which love and lust are attached to those of the same gender (from Greek *homos* (same) + *philia* (love).

Homophobia: A term that has commonly come to refer to prejudice against people who are homophilic (from Greek *homos* (same) + *phobos* (fear or fright). It should not be considered a clinical phobia.

Homosexual: Sexual contacts with people of the same gender; it may involve either genital acts or a long-term affectional-erotic status. (Because the term has multiple meanings, its use as an adjective is often unclear, e.g., homosexual rape, homosexual spokesperson, homosexual partner.)

Lesbian: Term for a woman whose affectional-erotic status and life-style reflect homophilia.

Sexual orientation: The relative balance between an individual's homophilia and heterophilia, viewed as separate parallel dimensions. It reflects one's affectional-erotic attraction to the same gender, other gender, or to both women and men.

I

The Meaning of
Sexual Orientation

Affectional, erotic, and sexual preferences can be understood only within the social milieu in which the individual is embedded at a particular historical moment. Sociohistorical changes have transformed the meaning of homosexuality from its medical classification in 1869 by Benkert as one of many forms of sexual perversion (Plummer 1984). A few years ago it was conceptualized as a minority status in Donald Webster Cory's 1951 book *Homosexual in America* (Kameny 1971). More recently, it has begun to be seen as a characteristic that defines a diverse, multiethnic, and multiracial community not only with a history but also with shared political and social concerns.

One particularly important influence in the process of reconceptualizing sexual orientation from an individual pathology to membership in a supportive community has been the feminist movement. It has challenged ideas about sexuality by deconstructing the concept of gender and its many assumptions. The movement has reduced the stigma surrounding lesbianism by defining women's affection along a broad continuum, by offering a sense of solidarity, positive role models, and community (Browning, Reynolds, and Dworkin 1991; Sophie 1985/1986).

The ideology of the lesbian-feminist movement has had an important influence on many lesbian communities and offered a contrast to the male-dominated gay liberation movement. For many gay men, liberation meant freedom from harassment and the power to exercise sexual freedom; for lesbian feminists, it meant resisting patriarchal oppression and developing new forms of intimacy (Pearlman 1987; Raymond 1986). Faderman (1984) coined the term *new gay lesbians* to refer to those women who define themselves as lesbians through the feminist movement. Other lesbians view their sexual identity as a reaction against patriarchal oppression. It is possible that some gay men are developing this awareness also, since the patriarchy clearly are heterosexual males. We discuss issues of diversity in terms of gender and ethnic minorities within the gay and lesbian community in detail in parts 4 and 5. In the future, the goals of lesbians and gay men may converge and gender differences may be recognized as an important strength.

As a result of political activism and accumulating empirical evidence that failed to link homosexuality with mental illness or emotional instability (e.g., Hooker 1957), the American Psychiatric Association voted to remove homosexuality from the list of mental illnesses in 1973 (Bayer 1981). At the same time, a lesbian/gay affirmative approach in psychology emerged that promoted the view that same-gender sexual orientation is a natural variant in the expression of normal erotic attractions and emotional commitment (Gonsiorek 1988). No longer deemed an illness, lesbian and gay life is now studied by psychologists to understand its characteristics, strengths, and the various problems of living associated with being lesbian or gay in a nonsupportive or hostile society.

In today's social context, the term *homosexuality* is ambiguous, and care should be taken to avoid heterosexist bias in language. For example, the American Psychological Association Committee on Lesbian and Gay Concerns suggested:

> The word *homosexual* has several problems of designation. First, it may perpetuate negative stereotypes because of its historical associations with pathology and criminal behavior. Second, it is ambiguous in reference because it is often assumed to refer exclusively to men and thus renders lesbians invisible. Third, it is often unclear. (Committee on Lesbian and Gay Concerns 1991:973)

The risk of ambiguity becomes even greater when other cultures or other historical periods are compared with our own (cf. Blackwood 1985). Can we validly compare same-gender sexual behavior in ancient Greece with gay men today? Is the similarity between the love poetry of Sappho and that of modern lesbian poets just coincidence? What is it about sexual orientation that forms a link between those people who share a same-gender sexual or affectional attraction?

In this part we focus on three different levels of meaning for the term *sexual orientation*. The first is the sociocultural view that sexual orientation has a particular meaning because one's social environment imposes that meaning. This perspective may be seen as a macroview, or as a political analysis. It is most powerfully seen from a historical review of the evolution and emergence of a politically active lesbian and gay male community. The underlying theme is that lesbians and gay men have come out of hiding and come together because heterosexist values in our culture have not permitted their form of individuality, and have not recognized this aspect of human diversity as equally acceptable to heterosexuality.

The process of coming together has reflected historical influences, such as the civil rights movement and the women's movement. It was stimulated, however, by the mobilization of armed forces to fight in World War II. Thus, we begin with a review of these influences using the context of the cultural milieu of San Francisco. D'Emilio traces the emergence of modern gay and lesbian political consciousness from the catalytic effect of World War II to the 1980s. In this analysis, one sees clearly the evolution of gay people from isolated individuals who performed "homosexual acts" to a politically powerful community that was suddenly overthrown in a coup d'état by an assassination committed by a leader of the heterosexist opposition. Following a night of rioting and police retribution, the gay and lesbian community in San Francisco eventually renewed its political strength. During the 1980s that strength was vital for confronting the advent of the cataclysmic epidemic of acquired immune deficiency syndrome and the conditions associated with infection by the human immunodeficiency virus (HIV/AIDS).

The second level of analysis of the meaning of sexual orientation might be termed *microanalysis*, or individual psychology. Beginning with the classic studies by Kinsey and his associates, an individual's sexual orientation has been conceptualized as a continuum from exclusive homosexuality to exclusive heterosexuality, with bisexuality in between. Implicit in that concept is the assumption that the more homosexual one is, the less heterosexual one can be, and vice versa. A different perspective on the meaning of sexual orientation is presented in the second selection by Shively and De Cecco. The authors separated sexual orientation from biological sex and from gender identity—long thought to be related to homosexuality. Moreover, Shively and De Cecco separated the concept of homosexuality from heterosexuality, placing each on a separate continuum. In addition they differentiated between physical and affectional attractions, allowing the possibility that one's erotic imagery might differ from one's physical behavior (so that, for example, one or both partners in male-male sex (for example, in a prison) might engage in homosexual behavior while having a heterosexual fantasy; and a heterosexually married lesbian might do the opposite). This view clearly shatters the myth that there is a single concept of "homosexuality," or that it reflects an inappropriate gender identity.

The third perspective reflects an interaction between the sociopolitical and the psychological viewpoints. One concept that has emerged that exemplifies this level of analysis is heterosexual bias, or heterosexism. We conclude this first part with a close examination of this concept, which may be ultimately the key to perceiving the cultural meaning of sexual orientation. As Herek points out in this article, individuals have come to be defined by what they do (or what they would like to do) in the privacy of their own affectional and sexual lives. This "master status" takes precedence over everything else about them, so that even gender, race, and age become subordinate to the individual's sexual orientation. One result is social permission by our heterosexist society to commit violence against lesbians and gay men, to express disgust in public about them and their behavior, and to avoid endorsement of their sexuality even while supporting their civil rights. Except for openly gay and lesbian leaders, most liberals do not "endorse the homosexual life-style" because it has been defined as this overarching social status that is devalued and used as a foil to define normal heterosexuality.

Reconceptualizing sexual orientation will allow individuals to consider options and to construct sexual identities they did not consider before (Herdt 1989). These changes also have a potentially beneficial impact on heterosexuals. As society's views shift to include greater visibility of lesbians and gay men and a reconceptualization of homosexuality toward natural variation instead of mental disorder, it makes sexual orientation a more salient aspect of one's identity (instead of assuming one's heterosexuality is a normative characteristic). This change may result in greater flexibility of gender roles and increased regard for human diversity.

CONTEMPORARY ISSUE: OUTING

Outing is the contemporary term for revealing someone's homosexuality. A recent example is an assistant to the U.S. secretary of defense. The man, who was identified in a national gay/lesbian newspaper, was in a position of potential influence in the Department of Defense, which has wreaked havoc on the lives of a large number of lesbians and gay men because the armed forces excludes them from service and has discharged and harassed any who are discovered or disclose themselves.

Outing is usually done in a public manner, such as by a newspaper or magazine report about someone who is known privately—but not publicly—to be gay or lesbian. It may be viewed as imposing the stigma of homosexuality—or the open identification as a member of the lesbian and gay male community—on someone against their wishes. Persons who are likely to be outed are those whose position of power or visibility is at odds with the political goals of the lesbian and gay male community.

In general, positions of power and prestige in our society appear to be protected by a glass ceiling above which access is granted primarily to white heterosexual males. The same processes that restrict access to women and to people of color also restrict access for lesbians and gay men. The restrictions are subtle and complex (Levine and Leonard 1984; Morgan and Brown 1991; Stewart 1991). The result is that those lesbians and gay men who do reach positions of high power tend to have kept their sexual orientation secret and resist disclosing it for fear of jeopardizing their position.

The argument against outing, of course, is that all persons have a right to privacy. Gay men and lesbians can lose their job, marriage, custody of children, and support of family members if their sexual orientation becomes known. It seems ironic that the gay community could tolerate any form of outing. Moreover, some lesbian and gay individuals can achieve greater power if they are not open; if their sexual orientation is revealed, they may lose all influence. Some closeted persons therefore believe that they can do more good for the lesbian and gay movement if they are able to maintain their privacy.

Although studies have found that being open is usually beneficial to one's mental health, no research has focused on the mental health consequences of having been outed. Do they parallel the benefits that have been found for persons who reveal their sexual orientation voluntarily; or would the shock and disruption that results be more significant than the increased integrity and reduced stress that may eventually result from being open? Some openly lesbian and gay leaders appear to maintain or even enhance their power over time, even if their sexual identity were disclosed by others. A study of the skills involved in this process would be beneficial. We discuss the general topic of identity development and disclosure in part 3.

REFERENCES

Bayer, R. 1981. *Homosexuality and American Psychiatry: The Politics of Diagnosis.* New York: Basic Books.

Blackwood, E. 1985. Breaking the mirror: The construction of lesbianism and the anthropological discourse of homosexuality. *Journal of Homosexuality* 11(3/4):1–17.

Browning, C., A. L. Reynolds, and S. H. Dworkin. 1991. Affirmative psychotherapy for lesbian women. *The Counseling Psychologist* 19(2):177–96.

Committee on Lesbian and Gay Concerns. 1991. Avoiding heterosexual bias in language. *American Psychologist* 46:973–74.

Faderman, L. 1984. The "new gay" lesbian. *Journal of Homosexuality* 10(3/4):85–95.

Gonsiorek, J. C. 1988. Current and future directions in gay/lesbian affirmative mental health practice. In M. Shernoff and W. A. Scott, eds., *Sourcebook on Lesbian/Gay Healthcare*, pp. 107–13. Washington, D.C.: National Lesbian and Gay Health Foundation.

Herdt, G. 1989. Introduction: Gay and lesbian youth, emergent identities, and cultural scenes at home and abroad. *Journal of Homosexuality* 17(1/2):1–42.

Hooker, E. 1957. The adjustment of the male overt homosexual. *Journal of Projective Techniques* 21:18–31.

Kameny, F. E. 1971. Homosexuals as a minority group. In E. Sagarin, ed., *The Other Minorities*, pp. 50–65. Waltham, Mass: Ginn.

Levine, M. P., and R. Leonard. 1984. Discrimination against lesbians in the work force. *Signs: Journal of Women in Culture and Society* 9:700–10.

Morgan, K. S., and L. S. Brown. 1991. Lesbian career development, work behavior, and vocational counseling. *Counseling Psychologist* 19:273–91.

Pearlman, S. F. 1987. The saga of continuing clash in lesbian community, or will an army of ex-lovers fail? In Boston Lesbian Psychologies Collective, eds., *Lesbian Psychologies: Explorations and Challenges*, pp. 313–26. Urbana: University of Illinois Press.

Plummer, K. 1984. Sexual diversity: A sociological perspective. In K. Howells, ed., *The Psychology of Sexual Diversity*, pp. 219–53. Oxford: Basil Blackwell.

Raymond, J. G. 1986. *A Passion for Friends: Toward a Philosophy of Female Affection.* Boston: Beacon.

Sophie, J. 1985/1986. A critical examination of stage theories of lesbian identity development. *Journal of Homosexuality* 12(2):39–51.

Stewart, T. A. 1991. Gay in corporate America. *Fortune* (December 16):42–56.

1

Gay Politics and Community in San Francisco Since World War II

John D'Emilio

In the last two decades, social historians have increasingly turned to the writing of community histories of ethnic and racial groups, such as the Blacks of Cleveland, the Italians of Chicago, and the Jews of New York. Historians of the gay and lesbian experience are beginning to do the same. In the following essay, John D'Emilio focuses attention on San Francisco, a city especially identified with the gay experience. He traces the relationship between community development and political mobilization since World War II, mapping the intricate ways in which community life and politics interact.

For gay men and lesbians, San Francisco has become akin to what Rome is for Catholics: a lot of us live there and many more have made the pilgrimage. The gay male subculture in San Francisco is more visible and more complex than in any other city; lesbians in the Bay Area also sustain more institutions than do their sisters elsewhere. San Francisco is one of the very few places where lesbians are residentially concentrated enough to be visible. For gay men and lesbians, San Francisco is a special place.

The gay community in San Francisco and its politics have been a long time in the making. Surveying its history can tell us much not just about one city, but about the emergence of sexual minorities generally, about shifting forms of oppression, and about changing political strategies.

THE HISTORICAL BACKGROUND

The distinction between behavior and identity is critical to an understanding of contemporary gay male and lesbian life. Jeffrey Weeks described it well in *Coming Out: Homosexual Politics in Britain.* "Homosexuality has existed throughout history," he wrote. "But what have varied enormously are the ways in which various societies have regarded homosexuality, the meanings they have attached to it, and how those who were engaged in homosexual activity viewed themselves. . . . As a starting point we have to distinguish between homosexual behavior, which is universal, and a homosexual identity, which is historically specific."[1]

In colonial America, in the family-centered household economy of the north, heterosexual relations and individual survival meshed, as production was based on the cooperative labor of husband, wife, and their children. Where forced labor predominated, White indentured servants and Black slaves were deprived of the most basic control of their own bodies. In either setting, the presence of lesbians and gay men was literally inconceivable. Though evidence of homosexual activity in the colonial era survives (mainly through the court records that detailed its punishment), nothing indicates that men or women could make their erotic/emotional attraction for the same sex into a personal identity. The prevailing ideology reflected the facts of social existence. Homosexual behavior was labeled a sin and a crime, a discrete act for which the perpetrator received punishment, in this world and the next. In preindustrial America, heterosexuality remained undefined because it was truly the only way of life.[2]

The decisive shift in the nineteenth century to industrial capitalism provided the conditions for a homosexual and lesbian identity to emerge. As a free-labor system, capitalism pulled men and women out of the home and into the marketplace. Throughout the nineteenth and twentieth centuries, capital expanded its sway over more aspects of material life and began producing as commodities goods that were once made in the home. Free labor and the expansion of commodity production created the context in which an autonomous personal life could develop. Affection, personal relationships, and sexuality increasingly entered the realm of "choice," seemingly independent and disconnected from how one organized the production of goods necessary for survival. Under these conditions, men and women could fashion an identity and way of life out of their sexual and emotional attraction to members of the same sex. As industrial capitalism extended its hegemony, the potential for homosexual desire to coalesce into an identity grew. Not only had it become possible to be a lesbian or a homosexual: as time passed, more and more men and women could embody that potential.[3]

Beginning in the last third of the nineteenth century, evidence points to the appearance of men and women for whom same-sex erotic interests became an organizing principle for their personal life. Meeting places, rudimentary institutions, and friendship networks dotted the urban landscape. The medical profession "discovered" the homosexual, a new, exotic human type. The lead taken by the medical profession in reconceptualizing homosexuality as a condition that inheres in a person, rather than as a criminal, sinful act, was less a sign of scientific progress than an ideological response to a changing social reality: Some women and men were structuring their lives in a new way. During the first half of the twentieth century, the institutions and networks that constituted the subcultures of gay men and lesbians slowly grew, stabilized, and differentiated themselves. This process occurred in an oppressive context. Those who engaged in homosexual activity were severely punished if they were caught; the culture devalued homosexual expression in any form; and lesbians and gay men were denied information about the lives of their own kind and about their sexuality.[4]

Capitalist society differentiates and discriminates according to gender, class, and, race. The evolution of gay life reflects those processes. For instance, in building on its patriarchal origins, capitalism drew more men than women out of the home and into the paid labor force, and at higher wages. The potential for men to live outside the heterosexual family unit has been, consequently, proportionately greater and the difference is reflected in the contrasting incidence rates for homosexuality among men and women in the Kinsey studies. Also, because the public space of cities has traditionally been male space, it is not surprising that gay male life has been significantly more public than lesbian life.[5]

POSTWAR SAN FRANCISCO

The slow, gradual evolution of a gay identity and of urban gay subcultures was immeasurably hastened by the intervention of World War II. The social disruption of the war years allowed the almost imperceptible changes of several generations to coalesce into a qualitatively new shape. World War II was something of a nationwide coming-out experience. It properly marks the beginning of the nation's, and San Francisco's, modern gay history.[6]

The war uprooted tens of millions of American men and women, plucking them from families, small towns, and the ethnic neighborhoods of large cities and depositing them in a variety of sex-segregated, nonfamilial environments. Most obvious among these were the armed services, but the home front also departed from the cosexual, heterosexual norm of peacetime society with millions of women entering the labor force, often working and lodging in all-female space. Young men and women who, in normal times, might have moved directly from their parents' home into one with their spouse, experienced years of living away from kin, and away from the intimate company of the opposite sex. For a generation of Americans, World War II created a setting in which to experience same-sex love, affection, and sexuality, and to discover and participate in the group life of gay men and women. For some it simply confirmed a way of living and loving they had already chosen. For others, it gave meaning to little-understood desires, introduced them to men and women with similar feelings, and thus allowed them to "come out." For still others, the sexual underside of the war years provided experiences they otherwise would not have had and that they left behind when the war ended.[7]

If the war years allowed large numbers of lesbians and gay men to discover their sexuality and each other, repression in the postwar decade heightened consciousness of belonging to a group. One component of cold war politics was the drive to reconstruct traditional gender roles and patterns of sexual behavior. Women experienced intense pressure to leave the labor force and return home to the role of wife and mother. Homosexuals and lesbians found themselves under virulent attack: purges from the armed forces; congressional investigations into government employment of "perverts"; disbarment from federal jobs; widespread FBI surveillance; state sexual psychopath laws; stepped-up harassment from urban police forces; and inflammatory headlines warning readers of the sex "deviates" in their midst. The tightening web of oppression in McCarthy's America helped to create the minority it was meant to isolate.[8]

These events also decisively shaped the gay history of San Francisco, initiating a process that has made it a unique place for lesbians and gay men. As a major port of departure and return for servicemen and women destined for the Pacific theater (and, later, for the postwar occupation of Japan and the fighting in Korea), and as an important center of war industry, the Bay Area's charm and physical beauty were exposed to large numbers of young, mobile Americans. Many stayed after demobilization; others later returned. Between 1940 and 1950 the population of San Francisco, which had declined during the 1930s, grew by more than 125,000.

The growth included a disproportionate number of lesbians and gay men. The sporadic, unpredictable purges from the armed forces in the Pacific deposited lesbians and homosexuals, sometimes hundreds at a time, in San Francisco with dishonorable discharges. Unable or unwilling to return home in disgrace to family and friends, they stayed to carve out a new gay life. California, moreover, was the one state whose courts upheld the right of homosexuals to congregate in bars and other public establishments. Though the police found ways around the decision and continued to harass gay bars, the ruling gave to bars in San Francisco a tiny measure of security lacking elsewhere. By the late 1950s about thirty gay male and lesbian bars existed in the city. Such small advantages were significant, and over the years created a qualitative difference, in the shape of gay life. Census statistics hint at the degree to which San Francisco was attracting a gay populace. From 1950 to 1960 the number of single-person households doubled, accounting for 38 percent of the city's residence units.[9]

Under the combined impact of the war, the publication of the Kinsey studies, the persecutions of the McCarthy era, and the wide currency that a growing civil rights movement was giving to the concept of minority group status, some gay men and lesbians began building a political movement of their own. In 1950, a small group of male homosexuals who were members of the Communist party or fellow-travelers formed the Mattachine Society in Los Angeles. Initially a secret underground organization, it developed a radical analysis of homosexuals as an oppressed minority and sought to build a mass movement of homosexuals working for their own emancipation. Though the founders were eventually purged and the philosophy and goals of the group transformed, the Mattachine did, at least, survive. In 1953 a branch was formed in San Francisco. Three years later, the organization's national office moved there and its monthly magazine, *Mattachine Review*, was published out of San Francisco. In 1955 in San Francisco, several lesbians founded the Daughters of Bilitis (DOB), a lesbian political group. DOB also published a monthly magazine, *The Ladder*, and tried, with limited success, to set up chapters in other cities.[10]

Throughout the 1950s, the "homophile" movement remained small and fragile. The combined membership of DOB and Mattachine in San Francisco probably never exceeded two hundred, yet no other American city reached even that number. Hostile as the social climate of the 1950s was to a gay movement, and notwithstanding the personal courage that involvement required, the feeble size of the movement stemmed in no small part from the political choices made by homophile leaders. Mattachine and DOB reflected (after its radical founders were purged) the accommodationist, conformist spirit of the Eisenhower era. They assiduously cultivated an image of middle-class respectability and denied that they were organizations of homosexuals, instead claiming that they were concerned with the problem of the "variant." They expected social change to come through the good offices of professionals. They saw their task primarily as one of educating the professionals who influenced public opinion and only secondarily as one of organizing lesbians and gay men. Moreover, in defining prejudice and misinformation as the problem, both DOB and Mattachine often found themselves blaming the victim. DOB regularly counseled lesbians to grow their hair long and wear dresses, and Mattachine firmly dissociated itself from the stereotypical promiscuous sexuality of male homosexuals, in one instance even applauding police for rounding up gay men who cruised a railroad terminal. Neither organization had kind words for the milieu of the gay bars, though they would have done well to consider why the bars were packed while their membership rolls remained tiny.[11]

Despite these limitations, one cannot dismiss the work of DOB and Mattachine in making San Francisco what it is today. More copies of *The Ladder* and *Mattachine Review* were distributed in San Francisco than elsewhere. The city had more women and men doing gay "political" work than any other. They made contact with a significant number of professionals and initiated a dialogue that was a crucial step in changing antigay attitudes. As the national headquarters of both organizations, San Francisco attracted gay men and lesbians.

Though a militant, grass-roots nationwide liberation movement of lesbians and gay men did not emerge until the end of the 1960s, San Francisco alone witnessed the beginnings of militancy and a mass politics several years earlier. San Francisco was the first city to see the barrier between the movement and the gay subculture break down. The impetus for this pre-Stonewall wave of gay politics emerged not from homophile leaders but from the bar subculture, and resulted from a set of circumstances unique to San Francisco.[12]

San Francisco in the 1940s and 1950s was the setting for an underground literary movement of poets and writers who dissented from the dominant ethos of cold war America, and who expressed through verse their opposition to the conformity and consumerism of the postwar era. By the mid-1950s, the bohemian literary scene in North Beach began attracting beat writers like Allen Ginsberg. Word of what was happening spread, and the San Francisco poets slowly reached a wider audience.

After 1957, however, what began as a small, underground movement was suddenly transmuted by the media into a nationwide generational rebellion against everything that America held sacred. The summer of 1958 witnessed the trial of Lawrence Ferlinghetti, the owner of City Lights bookstore, on charges of selling obscene literature (Ginsberg's *Howl*). Simultaneously, Kerouac's *On the Road* was published. Over the next two years the media turned a spotlight on the beat rebellion and on North

Beach, the setting of the most visible, concentrated beat subculture. The sensationalistic portrayal of them quickly overshadowed the reality. As writers and as a social movement, they received almost universal condemnation. *Look* magazine accused the beats of turning "the average American's value scale ... inside out." The local press descended on North Beach, with the *Examiner* and the *Chronicle* running lurid series that exposed the boozing, drug-crazed, orgiastic, and sexually perverse life of San Francisco's beatniks. In a way that tended to become self-fulfilling, North Beach was labeled the "international headquarters" of the beat generation.[13]

The visibility of the beat subculture in North Beach had a major impact on gay consciousness in San Francisco. Many of the central figures of the literary renaissance in San Francisco were, in fact, gay men—Robert Duncan, Jack Spicer, Robin Blaser, and, of course, Ginsberg—and through their work they carved out a male homosexual cultural space. Ginsberg's *Howl*, a local best-seller, openly acknowledged male homosexuality. In describing gay male sex as joyous, delightful, and even holy, Ginsberg did, in fact, turn American values inside out. The geography of the two subcultures, moreover, overlapped considerably. Most important, the philosophy behind the beat protest resonated with the experience of gays in the 1950s. The beats were rebelling against the "straight" ethos of cold war society—career, home and family, suburban life—an ethos that excluded lesbians and gay men. The beats provided a different lens through which homosexuals and lesbians could view their lives-as a form of protest against a stultifying life-style and set of values.

While the beats exerted their subtle influence on the self-image of the city's gay population, two homosexual-related scandals rocked the city. In the midst of the 1959 mayoral campaign, one of the candidates accused the incumbent mayor and his chief of police of allowing San Francisco to become "the national headquarters of the organized homosexuals in the United States." The charges, based on the fact that Mattachine and DOB were located in San Francisco, made front-page headlines for several days. Political figures and the local press vigorously denied the charges but the affair made the entire city aware of the homophile organizations in its midst.[14]

The following spring, the city was treated to another extensive discussion of the gay presence in San Francisco when a "gayola" scandal hit the police department. Several gay bar owners reported to the district attorney a long history of extortion by the police. One detective and state liquor department investigator were caught with marked money and pleaded guilty. Several other indicted officers opted for a jury trial that dragged on throughout the summer. All of them were acquitted, but the scandal seriously embarrassed the police department and the administration.[15]

Taken together, the beat phenomenon and the homosexual scandals were giving San Francisco an unwelcome reputation as the home for the nation's "deviates" and "rebels." By 1959 the police had increased their patrols in North Beach and were systematically harassing beat gathering places and individuals. The following year, immediately after the conclusion of the gayola trials, the police, with the support and encouragement of the mayor, shifted their attention to the city's gay population. Felony convictions of gay men, which stood at zero in the first half of 1960, rose to twenty-nine in the next six months and jumped to seventy-six in the first six months of 1961. Misdemeanor charges against gay women and men stemming from sweeps of the bars ran at an estimated forty to sixty per week during 1961. By October the state alcoholic beverage control department had revoked the licenses of twelve of the city's thirty gay bars and had initiated proceedings against another fifteen. Every one of the bars that testified against the police department during the gayola inquiry was shut down. The police, backed by the city's press, also intensified surveillance of gay male cruising areas. Vice squad officers raided the theaters showing male homosexual pornographic films and confiscated thousands of gay male and lesbian pulp fiction.[16]

Police harassment of gay bars was not new. In the 1950s it was endemic to the gay male and lesbian subculture of American cities. What was novel about the San Francisco police crackdown was the social context in which it took place. The scandals of 1959 and 1960 led to an unprecedented degree of public discussion of homosexuality. Just as important, the stepped-up harassment followed on the growing awareness of the beat rebellion and its subtle impact on gay consciousness in San Francisco. Thus, the conditions were present to encourage a political response to the antigay campaign.

Both DOB and Mattachine were too enmeshed in the accommodationist politics of the 1950s to resist attacks on aspects of gay life that both organizations deplored as unseemly. Instead, the first wave of rebellion emerged directly out of the bar subculture and out of the one bar, the Black Cat, where gay men, bohemian nonconformity, and police harassment most clearly converged. Located on Montgomery Street a few blocks from the center of North Beach, the Black Cat had a long history as a bohemian meeting place. In the 1940s the character of the bar began to change and it became more clearly a gay male bar. But it retained a special flavor. Allen Ginsberg described it as "the greatest gay bar in America . . . totally open, bohemian. . . . All the gay screaming queens would come, the heterosexual gray flannel suit types, longshoremen. All the poets went there." For more than fifteen years, beginning in the late 1940s, its owner, Sol Stoumen, steadfastly engaged in a court fight against the state liquor board to stay open, spending more than \$38,000 to finance his protracted court battle.[17]

During the 1950s, the Black Cat had a drag entertainer, José Sarria, who staged satirical operas on Sunday afternoons that drew an overflow crowd. Sarria took a traditional, sometimes self-deprecating form of gay male humor camp and drag and transformed it into political theater. Outrageously dressed in female attire, he would perform Carmen, but Carmen as a homosexual hiding in the bushes trying to avoid capture by the vice squad. For years, Sarria ended his show without satire. As George Mendenhall, a pre-Stonewall activist, recalled it:

> José would make these political comments about our rights as homosexuals and at the end . . . of every concert, he would have everybody in the room stand, and we would put our arms around each other and sing, "God Save Us Nelly Queens." It sounds silly, but if you lived at that time and had the oppression coming down from the police department and from society, . . . to be able to put your arms around other gay men and sing "God Save Us Nelly Queens." . . . We were not really saying "God Save Us Nelly Queens." We were saying, "We have our rights, too."[18]

In 1961, at the height of the police crackdown, Sarria decided to run for city supervisor. He had no chance of winning, but victory was not his goal: "I was trying to prove to my gay audience," he recalled, "that I had the right, being as notorious and gay as I was, to run for public office, because people in those days didn't believe you had rights." Sarria's operas made him the best-known gay man in San Francisco; his reputation extended to the entire bar-going population. Though he collected only six thousand votes, his candidacy was the hot topic in the bars that fall, forcing patrons to think about their lives and their sexual orientation in political terms.[19]

Sarria's candidacy set in motion developments that fed lesbian and gay political activity in San Francisco throughout the 1960s. During his campaign, a group of gay men began publishing a biweekly newspaper that they distributed in the bars. Financed by advertising from gay tavern owners, the League for Civil Education (LCE) *News* used a muckraking style to expose gay oppression. Headlines such as "SFPD ATTACKS

HOMOS" and "WE MUST FIGHT NOW!" fueled an ongoing discussion of police" abuses among bar patrons. The LCE *News* encouraged gays to vote as a bloc and sponsored registration drives. By 1963 candidates for public office were taking advertisements in the paper. In 1962 several gay bar owners formed the Tavern Guild as a defense organization to resist attacks from the state. In 1964 some members of the Tavern Guild and a few other friends founded the Society for Individual Rights (SIR). SIR was virtually alone among pre-Stonewall gay male homophile organizations in legitimizing the social needs of homosexuals. In addition to voter registration, candidates' nights during election time, public picketing, and other "political" activity, SIR sponsored dances, bridge clubs, and picnics, provided venereal disease testing, and opened a community center. Its meetings often attracted more than two hundred people, and by 1968 it had a membership of almost a thousand, making it far and away the largest male homophile organization in the country.

By the mid-1960s, lesbians and gay men in San Francisco were breaking out of the isolation that oppression had imposed on them. In 1964 Glide Memorial Methodist Church, whose social-action ministry in the Tenderloin forced it to confront the situation of young male hustlers, opened a dialogue with the city's homophile organizations. Out of it came the Council on Religion and the Homosexual (CRH). The ministers witnessed a vivid display of gay oppression when they sponsored a New Year's Eve dance for San Francisco's gay community. The San Francisco Police Department was there to photograph people as they entered California Hall and to arrest several "chaperones" for "obstructing" police officers. The police came under heavy attack from the press, the American Civil Liberties Union (ACLU) took the case, and a municipal judge dismissed all charges and reprimanded the police. Thereafter, a segment of the city's Protestant clergy spoke out for gay rights "and initiated discussions of homosexuality within their denominations. Phyllis Lyon of DOB was hired to run CRH's educational program. In 1965 Del Martin of DOB helped organize Citizens Alert, a twenty-four-hour hotline to respond to incidents of police brutality. In 1966 DOB planned ten days of public forums at which city officials addressed themselves to gay concerns. Homophile groups cooperatively sponsored candidates' nights each year, and local politicians began to court the gay vote. Some, like state legislator Willie Brown, enthusiastically took up gay concerns.[20]

Unlike the Stonewall Riot of 1969, the impact of Sarria's symbolic candidacy remained confined to San Francisco. The city's situation was too unique, gay men and lesbians in the rest of the country still too isolated and invisible, for it to have anything more than a local effect. At the end of the 1960s, news of a gay riot in New York could spread rapidly through the networks of communication created by the mass movements of the decade. In 1961, with the exception of the southern civil rights movement, those movements and those channels for disseminating information did not exist. And the absence of a nationwide gay movement placed limits, in turn, on how far gay politics in San Francisco could develop.

There were, however, additional reasons why, on a local level, the discontent within the bars was channeled into reform politics. SIR and the Tavern Guild maintained a close working relationship (the two had an overlapping leadership), and SIR relied on the Guild for much of its funds and for publicity. Bar owners wanted police harassment of their businesses to end; once that goal had been achieved, as it largely had been by about 1966, their interest in politics waned and their needs increasingly diverged from patrons who faced job discrimination and police harassment in other urban spaces. The dependence on gay entrepreneurs encouraged SIR's leaders not to rock the boat. Those gay men for whom the beats' cultural protest and glorification of nonconformity had originally struck a responsive chord found little in SIR to claim their allegiance. Instead, the heirs of the beats—the burgeoning hippie movement and counterculture in the Bay Area—offered them a more hospitable home. By the late 1960s gay politics in San Francisco had lost its dynamism.

Homophile politics in San Francisco remained within the limits of reformism during the 1960s and actively involved only a small fraction of its potential constituency. At most, two thousand men and women had organizational affiliation and of these only a few dozen could be considered hard-core activists. Yet, the movement had achieved a level of visibility unmatched elsewhere. By the late 1960s mass magazines were referring to San Francisco as the gay capital of the United States. When the Stonewall Riot sparked a gay liberation movement, San Francisco's lesbian and gay male community could assume a leading role.

THE GROWTH OF THE GAY LIBERATION MOVEMENT

The Stonewall Riot in New York in June 1969 was able to inspire a nationwide grass-roots liberation movement because of the mass radical movements that preceded it. Black militants provided a model of an oppressed minority that transformed their "stigma" into a source of pride and strength. The New Left, antiwar, and student movements popularized a critique of American society and a confrontational style of political action. The counterculture encouraged the rejection of the values and life-style of the middle class, especially its sexual mores. Above all, the women's liberation movement provided a political analysis of sex roles and sexism.

Stonewall initiated a qualitatively different phase of gay and lesbian politics. Two aspects deserve emphasis. One is the notion of coming out, which served both as a goal and a strategy. Coming out became a pro-foundly political step that an individual could take. It promised an imme-diate improvement in one's life, a huge step forward in shedding the self-hatred and internalized oppression imposed by a homophobic society. Coming out also became the key strategy for building a mass movement. Gay women and men who came out crossed a critical dividing line. They relinquished invisibility, made themselves vulnerable to attack, and became invested in the success of the movement. Visible lesbians and gay men, moreover, served as magnets that drew others to them.

Coming out quickly captured the imagination of tens of thousands, perhaps hundreds of thousands, of lesbians and gay men. A mass move-ment was born almost overnight. On the eve of Stonewall, after almost twenty years of homophile politics, fewer than fifty organizations existed. By 1973 more than eight hundred lesbian and gay male groups were scattered across the country. The largest pre-Stonewall homophile dem-onstrations attracted only a few dozen people. In June 1970 five thousand women and men marched in New York to commemorate the Stonewall Rebellion. By the mid-1970s, the yearly marches in several cities were larger than any other political demonstrations since the decline of the civil rights and antiwar movements. Lesbians and gay men created publications and independent presses, record companies, coffeehouses, community centers, counseling services, health clinics, and professional associations.[21]

A second critical feature of the post-Stonewall era was the emergence of a lesbian movement. Lesbians were but a small fraction of the tiny homophile movement. The almost simultaneous birth of women's liber-ation and gay liberation propelled large numbers of lesbians into liberation politics. Lesbians were active both in early gay liberation groups and in feminist organizations. By 1970 the experience of sexism in gay liberation and of heterosexism in women's liberation inspired many lesbians to form organizations of their own, such as Radicalesbians in New York, the Col-lective in Washington, D.C., and Gay Women's Liberation in San Fran-cisco. Lesbian-feminism pushed the analysis of sexism and heterosexism beyond where either the women's or gay movement ventured and so cogently related the two systems of oppression that sectors of the women's movement and gay movement had to incorporate lesbian-feminist analysis into their political practice.[22]

Though gay liberation and women's liberation each played an important role in the emergence of a lesbian-feminist movement, in certain ways the latter exerted a special influence. The feminist movement provided the physical and psychic space for growing numbers of women to come out. As women explored their oppression together, it became easier to acknowledge their love for other women and to embrace "woman-identification." Many lesbians were already living independent, autonomous lives: unencumbered by primary sexual and emotional attachments to men, lesbians had the freedom to explore the farthest reaches of a feminist future. They also had the inclination and need to build and sustain a network of institutions—coffeehouses, clinics, shelters, record companies, presses, schools, and communes—that continually nourished the growth of a lesbian-feminist politics. As opponents of feminism were quick to realize, the women's movement was, in fact, a "breeding ground" for lesbians.

Only a minority of lesbians and gay men joined organizations, but that minority decisively affected the lives of a much larger number. Through coming out and its example of gay pride, through the vastly increased flow of information that an activist minority stimulated, and especially through the inhibitions on police harassment that militancy imposed, lesbian and gay liberation transformed the self-image of many and offered the hope of a better life even to those who had never attended a meeting or participated in a demonstration.

In concrete terms a better life often translated into a decision to move to one of the handful of large cities known to have a well-developed gay subculture. America in the 1970s saw a massive sexual migration set in motion by the lesbian and gay movements. Here, San Francisco had a running start on every other city. Homophile groups were already getting attention from liberal politicians and had already limited police harassment of bars. Magazines played up San Francisco's reputation as a city that tolerated gays. The 1960s, moreover, established the Bay Area as an enclave of radical and life-style politics. The women's movement in the Bay Area, though not free of gay-straight conflict, was noticeably more hospitable to lesbians than elsewhere. While the New York chapter of the National Organization for Women (NOW), for instance, was purging lesbians from its ranks, the San Francisco chapter was pushing for a lesbian rights resolution at the organization's 1971 national convention.

By the mid-1970s San Francisco had become, in comparison with the rest of the country, a liberated zone for lesbians and gay men. It had the largest number and widest variety of organizations and institutions. An enormous in-migration had created a new social phenomenon—residential areas that were visibly gay in composition: Duboce Triangle, Noe Valley, and the Upper Mission for lesbians; the Haight, Folsom, and above all the Castro for gay men. Geographic concentration offered the opportunity for local political power that invisibility precluded.

The explosive growth of the gay community and its political activism also made internal differences visible. For some gay men liberation meant freedom from harassment; for Radicalesbians it meant overthrowing the patriarchy. Bay Area Gay Liberation participated in anti-imperialist coalitions while members of the Alice B. Toklas Democratic Club sought to climb within the Democratic party hierarchy. The interests of gay entrepreneurs in the Castro clashed with those of their gay employees. Gay male real-estate speculators displayed little concern for "brothers" who could not pay the skyrocketing rents. Gay men and women of color found themselves displaced by more privileged members of the community as gentrification spread to more and more neighborhoods. Sexual orientation created a kind of unity, but other aspects of identity brought to the surface conflicting needs and interests.

COMMUNITY AND POWER IN
AN AGE OF ADVERSITY

The second half of the 1970s witnessed a rapid coming of age of gay political force in San Francisco. In 1975 George Moscone, a liberal state senator with a progay voting record, was elected mayor by a narrow margin of three thousand votes. Moscone credited gays with providing his margin of victory and included gays among the constituencies to be courted with political appointments. In November 1976 gay residential areas voted heavily for Proposition T, which mandated district elections for city supervisors. The following year Harvey Milk, a political outsider with few ties to the gay Democratic "establishment," won election from District 5, which included the Castro, Noe Valley, and the Haight. In June 1976 San Francisco surpassed New York in the size of its Gay Freedom Day march. The turnout of more than ninety thousand alerted politicians to the potential significance of the gay vote.[23]

The antigay backlash of the New Right provided the stimulus that seemed to transform that potential into a force with real power. The repeal of gay rights ordinances in Dade County, Florida, and in Saint Paul,

Wichita, and Eugene, Oregon, in 1977 and 1978, fueled a repressive legislative initiative in California. John Briggs, an ultraconservative state senator from Orange County with aspirations for higher office, announced plans to introduce legislation to prohibit gays from teaching in the public schools. When it became obvious that the legislation had no chance of passage, Briggs shifted tactics and mounted a campaign to have his proposal placed on the ballot as a statewide initiative. California voters would have to decide whether lesbians and gay men, as well as anyone who publicly or privately advocated or encouraged homosexual conduct, should be dismissed from jobs in the public school system.

The Briggs initiative ("Proposition 6" on the ballot) stimulated the most far-reaching and sustained gay organizing campaign in history. A bewildering array of organizations came into existence in every part of the state, with a wide range of political perspectives. Unlike the previous campaigns in other cities — low-key, respectable, "human rights" in emphasis—many in the anti-Briggs effort decided to confront issues of homophobia and sexuality directly, to link the antigay initiative with Proposition 7, a measure to reinstitute the death penalty, and to discuss the Briggs initiative as one part of a New Right strategy to attack racial minorities, women, and workers. The San Francisco lesbian and gay communities were in the forefront of the more radical approach to the anti-Briggs campaign.[24]

The mobilization of San Francisco's lesbians and gay men against Briggs secured other important gains and provided further evidence of growing gay power. The "Prop 6 campaign" forced most of the city's politicians to take a progay stand, however tenuous and opportunistic. In March 1978, after years of effort, a comprehensive gay rights ordinance was passed by the Board of Supervisors. The city allocated public funds for Gay Freedom Day activities; 300,000 people assembled for the rally at civic center. San Francisco's police chief, Charles Gain, announced a drive to recruit lesbians and gay men for the police force and urged gays already in the department to come out.

The anti-Briggs campaign also had a profound effect on the political career and image of Harvey Milk, San Francisco's gay supervisor. Milk was not the "leader" of the "No on 6" effort. But as the state's only openly gay elected official Milk was uniquely visible. This gave him a degree of political leverage that most local politicians only dream of attaining. He matured as a political leader, became more than a gay spokesperson, and began moving beyond liberalism. He worked hard to cement a coalition among gays, racial minorities, and the elderly. He became a strong advocate of rent control, opposed the redevelopment plans being pushed by downtown corporate interests, and introduced a resolution to have the South African consulate in San Francisco closed. During 1978 he helped to push Moscone away from mainstream liberalism and toward a populist-style coalition politics. By the time of the November election, Milk had become one of the most popular politicians in San Francisco and had achieved wide voter recognition throughout the state.

The November balloting brought a decisive victory to California's lesbians and gay men. Almost 60 percent of the electorate voted no on Proposition 6. In San Francisco the figure was 75 percent, with only a handful of the city's nine hundred precincts supporting the measure. The California victory was enormously significant in checking the mood of gloom and despair that was infecting the lesbian and gay movement throughout the country. Locally, it stimulated celebrations and fueled a sense of growing, almost unstoppable, power. Then, less than three weeks later, Milk and Moscone were assassinated by former city supervisor Dan White.

The day after the murders, the *Chronicle* called them "politically motivated." The truth of that charge was apparent. White, a veteran, former police officer, and firefighter, was the most conservative member of the Board of Supervisors and notoriously antigay. His 1977 campaign included rhetorical attacks on "social deviates." The only supervisor to vote against the gay rights ordinance, he also supported the Briggs initiative. Milk stood at opposite ends of the political spectrum represented on the Board of Supervisors. The assassination of Milk and Moscone effected a political coup in San Francisco. There were no progressive Democrats of comparable stature to replace them. Dianne Feinstein, closely allied to downtown business interests and a mentor of Dan White, became mayor.

The assassination made clear that gay power in San Francisco, though real, was also fragile. The political momentum generated among lesbians and gay men in San Francisco by the antigay backlash, and the gains made in the city during 1977–78, had tended to obscure the extent of homophobia in San Francisco. When Sheriff Hongisto campaigned for gays in Miami, for instance, the deputy sheriffs' association sent a telegram of support to Anita Bryant. Police chief Charles Gain's drive to recruit lesbian and gay cops aroused the ire of the rank and file. A few days after the massive 1977 Gay Freedom Day march, five gay businesses on Castro Street were bombed. While the Board of Supervisors debated the gay rights ordinance, arsonists were setting fires to gay-owned stores in the south-of-Market Folsom area. Throughout 1977 and 1978, street violence against lesbians and gay men was a pervasive problem. A few days after becoming mayor, Feinstein warned the gay community that it was a minority in a heterosexual society and had to respect the sensibilities and standards of the majority.

For a time it seemed as if gay men and lesbians were about to lose the ground they had gained. In December 1978 an antipornography bill introduced by Feinstein became law and the district attorney's office began an investigation and crackdown against gay male bookstores and theaters. In January police officers assaulted and arrested two women as they left Amelia's, a lesbian bar in the Upper Mission. In March a group of drunken off-duty police burst into Peg's Place, a lesbian bar in the Richmond, and indiscriminately attacked patrons. The police began harassing gay male leather bars in the Folsom area and hassling young gays on Polk Street. The plan of these attacks was clear: leave the Castro, the heavily gay male area, alone, but attack the "periphery" of the gay subculture—lesbian rather than gay male bars, gay youth rather than adults, sadomasochists rather than ordinary gays, "porn" stores and theaters rather than "good gay" meeting places.

Then came the Dan White murder trial: an all-White, all-straight jury; a prosecutor who never mentioned the political antagonisms between White and Milk and therefore could not prove premeditation; a taped confession, taken by White's former softball coach, that made jurors weep in sympathy for the defendant; and prosecution witnesses, like Mayor Feinstein, who praised the moral character of the killer. Throughout the trial the local press was unusually sympathetic toward the assassin of the city's mayor and gay supervisor. Cops were reported to be wearing "Free Dan White" t-shirts; a local reporter told me that when the manslaughter verdict (the lightest possible conviction) was announced, "Oh Danny Boy" was played on the police radio.[25]

The manslaughter verdict of May 21, 1979, sparked a riot, but did not cause the riot. The actions of the five to ten thousand gay men and women at City Hall that night were caused by six months of accumulating anger over police harassment and violence, street attacks, and an increasingly hostile city administration. The riot was the response of a community that had worked hard for its victories and then, after its greatest triumph, watched its dreams shattered by bullets from an assassin who represented everything that lesbians and gay men were fighting against.

Gay men and women at city hall attacked property; later that night, after the rioting was over, the police smashed heads. Rank-and-file police, packed into squad cars and vans, and encouraged by their officers, arrived on Castro Street and produced a terrifying display of indiscriminate violence. They charged into the Elephant Walk, a popular bar, smashing windows and upsetting tables. Screaming "dirty cocksuckers" and "sick faggots," and "we lost the battle of city hall; we won't lose this one," they attacked the bar's patrons. Others went marauding through the street, bloodying the faces of passersby. For two hours Castro Street was a virtual war zone, with the police on the offensive.

The anger that the Dan White verdict unleashed made it clear that the gay community in San Francisco was not about to relinquish its political power. By the end of the 1970s, the web of institutions in the community was too dense to be sundered by an assassin's bullet. Indeed, over the next few years gay men and lesbians were incorporated into the political life of the city as never before. Many elected officials, particularly liberal Democrats, routinely hired liaisons to the community, while others made use of gay political leadership on their staffs. Some lesbians and gay men were elected to minor posts in the city; many more were appointed to municipal regulatory boards.

The strength of the community became apparent during the 1980s when it was hit by the AIDS crisis. The lethal syndrome first came to light in 1981. The virus that seemed to cause the breakdown of the immune system was spread by blood and semen. The network of sexual meeting places that fostered recreational sex among gay men provided a hospitable environment for the rapid spread of the virus, and the AIDS caseload grew exponentially. By 1987 there were more than forty-five thousand cases in the nation and more than forty-four hundred in San Francisco. The overwhelming majority of the San Francisco cases were among gay men. Death became endemic, with survivors wondering if they would be next. A community that was bound together by an exuberant sexuality was forced to engage in serious soul-searching and to question what kind of future beckoned.[26]

Although AIDS was an unparalleled tragedy for the gay community around the nation, it also fostered a heightened level of political organizing. Wherever cases appeared in significant numbers, new organizations sprang to life to deal with the suffering. By the mid-1980s AIDS was pushing gay issues toward the center of public debate. Groups that formed to provide social services soon found it necessary to plunge into the political arena to demand more funding for research and support services, to lobby for protection against discrimination, and to ward off the Orwellian proposals of right-wing pressure groups. The March on Washington in October 1987, in which 600,000 gay men, lesbians, and their allies converged on the nation's capital, testified to the depth of anger and political militancy that the AIDS crisis had generated.

As with so many other areas, the San Francisco community emerged as a leader in the response to AIDS. The city government, prodded by its highly visible gay constituency, provided proportionately more money more quickly than any other municipality. Support services proliferated, both on the part of government agencies and within the gay community itself. San Franciscans were saturated with educational materials and campaigns about safer sex; the incidence of diseases, such as syphilis and gonorrhea, plummeted as gay men altered their sexual habits to protect themselves. And a gay political leader in San Francisco, Cleve Jones, conceived and organized the "Names Project," a memorial quilt to those who died from AIDS that captured the attention and the sympathy of the nation.

But it would be wrong to overstate the political strength of lesbians and gay men in the city in the mid-1980s. For one, the San Francisco community existed in a larger social and political environment in which homophobia remained entrenched. The Reagan administration and the New Right continued to shape the national agenda to which gay activists had to react; in California, a conservative Republican governor, George Deukmejian, stymied progress at the state level. Within San Francisco itself, the community remained divided by political persuasion as well as identity. The progressive Harvey Milk Democratic Club and Stonewall Democratic Club engaged in rivalry with the more moderate Alice B. Toklas Club. Gender, class, and racial identities shaped sometimes conflicting priorities among the gay population. Antigay violence, stimulated by AIDS, persisted as a problem, and the police were still not reliable defenders of the gay community.

Still, the previous few decades had witnessed a profound and lasting change in San Francisco (and in the nation at large). What was once a despised identity had become the basis for an urban community, sharing many of the characteristics of more traditional ethnic groupings. And the community had, in turn, spawned a vigorous politics that gave it unusual national influence and served as a beacon of hope for others.

NOTES

1. Jeffrey Weeks, *Coming Out: Homosexual Politics in Britain from the Nineteenth Century to the Present* (London, 1977), pp. 2–3.

2. The best treatment of colonial America is Jonathan Ned Katz, *Gay/Lesbian Almanac* (New York, 1983), pp. 23–133.

3. See John D'Emilio, "Capitalism and Gay Identity," in Ann Snitow, Christine Stansell, and Sharon Thompson, eds., *Powers of Desire: The Politics of Sexuality* (New

York, 1983), pp. 100–13; and Eli Zaretsky, *Capitalism, the Family and Personal Life* (New York, 1976).

4. On the medical model and the changing social expression of homosexuality see Katz, *Gay/Lesbian Almanac*, pp. 173–74, and *Gay American History* (New York, 1976), pp. 129–207; George Chauncey, Jr., "From Sexual Inversion to Homosexuality: Medicine and the Changing Conceptualization of Female Deviance," *Salmagundi* 58/59 (Fall 1982/Winter 1983):114–46; and Lillian Faderman, *Surpassing the Love of Men* (New York, 1981).

5. For a sense of the varieties of gay and lesbian experience see Eric Garber, "A Spectacle in Color: The Lesbian and Gay Subculture of Jazz Age Harlem," in Martin Duberman, Martha Vicinus, and George Chauncey, Jr., eds., *Hidden from History: Reclaiming the Gay and Lesbian Past* (New York, 1989), pp. 318–31; George Chauncey, Jr., "Christian Brotherhood or Sexual Perversion?: Homosexual Identities and the Construction of Sexual Boundaries in the World War I Era," in Duberman, Vicinus, and Chauncey, *Hidden from History*, pp. 294–317; and Faderman, *Surpassing the Love of Men.*

6. Much of the evidence and the argument about postwar San Francisco's gay community and its politics is taken from John D'Emilio, *Sexual Politics, Sexual Communities: The Making of a Homosexual Minority in the United States, 1940–1970* (Chicago, 1983).

7. Ibid., pp. 23–29; Allan Bérubé, "Marching to a Different Drummer: Lesbian and Gay GIs in World War II," in Duberman, Vicinus, and Chauncey, *Hidden from History*, pp. 383–94; and "Coming Out Under Fire," *Mother Jones*, February–March 1983, pp. 23–29, 45.

8. D'Emilio, *Sexual Politics, Sexual Communities*, pp. 40–53; Allan Bérubé and John D'Emilio, "The Military and Lesbians During the McCarthy Years, *Signs* 9:759–75, 1986; John D'Emilio, "The Homosexual Menace: The Politics of Sexuality in Cold War America," in Kathy Peiss and Christina Simmons, eds., *Passion and Power* (Philadelphia, 1989); Katz, *Gay American History*, pp. 91–108.

9. See the interview with Pat Bond in Nancy Adair and Casey Adair, *Word Is Out* (San Francisco, 1978), pp. 55–65; D'Emilio, *Sexual Politics, Sexual Communities*, pp. 182–85.

10. D'Emilio, *Sexual Politics, Sexual Communities*, pp. 57–107; Del Martin and Phyllis Lyon, *Lesbian/Woman* (San Francisco, 1972).

11. D'Emilio, *Sexual Politics, Sexual Communities*, pp. 108–25. The political perspective of the homophile movement in the 1950s can be gleaned from a reading of its three periodicals: *Mattachine Review, The Ladder*, and *ONE.*

12. The discussion of events in San Francisco in the 1960s is drawn from D'Emilio, *Sexual Politics, Sexual Communities*, pp. 176–95.

13. *Look*, August 19, 1958, pp. 64ff. On the Beats see Bruce Cook, *The Beat Generation* (New York, 1971); John Tytell, *Naked Angels* (New York, 1976); and Dennis McNally, *Desolate Angel: Jack Kerouac, the Beat Generation, and America* (New York, 1979).

14. On the election controversy see the San Francisco *Progress*, October 7, 1959, where the original charges were made, and the *News-Call-Bulletin*, the *Examiner*, and the *Chronicle*, October 9, 1959, and the days following.

15. The gayola scandal received extensive coverage in San Francisco's newspapers from May through August 1960.

16. D'Emilio, *Sexual Politics, Sexual Communities*, pp. 183–85.

17. *Allen Ginsberg: Gay Sunshine Interview with Allen Young* (Bolinas, Calif., 1974), pp. 11–12; *Stoumen v. Reilly*, 234 P. 2d 969.

18. Adair and Adair, *Word Is Out*, pp. 73–74.

19. "Gay Life in the 1950s: Interview with José Sarria," KPFA-FM, Berkeley, Calif., March 14, 1979.

20. D'Emilio, *Sexual Politics, Sexual Communities*, pp. 188–95.

21. On gay liberation see Dennis Altman, *Homosexual Oppression and Liberation* (New York, 1972); Toby Marotta, *The Politics of Homosexuality* (Boston, 1981); Donn Teal, *The Gay Militants* (New York, 1971); Karla Jay and Allen Young, eds., *Out of the Closets: Voices of Gay Liberation* (New York, 1972); and Laud Humphreys, *Out of the Closets* (Englewood Cliffs, N.J., 1972).

22. On lesbian-feminism see Jay and Young, *Out of the Closets*, especially pp. 172–203; Sidney Abbott and Barbara Love, *Sappho Was a Right-On Woman* (New York, 1972); Nancy Myron and Charlotte Bunch, eds., *Lesbianism and the Women's Movement* (Baltimore, 1975); and Jill Johnston, *Lesbian Nation* (New York, 1973).

23. On San Francisco in the 1970s see, especially, Randy Shilts, *The Mayor of Castro Street* (New York, 1982), and Frances FitzGerald, *Cities on a Hill* (New York, 1987).

24. See Shilts, *The Mayor of Castro Street*, and Amber Hollibaugh, "Sexuality and the State," *Socialist Review* 45 (May–June 1979):55–72.

25. The discussion of events surrounding the trial and the verdict is taken from personal observation, conversations, and a reading of San Francisco papers during a long stay in San Francisco in 1979.

26. The literature on AIDS is already immense but see, especially, Dennis Altman, *AIDS in the Mind of America* (Garden City, N.Y., 1986); Cindy Patton, *Sex and Germs* (Boston, 1985); and Randy Shilts, *And the Band Played On* (New York, 1987).

2

Components of Sexual Identity

Michael G. Shively and John P. De Cecco

This paper examines the four components of sexual identity: biological sex, gender identity, social sex-role, and sexual orientation. Theories about the development of each component and how they combine and conflict to form the individual's sexual identity are discussed. As defined here, social sex-role includes the individual's femininity and masculinity. Sexual orientation includes the individual's physical and affectional sexual preferences for relationships with members of the same and/or opposite biological sex. This paper may help to clarify meanings of the following terms used in research on sexual identity: sex, gender, femininity, masculinity, heterosexuality, *and* homosexuality.

The purpose of this paper is to discuss the psychological components of sexual identity. In addition to the biological sex of the individual these components are: a) gender identity, b) social sex-role, and c) sexual orientation. Theories about the development of each component and how they combine and conflict to form the individual's sexual identity will also be discussed.

BIOLOGICAL SEX

At birth each individual is classified by biological sex. The doctor tells the parents that the neonate is a boy or girl. Most often it is an easy process to ascertain the biological sex—the doctor simply looks. In more difficult cases there are seven criteria (table 2.1) used in determining the biological sex of the child.

TABLE 2.1
Criteria Used in Determining the Biological Sex of Sexually Ambiguous Children

Criteria	Examples
Chromosomal configuration	XX female
	XY male
Gonads	Ovaries or testes
Internal reproductive structures	Uterus or prostate, etc.
External genitalia	Clitoris and labia or
	penis and scrotum
Hormonal secretions	Estrogens—female
	Androgens—male
Sex assigned at birth	Girl or boy
Psychological sex—gender identity	Female or male

GENDER IDENTITY

The first psychological component of sexual identity to develop is gender identity. Green (1974) defines this component as the "individual's basic conviction of being male or female." This conviction is not entirely contingent on the individual's biological sex. Occasionally boys develop the conviction of being female and girls of being male. It is generally thought that gender identity develops between birth and three years of age (Green 1974; Money and Tucker 1975). Gender identity is usually present by the time the child begins to talk.

The exact process by which young boys come to see themselves as males and young girls come to see themselves as females is not known. It seems probable that from birth male infants are socialized as boys and female infants are socialized as girls (Maccoby and Jacklin 1974; Money and Tucker 1975; Sears 1965). The relative contribution of biological development and social learning to the formation of gender identity is now being studied (e.g., Green 1974; Money and Ehrhardt 1972).

When there is a conflict between biological sex and gender identity, one way the individual may resolve the conflict is by undergoing surgery whereby biological sex is modified to be congruent with gender identity. Individuals who have undergone this operation are known as transsexuals.

Biological sex is a way in which individuals are identified by themselves and by others. Gender identity is part of the individual's self-identification.

SOCIAL SEX-ROLE

The second component of sexual identity to develop is social sex-role. It refers to characteristics that are culturally associated with men or with women. These characteristics are perceived as stereotypically masculine or feminine.

Social sex-role is largely tied to characteristics of appearance, behavior, and personality. Based on cultural norms, individuals are "expected" to behave in socially stereotypical ways that are associated with their biological sex. That is, males are expected to act in ways that will be seen as masculine, and females in ways that will be seen as feminine. Behaviors that deviate from these stereotypes are viewed as inappropriate.

Social sex-role formation generally occurs between the ages of three and seven years. Kagan (1958) explains the development of this component by using social learning theory. Social sex-roles are acquired by: a) children wanting approval; b) adult caretakers giving children approval for developing stereotypic behavior; and c) males learning to behave like boys, and females like girls. Social sex-roles are also acquired by the relationship of the child to the adult caretaker who is modeling behavior. Kagan describes the relationship of the child to the caretaker model: a) the model must be perceived by the child as nurturant; b) the model must be in command of resources desired by the child; and c) the child must perceive some objective bases of similarity between himself or herself and the model.

Masculinity and femininity can be viewed as one continuum (bipolar) or as two independent continua. If viewed as bipolar, the individual expresses masculinity at the expense of femininity and femininity at the expense of masculinity. Figure 2.1 shows a bipolar conception of social sex-role. Pilot data gathered in a study of the relationship between social sex-role and the abridgment of civil liberties indicated that respondents saw the presence of masculinity in both heterosexual and homosexual men and women as the absence of femininity (De Cecco et al. 1975).

Masculinity and femininity can also be viewed as independent continua

Figure 2.1. Masculinity-Femininity Continuum

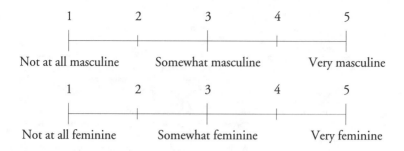

Figure 2.2. Masculinity-Femininity Continua

(Bem 1974). As shown in figure 2.2, these two continua describe both qualitative and quantitative differences in masculinity and femininity. Qualitatively, an individual male or female can be seen as masculine, feminine, or both masculine and feminine. Quantitatively, masculinity and femininity can range from very much to very little. There are individuals who can be seen as equally masculine and feminine. Bem has called these individuals androgynous. Spence, Helmreich, and Stapp (1975) have called individuals who are both very masculine and very feminine androgynous. They have called those individuals who are not at all masculine or feminine "undifferentiated" in social sex-role.

Adults use internalized stereotypes to make judgments about their own and others' relative masculinity and femininity. Listed in table 2.2 are the ten major categories of social sex-role characteristics that White middle-class adults are known to use in making discriminations about masculinity and femininity (Shively and Rudolph 1977). Physical attributes, mannerisms, speech, and personality traits are the categories most emphasized in making discriminations about the masculinity and femininity of individuals.

In some individuals conflicts arise between biological sex and social sex-role. Green (1974), Green and Money (1969), Rekers and Lovaas (1974), and Rekers et al. (1976) have studied boys who developed behavior that was considered very feminine. One way an individual may resolve this conflict is by becoming a transvestite, a person who dresses in clothing ordinarily worn by a person of the biological sex opposite to his or her own.

In other individuals there may be conflict between gender identity and social sex-role. These individuals may be men who are seen by others as masculine but see themselves as females, or women who are seen by others as feminine but see themselves as males. For these individuals, behaving as transvestites may be preliminary to their becoming transsexuals.

TABLE 2.2
Categories and Characteristics of Social Sex Role

Categories	Examples
Physical attributes	The physical traits that an individual is born with or develops. Mostly secondary sexual characteristics (e.g., presence or absence of body hair, breasts).
Physical condition	Healthy men are seen as more masculine and healthy women are seen as more feminine than are unhealthy men and women. Women who have an average body weight for their body build are seen as more feminine than are very thin or obese women.
Mannerisms	The way in which an individual moves, sits, or stands. Men who move their hands in an uncontrolled manner are seen as more feminine than masculine.
Adornment	The kind of things an individual chooses to put on his/her body (e.g., clothing, jewelry).
Personality traits	Men are seen as masculine when they are assertive and confident, women as feminine when they are soft, discreet, and sociable.
Grooming	Personal cleanliness, hairstyle, etc. Men and women are seen as more masculine and feminine, respectively, if they are reasonably well kept.
Speech and vocabulary	The inflection of the voice—pitch, tone, etc. The words used in speaking (e.g., slang).
Social interaction	An individual's behavior toward persons of the same or opposite sex in social situations.
Interests	An individual's employment and what his/her interests are apart from work (e.g., opera or baseball games).
Habits	Smoking, drinking alcohol, nail biting, etc.

SEXUAL ORIENTATION

The third component of sexual identity to develop is sexual orientation. Previous research on sexual orientation has been based on a bipolar view as shown in figure 2.3 (e.g., Bell 1973; Bieber 1976; Bieber et al. 1962; Kinsey, Pomeroy, and Martin 1948; Kinsey et al. 1953). In this conception an individual expresses one orientation at the expense of the other.

Sexual orientation can be viewed as having two aspects. One is physical preference, the other is affectional preference. Physical preference refers to the individual's preference for male and/or female sexual partners. Affec-

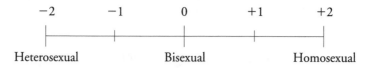

Figure 2.3. Bipolar Model of Sexual Orientation

tional preference refers to an individual's preference for male and/or female emotional partners.

Physical preference can be viewed as two independent continua of heterosexuality and homosexuality (see figure 2.4). For each individual there is one continuum for physical heterosexuality and another for physical homosexuality. Qualitatively, individuals can be seen as heterosexual, homosexual, or both heterosexual and homosexual. Quantitatively, individuals can be seen as having heterosexuality and homosexuality ranging from very much to very little.

Affectional preference, in similar fashion, can be viewed as two independent continua of affectional heterosexuality and affectional homosexuality. Figure 2.5 shows the two continua and the relationship of one continuum to the other.

The bipolar view of sexual orientation is restricted to physical expression and suggests that homosexuality is expressed at the expense of heterosexuality, or heterosexuality is expressed at the expense of homosexuality. A theory that includes both the physical and affectional expression of sexual orientation allows an examination of a greater variety of ways of expressing sexuality.

In the physical-affectional theory of sexual orientation, conflicts can occur a) between physical and affectional expression, b) between homosexual and heterosexual physical sexuality, and c) between homosexual and

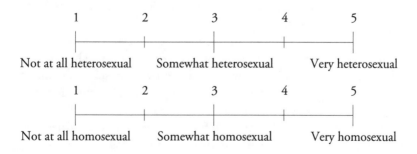

Figure 2.4. Physical Preference: Heterosexuality-Homosexuality Continua

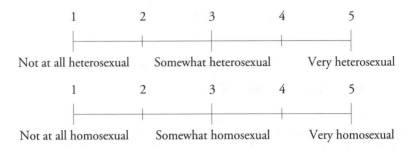

Figure 2.5. Affectional Preference: Heterosexuality-Homosexuality Continua

heterosexual affectional sexuality. These conflicts may be resolved at two levels, behavior and fantasy. The behavioral level is generally observed and used to identify sexual orientation. The fantasy level is examined by the therapist and the patient and sometimes used by them to identify sexual orientation. A complete identification of the individual's sexual orientation should include both behavior and fantasy. Behavior and fantasy can occur in the same or different orientations. Because sexual attraction is very powerful it is possible that neither sexual orientation is ultimately surrendered by the individual. Freud (1922, 1938) believed that children are originally bisexual. Oedipal theory is based on a bipolar conception of sexual orientation and emphasizes heterosexual resolutions. These resolutions are the ones that are institutionalized and have social approval.

The development of sexual orientation probably parallels, but is not synchronous with, the development of social sex role. The development of the physical and affectional aspects of sexual orientation may also be asynchronous. The affectional aspect of the parents' sexual orientation is usually more open to observation by the child than the physical aspect. Therefore, the emotional aspect of the child's sexual orientation may develop at a faster rate than the physical aspect. The emotional aspect may develop more rapidly in childhood, and the physical aspect may develop more rapidly in adolescence.

There are several types of conflicts that can develop between sexual orientation and the other components of sexual identity. The most generally recognized conflict is between biological sex and sexual orientation. A heterosexual physical orientation is biologically and culturally tied to procreation. One way this conflict between having and not having children may be resolved is by differentiating the two aspects of sexual orientation. Whereas procreation is one important reason for sexual intercourse, physical pleasure and emotional intimacy are other important reasons.

There are no studies at present on conflicts between sexual orientation and gender identity. In theory, men or women who choose persons of the same biological sex for sexual expression may be in conflict over their gender identity if they believe they are behaving as people of the opposite biological sex.

De Cecco and Shively (in press a, b) are studying conflicts that arise between sexual orientation and social sex-role. In intimate relationships, men tend to have conflicts over issues of power, and women over issues of dependency. Power represents the socialized masculine role. Dependency represents the socialized feminine role.

The three psychological components of sexual identity have been discussed: gender identity, social sex-role, and sexual orientation. Theories about the development of each component have also been discussed. Some of the conflicts that can occur between biological sex and one or more of these components have been identified.

REFERENCES

Bell, A. 1973. Homosexualities: Their range and character. In J. K. Cole and R. Dienstbier, eds., *Nebraska Symposium on Motivation*, vol. 21. Lincoln: University of Nebraska Press.

Bem, S. L. 1974. The measurement of psychological androgyny. *Journal of Consulting and Clinical Psychology* 2:155–62.

Bieber, I. 1976. A discussion of "Homosexuality: The ethical challenge." *Journal of Consulting and Clinical Psychology* 44(2):163–66.

Bieber, I., H. J. Dain, P. R. Dince, M. D. Drelich, H. G. Grand, R. H. Gundlach, M. V. Kremer, A. A. Rifkin, C. B. Wilber, and T. B. Bieber. 1962. *Homosexuality: A Psychoanalytic Study of Male Homosexuals*. New York: Basic Books.

De Cecco, J. P., and M. G. Shively. In press (a). Children's development: Social sex-role and hetero-homosexual orientation. In *The Sexual and Gender Development of Young Children*. Oremland and Oremland.

De Cecco, J. P., and M. G. Shively. In press (b). Conflicts over rights and needs in homosexual relationships. In *The Gay Academic*. Homewood, Ill.: ETC Press.

De Cecco, J., M. Shively, F. Minnigerode, M. Adelman, J. Rudolph, O. Glover, and M. Figliulo. 1975. *Civil Liberties of Homosexual Men and Women*. Grant 1-RO-1-MH-6740–01-SP, Department of Health, Education, and Welfare, National Institute of Mental Health.

Freud. S. 1922. *Beyond the Pleasure Principle*. London: Hogarth Press.

Freud, S. 1938. *Three Contributions to the Theory of Sex in the Basic Writings of Sigmund Freud*. Edited and translated by A. A. Brill. New York: Modern Library.

Green, R. 1974. *Sexual Identity Conflict in Children and Adults*. New York: Basic Books.

Green, R., and J. Money, eds. 1969. *Transsexualism and Sex Reassignment.* Baltimore: Johns Hopkins University Press.

Kagan, J. 1958. The concept of identification. *Psychological Review* 65:296–305.

Kinsey, A., W. Pomeroy, and C. Martin. *Sexual Behavior in the Human Male.* Philadelphia: W. B. Saunders.

Kinsey, A. C., W. B. Pomeroy, C. E. Martin, and P. H. Gebhard. 1953. *Sexual Behavior in the Human Female.* Philadelphia: W. B. Saunders.

Maccoby, E. E., and C. N. Jacklin. 1974. *Psychology of Sex Differences.* Stanford, Calif.: Stanford University Press.

Money, J., and A. A. Ehrhardt. 1972. *Man and Woman, Boy and Girl: The Differentiation and Dimorphism of Gender Identity from Conception to Maturity.* Baltimore: Johns Hopkins University Press.

Money, J., and P. Tucker. 1975. *Sexual Signatures: On Being a Man or a Woman.* Boston: Little, Brown.

Rekers, G. A., and O. I. Lovaas. 1974. Behavioral treatment of deviant sex-role behaviors in a male child. *Journal of Applied Behavioral Analysis* 7:173–90.

Rekers, G. A., et al. 1976. Childhood gender identity change: Operant control over sex-typed play and mannerisms. *Journal of Behavior Therapy and Experimental Psychiatry* 7:51–57.

Sears, R. 1965. Development of gender role. In F. A. Beach, ed., *Sex and Behavior,* pp. 133–63. New York: Wiley.

Shively, M. G., and J. R. Rudolph. 1977. Stereotypes of femininity and masculinity. Master's thesis, San Francisco State University.

Spence, J., R. Helmreich, and J. Stapp. 1975. Ratings of self and peers on sex-role attributes and their relationship to self-esteem and conceptions of masculinity and femininity. *Journal of Personality and Social Psychology* 32:29–39.

3

The Context of Antigay Violence: Notes on Cultural and Psychological Heterosexism

Gregory M. Herek

Hate crimes against lesbians and gay men occur within a broader cultural context that is permeated by heterosexism. Heterosexism is defined here as an ideological system that denies, denigrates, and stigmatizes any nonheterosexual form of behavior, identity, relationship, or community. It operates principally by rendering homosexuality invisible and, when this fails, by trivializing, repressing, or stigmatizing it. This article focuses on the nexus between cultural heterosexism and individual prejudice against lesbians and gay men. Key components of the ideologies of sex and gender from which heterosexism derives are identified: a) the personal-public dichotomy, b) the stigmatization of particular forms of sexuality, and c) the linkage of heterosexuality to gender-role conformity. Supported by these ideological underpinnings, cultural heterosexism fosters individual antigay attitudes by providing a ready-made system of values and stereotypical beliefs that justify such prejudice as "natural." By imbuing homosexuality with a variety of symbolic meanings, cultural heterosexism enables expressions of individual prejudice to serve various psychological functions. Further, by discouraging lesbians and gay men from coming out to others, heterosexism perpetuates itself. Recent social trends that may affect the ideology of heterosexism are identified, and their potential for reducing antigay prejudice is discussed.

Hate crimes against lesbians and gay men in the United States must be understood in context: antigay violence is a logical, albeit extreme, extension of the heterosexism that pervades American society. *Heterosexism* is defined here as an ideological system that denies, denigrates, and stigmatizes any nonheterosexual form of behavior, identity, relationship, or community. Like racism, sexism, and other ideologies of oppression, hetero-sexism is manifested both in societal customs and institutions, such as religion and the legal system (referred to here as *cultural heterosexism*) and in individual attitudes and behaviors (referred to here as *psychological heterosexism*).

The present article has four goals. First, it describes cultural heterosexism in the United States today as the backdrop against which antigay violence occurs. Second, it explores how key components of the cultural ideologies of sexuality and gender foster heterosexism and, ultimately, antigay violence. These components of ideology are conceptualized here as underpinning antigay hostility by creating conditions in which gay people remain largely invisible while the concept of homosexuality is imbued with various symbolic statuses (e.g., deviance, sickness, evil). Third, the article describes how these symbolic statuses, rather than interactive experiences with gay persons, form the basis for most heterosexuals' attitudes and how, as a result, those attitudes function primarily to fulfill psychosocial needs. Finally, the article considers how societal transformations now in progress might affect cultural heterosexism and its underlying ideologies. The overall question to be addressed is not so much *why* homosexuality is stigmatized in American society, but rather *how* heterosexism is transmitted through cultural institutions and individual experience.

INSTITUTIONAL MANIFESTATIONS OF CULTURAL HETEROSEXISM

Cultural heterosexism is like the air we breathe: It is so ubiquitous that it is hardly noticeable. Even a cursory survey of American society reveals that homosexuality is largely hidden and, when publicly recognized, is usually condemned or stigmatized. This alternation between invisibility and condemnation is readily apparent in four major societal institutions: religion, the law, psychiatry and psychology, and mass media.

In prescribing guidelines for moral living, modern Christian and Jewish religious institutions stress the inherent virtue of committed marital relationships through which children are conceived and raised in the faith. Marriages are heterosexual by definition; homosexual behavior is widely condemned; same-sex relationships and families are not recognized (see Boswell 1980, for historical background). Some denominations and congregations recently have adopted more accepting positions concerning homosexuality. They have opposed discrimination, allowed gay people to join the clergy and, in rare cases, blessed gay relationships (e.g., Diamond

1989; Fernandez 1990; Goldman 1989; Lattin 1988). Others, however, have reaffirmed and even intensified their rejection. The Catholic church, for example, officially opposed extending civil rights protection to gay people in a Vatican statement that also was widely interpreted as condoning antigay violence: "When civil legislation is introduced to protect behavior to which no one has any conceivable right, neither the Church nor society at large should be surprised when other distorted notions and practices gain ground, and irrational and violent reactions increase" (Congregation for the Doctrine of the Faith 1986, par. 10). In the third paragraph of that document, homosexual feelings are described as "ordered toward an intrinsic moral evil," which leads to the conclusion that homosexuality "itself must be seen as an objective disorder."

Gay men and lesbians also remain largely outside the law (Melton 1989). Except in two states (Wisconsin and Massachusetts) and a few dozen municipalities (e.g., San Francisco, New York City, Chicago), legal protections do not exist for gay people in employment, housing, or services. Gay relationships have no legal status, and lesbian and gay male parents often lose legal custody of their children when their homosexuality becomes known (Falk 1989). The right of states to outlaw homosexual behavior was upheld by the U.S. Supreme Court in 1986 (*Bowers v. Hardwick* 1986). In a clear illustration of the linkage between legal philosophies and religious teachings, Justices White and Burger refused to find a constitutional right for adults to engage privately in consenting homosexual behavior, based on the fact that legal proscriptions against sodomy have "ancient roots" and that condemnation of homosexuality "is firmly rooted in Judeo-Christian moral and ethical standards" (*Bowers v. Hardwick* 1986).

In contrast to other institutions, the mental health field has made homosexuality highly visible; this visibility, however, has been within a discourse of pathology. Despite Freud's refusal to label homosexuality a sickness, mainstream American psychiatry and psychoanalysis spent much of the twentieth century seeking its "cure" (Bayer 1987). When finally subjected to rigorous scientific testing, however, the linkage of homosexuality with psychopathology proved to be wrong (Gonsiorek 1982; Gonsiorek and Weinrich 1991; Hooker 1957). Consequently, the American Psychiatric Association finally dropped homosexuality as a diagnosis from its Diagnostic and Statistical Manual in 1974 (Bayer 1987). Since then, the American Psychological Association (APA) has led other scientific and professional organizations in removing the stigma so long associated with homosexuality (e.g., APA 1975). Nevertheless, the International Classification of Diseases (ICD) continues to label homosexuality as a mental illness, and the language of pathology still infuses popular perceptions.

A fourth institution that reflects and perpetuates cultural heterosexism is the electronic mass media. Mirroring society, media portrayals of homosexuality are relatively infrequent and typically are negative when they occur. Russo's (1981) study of Hollywood films, for example, demonstrated that most homosexual characters die before the end of the movie, usually from suicide or murder. In children's cartoons, characters whose homosexuality is implied through their violation of gender roles long have been targeted for ridicule, contempt, and violence (Russo 1989). Even when gay characters have been portrayed positively in more recent films and television programs, they almost always appear in a story *because* they are gay (i.e., because their homosexuality is important to the plot; Gross 1984). Thus all characters are heterosexual unless explicitly identified as homosexual, in which case the story focuses on their sexuality rather than their day-to-day nonsexual lives.

As these examples show, homosexuality is alternately rendered invisible and condemned by cultural institutions. Psychological heterosexism parallels this process: most heterosexuals perceive the world entirely in heterosexual terms until confronted with evidence of homosexuality, at which time they respond with some combination of discomfort, confusion, condemnation, hostility, and disgust. In the next section, the ideological systems that underlie this dual negation are explored.

CULTURAL IDEOLOGIES OF SEXUALITY AND GENDER

A cultural ideology is defined here as a system of beliefs, values, and customs that form the basis for group members' shared perceptions of social reality. It reflects a consensual worldview and the institutions based on it, both of which evolve continuously through social interaction.[1] Heterosexism is one component of the broader and overlapping ideologies of sexuality and gender.[2] Although these ideologies vary across groups within American society, the twin themes of denial and stigmatization concerning homosexuality recur repeatedly. In this section, the roots of those themes are considered for each ideology.

HETEROSEXISM, SEXUALITY, AND SOCIOEROTIC IDENTITY

Since the nineteenth century, Western societies have come to define who people *are* in terms of what they *do* sexually, giving rise to social categories based on sexual behavior and preference. The social roles and psychosocial identities deriving from these categories are referred to here as "socioerotic identities." Historically, socioerotic identities became incorporated into the Western worldview as various economic and social changes permitted individuals to leave traditional kin-based lives in order to seek out others with sexual proclivities like their own (D'Emilio 1983; Weeks 1977). This trend coincided with shifts in social consensus about the primary goal and cultural focus of sexuality: from reproduction to intimacy and personal happiness, and from family and community to the individual (D'Emilio and Freedman 1988).

Social categories developed to describe those who transgressed the boundaries of existing marital and reproductive roles, namely, homosexuals and bisexuals. These are master statuses to which all other characteristics of an individual are subordinated in others' perceptions (Becker 1963). From the first, the modern concept of "the homosexual" developed more in opposition to "normalcy" than to heterosexuality per se, and was stigmatized as sinful, illegal, and sick (D'Emilio and Freedman 1988; Duberman, Vicinus, and Chauncey 1989; Foucault 1978; Plummer 1981; Weeks 1977).

In theory, all members of society can be categorized according to their socioerotic identity. Just as White Americans, however, typically do not think of themselves as White (e.g., Wellman 1971), and men usually can think of themselves as human beings rather than as males (e.g., De Beauvoir 1953), so heterosexuals can think of themselves as husbands or wives, fathers or mothers. Those identities largely negate the experiences of gay and bisexual people, however. Like members of other minorities, they must define themselves in terms of the characteristic (sexual orientation) that relegates them to unequal status and sets them in opposition to the dominant group. Socioerotic identity, based as it is entirely on sexuality, is inherently problematic for at least two reasons. First, it constitutes a public manifestation of what society prescribes should be private, namely, sexuality. Second, because homosexual behavior is regarded negatively by society, an identity based on such behavior is inevitably stigmatized.

Privatization and Invisibility: The Personal-Public Dichotomy. In a questionnaire study of heterosexuals' attitudes toward lesbians and gay men (Herek 1987), one college student wrote: "Homosexuals would be more acceptable if they wouldn't flaunt their homosexuality." Another student wrote: "Gay people have a right to live their own lives as long as they keep it to themselves and don't display the fact in public." Expressing a sentiment widespread in American society, these comments reflect an important component of sexual ideology: the belief that sexuality belongs only in the personal or private sphere of life. This aspect of sexual ideology perpetuates homosexuality's invisibility and creates a basis for stigmatizing it when it becomes visible.

The cultural dichotomy between public and private spheres of life, with sexual intimacy and pleasure relegated to the latter, has developed fairly recently in historical terms (D'Emilio and Freedman 1988). Ostensibly, all sexuality is privatized. Private heterosexuality, however, has public counterparts through which it is implicitly affirmed. The institutions of marriage publicly legitimizes heterosexual partnerships through such mechanisms as wedding rituals, tax and inheritance laws, employee benefits programs, and immigration and naturalization policies. The institutions of parenthood and the family are heterosexually identified: the birth of children (which implicitly is interpreted as affirming the parents' heterosexuality) is recognized by the larger community through birth announcements, gift-giving, religious rituals, tax deductions, and other customs.

Homosexuality, however, has no corresponding public institutions. Because same-sex marriage is illegal, gay relationships and families remain hidden. When gay people engage in behaviors that parallel those allowed to heterosexuals, they make public what society prescribes should be private. They are accused of "flaunting" their sexuality and thereby are perceived as deserving or even "asking for" retribution, harassment, or assault.

For example, displaying a photograph of one's (heterosexual) spouse in the workplace implicitly conveys information to others about one's private sexual behavior. Yet, because that spouse has a public identity as husband or wife, most onlookers (if they even notice the photo) do not think of the person pictured primarily in sexual terms. Rather, their interest centers on the partner's physical appearance, social status, occupation, and personality. They do not perceive the photograph's display to constitute an inappropriate intrusion of the private sphere into public life. When the photograph is of a same-sex partner, in contrast, everyone is likely to notice. The partner's gender overwhelms all other information about her or him. The sexual component of the relationship is no longer mundane and implicit; the private-public barrier is perceived to have been violated. The seemingly innocent act of displaying a partner's photograph fundamentally changes one's status and relationships.

Sexualization and Stigmatization. Heterosexism derives, in part, from cultural negativity toward particular forms of sexuality. As Rubin (1984) summarized, "normal" sexuality "should ideally be heterosexual, marital, monogamous, reproductive, and noncommercial. It should be coupled, relational, within the same generation, and occur at home. It should not involve pornography, fetish objects, sex toys of any sort, or roles other than male and female" (pp. 280–81).

Gay sexuality violates many of these rules. It is not reproductive by definition and not marital by statute. Many gay relationships are not sexually exclusive (Bell & Weinberg 1978). Some homosexual men have staked out "cruising areas" for sexual behavior that are semipublic (Humphreys 1970; Altman 1982). Because of the culture's abiding suspicion of and hostility toward such "merely" pleasurable sexuality,[3] gay sexuality is " 'bad,' 'abnormal,' or 'unnatural' " (Rubin 1984:281).

Not only are gay people reduced to their socioerotic identity, but that identity is equated with deviance and abnormality. Further, it is stereotyped as pathological, predatory, compulsively promiscuous (Adam 1978; Herek 1991). At best, gay people are perceived as basing their identity and life-style on a trivial pursuit, namely, sexual pleasure. At the worst, homosexuality is stigmatized as inherently sick or dangerous, and worthy of punishment through legal (through the criminal justice system) or extralegal (in the form of antigay hate crimes) means.

HETEROSEXISM AND GENDER

Whereas biological sex is about physiology, gender is about behavior. The ideology of gender is a set of shared beliefs, values, and customs concerning "masculinity" and "femininity." Children internalize the rules for behavior prescribed by this cultural ideology in the course of defining their gender identity (i.e., their core sense of self as a man or woman, e.g., Money 1987; Money and Ehrhardt 1972). Because they are learned at a very early age, the meanings attached to masculinity and femininity subsequently seem "natural" rather than socially constructed.

Although gender identity is distinct from socioerotic identity (the sense of self as heterosexual, homosexual, or bisexual), the two are closely related.[4] Heterosexuality is equated ideologically with "normal" masculinity and "normal" femininity, whereas homosexuality is equated with violating norms of gender. Although no inherent connection exists between sexual behavior and gender conformity, gay men are widely stereotyped as highly effeminate, and lesbians as hypermasculine (Herek 1984, 1986a, 1991). This ideological linkage between sexuality and gender has at least three consequences.

First, gay people are stigmatized not only for their erotic behaviors, but also for their perceived violation of gender norms. Second, because homosexuality is associated with deviation from something so "natural" as masculinity or femininity, its labeling as abnormal receives further justification. Heterosexuals with deep-seated insecurities concerning their own ability to conform to cultural standards for masculinity or femininity may even perceive homosexuality as threatening their sense of self as a man or woman.

Third, a dual pattern of denial and condemnation is associated with gender which parallels that previously described for cultural heterosexism. People who do not conform to gender roles—regardless of their actual sexual orientation—are often labeled as homosexual and stigmatized or attacked. Fear of such labeling leads heterosexuals and homosexuals alike to monitor their own behavior carefully to avoid any appearance of gender nonconformity (e.g., Lehne 1976).

PSYCHOLOGICAL HETEROSEXISM

The foundation of psychological heterosexism—the individual manifestation of antigay prejudice—is laid down early in life. Long before children know anything about homosexuality or heterosexuality per se, they learn to prize what their parents and peers define as "good" and "normal." They learn moral values, attitudes toward the body and sexuality, and the distinction between private and public. They develop a gender identity and internalize negative feelings and stereotypical beliefs about those who violate gender roles. They learn to value acceptance from peers and adults, and acquire strategies for winning it. They learn the benefits and costs associated with multiple social roles, including those of the "normal" and its counterpart, the deviant. They learn the social attitudes associated with race, gender, and those who are different or "queer," long before they understand that *queer* is an epithet for homosexuals (Goffman 1963; Katz 1976).

Because of homosexuality's cultural invisibility, relatively few children are likely to have personal contact with someone who is openly gay while learning these concepts (Schneider and Lewis 1984). Consequently, rather than defining homosexuality as a characteristic associated with flesh-and-blood human beings, most people respond to it primarily as a symbol: the embodiment of such concepts as "sin," "sickness," "predator," "outsider," or whatever else an individual considers to be the opposite of her- or himself, or set apart from her or his community. Whereas attitudes toward people with whom one has direct experience function primarily to organize and make sense of that experience, attitudes toward symbols serve a variety of expressive needs. At least three functions are served by psychological heterosexism (Herek 1986b, 1987).

First, antigay prejudice may serve a *value-expressive* function, helping individuals to affirm who they are by expressing important personal values. For example, a fundamentalist Christian may express hostile attitudes toward gay people as a way of affirming her or his own Christianity. She or he opposes homosexuality because such opposition is an integral part of being a good Christian, which is of central importance to feeling good about oneself. The same individuals would express similar hostility toward other groups if they were similarly defined in religious terms. Violence also may serve a value-expressive function for the perpetrator. For example, members of hate groups, such as the Ku Klux Klan, appeal to moral authority in their antigay rhetoric (see Segrest and Zeskind 1989).

Antigay prejudice can also serve a *social-expressive* function by helping individuals to win approval from important others (e.g., peers, family, neighbors) and thereby increase their own self-esteem. As with the value-expressive function, lesbians and gay men are treated as abstract concepts. With social-expressive prejudice, they are the epitome of outsiders; attacking them solidifies one's own status as an insider, one who belongs to the group. Expressing antigay attitudes or violently attacking gay people thus leads to being accepted and liked, which are of central importance to the individual. For example, some assailants in antigay street assaults view the attack primarily as a way of demonstrating their loyalty and increasing group solidarity (Weissman 1978). Perpetrators in male-male rapes and sexual assaults also have been observed to be motivated by needs to maintain status and affiliation with peers (Groth and Burgess 1980).

Antigay prejudice also may serve a *defensive* function by reducing the anxiety that results from unconscious psychological conflicts (e.g., those associated with one's own sexuality or gender). The defensive function is summarized in the popular notion that people who express antigay prejudice actually are revealing their own latent homosexuality. For people with defensive attitudes, lesbians or gay men symbolize unacceptable parts of the self (e.g., the feminine man, the masculine woman). Expressing antigay hostility is a strategy for avoiding an internal conflict by externalizing it to a suitable symbol which then is attacked. Antigay assaults, for example, may provide a means for young males to affirm their masculinity (consciously or not) by attacking someone who symbolizes an unacceptable aspect of their own personalities (e.g., homoerotic feelings or tendencies toward effeminacy). Similarly, some perpetrators in male-male sexual assaults apparently wished to punish the victim as a way of dealing with their own unresolved and conflictual sexual interests (Groth and Burgess 1980).

Antigay hostility thus functions to define who one *is* by identifying gay people as a symbol of what one is *not* and directing hostility toward them. With the value-expressive function, prejudice defines the world according to principles of good and evil, right and wrong; by opposing the embodiment of evil (gay people), one affirms one's own goodness. With the social-expressive function, prejudice defines the ingroup and outgroup; by denigrating outsiders (lesbians and gay men), one affirms one's own status as an insider. With the defensive function, prejudice defines the self and the "not-self"; by attacking gay people, one symbolically (and unconsciously) attacks the unacceptable or bad aspects of self.

Psychological heterosexism can serve these functions only when cultural ideology converges with psychological needs. Antigay prejudice can be value-expressive only to the extent that an individual's self-concept is tied to particular values that have become socially identified as antithetical to homosexuality. It can be social-expressive only insofar as an individual's social group rejects gay people and the individual strongly needs to be accepted by members of that group. It can be defensive only when lesbians and gay men are culturally defined in a way that links them to an individual's own psychological conflicts.

Gay people can fulfill these symbolic roles only so long as they remain abstract concepts for the prejudiced heterosexual person, rather than flesh-and-blood human beings. Having a close friend, coworker, or family member who is openly gay can eventually change a prejudiced person's perception of homosexuality from a value-laden symbolic construct to a mere demographic characteristic, like hair color or political party affiliation. By coming out to others, lesbians and gay men disrupt the functions previously served by antigay attitudes. When heterosexuals learn that someone about whom they care is gay, formerly functional prejudice can quickly become dysfunctional: the untruth in stereotypes becomes obvious, social norms are perceived to have changed, and traditional moral values concerning sexuality are challenged by their juxtaposition against the heterosexual person's past experience with, knowledge about, and feelings of love for the specific gay man or lesbian. Thus, as with other forms of prejudice, interpersonal contact between gay people and heterosexuals under favorable conditions is one of the most effective ways of reducing psychological heterosexism (Allport 1954; Amir 1976; Herek 1991; Schneider and Lewis 1984).

Coming out, however, is difficult and possibly dangerous. It requires making public an aspect of oneself that society perceives as appropriately kept private. It can mean being defined exclusively in terms of sexuality by strangers, friends, and family. It also can mean being newly perceived as possessing some sort of disability or handicap, an inability to be what one should be as man or woman. In the worst situations, it means being completely rejected or even attacked by those to whom one has come out.

Many gay people remain in the closet because they fear these negative interpersonal consequences, as well as discrimination and stigmatization. Additionally, having continually to overcome invisibility is itself a frustrating experience; allowing others to assume that one is heterosexual often is the path of least resistance. Consequently, most heterosexuals' attitudes and behavior toward gay people remain uninformed by personal interactions and instead are driven by the cultural ideologies of sexuality and gender.

TRANSFORMATIONS IN HETEROSEXIST IDEOLOGY: IMPORTANT RECENT TRENDS

The feminist and gay movements, coupled with the struggles for civil rights for racial minorities, have had a profound impact on socioerotic self-definitions, perceptions of the public and the private, and gender roles during the past twenty-five years (Adam 1987; Altman 1982). Additionally, lesbians and gay men have achieved increasing visibility through community action and by individually coming out. Since the early 1980s, the AIDS epidemic has influenced this process in ways that perhaps will not be recognized for years. In the final section of this article some of these changes and their possible implications for cultural and psychological heterosexism are briefly considered.

HETEROSEXISM AND SEXUALITY

From Private to Public. Through intense political struggle, lesbians and gay men have begun to make what previously was the private world of homosexuality a focus for public discourse. This discourse has itself evolved. The liberationist approach of the early 1970s, which celebrated a polymorphously perverse sexuality, has yielded to a paradigm that defines homosexuals as members of a minority community similar to ethnic groups (Altman 1982; Levine 1979; Murray 1979). Lesbians and gay men now are often perceived as a quasi-ethnic minority group struggling for civil rights (Herek 1991). Consequently, gay people are beginning to attain the rudiments of a public identity that is based on community membership as well as individual sexual behavior.

This public identity also has begun to include relational and parental roles. Lesbian and gay male relationships, long hidden from heterosexual society, have become increasingly visible. Growing numbers of openly gay people are raising children, thereby defining parenthood as a component of their gay identity (e.g., Kolata 1989). Some official recognition has been accorded to gay families. A New York Supreme Court, for example, ruled that a gay lover constitutes family for purposes of rent control laws (Gutis 1989). Former New York mayor Koch expanded benefits, such as funeral leave, to include gay city employees ("Koch to Add Rights for Domestic Couples," 1989). In 1989, San Francisco Mayor Art Agnos signed a domestic partners bill that created a mechanism for members of an unmarried couple (gay or heterosexual) to register their relationship legally, and extended to domestic partners the same considerations provided by the city to married partners (Keane 1989). Opposition to societal recognition of gay families has been vigorous. The 1989 San Francisco domestic partners bill, which closely resembled an ordinance vetoed seven years earlier by then-Mayor Feinstein, was defeated by city voters in a subsequent referendum. Both the mayoral veto and the referendum were heavily influenced by religious groups (Rannells 1982; Sandalow and Herscher 1989).

The AIDS epidemic has given further visibility to gay relationships and communities. Media coverage has included reporting on the devoted care that gay men with AIDS have received from their lovers and gay families, often while their biological relatives rejected them because of their homosexuality. Such portrayals, along with increasingly frequent personal interactions as more gay people come out in response to the epidemic, undoubtedly have changed public perceptions of gay relationships— showing both that they exist and that they can include such socially valued attributes as self-sacrifice and commitment.

Thus, recognition and legitimation of gay communities, relationships, and families have begun to infiltrate American society. Gay men and women have increasing access to public identities that allow them to affirm their sexual orientation on the basis of community membership and relational commitment but without violating privacy barriers or being "merely" sexual. Public debate is expanding to include a discourse on community and family, as well as sexual self-expression.

The Legitimizing of Socioerotic Identities. Because it is a public manifestation of what society prescribes should be private, socioerotic identity
heretofore has been inherently stigmatized. This may change, however, as
heterosexuals increasingly feel forced to make their own socioerotic identities explicit. Individual Whites often become aware of their own racial
identity for the first time when they are surrounded by highly visible racial
minority cultures (e.g., Walsh 1990). Similarly, as gay relationships and
families become increasingly visible, individual heterosexuals may experience greater pressure to assert and prove their socioerotic identity rather
than simply defining themselves in terms of marital and familial status.
As a result, socioerotic identity may become less trivialized and accorded
greater importance by heterosexual society. Ironically, it may simultaneously become less salient to lesbians and gay men who will have relational,
familial, and community-based identities newly available to them. To the
extent that homosexuality remains stigmatized, this process may have a
negative consequence, at least in the short term: pressures to affirm one's
heterosexuality may become even more intense for adolescents and young
adults, especially males. In the absence of effective prevention programs,
this pressure may foster an increase in antigay attacks by young males
strongly concerned about their own sexuality and social acceptance.

HETEROSEXISM AND GENDER

An early goal of the gay movement was to foster sexual liberation, which
required, in part, the breaking down of rigid gender roles (e.g, Altman
1971). Although the range of experiences available to each gender has
expanded somewhat, the importance of gender conformity remains relatively unchanged: people who seriously transgress gender roles (e.g., "drag
queens" and "bar dykes") remain at the low end of the hierarchy of accept-
ability (among gay people as well as among heterosexuals). But a change
has occurred, albeit not the one originally foreseen by gay liberationists:
the traditional equation of homosexuality with gender norm violation
appears to be weakening.

As heterosexual Americans have begun to have more contact with
openly gay people, the inaccuracy of stereotypes associating a homosexual
orientation with the adoption of cross-gender mannerisms and behavior
has become more evident. As conceptualizations of gay people become
more complex and differentiated, global stereotypes (such as the "sissy"
and the "bull dyke") are being replaced by multiple subcategories of var-

ious "types" common in gay communities (e.g., "lipstick lesbian," "homo politico," "clone"). Heterosexuals may well continue to dislike effeminate men and masculine women (as do some gay people), but may not equate this with dislike of all homosexuals. As a result, gay people whose outward behavior conforms to cultural conceptions of masculinity and femininity may achieve greater acceptance (Rubin 1984).

Symbolism and Attitudes

As a consequence of the gay political movement, heterosexuals now can have positive attitudes toward gay people that are psychologically functional in ways not previously possible. Because of its identification with movements for racial equality and women's rights, as well as the rights of privacy and free speech, the movement for gay civil rights increasingly has become a respectable progressive political cause. Consequently, heterosexuals who identify themselves as liberals, feminists, and civil libertarians can express support for gay rights as a way of affirming their social identities (a value-expressive function). This equation of the gay community with notions of political progressivism receives impetus when bigoted individuals and hate groups identify gay people as targets comparable to Blacks and Jews (Segrest and Zeskind 1989). Ironically, such attacks may permit positive attitudes toward gay people to serve both value-expressive and social-expressive functions as many members of society express their distaste for such bigotry and distance themselves from the groups that promulgate it. If uncoupling of gender and sexuality becomes widespread, the cultural basis for defensive antigay prejudice also may diminish as gay people become less suitable symbols for externalizing anxiety about one's own gender identity.

Additionally, AIDS has affected the symbolic status of homosexuality in American culture in both negative and positive ways. By linking stigmatized sexual behavior with death, the popular view of AIDS in the United States reinforces both a moralistic condemnation of homosexuality and individual feelings of defensiveness. Gay people (lesbians have not been differentiated from gay men in popular discourse on AIDS) are viewed by many as receiving just punishment for their sins, and homosexuality is equated with death (Herek and Glunt 1988). Yet, the AIDS epidemic also has led many heterosexuals to confront their own attitudes toward homosexuality for the first time. Because AIDS has made gay people more visible, more heterosexuals have had to articulate their own feelings about homosexuality, often in relation to a gay loved one.

CONCLUSION

Antigay violence and victimization in the United States today cannot adequately be understood apart from cultural heterosexism. By alternately denying and stigmatizing homosexuality, this ideology fosters the individual antigay prejudice that makes victimization of lesbians and gay men possible. The analysis presented here highlights the necessity of a comprehensive approach to eliminating antigay violence. Interventions that focus specifically on violence and victimization clearly are needed (e.g., Berrill and Herek 1990; Garnets, Herek, and Levy 1990; Wertheimer 1990). These efforts, however, will not be sufficient to eliminate the ultimate causes of antigay violence. Making lesbians and gay men visible and removing the stigma that has so long been attached to a homosexual orientation will require institutional changes (e.g., Berrill and Herek 1990), as well as personal interventions (Herek 1991). Societal transformations have begun in the past few decades that eventually may shake the foundations of cultural and psychological heterosexism. Perhaps most important of these has been the widespread emergence of lesbians and gay men from invisibility into public life. By discouraging and directly punishing this emergence, antigay violence functions to perpetuate heterosexism, as well as to express it. Eradicating heterosexism, therefore, inevitably requires confronting violence against lesbians and gay men. Eliminating antigay violence, in turn, requires an attack on heterosexism.

ACKNOWLEDGMENTS

The author thanks Kevin Berrill, Howard Ehrlich, Linda Garnets, Barrie Levy, R. Anthony Reese, and Theresa Reid for their thoughtful comments on earlier versions of this article.

NOTES

1. The term *ideology* has been used differently by philosophers, sociologists, political scientists, psychologists, and others (see Drucker 1974; Lane 1962). The usage here derives primarily from a social psychological approach to cultural systems of values and beliefs.

2. Some confusion arises in discussing these two ideologies because the word *sex* in the English language refers both to gender ("the female sex," "the male sex") and to erotic activity and desire ("to have sex"). As Rubin (1984) noted, this dual defi-

nition "reflects a cultural assumption that sexuality is reducible to sexual intercourse and that it is a function of the relations between women and men" (p. 307). Although teasing apart the two ideologies clearly would be a valuable endeavor, such a task is beyond the scope of this article. For purposes of clarity, reference will be made to the "ideologies of sex and gender" when discussing components that seem common to both.

3. As Rubin (1984) notes, a telling illustration of this discomfort with "merely" pleasurable sexuality is the perseverance of obscenity statutes, which outlaw production and commercial distribution of materials whose sole purpose is sexual arousal (without artistic, scientific, or other purposes).

4. Whether or not the cultural organization of sexuality can be understood apart from that of gender is a topic for debate. Some authors have asserted that heterosexism can be analyzed only as part of the cultural ideology of gender (e.g., Rich 1980), whereas others have argued for the necessity of analytically separating sexuality from gender in order to understand the distinct (though related) social organization of each (Rubin 1984).

REFERENCES

Adam, B. D. 1978. *The Survival of Domination.* New York: Elsevier North-Holland.

Adam, B. D. 1987. *The Rise of a Gay and Lesbian Movement.* Boston: Twayne.

Allport, G. 1954. *The Nature of Prejudice.* New York: Addison-Wesley.

Altman, D. 1971. *Homosexual: Oppression and Liberation.* New York: Outerbridge and Dienstfrey.

Altman, D. 1982. *The Homosexualization of America, the Americanization of the Homosexual.* New York: St. Martin's.

American Psychological Association. 1975. Minutes of the Council of Representatives. *American Psychologist* 30:633.

Amir, Y. 1976. The role of intergroup contact in change of prejudice and intergroup relations. In P. Katz, ed., *Towards the Elimination of Racism,* pp. 245–308. New York: Pergamon.

Bayer, R. 1987. *Homosexuality and American Psychiatry: The Politics of Diagnosis.* 2d ed. Princeton, N.J.: Princeton University Press.

Becker, H. S. 1963. *Outsiders: Studies in the Sociology of Deviance.* New York: Free Press.

Bell, A. P., and M. S. Weinberg. 1978. *Homosexualities: A Study of Diversity among Men and Women.* New York: Simon and Schuster.

Berrill, K. T., and G. M. Herek. 1990. Primary and secondary victimization in anti-gay hate crimes: Official response and policy. *Journal of Interpersonal Violence* 5:401–13.

Boswell, J. 1980. *Christianity, Social Tolerance, and Homosexuality: Gay People in Western Europe from the Beginning of the Christian Era to the Fourteenth Century.* Chicago: University of Chicago Press.

Bowers v. Hardwick, 478 U.S. 186 (1986).

Congregation for the Doctrine of the Faith. 1986. *Letter to the Bishops of the Catholic Church on the Pastoral Care of Homosexual Persons.* Vatican City: Congregation for the Doctrine of the Faith.

de Beauvoir, S. 1953. *The Second Sex.* New York: Alfred A. Knopf.

D'Emilio, J. 1983. *Sexual Politics, Sexual Communities: The Making of a Homosexual Minority in the United States, 1940–1970.* Chicago: University of Chicago Press.

D'Emilio, J., and E. B. Freedman. 1988. *Intimate Matters: A History of Sexuality in America.* New York: Harper and Row.

Diamond, R. 1989. First gay Episcopal priest is ordained. *San Francisco Examiner* (December 17):A-6.

Drucker, H. M. 1974. *The Political Uses of Ideology.* London: Macmillan.

Duberman, M. B., M. Vicinus, and G. Chauncey, Jr. 1989. *Hidden from History: Reclaiming the Gay and Lesbian Past.* New York: New American Library.

Falk, P. 1989. Lesbian mothers: Psychosocial assumptions in family law. *American Psychologist* 44(6):941–47.

Fernandez, E. 1990. Gays ordained as ministers in affront to ban. *San Francisco Examiner* (January 21):B-1.

Foucault, M. 1978. *The History of Sexuality.* Vol. 1: *An Introduction.* Translated by R. Hurley. New York: Pantheon. (Originally published 1976.)

Garnets, L., G. M. Herek, and B. Levy. 1990. Violence and victimization of lesbians and gay men: Mental health consequences. *Journal of Interpersonal Violence* 5:366–83.

Goffman, E. 1963. *Stigma: Note on the Management of Spoiled Identity.* Englewood Cliffs, NJ: Prentice-Hall.

Goldman, A. L. 1989. Reform conference debates allowing homosexuals to become rabbis. *New York Times,* June 27, p. A-8.

Gonsiorek, J. C. 1992. Results of psychological testing on homosexual populations. *American Behavioral Scientist* 25:385–96.

Gonsiorek, J. C., and J. D. Weinrich. 1991. *Homosexuality: Social, Psychological, and Biological Issues.* 2d ed. Newbury Park, Calif.: Sage.

Gross, L. 1984. The cultivation of intolerance: Television, Blacks, and gays. In G. Melischek, K. E. Rosengren, and J. Stappers, eds., *Cultural Indicators: An International Symposium,* pp. 345–63. Osterreichischen Akademie der Wissenschaften.

Groth, A. N., and A. W. Burgess. 1980. Male rape: Offenders and victims. *American Journal of Psychiatry* 137(7):806–10.

Gutis, P. S. 1989. Court widens family definition to gay couples living together. *New York Times* (July 7):A-1, A-13.

Herek, G. M. 1984. Beyond "homophobia": A social psychological perspective on attitudes toward lesbians and gay men. *Journal of Homosexuality* 10(1/2):1–21.

Herek, G. M. 1986a. On heterosexual masculinity: Some psychical consequences of the social construction of gender and sexuality. *American Behavioral Scientist* 29:563–77.

Herek, G. M. 1986b. The instrumentality of attitudes: Toward a neofunctional theory. *Journal of Social Issues* 42(2):99–114.

Herek, G. M. 1987. Can functions be measured? A new perspective on the functional approach to attitudes. *Social Psychology Quarterly* 50:285–303.

Herek, G. M. 1991. Stigma, prejudice, and violence against lesbians and gay men. In J. Gonsiorek and J. Weinrich, eds., *Homosexuality: Social, Psychological, and Biological Issues.* 2d ed. Newbury Park, Calif.: Sage.

Herek, G. M., and E. K. Glunt. 1988. An epidemic of stigma: Public reactions to AIDS. *American Psychologist* 43:886–91.

Hooker, E. 1957. The adjustment of the male overt homosexual. *Journal of Projective Techniques* 21:18–31.

Humphreys, L. 1970. *Tearoom Trade: Impersonal Sex in Public Places.* New York: Aldine.

Katz, P. A. 1976. The acquisition of racial attitudes in children. In P. A. Katz, ed., *Towards the Elimination of Racism,* pp. 125–54. New York: Pergamon.

Keane, T. G. 1989. SF supervisors OK law on "domestic partners." *San Francisco Chronicle* (May 23):A-1.

Koch to add rights for domestic couples. 1989. *San Francisco Examiner* (July 9):A-4.

Kolata, G. 1989. Lesbian partners find the means to be parents. *New York Times* (January 30).

Lane, R. E. 1962. *Political Ideology.* New York: Free Press.

Lattin, D. 1988. Episcopalians endorse gay "marriages." *San Francisco Chronicle* (October):A-8.

Lehne, G. 1976. Homophobia among men. In D. David and R. Brannon, eds., *The Forty-Nine Percent Majority: The Male Sex Role,* pp. 68–88. Reading, Mass.: Addison-Wesley.

Levine, M. P. 1979. Gay ghetto. In M. P. Levine, ed., *Gay Men: The Sociology of Male Homosexuality,* pp. 182–204. New York: Harper and Row.

Melton, G. B. 1989. Public policy and private prejudice: Psychology and law on gay rights. *American Psychologist* 44(6):933–40.

Money, J. 1987. Sin, sickness, or status? Gender identity and psychoneuroendocrinology. *American Psychologist* 42:384–99.

Money, J., and A. E. Ehrhardt. 1972. *Man and Woman, Boy and Girl: Differentiation and Dimorphism of Gender Identity from Conception to Maturity.* Baltimore: Johns Hopkins University Press.

Murray, S. 0. 1979. The institutional elaboration of a quasi-ethnic community. *International Review of Modern Sociology* 9:165–77.

Plummer, K., ed. 1981. *The Making of the Modern Homosexual.* London: Hutchinson.

Rannells, J. 1982. Live-in lover plan vetoed. *San Francisco Chronicle* (December 10):A-1.

Rich, A. 1980. Compulsory heterosexuality and lesbian existence. *Signs* 3(4):631–60.

Rubin, G. G. 1984. Thinking sex: Notes for a radical theory of the politics of sexuality. In C. S. Vance, ed., *Pleasure and Danger: Exploring Female Sexuality,* pp. 267–319. Boston: Routledge and Kegan Paul.

Russo, V. 1981. *The Celluloid Closet: Homosexuality in the Movies.* New York: Harper and Row.

Russo, V. 1989. Nelly toons: A look at animated sissies. Introduction to a program at the 13th Lesbian and Gay Film Festival, Castro Theater, San Francisco, June.

Sandalow, M., and E. Herscher. 1989. Prop. S defeat a serious blow to gay power. *San Francisco Chronicle* (November 9):A-1, A-26.

Schneider, W., and I. A. Lewis. 1984. The straight story on homosexuality and gay rights. *Public Opinion* (February):16–20, 59–60.

Segrest, M., and L. Zeskind. 1989. *Quarantines and Death: The Far Right's Homophobic Agenda.* Atlanta: Center for Democratic Renewal.

Walsh, J. 1990. School colors. *San Francisco Examiner* (February 4):"This World" section, pp. 9–11.

Weeks, J. 1977. *Coming Out: Homosexual Politics in Britain, from the Nineteenth Century to the Present.* London: Quartet.

Weissman, E. 1978. Kids who attack gays. *Christopher Street* (August):9–13.

Wellman, B. 1971. Social identities in black and white. *Sociological Inquiry* 41:57–66.

Wertheimer, D. M. 1990. Treatment and service interventions for lesbian and gay male crime victims. *Journal of Interpersonal Violence* 5:384–400.

II

Origins of Sexual Orientation

As long as sexual orientation is a master status in our society that over-whelms all other characteristics of the individual, the question about the causes of this condition will be of concern. To date it has been possible only to reframe the question from a focus on the causes of homosexuality to the origins of sexual orientation in general. Even so, bisexual orientation has received little serious attention, and often persons with some homo-sexual erotic imagery or behavior are combined with the more exclusively homosexual sample. In short, the focus is: why isn't everyone heterosexual?

The issue is made more complex by the fact that male homosexuality is especially perplexing in our heterosexist culture. On the one hand, het-erosexuality is usually defined by the avoidance of anything associated with homosexuality, so why would a sane man become the antithesis of eve-rything he has been taught is normal? On the other hand, many find it even more perplexing to think that a man would give up his male heter-osexual privilege in a society that is dominated by White male heterosex-uals. Obviously, something must be wrong. This point of view is consis-tent with the observation that gay men usually believe that they have no choice about their sexual orientation, and if they could choose, many would prefer to be heterosexual—at least when they first recognize the implications of their sexual feelings.

The situation is less clearly defined for lesbians. Perhaps because women are usually denied access to male privileges, and female roles tend to be devalued and regarded as less important in our sexist culture, there appears to be only modest interest in the question of why women become lesbian. Often women are not included in studies, or are only a heterosexual control group for the homosexual and heterosexual men. Moreover, many lesbians believe that sexual orientation is a matter of choice or preference instead of an unchanging characteristic of individuals. In contrast, men typically think of sexual orientation as an essential characteristic of themselves, and one over which they have little choice. It is not clear whether this difference reflects sociocultural factors, or is a gender difference in sexual orientation.

The first two articles in this part illustrate these points. Richardson adopts a sociological perspective to examine the social construction of sexual orientation. This model seems especially compatible for those persons who feel they have some degree of voluntary choice about their sexual orientation. Moreover, this approach points out the ways in which individuals and cultures construct the meanings of sexuality.

Money provides a detailed examination of the process by which prenatal development affects an individual's physical sex/gender, and the complex relationship between prenatal influences, postnatal influences, and an individual's gender identity/role; possibly sexual orientation is affected as well. This psychobiological approach is compatible with the viewpoint that one's sexuality is relatively fixed and an essential characteristic of one's identity. It also provides a framework for understanding the flexibility of sexual orientation, including bisexuality. Because Money's perspective is based on his research with atypical prenatal development, his work has been criticized to the extent that he views homosexuality as atypical, and that he uses as a norm stereotypic heterosexual behavior for masculinity and femininity. Readers who view sexual orientation as a matter of choice may find Money's perspective incompatible with their own. His perspective is a useful one, however, because research will continue to seek possible biological origins of sexual orientation (cf. LeVay 1991). Thus, it is necessary to understand the biological processes by which differences and similarities arise between males and females in prenatal development.

Bisexuals are a group that appear to be less restricted by gender in their sexual and affectional attractions than either lesbians or gay men, and their development of sexual orientation appears to differ from that of gay men and lesbians. For example, Bell, Weinberg, and Hammersmith (1981) found that unlike gay men, bisexual males tended not to report feeling sexually different in childhood; both male and female bisexuals were less likely to have established their adult sexual preference by age nineteen, and they were more likely to have been influenced by sexual learning than were lesbians and gay men. Moreover, some bisexual women and men tend to be attracted to persons of both genders, attending more to the characteristics of the person than to his or her gender. Others are sequential bisexuals—alternating same- and other-gender affectional and sexual relationships.

> Dan was in his late twenties when I first interviewed him. He and his wife had good communication; both were sensitive persons, and well-educated. But Dan was worried that the majority of his sexual dreams and fantasies were of homosexual relationships. He joined a support-group for married bisexual men. Two years later I learned he had left his wife and was living in the gay community. Though most of his sexual activity was now with men, he reported that many of his fantasies and sexual dreams were now of women. (Matteson 1987:139)

Masters and Johnson (1979) provided some interesting information about the interaction of gender and sexuality for bisexuals. Their study restricted the sample to those men and women who had equal sexual attraction to women and men and who reported no interest in a continuing emotional relationship with a partner. This atypical sample was paired with homosexual and heterosexual assigned partners and observed while engaging in assigned sexual interactions. No differences in sexual response were found among the men and women between their heterosexual and homosexual experiences. Moreover, the patterns were similar to those displayed by the homosexual and heterosexual couples in other phases of the research. The procedure, however, provided a fascinating laboratory for the study of gender differences in sexual behavior. For example, the same bisexual men moved more quickly toward orgasm with heterosexual female partners than with homosexual male partners. Similarly, the same bisexual women engaged in mutual "my turn, your turn" sexual interaction with homosexual female partners, but let the heterosexual male partners "set the pace throughout the entire sexual interaction" (p. 169). These sexual patterns were similar to those of gay men and lesbians in another part of the study with partners of the same gender, and were similar to the pattern of heterosexuals with partners of the other gender. Clearly, bisexuality appears to be different from either homosexuality or heterosexuality in subtle ways.

Blumstein and Schwartz conducted a pioneering study on bisexual men and women reprinted here that represents a useful introduction to this understudied sexual orientation. Today a growing movement of bisexuals is seeking more visible inclusion in the lesbian and gay community. In a manner parallel to the earlier struggle for adding "lesbian" to gay, one goal is to add "bisexual" into the names of lesbian, bisexual, and gay community groups.

Before we conclude this introduction, however, let us briefly state our synthesis of the various points of view about the origins of sexual orientation. Overall, our perspective is that the mix of multiple influences on one's sexual orientation—such as biology, experiences, or choice—differs from one individual to another. Moreover, the development of sexual orientation appears to differ for women and men, and for persons in differing cultures. Also, sexual orientation — liking one gender or another—is only one aspect of an individual's pattern of sexuality.

Our earlier discussion suggested that there are two major differing theoretical frameworks for viewing the nature and origin of sexual orientation. One view is that it represents an essential characteristic of an individual (cf. Weinrich and Williams 1991). For example, a major contemporary view of sexual orientation development is that it reflects an interaction between some sort of inborn predisposition to learn sexual-erotic responses and key experiences at critical times in development (Money 1988). A parallel with language development may be apt because erotic feelings can operate as a kind of encoded language of sexuality and intimacy that frames the ways in which these experiences are conceptualized. Moreover, like language, more than one sexual orientation could be mastered.

In contrast to the essentialist view, other social scientists argue that sexual orientation is a social construction. Regardless of the origin of one's sexual and affectional preferences, it is the social meaning attached to them that is critical. At the core of this constructionist view is the idea that all individuals construct their own identity. Although this process is influenced by individual characteristics and by society norms, the self-creating and re-creating process can transcend these limits. This implies that one may choose one's sexual orientation through conscious choice, possibly influenced by political ideology, group loyalty to the family or nation, religious inspiration, or other powerful factors that influence one's construction of social reality. Moreover, social scripts that outline ways to fall in love, engage in sex, and live happily ever after are important for defining and understanding sexual and affectional responses. Such scripts are social constructions, to be sure, but they are enacted by a unique individual in idiosyncratic ways. The social construction and individual creation of sexual and affectional scripts is basic to understanding sexual orientation (Gagnon 1990; Golden 1987; Risman and Schwartz 1988; Tiefer 1987).

This idea of social scripts provides a link between the constructionist position and the essentialist view. That is, the script, like language, results from an interaction between an individual actor or speaker and the sociocultural context or language. Likewise, sexual orientation can be seen as a reflection of the unique characteristics of the individual interacting with the socially defined meanings of sexual orientation.

Therefore, we conclude that the origins of sexual orientation involve both the individual and society. Perhaps the best expression of this interactive view of the origin of sexual orientation has been proposed by Money's (1988) term *lovemap* as a counterpart to language that is established in children at a young age. In brief, the result of an interaction between individual development and the social construction of sexuality is that each individual develops a lovemap that is unique, similar to one's voice quality or accent. It reflects not only the preferred gender of one's sexual-affectional attraction, but also specific characteristics of attractive people, and possibly also desired sexual or emotional activities. An individual's unique lovemap encompasses one's entire emotional and erotic turn-ons and fantasies; it is as unique as one's voice print or fingerprint. Thus, sexual orientation is only one aspect of one's lovemap. It is our culture that has made this a major social concern, or master status. Perhaps this will change. Only a few decades ago (1947) the Supreme Court struck down laws that forbid interracial marriages. Then, lovemaps that contained attractions to persons of different races were stigmatized in ways similar to that of lesbians and gay men today.

CONTEMPORARY ISSUE: CHOICE
VERSUS NO CHOICE

There is currently a debate concerning the extent of choice versus no choice in the nature of sexual orientation. Whether sexual orientation is in some sense as fixed and immutable as race, eye color, height, or gender is of considerable interest in the political debate about the meaning of sexual orientation. The debate centers on the fact that in most states sexual orientation can be the basis for legal discrimination.

The no-choice position is that if sexual orientation is determined, perhaps as some essential part of oneself, such as one's race, then civil rights protections would be granted more readily. In contrast, persons who believe sexual orientation is a matter of choice imply that people have voluntarily chosen to subject themselves to stigma and oppression and therefore do not require legal protections, since they could choose to conform to the majority position. Likewise, some religious leaders believe that homosexuality is a sinful behavior that can be changed through some kind of religious practice.

A middle point in the debate—that sexual orientation is at least as stable and no more a matter of choice than one's religion, which is a protected category with regard to civil rights in the United States, and for some may be as immutable as one's race, which also is a protected category—seems not to be widely recognized (Kimmel and Weiner 1985:377; van Gelder 1991).

There is more that this issue touches off, however. For example, when a careful scientific research project finds a difference between gay men and heterosexual men in the brain, or in some biochemical process, media attention focuses on the possible significance of these findings. No matter how carefully phrased, with caveats and concerns about the need to replicate the research, suddenly it is assumed that a clue to the cause of homosexuality has been found. To understand the peculiarity of this, consider instead that the research had found a similar difference between persons who were gifted violinists and those who were without musical talent. Would attention suddenly focus on the "no-choice" origin of musical giftedness?

Obviously, the underlying theme is one of heterosexist bias. If the origin of homosexuality is found, then maybe it can be cured or prevented—unlike musical gifts, which we recognize as part of the mosaic of human diversity.

A final caution is in order with regard to this debate. Essentially all of the studies that have proposed some biological or biochemical difference between persons with a homosexual orientation and those with a heterosexual orientation have not been replicated successfully. The findings are reported in the media when they are first discovered; but the lack of replication is seldom reported as prominently, and often goes unnoted.

REFERENCES

Bell, A. P., M. S. Weinberg, and S. K. Hammersmith. 1981. *Sexual Preference: Its Development in Men and Women.* Bloomington: Indiana University Press.

Gagnon, J. H. 1990. Gender preference in erotic relations: The Kinsey scale and sexual scripts. In D. P. McWhirter, S. A. Sanders, and J. M. Reinisch, eds., *Homosexuality/Heterosexuality,* pp. 177–207. New York: Oxford University Press.

Golden, C. 1987. Diversity and variability in women's sexual identities. In Boston Lesbian Psychologies Collective, ed., *Lesbian Psychologies: Explorations and Challenges,* pp. 19–34. Urbana: University of Illinois Press.

Kimmel, D. C., and I. B. Weiner. 1985. *Adolescence: A Developmental Transition.* Hillsdale, N.J.: Erlbaum.

LeVay, S. 1991. A difference in hypothalamic structure between heterosexual and homosexual men. *Science* 253:1034–37.

Masters, W. H., and V. E. Johnson. 1979. *Homosexuality in Perspective.* Boston: Little, Brown.

Matteson, D. R. 1987. The heterosexually married gay and lesbian parent. In F. W. Bozett, ed., *Gay and Lesbian Parents,* pp. 138–61. New York: Praeger.

Money, J. 1988. *Gay, Straight, and In-Between: The Sexology of Erotic Orientation.* New York: Oxford University Press.

Risman, B., and P. Schwartz. 1988. Sociological research on male and female homosexuality. *Annual Review of Sociology* 14:125–47.

Tiefer, L. 1987. Social constructionism and the study of human sexuality. In P. Shaver and C. Hendrick, eds., *Reviews of Social and Personality Psychology,* pp. 70–94. Beverly Hills, Calif.: Sage.

van Gelder, L. 1991. The "born that way" trap. *Ms.* 1(6) (May/June):86–87.

Weinrich, J. D., and W. L. Williams. 1991. Strange customs, familiar lives: Homosexualities in other cultures. In J. C. Gonsiorek and J. D. Weinrich, eds., *Homosexuality: Research Implications for Public Policy,* pp. 44–59. Newbury Park, Calif.: Sage.

4

Recent Challenges to Traditional Assumptions about Homosexuality: Some Implications for Practice

Diane Richardson

During the last decade there has been a change in professional attitudes toward homosexuality reflected in the development of new models of treatment. Rather than offering a cure the aim is to help homosexuals adjust positively to their orientation. Such attitudinal change on the part of the practitioners has not, in the main, questioned the fundamental assumptions of theories that seek to explain homosexuality. Recent theoretical inquiry into homosexuality, however, has done this, posing an important challenge to the traditionally held view that people have an essential sexuality that is either homosexual or heterosexual and that remains fixed and unchanging throughout their lives. This paper addresses some of the more important clinical implications of these recent developments, in particular, the suggestion that "the homosexual" as a certain type of person is an "invention." In addition, the therapeutic value and difficulties associated with an acknowledgment that sexual preference and identity may change over time are considered. Finally, there is consideration of what the goals should be in the case of the person who seeks professional help in changing from a homosexual to a heterosexual orientation.

Prior to the early 1970s the view of homosexuality as a mental disorder predetermined the goals of treatment for practitioners. The aim was to provide patients with a "cure" for their psychopathological condition. Therapeutic success was usually defined as the elimination of homosexual behavior.

Over the past decade this situation has changed. There has been an emergence of viewpoints that have sought to reconceptualize ideas about mental health and homosexuality; the feminist and gay movements have directly challenged the view of homosexuality as a sickness. In the face of such social change several professional bodies have recognized the need to move away from a sickness model of homosexuality, and one of the steps toward achieving this was the deletion in 1973 of homosexuality per se from the American Psychiatric Association's official list of mental diseases.

Although there has been no public declaration comparable to this in England, during the last decade many clinicians have begun to accept new models of treatment with their homosexual patients based on enhancing homosexual functioning rather than trying to eliminate it. Indeed, many clinicians would now define their therapeutic role with homosexuals as one of providing "skills to ensure adjustment in their chosen sexual orientation" (Higginbottom and Farkas 1977). An example of such professional liberalism was provided by Duehn and Mayadas (1976), who used an assertion training program to help a male homosexual cope with the social and interpersonal problems associated with his decision to reveal his homosexuality to others.

Research supports this move away from a disease-oriented approach to homosexuality. Numerous studies on a variety of samples have consistently concluded that there is no difference in psychological adjustment between homosexuals and heterosexuals (Gonsiorek 1982; Meredith and Reister 1980). This is not to say that psychologically disturbed individuals who happen to be homosexual do not exist, nor that certain individuals may, in a stigmatizing situation, have problems associated with being homosexual, but rather that homosexuality per se is unrelated to psychological adjustment.

Despite supportive evidence for a move away from psychopathological models of homosexuality, not all therapists accept such changes. Instead, they may continue to uphold the view that homosexuality is an important and serious mental disorder (e.g., Socarides 1979). A range of views about homosexuality therefore currently inform therapeutic practice. Even among therapists who have come to regard homosexuality as "nonpathological" there will be important differences in the extent to which they reject not merely a pathological *attitude* toward homosexuality but, equally important, the causal models on which they predicate such attitudes. Indeed, I would argue that the greatest changes that have taken place among therapists with regard to homosexuality have been largely attitudinal, rather than analytical. In other words, while many therapists, in coming to "accept" their homosexual patients, have forsaken a pathological view of homosexuality, considerably fewer have relinquished models of explanation that regard homosexuality as the end product of an immature/abnormal psychosexual development. This may be due, in part, to the fact that no single model has replaced the disease-oriented model of homosexuality. In recent years, however, new ways of thinking about homosexuality have begun to emerge that require us to face the contradictions inherent in the therapist saying, "I accept you," while at the same time maintaining a pathological model of explanation.

OLD IDEAS AND NEW REALITIES

Homosexuality traditionally has been defined as an essential and permanent aspect of being, that is, as the sexual orientation[1] of a minority group of individuals. Sexual orientation explains sexual identification and erotic attraction. As "a homosexual" one will experience erotic attraction to the same sex and will come to identify oneself as homosexual. Such assumptions have dominated the way in which practitioners have responded to homosexual interests and activities. Theories appearing in recent years that challenge these fundamentals have important implications for clinical practice.

Broadly speaking, two major developments in the literature on homosexuality have emerged in recent years that have posed a serious challenge to the traditional approach. One of these has been the emergence of concepts and studies that have directly challenged the view that homosexuality is an essential personality characteristic of a particular subgroup of people. This notion of "the homosexual" is, Plummer (1981) suggested, an "invention": it is a categorization specific to certain societies and particular historical periods. On this basis it is not possible to make a direct comparison between "homosexuality" in present day Western society with "homosexuality" in different cultures and historical periods as, say, Whitam did in viewing homosexuality as a natural, universal condition (Whitam 1980). Although the physical actions involved may be similar, the social and subjective meanings assigned to such actions are likely to vary considerably.[2]

Other studies by sociologists and social historians (e.g., Foucault 1979; McIntosh 1968; Weeks 1981, 1982) have supported the claim that, in Europe at least, the notion of "the homosexual" as a type of person is a relatively recent development. Weeks (1981), for instance, convincingly argued that the conceptualization of *individuals*, rather than certain *activities*, as homosexual only began to develop in England toward the latter part of the nineteenth century.

One of the important implications of this recent work has been that it highlights the need to distinguish between homosexual attraction and activity as compared with homosexual categorizations and identities. Traditional accounts of homosexuality imply that labeling oneself as essentially homosexual, heterosexual, or bisexual is a universal feature of human psychosexual development, something we all inevitably go through, independent of the culture or historical period we live in. What is being suggested here is that without the existence of a specific category of persons labeled as homosexuals there can be no development of a discrete homosexual identity.

Even within Western society, however, where there clearly does exist a notion of "the homosexual," we should take great care as clinicians to distinguish between homosexual attraction and activity and the category of homosexual. Various studies (e.g., Bell and Weinberg 1978; Ponse 1978; Weinberg 1978) have indicated that there is no necessary relationship between a particular pattern of sexual behavior and a particular sexual identity. What is crucial, it has been argued, is the particular meaning that individuals ascribe to their sexual feelings and activities, which will depend not only on the specific situation in which sexual conduct occurs, but also on the significance of sexual orientation in a particular historical, social, and cultural context (Weinberg 1978). What this means in practice is that we need to pay much more attention to the ways in which individuals interpret their sexual fantasies and activities *for themselves.* In the past, clinical "treatment" of homosexuals, with its emphasis on sexual acts, has failed to do this, being rather more concerned with the *therapist's view* of whether or not the individual's homosexual interests and activities constitute "real" homosexuality. Indeed, many clinicians, including those who no longer offer a "cure," still regard it as a major part of their therapeutic role to provide patients with an interpretation of their homosexual feelings and behavior and, eventually, a label.

Interest in the way in which individuals come to label themselves as "essentially" either homosexual, heterosexual, or bisexual represents the other major development in the study of homosexuality in recent years. Little attention has been paid to sexual identity in the past, the traditional assumption being that a person's sexual identity simply "emerges," sometime during adolescence, as a natural outcome of sexual orientation.[3] In addition, the stability of sexual identity has simply been assumed within traditional accounts, as part and parcel of the belief in a stable underlying sexual orientation upon which a person's sexual identity is founded.

Beginning in the 1970s, this view has been challenged by research studies (e.g., Dank 1971; Plummer 1975; Troiden 1979; and Weinberg 1978) which, in suggesting that our sexual identities are socially constructed, have focused on the need to elaborate the complex cognitive processes by which we come to interpret our sexual selves and take on an identity. While acknowledging that for most people identification as homosexual or heterosexual is a central and stable aspect of their self-identity, such an approach implies that we cannot simply assume this to be the case. We need to consider the processes whereby, for each individual, either stability *or change* of sexual identity occurs. We must, in other words, address ourselves not only to the question of how individuals develop a heterosexual or homosexual identity, but also how they do, or do not, maintain this identity thereafter. As a limited number of studies have shown (e.g., Pattison and Pattison 1980; Ponse 1978), despite the widespread belief that sexual "orientation" is a permanent characteristic, individuals may undergo one or more redefinitions of sexual identity during their lifetime.

Finally, in considering recent developments in the literature, some writers have questioned not only the relevance of assuming the natural existence of the categories homosexual, heterosexual, and bisexual, but also the assumption that sexual desire itself is a natural and universal phenomenon. This fundamental challenge to traditional accounts of psychosexual development has come from three different theoretical approaches to understanding sexuality: the interactionist (e.g., Gagnon and Simon 1973; Gagnon 1973), the discursive (e.g., Foucault 1979), and the psychoanalytic (e.g., Lacan 1977). Such contributions pose an important challenge to what for many of us is the very foundation stone of our thinking about sexuality. At the present time, however, neither the theoretical nor the therapeutic implications of such developments for our understanding of homosexuality have been fully explored.[4]

THERAPEUTIC IMPLICATIONS OF RECENT CONCEPTUAL DEVELOPMENTS

It is by questioning the view that people have a core sexuality that is either homosexual or heterosexual, a fixed and unchanging "essence," that recent researchers into homosexuality (e.g., Plummer 1981; Ponse 1978; Richardson and Hart 1981; Weeks 1981) have posed the most important theoretical, social, and political challenges. Of prime consideration in this article are the clinical implications of such developments, of which very little has so far been written (e.g., Hart 1984; Plummer 1981).

Clinicians face a dilemma if they accept the view that, far from being a universal categorization that is predetermined by nature, homosexuality is a fiction. Once homosexuality is defined within society as a way of being, people will frequently reconstruct their past in keeping with their present identification as homosexual (Richardson 1981). This may take the form of their saying "I must really have been gay all along," it being a case of their "real" selves having been "suppressed" until they identified themselves as homosexual. This process of reconstruction may still occur even where it runs counter to a previous identification as heterosexual and a prior absence of homosexual attraction (Ponse 1978). Thus, a person who has lived forty or fifty years as a "happy heterosexual" may come to view this period of their life as a "falsity," in an effort to preserve the notion of being one way sexually.

For the practitioner who rejects the view that being homosexual or heterosexual is an essential and fixed part of human nature, there remains the reality that this is how the majority of patients construct their sexuality. Moreover, many patients seek out professional help exactly for the reason that they feel a great deal of anxiety "not knowing what they really are." The implication is that if they are not really homosexual, then they need not worry about their homosexual desires. If, however, they are really homosexual, then they must deal with their feelings, either by "coming to terms with themselves" and acting on them, or by trying to ignore or get rid of them. Either way, what individuals in this position are most likely to want from professional or self-help is the ascription of a label that will give meaning to their experiences and feelings.

Given all the social pressures on individuals to categorize themselves and others as one thing or another sexually, practitioners must choose their responses carefully. As Plummer suggested, faced with this "paradox of categorization":

> The task of practitioners is not an easy one: to label too soon may prematurely close possibilities, and to label too late may add to the weight of suffering. . . . On the one hand, labels are useful devices—they give order to chaos, structure to openness, security to confusion. Knowing that one is gay is much more comforting than living with the precariousness of confused sexual identities. On the other hand, labels are destructive devices—they restrict where other choices are possible, they control and limit possible variety, they narrow human experimentation. In the short run, labels are comforting; in the long run, they are destructive. (1981: 108–9)

To avoid sexual categorization is extremely difficult in a world that places so much importance on the gender of one's sexual partner, real or fantasized. Still, we should be fully aware of the costs and benefits for individuals of this self-labeling. For the therapist it is important to explore the meaning and significance that a homosexual identification holds for each individual, in the context of their current life-style, self-identity, and visions of the future.

Implicit in what I am suggesting is that the meaning of sexual feelings, fantasies, behaviors, and sexual identity itself may change over time. Some of these changes may be related to aging, personal experiences, changing views of the self, and wider social changes in the meaning of sexual behavior and identities. We also need to acknowledge that sexual preferences and identities may themselves change over time. Although this is a relatively unresearched area, the Kinsey studies of female and male sexuality did provide evidence that, for some individuals, sexual preferences did not continue along a habitual and unchanging path during the life cycle (Kinsey, Pomeroy, and Martin 1948; Kinsey et al. 1953). It was, Kinsey claimed, perfectly possible for an exclusively heterosexual pattern of sexual behavior to be replaced at a later period of the life span by more or less exclusive homosexual activity (Kinsey 1941). Thus, a person could have no homosexual relationships until, say, the third or fourth decade of life, and thereafter remain more or less exclusively homosexual. More recent research has also indicated that some individuals may undergo a genuine change of sexual identity during their lives (e.g., Pattison and Pattison 1980; Ponse 1978).

Such challenges to the view that homosexuality is a permanent condition have important implications for practice, especially as it is precisely the issue of permanency that is so often a cause for concern both for the patient and the therapist, who must decide what, if any, help to offer. A good example is the professional concern in offering help to adolescents who think they "might be gay." Despite the appeals made for legal constraints on practice, such concerns instead are frequently grounded in worries about what the long-term implications of engaging in homosexual relationships may be for adolescents. Adolescents may not always share such worries. As one young woman clearly stated when asked if she thought that by opting to have a homosexual relationship she would end up being a homosexual for the rest of her life: "I don't know, you can't say. In any case, it doesn't really matter. *You know what you want now.*"

For those who do believe that homosexuality is a permanent and life-long state, we need to recognize that there may be a considerable amount of anxiety experienced in those situations where they are "encouraged" to view their feelings of same-sex attraction as homosexual precisely because they fear that for them to do so would mark the beginning of a lifelong stigmatized existence. These fears and anxieties may be compounded if they also believe that sexuality is beyond voluntary control. The way people deal with these feelings will vary, although Seligman suggested that when people perceive situations as beyond their control, they are likely to experience helplessness and depression (Seligman 1975).

One of the clinical implications of seeing sexual identity and sexual preference as potentially open to change is that it may be possible to relieve the worry of those individuals who believe that having a homosexual identity is a lifetime career. Again, there are important therapeutic dilemmas inherent in the adoption of such a position given that, for some people, the notion that homosexuality is a permanent condition provides both a way to accept themselves and to manage being stigmatized by society. It enables them to argue that, because they cannot help being what they are and cannot change, they should not be discriminated against.[5] Such a response is understandable. As members of a stigmatized and oppressed group in society, homosexuals often experience their identity as one they fought hard for and as one in need of protection. To suggest, therefore, that being a homosexual is not necessarily a lifetime career may spark anger and hostility, rather than relief. I have a good deal of sympathy for the person who responds in this way, given that denial is a common experience for women and men who state that they might be homosexual. Moreover, a major part of this process of denial for the individual may be the experience of being told by significant others—and here I would include practitioners—that they can, and in all likelihood probably will, change: "You're not really homosexual, it's just a phase/stage of life that you're going through."

In rejecting or moving away from a traditional view of homosexuality as a permanent "condition," therefore, therapists need to be highly conscious of the important issues that an acknowledgment of the possibility of either stability *or* change raises. These are perhaps thrown into sharpest relief by a consideration of what the goals for "treatment" should be in the case of the person who seeks professional help in changing from homosexual to heterosexual. In such cases one could argue that, despite no longer viewing homosexuality as a sickness, the therapist should adopt a "value-free" position and, in accepting the client's decision, offer a treatment program based on helping the individual shift from a homosexual to a heterosexual orientation and life-style (e.g., Masters and Johnson 1979). On the other hand, one might want to warn against offering treatment to aid such change. Interestingly, this response may stem from very different theoretical beliefs about homosexuality. Certain practitioners may be wary of encouraging individuals in their desire for change for the very reason that they do not believe "real" change is possible. Working within a traditional theoretical framework in which sexual orientation is regarded as an essential and relatively permanent aspect of personality structure, they would question whether "it is beneficial to change a person's sexual behavior to something that is incongruent with their sexual orientation" (Coleman 1982).

One could, however, adopt a very different theoretical position, one that views sexual orientation and sexual identity as a dynamic *process* of change and yet denies help to the homosexual person who wants to change. The argument for such a response is that as a stigmatized and oppressed group, homosexuals are likely to have experienced considerable social and societal pressure to change. What the person who seeks change is likely to be expressing, therefore, is not the freely chosen desire to change but guilt that what they "are" is socially unacceptable, and therefore they *ought* to change.

Silverstein endorsed this argument in suggesting that the first thing therapists should do with those patients who express a wish to change is to desensitize them to their guilt about their homosexuality (Silverstein 1972). In addition, he suggested that therapists should discover what the person means when they say they want to change, since again their reason may be rooted in negative and erroneous beliefs about homosexuality. Only after the therapist has helped the patient face up to and accept his or her feelings of homosexual attraction should the therapist encourage any talk of change (Silverstein 1977). Even then, Davidson (1982) argued, mental health practitioners ought not to offer help to homosexuals wanting to change unless they are also willing to "propose that a concerted program of clinical research be encouraged for the development of maximally effective procedures to help heterosexually oriented people become homosexually oriented, if it can somehow be determined that *they really want to*" (p. 96).

I would argue with Davidson that therapists certainly should consider the possibility that many of their heterosexual patients may wish to change, or at least expand, their sexual repertoires, just as some homosexuals may want to change theirs. Despite the likelihood that such wishes have been expressed during therapy, the fact is that it is never reported, according to Pillard (1982), "no doubt because such a development would be considered a reflection on the competence of the therapist" (p. 110).

These therapeutic conflicts notwithstanding, one of the important implications for practice of viewing sexual identity as an ongoing process is that this view acknowledges that the reasons for a person "being homosexual," and what this means to them, may change. Similarly, the reasons why a person comes to identify as homosexual in the first place may not be the reasons why they still continue to do so. More generally, such a perspective increases the possibility of being able to see sexual attraction and sexual identity as part of a person's *total* identity and life-style, rather than as purely the indivual's sexual preference. This may be important in helping people feel that they have some degree of responsibility and control over the relationships they decide to have, albeit within particular social and personal constraints. This may be an extremely useful therapeutic resource when faced with the person who feels "doomed" to be homosexual and cannot accept it, or with the person who seeks change by saying "I've never wanted to be homosexual; all my life I've desperately wanted to be heterosexual." In the latter case it would be important to explore with the client not only the reasons why he or she wishes to change, but what, in fact, a change of identity would mean. One of the ways this might be achieved is for the therapist to explore with the individual the important reasons why, in the context of their current view of themselves, their life-style, and their future opportunities, any change in sexual identity might involve social and personal loss. In so doing, the important factors that, despite their negative feelings, are currently important in their maintaining a homosexual identity may be revealed. Patients should explore the reasons why change would be difficult and unrealistic, as well as incurring certain important losses, unless they undertook a considerable restructuring of their total view of themselves and their life-style. These difficulties and losses may not be specifically sexual. It may be that a major influence on their maintaining a homosexual identity is that the homosexual subculture provides them with a supportive friendship network that they do not see as being readily available elsewhere and do not wish to lose. Not only may such an analysis increase the patients' feelings that they have some control over the relationships they form, in focusing on the current costs and benefits for them of being homosexual, but also it may enable them to pay attention to both negative and positive aspects of their sexual identity. This will be particularly important in cases where the person has problems of self-esteem and self-worth.

SUMMARY AND CONCLUSIONS

At a theoretical level, one of the most obvious and important implications of recent research into homosexuality is the questions it raises for the view that homosexuality is an inherent aspect of both the structure of society and of individual personality, a view that has dominated the medical and psychiatric discourse on sex. In this article, and in more detail elsewhere (Richardson 1984), I have tried to demonstrate that we have now reached a stage in theorizing about homosexuality where we can no longer continue to dismiss the theoretical difficulties that an essentialist view of sexuality poses. A fundamental reappraisal of theoretical beliefs about homosexuality is required.

Clinicians need to consider the therapeutic implications of such a reappraisal. Although this will not be easy, this should deter us neither from a careful evaluation of recent research into homosexuality nor from a full consideration of the therapeutic advantages and difficulties that may ensue in attempting to translate nonessentialist ideas into practice.

NOTES

1. Initially, it would seem that it was not so much the concept of sexual orientation that dominated medical and psychiatric theorizing on the subject of homosexuality, as it was the concept of gender inversion (Marshall 1981).

2. This also may be disputed, however. Although the available data on sexual conduct are limited, certain writers have suggested that sexual activity is motivated, coordinated, and organized by culturally and historically specific erotic scripts (e.g., Gagnon and Simon 1973; Gagnon 1973). What is viewed as "typical" homosexual activity in San Francisco in the 1980s, therefore, may well be very different in terms of the form, frequency, type, and order of homosexual acts "typically" performed, say, in ancient Greece.

3. The possible exception to this, where a homosexual identity does not follow on "inevitably" from a homosexual orientation, is accounted for by the concept of latent homosexuality. In this instance it is assumed that although the individual has a homosexual orientation, the self-awareness of this is repressed, and the individual comes to see him- or herself "inaccurately" as heterosexual.

4. Where the questioning of an instinctual sexual drive does seem to have rather more obvious applicability is in cases of sexual misconduct, where the explanation often given is in terms of a lack of cognitive control over basic and instinctual sexual needs. Rape is the most obvious example, and the notion of "situational" homosexuality in men is another.

5. Such arguments have been used in the past as a rationale for social acceptance and reform. For example, deterministic assumptions about the permanency of the homosexual "condition" were important in the reasoning of the Wolfenden report, which recommended the 1967 law reforms on male homosexuality in England and Wales.

REFERENCES

Bell, A. P.. and M. S. Weinberg. 1978. *Homosexualities: A Study of Diversity among Men and Women.* London: Mitchell Beazley.

Coleman. E. 1982. Changing approaches to the treatment of homosexuality: A review. In J. D. Weinrich, J. C. Gonsiorek, and M. E. Hotvedt, eds., *Homosexuality: Social, Psychological, and Biological Issues,* pp. 81–88. Beverly Hills, Calif.: Sage.

Dank, B. M. 1971. Coming out in the gay world. Psychiatry 34:180–97.

Davidson, G. C. 1982. Politics, ethics and therapy for homosexuality. In W. Paul, J. D. Weinrich, J. C. Gonsiorek, and M. E. Hotvedt, eds., *Homosexuality: Social, Psychological, and Biological Issues*, pp. 89–98. Beverly Hills, Calif.: Sage.

Duehn, W. D., and N. S. Mayadas. 1976. The use of stimulus/modeling videotapes in assertiveness training for homosexuals. *Journal of Homosexuality* 1:373–81.

Foucault, M. 1979. *The History of Sexuality.* Vol. 1. London: Allen Lane.

Gagnon. J. H. 1973. Scripts and coordination of sexual conduct. In J. K. Cole and R. Dienstbier, eds., *Nebraska Symposium on Motivation*, pp. 27–59. Lincoln: University of Nebraska Press.

Gagnon, J. H.. and W. Simon. 1973. *Sexual Conduct: The Social Sources of Human Sexuality.* London: Hutchinson.

Gonsiorek, J. C. 1982. Results of psychological testing on homosexual populations. In W. Paul, J. D. Weinrich, J. C. Gonsiorek, and M. E. Hotvedt, eds., *Homosexuality: Social, Psychological, and Biological Issues*, pp. 71–80. Beverly Hills, Calif.: Sage.

Hart, J. 1984. Therapeutic implications of viewing sexual identity in terms of essentialist and constructionist theories. *Journal of Homosexuality* 9(4):39–51.

Higginbottom, H. N., and G. M. Farkas. 1977. Basic and applied research in human sexuality: Current limitations and future directions in sex therapy. In J. F. Fischer and H. L. Gochros, eds., *Handbook of Behavior Therapy with Sexual Problems*, pp. 38–50. New York: Pergamon Press.

Kinsey, A. C. 1941. Criteria for a hormonal explanation of the homosexual. *Journal of Clinical Endocrinology* 1:424–28.

Kinsey, A. C., W. B. Pomeroy, and C. E. Martin. 1948. *Sexual Behavior in the Human Male.* Philadelphia: W. B. Saunders.

Kinsey, A. C., W. B. Pomeroy, M. E. Clyde, and P. H. Gebhard. 1953. *Sexual Behavior in the Human Female.* Philadelphia: W. B. Saunders.

Lacan, J. 1977. *The Four Fundamental Concepts of Psychoanalysis.* London: Hogarth Press.

McIntosh, M. 1968. The homosexual role. *Social Problems* 16:181–92.

Marshall, J. 1981. Pansies, perverts and macho men: Changing conceptions of male homosexuality. In K. Plummer, ed., *The Making of the Modern Homosexual*, pp. 133–54. London: Hutchinson.

Masters, W. M., and V. E. Johnson. 1979. *Homosexuality in Perspective.* Boston: Little, Brown.

Meredith, R. L., and R. W. Reister. 1980. Psychotherapy, responsibility and homosexuality: Clinical examination of socially deviant behavior. *Professional Psychology* 11:174–93.

Pattison, E. M., and M. L. Pattison. 1980. "Ex-gays": Religiously mediated change in homosexuals. *American Journal of Psychiatry* 137:1553–62.

Pillard, R. C. 1982. Psychotherapeutic treatment for the invisible minority. In W. Paul, J. D. Weinrich, J. C. Gonsiorek, and M. E. Hotvedt, eds., *Homosexuality: Social, Psychological, and Biological Issues*, pp. 99–113. Beverly Hills, Calif.: Sage.

Plummer, K. 1975. *Sexual Stigma: An Interactionist Account.* London: Routledge and Kegan Paul.

Plummer, K. 1981. Going gay: Identities, life cycles and life styles in the male gay world. In J. Hart and D. Richardson, eds., *The Theory and Practices of Homosexuality*, pp. 93–110. London: Routledge and Kegan Paul.

Ponse, B. 1978. *Identities in the Lesbian World: The Social Construction of Self.* Westport, Conn.: Greenwood Press.

Richardson, D. 1981. Lesbian identities. In J. Hart and D. Richardson, eds., *The Theory and Practice of Homosexuality*, pp. 111–24. London: Routledge and Kegan Paul.

Richardson, D. 1984. The dilemma of essentiality in homosexual theory. *Journal of Homosexuality* 9(2/3):79–90.

Richardson, D., and J. Hart. 1981. The development and maintenance of a homosexual identity. In J. Hart and D. Richardson, eds., *The Theory and Practice of Homosexuality*, pp. 73–92. London: Routledge and Kegan Paul.

Seligman, M. E. P. 1975. *Helplessness: On Depression, Development, and Death.* London: Freeman.

Silverstein, C. 1972. Behavior modification and the gay community. Paper presented at the annual convention of the Association for Advancement of Behavior Therapy, New York, October.

Silverstein, C. 1977. Homosexuality and the ethics of behavioral intervention. *Journal of Homosexuality* 2:205–11.

Socarides, C. W. 1979. The psychoanalytic theory of homosexuality, with special reference to therapy. In I. Rosen, ed., *Sexual Deviation*, 2d ed., pp. 243–77. Oxford: Oxford University Press.

Troiden, R. R. 1979. Becoming homosexual: A model of gay identity acquisition. *Psychiatry* 42:363–73.

Weeks, J. 1981. Discourse, desire and sexual deviance: Some problems in a history of homosexuality. In K. Plummer, ed., *The Making of the Modern Homosexual*, pp. 76–111 (London: Hutchinson).

Weeks, J. 1982. *Sex, Politics, and Society.* London: Longman.

Weinberg, T. 1978. On "doing" and "being" gay: Sexual behavior and homosexual male self-identity. *Journal of Homosexuality* 4:143–56.

Whitam, F. L. 1980. The prehomosexual male child in three societies. *Archives of Sexual Behavior* 9:87–100.

5

Sin, Sickness, or Status?
Homosexual Gender Identity
and Psychoneuroendocrinology

John Money

Devised animal experiments show conclusively that sex hormones influence the male/female dimorphism of the brain, prenatally, in four possible ways, namely, masculinizing, demasculinizing, feminizing, and defeminizing. The human counterparts of devised animal experiments are clinical intersexual (hermaphroditic) syndromes that occur spontaneously as experiments of nature. The two sources of data supplement one another. Both lead to the conclusion that prenatal hormonalization of the brain influences the subsequent sexual status or orientation as bisexual, heterosexual, or homosexual. This effect is more robotlike in subprimate than in primate species. As in subhuman primates, in the human species sexuoerotic status is dependent not only on prenatal hormonalization, but also on postnatal socialization effects. There are several different human hermaphroditic syndromes each of which makes its own specific contribution to the science of homosexology and to the understanding of genetic, prenatal-hormonal, pubertal-hormonal, and socialization determinants of being gay, straight, or bisexual. In combination, they indicate that sexual orientation is not under the direct governance of chromosomes and genes, and that, whereas it is not foreordained by prenatal brain hormonalization, it is influenced thereby, and is also strongly dependent on postnatal socialization. The latter is, like native language, programmed into the brain through the senses. Postnatal programming may become incorporated into the brain's immutable biology.

HISTORICAL AND CULTURAL RELATIVITY

The phenomenon that is today named homosexuality did not have that name until it was coined by K. M. Benkert, writing under the pseudonym of Kertbeny, in 1869. Though he applied the term *homosexuality* to both males and females, he defined it on the criterion of erectile failure:

In addition to the normal sexual urge in men and women, Nature in her sovereign mood has endowed at birth certain male and female individuals with the homosexual urge, thus placing them in a sexual bondage which renders them physically and psychically incapable—even with the best intention—of normal erection. This urge creates in advance a direct horror of the opposite sex, and the victim of this passion finds it impossible to suppress the feeling which individuals of his own sex exercise upon him. (Benkert 1869, quoted in Bullough 1976:637)

Instead of the criterion of genital sexuality, as in homo*sexual,* Benkert could have used the criterion of falling in love, as in homo*philic,* or the criterion of being attracted to those of the same sex, as in homo*genic.* Both terms were proposed by others, but homosexual won the day, probably because it was taken up in the early years of the twentieth century by Havelock Ellis and Magnus Hirschfeld (Ellis 1942; Hirschfeld 1948). Neither of these two writers recognized that the ethnocentricity of Benkert's definition of homosexuality as a sickness, though freeing it from being a sin or a crime, confines it too narrowly to pathological deviancy. It leaves no place for homosexuality as a status that is culturally ordained to be normal and healthy, as it is in societies that have, since time immemorial, institutionalized bisexuality. In bisexuality, homosexuality and heterosexuality may coexist concurrently, or they may be sequential, with a homosexual phase of development antecedent to heterosexuality and marriage. Concurrent bisexuality was exemplified in classical Athenian culture (Bullough 1976). Sequential bisexuality is exemplified in various tribal Melanesian and related cultures.

There is a vast area of the world, stretching from the northwestern tip of Sumatra through Papua, New Guinea to the outlying islands of Melanesia in the Pacific, in which the social institutionalization of homosexuality is shared by various ethnic and tribal people (Herdt 1984; Money and Ehrhardt 1972). More precisely, it is sequential bisexuality that is institutionalized in these societies. Their cultural tradition dictates that males between the ages of nine and nineteen reside no longer with their families but in the single longhouse in the village center where males congregate. Until the age of nineteen, the prescribed age of marriage, they all participate in homosexual activities. After marriage, homosexual activity either ceases or is sporadic.

The Sambia people (Herdt 1981) of the eastern highlands of New Guinea are among those whose traditional folk wisdom provided a rationale for the policy of prepubertal homosexuality. According to this wisdom, a prepubertal boy must leave the society of his mother and sisters and enter the secret society of men in order to achieve the fierce manhood of a head hunter. Whereas in infancy he must have been fed woman's milk in order to grow, in the secret society of men he must be fed men's milk— that is, the semen of mature youths and unmarried men—in order to become pubertal and grow mature himself. It is the duty of the young bachelors to feed him their semen. They are obliged to practice institutionalized pedophilia. For them to give their semen to another who could already ejaculate his own is forbidden, for it robs a prepubertal boy of the substance he requires to become an adult. When a bachelor reaches the marrying age, his family negotiates the procurement of a wife and arranges the marriage. He then embarks on the heterosexual phase of his career. He could not, however, have become a complete man on the basis of heterosexual experience alone. Full manhood necessitates a prior phase of exclusively homosexual experience. Thus, homosexuality is universalized and is a defining characteristic of head-hunting, macho manhood.

In Sambia culture, omission of, rather than participation in, the homosexual developmental phase would be classified as sporadic in occurrence, if it occurred at all, and would stigmatize a man as deviant. In our own culture, by contrast, it is homosexual participation that is classified as sporadic and stigmatized as a deviancy in need of explanation. For us, heterosexuality, like health, is taken as a verity that needs no explanation, other than being attributed to the immutability of the natural order of things. Because heterosexuality needs no explanation, then in bisexuality the homosexual component alone needs explanation. Consequently, there has been no satisfactory place for bisexuality in theoretical sexology. The universalization of sequential bisexuality, as in the Sambia tradition, is unexplainable in homosexual theory that is based exclusively on the concept of homosexuality as sporadic in occurrence and pathologically deviant (Stoller and Herdt 1985).

Institutionalized homosexuality, in serial sequence among the Sambia and other tribal peoples, must be taken into account in any theory that proposes to explain homosexuality. The theory will be deficient unless it takes heterosexuality into account also. Culturally institutionalized bisexuality signifies either that bisexuality is a universal potential to which any member of the human species can be acculturated or that bisexuality is a unique potential of those cultures whose members have become selectively inbred for it. There are no data that give conclusive and absolute support to either alternative. Genetically pure inbred strains, however, are an ideal of animal husbandry, not of human social and sexual interaction. Therefore, it is likely that acculturation to bisexuality is less a concomitant of inbreeding than it is of the bisexual plasticity of all members of the human species. It is possible that bisexual plasticity may vary over the life span. Later in life it may give way to exclusive monosexuality or it may not.

PREFERENCE VERSUS STATUS OR ORIENTATION

In the human species, a person does not prefer to be homosexual instead of heterosexual, nor to be bisexual instead of monosexual. *Sexual preference* is a moral and political term. Conceptually it implies voluntary choice, that is, that one chooses, or prefers, to be homosexual instead of heterosexual or bisexual, and vice versa. Politically, *sexual preference* is a dangerous term, for it implies that if homosexuals choose their preference, then they can be legally forced, under threat of punishment, to choose to be heterosexual.

The concept of voluntary choice is as much in error here as in its application to handedness or to native language. You do not choose your native language as a preference, even though you are born without it. You assimilate it into a brain prenatally made ready to receive a native language from those who constitute your primate troop and who speak it to you and listen to you when you speak it. Once assimilated through the ears into the brain, a native language becomes securely locked in—as securely as if it had been phylogenetically preordained to be locked in prenatally by a process of genetic determinism or by the determinism of fetal hormonal or other brain chemistries. So also, sexual status or orientation, whatever its genesis, may become assimilated and locked into the brain as monosexually homosexual or heterosexual or as bisexually a mixture of both.

A sexual status (or orientation) is not the same as a sexual act. It is possible to participate in, or be subjected to, a homosexual act or acts without, thereby, becoming predestined to have, as a consequence, a homosexual status, and vice versa with heterosexuality. The "Skyscraper Test" exemplifies the difference between act and status. One of the versions of this test applies to a person with a homosexual status who is atop the Empire State Building or other high building and is pushed to the edge of the parapet by a gun-toting, crazed sex terrorist with a heterosexual status. Suppose the homosexual is a man and the terrorist a woman who demands that he perform oral sex with her or go over the edge. To save his life, he might do it. If so, he would have performed a heterosexual act, but he would not have changed to have a heterosexual status. The same would apply, vice versa, if the tourist was a straight man and the terrorist a gay man, and so on.

This Skyscraper Test, by dramatizing the difference between act and status, points to the criterion of falling in love as the definitive criterion of homosexual, heterosexual, and bisexual status. A person with a homosexual status is one who has the potential to fall in love only with someone who has the same genital and bodily morphology as the self. For a heterosexual, the morphology must be that of a person of the other sex. For the bisexual, it may be either.

It is not necessary for the masculine or feminine bodily morphology of the partner to be concordant with the chromosomal sex, the gonadal sex, or the sex of the internal reproductive anatomy. For example, a male-to-female, sex-reassigned transsexual with the body morphology transformed to be female in appearance is responded to as a woman—and vice versa in female-to-male transsexualism.

Discordance between the body morphology and other variables of sex occurs also in some cases of intersexuality. For example, it is possible to be born with a penis and empty scrotum and to grow up with a fully virilized body and mentality, both discordant with the genetic sex (46, XX), the gonadal sex (two normal ovaries), and the internal sexual structures (uterus and oviducts). Conversely, it is possible to be born with a female vulva and to grow up with a fully feminized body and mentality, both discordant with the genetic sex (46, XY), the gonadal sex (two testes), and the internal sexual structures (vestigated feminine mullerian-duct structures and differentiated masculine wolffian-duct structures). Clinical photographic examples of these syndromes, and many others, are reproduced in Money (1968b, 1974).

The 46, XX intersexed man who falls in love with and has a sex life with a 46, XX normal woman is regarded by everyone as heterosexual, and so is his partner. The criterion of their heterosexuality is the sexual morphology of their bodies and the masculinity or femininity of their mentality and behavior, not the sex of their chromosomes, gonads, or internal organs. The same principle applies conversely in the case of the feminized 46, XY intersexed woman whose sex life is with a normal 46, XY man.

EVOLUTIONARY BISEXUALITY

Any theory of the genesis of either exclusive homosexuality or exclusive heterosexuality must address primarily the genesis of bisexuality. Monosexuality, whether homosexual or heterosexual, is secondary and a derivative of the primary bisexual or ambisexual potential. Ambisexuality has its origins in evolutionary biology and in the embryology of sexual differentiation.

Ambisexuality has many manifestations in evolutionary biology. Oysters, garden worms, and snails, for example, are ambisexual. They are also classified as bisexual and as hermaphroditic. Many species of fish are capable of changing their sex from female to male, or from male to female, and in some species more than once (Chan 1977). The change is so complete that the fish spends part of its life breeding as a male with testicles that make sperm and part as a female with ovaries that make eggs—an exceptionally thorough degree of sequential bisexuality.

A species of whiptail lizard from the Southwest, *Cnemedophorus uniparens*, offers a unique contribution to bisexual theory (Crews 1982, in press). This species has neither males nor females but is monecious and parthenogenic. Nonetheless, as judged by comparison with closely related two-sexed whiptail species, each individual lizard is able at different times to behave as if a male and as if a female in mating. The one in whom a clutch of eggs is ripening, ready to be laid in the sand for sun-hatching, is mounted by a mate whose ovaries are in a dormant, nonovulatory phase. This enactment is believed to affect the hormonal function of the pituitary of the ovulating lizard and to facilitate reproduction. At a later date, their roles reverse.

In this parthenogenic reptilian species, the brain is bisexual or ambisexual, even though the pelvic reproductive anatomy is not. According to MacLean's evolutionary theory of the triune brain, the mammalian brain is made up of an evolutionarily ancient reptilian brain overlaid by a paleocortex that is shared by all mammals, and that, in turn, is overlaid by the neocortex, which is most highly evolved in the human species (MacLean 1972). Thus, the behavioral bisexuality of parthenogenic whiptail lizards may provide a key to understanding the bisexual potential of mammalian species.

It has long been known that the mammalian embryo, in the early stages of its development, is sexually bipotential. The undifferentiated gonads differentiate into either testes or ovaries. Thereafter, the Eve principle triumphs over the Adam principle: sexual differentiation proceeds to be that of a female unless masculinizing hormones are added, normally by being secreted by the fetal testes. One of the two masculinizing hormones from the fetal testes is actually a defeminizing hormone, MIH (mullerian-inhibiting hormone). It has a brief life span during which it vestigiates the two mullerian ducts and prevents them from developing into a uterus and fallopian tubes (oviducts). The other hormone masculinizes. It is testosterone (or one of its metabolites). It presides over the two wolffian ducts and directs their development into the male internal accessory organs, including the prostate gland and seminal vesicles.

Differentiation of the internal genitalia is ambitypic. That is, the male and female anlagen are both present to begin with, after which one set vestigiates while the other set proliferates (figure 5.1). By contrast, differ-

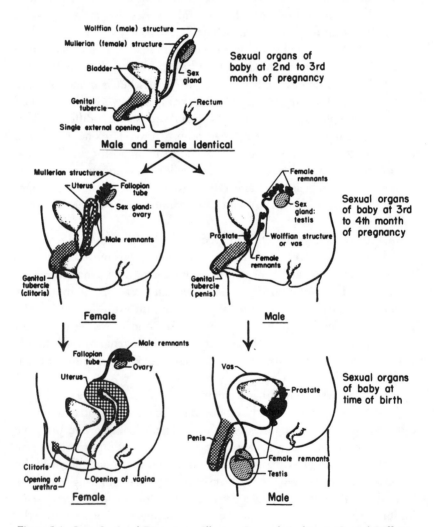

Figure 5.1. Cross-Sectional Diagrams to Illustrate Internal, Ambitypic Genital Differentiation in the Human Fetus

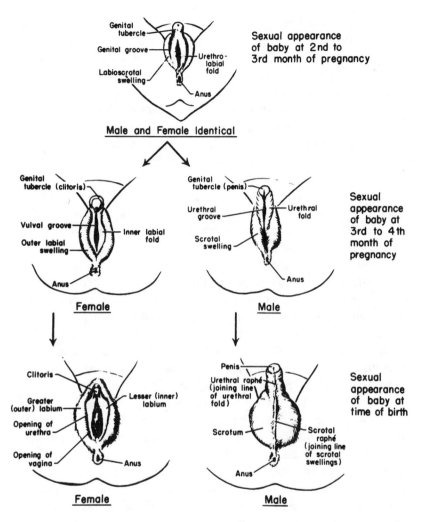

Figure 5.2. Diagrams to Illustrate External, Unitypic Genital Differentiation in the Human Fetus.

entiation of the external genitalia is unitypic. That is, there is a single set of anlagen that have two possible destinies, namely, to become either male or female (figure 5.2). Thus, the clitoris and the penis are homologues of one another, as are the clitoral hood and the penile foreskin. The tissues that become the labia minora in the female wrap around the penis in the male and fuse along the midline of the underside to form the tubular urethra. The swellings that otherwise form the divided labia majora of the female fuse in the midline to form the scrotum of the male.

The Adam principle as applied to hormonal induction of sexual dimorphism of the genitalia applies also to dimorphism of the brain and its governance of the genitalia and their functioning. According to present evidence, hormone-induced brain dimorphism takes place later than that of the genitalia, and, dependent on the species, may extend into the first few days or weeks of postnatal life. The primary masculinizing hormone is testosterone, though it is not necessarily used in all parts of the brain as such. Within brain cells themselves, as within cells of the pelvic genitalia, it may be reduced to dihydrotestosterone. Paradoxically, it may also exert its masculinizing action only if first aromatized into estradiol, one of the sex steroids that received its name when it was considered to be exclusively an estrogenic, feminizing hormone. In both sexes, estradiol is metabolized from testosterone, which, in turn, is metabolized from progesterone, of which the antecedent is the steroidal substance, cholesterol, from which all of the steroidal hormones are derived.

On the basis of animal experimental studies of the effects of prenatal brain hormonalization on subsequent sexually dimorphic behavior, it is now generally acknowledged that the converse of brain masculinization is not feminization but demasculinization. The converse of feminization is defeminization. It is possible for masculinization to take place without defeminization, and for feminization to take place without demasculinization (Baum 1979; Baum et al. 1982; Beach 1975; Ward 1972, 1984; Ward and Weisz 1980; Whalen and Edwards 1967). That means that the differentiation of sexual dimorphism in the brain is not unitypic, like that of the external genitalia, but ambitypic, like that of the internal genitalia. Ambitypic differentiation allows for the possible coexistence of both masculine and feminine nuclei and pathways, and the behavior they govern, in some if not all parts of the brain. The two need not necessarily have equality. One may be more dominant than the other. To illustrate, when cows in a herd are in season, the central nervous system functions in such a way as to permit cow to mount cow, whereas when a bull is present, the cow is receptive and the bull does the mounting. Mounting is traditionally defined as masculine behavior, but it would be more accurately defined as ambisexual, because it is shared by both sexes. On the criterion of mounting, cows are bisexual insofar as they mount and are mounted. Bulls are less so, insofar as they are seldom mounted.

The first evidence of the hormonal induction of sexual dimorphism in the brain was inferred from its effects on behavior. The first experiment was done by Eugen Steinach early in the twentieth century (Steinach 1940). He demonstrated that the mating behavior of female guinea pigs would be masculinized if, in fetal life, they had been exposed to male hormone injected into the pregnant mother. The theoretical implications of Steinach's finding were too advanced for their time. They lay dormant until William C. Young replicated the experiment in the 1950s (Young, Goy, and Phoenix 1964). Since then, a whole new science of hormone-brain-behavior dimorphism has developed.

By the 1970s it had become evident that hormone mediated dimorphism of the brain was no longer an inference based on sexually dimorphic behavior, but an actuality that could be neuroanatomically demonstrated directly in brain tissue. In 1969 Dörner and Staudt reported that the nuclear volume of nerve cells in the preoptic area and ventromedial nucleus in the rat hypothalamus was larger in females than in males and that androgen administered in late prenatal and early neonatal life would reduce the volume of these cells in females and castrated males. In 1971 Raisman and Field reported their discovery of sexual dimorphism in the dendritic synapses of the preoptic area of the rat brain. Thus began a new era of research into the prenatal hormone determinants of sex differences in the neuroanatomy of those regions of the brain that mediate mating behavior (see reviews by Arnold and Gorski 1984; De Voogd 1986; De Vries et al. 1984).

Confirmatory findings followed in quick succession. In rats, Gorski and his research colleagues found and named the sexually dimorphic nucleus of the preoptic area (SDN-POA; Gorski et al. 1978). Corresponding sexually dimorphic tissues in the human brain Gorski referred to as interstitial nuclei of the anterior hypothalamus. The SDN-POA of male rats is bigger than that of females and becomes so under the influence of steroid hormone from the testes (testosterone or its metabolite, estradiol) during the critical period of the first few days after birth (Döhler et al. 1982). Also in rats, Breedlove and Arnold (1980) discovered sexual dimorphism in the number of motor neurons innervating the perineal muscles and that it is during the critical period of the first few days after birth that the larger number of these motor neurons in males is produced by the presence of steroid hormone from the testes (Breedlove 1986).

In songbirds, as well as in rats, the presence of testicular hormone during a brief critical period proved to be the determinant in the male brain of the neuroanatomy that governs song (Nottebohm and Arnold 1976). In the zebra finch, testicular hormone exerts its masculinizing effect once and forever during the early critical period. There is no backtracking. The song pattern of the first spring singing season persists unchanged in subsequent years. In the canary, by contrast, the entire process is reactivated each spring, which allows the male to change his song and learn a new one each year instead of having only the one that he learned in the first year of life. An adult female, provided she is treated with steroid hormone, is able to learn a song for the first time as an adult. Learning the song first as a newly hatched nestling is not imperative. Male songbirds copy the song they hear in the nest even though they do not sing it until weeks later.

The findings with respect to canary song demonstrate a type of sexual dimorphism in which the ambisexual window is not forever closed after the neonatal critical period, but is reopened annually. Thus, a canary of either sex may sing one year but not the next, depending on the degree of steroidal hormonalization of the sexually dimorphic brain in the springtime of each year. As songsters, canaries thus have the possibility of being serially, rather than concurrently, bisexual.

Concurrent bisexuality would require two coexistent, dimorphic neuroanatomical systems, one subserving masculine and one feminine dimorphism of behavior, for example, mounting and lordosing, respectively. In rat experiments, Nordeen and Yahr (1982) found such a duality in the form of hemispheric asymmetry in the neighborhood of the sexually dimorphic nucleus of the preoptic area of the hypothalamus. They implanted pellets of the steroid hormone estradiol separately into the left and right sides of the hypothalamus of newborn female rat pups. The subsequent effect of the hormone on the left side was to defeminize— that is, to suppress lordosis—and on the right side to masculinize—that is, to facilitate mounting behavior—after the rats became mature.

The lateral distribution in the brain of masculine to the right and feminine to the left means that the two sides may develop to be either concordant (one masculinized and the other defeminized, or one feminized and the other demasculinized) or discordant (one masculinized and the other feminized, or one demasculinized and the other defeminized). Disparities may come into being on the basis of the amount of hormone needed by and available to each side; the timing of its availability to each side; the synchrony or dissynchrony of the hormonal programming on each side; and the pulsatility or continuity of the hormonal supply on each side. Thus, there are alternative ways in which one side could be rendered masculine and the other feminine to a sufficient degree to constitute bisexuality. Likewise, there are alternative ways in which the brain may be masculinized when the genitals are feminized, or vice versa, so as to constitute homosexuality.

These alternative ways of predisposing the brain to be either bisexual or homosexual can, of course, be manipulated experimentally. They may also occur adventitiously as an unrecognized side effect of hormone imbalance secondary to nutritional, medicinal, or endocrine changes, including stress-derived changes, in the pregnant mother's bloodstream. Sleeping pills containing barbiturate, for example, may have a demasculinizing effect on the brain of the human fetus, because the drug has been shown to have such an effect on male rat pups (reviewed in Reinisch and Saunders 1982). Also in rats, maternal stress that alters maternal adrenocortical hormones may exert a prenatal demasculinizing effect on male pups, subsequently evident in their bisexual and homosexual mating behavior (Ward 1984).

The dramatic power of the steroid hormones in prenatal life to foreordain the sexual orientation and mating behavior of adult life has been illustrated in several laboratory species in experiments in which fetal females are hormonally masculinized or males demasculinized. The hormonal intervention may be timed so as to change the sex first of the external genitalia and then of the brain or to spare the external genitalia and change the brain only.

There is a remarkable film (Short and Clarke, undated; see Clarke 1977) that shows how the brains and behavior of ewe lambs, independently of their bodies, can be masculinized in utero by injecting the pregnant mother with testosterone at the critical period of gestation, Day 50 and thereafter. The lamb grows up to be a lesbian ewe. Its brain is so effectively masculinized that its mating behavior (and its urinating behavior also), including mating rivalry and the proceptive courtship ritual, is exactly like that of a ram, even though, at the same time, its own ovaries are secreting estrogen, not androgen. Moreover, the normal rams and ewes of the flock respond to the lesbian ewe's masculinized mating behavior as if it were that of a normal ram.

Sheep, cattle, and swine (reviewed by D'Occhio and Ford, in press) and other four-legged species are, more or less, hormonal robots insofar as a masculine or a feminine mating pattern can be foreordained on the basis of regulating the prenatal hormonalization of the brain. Even among sheep, however, the final outcome will be influenced by whether the lamb grew up in a normal flock of ewes and rams or in a sex-segregated herd. Mates are even more influenced by the social conditions of growing up and are less subject to hormonal robotization.

In the now well-known hermaphrodite experiments from the primate research centers in Oregon and Wisconsin, female rhesus monkeys were masculinized prenatally so that they were born with a penis and empty scrotum. Though they engaged in tomboyish play in childhood, unlike the sheep they did not grow up to mature sexually as lesbians. According to the evidence available, the postpubertal sexological outcome of prenatal hormonalization was modulated, in some degree, by the social conditions of their rearing in a coeducational, as opposed to an all-male or all-female, group of age mates (Goldfoot 1977; Goldfoot and Neff in press; Goldfoot and Wallen 1978; Goldfoot et al. 1984).

Social rearing was not, however, the only factor that influenced the sexological outcome. Other factors proved to be age at testing; whether intact or castrated; if castrated, whether primed with estradiol or testosterone as a replacement hormone; hormonal dosage; and sex of the partner (Phoenix and Chambers 1982; Phoenix, Jensen, and Chambers 1983). Taking into consideration these different variables, it has become evident that masculinized mating behavior, with an estrus female partner, may be a sequel to prenatal hormonal masculinization but is far from being an inevitable one, irrespective of whether the hermaphroditic animals had their own ovaries intact or had been ovariectomized and treated with replacement estradiol or with replacement testosterone. On testosterone, the younger they were, the more they were likely to get an erection, but the prevalence of intromission and of the movements of ejaculation (without semen) was, though not zero, very low.

There were no youthful tests of the effect of prenatal masculinizing on the effect of pairing the hermaphrodite with a male partner. The hermaphrodites had no external vaginal opening and could not be given one by plastic surgery because they would have mutilated the postsurgical wound. Themselves aggressive, the hermaphrodites were at risk of attacking and of being attacked by a male partner. At a later age, this risk was circumvented by using partners of proven gentleness, namely, aged monkey eunuchs treated with testosterone. The hermaphrodites and the control females were treated with estradiol, because both groups had a history of having been ovariectomized. In this experiment, the hermaphrodites were sexologically not different from the controls in responding to the males as females. The males mounted them both but were able to achieve intromission and ejaculation only with the control females, in view of the fact that the hermaphrodites had no vaginal opening.

The conclusion from the foregoing is that, in a primate species, prenatal hormonal masculinization a) although it is compatible with subsequent mating, does not ensure it, and b) although it does not guarantee feminized mating, does not obliterate it. Masculinized and feminized mating responses may coexist in an experimentally manipulated manifestation of monkey bisexuality.

INTERSEXUALITY AND BISEXUALITY

Although the sequential influence of prenatal hormonal and postnatal rearing effects cannot be studied experimentally by inducing intersexuality in human beings, it can be studied in the so-called experiments of nature, namely, the syndromes of intersexual and other birth defects of the sex organs. These are the syndromes that are known collectively by the term *hermaphroditism*, as well as by its synonym *intersexuality*. They are augmented by syndromes of agenesis of the sex organs, as in congenital absence of the penis and in congenital micropenis, and by syndromes of traumatic or surgical loss of the genitalia.

By definition, intersexuality, and likewise its synonym, hermaphroditism, signifies ambiguity as to whether an individual is male or female. In the human species, as in all mammals, it is not possible to be both male and female, either simultaneously or sequentially. Intersexual ambiguity means, therefore, that the multiple criteria of sex are not consistently either all male or all female, but that there is some degree of inconsistency or incongruity among them. The criteria of sex are as follows (Money 1955; Money, Hampson, and Hampson 1955): chromosomal sex, H-Y antigenic sex, gonadal sex, prenatal hormonal sex, internal genital sex, external genital sex, pubertal hormonal sex, assigned sex and rearing, and gender-identity/role (G-I/R; see also *Dorland's Illustrated Medical Dictionary* 1981).

In some instances, intersexuality is concealed: the external genitalia appear to conform to the criterion of being either male or female but are inconsistent with all or part of the internal reproductive anatomy. In other instances, intersexuality is visible as ambiguity of the external genitals: what might be a penile clitoris might also be a clitoridic penis, and what might be labial fusion might also be a labioscrotum. Internally, the reproductive structures may be predominantly either male or female.

Discordances among the criteria of sex, as manifest in intersex syndromes, can be explained embryologically in terms of the Adam/Eve principle, as mentioned earlier. Incomplete or partial masculinization of the external genitalia leaves a protuberant penoclitoris (or clitoropenis) with an open gutter on its underside and a urogenital opening or funnel at its base. This ambiguous condition is named hypospadias if the individual is designated as a male and surgically corrected as a male. Correspondingly, the same condition is named partial urogenital fusion with clitoromegaly if the individual is designated as a female and surgically corrected as a female. In such among the newborn, the final intersexual (or hermaphroditic) diagnosis cannot be established by visually inspecting the "unfinished," birth-defective genitalia. The diagnosis is not necessarily the final criterion of the sex to which the baby would best be assigned, reared, and clinically habilitated. It is on this account, and because, historically, medical opinion has not been unanimous regarding the sex of assignment in cases of birth defect of the sex organs, that science has serendipitously been provided with matched pairs of two or more cases that are concordant for prenatal history and diagnosis but discordant for postnatal history and treatment.

There are two grand strategies for utilizing intersexual cases to investigate the genesis of homosexual, bisexual, or heterosexual status. One is the group-comparison method. The other is the matched-pair method.

The group-comparison strategy requires a sufficient number of individuals with the same diagnosis to constitute a diagnostically homogeneous sample—homogeneous for intersexual diagnosis. It is compared to either a matched clinical control group or a matched normal control group, or both. The clinical control group is homogeneous for its own diagnosis, which is specifically selected because of either its similarity to or divergence from the primary research sample. The investigative design allows status (or orientation) in adulthood as homosexual, bisexual, or heterosexual to be the dependent variable. It is compared with the other variables or determinants of sex from conception on, namely, chromosomal sex, H-Y antigen, gonadal sex, prenatal hormonal sex, internal morphologic sex, external morphologic sex, assigned sex and rearing, and pubertal hormonal sex.

The paired-comparison strategy matches pairs or sets of pairs of individuals who are intersexually concordant for prenatal etiology and diagnosis but discordant for sex of assignment and rearing, and compares them with respect to adult homosexual, bisexual, or heterosexual status. The paired-comparison strategy may also be applied to intersexed individuals who are concordant for sex of rearing and for some, though not all, of the other variables of sex—for example, genetic sex and gonadal sex may be male in one case (androgen-insensitivity syndrome) and female in another (Rokitansky syndrome), with the other variables of sex in both cases being female.

In the nineteenth century, the nomenclature of intersexuality was assigned on the criterion of the gonads (Klebs 1876). When both ovarian and testicular tissues were found, either separately or combined in an ovotestis, the diagnosis was true hermaphroditism. If both gonads were ovarian, the diagnosis was female pseudohermaphroditism, and if both were testicular, male pseudohermaphroditism. Today the prefix "pseudo-" is falling into disuse because it is redundant and also incorrectly implies that the condition is not authentically intersexual. Today, it is also known that intersexuality may exist in the presence of vestigial gonads that are neither ovarian nor testicular. Contemporary classification of intersexuality tends increasingly to reflect advances in etiological knowledge of inborn errors of hormonal synthesis (21-hydroxylase deficiency in female hermaphroditism, and 5-reductase deficiency in male hermaphroditism, for example) or hormonal metabolism (intracellular inability to use androgen in the androgen-insensitivity syndrome of male hermaphroditism, for example).

A diagnosis on the basis of endocrine etiology is currently more readily established in female rather than in male hermaphroditism, true hermaphroditism, or agonadal hermaphroditism. Especially in the case of male hermaphroditism, the method of establishing an etiological diagnosis today is not a routine procedure, but a research laboratory one. In addition, there are some cases of male hermaphroditism for which an etiological diagnosis has not yet been established. Thus, for a given etiological diagnosis, the available sample may be small, in which case the paired-comparison strategy takes precedence over the group-comparison strategy. In female hermaphroditism, by contrast, there are fewer limitations on assembling a larger sample group, specifically in the case of the adrenogenital syndrome, the most prevalent form of female hermaphroditism. Some less common varieties of female hermaphroditism do exist, however, as discussed in the following sections.

ANDROGEN-INDUCED HERMAPHRODITISM

The least commonly recorded variety of female hermaphroditism is that in which an embryonically normal female is hormonally masculinized prenatally in fetal life by an excess of androgen that passes through the placenta from the mother's bloodstream. The excess androgen has its most likely source in an androgen-secreting ovarian or adrenocortical tumor that becomes hormonally active in the mother during the course of the pregnancy. In the fetus, embryonic differentiation of fertile ovaries is not affected. Unlike testes, ovaries make no mullerian-inhibiting hormone, so the mullerian ducts do not vestigiate but differentiate into a uterus and oviducts. Differentiation of the external genitalia, by contrast, is profoundly altered by the excess of androgen. The clitoris becomes hypertrophied so as to become a penile clitoris with incomplete fusion and a urogenital sinus or, if fusion is complete, a penis with urethra and an empty scrotum.

According to the principle of the statistics of extremes, only one case of this type would be needed to break the stranglehold of the traditional dogma that sexual orientation and erotic status in adulthood are innately and genetically preordained by the gonads and their hormonal functioning at puberty. To break the stranglehold, it would be necessary to have a case in which, at birth, the baby was assigned, reared, and clinically habilitated as a boy. The latter would entail surgery to masculinize the external genitalia. To prevent hormonal feminization (breasts and menses) at puberty would require either surgical removal of the ovaries or treatment with testosterone to suppress their secretion of female hormones. Testosterone treatment would induce pubertal virilization. It would then be necessary to follow the case to adulthood in order to establish that the erotosexual status and sex life were those of a man.

That was, indeed, the outcome not only in one such case (Money 1967; Money et al. 1955) but in two, the second unpublished. In each case, the individual grew up to be an adult who was universally accepted by his professional peers and friends as a man, by his wife as a husband, and by his adopted children as a father, not notably different from other fathers in the kinship or the community. Absolutely no one ever thought of either of these individuals as being lesbian, or even as bisexual.

Their lives have great value for homosexological theory. With a different postnatal social and clinical history, they could have grown up, as others like them have done, to become women, wives, and mothers who carried their own pregnancies. Instead, they grew to adulthood with a heterosexual orientation or status as men. Their masculine orientation may have been facilitated by some degree of prenatal hormonal masculinization of the brain in parallel with the prenatal hormonal masculinization of the external genitals. It may also have been facilitated by the clinical intervention, at the time of the spontaneous onset of ovarian puberty, to arrest breast enlargement and put an end to menstruation through the penis. Hormones and surgery notwithstanding, their adult status as men was certainly not only facilitated by but developmentally engendered by the cumulative influences of their having been reared and socialized as boys.

Cases like these two demonstrate that both prenatal hormonal and postnatal social factors contribute to adult erotosexual status; but they do not spell out the details as they might apply to nonintersexed, morphologically normal girls who grow up, in the absence of hormonal masculinization, to be lesbians. No one yet knows what, if any, covert prenatal hormonal influences may predispose to lesbianism in anatomically normal girls. In addition, no one yet knows the social-learning formula, if there is one, that will unfailingly guarantee lesbianism as the outcome, with or without a predisposition. Conjectures and hypotheses that have been put forward have not been confirmed. They exist only as doctrines and dogmas.

PROGESTIN-INDUCED HERMAPHRODITISM

There is one form of human intersexuality that resembles an experiment of nature but is actually an experiment of iatrogenic trial and error. The error in this instance occurred when in the 1940s newly synthesized steroid hormones came on the market (McGarry 1987). Though they eventually proved to share both androgenic and progestinic properties, as well as chemical structure, they were initially prescribed as a progesterone substitute in the belief, false as it turned out, that they would prevent threatened miscarriage. In a small minority of unexplained cases, the external sex organs of a female fetus were masculinized, so that they had an intersexual external genital appearance. With rare exceptions, the babies were assigned and surgically corrected as girls. They needed no hormonal treatment to develop at puberty as females. During childhood they had a penchant for tomboyism (Ehrhardt and Money 1967), which suggested the possibility (wrongly as it turned out) of a sufficient degree of brain masculinization that they might, in adolescence, have bisexual imagery, ideation, and experience.

It was possible to obtain a follow-up on eleven of these individuals in adulthood (Money and Mathews 1982). The finding at this time was that their earlier tomboyism had not persisted and that they had only heterosexual imagery, ideation, and practice, with no homosexual inclinations. They were more interested in marriage and motherhood than in a nonmaternal career.

Evidently, the synthetic hormone that masculinized their external genitalia did not have a lasting masculinizing effect on that part of the brain that, at puberty and thereafter, governs sexuality. Possibly the prenatal hormonal effect was too weak or did not persist long enough to have an enduring effect on the brain. Another possibility is that hormonally sensitive brain cells did not recognize and were unable to respond to the synthetic hormone, whereas the cells of the developing external sex organs were able to do so. Whatever the explanation, the heterosexual outcome in the progestin-induced syndrome of female hermaphroditism was not replicated in the adrenocortical-induced syndrome (adrenogenital syndrome) of female hermaphroditism.

ADRENOGENITAL SYNDROME

The adrenogenital syndrome is also known as congenital adrenal hyperplasia (CAH) and congenital virilizing adrenal hyperplasia (CVAH). Inclusion of the term *virilizing* denotes the fact that if left untreated the syndrome induces the onset of puberty as early as the age of eighteen months and that it is invariably masculinizing in both sexes. During fetal life and continuously thereafter, unless corrected, the masculinizing hormone is secreted instead of cortisol by the affected individual's own adrenocortices in response to a recessively transmitted genetic error of cortisol synthesis. The error takes various forms, of which the most common is the 21-hydroxylase deficiency.

In fetal life, 21-hydroxylase deficiency does not alter the masculine differentiation of the chromosomally (46, XY) and gonadally (testicular) male fetus. By contrast, 21-hydroxylase deficiency has a profound effect in altering the feminizing differentiation of the chromosomally (46, XX) and gonadally (ovarian) female fetus, namely, by inducing masculinization of the external genitalia. The internal genitalia, which differentiate earlier, escape alteration. Masculinization of the external genitalia may be so extreme that the clitoris and its hood and labia minora become a normal penis with foreskin and covered urethra opening at the tip of the glans. The divided labia majora fuse and they do so completely, so as to become an empty scrotum when the formation of the penis is complete, thus producing normal appearing external genitalia except for the missing testes. In the least extreme degree of masculinization, the sole evidence may be clitoral enlargement. Between the two extremes are various degrees of clitoromegaly plus external urogenital closure, with resultant ambiguity as to the sex of the newborn baby. On the basis of visual inspection alone it cannot be decided whether the surgical correction should be designed to make the ambiguous organs more feminine or more masculine. At different times and places, and for different reasons, each decision has been made. Here, as in other syndromes, the outcome is of great relevance to the theory of homosexology.

The 21-hydroxylase deficiency in a chromosomally 46, XX, gonadal female born with a penis and empty scrotum is one of the intersexual conditions that holds a key to the very definition of homosexuality. Some such individuals have been assigned and reared as boys, either because they were given a diagnosis of undescended testes, or because, in the era prior to 1950, there was no known treatment to prevent the relentless and precocious progress of pubertal virilization (Money and Daléry 1977). Such a boy encounters no unusual hazards in growing up to have an adolescent romantic and erotosexual life with a female partner and, in adulthood, to become a husband and a father by either donor insemination or adoption. Yet, like his wife, he was born as a genetic female with two ovaries and female reproductive organs internally. Had his case been differently managed endocrinologically and surgically, he could have become pregnant and delivered a live baby by Caesarian section. Hence the question: are he and his wife both lesbians?

The answer is that they are not. This is another of the cases that confirm the proposition that, in general usage, homosexuality is not defined on the basis of the chromosomal sex, nor of any of the internal and concealed variables of sex. Instead, it is defined on the basis of the external sexual anatomy and the sexual characteristics of the body in general. Two people are identified as having a homosexual encounter or relationship provided that their external sex organs are anatomically of the same sex, regardless of how different they may be in secondary sexual characteristics. The 46, XX gonadal female with a penis and empty scrotum, assigned and reared as a boy, would be classified as homosexual if he had an affair with another person with a penis. If he did something so far unheard of, however, namely undergo surgical sex reassignment and then continue the affair with the same lover, then the relationship would be redefined as heterosexual. Hormonal treatment alone, even if it brought about breast growth and menstruation through the penis, would not suffice to change the definition of the relationship from homosexual to heterosexual. Only one partner should have a penis to permit a relationship to be defined as heterosexual, and, vice versa, only one should have a vulva.

Social conformity to the cultural criterion of femininity (or, vice versa, masculinity) does not, per se, override the genital criterion of homosexuality. To illustrate: in the case of a morphologically normal male who is a female impersonator, no matter how ladylike the appearance, or how hormonally feminized the body, the impersonator who is a lady with a penis is still regarded morally and legally as a homosexual (or perhaps as a preoperative transsexual) if she has a sexual partner who also has a penis. Her syndrome is gynemimesis—the miming of a female by a person who has a penis (Money and Lamacz 1984).

The syndrome of gynemimesis, otherwise known as syndrome of the lady with a penis, has not yet been known to have occurred in association with a diagnosis of 46, XX, CVAH with a penis. Quite to the contrary, congenital virilizing adrenal hyperplasia seems to blockade, utterly, the possibility of gynemimesis (Money and Lewis 1982). The responsible blocking factor is, presumably, the high degree of prenatal androgenization which, by inference, masculinizes the sexual brain as well as the external genitalia. The effect of prenatal adrogenization may completely override the effect of pubertal feminization, according to the evidence of a unique case of the 46, XX adrenogenital syndrome (Money 1974).

In this case the baby was one of those born with a fully formed penis and empty scrotum. The diagnosis was not changed from male with undescended testes until age ten, when it was established as congenital virilizing adrenal hyperplasia in a genetic and gonadal female hermaphrodite. On the basis of an erroneous belief that hormones would feminize the mind as well as the body, and without his own consent, the boy's local physician gave him hormonal treatment with cortisol, thus releasing his ovaries to secrete their own feminizing hormones of puberty. His breasts developed and heralded the approach of first menstruation, through the penis. He was mortified.

Behaviorally he was very much a macho boy. His parents said he was the very antithesis of his sister. His mother discovered a love letter he had written to his girlfriend. She and his father agreed that to convert him to a girl (despite the fact that he had two ovaries and no testes) would be the equivalent of forcing him to be a lesbian, with a girlfriend as a lover. They saw no point in forcing him to have his penis amputated as the first step in surgical feminization, nor in forcing him to take hormonal treatments that would enlarge his breasts and induce menstruation but would not demasculinize his voice or body hair. They decided, instead, to seek a second opinion regarding masculinizing treatment. They were, of course, correct. They had a son, not a daughter, irrespective of his clinical diagnosis as a female hermaphrodite with two ovaries and 46, XX chromosomes. He had the sexual orientation of a heterosexual boy. It was too late to change it by edict or by any known method of intervention.

This particular boy had missed being diagnosed neonatally because his life was not threatened by the salt-losing symptom associated with one variant of adrenal hyperplasia. Babies who are salt-losers are diagnosed. Otherwise they die. Some of them have had a penis and empty scrotum, and some an enlarged clitoris, variable in size, with incomplete labioscrotal fusion. In either case, today's standard pediatric recommendation is to assign the child as a girl or, in some instances, to make a reassignment if the child had initially been announced as a boy. Assignment as a girl entails surgical feminization of the genitalia. It entails also antimasculinizing hormonal treatment with a substitute for the missing adrenal glucocorticoid, cortisol, throughout life. This treatment, which arrests the continuation of masculinization, postnatally, and permits puberty to be feminizing, was discovered only in 1950. Thus, the first generation of babies to be treated with cortisol now constitute the first generation of young adults whose prenatal history of masculinization was not followed by a history of postnatal virilization. With respect to homosexology, they provide an opportunity to investigate the role of hormonal masculinization that is prenatal only, and not also postnatal, relative to sexual orientation as homosexual, bisexual, or heterosexual.

On the basis of longitudinal follow-up findings (Money, Schwartz, and Lewis 1984), it does appear that prenatal hormonal masculinization may have the same long-term sexological effect on 46, XX, adrenogenital babies who are clinically habilitated as girls as it does on those who are clinically habilitated as boys; that is, both are able to grow up to be romantically and sexually attracted to girls. In the case of those who grow up as boys, this predisposition is unhindered. It is incorporated into the postnatal effects of clinical and social masculinization, so that the ultimate outcome is socially approved heterosexuality as a male.

By contrast, in the case of those who grow up as girls, the predisposition set by prenatal hormonal masculinization is at odds with postnatal effects of clinical and social feminization. In adulthood, the ultimate outcome is heterogenously distributed between heterosexuality, bisexuality, or homosexuality as a female. In a sample of thirty follow-up cases, the actual percentages were: heterosexual, 40 percent (n = 12); bisexual, 20 percent (n = 6); homosexual, 17 percent (n = 5); and noncommittal, 23 percent (n = 7)—all grossly different from the control group (n = 27), x^2 (1, n = 57) = 18.5; p <.001. If the noncommittal group is omitted and the percentages recalculated, then 48 percent (n = 11) classified themselves as bisexual on the basis of imagery and/or activity, of whom five classified themselves as predominantly or exclusively lesbian as adults. This proportion, 48 percent, is similar to that obtained in an earlier study (Ehrhardt, Evers, and Money 1968) of 23 women who grew up in the pre-1950, precortisol era and who were, therefore, highly masculinized in physique. Evidently the high degree of masculinization that these 23 women underwent postnatally did not augment the predisposition set by prenatal masculinization. In CVAH syndrome, prenatal brain masculinization alone is sufficient to predispose to a bisexual or lesbian orientation.

One young woman in this CVAH follow-up study who did develop a lesbian orientation said, after having had two different boyfriends with whom she attempted in vain to relate in sexual intercourse, that she had to admit that she could fall in love only with another woman, not a man. She became lovesick over a girlfriend who, though her close companion, was unable to fall in love homosexually, only heterosexually. Driven to the despair of love unrequited, worsened by adversarial parents, the CVAH girl drove her car into isolated swamp country, and there was found, two weeks later, dead of self-inflicted gunshot wounds.

In the target tissues of the brain, the site where prenatal hormonal masculinization is translated into a predisposition toward subsequent bisexuality or homosexuality has not been demonstrated in the human species. One must infer, on the basis of studies of laboratory animals, that the site of masculinization is in the limbic system or paleocortex, intimately connected with the hypothalamus. In the adrenogenital syndrome, there is as yet no way of identifying either a timing or a dose-response effect that would distinguish those who eventually become bisexual from those who become monosexual as either homosexual or heterosexual. The difference might not prove to be exclusively prenatal, but postnatal also, in the overlay of developmental events and experiences that augment a prenatally established disposition that, by itself alone, would be too weak to preordain the status of adult sexual orientation.

ADOLESCENT GYNECOMASTIA

The adrenogenital syndrome occurs in 46, XY gonadal males, as well as in 46, XX gonadal females. Since 1950, the year when treatment became available, CVAH boys have been hormonally regulated with cortisol so that they do not undergo a precociously virilizing puberty which, in older texts, was termed the infant Hercules syndrome. Before birth, however, their own bodies made a flood of male hormone of adrenocortical origin, which exposed the brain to a supramasculinizing level of the hormone.

Youths with a history of the treated adrenogenital syndrome (n = 8) were selected in their late teenage years or in early adulthood as suitable for a contrast group of controls for youths (n = 10) who at puberty developed breast enlargement like that of a girl (Money and Lewis 1982). The latter condition, idiopathic adolescent gynecomastia, is of unknown etiology. One possibility is that the glandular tissue behind the nipple is unduly sensitive to estrogen in the amount normally secreted by the male's testicles. An alternative possibility is that the same tissue is unduly resistant to the effect of testosterone in overriding the effect of estrogen. Before puberty, there are no signs of unusual body development. Retrospectively, no evidence has been obtained that would point to unusual hormonal functioning in prenatal life, and no cases have turned up in prospective studies. Thus, there is no evidence, one way or the other, of the possibility of deficient brain masculinization, nor of a demasculinizing process, prenatally. Similarly, because there is no evidence for or against brain feminization prenatally, there is no evidence for or against brain ambisexualization.

The ten boys with adolescent gynecomastia constituted an unbiased and geographically available sample from a larger clinic list. Three of them proved to have a homosexual status, about which they talked openly. Long before puberty they had been stigmatized as sissy by their peers and recognized as atypical adults. Their boyhood lives had been marked by family adversity. Some of the CVAH boys also experienced family adversity. Nonetheless, there was no evidence of either a homosexual or bisexual status in any CVAH boy.

Thus, one may assume that with a history of hormonal supramasculinization prenatally, the CVAH syndrome boys had no leeway to develop other than heterosexually, no matter what. By contrast, one may assume that the boys who were destined to develop breasts were destined also to have leeway to veer toward homosexuality, provided other circumstances so conspired. It is possible that in prenatal life their brains were insufficiently responsive to androgen or in some other way were suboptimally masculinized hormonally. It will require a new and advanced research technology before this issue can be addressed.

It may be argued that the sample size in this study, being small, may have produced a fortuitous finding that will fail to be replicated. That argument is refuted by the data from the full list of patients from which the study sample was drawn. Among the thirty-three CVAH males, there was only one known instance of a homosexual status. The patient had a rare, asymptomatic case of CVAH which would not have been ascertained except for the fact that he was a cousin of two CVAH brothers and participated in a pedigree study. Among the forty-one adolescent gynecomastia males, there were eight who had homosexual (or bisexual) imagery and ideation. One of them was explicit in disclosing details of actual homosexual participation. One youth, struggling to resolve his dilemma, declared that if he could not become heterosexual, he would become either a priest with an abstinent sex life or a male-to-female transsexual. Instead, he became reconciled to being a practicing gay male.

ANDROGEN-INSENSITIVITY SYNDROME

Whereas the adrenogenital syndrome is characterized by prenatal supra-masculinization, the reverse applies to the androgen-insensitivity syndrome (AIS), formerly known as the testicular-feminizing syndrome. Inframasculinization characterizes partial androgen insensitivity, whereas complete antimasculinization characterizes complete androgen insensitivity. It is for this reason that patients with the complete syndrome of androgen insensitivity were selected to constitute the clinical contrast group of controls for the women with the 46, XX adrenogenital syndrome mentioned earlier.

The complete androgen-insensitivity syndrome occurs in girls and women who, paradoxically, are chromosomally 46, XY and whose gonads are histologically testicular, though without spermatogenesis and without the capacity to do the work of testes. Their incapacitation stems from a genetically transmitted, X-linked recessive error that blocks, in all cells of the body, either the uptake or the utilization of the hormone, testosterone. Secreted by the testes. Unable to use testosterone in both prenatal and postnatal life, the body fails to masculinize. Confronted with that failure, nature reverts to her primal template which is to construct not Adam, but Eve. In fetal life, this reversion takes place after the gonads have formed and secreted their antimullerian hormone, which blocks the growth of the mullerian ducts into a uterus and fallopian tubes. Thereafter, no further masculinization occurs, so that the baby is born as Eve, but without Eve's internal reproductive organs. The vagina is present, but lacks depth until dilated. The vulva appears normally female except that, in adulthood, pubic hair is sparse or absent. Pubic and axillary hair follicles, unable to utilize androgen, are unable to grow hair. At puberty, the breasts develop and the body feminizes in contour under the influence of the amount of testicular estrogen that normally circulates in the bloodstream of all males.

Two characteristics of the syndrome most commonly responsible for bringing the individual to medical attention are the shallow or atresic vagina and the failure to menstruate. These same two characteristics, vaginal atresia and amenorrhea, secondary to congenital absence of the uterus and fallopian tubes, are found also in women who are chromosomally 46, XX and gonadally female with a diagnosis of Rokitansky syndrome (or Mayer-Rokitansky-Küster [MRK] syndrome).

The two syndromes, AIS and MRK, are admirably suited to be clinical contrast or control groups for one another, because they are similar on all counts except chromosomal sex, gonadal sex, and hormonal cyclicity. A comparative study of an unbiased sample of eighteen women (Lewis and Money 1983; Money and Lewis 1983), nine in each diagnostic group, showed the two groups to be identical on a range of erotosexual variables.

All eighteen were exclusively heterosexual as women in imagery, ideation, and practice. The significance of this finding for homosexology is that it rules out three of the criteria of female sex—namely, chromosomal status, gonadal status, and hormonal cyclicity—as essential to the development of a feminine sexual orientation, because the two groups were antithetical on these three variables. The variables that they shared in common as heterosexual women were female external genital anatomy and body build, spontaneous hormonal feminization of the body at puberty, and a history of having been assigned and reared as girls.

Androgen insensitivity is another of the syndromes that points to the definition of homosexuality as sexual and erotic expression between two people who have the same external genital anatomy and body morphology. No one would ever consider a married androgen-insensitive mother with two adopted children a male homosexual simply because her husband had the same chromosomal sex as she has and the same gonadal sex as she had preoperatively. Common sense demands that she be accorded the same heterosexual status as her Rokitansky-woman counterpart.

The similarity between the two syndromes proved to be so perfect that it was, in fact, quite in order to combine the two diagnoses in order to get a sufficiently large control group for the aforementioned study of thirty adrenogenital women.

MALE HERMAPHRODITISM

Partial androgen insensitivity in a 46, XY fetus allows the Eve principle to take over partially. So also does partial androgen insufficiency. In both instances, the baby is born with a birth defect of the external sex organs, so that the genital appearance is ambiguously hermaphroditic or intersexed. Some such babies have been assigned and reared as boys, and some as girls. At puberty, irrespective of their sex of rearing, some have undergone spontaneous hormonal feminization and developed breasts. They do not menstruate, as they lack a uterus. The masculinizing puberty of those who do not feminize is likely to be partial or eunuchoidal, rather than complete.

In androgen-insensitivity cases, when the individual's own hormonal puberty is inadequate, hormonal treatment to bring about feminization is successful, whereas treatment to bring about masculinization is unsatisfactory. The consequences are dire if the partially androgen-insensitive individual has been assigned and reared to live as a boy, because he forever fails to gain the bodily appearance of masculine maturity. If he has grown up to the age of puberty self-identified as a boy, and if his imagery and ideation are heterosexually masculine, then it is impossible for him to espouse the rational logic of becoming hormonally and surgically reassigned to live as a woman, even if, untreated, he has already developed breasts and a feminine body morphology. To impose feminizing surgery of his genitalia would be totally incompatible with the history of the multiple operations to which his penis had already been subjected in order to affirm genital masculinity and to permit urination as a male.

In the annals of male hermaphroditism, cases of sex reassignment from male to female are rare, even in cases of impaired masculine bodily maturation on the basis of partial androgen insensitivity (Money and Norman, in press), whereas sex reassignment from female to male is not so rare (Money, Devore, and Norman 1986). The parallel phenomenon occurs in female hermaphroditism insofar as a sex reassignment from female to male is virtually unheard of, no matter how extensive the degree of masculinization (Money 1968a). There is, however, no corresponding parallel in female hermaphroditism with respect to the prevalence of reassignment from male to female, the explanation being that only a few female hermaphrodites are reared as boys. Even if they are announced as boys neonatally, a reannouncement is likely to follow soon thereafter. The explanation lies in the fact that female hermaphroditism is almost always associated with the adrenogenital syndrome, which produces a sufficiency of complicating symptoms—especially severe salt loss, which is lethal if not neonatally detected and treated—to lead to the neonatal diagnosis of gonadal sex (ovarian) and chromosomal sex (46, XX).

There is absolutely no doubt that in the traditional wisdom of most parents and their religious advisors, as well as of many doctors, primacy is attributed to chromosomal and gonadal sex, and to the prospect of fertility, as the criteria on which to decide the sex of assignment. Surgically, it is technically more feasible to demasculinize and feminize the external genitalia than it is to defeminize and masculinize them. Thus, the greater simplicity of feminizing corrective surgery also is a criterion in announcing the sex of a female hermaphrodite as female. This criterion is quite often disregarded in announcing or reannouncing the sex of a chromosomally and gonadally diagnosed male hermaphrodite as a boy. As a consequence, he may be nosocomially traumatized by multiple surgical admissions in childhood, only to have, in adulthood, a small and deformed penis inadequate for copulation (Money and Lamacz 1986) and possibly for urination as well.

The primacy accorded the chromosomal sex and, more especially, the gonadal sex as the ultimate criteria by which to decide the sex of a hermaphrodite child influences the destiny of the male hermaphroditic child at any age. For the baby assigned and reared as a girl and not diagnosed as gonadally and chromosomally male until later in life, the diagnosis may lead to an imposed sex reassignment. Or, if in childhood or adolescence, the male hermaphrodite living as a girl is ambivalent about or rejects her status as a girl, the covert if not the overt influence of the primacy of the chromosomal and gonadal criteria tips the scales in favor of permitting a sex reassignment that would otherwise be vetoed. Sex reassignment would be vetoed in the corresponding case of a male hermaphrodite living as a boy and ambivalent about or rejecting his status as a boy. In the same way, sex reassignment from girl to boy would be vetoed for a female hermaphrodite (Jones 1979; Money 1968a).

Sex is a binary system: male and female. A hermaphroditic child who grows up ambivalent about his or her status in the sex of assignment has effectively only one alternative, namely, to change to the other sex. If this alternative is congruous with the criteria of the agents of society, including parents and professionals, who set the rules as to who may change, then sex reassignment is more likely to be permitted or endorsed.

A hermaphroditic individual's nonconformity with respect to his or her status in the sex of assignment and rearing manifests itself in nonconformity regarding social and legal stereotypes with respect to the male-female division of labor, play, education, dress, adornment, wealth, and so forth, but more specifically with respect to the imagery, ideation, and practices of falling in love and having a sex life. In the love life and in the sex life, nonconformity may be manifested as bisexuality, or as homosexuality defined on the criterion of assigned sex, or as a change of sexual status through sex reassignment.

With respect to homosexology, it is of major theoretical significance not that some male hermaphrodites, assigned and clinically habilitated as girls, grow up to be bisexual, homosexual, or sex reassigned, but that others grow up with a heterosexual status as women who have men as romantic partners and husbands. Unless informed of the clinical history and intersex diagnosis of these women, other people do not suspect anything amiss, nor do they have reason to do so. Socially and in bodily appearance, as well as romantically and in the sex life, the male hermaphrodite success-fully habilitated as a woman is not conspicuous and identifiable among other women. The same applies also to the related birth defect of micro-penis (Money 1984). Both types of cases further substantiate the principle, aforementioned, that homosexuality is defined in terms of the genital and body morphology of the two partners, not in terms of the chromosomal sex, nor of the sex of the gonads. Correspondingly, of course, heterosex-uality is also defined on the criterion that the two partners do not have the same kind of genital and overall body conformation. Thus, the woman with a history of having been treated for either male hermaphroditism or micropenis is defined as heterosexual, regardless of her chromosomal or gonadal status, provided her habilitation has been to develop from girl-hood to womanhood with a romantic and erotic life shared with at least one boyfriend or husband. By contrast, this same woman, with her history of having been reared as a girl, would be defined as homosexual and a lesbian if she had grown up to be attracted erotically only to another woman and to be repelled by the advances of a would-be boyfriend whose attraction to her she would personally equate, in her own case, with the homosexuality of two men being together. She might resolve her dilemma by changing to live as a man with a woman lover, or she might continue to live as a woman with a woman lover and be known in society as a lesbian, or with both a man and a woman lover and be known as bisexual. Each outcome would qualify as a manifestation of some degree of gender transposition away from the ideological norm of femininity toward the ideological norm of masculinity. The criterion standard is the ideological, not the statistical, norm. The extreme degree of transposition is sex reas-signment. Living as a lesbian is a lesser degree of transposition, and as a bisexual lesser still.

The prevalence of gender transposition was the object of a study (Money et al. 1986) of adult patients (n = 32) with a history of having been diagnosed as male hermaphrodites, assigned as girls, reared as girls, and clinically habilitated to live as girls and women. In this study, sex reassignment from female to male was classified as a gender transposition phenomenon, as were imagery and ideation or actual experience of attrac-tion to a female either exclusively, as a lesbian, or bisexually.

The high proportion of patients (n = 15) who were classified as man-ifesting a transposition phenomenon is, in part, an artifact of sampling, because one reason for a patient's referral to Johns Hopkins was the pres-ence of a transposition dilemma. Thus, the ratio of 15:17 exaggerates the prevalence of transposition in the syndromes of male hermaphroditism at large. That proved to be an advantage for present purposes, as it provides a nice balance of cases among which to search for correlates or determinants of the phenomenon of transposition.

The only variable that proved to be significantly correlated (x^2 [1, n = 32] = 10.98, $p <.001$) with transposition phenomena was a history of stigmatization during the childhood years. Stigmatization at home took the form of never mentioning the unspeakable birth defect, never explaining frequent clinic checkups or anything else connected with the defect, and never allowing the genitalia to be exposed except medically. Among peers it took the form of being teased as a sexual freak on the basis of a leakage of information about either the genital condition or the neonatal history of indeterminacy regarding the sex of announcement or reannouncement.

The stigmatization effect proved to be prepubertal in origin and not related to the incongruity of undergoing a masculinizing or eunuchoidal puberty instead of a feminizing one. Those children who would masculinize at puberty are presumed to have been more likely than the pubertal feminizers to have undergone stronger hormonal brain masculinization, prenatally. Childhood stigmatization, however, did not happen exclusively to the future pubertal masculinizers. This finding seems to rule out the possibility that prenatal brain masculinization might somehow or other have preordained an early behavioral manifestation of a gender transposition, such as uncompromising tomboyism of behavior, that would provoke teasing and stigmatization during childhood. Moreover, if a girl is tomboyish in her behavior and a winner in athletics, her success builds self-esteem and inures her against the otherwise deleterious effects of teasing and stigmatization.

A male hermaphrodite with a history of having been assigned as a girl, and of subsequently having subjectively sensed the prospect or realization of a sexual relationship with a man as homosexual, is cited as a triumph of nature over nurture by those who label themselves as biological determinists. To maintain the triumph, however, they neglect or discard the converse evidence of cases in which nurture may be said to triumph over nature.

The example most quoted by the naturists is that of a pedigree of male hermaphrodites in an inbred population inhabiting three isolated mountain villages in the Dominican Republic (Imperato-McGinley et al. 1974; Imperato-McGinley and Peterson 1976; Imperato-McGinley et al. 1979).

The biochemical error responsible for the intersexed condition is 5-reductase deficiency. At birth the defective sex organs resemble those of a female more than those of a male.

In the first generation of intersexed births, affected babies were assigned as girls. When they reached the age of puberty they failed to feminize, but, instead, developed in a eunuchoid, masculine way. The clitoridic organ enlarged and protruded sufficiently so as to qualify in some instances as a small, hypospadiac penis that would require surgery to release it for copulatory use.

Because all of the intersexed children had the same condition, they all developed in the same nonfeminine way. Subsequently, therefore, newborn intersex babies were assigned as boys. Those who had already grown up were more readily tolerated in the village if they changed to live and earn a living as men, and perhaps to try to have the sex life of a man. In the absence of local hospital facilities, there was no hormonal treatment available either to feminize or to better masculinize the body, and there was no available corrective surgery for the deformed sex organs.

Imperato-McGinley and her coauthors proposed the hypothesis that the testosterone of puberty had a masculinizing effect not only on the body, including the sex organs, but also on the mind, including the sex drive. Hence the changing of sex.

There is a flaw in the biological reductionism of this hypothesis: it ignores the nonhormonal variables that affected the intersexed children's lives. Though assigned to live as girls, they were stigmatized as freaks by being known pejoratively as *guevodoces*, translated literally as "eggs at twelve," for which the idiomatic English is "balls (testicles) at twelve." They were also known as *machi hembra*, which translates as "macho miss" with its strong implication of half-girl, half-boy freakishness, as well as of being tomboyish. There was no possibility in a traditional Hispanic village culture for such a person to be a wife and mother, and there was no other role for a woman except to be an economic liability as an unmarriageable freak supported by her family. The alternative was to adapt as well as possible to being a man.

A consideration of the sociological variables in these cases of 5-reductase deficiency does not exclude the possibility that they were superimposed on a substrate somehow made compliantly masculine by reason of the 5-reductase deficiency. The ideal test, in the best of all possible experimental designs, would be to have as a control group another pedigree, in another location, where all cases would be clinically and socially habilitated as girls from birth on, beginning with surgical feminization of the genitalia in early infancy. The onset of puberty would be clinically regulated and would be exclusively feminine. Vaginoplasty, if required, would be available on an elective basis as soon as the body was adolescently mature. Individual cases of 5-reductase deficiency have been treated in this way. The outcome is not as in the Dominican pedigree. The girl becomes a woman and has a heterosexual status as a woman, even though it is contradictory to her chromosomal and gonadal sexual status.

The Dominican Republic pedigree does not stand up to the claim of being unique in demonstrating the triumph of nature over nurture. On the contrary, it demonstrates, as do all other examples of intersexuality, that the status of sexual orientation in adulthood cannot be attributed to any variable that is either exclusively nature or exclusively nurture. By itself alone, testosterone at puberty cannot be held responsible for male heterosexuality in 5-reductase deficient hermaphroditism. That would be tantamount to claiming that testosterone is responsible for all male heterosexuality. If that were so, then the vast majority of homosexual men would be heterosexual, because they also have a normal level of testosterone. Similarly, the vast majority of male-to-female transsexuals would be heterosexually normal men, because they also have a normal level of testosterone prior to reassignment.

It is a basic requirement of any theory that it cannot be used to explain one set of data if that explanation is inconsistent with, or totally contradicted by, a related set of data. Imperato-McGinley's theory fails to satisfy this requirement. It fails to take into account gender transpositions not associated with the 5-reductase syndrome.

EPILOGUE AND SYNOPSIS

In the culture of the West, we characterize homosexuality as sporadic and pathological in occurrence. Elsewhere, as among the Sambia of New Guinea, homosexuality is characterized as a phase of universalized sequential bisexuality, the absence of which is sporadic and pathological in occurrence. A theory of homosexuality must encompass both manifestations.

Human sexological syndromes in the clinic represent experiments of nature that are the counterpart of animal sexological syndromes induced experimentally in the laboratory. Despite species differences and variations, data from these two sources are mutually compatible. They indicate that, in all species, the differentiation of sexual orientation or status as either bisexual or monosexual (i.e., exclusively heterosexual or homosexual) is sequential. Prenatally, and with a possible brief neonatal extension, differentiation begins under the aegis not of genetics but of brain hormonalization and continues postnatally under the aegis of the senses and social communication and learning.

Dimorphic hormonalization of the brain prenatally takes place under the influence of a steroidal hormone. Normally it is testosterone, secreted by the fetal testes. Some target cells receive testosterone and change it into one of its metabolites, notably estradiol and dihydrotestosterone. Steroidal hormone masculinizes and defeminizes. Its lack or insufficiency demasculinizes and feminizes. It is possible for masculinization and feminization both to coexist to some degree, with consequent bisexual rather than monosexual manifestations of behavior.

Whereas brain dimorphism formerly was inferred from its effects in producing male/female dimorphism of behavior, in recent years it has been directly demonstrated in neuroanatomical structures that differ in the brains of males and females, especially in the region of the hypothalamus.

In subprimate species, prenatal hormonal differentiation of the brain preordains subsequent mating behavior as male or female more inexorably than is the case in primate species, especially the human species. Even in subprimates, however, the final outcome is not immune to postnatal modulation by variations in the circumstances of infant care and social contact. In primates, as compared to subprimates, the influence of prenatal and neonatal hormonalization is more susceptible to subsequent superimposed variations in social communication and learning. In particular, juvenile sexual rehearsal play is prerequisite to both masculinized and feminized proficiency in adult mating skill.

In the human species, there are only a few, infrequently occurring clinical syndromes in which it is possible to reconstruct the prenatal and neonatal hormonal history and relate it to subsequent orientation as heterosexual, bisexual, or homosexual. In other homosexual and bisexual people, one may conjecture the possibility of unsuspected nutritional, medicinal, or hormonal changes, including stress-derived changes in the chemistries of the pregnant mother's bloodstream—changes that may induce a masculinizing or demasculinizing, feminizing or defeminizing effect on sexual differentiation of the baby's brain. Prenatal maternal stress, for example, is known to have a demasculinizing effect on rat pups; likewise, barbiturates ingested by the mother are demasculinizing.

With respect to orientation as homosexual or bisexual, there is no human evidence that prenatal hormonalization alone, independently of postnatal history, inexorably preordains either orientation. Rather, neonatal antecedents may facilitate a homosexual or bisexual orientation, provided the postnatal determinants in the social and communicational history are also facilitative.

Logically, there is a possibility that the postnatal determinants may need no facilitation from prenatal ones. Defense of this proposition precipitates, yet once again, the obsolete nature-nurture debate, with no resolution. On the issue of the determinants of sexual orientation as homosexual, bisexual, or heterosexual, the only scholarly position is to allow that prenatal and postnatal determinants are not mutually exclusive. When nature and nurture interact at critical developmental periods, the residual products may persist immutably. It will require new methodology and new increments of empirical data before the full catalogue of these residuals can be specified.

Meanwhile, it is counterproductive to characterize prenatal determinants of sexual orientation as biological, and postnatal determinants as not. The postnatal determinants that enter the brain through the senses by way of social communication and learning also are biological, for there is a biology of learning and remembering. That which is not biological is occult, mystical, or, to coin a term, *spookological.* Homosexology, the science of orientation or status as homosexual or bisexual rather than heterosexual, is not a science of spooks.

REFERENCES

Arnold, A. P., and R. A. Gorski. 1984. Gonadal steroid induction of structural sex differences in the central nervous system. *Annual Review of Neuroscience* 7:413–42.
Baum, M. J. 1979. Differentiation of coital behavior in mammals: A comparative analysis. *Neuroscience and Biobehavioral Reviews* 3:265–84.
Baum, M. J., C. A. Gallagher, J. T. Martin, and D. A. Damassa. 1982. Effects of testosterone, dihydrotestosterone, or estradiol administered neonatally on sexual behavior of female ferrets. *Endocrinology* 111:773–80.
Beach, F. A. 1975. Hormonal modification of sexually dimorphic behavior. *Psychoneuroendocrinology* 1:3–23.
Breedlove, S. M. 1986. Cellular analyses of hormone influence on motoneuronal development and function. *Journal of Neurobiology* 17:157–76.
Breedlove. S. M., and A. P. Arnold. 1980. Hormone accumulation in a sexually dimorphic motor nucleus of the rat spinal cord. *Science* 210:564–66.
Bullough, V. L. 1976. *Sexual Variance in Society and History.* New York: Wiley.
Chan, S. T. H. 1977. Spontaneous sex reversal in fishes. In J. Money and H. Musaph, eds., *Handbook of Sexology*, pp. 91–105. Amsterdam: Excerpta Medica.
Clarke, I. J. 1977. The sexual behavior of prenatally androgenized ewes observed in the field. *Journal of Reproduction and Fertility* 49:311–15.

Crews, D. 1982. On the origin of sexual behavior. *Psychoneuroendocrinology* 7:259–70.

Crews. D. In press. Functional associations in behavioral endocrinology. In J. M. Reinisch, L. A. Rosenblum, and S. A. Sanders, eds., *Masculinity/Femininity: Concepts and Definitions.* New York: Oxford University Press.

De Voogd, T. J. 1986. Steroid interactions with structure and function of avian song control regions. *Journal of Neurobiology* 17:177–201.

De Vries, G. J., J. P. C. De Brun, H. B. M. Uylings, and M. A. Corner, eds. 1984. *Sex Differences in the Brain: Relation Between Structure and Function.* Amsterdam: Elsevier.

D'Occhio, M. J., and J. J. Ford. In press. Contribution of studies in cattle, sheep and swine to our understanding of the role of gonadal hormones in processes of sexual differentiation and adult sexual behavior In J. M. A. Sitsen, ed., *Handbook of Sexology,* vol. 7. Amsterdam: Elsevier.

Dörner, G., and J. Staudt. 1969. Perinatal structural sex differentiation of the hypothalamus in rats. *Endocrinology* 5:103–6.

Döhler, K. D., A. Coquelin, F. Davis, M. Hines, J. E. Shryne, and R. A. Gorski. 1982. Differentiation of the sexually dimorphic nucleus in the preoptic area of the rat brain is determined by the perinatal hormone environment. *Neuroscience Letters* 33:295–98.

Dorland's Illustrated Medical Dictionary. 1981. 26th ed. Philadelphia: W. B. Saunders.

Ellis, H. 1942. *Studies in the Psychology of Sex.* Vols. 1 and 2. New York: Random House.

Ehrhardt, A. A., K. Evers, and J. Money. 1968. Influence of androgen and some aspects of sexually dimorphic behavior in women with late-treated adrenogenital syndrome. *Johns Hopkins Medical Journal* 123:115–22.

Ehrhardt, A. A., and J. Money. 1967. Progestin-induced hermaphroditism: IQ and psychosexual identity in a study of ten girls. *Journal of Sex Research* 3:83–100.

Goldfoot, D. A. 1977. Sociosexual behaviors of nonhuman primates during development and maturity: Social and hormonal relationships. In A. M. Schrier, ed., *Behavioral Primatology: Advances in Research and Theory,* vol. 1, pp. 139–84. Hillsdale, N.J.: Erlbaum.

Goldfoot, D. A. and D. A. Neff. In press. On measuring behavioral sex differences in social contexts. In J. M. Reinisch, L. A. Rosenblum, and S. A. Sanders, eds., *Masculinity/Femininity: Basic Perspectives.* New York: Oxford University Press.

Goldfoot, D. A., and K. Wallen. 1978. Development of gender role behaviors in heterosexual and isosexual groups of infant rhesus monkeys. In D. J. Chivers and J. Herbert, eds., *Recent Advances in Primatology,* vol. 1, *Behaviour,* pp. 155–59. London: Academic Press.

Goldfoot, D. A., K. Wallen, D. A. Neff, M. C. McBriar, and R. W. Goy. 1984. Social influences upon the display of sexually dimorphic behavior in rhesus monkeys: Isosexual rearing. *Archives of Sexual Behavior* 13:395–412.

Gorski, R. A., J. H. Gordon, J. E. Shryne, and A. M. Southam. 1978. Evidence for a morphological sex difference within the medial preoptic area of the rat brain. *Brain Research* 148:333–46.

Herdt, G. H. 1981. *Guardians of the Flutes: Idioms of Masculinity.* New York: McGraw-Hill.

Herdt, G. H., ed. 1984. *Ritualized Homosexuality in Melanesia.* Berkeley: University of California Press.

Hirschfeld, M. 1948. *Sexual Anomalies: The Origins, Nature and Treatment of Sexual Disorders.* New York: Emerson Books.

Imperato-McGinley, J., L. Guerrero, T. Gautier, and R. E. Peterson. 1974. Steroid 5-reductase deficiency in man: An inherited form of male pseudohermaphroditism. *Science* 186:1213–15.

Imperato-McGinley, J., and R. E. Peterson. 1976. Male pseudohermaphroditism: The complexities of male phenotypic development. *American Journal of Medicine* 61:251–72.

Imperato-McGinley, J., R. E. Peterson, T. Gautier, and E. Sturla. 1979. Androgens and the evolution of male-gender identity among male pseudohermaphrodites with 5-reductase deficiency. *New England Journal of Medicine* 300:1233–37.

Jones, H. W., Jr. 1979. A long look at the adrenogenital syndrome. *Johns Hopkins Medical Journal* 145:143–49.

Klebs, E. 1876. *Handbuch der Pathologischen Anatomie.* Berlin: A. Herschwald.

Lewis, V. G., and J. Money. 1983. Gender-identity/role: G-I/R Part A: XY (androgen-insensitivity) syndrome and XX (Rokitansky) syndrome of vaginal atresia compared. In L. Dennerstein and G. Burrows, eds., *Handbook of Psychosomatic Obstetrics and Gynaecology,* pp. 51–60. Amsterdam/New York/Oxford: Elsevier Biomedical Press.

MacLean, P. D. 1972. A triune concept of the brain and behavior. In T. Boag, ed., *The Hincks Memorial Lectures.* Toronto: Toronto University Press.

McGarry, J. M. 1987. The discovery of the contraceptive. *British Journal of Sexual Medicine* 14:6–8.

Money, J. 1955. Hermaphroditism, gender and precocity in hyperadrenocorticism: Psychologic findings. *Bulletin of The Johns Hopkins Hospital* 96:253–64.

Money, J. 1967. Hermaphroditism: An inquiry into the nature of a human paradox. Doctoral dissertation, Harvard University, University Microfilms No. 65–6698.

Money, J. 1968a. Psychologic approach to psychosexual misidentity with elective mutism: Sex reassignment in two cases of hyperadrenocortical hermaphroditism. *Clinical Pediatrics* 7:331–39.

Money, J. 1968b. *Sex Errors of the Body: Dilemmas, Education, Counseling.* Baltimore: Johns Hopkins University Press.

Money, J. 1974. Prenatal hormones and postnatal socialization in gender identity differentiation. In *Nebraska Symposium on Motivation,* vol. 21, pp. 221–95. Lincoln: University of Nebraska Press.

Money, J. 1984. Family and gender-identity/role. Parts I–III. *International Journal of Family Psychiatry* 5:317–81.

Money, J., and J. Daléry. 1977. Hyperadrenocortical 46, XX hermaphroditism with penile urethra. Psychological studies in seven cases, three marked as boys, four as girls. In P. A. Lee, L. P. Plotnick, A. A. Kowarski, and C. J. Migeon, eds., *Congenital Adrenal Hyperplasia,* pp. 433–46. Baltimore: University Park Press.

Money, J., H. Devore, and B. F. Norman. 1986. Gender identity and gender transposition: Longitudinal study of 32 male hermaphrodites assigned as girls. *Journal of Sex and Marital Therapy* 12:165–81.

Money, J., and A. A. Ehrhardt. 1972. Gender-dimorphic behavior and fetal sex hormones. In E. B. Astwood, ed., *Recent Progress in Hormone Research*, vol. 28, pp. 735–54. New York: Academic Press.

Money, J., J. G. Hampson, and J. L. Hampson. 1955. An examination of some basic sexual concepts: The evidence of human hermaphroditism. *Bulletin of The Johns Hopkins Hospital* 97:301–19.

Money, J., and M. Lamacz. 1984. Gynemimesis and gynemimetophilia: Individual and cross-cultural manifestations of a gender coping strategy hitherto unnamed. *Comprehensive Psychiatry* 25:392–403.

Money, J., and M. Lamacz. 1986. Nosocomial stress and abuse exemplified in a case of male hermaphroditism from infancy through adulthood: Coping strategies and prevention. *International Journal of Family Psychiatry* 7:71–105.

Money, J,. and V. G. Lewis. 1982. Homosexual/heterosexual status in boys at puberty: Idiopathic adolescent gynecomastia and congenital virilizing adrenocorticism compared. *Psychoneuroendocrinology* 7:339–46.

Money, J., and V. G. Lewis. 1983. Gender-identity/role: G-I/R Part B: A multiple sequential model of differentiation. In L. Dennerstein and G. Burrows, eds., *Handbook of Psychosomatic Obstetrics and Gynaecology*, pp. 61–67. Amsterdam/New York/Oxford, England: Elsevier Biomedical Press.

Money, J., and D. Mathews. 1982. Prenatal exposure to virilizing progestins: An adult follow-up study of twelve women. *Archives of Sexual Behavior* 11:73–83.

Money, J., and B. F. Norman. In press. Gender identity and gender transposition: Longitudinal outcome study of 24 male hermaphrodites assigned as boys. *Journal of Sex and Marital Therapy* 13.

Money, J., M. Schwartz, and V. G. Lewis. 1984. Adult erotosexual status and fetal hormonal masculinization and demasculinization: 46, XX congenital virilizing adrenal hyperplasia and 46, XY androgen-insensitivity syndrome compared. *Psychoneuroendocrinology* 9:405–14.

Nordeen, E. J., and P. Yahr. 1982. Hemispheric asymmetries in the behavioral and hormonal effects of sexually differentiating mammalian brain. *Science* 218:391.

Nottebohm, F., and A. P. Arnold. 1976. Sexual dimorphism in vocal control areas of the song-bird brain. *Science* 194:211–13.

Phoenix, C. H., and K. C. Chambers. 1982. Sexual behaviour in adult gonadectomized female pseudohermaphrodite, female, and male rhesus macaques (Macaca mulatta) treated with estradiol benzoate and testosterone propionate. *Journal of Comprehensive Physiology* 96:823–33.

Phoenix, C., J. N. Jensen, and K. C. Chambers. 1983. Female sexual behavior displayed by androgenized female rhesus monkeys. *Hormones and Behavior* 17:146–51.

Raisman, C., and P. M. Field. 1971. Sexual dimorphism in the preoptic area of the rat. *Science* 173:731–33.

Reinisch, J. M. and S. A. Sanders. 1982. Early barbiturate exposure: The brain, sexually dimorphic behavior, and learning. *Neuroscience and Biobehavioral Reviews* 6:311–19.

Short, R. V., and I. J. Clarke. Undated. *Masculinization of the Female Sheep* (film). Distributed by MRC Reproductive Biology Unit, Edinburgh.

Steinach, E. 1940. *Sex and Life. Forty Years of Biological and Medical Experiments.* New York: Viking Press.

Stoller, R. J., and G. H. Herdt. 1985. Theories of origins of male homosexuality. *Archives of General Psychiatry* 42:399–404.

Ward, I. L. 1972. Prenatal stress feminizes and demasculinizes the behavior of males. *Science* 175:82–84.

Ward, I. L. 1984. The prenatal stress syndrome: Current status. *Psychoneuroendocrinology* 9:3–11.

Ward, I. L., and J. Weisz. 1980. Maternal stress alters plasma testosterone in fetal males. *Science* 207:328–29.

Whalen, R. E. and D. A. Edwards. 1967. Hormonal determinants of the development of masculine and feminine behavior in male and female rats. *Anatomical Record* 157:173–80.

Young, W. C., R. W. Goy, and C. H. Phoenix. 1964. Hormones and sexual behavior. *Science* 143:212–18.

6

Bisexuality: Some Social Psychological Issues

Philip W. Blumstein and Pepper Schwartz

This article presents an overview of our interview study with 156 men and women having a history of more than incidental sexual experience with both men and women. Data from other studies that point to the existence of bisexuality are reviewed and suggestions are made about why bisexuality has not been incorporated into scientific thinking about sexuality. Our study is described and some of the findings are presented to address the following questions: how does bisexuality fit into the erotic careers of respondents? What factors contribute to the adoption of bisexual self-identification? What circumstances are conducive to the development of bisexuality in individuals? What are the differences between the processes of becoming a bisexual female and becoming a bisexual male?

The scientific study of human sexuality has not reached a stage of conceptual maturity. Any scientific endeavor must, as an important early step, develop a workable number of abstractions to simplify a complex universe of phenomena. The study of sexuality has had little success at such a task because it has failed to address an even more fundamental problem, that is, to recognize and map the complexity and diversity of the very sexual phenomena under scrutiny. It is not difficult to understand why sex research is replete with oversimplifications masquerading as scientific abstractions. By and large, investigators working with sexual data have accepted uncritically the pervasive cultural understandings of sexuality, and have assumed there to be a simple and "correct" conceptual scheme readily modifiable to the requirements of scientific rigor. As a result of our continuing study of sexual identity we have been led to quite the opposite view, and have become disaffected with scientific conceptions that simply reflect the prejudices of folk wisdom. Indeed, the most fundamental conclusion from our research has been that the closer we probe such questions as how people come to define themselves sexually or how their erotic and affectional biographies are structured, the more—not less—the data defy organization in terms of the classical simplicities.

Escaping scientists' borrowed conceptions of sexuality is difficult indeed, because these lay notions, we feel, play an important part in shaping the actual sexual data themselves. We take the simple position that personal views about sexuality in the abstract reflect wider cultural understandings, and affect, in turn, the concrete constructions people place on their own feelings and experiences, and thereby affect their behavior. So it is essential to accept cultural understandings of sexuality as crucial data, while at the same time rejecting the scientific validity of their underlying premises.

Guiding our primary cultural understandings concerning sexuality are three related dichotomies: gender (female versus male), sex role (feminine versus masculine), and affectional preference (homosexual versus heterosexual). Although departures from these dichotomies can be accommodated (e.g., transsexualism has been allowed to emerge as both a concept and as an empirical reality), the very extraordinariness that accompanies such departures reflects and reinforces the cultural simplifications.

Bisexuality is another conceptual loose end that has been forced into a precarious niche in an otherwise neat conceptual apparatus. That some people do not limit their lifetime of sexual experiences to one sex or the other is certainly not new. In fact, sex researchers over the years have presented compelling evidence of bisexuality in both our own culture and elsewhere around the world (Ford and Beach 1951). Nevertheless, it seems clear that such behavior has been seen as a curiosity, and no attempt has been made to integrate the occasional data on bisexuality into any coherent scientific view of sexuality, nor to modify the hegemony of dichotomous concepts.

As far back as 1948 Kinsey admonished sex researchers to think of sexuality in general, and sex-object choice in particular, in terms of a continuum rather than as a rigid set of dichotomous categories (Kinsey, Pomeroy, and Martin 1948). His studies found that "37 percent of the total male population had at least some overt homosexual experience to the point of orgasm between adolescence and old age," and that between 8 percent and 20 percent of females (depending on marital status and education) had made at least incidental homosexual responses or contacts in each of the years between twenty and thirty-five years of age (Kinsey et al. 1953). These data, as revolutionary as they were, need to be contrasted with the findings that only 4 percent of Kinsey's White males and between 0.3 percent and 3 percent of his females were exclusively homosexual after the onset of adolescence. The inescapable — but often escaped—conclusions from Kinsey et al.'s findings are that a mix of homosexual and heterosexual behavior in a person's erotic biography is a common occurrence, and that it is entirely possible to engage in anywhere from a little to a great deal of homosexual behavior without adopting a homosexual life-style.

The implications of viewing human sexuality as being plastic and malleable have never really been exploited. Even the word bisexuality gives a misleading sense of fixedness to sex-object choice, suggesting, as it does, a person in the middle, equidistant from heterosexuality and from homosexuality, equally erotically disposed to one gender or the other. Our data show that exceedingly few people come so neatly packaged. Thus, if we were to be really true to Kinsey's idea of a sexual continuum, we would instead use the preferable term *ambisexuality*, connoting a person's ability to eroticize both genders under some circumstances. The term *bisexuality* seems, however, to have become entrenched in our language, and so we will have to settle for it, rather than the term Kinsey would have preferred. Indeed, even though we are indebted to Kinsey for his insistence on a homosexual/heterosexual continuum, we must emphasize that this view also misleads by focusing on the individual, with his or her sexual "place" as a unit of conceptualization, rather than on the sexual behavior (with all its antecedents and subjective meanings) as a unit for theorizing.

Kinsey et al.'s data were not the only ones indicating that homosexual and heterosexual behavior could be incorporated in a single sexual career. Other studies have pointed to a bisexual phenomenon, although they have never dealt with the question of bisexuality per se. McCaghy and Skipper (1969) argued, for example, that because of the social organization of the occupation of striptease, many of the women become involved in homosexual relationships, although they often continue to have heterosexual involvements. Furthermore, it has been well documented that women in correctional institutions commonly develop homosexual relationships within a well-articulated, quasi-kinship system (Giallombardo 1966, 1974; Ward and Kassebaum 1965). While the homosexual liaisons seem to be important for the psychological well-being of the inmates and serve as a major foundation for the social organization of the institutions, the homosexuality is for most inmates situational. Most of those women and girls who were committed to a heterosexual life-style before incarceration return to the same pattern upon release.

The existence in our society of bisexuality in males has received some-what greater documentation. Studies of prisoners (Kirkham 1971; Lindner 1948; Sykes 1958) have repeatedly shown a fair incidence of homosexual behavior and the development of homosexual liaisons among men who had no prior homosexual experience and who would return to exclusive heterosexuality upon release. A study of brief homosexual encounters in public rest rooms (Humphreys 1970) demonstrated that a sizeable number of men who take part in "tearoom" activities are heterosexually married and do not consider themselves to be homosexual. Ross (1971) has reported that some of the men in his sample of self-identified homosexual men who were married to women had ongoing sexual relationships with their wives. Reiss (1961) interviewed teenage male prostitutes who engaged in homosexual relations with adult men, while maintaining a heterosexual self-perception and an otherwise heterosexual career. Reiss viewed this duality as a reflection of the legitimizing effects of peer group norms, the depersonalized nature of the sexual relations, and the financial gain that could be used as a neutralization technique.

What has been obscured in all of this haphazard treatment of bisexuality is that these sexual data can be used to address more general questions of theoretical importance. Bisexuality illustrates and illuminates important facets of processes of self-labeling, of the plasticity of human sexuality, and of the differences between the erotic and emotional socialization of men and women in our society.

THE PRESENT STUDY

In our study of bisexuality, we were interested in four major questions. First, in deference to Kinsey et al.'s observation of sexual fluidity, we were particularly interested in how sexual object choice develops, and how this development fits into the individual's life experiences. Is bisexuality, for example, a continuous theme throughout a person's life, foreordained by events occurring in childhood and adolescence—as much of psychosexual theory (e.g., Fenichel 1945) would argue—or does it emerge and change with the buffeting of events and circumstances throughout the life cycle? The second question of interest was that of self-definition. When does a pattern of sexual or other social behaviors give rise to a person's sense of his or her sexual identity, and when are they simply behaviors with no further implications? Our third concern was with the circumstances and conditions that either encourage or allow, discourage or prevent, the devel-opment of bisexual behavior. And, finally, our fourth interest was in how these three issues—continuity, self-definition, and causal factors—would differ between males and females in our society. What might a comparison of the processes of becoming a bisexual woman and the processes of becoming a bisexual male tell us about male and female sexuality in general?

Our observations in response to these four questions are based on lengthy semistructured interviews with 156 people (equally divided between men and women), who had more than incidental sexual experience with both men and women. We also interviewed a number of persons who had strong feelings about bisexuality as it pertained either to their own lives or to groups to which they belonged. The interviews were conducted in Seattle, New York, Berkeley, San Francisco, and a few other locations between 1973 and 1975. The respondents ranged in age from nineteen to sixty-two, and reflected a broad spectrum of occupations, educational levels, and sexual histories. Most of those interviewed were recruited through advertisements in taverns, restaurants, churches, universities, voluntary associations, and even a few embryonic bisexual rap groups. A large number of respondents were from a "snowball" sample or were personal contacts of the authors. The interviews generally lasted between one-and-one-half hours and three hours and were tape-recorded. They covered the following areas of the respondents' lives: sexual and romantic history, family relationships and background, preferred sexual behaviors and fantasies, and, most important, critical events in the formation of a sexual identity and the development of a sexual career. These interviews were conducted against a backdrop of several years of formal and informal observation and interviews with self-identified male and female homosexuals.

While our respondents constitute a diverse and heterogeneous group, they are certainly not representative of anything but themselves. It is quite inappropriate to think in terms of random sampling of a specifiable universe of persons when dealing with underground populations or sexual minorities (Bell 1974; Weinberg 1970), and it was our intention to find any bisexuals we could and explore with them any themes they might have shared in their sociosexual development. Because the sample was heterogeneous we are quite confident that we are not simply describing the idiosyncrasies of a unique set of persons, and that we are able to suggest some regularities that exist among a broad group of people in the present cultural and historical context. But we also feel that to place great stock in the frequencies of response patterns would give a misleading sense of concreteness to what we have observed. Therefore, we have chosen to present data only when patterns occurred with sufficient regularity to deserve interpretation, and to present data in the form of verbatim responses that represent (perhaps with a prejudice to more articulate statements) a class of responses that were found among a sizeable number of respondents. In this article we present a general discussion of how our interview data were used to address the four guiding questions outlined above. (For other treatments of this material see Blumstein and Schwartz 1976b, in press.)

THE EROTIC BIOGRAPHY OF RESPONDENTS

We found no such thing as a prototypic bisexual career. This is not to say there are no patterns to the lives of our respondents, but rather no single or small number of patterns seems to predominate among those who call themselves bisexual, or among those whose behavior might be given that label. For example, a sizeable number of male respondents and the majority of the females had no homosexual experiences prior to adulthood. Furthermore, the occurrence of family patterns often claimed to predict a nonheterosexual adaptation (e.g., boys with weak distant fathers and overwhelming mothers) was quite rare. A few respondents had early sexual experiences that might be termed traumatic, but their adult lives had little else in common. Major themes in psychosexual theory were of little utility in understanding our respondents.

Perhaps the most interesting finding was that many respondents, who had once seemed well along the road to a life of exclusive heterosexuality or of exclusive homosexuality, made major changes in sex-object choice. For example, early in the study we interviewed a young professional woman who referred to herself as "purely and simply gay," even though she had sexual experience with men. In recounting her life history she mentioned that at the age of seven or eight she habitually initiated sexual contacts with her friends at pajama parties. Eventually one girl's mother learned about it, and our respondent was castigated by her friends' families, her friends, and her own family. If that stigmatizing experience were not enough to plant the seeds of a deviant self-definition, in adolescence she was the victim of a brutal sexual assault by a group of boys. She pointed to both of these experiences as the basis for why she had become a lesbian ten years prior to the interview. We found her analysis convincing as it was so consistent with prevailing views on the psychodevelopment of lesbianism (e.g., Wilbur 1965). Then, a year later she wrote to tell us she was in love with a man and they planned to marry.

Clearly, this woman's early experiences, as well as her ten years of lesbian relationships and her active adherence to a lesbian self-label, did not guarantee that she would not experience a significant change in her life. Other interviews like this one, some starting with homosexual identification, some with heterosexual, suggested to us that while childhood and adolescent experiences do have a place in developing sexuality, their effects are far from immutable. For the majority of respondents, pivotal sexual experiences occurred in adulthood, and those whose experiences or fantasies stemmed from adolescence or childhood were no more or less likely to make a subsequent change than was the larger group.

We were continually surprised at how discontinuous our respondents' erotic biographies could be. For example, a number of men who had decided they were homosexual at an early age and lived in almost exclusively homosexual networks later met women with whom they had sexual relationships for the first time in their lives. A large number of both male and female respondents had made at least one full circle—an affair with a man, then one with a woman, and finally back to a man, or vice versa. For example, one woman, about forty-five years of age, had been married and had three children. After divorcing and having several heterosexual relationships, she fell in love with another woman of her own age, and they began the first homosexual relationship that either of them had experienced. Neither had ever had any homosexual fantasies prior to their meeting. After a three-year relationship, they broke up and our respondent had a number of brief affairs with both women and men. Our interview captured her at this point in her life, but she reflected that in each of her relationships she considered herself to be what was implied by the gender of the person with whom she was amorously involved: homosexual when with a woman, heterosexual when with a man. She wondered aloud whether perhaps bisexual might be a more appropriate term.

It is clear from these cases that it was crucial for us to have the respondent's retrospective report, as well as some longitudinal data. Fortunately, we were able to retain contact after the interview with about a quarter of our sample. It is misleading to try to understand anything about the achievement of sexual identity or about the importance of sexual events in a person's life without longitudinal observation. Speaking to respondents more than once was important, too, because they often tended to see more continuity in their lives than we found. It was common for them to say that prior changes in sex-object choice were part of a past history of self-misperception, and that they had finally found their sexual "place." A follow-up interview often contradicted their assertions.

Our conclusion was that classical notions of the immutability of adult sexual preference are an overstatement and often misleading. Because of the unrepresentativeness of our sample, we cannot speculate about how widespread such erotic malleability is in our society. Perhaps many people have undergone major life changes. The ease with which we found respondents with such a background suggests that it is more than a rare occurrence. Perhaps many people could experience such monumental changes if they were not insulated from precipitating circumstances; or perhaps the vast majority would not be subject to such changes under any circumstances. If future research proves bisexual potential to be relatively rare, then classic developmentalist approaches that view childhood socialization to be all-important will be vindicated. If, on the other hand, the potential is not uncommon, then approaches that emphasize the situational emergence of human behavior will be supported. From our data we conclude that a) sex-object choice and sexual identification can change in many ways and many times over the lifecycle; b) the individual is often unaware of his or her ability to change; and c) childhood and adolescent experiences are not the final determinants of adult sexuality.

SEXUAL BEHAVIOR AND SEXUAL IDENTITY

In our early interviews it became clear that people often adopted homosexual or bisexual self-identifications without having any homosexual experience. It was equally clear that, for many people, extensive homosexual experience had no effect on their heterosexual identity. For example, one male respondent recalled:

> I had this affair with a gay guy for almost a year. We were good friends and we became identified as a couple after a while. I think he basically saw me as a straight person who was kind of stepping over the imaginary line for a while. I was also sleeping with a woman, and, while I liked them both, I thought I was heterosexual as a person.

Another female respondent recalled her first homosexual encounter:

> It was a great experience. I think everyone should have it. Before this happened, I was really hung up. When I got involved with another woman, I realized how nice it was. It was really enlightening. I think heterosexually though, so I don't feel any big drives to repeat it. But I probably will if the opportunity comes along.

Still other respondents could have a single erotic encounter with a person of either the same or opposite gender and decide unequivocally what they "really were." As one woman reported:

> The first time Linda touched me, I went weak. The men I had made love with were so clumsy and awkward by comparison. I just realized who I was, that I was gay, and men were OK, but not the main thing.

On the other hand, experience with both genders could be seen as confirmation of a bisexual identity. One respondent told us how it had seemed reasonable to him:

> "Well," I thought as this guy climbed in my bed, "What the hell? Why shouldn't I? There's no reason why I should cut off my nose to spite my face. It's going to be fun; it's been fun before, and why can't I have the best of both possible worlds?" Bisexuality seemed like me.

We feel that certain conditions were significant in making a sexual event either crucial or irrelevant in the process of assuming sexual identity.

LABELING

Consistent with what sociologists have noted in regard to other self-definitions (Becker 1973), events or behaviors that produced a public reaction or otherwise affected the reactions other people made to our respondents were important in providing a bisexual (or homosexual or heterosexual) self-definition. Such events were particularly significant during adolescence, when peer-group definitions have tremendous power over people. Several male respondents, who had been labeled the "class sissy," had felt that surely they must be sexually odd, and that their oddness was recognized by their peers. They had believed that their peers knew more about them than they had known themselves, and this was often self-fulfilling when it came to sex-object choice. It is noteworthy that such labeling processes seemed to be more important for males than for females in the assumption of a homosexual or bisexual identity in adulthood. In contrast, boys and girls who escaped such labeling, even though some of their behavior might be homosexual, seemed somewhat less apt to apply deviant labels to themselves. For example, we interviewed two men who had been successful high school athletes. They shared a sexual relationship throughout high school and also had sexual relations with girls. They were never ridiculed or stigmatized in high school, even though their inseparability was well known. Because so much of these men's behavior was considered sex-role appropriate, they escaped a homosexual label from others who might suspect their relationship. The two continued their homosexual activities into adulthood, one finally deciding he was homosexual, the other preferring to be bisexual.

CONFLICTING EVENTS

The ability to perform sexually with a person of the opposite gender was not sufficient to inhibit the adoption of a homosexual identity, nor was it necessary for a bisexual identification. But it did seem to increase the likelihood of the latter. Many respondents seemed to be caught up in dichotomous thinking about sexuality, and struggled to resolve conflicting events (sexual experiences, attraction, or fantasies directed at both genders) by emphasizing one set of events as more plausible than the other. Commonly, one set of explanatory events was adduced for one's heterosexual behavior and a completely different set for one's homosexual behavior. For example, a male respondent reported:

> I'm straight, but I need outlets when I'm away from home and times like that. And it's easier to get with men than women. So I go into the park, or at a rest station on the highway and get a man to blow me. I would never stay the night with one of them, or get to know them. It's just a release. It's not like sex with my wife. It's just a way to get what you need without making it a big deal. And it feels less like cheating.

While attempts to balance the two sets of conflicting information might have offered the chance of deciding one was bisexual, for most of our respondents (especially men) fairly strong heterosexual feelings and a good deal of heterosexual experience from an early age were necessary for a bisexual identification to compete with a homosexual identity. Our cultural logic holds that it is almost impossible to have only some homosexual feelings. The idea is seldom questioned that a single homosexual act or strong homosexual feelings reveal the "true person." Hence, since we have no imagery for partial states of being, the individual often reinterprets past events as further confirmation of his or her undeniable homosexuality. As one male respondent said:

> I was married for four years when I started to have these fantasies about a guy I worked with. I would get these fantasies and I would have to masturbate. I think that this was just the most mature crush I had, because

when I think back on it, there had been lots of others, although I didn't know what they were then. I began to think I was homosexual about this time, even though I was still sleeping with my wife and enjoying it. But I felt guilty, and I was worried she would find out what I really was.

Of course, interpretations of respondents' erotic recollections are indeed risky, and commonly the present shapes the past more than the reverse. Nevertheless, it seemed clear that most respondents actively searched their memories for significant events that would help confirm their lay hypotheses concerning present events and feelings.

Among our interviewees, it seems that sexual attraction, as well as enjoyable sexual experience with both genders, helped people adopt a bisexual identity. Another factor was the emotional response to persons of either gender. Whom a person loved seemed to have an impact somewhat independent of whom that person eroticized. This was particularly true of women, since love and sexuality are customarily such interwoven themes in female erotic socialization. But it was also true of a sizeable number of males. It was not uncommon for a nonsexual but deeply emotional attachment between two people of the same gender who had no prior homosexual feelings to develop into a sexual relationship, and sometimes a shift to a bisexual identification for both partners. On the other hand, if a person (mostly men) could relate sexually to men and women but could only love one or the other, then that person would not likely assume a bisexual label.

REFERENCE GROUP CONTACT

Sexual behavior and sexual identification both seem to vary by whether the respondent was a social isolate, was involved in an ongoing relationship, or was part of a sexual community. By the latter we mean subcultural groups that have formed and organized around members' sexual similarities, such as the various gay subcultures. So, for example, some respondents were strongly committed to particular homosexual relationships for a number of years without assuming a homosexual identity if they were not involved in the gay community. When most of their friends were homosexual, respondents were likely to be treated as homosexual and come to define themselves as such.

Our conclusion, after noticing the regularity in the differences of sexual identity depending on subculture membership and involvement, was that the social ratification of identities provided by such groups can be very powerful (Berger and Luckmann 1966). Respondents who were ambivalent or questioning about their bisexual attractions or behaviors often encountered people in the gay world who could provide easy vocabularies for interpreting these feelings and acts (Blumstein and Schwartz 1976a, b, in press). Sometimes they were told that heterosexual attractions were only a cop-out or an aspect of false consciousness, that the respondent was really denying his or her true sexuality, being unwilling to come to grips with being a homosexual. After varying amounts of personal struggle, some respondents found this explanation plausible and moved toward adoption of a homosexual identity, developed a gay life-style, and concentrated on homosexual relationships. Others, finding the gay world unsympathetic or incredulous when it came to their bisexuality, either left the community for periods of time or kept their bisexual feelings private. For example, one woman who had a lesbian identification fell in love with a man and felt compelled to leave her women's collective because the other members would not grant support or legitimacy for her new relationship and asserted that it was simply "neurotic acting out."

We do not mean to paint the homosexual communities as villains in thwarting people's bisexuality. Indeed, respondents were much more likely to report hostility to their life-styles among heterosexuals (who could not appreciate the distinction between bisexual and homosexual) than among homosexuals, and many reported a great deal of support for a bisexual identification among homosexual friends. But in both the straight and gay communities, the fact that respondents had homosexual relationships tended to define an identity for them, while their heterosexual relationships were considered somehow irrelevant or a passing fancy.

The final step, we began to see, especially in the San Francisco area, was a deliberate attempt to create a bisexual community, where members could come together to give mutual support and to share with one another a collective wisdom for developing a bisexual life-style. Although it is premature to know, it seems likely that such institutions as bisexual rap groups will increasingly support people's assumption of a bisexual identification.

CIRCUMSTANCES CONDUCIVE TO BISEXUALITY

While there is a wide array of situations or conditions that serve to introduce people to novel sexual experiences, we found three themes to be particularly prevalent among our respondents. The first of these was experimentation in a friendship context. Many respondents (especially women) progressed to a sexual involvement from an intense emotional attachment with a person of the gender they had never before eroticized. A male with a homosexual identification might develop a casual experimental heterosexual relationship with a close woman friend at a point in his life where he seemed perfectly comfortable with his homosexuality. Several previously heterosexual men who came to a bisexual identity in their thirties reported that they had had early homosexual experiences with close teen-age friends when heterosexual relations were somewhat limited. They had treated these experiences as irrelevant teen-age play, until adult experiences precipitated reconsideration. A few respondents with no previous homosexual experience reported that they were able to eroticize adult male friendships. A few lesbians reported being able to develop sexual involvements with male friends, especially homosexual men whose sexual politics they found less objectionable. The most common finding, however, was that previously heterosexual women who developed deep attachments to other women, for example, as college roommates or later in life when involved in the women's movement, ultimately shifted these feelings into the erotic arena and began long-term homosexual relationships.

Bisexual encounters also emerged frequently in such liberal hedonistic environments as group sex, "three ways," and other combinations. These often proved a less threatening arena for sexual experimentation for heterosexuals than would a dyadic homosexual encounter. Females found these experiences less difficult than males, who were customarily the instigators of the event. These occurrences were understood to be pleasure seeking in a diffuse sense, rather than a specific act with stigmatizing implications for one's sexual identity. Focus was on the good feelings rather than on the gender of the person providing them.

The third pattern was supported by a number of erotically based ideological positions. For example, some people came to a bisexual identification (occasionally without any corresponding behavior) because of adherence to a belief in humanistic libertarianism. They felt that everyone should be free and able to love everyone in a perfect erotic utopia. For them, love meant sex, which was seen as a means of communication and "becoming human." Encounter groups or group massages often progressed to a sexual stage. As one respondent explained, "It only made sense. We had all been psych majors, and every psych major learns that we are all inherently bisexual." How much of this ideology preceded the behavior and how much provided post hoc legitimacy is, of course, difficult to assess.

Many of the women in our study decided to experiment with homosexual relationships because they felt encouraged by the tenets of the women's movement to examine their feelings toward other women and to learn to be close to them. The movement had encouraged them to respect and like other women, and for many this novel feeling was closely akin to the feelings they had felt with those men whom they had eroticized. Sometimes these women instigated sexual encounters for ideological rather than erotic reasons, but soon developed erotic responses and became more generally physically attracted to other women. In some cases the homosexual attraction became a dominating force in the women's's lives; in other cases it coexisted with heterosexual responses; and in still other cases it never established any prominence and homosexual behavior was discontinued (although a political bisexual self-identification was sometimes retained).

DIFFERENCES BETWEEN WOMEN AND MEN

There were a great many differences in the bisexual behavior of male and female respondents, which seemed quite consistent with what we know about general patterns of male and female sexuality (Gagnon and Simon 1973). Most prominently, men and women differed in the ease with which they incorporated homosexual activity into their lives. Women found initial experiences much less traumatic than men did, and they were less likely to allow a single experience or a few experiences to lead them to an exclusively homosexual identification. Women often felt that such activities were a natural extension of female affectionate behavior and did not have implications for their sexuality. Men, on the other hand, were much more preoccupied with what the experience meant for their masculinity, sometimes fearing that they might never again be able to respond erotically to a woman. Some men insulated themselves from the homosexual implications of homosexual behavior by exclusively engaging in either impersonal sex, as in public rest rooms (Humphreys 1970), or in homosexual acts where they took what they considered to be the masculine role, that is, the inserter role in fellatio or sodomy. As one man recounted, "There are four kinds of men: men who screw women, men who screw men and women, men who screw men, and then there are the queers (i.e., the ones who get screwed)."

For men, both their first heterosexual and first homosexual experiences were likely to be with strangers (prostitutes, "bad girls," homosexual tricks), whom they would probably never see again. The predominant pattern among women was for sex to occur with a close friend, and this to them was a natural and logical outgrowth of a strong emotional attachment. The realization that they were in love with a person (of the same or opposite gender) was often a prerequisite for sexual attraction, sexual behavior, or a change in sexual identity.

Males reported much more difficulty coping with homosexual behavior and developing a homosexual identification than women did. We attribute this to the stigma attached to homosexuality among American men (more than among women). Masculinity is a major element in men's sense of self-worth, and homosexuality, in the popular imagination, implies impaired masculinity.

CONCLUSION

This study has been part of our ongoing research on sexual identity and how it reflects the interaction of social forces, cultural perspectives, and psychological processes. We chose bisexuality as a vehicle of inquiry because we feel it has a strategic capacity for illuminating more general issues in the study of human sexuality. We view our research as exploratory, but we feel that when more investigators have addressed themselves to the phenomenon of bisexuality the accumulated evidence will help transform the way science views human sexuality. We anticipate that the perspective that emerges will reflect a number of thematic questions. What is the nature of the relationship between people's sexual experiences and the ways they make sense of their sexuality? How do cultural and subcultural understandings regarding sexuality affect sexual experience and sexual identification? How much of sexuality can be understood by focusing on the continuities among males and the continuities among females, irrespective of affectional preference or sexual life-style? How much of adult sexuality is determined by socialization experiences and how much reflects adult experiences and events? And, finally, what do the answers to these questions tell us about the variability and plasticity of sexual behavior and sexual definitions?

REFERENCES

Becker, H. S. 1973. *Outsiders: Studies in the Sociology of Deviance.* Rev. ed. New York: Free Press.

Bell, A. P. 1974. Homosexualities: Their range and character. In *Nebraska Symposium on Motivation.* Lincoln: University of Nebraska Press.

Berger, P. L., and T. Luckmann. 1966. *The Social Construction of Reality: A Treatise in the Sociology of Knowledge.* Garden City, N.Y.: Doubleday.

Blumstein, P. W., and P. Schwartz. 1976a. Bisexuality. Paper presented at the meeting of the American Sociological Association, New York, August.

Blumstein, P. W., and P. Schwartz. 1976b. Bisexuality in women. *Archives of Sexual Behavior* 5:171–81.

Blumstein, P. W., and P. Schwartz. In press. Bisexuality in men. *Urban Life*.

Fenichel, 0. 1945. *The Psychoanalytic Theory of Neurosis*. New York: Norton.

Ford, C. S., and F. A. Beach. 1951. *Patterns of Sexual Behavior*. New York: Harper and Row.

Gagnon, J. H., and W. Simon. 1973. *Sexual Conduct: The Social Sources of Human Sexuality*. Chicago: Aldine.

Giallombardo, R. 1966. *Society of Women*. New York: Wiley.

Giallombardo, R. 1974. *The Social World of Imprisoned Girls*. New York: Wiley.

Humphreys, L. 1970. *Tearoom Trade: Impersonal Sex in Public Restrooms*. Chicago: Aldine.

Kinsey, A. C., W. B. Pomeroy, and C. E. Martin. 1948. *Sexual Behavior in the Human Male*. Philadelphia: W. B. Saunders.

Kinsey, A. C., W. B. Pomeroy, C. E. Martin, and P. H. Gebhard. 1953. *Sexual Behavior in the Human Female*. Philadelphia: W. B. Saunders.

Kirkham, G. L. 1971. Homosexuality in prison. In J. M. Henslin, ed., *Studies in the Sociology of Sex*. New York: Appleton-Century-Crofts.

Lindner, R. 1948. Sexual behavior in penal institutions. In A. Deutsch, ed., *Sex Habits of American Men*. New York: Prentice-Hall.

McCaghy, C. H., and J. K. Skipper, Jr. 1969. Lesbian behavior as an adaptation to the occupation of stripping. *Social Problems* 17:262–70.

Reiss, A. J., Jr. 1961. The social integration of queers and peers. *Social Problems* 9:102–20.

Ross, H. L. 1971. Modes of adjustment of married homosexuals. *Social Problems* 18:385–93.

Sykes, G. 1958. *The Society of Captives*. Princeton, N.J.: Princeton University Press.

Ward, D. A., and G. G. Kassebaum. 1965. *Women's Prison: Sex and Social Structure*. Chicago: Aldine.

Weinberg, M. S. 1970. Homosexual samples: Differences and similarities. *Journal of Sex Research* 6:312–25.

Wilbur, C. B. 1965. Clinical aspects of female homosexuality. In J. Marmor, ed., *Sexual Inversion: The Multiple Roots of Homosexuality*. New York: Basic Books.

III
Identity Development and Stigma Management

A normal part of adolescence is the development of a sense of identity. The enduring sense of self that is continuous over time involves, among other aspects, a sense of who one is with regard to sexual, affectional, and erotic relationships with others. Thus, the development of a sense of identity is complicated for lesbians and gay men since heterosexist biases devalue same-gender erotic and affectional feelings. The process of developing a positive sense of identity in the social context of negative values about a core aspect of oneself has received a great deal of attention in the psychological literature. Troiden's article summarizes this area.

It is useful to contrast the development of gay male and lesbian identity with the development of identity as a racial or ethnic minority. Differences and similarities are both important. Similar developmental stages have been found in the process of forming a sexual and a racial/ethnic identity. The primary task of each involves the transformation of a negative, stigmatized identity into a positive one:

> Both models describe one or several stages of intense confusion and at least one stage of complete separatism from and rejection of all representatives of the dominant society. The final stage for both models implies the acceptance of one's own identity, a committed attitude against oppression, and

an ability to synthesize the best values of both perspectives and to communicate with members of the dominant group. (Espín 1987:39)

A racial or ethnic identity, however, is an ascribed status that is recognized and acknowledged from birth, while sexual identity is an achieved status that is generally not discovered until adolescence or adulthood. On the one hand, lesbians and gay men are better able to hide their stigmatized identity from others and even from themselves, but on the other hand, ethnic and racial minority groups have group support from earliest childhood for their emerging identity.

Various stage theories are often employed to describe the process of identity development. As with all stage theories, individual variation, gender differences, and the interaction with ethnic and cultural minority status complicate the theory and are not adequately represented by the general stage model. Subsequent parts of this book will elaborate on gender and ethnic diversity within the context of these general models presented in this part.

Subtle variations may also be important. For example, in some urban areas a visible lesbian and gay community exists, so that one not only comes out but also comes into a community of support. This is not available in most rural areas and thus represents another difference in the identity formation process. Moreover, some support groups for women provide a kind of community that differs in its support for same-gender self-affirmation than is true in many male communities. This difference reflects both the emergence of the feminist movement and the dual oppression of lesbians as members of stigmatized minorities based on gender and sexual orientation.

An aspect of the complex sequence of events involved in coming out is identity disclosure, a lifelong process of explicitly revealing one's sexual identity to others. Managing outness, that is, one's openness about one's gay or lesbian identity, is an important aspect of management of potentially stigmatizing information concerning one's homosexuality. Coming out to others is usually a relatively late event in gay male and lesbian identity formation. It has no counterpart in the lives of nongay people, although some parallels may exist, such as disclosing previously hidden identities or private experiences.

An ongoing dilemma of whether to tell or not to tell frequently faces gay men and lesbians in situations where heterosexuality is assumed. De Monteflores points out that lesbians and gay men often function in two distinct worlds in order to avoid the stigma associated with homosexuality.

They separate the heterosexual from the gay and place clear boundaries between them. A variety of strategies are often employed to manage the stigma and to cross this boundary between the two worlds. Ideally, the process of coming out eradicates the boundary so that one may be known as lesbian or gay in all major areas of life, including family and work.

Even when gay men and lesbians accept their sexual identity and are open in major areas of life, there also remains good reasons for them to conceal under some circumstances (Cain 1991). Realistic costs and benefits exist when coming out so that many gay men and lesbians are out in certain areas of their lives, but not in others. Typical examples might be in situations where there is the threat of antilesbian or antigay violence or in situations where being assumed to be heterosexual would have short-term beneficial consequences in family or social interactions. "The often harsh social realities of public disclosure conflict with the cultural expectations that gay men [and lesbians] ought to disclose their homosexuality and that openness is good and beneficial" (Cain 1991:72). Nonetheless, individuals in positions of public prestige and importance who choose to remain closed about their sexual identity risk outing as a result of their perceived impact on lesbian and gay issues.

Fewer than 50 percent of lesbians and gay men who have been surveyed reported that they have disclosed their sexual identity to their parents (Bell and Weinberg 1978; Cramer and Roach 1988; Remafedi 1987). Revealing one's sexual orientation to one's family often initiates a family crisis. In many respects, a family's process of coming to terms with their child's being gay or lesbian parallels the stages of coming out that individual lesbians and gay men experience. Strommen's article discusses these issues in detail.

Disclosure of one's sexual orientation to a spouse if heterosexually married or to one's children raises another set of complex issues. Two patterns of couple adaptations to such disclosures have been reported (Matteson 1987). The first pattern involves a "conspiracy of silence" (Bozett 1982) in which the spouse tends to be secretive about homosexual feelings and behavior and to compartmentalize his or her life into distinct and conflicting identities. The second pattern involves couples who stay together and who undergo a developmental process over several years from disclosure to renegotiation and stabilization of the relationship.

Little systematic research has been conducted to understand how children cope with a parent's disclosure of being gay or bisexual. These issues will be discussed in more detail in the part on relationships and parenthood.

Since lesbians and gay men generally work in settings that reflect heterosexual norms of interaction, they learn to manage their identity in work
settings. Decisions about workplace openness affect both the process of
vocational/career development, as well as management of identity and
stigma within the work setting. Coming out at work involves a complicated assessment of the relative safety, sanctions, and interpersonal support. Often there are both real and anticipated negative consequences.
Nonetheless, lesbians and gay men report that disclosure of their sexual
orientation at work allows the possibility of integration into the workplace
with less anxiety and greater self-confidence. The article by Morgan and
Brown expands on these points.

CONTEMPORARY ISSUE: DIFFERENCES BETWEEN THE OLDER AND YOUNGER GENERATIONS

A few years ago only a small number of lesbians and gay men felt comfortable coming out, especially at work or in the family. Those who did
often were in stigmatized occupations, stereotypically associated with gay
men and lesbians. Today, lesbians and gay males are openly demanding
spouse health insurance benefits, equal access to all social institutions, and
full recognition as couples, families, and workers.

This sudden and dramatic historic shift has affected different generations of lesbians and gay men differently. Not surprisingly, younger persons were affected earlier in life by these changes and many have little
experience with the kind of stigma and hiding that was typical only a
decade or two ago. One potential outcome of this cohort difference
between older and younger generations of gay men and lesbians would be
a wedge between the young, proud, open, assertive groups and the older,
secretive, stigmatized survivors of the old days. Some have even expressed
an envy of being young and gay today. This envy came to an abrupt end,
however, with the beginnings of the AIDS epidemic that clearly has struck
the younger segment of the population most severely.

Today it appears that the younger generation are beginning also to
think of themselves as survivors and are looking to the older generation
for clues to survivorship and a greater sense of historical continuity. Thus,
there may be the potential for forming new bonds across the generations.
The older generation is of course benefiting from the changes, and the
benefits for them are in many ways as profound as for the younger people.
Thus, as conditions are improving for all lesbians and gay men, all generations are profiting and are freer to provide support and comfort openly
to each other.

REFERENCES

Bell, A. P. & M. W. Weinberg. 1978. *Homosexualities: A Study of Diversity among Men and Women.* New York: Simon and Schuster.

Bozett, F. W. 1982. Heterogeneous couples in heterosexual marriages. *Journal of Marital and Sexual Therapy* 8:81–89.

Cain, R. 1991. Stigma management and gay identity development. *Social Work* 36(1):67–73.

Cramer, D. W., and A. S. Roach. 1988. Coming out to mom and dad: A study of gay males and their relationships with their parents. *Journal of Homosexuality* 15(3–4):79–91.

Espín, O. M. 1987. Issues of identity in the psychology of Latina lesbians. In the Boston Lesbian Psychologies Collective, eds., *Lesbian Psychologies: Explorations and Challenges,* pp. 35–51. Urbana: University of Illinois Press.

Matteson, D. R. 1987. The heterosexually married gay and lesbian parent. In F. W. Bozett, ed., *Gay and Lesbian Parents,* pp.138–61. New York: Praeger.

Remafedi, G. 1987. Male homosexuality: The adolescent's perspective. *Pediatrics* 79:326–30.

7

The Formation of Homosexual Identities

Richard R. Troiden

This article uses sociological theory to develop an ideal-typical model of homosexual identity formation. The four-stage model outlined here represents a synthesis and an elaboration on previous research and theorizing on homosexual identity development. The model describes how committed homosexuals—lesbians and gay males who see themselves as homosexual and adopt corresponding life-styles—recall having acquired their homosexual identities. More specifically, a sociological perspective toward sexuality is introduced; key concepts of self-concept, identity, and homosexual identity are differentiated; ideal types are defined and described; homosexual identity formation literature is summarized; a four-stage, ideal-typical model of homosexual identity formation is presented; and qualifications to the model are described. Often repeated themes in the life histories of gay males and lesbians, clustered according to life stages, provide the content and characteristics of each stage.

THEORETICAL PERSPECTIVE

Sexual conduct is primarily social in origin (Gagnon 1977; Gagnon and Simon 1973; Plummer 1975; Ponse 1978; Simon and Gagnon 1984). Existing sociocultural arrangements define what sexuality is, the purposes it serves, its manner of expression, and what it means to be sexual.

People learn to be sexual pretty much as they learn everything else. Women and men are born with an open-ended, diffuse, and relatively fluid capacity for bodily pleasure that is shaped and expressed through sexual scripts. These scripts are learned and organized during adolescence along lines previously laid down during gender-role socialization. Males, for example, are taught to see sex in active, genitally focused, and goal-oriented terms; females are encouraged to view sexuality in reactive, emotionally focused, and process-oriented ways (Laws and Schwartz 1977; Levine 1987).

Sexual scripts are articulated by the wider culture and are similar to blueprints: they shape, direct, and focus sexual conduct by providing sexuality with its affective and cognitive boundaries (Gagnon and Simon 1973). Sexual scripts provide sexuality with its affective or emotional boundaries by specifying what kinds of feelings are sexual. "The mind has to define something as 'sexual' before it is sexual in its consequences" (Plummer 1975:30). In addition, sexual scripts designate the cognitive limits of sexuality by indicating appropriate and inappropriate sexual partners (*the whos*), proper and improper sexual behavior (*the whats*), permissible and nonpermissible settings for sex (*the wheres*), positively and negatively sanctioned motives for sex (*the whys*), and appropriate and inappropriate sexual techniques (*the hows*) (Gagnon 1977; Gagnon and Simon 1973; Simon and Gagnon 1984). This is not to deny a biological substratum to sexuality, but to emphasize the powerful role of social forces in shaping sexual conduct. Because sexual learning occurs within specific historical eras and sociocultural settings, sexual conduct and its meanings vary across history and among cultures.

Today, in the research tradition established by Alfred Kinsey and his associates (Kinsey, Pomeroy, and Martin 1948; Kinsey et al. 1953), sexuality experts generally view heterosexuality and homosexuality as matters of degree rather than kind. People are described as occupying various points along a continuum in their sexual behaviors and responsiveness from exclusive heterosexuality (Kinsey 0s) through bisexuality (Kinsey 3s) to exclusive homosexuality (Kinsey 6s). Whether sexual orientations are established before birth (Bell, Weinberg, and Hammersmith 1981a, b; Whitam and Mathy 1986), grow out of gender-role preferences established between the ages of three and nine (Harry 1982), or are organized out of experiences gained with gender roles and their related sexual scripts (Gagnon and Simon 1973), the meanings of sexual feelings are neither self-evident nor translated directly into the consciousness. People construct their sexual feelings to the extent that they actively interpret, define, and make sense of their erotic yearnings using systems of sexual meanings articulated by the wider culture.

Sexual identities, that is, perceptions of self as homosexual, heterosexual, or bisexual in relation to sexual and romantic contexts, are constructed similarly. People learn to identify and label their sexual feelings through experiences gained with gender roles and their related sexual scripts.

Women and men decide what types of feelings they have, their significance and predominance, and whether they are personally relevant and salient enough to warrant self-definition as heterosexual, homosexual, or bisexual. I shall describe how committed lesbians and gay males recall having constructed their homosexual identities after I have differentiated key theoretical concepts, discussed ideal types, and briefly summarized the homosexual identity formation literature.

KEY CONCEPTS

The differences between self-concept and identity are revealed in the ways the two concepts are defined. Self-concept refers to people's mental images of themselves: what they think they are like as people. Defined in this way, self-concept is similar to the concept of identity as used traditionally by psychologists. Identity, on the other hand, refers to perceptions of self that are thought to represent the self definitively in specific social settings (such as the "doctor" identity at work, the "spouse" identity at home). Self-concept is broader in scope than identity and encompasses a wider range of social categories; identity encompasses only situationally relevant dimensions of self-concept. Stated somewhat differently, self-concept and identity differ in the sense that identity requires reference to a specific social setting (imagined or real), and self-concept does not (Troiden 1984/ 1985).

Social situations are structured normatively: people's expectations of how they and others should act often depend on the contexts in which they find themselves. Situationally based expectations place limits on the range of identities and roles that may legitimately be expressed: identities are mobilized in situations where they are relevant. Once removed from a situation, the relevant identity becomes dormant or latent: part of the bundle of potentially relevant identities that make up a person's self-concept.

Identities perceived and experienced as relevant in many social situations are transsituational identities. The stigma surrounding homosexuality and the perceived need to keep homosexuality a secret may infuse homosexual identities with transsituational significance.

The homosexual identity is one of several identities incorporated into a person's self-concept. A homosexual identity is a perception of self as homosexual in relation to romantic or sexual situations. A perception of self as homosexual is an attitude, a potential line of action toward self and others, that is mobilized in settings (imagined or real) that are defined as sexual or romantic. Depending on the context, the homosexual identity may function as a self-identity, a perceived identity, a presented identity, or all three (Cass 1983/1984).

The homosexual identity is a *self-identity* when people see themselves as homosexual in relation to romantic and sexual settings. It is a *perceived identity* in situations where people think or know that others view them as homosexual. It is a *presented identity* when people present or announce themselves as homosexual in concrete social settings. Homosexual identities are most fully realized, that is, brought into concrete existence, in situations where self-identity, perceived identity, and presented identity coincide— where an agreement exists between who people think they are, who they claim they are, and how others view them.

IDEAL TYPES

Ideal types are not real; nothing and nobody fits them exactly. They represent abstractions based on concrete observations of the phenomena under investigation. Ideal types are heuristic devices, ways of organizing materials for analytical and comparative purposes, and are used as benchmarks against which one describes, compares, and tests hypotheses relating to empirical reality (Theodorson and Theodorson 1969). Described somewhat differently, they are frameworks for ordering observations logically. Ideal types are similar to stereotypes, except that they are examined and refined continuously to correspond more closely to the empirical reality they try to represent. At best, ideal models capture general patterns: variations are expected and explained, and often lead to revisions of ideal types.

The four-stage model of homosexual identity formation outlined here describes only general patterns encountered by committed homosexuals. Often-repeated themes in the life histories of lesbians and gay males, clustered according to life stages, provide the content and characteristics of each stage. Progress through the various stages increases the probability of homosexual identity formation, but does not determine it fully. A shifting effect is involved: some men and women "drift away" at various points before stage four. Only a small portion of all people who have homosexual experiences ever adopt lesbian or gay identities and corresponding lifestyles (Kinsey, Pomeroy, and Martin 1948; Kinsey et al. 1953).

Homosexual identity formation is not conceptualized here as a linear, step-by-step process in which one stage precedes another and one necessarily builds on another, with fluctuations written off as developmental regressions. Instead, the process of homosexual identity formation is likened to a horizontal spiral, like a spring lying on its side (McWhirter and Mattison, 1984). Progress through the stages occurs in back-and-forth, up-and-down ways; the characteristics of stages overlap and recur in somewhat different ways for different people. In many cases, stages are encountered in consecutive order, but in some instances they are merged, glossed over, bypassed, or realized simultaneously.

LITERATURE SUMMARY

During the past decade, several investigators have proposed theoretical models that attempt to explain the formation of homosexual identities (Cass 1979, 1984; Coleman 1982; Lee 1977; Ponse 1978; Schäfer 1976; Troiden 1977, 1979; Weinberg 1977, 1978). Although the various models propose different numbers of stages to explain homosexual identity formation, they describe strikingly similar patterns of growth and change as major hallmarks of homosexual identity development.

First, nearly all models view homosexual identity formation as taking place against a backdrop of stigma. The stigma surrounding homosexuality affects both the formation and expression of homosexual identities. Second, homosexual identities are described as developing over a protracted period and involving a number of "growth points or changes" that may be ordered into a series of stages (Cass 1984). Third, homosexual identity formation involves increasing acceptance of the label "homosexual" as applied to the self. Fourth, although coming out begins when individuals define themselves to themselves as homosexual, lesbians and gay males typically report an increased desire over time to disclose their homosexual identity to at least some members of an expanding series of audiences. Thus, coming out, or identity disclosure, takes place at a number of levels: to self, to other homosexuals, to heterosexual friends, to family, to coworkers, and to the public at large (Coleman 1982; Lee 1977). Fifth, lesbians and gays develop "increasingly personalized and frequent" social contacts with other homosexuals over time (Cass 1984).

The four-stage model developed here is a revision of my earlier work, which synthesized and elaborated Plummer's (1975) model of "becoming homosexual." The revised model incorporates insights provided by Barbara Ponse's (1978) and Vivienne Cass's (1979, 1984) theorizing and research on homosexual identity formation. The first stage, sensitization, is borrowed from Plummer. Stage two, identity confusion, combines insights borrowed from Plummer, Cass, and my earlier model. The third stage, identity assumption, incorporates Cass's hypothesized stages of identity tolerance and acceptance. The fourth stage, commitment, posits identity disclosure (Cass 1979, 1984) as an identity option (rather than as a separate stage) and as an external indicator of commitment to homosexuality as a way of life. Theoretical insights borrowed from Ponse (1978) are incorporated throughout the model. (See Troiden 1988, for an extended description and criticism of the various models of homosexual identity formation.)

THE MODEL

Sociological analysis of homosexual identity formation begins with an examination of social contexts and patterns of interaction that make homosexuality personally relevant. "Becoming homosexual" involves the accumulation of a series of sexual meanings that predispose people to identify themselves subsequently as homosexual (Plummer 1975). The meanings of feelings or activities, sexual or otherwise, are not self-evident. Before people can identify themselves in terms of a social condition or category, they must a) learn that a social category representing the activity or feelings exists (e.g., homosexual preferences or behavior); b) learn that other people occupy the social category (e.g., that homosexuals exist as a group); c) learn that their own socially constructed needs and interests are more similar to those who occupy the social category than they are different; d) begin to identify with those included in the social category; e) decide that they qualify for membership in the social category on the basis of activity and feelings in various settings; f) elect to label themselves in terms of the social category, that is, define themselves as "being" the social category in contexts where category membership is relevant (e.g., self-definition as homosexual); and g) incorporate and absorb these situationally linked identities into their self-concepts over time (Lofland 1969; McCall and Simmons 1966; Simmons 1965).

Stage One: Sensitization

The *sensitization* stage occurs before puberty. At this time, most lesbians and gay males do not see homosexuality as personally relevant, that is, they assume they are heterosexual, if they think about their sexual status at all. Lesbians and gay males, however, typically acquire social experiences during their childhood that serve later as bases for seeing homosexuality as personally relevant, that lend support to emerging perceptions of themselves as possibly homosexual. In short, childhood experiences sensitize lesbians and gay males to subsequent self-definition as homosexual.

Sensitization is characterized by generalized feelings of marginality, and perceptions of being different from same-sex peers. The following comments illustrate the forms that these childhood feelings of difference assumed for lesbians: "I wasn't interested in boys"; "I was more interested in the arts and in intellectual things"; "I was very shy and unaggressive"; "I felt different: unfeminine, ungraceful, not very pretty, kind of a mess"; "I was becoming aware of my homosexuality. It's a staggering thing for a kid that age to live with"; "I was more masculine, more independent, more aggressive, more outdoorish"; and "I didn't express myself the way other girls would. For example, I never showed my feelings. I wasn't emotional" (Bell, Weinberg, and Hammersmith 1981a:148, 156).

Similar themes of childhood marginality are echoed in the comments of gay males: "I had a keener interest in the arts"; "I couldn't stand sports, so naturally that made me different. A ball thrown at me was like a bomb"; "I never learned to fight"; "I wasn't interested in laying girls in the cornfields. It turned me off completely"; "I just didn't feel I was like other boys. I was very fond of pretty things like ribbons and flowers and music"; "I began to get feelings I was gay. I'd notice other boys' bodies in the gym and masturbate excessively"; "I was indifferent to boys' games, like cops and robbers. I was more interested in watching insects and reflecting on certain things"; and "I was called the sissy of the family. I had been very pointedly told that I was effeminate" (Bell, Weinberg, and Hammersmith 1981a:74, 86).

Research by Bell, Weinberg, and Hammersmith (1981a) found that homosexual males (n = 573) were almost two times more likely (72 percent versus 39 percent) than heterosexual controls (n = 284) to report feeling "very much or somewhat" different from other boys during grade school (grades 1–8). Lesbians (n = 229) were also more likely than heterosexual controls (n = 101) to have felt "somewhat or very much" different from other girls during grade school (72 percent versus 54 percent).

Childhood social experiences play a larger role in generating perceptions of difference during sensitization than events encountered in the spheres of emotionality or genitality. Both lesbians and gay males in the Bell, Weinberg, and Hammersmith (1981a) sample saw gender-neutral or gender-inappropriate interests, or behaviors, or both as generating their feelings of marginality (the social realm). Only a minority of the lesbians and gay males felt different because of same-sex attractions (the emotional realm) or sexual activities (the genital realm).

More specifically, lesbians in the Bell, Weinberg, and Hammersmith (1981a) study were more likely than heterosexual controls to say they felt different because they were more "masculine" than other girls (34 percent versus 9 percent), because they were more interested in sports (20 percent versus 2 percent), or because they had homosexual interests, or lacked heterosexual interests, or both (15 percent versus 2 percent). Moreover, fewer lesbians than heterosexual controls (13 percent versus 55 percent) reported having enjoyed typical girls' activities (e.g., hopscotch, jacks, playing house), but lesbians were much more likely (71 percent versus 28 percent) to say they enjoyed typical boys' activities (e.g., baseball, football).

In a similar vein, homosexual males were more likely than heterosexual controls to report that they felt odd because they did not like sports (48 percent versus 21 percent), or were "feminine" (23 percent versus 1 percent), or were not sexually interested in girls, or because they were sexually interested in other boys (18 percent versus 1 percent). Gay males were also significantly more likely than heterosexual controls (68 percent versus 34 percent) to report having enjoyed solitary activities associated only indirectly with gender (e.g., reading, drawing, music). Moreover, homosexual males were much less likely than heterosexual controls (11 percent versus 70 percent) to report having enjoyed boys' activities (e.g., football, baseball) "very much" during childhood.

Although a sense of being different and set apart from same-sex age mates is a persistent theme in the childhood experiences of lesbians and gay males, research indicates that only a minority of gay males (20 percent) and lesbians (20 percent) begin to see themselves as sexually different before age twelve, and fewer still, only 4 percent of the females and 4 percent of the males, label this difference as "homosexual" while they are children (Bell, Weinberg, and Hammersmith 1981b:82–83). It is not surprising that "prehomosexuals" used gender metaphors, rather than sexual metaphors, to interpret and explain their childhood feelings of difference: the mastery of gender roles, rather than sexual scripts, is emphasized during childhood (Doyle 1983; Tavris and Wade 1984). Although they may have engaged in heterosexual or homosexual sex play, children do not appear to define their sexual experimentation in heterosexual or homosexual terms. The socially created categories of homosexual, heterosexual, and bisexual hold little or no significance for them. Physical acts become meaningful only when they are embedded in sexual scripts, which are acquired during adolescence (Gagnon and Simon 1973). For these reasons prehomosexuals rarely wonder, "Am I a homosexual?" or believe that homosexuality has anything to do with them personally while they are children.

The significance of sensitization resides in the meanings attached subsequently to childhood experiences, rather than the experiences themselves. Since sociocultural arrangements in Anglo-American society articulate linkages between gender-inappropriate behavior and homosexuality, gender-neutral or gender-atypical activities and interests during childhood provide many women and men with a potential basis for subsequent interpretations of self as possibly homosexual. Childhood experiences gained in social, emotional, and genital realms come to be invested with homosexual significance during adolescence. The reinterpretation of past events as indicating a homosexual potential appears to be a necessary (but not sufficient) condition for the eventual adoption of homosexual identities.

STAGE TWO: IDENTITY CONFUSION

Lesbians and gay males typically begin to personalize homosexuality during adolescence, when they begin to reflect on the idea that their feelings, behaviors, or both could be regarded as homosexual. The thought that they are potentially homosexual is dissonant with previously held self-images. The hallmark of this stage is *identity confusion*, inner turmoil and uncertainty surrounding their ambiguous sexual status. The sexual identities of lesbians and gay males are in limbo: they can no longer take their heterosexual identities as given, but they have yet to develop perceptions of themselves as homosexual.

Cass (1984) describes the early phase of identity confusion in the following way: "You are not sure who you are. You are confused about what sort of person you are and where your life is going. You ask yourself the questions "Who am I?," "Am I a homosexual?," "Am I really a heterosexual?" (p. 156). By middle to late adolescence, a perception of self as "probably" homosexual begins to emerge. Gay males begin to suspect that they "might" be homosexual at an average age of seventeen (Troiden 1977, 1979; Troiden and Goode 1980); lesbians at an average age of eighteen (Schäfer 1976). Cass (1984:156) describes the later phase of identity confusion in the following manner:

> You feel that you *probably* are a homosexual, although you're not definitely sure. You feel distant or cut off from [other people]. You are beginning to think that it might help to meet other homosexuals but you're not sure whether you really want to or not. You prefer to put on a front of being completely heterosexual.

Several factors are responsible for the identity confusion experienced during this phase: a) altered perceptions of self; b) the experience of heterosexual and homosexual arousal and behavior; c) the stigma surrounding homosexuality; and d) inaccurate knowledge about homosexuals and homosexuality.

Altered perceptions of self are partly responsible for the identity confusion experienced during this phase. Childhood perceptions of self as different crystallize into perceptions of self as sexually different after the onset of adolescence. Whereas only 20 percent of the lesbians and the gay males in the Bell, Weinberg, and Hammersmith (1981a) study saw themselves as sexually different before age twelve, 74 percent of the lesbians and 84 percent of the gay males felt sexually different by age nineteen, as compared to only 10 percent of the heterosexual female controls and 11 percent of the heterosexual male controls. For both homosexual women and men, the most frequently cited reasons for feeling sexually different were either homosexual interests, or the lack of heterosexual interests, or both. Gender atypicality was mentioned, but not as frequently. Thus, genital and emotional experiences, more than social experiences, seem to precipitate perceptions of self as sexually different during the stage of identity confusion.

Another source of identity confusion is found in the realm of sexual experience itself. Recent investigations of homosexuality have revealed consistently that homosexuals exhibit greater variability in their childhood and adolescent sexual feelings and behaviors than heterosexuals (Bell and Weinberg 1978; Bell, Weinberg, and Hammersmith 1981a; Saghir and Robins 1973; Schäfer 1976; Weinberg and Williams 1974). By early to middle adolescence, most lesbians and gay males have experienced both heterosexual and homosexual arousal and behavior. Only a minority of the Bell, Weinberg, and Hammersmith (1981b) sample, for example, 28 percent of the gay males and 21 percent of the lesbians, were never sexually aroused by the opposite sex, and only 21 percent of the males and 12 percent of the females reported never having an opposite-sex encounter that they or others considered sexual. Thus, significant majorities of lesbians and gay males experience heterosexual and homosexual arousal and behavior before age nineteen. Because Anglo-American society portrays people as either homosexual or heterosexual, it is not surprising that adolescent lesbians and gay males are uncertain and confused regarding their sexual orientations.

As a general rule, gay males are aware of their same-sex attractions at earlier ages than lesbians are. Males report awareness of their same-sex feelings at an average age of thirteen (Bell, Weinberg, and Hammersmith 1981a; Dank 1971; Kooden et al. 1979; McDonald 1982). The corresponding average age for lesbians is between fourteen and sixteen (Bell, Weinberg, and Hammersmith 1981a; Riddle and Morin 1977). Gay males first act on their sexual feelings at an average age of fifteen (Bell, Weinberg, and Hammersmith 1981a; Kooden et al. 1979; McDonald 1982; Troiden 1977, 1979; Troiden and Goode 1980), whereas lesbians first act on their sexual feelings at an average age of twenty, four to six years after the first awareness of their same-sex attractions (Bell, Weinberg, and Hammersmith 1981a; Riddle and Morin 1977; Schäfer 1976).

The stigma surrounding homosexuality also contributes to identity confusion because it discourages adolescent (and some adult) lesbians and gay males from discussing their emerging sexual desires, or activities, or both with either age mates or families. As Plummer (1975) has noted, the societal condemnation of homosexuality creates problems of guilt, secrecy, and difficulty in gaining access to other homosexuals. Moreover, the emphasis placed on gender roles and the general privatization of sexuality compounds the experience of identity confusion and aloneness.

Ignorance and inaccurate knowledge about homosexuality also contribute to identity confusion. People are unlikely to identify themselves in terms of a social category as long as they are unaware that the category exists, lack accurate information about the kinds of people who occupy the category, or believe they have nothing in common with category members (Lofland 1969). In other words, before they can see themselves as homosexual, people must realize that homosexuality and homosexuals exist, learn what homosexuals are actually like as people, and be able to perceive similarities between their own desires and behaviors and those of people labeled socially as homosexual. Today, accurate information about homosexuality has been circulated and distributed throughout society, making it easier to identify homosexual elements in feelings and activities (Dank 1971; Troiden 1979; Troiden and Goode 1980). Lesbians and gay males first understand what the term "homosexual" means at approximately the same time, at the average ages of sixteen or seventeen, respectively (Riddle and Morin 1977). Knowledge of what the term *homosexual* means may be acquired more rapidly in urban areas, where homosexuality is more likely to be discussed, than in rural areas, where conversation is less apt to focus on the topic.

Lesbians and gay males typically respond to identity confusion by adopting one or more of the following strategies: a) denial (Goode 1984; Troiden 1977); b) repair (Humphreys 1972); c) avoidance (Cass 1979); d) redefinition (Cass 1979; Troiden 1977); and e) acceptance (Cass 1979; Troiden 1977).

Lesbians and gay males who use *denial,* deny the homosexual component to their feelings, fantasies, or activities.

Repair involves wholesale attempts to eradicate homosexual feelings and behaviors. Professional help is sought to eliminate the homosexual feelings, fantasies, or activities.

Avoidance is a third overall strategy for dealing with identity confusion (Cass 1979). Although avoidant women and men recognize that their behavior, thoughts, or fantasies are homosexual, they see them as unacceptable, as things to be avoided. Avoidance may assume at least one of six forms.

First, some adolescent (and adult) men and women inhibit behaviors or interests they have learned to associate with homosexuality: "I thought my sexual interest in other girls would go away if I paid more attention to boys and concentrated more on being feminine"; "I figured I'd go straight and develop more of an interest in girls if I got even more involved in sports and didn't spend as much time on my art".

A second avoidance strategy involves limiting one's exposure to the opposite sex to prevent peers or family from learning about one's relative lack of heterosexual responsiveness: "I hated dating. I was always afraid I wouldn't get erect when we petted and kissed and that the girls would find out I was probably gay"; "I felt really weird compared to the other girls. I couldn't understand why they thought guys were so great. I dated to keep my parents off my back".

A third avoidance strategy involves avoiding exposure to information about homosexuality. People may avoid accurate information because they fear that the information may confirm their suspected homosexuality: "Your first lecture on homosexuality awakened my fears of being homosexual. I cut class during the homosexuality section and skipped the assigned readings. I just couldn't accept the idea of being a lesbian"; "One ingenious defense was to remain as ignorant as possible on the subject of homosexuality. No one would ever catch me at the 'Ho' drawer of the New York Public Library card catalog" (Reid 1973:40).

A fourth avoidance strategy involves assuming antihomosexual postures. Some adolescent (and adult) women and men distance themselves from their own homoerotic feelings by attacking and ridiculing known homosexuals: "At one time I hated myself because of my sexual feelings for men. I'm ashamed to admit that I made a nellie guy's life miserable because of it"; "I really put down masculine acting women until I came out and realized that not all lesbians act that way and that many straight women do".

Heterosexual immersion is a fifth avoidance strategy. Some teenaged lesbians and gay males establish heterosexual involvements at varying levels of intimacy in order to eliminate their "inappropriate" sexual interests: "I thought my homosexual feelings would go away if I dated a lot and had sex with as many women as possible"; "I thought my attraction to women was a passing phase and would go away once I started having intercourse with my boyfriend". In some cases, an adolescent girl may purposely become pregnant as a means of "proving" that she couldn't possibly be homosexual.

A sixth avoidance strategy involves escapism. Some adolescent lesbians and gay males avoid confronting their homoerotic feelings through the use and abuse of chemical substances. Getting "high" on drugs provides temporary relief from feelings of identity confusion, and may be used to justify sexual feelings and behaviors ordinarily viewed as unacceptable.

A fourth general means of reducing identity confusion involves *redefining* behavior, feelings, or context along more conventional lines. Redefinition is reflected through the use of special case, ambisexual, temporary identity (Cass 1979), or situational strategies.

In the special case strategy, homosexual behavior and feelings are seen as an isolated case, a one-time occurrence, part of a special, never-to-be-repeated relationship: "I never thought of my feelings and our lovemaking as lesbian. The whole experience was too beautiful for it to be something so ugly. I didn't think I could ever have those feelings for another woman".

Defining the self as ambisexual is another redefinitional strategy: "I guess I'm attracted to both women and men". This strategy may or may not reflect an individual's actual sexual interests.

A third redefinitional response is the temporary identity strategy. Here, people see their homosexual feelings and behaviors as stages or phases of development that will pass in time: "I'm just passing through a phase, I'm really not homosexual".

People who adopt the situational redefinitional strategy define the situation, rather than themselves, as responsible for the homosexual activity or feelings: "It only happened because I was drunk"; "It would never have happened if I hadn't been sent to prison."

A fifth overall strategy is *acceptance.* With acceptance, men and women acknowledge that their behavior, feelings, or fantasies may be homosexual and seek out additional sources of information to learn more about their sexual feelings. For men and women who always felt different because they felt that their thoughts, feelings, and behaviors were at odds with others of their sex, the gradual realization that homosexuals exist as a social category and that they are "probably" homosexual diminishes their sense of isolation. The homosexual category provides them with a label for their difference. "From the time I was quite young I felt different from other girls and I felt more masculine than feminine. When I learned that lesbians existed I had a word that explained why I was different from other girls". "The first name I had for what I was, was 'cocksucker.' 'Cocksucker' was an awful word the way they used it, but it meant that my condition was namable. I finally had a name for all those feelings. I wasn't nothing" (Reinhart 1982:26).

Perceptions of self anchored in the strategies of denial, repair, avoidance, or redefinition may be sustained for months, years, or permanently. Bisexual (ambisexual) perceptions of self, for example, a redefinitional strategy, may be maintained or undermined by a person's social roles, position in the social structure, intimate relationships, and by the perceived strength, persistence, and salience of the homosexual feelings. Although individuals may use several different stigma-management strategies, they characteristically use some more than others.

Stage Three: Identity Assumption

Despite differences in stigma-management strategies, a significant number of women and men progress to *identity assumption*, the third stage of homosexual identity formation, during or after late adolescence. In this stage, the homosexual identity becomes both a self-identity and a presented identity, at least to other homosexuals. Defining the self as homosexual and presenting the self as homosexual to other homosexuals are the first stages in a larger process of identity disclosure called "coming out" (Coleman 1982; Lee 1977). The earmarks of this stage are self-definition as homosexual, identity tolerance and acceptance, regular association with other homosexuals, sexual experimentation, and exploration of the homosexual subculture.

Lesbians and gay males typically define themselves as homosexual at different ages and in different contexts. Retrospective studies of adult homosexuals suggest that gay males arrive at homosexual self-definitions between the ages of nineteen and twenty-one, on the average (Dank 1971; Harry and DeVall 1978; Kooden et al. 1979; McDonald 1982; Troiden 1979). Retrospective studies involving small samples of adolescent gay males indicate a younger age at the time of self-identification as homosexual: age fourteen, on the average (Remafedi 1987). Adult lesbians recall reaching homosexual self-definitions slightly later, between the average ages of twenty-one and twenty-three (Califia 1979; Riddle and Morin 1977; Schäfer 1976; Smith 1980).

The contexts in which homosexual self-definition occurs also vary between the sexes. Lesbians typically arrive at homosexual self-definitions in contexts of intense affectionate involvements with other women (Cronin 1974; Schäfer 1976). Seventy-six percent of the lesbians interviewed by Cronin, for example, defined themselves as lesbian in contexts of meaningful emotional involvements with other women. Gay males, on the other hand, are more likely to arrive at homosexual self-definitions in sociosexual contexts where homosexual men are reputed to gather for sexual purposes: gay bars, parties, parks, YMCAs, and men's rooms (Dank 1971; Troiden 1979; Warren 1974). Only a minority of gay males, roughly 20 percent, appear to define themselves in contexts of same-sex love relationships (Dank 1971; McDonald 1982; Troiden 1979). Today, I suspect that young men are more likely to arrive at homosexual self-definitions in romantic contexts than in sexual settings. For many men, the possibility of AIDS infection has reduced the perceived desirability of sexual experimentation.

Patterns laid down during sex-role socialization explain why lesbians define themselves in emotional contexts and why gay males do so in sociosexual contexts: "Male sexuality is seen as active, initiatory, demanding of immediate gratification, and divorced from emotional attachment; female sexuality emphasizes feelings and minimizes the importance of immediate sexual activity" (de Monteflores and Schultz 1978). For males, admitting a desire for homosexual activity implies the label of homosexual; for females, intense emotional involvement with the same sex has similar implications.

Although homosexual identities are assumed during this stage, they are tolerated initially rather than accepted. Cass (1984:156) describes people who tolerate their homosexual identities as follows:

> You feel sure you're a homosexual and you put up with, or tolerate this. You see yourself as a homosexual for now but are not sure about how you will be in the future. You usually take care to put across a heterosexual image. You sometimes mix socially with homosexuals, or would like to do this. You feel a need to meet others like yourself.

Self-definition as homosexual may occur just before, at the same time as, or shortly after first social contact with other homosexuals (Cronin 1974; Dank 1971; Ponse 1978; Troiden 1977, 1979; Weinberg 1977, 1978). Initial contacts may have been engineered consciously (e.g., deciding to go to a homosexual bar) or accidentally (e.g., learning that a respected friend is homosexual). Only a minority of lesbians and gay males appear to define themselves as homosexual without having direct contact with one or more homosexuals. Self-designation as homosexual in the absence of affiliation with other homosexuals (e.g., as a consequence of reading about homosexuality) has been referred to as *disembodied affiliation* (Ponse 1978).

The quality of a person's initial contacts with homosexuals is extremely important (Cass 1979). If initial contacts are negative, further contact with homosexuals may be avoided and nonhomosexual perceptions of self will persist, maintained through the strategies of denial, repair, ambisexuality, or temporary identity described earlier. Perceptions of the increased risks of living as a homosexual (e.g., fear of blackmail or AIDS) in a homophobic society may also encourage individuals to cling to nonhomosexual self-perceptions.

Positive contacts with homosexuals, on the other hand, facilitate homosexual identity formation. Favorable contacts provide lesbians and gay males with the opportunity to obtain information about homosexuality at first hand. Direct positive exposure provides a basis for reexamining and reevaluating their own ideas about homosexuality, and for seeing similarities between themselves and those labeled "homosexual." The meanings attributed to the homosexual label begin to change in a more favorable direction.

Personally meaningful contacts with experienced homosexuals also enable neophytes to see that homosexuality is socially organized, and that a group exists to which they may belong, which diminishes feelings of solitude and alienation. Experienced homosexuals provide neophytes with role models from whom they learn: a) strategies for stigma management; b) rationalizations that legitimize homosexuality and neutralize guilt feelings; c) the range of identities and roles available to homosexuals; and d) the norms governing homosexual conduct.

Once they adopt homosexual identities, lesbians and gay males are confronted with the issue of stigma and its management. They may adopt one of several stigma-evasion strategies during identity assumption: capitulation, minstrelization, passing, and group alignment (Humphreys 1972).

Women and men who *capitulate* avoid homosexual activity because they have internalized a stigmatizing view of homosexuality. The persistence of homosexual feelings in the absence of homosexual activity, however, may lead them to experience self-hatred and despair.

Individuals who use *minstrelization* express their homosexuality along lines etched out by the popular culture. They behave as the wider culture expects them to behave, in highly stereotyped, gender-inappropriate fashions.

Passing as heterosexual is probably the most common stigma-evasion strategy (Humphreys 1972). Women and men who pass as heterosexual define themselves as homosexual, but conceal their sexual preferences and behavior from heterosexual family, friends, and colleagues, "by careful, even torturous, control of information" (Humphreys 1972:138). Passers lead "double lives," that is, they segregate their social worlds into heterosexual and homosexual spheres and hope the two never collide.

Group alignment is also adopted commonly by neophyte homosexuals to evade stigma. Men and women who evade stigma through affiliation become actively involved in the homosexual community. The perception of "belonging" to a world of others situated similarly eases the pain of stigma. Other homosexuals are looked upon as sources of social and emotional support, as well as sexual gratification. Yet, an awareness of "belonging" to the homosexual subculture also fosters an awareness of "not belonging," perceptions of being excluded from the worlds of opposite-sex dating, marriage, and parenthood. As Ponse (1978) has noted, people may deal with this alienation by immersing themselves completely in the homosexual subculture, by avoiding heterosexual settings that remind them of their stigma, by normalizing their behaviors (i.e., minimizing the differences between heterosexuals and homosexuals), or by aristocratizing their behaviors (i.e., attaching a special significance to homosexual experience). Other lesbians and gay males may nihilize heterosexual experience, that is, define heterosexual patterns as deviant (Warren 1974).

To recapitulate, positive homosexual experiences facilitate homosexual self-definition; unrewarding experiences reinforce negative attitudes toward homosexuality. Undesirable homosexual experiences may prompt people to reject the identity ("I am not homosexual"), abandon the behavior ("I'm not really homosexual if I avoid the behavior"), or reject both identity and behavior ("I'm not homosexual. I can learn to behave heterosexually").

By the end of the identity assumption stage, people begin to accept themselves as homosexual. Cass describes acceptance of the homosexual identity as follows:

> You are quite sure you are a homosexual and you accept this fairly happily. You are prepared to tell a few people about being a homosexual but you

carefully select whom you will tell. You adopt an attitude of fitting in where you live and work. You can't see any point in confronting people with your homosexuality if it's going to embarrass all concerned. (1984:156)

STAGE FOUR: COMMITMENT

A commitment is a feeling of obligation to follow a particular course of action (Theodorson and Theodorson 1969). In the homosexual context, *commitment* involves adopting homosexuality as a way of life. For the committed homosexual, "it becomes easier, more attractive, less costly to remain a homosexual" than to try to function as a heterosexual (Plummer 1975:150). Entering a same-sex love relationship marks the onset of commitment (Coleman 1982; Troiden 1979).

The main characteristics of the commitment stage are self-acceptance and comfort with the homosexual identity and role. Commitment has both internal and external dimensions. It is indicated *internally* by: a) the fusion of sexuality and emotionality into a significant whole; b) a shift in the meanings attached to homosexual identities; c) a perception of the homosexual identity as a valid self-identity; d) expressed satisfaction with the homosexual identity; and e) increased happiness after self-defining as homosexual. It is indicated *externally* by: a) same-sex love relationships; b) disclosure of the homosexual identity to nonhomosexual audiences; and c) a shift in the type of stigma-management strategies.

The fusion of same-sex sexuality and emotionality into a meaningful whole is one internal measure of a person's commitment to homosexuality as a way of life (Coleman 1982; Warren 1974; Troiden 1979). The same sex is redefined as a legitimate source of love and romance, as well as sexual gratification. Homosexuals themselves see same-sex romantic preferences as differentiating "true" homosexuals from those who are merely experimenting (Warren 1974).

Another internal measure of commitment to homosexuality as a way of life is reflected by the meanings attached by homosexuals to the homosexual identity. The homosexual subculture encourages both lesbians and gay males to perceive the homosexual identity as an "essential" identity, a "state of being" and "way of life" rather than merely a form of behavior or sexual orientation (Ponse 1978; Warren 1974; Warren and Ponse 1977). Lesbian feminists are especially likely to view lesbianism as all-encompassing: "A lesbian's entire sense of self centers on women. While sexual energies are not discounted, alone they do not create the lesbian feminist" (Faderman 1984/1985:87).

The perception of the homosexual identity as a valid self-identity is also a sign of internal commitment. Homosexual identities and roles are seen as growing out of genuine, deep-seated needs and desires. Homosexual expression is reconceptualized as "natural" and "normal" for the self. Committed homosexuals find the homosexual identity "a more valid expression of the human condition than that afforded by a heterosexual one" (Humphreys 1979:242).

The degree of satisfaction people express about their present identities is another measure of internal commitment (Hammersmith and Weinberg 1973). When Bell and Weinberg (1978) asked their sample of homosexuals whether they would remain homosexual even if a magic pill would enable them to become heterosexual, 95 percent of the lesbians and 86 percent of the gay males claimed they would not take the magic pill. In addition, 73 percent of the gay males and 84 percent of the lesbians indicated they had "very little or no" regret about their homosexuality. Only 6 percent of the male and 2 percent of the female homosexuals felt "a great deal" of regret. Societal rejection, punitiveness, and the inability to have children were the most frequently mentioned sources of regret.

Increased happiness is another indication of an internal commitment to homosexuality. When asked, "At this time would you say you are more, less, or about as happy as you were prior to arriving at a homosexual self-definition?" 91 percent of the gay males I interviewed indicated they were more happy, 8 percent stated they were about as happy, and only one person said he was less happy (Troiden 1979).

A same-sex love relationship is one external sign of a commitment to homosexuality as a way of life, a concrete manifestation of a synthesis of same-sex emotionality and sexuality into a meaningful whole (Coleman 1982; Troiden 1977, 1979). Lesbians appear to enter their first same-sex love relationships between the average ages of twenty-two and twenty-three (Bell and Weinberg 1978; Riddle and Morin 1977), a year or less after they define themselves as lesbians. Gay males typically have their first love affairs between the average ages of twenty-one and twenty-four (Bell and Weinberg 1978: McDonald 1982; Troiden 1979), roughly two to five years after they define themselves as homosexual.

In keeping with their gender-role training, males are much more likely than lesbians are to gain sexual experiences with a variety of partners before focusing their attentions on one special person (Troiden 1979). Lesbians, on the other hand, are more likely to explore the homosexual community and gain sexual experiences in the context of emotional relationships with one woman or a series of special" women (Cronin 1974; Smith 1980).

Disclosure of the homosexual identity to heterosexual audiences is another external measure of commitment to homosexuality as a way of life. As mentioned earlier, coming out involves disclosure of the homosexual identity to some of an expanding series of audiences ranging from self, to other homosexuals, to heterosexual friends, family, or both, to coworkers, to employers, to public identification as homosexual by the media (Lee 1977).

Homosexual identity formation is characterized over time by an increasing desire to disclose the homosexual identity to nonhomosexual audiences (Cass 1984). Few people, however, disclose their homosexual identities to everybody in their social environments. Instead, they fluctuate "back and forth in degrees of openness, depending on personal, social, and professional factors" (de Monteflores and Schultz 1978).

Lesbians and gay males appear more likely to come out to siblings or close heterosexual friends, than to parents, coworkers, or employers. Fifty percent of the gay males and 62 percent of the lesbians interviewed by Bell and Weinberg (1978) said that they had told "some or all" of their siblings about their homosexuality. Regarding disclosure to heterosexual friends, 54 percent of the lesbians and 53 percent of the gay males claimed that "some or most" of their heterosexual friends knew about their homosexuality. Fewer had told their parents about their homosexuality. Forty-two percent of the gay males and 49 percent of the lesbians said they had come out to their mothers, and 37 percent of the lesbians and 31 percent of the gay males said that they had told their fathers.

Bell and Weinberg's (1978) respondents exercised even greater discretion in disclosing their homosexual identities to coworkers and employers. Sixty-two percent of the gay males and 76 percent of the lesbians stated that "few or none" of their coworkers knew they were homosexual, and 85 percent of the lesbians and 71 percent of the gay males claimed that their employers were unaware of their homosexuality. Lesbians and gay males appear reluctant to come out in the workplace for two reasons: fear of endangering job credibility or effectiveness, and fear of job or income loss (Kooden et al. 1979; Riddle and Morin 1977).

Those lesbians who disclose their homosexual identities to nongay friends begin to do so at an average age of twenty-eight (Riddle and Morin 1977); gay males between the average ages of twenty-three and twenty-eight (McDonald 1982; Riddle and Morin 1977). Gay males who disclose their homosexual identities to their parents do so at age twenty-eight, on the average; lesbians do so at an average age of thirty (Riddle and Morin 1977). Those who come out in professional settings do so at even later average ages, thirty-two for lesbians, thirty-one for gay males (Riddle and Morin 1977). The AIDS epidemic, however, has amplified the stigma surrounding homosexuality. As a result, younger gay males and lesbians may be less willing today than in the past to disclose their homosexual identities to nonhomosexual audiences.

A third external indicator of commitment is a shift in stigma management strategies. Covering (Humphreys 1972) and blending appear to replace passing and group alignment as the most common strategies, with a minority opting for conversion (Humphreys 1972).

Women and men who *cover* are ready to admit that they are homosexual (in many cases because it is obvious or known), but nonetheless take great pains to keep their homosexuality from looming large. They manage their homosexuality in ways meant to demonstrate that although they may be homosexual, they are nonetheless respectable. "Imitation of heterosexual marriage, along with other roles and life-styles designed to elicit praise from straight segments of society," typifies this form of stigma evasion (Humphreys 1972:139). Like people who blend, people who cover turn to other homosexuals for social and emotional support, as well as sexual gratification, and disclose their homosexual identities selectively to significant heterosexuals.

People who *blend* act in gender-appropriate ways and neither announce nor deny their homosexual identities to nonhomosexual others. They perceive their sexual orientations as irrelevant to the kinds of activities they undertake with heterosexuals, and cloak their private lives and sexuality with the shroud of silence. When quizzed or challenged about their sexual orientations or behavior, they are likely to respond: "What's it to you?" or "It's none of your business." Women and men who blend affiliate with the homosexual subculture and present themselves as homosexual to other gay males and lesbians, and to carefully selected nonhomosexuals.

Lesbians and gay males who *convert* acquire an ideology or worldview that not only destigmatizes homosexuality, but transforms it from a vice to a virtue, from a mark of shame to a mark of pride. People who convert confront rather than evade the homosexual stigma. Formally or informally, they attempt to inform the general public about the realities of homosexuality and the special contributions made to society by homosexuals. Their goal is to eliminate oppression through education and political change (e.g., equal rights in jobs and housing). A few lesbians and gay males adopt conversionist strategies during the identity assumption stage when they define themselves as homosexual.

Stigma-evasion strategies are situational rather than constant, that is, personal, social, or professional factors may prompt individuals to blend or cover in some situations, disclose their homosexual identity openly in others, and switch to conversionist modes in yet other contexts. Selective and relatively nonselective self-disclosure have important consequences for the self. Identity disclosure enables the homosexual identity to be more fully realized, that is, brought into concrete existence, in a wider range of contexts. A more complete integration between homosexuals' identities and their social worlds is made possible when they can see and present themselves as homosexual and can be viewed as such by others. Cass (1984:156) describes *identity synthesis* in the following way: "You are prepared to tell [almost] *anyone* that you are a homosexual. You are happy about the way you are but feel that being a homosexual is not the most important part of you. You mix socially with homosexuals and heterosexuals [with whom] you are open about your homosexuality."

In the final analysis, homosexual identity is emergent: never fully determined in a fixed or absolute sense, but always subject to modification and further change. Homosexual identity formation is continuous, a process of "becoming" that spans a lifetime, a process of "striving but never arriving" (Plummer 1975). For this reason, commitment to the homosexual identity and role is a matter of degree. Homosexuals span a continuum from low to high levels of commitment on both internal and external dimensions, which may vary across time and place. Thus, commitment is always somewhat inconsistent, strengthened, or weakened at various points and contexts by personal, social, or professional factors.

QUALIFICATIONS

More research is needed to determine more clearly the variables that help and hinder homosexual identity formation. A number of factors implicated in homosexual identity formation appear to influence the ages at which samples of homosexuals recall having experienced events related to homosexuality (e.g., first same-sex arousal, first same-sex sexual activity, homosexual self-definition, first same-sex love relationship). Below, I have indicated a number of issues in need of further attention and investigation.

First, the average ages outlined for each stage should be viewed as approximations or rough guidelines. Since these ages are based on averages, variations are expected and should not be treated as developmental regressions.

Second, sample characteristics may also influence reported rates of homosexual identity formation: the mean ages of respondents in the studies cited here vary, for example. In retrospective samples consisting of relatively older lesbians and gay males, the respondents recall having encountered various events (e.g., self-definition as homosexual) at relatively older ages than younger informants, thus raising the average ages at which the various events seem to occur. Older informants grew up during a time when homosexuality was rarely discussed, and then only in highly stereotypical terms.

Research obtained in the 1970s (Dank 1971; Troiden 1977, 1979; Troiden and Goode 1980) and 1980s (Remafedi 1987) indicates that adolescent lesbians and gay males today acquire their homosexual identities at younger average ages than did their older counterparts. More specifically, homosexuals under twenty-five recall having encountered the various events (e.g., first same-sex love relationship) associated with homosexual identity formation at significantly younger average ages than the ones reported here. Increased openness, tolerance, and accurate information about homosexuality may have made it easier to perceive similarities between self and "homosexuals."

On the other hand, the onset of the AIDS epidemic may have the opposite effect: it may delay homosexual identity formation (at least among males) because it has amplified the stigma surrounding homosexuality. The possibility of contracting AIDS may defensively motivate people to deny their erotic feelings, to delay acting on them, or to express them only in the context of committed love relationships. In addition, identity integration and a positive sense of homosexual identity may be undermined. To avoid being seen as potential disease carriers, lesbians and gay males may choose not to disclose their homosexual identities to non-homosexual audiences. Identity fear may replace identity pride. Fears of infection may promote erotophobia, a fear of sexual relations, and cause people to avoid homosexual behavior completely or to reduce their sexual experimentation.

Gender-inappropriate behavior (Harry 1982), adolescent homosexual arousal and activity, and an absence of heterosexual experiences (Troiden and Goode 1980) facilitate progress through the various stages. Gender-atypical, homosexually active, heterosexually inexperienced adolescent lesbians and gay males encounter less identity confusion than other "pre-homosexuals" because Anglo-American gender conventions articulate linkages between all three characteristics and adult homosexuality. Conversely, adolescent gay males and lesbians who are gender-typical, heterosexually active, and homosexually inexperienced encounter more confusion regarding their sexual identities because their characteristics are at variance with prevailing stereotypes.

Supportive family and friends may also facilitate homosexual identity formation. Individuals may feel more comfortable acting on their sexual feelings when they believe that those close to them will accept them for themselves. Conversely, lesbians and gay males with nonsupportive families and friends may find it more difficult to acknowledge and act on their sexual feelings. Fears of rejection appear to inhibit homosexual identity formation to various degrees.

Educational level and prevailing atmosphere of the workplace also facilitate or hinder homosexual identity formation. Highly educated lesbians and gay males in homophobic professions may fear that they have more to lose by acknowledging and acting on their sexual feelings than their less educated counterparts. Fears of job or income loss, or concerns about endangering professional credibility, inhibit homosexual identity formation (Kooden et al. 1979; Troiden 1977). Conversely, lesbians and gay males with less education, and those who work in more supportive occupational structures, may find it easier to act on and integrate their sexual feelings into their overall lives because they feel they have less to lose.

This article has developed an ideal-typical model of homosexual identity formation using a sociological perspective. The stigma surrounding homosexuality was shown to affect powerfully the formation and management of homosexual identities. Homosexual identity formation was described as occurring over a protracted period and involving a number of growth points or changes, which were ordered into a series of four ideal-typical stages. Among committed homosexuals, that is, lesbians and gay males who define themselves as homosexual and adopt corresponding life-styles, childhood perceptions of self as different crystallize into views of self as sexually different during middle to late adolescence. Positive contacts with other homosexuals facilitate self-definition and acceptance of self as homosexual. Continued involvement with the homosexual identity and role fosters commitment to homosexuality as a way of life and an increased desire to disclose the homosexual identity to nonhomosexual audiences. Selective and nonselective identity disclosure permit the homosexual identity to be realized more fully across a wider range of situations and contexts, which enables gay males and lesbians to integrate their homosexual self-identities more completely with their social worlds. Differences in gender-role socialization explain differences between gay males and lesbians in the homosexual identity formation process. The article concluded by indicating factors that may promote or hinder rates of homosexual identity formation and that are in need of further research.

ACKNOWLEDGMENT

The author wishes to thank Dr. Karen Feinberg for her editorial assistance.

REFERENCES

Bell, A. P., and M. S. Weinberg. 1978. *Homosexualities: A Study of Diversity among Men and Women.* New York: Simon and Schuster.

Bell, A. P., M. S. Weinberg, and S. K. Hammersmith. 1981a. *Sexual Preference: Its Development in Men and Women.* Bloomington: Indiana University Press.

Bell, A. P., M. S. Weinberg, and S. K. Hammersmith. 1981b. *Sexual Preference: Its Development in Men and Women: Statistical Appendix.* Bloomington: Indiana University Press.

Califia, P. 1979. Lesbian sexuality. *Journal of Homosexuality* 4:255–66.

Cass, V. C. 1979. Homosexual identity formation: A theoretical model. *Journal of Homosexuality* 4:219–35.

Cass, V. C. 1983/1984. Homosexual identity: A concept in need of definition. *Journal of Homosexuality* 9:105–26.

Cass, V. C. 1984. Homosexual identity formation: Testing a theoretical model. *Journal of Sex Research* 20:143–67.

Coleman, E. 1982. Developmental stages of the coming-out process. In W. Paul, J. D. Weinrich, J. C. Gonsiorek, and M. E. Hotvedt, eds., *Homosexuality: Social, Psychological and Biological Issues,* pp. 149–58. Beverly Hills, Calif.: Sage Publications.

Cronin, D. M. 1974. Coming out among lesbians. In E. Goode and R. R. Troiden, eds., *Sexual Deviance and Sexual Deviants,* pp. 268–77. New York: William Morrow.

Dank, B. M. 1971. Coming out in the gay world. *Psychiatry* 34:180–97.

de Monteflores, C., and S. J. Schultz. 1978. Coming out: Similarities and differences for lesbians and gay men. *Journal of Social Issues* 34:59–72.

Doyle, J. A. 1983. *The Male Experience.* Dubuque, Ia.: Wm. C. Brown.

Faderman, L. 1984/1985. The "new gay" lesbian. *Journal of Homosexuality* 10:85–95.

Gagnon, J. H. 1977. *Human Sexualities.* Glenview, Ill.: Scott, Foresman.

Gagnon, J. H., and W. Simon. 1973. *Sexual Conduct: The Social Sources of Human Sexuality.* Chicago: Aldine.

Goode, E. 1984. *Deviant Behavior.* 2d ed. Englewood Cliffs, N.J.: Prentice-Hall.

Hammersmith, S. K., and M. S. Weinberg. 1973. Homosexual identity: Commitment, adjustments, and significant others. *Sociometry* 36:56–78.

Harry, J. 1982. *Gay Children Grown Up: Gender Culture and Gender Deviance.* New York: Praeger.

Harry, J., and W. DeVall. 1978. *The Social Organization of Gay Males.* New York: Praeger.

Humphreys, L. 1972. *Out of the Closets: The Sociology of Homosexual Liberation.* Englewood Cliffs, N.J.: Prentice-Hall.

Humphreys, L. 1979. Being odd against all odds. In R. C. Federico, ed., *Sociology*, 2d ed., pp. 238–42. Reading, Mass.: Addison-Wesley.

Kinsey, A. C., W. B. Pomeroy, and C. E. Martin. 1948. *Sexual Behavior in the Human Male*. Philadelphia: W. B. Saunders.

Kinsey, A. C., W. B. Pomeroy, C. E. Martin, and P. H. Gebhard. 1953. *Sexual Behavior in the Human Female*. Philadelphia: W. B. Saunders.

Kooden, H. D., S. F. Morin, D. L. Riddle, M. Rogers, B. E. Strang, and F. Strassburger. 1979. *Removing the Stigma: Final Report of the Board of Social and Ethical Responsibility for Psychology's Task Force on the Status of Lesbian and Gay Male Psychologists*. Washington, D.C.: American Psychological Association.

Laws, J. L., and P. Schwartz. 1977. *Sexual Scripts: The Social Construction of Female Sexuality*. Hinsdale, Ill.: Dryden Press.

Lee, J. A. 1977. Going public: A study in the sociology of homosexual liberation. *Journal of Homosexuality* 3:49–78.

Levine, M. P. 1987. Gay macho: Ethnography of the homosexual clone. Doctoral dissertation, New York University.

Lofland, J. 1969. *Deviance and Identity*. Englewood Cliffs, N.J.: Prentice-Hall.

McCall, G. J., and J. L. Simmons. 1966. *Identities and Interactions: An Examination of Human Associations in Everyday Life*. New York: Free Press.

McDonald, G. J. 1982. Individual differences in the coming out process for gay men: Implications for theoretical models. *Journal of Homosexuality* 8:47–60.

McWhirter, D. P., and A. M. Mattison. 1984. *The Male Couple: How Relationships Develop*. Englewood Cliffs, N.J.: Prentice-Hall.

Minton, H. L., and G. J. McDonald. 1983/1984. Homosexual identity formation as a developmental process. *Journal of Homosexuality* 9:91–104.

Plummer, K. 1975. *Sexual Stigma: An Interactionist Account*. London: Routledge and Kegan Paul.

Ponse, B. 1978. *Identities in the Lesbian World: The Social Construction of Self*. Westport, Conn.: Greenwood Press.

Reid, J. 1973. *The Best Little Boy in the World*. New York: Putnam.

Reinhart, R. C. 1982. *A History of Shadows*. New York: Avon Books.

Remafedi, G. 1987. Male homosexuality: The adolescent's perspective. *Pediatrics* 79:326–30.

Riddle, D. I., and S. F. Morin. 1977. Removing the stigma: Data from individuals. *APA Monitor* 16 (November):28.

Saghir, M. T., and E. Robins. 1973. *Male and Female Homosexuality: A Comprehensive Investigation*. Baltimore: Williams and Wilkins.

Schäfer, S. 1976. Sexual and social problems among lesbians. *Journal of Sex Research* 12:50–69.

Simmons, J. L. 1965. Public stereotypes of deviants. *Social Problems* 13:223–32.

Simon, W., and J. H. Gagnon. 1984. Sexual scripts. *Society* 22:53–60.

Smith, K. S. 1980. Socialization, identity, and commitment: The case of female homosexuals. Master's thesis, Miami University.

Tavris, C., and C. Wade. 1984. *The Longest War: Sex Differences in Perspective*. New York: Harcourt Brace Jovanovich.

Theodorson, G. A., and A. G. Theodorson. 1969. *A Modern Dictionary of Sociology.* New York: Thomas Y. Crowell.

Troiden, R. R. 1977. Becoming homosexual: Research on acquiring a gay identity. Doctoral dissertation, State University of New York at Stony Brook.

Troiden, R. R. 1979. Becoming homosexual: A model of gay identity acquisition. *Psychiatry* 42:362–73.

Troiden, R. R. 1984/1985. Self, self-concept, identity, and homosexual identity: Constructs in need of definition and differentiation. *Journal of Homosexuality* 10:97–109.

Troiden, R. R. 1988. *Gay and Lesbian Identity: A Sociological Analysis.* New York: General Hall.

Troiden, R. R., and E. Goode. 1980. Variables related to the acquisition of a gay identity. *Journal of Homosexuality* 5:383–92.

Warren, C. A. B. 1974. *Identity and Community in the Gay World.* New York: Wiley.

Warren, C. A. B., and B. Ponse. 1977. The existential self in the gay world. In J. D. Douglas and J. M. Johnson. eds., *Existential Sociology,* pp. 273–89. New York: Cambridge University Press.

Weinberg, M. S., and C. J. Williams. 1974. *Male Homosexuals: Their Problems and Adaptations.* New York: Oxford University Press.

Weinberg, T. S. 1977. Becoming homosexual: Self-disclosure, self-identity, and self-maintenance. Doctoral dissertation, University of Connecticut.

Weinberg, T. S. 1978. On "doing" and "being" gay: Sexual behavior and homosexual male self-identity. *Journal of Homosexuality* 4:143–56.

Whitam, F. L., and R. M. Mathy. 1986. *Male Homosexuality in Four Societies: Brazil, Guatemala, the Philippines, and the United States.* New York: Praeger.

8

Notes on the Management
of Difference

Carmen de Monteflores

When a majority group assumes the power of instituting norms from which minority groups are seen to deviate, differences between these groups become institutionalized. Difference is then perceived as a deficit, or as a failure to meet the standards of the majority. The institutionalization of differences between individuals and between groups creates stereotypes which reduce the full humanity of the individual to a few selected deviant traits. The stereotyping of minority individuals and groups often leads to severe social limitations and to considerable psychological disempowerment.

Goffman (1963), in an insightful analysis of *stigma* and the management of spoiled identity, described the way in which perceived differences negatively affect an individual's self-concept and functioning. Goffman barely touches on what function the stigmatization process may serve in a society, however, and what might be the origin of our perception of differences. The purpose of this article is a) to develop a hypothesis regarding the origin and function of the institutionalization of difference between the majority group, which determines norms, and minority groups; b) to explore the strategies which minority individuals and groups may use to cope with institutionalized difference; and c) to explore the psychological implications of institutionalized difference and how they can be approached in psychotherapy.

ORIGIN OF OUR CONCEPT OF DIFFERENCE

The traits on which an identity of difference is based can be seen either as personal and chosen or as circumstantial and imposed. The tension between internalizing (ascribing choice) and externalizing (implicating circumstance) is one of the core conflicts in a minority identification and one of the thorniest issues in the practice of minority psychotherapy. There is a greater emphasis in current psychotherapy toward the internalization of responsibility, the rationale being that we can empower ourselves by recognizing that what we do to ourselves we can also undo. To the stigma of being the bearer of rejected traits of a society is added the secondary stigma of being seen as someone who does not choose to make himself, or herself, feel better, in essence as a malingerer.

I want to hypothesize that the illusion of absolute power over our intrapsychic lives, and to a large extent power over circumstance, is a class bias. Within a framework of opportunity, not to strive and make use of that opportunity is indeed a cause for shame. Within a framework of deprivation and limited resources, power is not assumed but is rather the basis of limits that define individual possibility. For rejected groups, power, and the power to change, is not an internal psychological reality; power is rather an external fact, often at odds with our needs.

This form of classism, the imposition of the views and values of one social class onto another, then becomes the model for dealing with difference. Goffman says:

> Society established the means of categorizing persons and the complement of attributes felt to be ordinary and natural for members of each of these categories. . . . When [a] stranger is present before us, evidence can arise of his possessing an attribute that makes him different from others in the category of *persons available for him* to be, and of a less desirable kind. . . . He is thus reduced in our minds from a whole and usual person to a tainted, discounted one. (1963:2–3; italics added)

I have emphasized the phrase "persons available for him to be" because there is here a strong implication of choice. All differences, including innate or circumstantial ones, are seen to some extent as chosen and therefore changeable.

To externalize all circumstance, on the other hand, and assume a lack of choice may render us even more powerless unless our assumed deficits are seen as potential sources of strength. This transformation of motive can be brought about by embracing and making a chronicle of our difference. Etiology then may be transformed into history. The confessional aspect of the coming out stories of all rejected groups speaks to a need to retrace one's history, revisit the sites and sounds, and make visible through anecdote and tale the workings of one's culture.

THE FUNCTION OF A CONCEPT OF DIFFERENCE

A recognition of how difference functions in the society is another aspect of the process of articulation and integration of difference as part of identity. What role does a particular minority group play in the societal "family"? Is this the group who feels? The group who is sexual? The group who nurtures? The group who is victimized? The group who creates change?

Minorities may function to remind the dominant class of their limits, their frailties, their fears. Minorities may be, in the Jungian sense, the "shadow" of a society in whom the disowned traits of a culture are reflected. For example, in recent years the larger society disowned both homosexuality and death by labeling AIDS as a "gay illness." It is easier for the dominant group in the society to assign sickness to gay men rather than to deal with fears about their own sexuality and death. On the other hand, the valuing of one's difference, as a member of a rejected minority, can lead to the valuing of difference itself, which is perhaps one of the most important contributions minorities can make to the larger society.

Goffman indicates that the stigmatized and the normal participate in a common process:

> Stigma involves not so much a set of concrete individuals who can be separated into two piles, the stigmatized and the normal, as a pervasive two-role social process in which every individual participates in both roles, at least in some connections and in some phases of life. The normal and the stigmatized are not persons but rather perspectives. (1963:137–38)

According to this view, the normal and the stigmatized can be seen to represent the forces of merging and differentiation in a society. Differentiation and merging are not only forces in the relationships between individuals but may also be central to the relationships between groups. Those who are different represent necessary discontinuities which produce creative tension, self-analysis, and change in a society. It is hoped, however, that the stigmatization of some groups is not a necessary part of the process of evolution of a society.

STRATEGIES FOR THE MANAGEMENT OF DIFFERENCE

When confronted with the fact of her or his institutionalized difference within a dominant culture, the individual, if not too damaged in the process, develops a variety of coping strategies. These strategies can be broadly categorized within a continuum of acceptance or rejection, merging or differentiating from the mainstream culture. Without attempting to be exhaustive, I will address four main strategies: a) assimilation, b) confrontation, c) ghettoization, and d) specialization. It should be noted that I am not suggesting a linear progression in the use of these strategies. Also, the relational aspects of some of these strategies will be explored in the second section of this article.

Assimilation

The core issue of assimilation is survival. The process of assimilation of all variant groups involves a need to learn the language of the dominant group, that is, the current modes of communicating and managing, in order to survive. Assimilation promotes a strengthening of external skills: the dress, organizational procedures, and the manners of the dominant culture are adopted. But, in this process, there can be a profound sense of self-betrayal as well, an inner unease, a disconnection with the values of one's culture of origin. An ambitious working-class lesbian who because of her intellectual ability is able to attend an upper-middle-class women's college may experience a sense of not belonging in that new environment and may also feel like an outsider in her own class group.

A static view of difference seems to be a part of a classist conceptualization. This conceptualization does not allow for the process of change that occurs as a result of interaction between groups or for the infinite variety that takes place when different groups or individuals meet. The static view manifests itself in a tendency to reinforce identity by reinforcing boundaries.

The struggle with boundaries is the essential drama of assimilation. Some lesbians come to psychotherapy feeling oppressed by what they describe as the pressure to conform to certain standards of dress in the lesbian community. They may feel, for example, that they are viewed with suspicion by members of their own group when they wear the standard feminine office attire. Latina lesbians who identify certain forms of dress with their affiliation with their Latina culture may feel a similar pressure from White women. A crisis of allegiance is then created, and an endless struggle for such individuals ensues between sameness and difference, allegiance and rejection both within groups and between groups.

The primary technique used in assimilation is passing. The process of assimilation always requires some degree of passing. Passing is ordinarily defined as appearing to be like the dominant group when one is not really a member of that group and as adopting the outer appearance of the dominant group in order to avoid direct rejection by it. I would like here to broaden the connotation of passing by defining it in a more positive and functional way as a process of managing the boundary between two groups and literally passing, or traversing, from one group to another.

As viewed here, boundary management is a central aspect of passing. Passing becomes dysfunctional only when the outer appearance and the inner feelings or beliefs become disconnected; when the mask acquires a life of its own. A very moving, vivid, and subtle portrayal of both the vicissitudes and the meaning of passing can be seen in the movies *La Cage aux Folles* and *La Cage aux Folles II*. In one scene, the central character, a male homosexual transvestite, attempts to show several heterosexual detectives how to pass as homosexuals. He demonstrates that there is a fine line, a boundary, between being feminine and being masculine, as well as between tragedy and wit, which he has developed into a high art.

On the other hand, to deny a basic sense of who we are by manipulating our appearance often leads to a splitting within ourselves, which, in turn, leaves us empty and ungrounded. A lesbian, for example, who because of a fear of loss of job and status chooses to remain closeted may manifest her deep sense of alienation in alcoholism.

Passing may not be consciously intentional, however. A hearing lesbian client who had been raised within the deaf culture, besides having a considerable amount of survivor guilt about being able to hear, was, in fact, in the position of being able to be within the hearing world and yet she experienced a great deal of self-betrayal and alienation about it as though she were passing. After a long period of working with her in psychotherapy, I was able to point out how our experiences had been similar, because I am a woman of color who appears to be White. With a sense of relief, she understood why she had cried profusely at a movie years earlier that had portrayed a Black woman who had a White child. This represented her own difference which she had not previously recognized. After this moment in therapy, she was better able to put her difference into perspective rather than to feel that she was a victim of it.

Another aspect of passing is qualifying difference. Within groups who have internalized negative stereotypes, a hierarchy of deficit is sometimes established. A common hierarchy is the color code, for people of color, stated as "lighter is better," and among lesbians, the less masculine women are often seen as more adjusted. They are the ones who elicit the surprised comment from heterosexuals, "You don't look like a lesbian." Among ethnic groups it may be viewed as better not to have the accent or the characteristic body features of the group. Among the disabled, individuals with less obvious disabilities may be more accepted; among the aged, the ones who "don't look their age" are praised.

There is in the very process of establishing a hierarchy an implied nega-tivization of the trait that determines the difference. Although a particular minority individual might feel relieved to be less affected by deviant traits than some of his or her counterparts are, use of this strategy ultimately requires a dissociation from the group of origin and an implied assumption of the superiority of those who do not possess the apparent deficit. The inferiority of the minority group based on characteristics of difference is thereby reinforced.

CONFRONTATION

Confrontation, the second strategy for managing differences, occurs, lit-erally, when we face up to and look at our difference. It requires an ack-nowledgment to ourselves of who we are. In this acknowledgment there is a profound self-affirmation. We become visible to ourselves first and then to others.

Coming out is the primary technique of confrontation used by rejected groups within a society. The process of coming out involves a transfor-mation: *the transformation of an apparent deficit into a strength.* This can be the means of healing by groups or individuals. It can be a core issue in psychotherapy for individuals, and a basis for the healing of a group at a social level.

Several elements mediate this transformation: a) a recognition that one is not alone with a difference, which leads to a bridging of isolation and eventually to a building of community and support; b) sadness and anger at the previous rejection by ourselves and others of significant parts of ourselves which are now valued; c) a recasting of the past and a reowning of origins and history; and d) some kind of public acknowledgment of a new awareness of a group identity.

As indicated elsewhere (de Monteflores and Schultz 1978), the process of coming out is a process of development of identity, but it does not follow a simple linear progression. Coming out is also affected by envi-ronmental factors, employment, survival needs, and the strength of affiliations to various support networks, such as family, ethnic groups, and class.

To see others like ourselves can be the first acknowledgment that our differences can be valuable. We begin to see what had been there all along but had remained hidden. For example, one lesbian reported: "I didn't know it then, but I was in love with my best woman friend in high school." Even the more visible traits, like color and disability, can become revealed in a new light. One client said: "All my relatives had different shades of skin color, but we never talked about it in the family. It didn't exist."

The image we see of ourselves through identification with others may be uncomfortable at first, because the ideal image, what we are supposed to look like or be like, is not there. In the process of coming out, there is a need to unlearn the traits that made assimilation possible. In addition, considerable anger may be experienced at having had to deny important aspects of ourselves that defined difference.

A role of being a "super-minority" person denouncing the dominant culture may be necessary for some, but for most it is only a transitional stance. Continuing a "more-oppressed-than-thou" attitude usually signals an impasse in the development of a mature identity. The mature identity necessarily includes a recognition of sameness as well as difference. The articulation of these attributes requires a certain flexibility in boundaries, which comes out of an inner sense of security about individual identity.

Ghettoization

By choice, or circumstance, or both, many individuals find themselves living a significant part of their lives within the confines, geographical as well as psychological, of a subculture with which they closely identify. Such ghettoization is the third way in which differences can be managed. The members of the ghetto participate in its causes and its feasts, its institutions, and its values and develop close networks of support. By doing so they acquire credibility within that group and, in turn, receive the support and protection of the group. There is always a potential for experiencing rejection by others when leaving the group. For example, a lesbian can walk hand in hand with a woman lover through various areas of a city and experience many different climates of acceptance. The distance or closeness between the two women can reflect the rejection experienced in each neighborhood.

Some religious or political separatist groups may appear to choose a geographical or psychological ghetto. Their identity is felt to depend on a strong boundary, which requires considerable energy to maintain by means of rules and prohibitions. Great attention is given by these groups to avoidance of being penetrated by other modes of existence and to preserving the subculture by externalization of values, such as regulated patterns of dress and behavior. In some rural lesbian communes, for example, boy children are excluded. In such communes an implied fear seems to exist that if gender boundaries are not strengthened the group will cease to exist.

In some subcultures the confines of the ghetto are largely psychological. In these subcultures, values may be more diffuse but also more pervasive. They may manifest in subtle patterns of behavior that are not experienced as chosen, such as use of space, time, and communication patterns. An example of such a pattern was given by a working class Latina lesbian client who indicated in psychotherapy that she had become aware of space as a class issue between herself and her upper-middle-class lover. When they fought, her lover always seemed to "want space" to think things over. The client felt that when she was growing up conflict had to be dealt with right there and then because there was no other place to go. For these two women their differing needs for psychological space seemed to be rooted, in part, in their economically based patterns of use of physical space.

The folk generalization regarding "colored-people time," or Latino time, or other valuing of time within subcultures points to some important different psychological conditioning regarding perception of time by non-white and other groups. Whorf (1956), for example, observes: "The Hopi language is seen to contain no words, grammatical forms, constructions or expressions that refer directly to what we call 'time,' or to past, present or future" (p. 57). This difference is, in part, associated among some groups with a greater emphasis on inner reality and inner rhythms rather than on external structure, demands, and schedules. When a Latina client, for example, arrives consistently late for psychotherapy, her behavior could represent a transference reaction, it could mean that she has not been socialized into therapy, or it could simply be that she is attending to other matters that are equally as important to her as this arbitrary fifty-minute hour. A therapist must discriminate between and relate these possibilities by careful assessment of the details. The point is that all such behavior is not merely "acting out" but may reflect meaningful differences between therapist and client.

In summary, it is important to acknowledge the value of ghettoization as a strategy that permits individuals and groups to validate and protect their different values and perceptions through solidarity with their group.

SPECIALIZATION

Another strategy for coping with differences is seeing oneself as special as a function of having unique and therefore superior qualities: for example, being exotic, having special talents as a group, being better for having suffered or for surviving suffering, and seeing oneself as belonging to a "chosen" or exiled group.

The Exotic. The exotic is an attractive mutation. To be seen as such permits a fleeting and flattering sense of superiority, which unfortunately derives largely from external form and appearance rather than from substance. For example, high-status colleges court minority students in much the same way as they court prize athletes. Representing the exploitation of deviant traits as exotic is the popularity of the film *La Cage Aux Folles* and the play *Torch Song Trilogy,* both about gay male transvestites, and of *Personal Best,* the film about lesbian athletes.

A gay male may be the subject of curiosity as a novelty at a heterosexual dinner party. Dwarfs were the fools and jesters of many courts. While internalizing a sense of being exotic can be temporarily enhancing for an individual and a way of coping with difference, however, it is ultimately self-devaluing. It is a collusion with a majority perspective which denies the real and rejected status of an individual or group who are different within the larger society.

Groups that are different are alternately denigrated and made exotic. The function of such a splitting of attitude may be to place the different individual or group in a realm outside ordinary human intercourse, in order both to distance from them and to make them appear inhuman. To be made inhuman is to be placed in a category in which exploitation can easily be rationalized. It is not as easy to abuse someone whom we regard as equally human as ourselves.

The Person of Special Talents. The recognition of special talents or qualities in a particular group also represents a double-edged sword; specialization is also limitation. Ascribing a set of special traits to a group is a curious form of splitting which often serves to keep that group in its place.

In a recent movie, *Educating Rita,* a working-class English woman goes back to school because she believes that learning will free her from the unnamed oppression she feels all around her. Her teacher is an alcoholic Oxford don who attempts to infantilize her. His ultimate maneuver is overprotection. He treats her as a sort of noble savage, whose special qualities of honesty, directness, and feeling need to be set apart to be preserved from extinction. Her fear is that she will lose her identity through contamination by middle-class values. But Rita has the strength to risk learning the ways of the educated classes in order to have choice in both worlds. Fortunately, she recognizes that if she were to rely only on the "special" qualities attributed to her by others, she would be severely limited in the society.

The Sufferer. Among rejected groups there can arise a culture of victimization and a sense of being morally better for having suffered. There can be an unspoken conspiracy between oppressor and victim, which can appear to be sadomasochistic in quality. The more the victim is abused, the more he or she feels superior.

Sometimes, in a culture of victimization, being a victim *is* the identity. A therapist can become a covictim and collaborator in this drama. She or he can be intimidated and made to feel guilty by a minority person who is immersed in his or her sense of victimization. For example, a lesbian of color psychologically terrorized her White lover with guilt. The politically conscious White woman could never understand enough to compensate for the deprivation of self-esteem that the Third World woman had experienced, nor for her real disempowerment in the society. It would have been easy in this situation for a therapist to confuse the client's disadvantaged position in the world with the client's personal dynamics. The latter required the client to visit on her White lover all the abuse she had received from the society. At that point in the development of her identity as a minority person, this lesbian client could see her lover only as the enemy.

The Survivor. Closely allied to victimization is a sense of having survived. The survivor has a profound sense of having faced ultimate horror and having been spared. There seems to be a curious dual sense of being special and at the same time being at the mercy of greater and uncontrollable forces that could strike again unpredictably.

The individual survivor also experiences guilt for not having had to go through the same horrors the others had to experience. Examples of the horrors individuals have survived include the experiences of gay and lesbian adolescents who are sent to mental institutions by their parents to be cured of their sexual preference; those of young people who are expelled from college for writing a love letter to a same-sex friend; and the pain of the men and women who are beaten on the streets, dishonorably discharged from the armed services, or humiliated in the school yard or on the streets because of their nonstereotypical appearance as men or women.

Some individuals in a minority group may feel that having survived such abuse imposes a special sense of obligation toward the less fortunate in the group. They may experience an obligation to help others also survive their oppression or to take action designed to prevent a recurrence of victimization.

The Chosen. Historically, Jews have seen themselves as members of a chosen group. Religious beliefs and cultural practices have permitted them to translate the attacks on their group into a special identity and sense of destiny.

This strategy of dealing with difference can also be seen in some other groups and individuals. It involves associating difference with some spiritual or religious dimension. Underlying this dimension seems to be an assumption that being set apart has a dual and almost paradoxical meaning: of being a "curse" but also a "gift," for which the individual becomes obligated and therefore needs to render service.

An individual example of this is the American Indian *berdache.* He was a homosexual, sometimes cross-dressed, and was often in the position of being seen as "a magical person who played an established role in their culture" (Evans 1978:101). George Caitlin, in the early nineteenth century, speaking of the Sioux, the Sacs, and the Foxes, suggested a connection between the sacred and the cursed in the *berdache:* "and he being the only one of the tribe submitting to this disgraceful degradation, is looked upon as *medicine* and sacred, and a feast is given to him annually" (Katz 1976:302). Difference can be so startling that it is seen as something outside the natural realm, and occasionally to explain the mystery of difference a supernatural dimension must be posited.

The Exile or Expatriate. Sometimes members of a minority group subscribe to a belief in a golden age. This attitude involves a longing for a kind of lost Eden, a country of origin, or a country of the future, a utopia where everything is always better than here and to which they expect eventually to return. This may be true of exiled Cubans or of lesbians returning to the islands of Lesbos. For some groups such a vision appears to contribute both cohesiveness and hope, especially when present circumstances are unfavorable and when there is a persistent sense of not belonging.

Identifying oneself as an exile preserves the feeling of not belonging, but it also transforms it. The belief "I do not belong here" becomes translated into "I do not belong here, but I belong elsewhere, and that other place is as good, if not better, than here." It is possible that the country of origin, real or imagined, becomes more idealized the further it is from immediate reality. Some disappointment is bound to occur if the exiled person permits herself actually to return to the longed-for place. The exiled person may discover that she has become, without realizing it, somewhat assimilated to her more recent environment. In addition, the exiled individual may go through repeated crises in which the feeling of not belonging becomes reinforced. The strategy then becomes an identity.

The marginality of the exile can involve a negative self-definition, or it can be used positively. As a positive aspect of identity, the exile realizes that she cannot ever go back home in a literal sense, and that the place of origin is not a location but rather a frame of reference that amplifies and enriches her perception of herself in the world. In this case, marginality can become a stance that permits a broader perspective with input from two or more cultures and therefore with the potential for new insights which can produce creative change in the larger society.

IMPLICATIONS FOR THERAPY

The previous discussion described, from a social psychology perspective, the strategies used by groups and by individuals within groups to manage difference. In the present section it will be suggested that there are links between some of the strategies described earlier, specifically, assimilation and confrontation, and essential processes in the development of individual identity, such as merging and differentiation. In addition, I will attempt in the following discussion to focus on the impact of institutionalization of difference on the intrapsychic functioning of individuals. The relevance of exploring differences between psychotherapist and client will also be discussed, particularly how this may contribute to the development of self-esteem and how it may challenge power assumptions inherent in the structure of therapy. The dyad of therapist and client will be seen as a microcosm of power issues in the society, with the therapist carrying the majority view.

THEORETICAL FRAMEWORK: SELF-PSYCHOLOGY

Since the negativization of difference is based on assumptions about power, specifically that power differentials exist between different economic classes and that one group has the power to set norms for the rest of the society, power then becomes a central issue in minority therapy. Power, within a social psychology perspective as described in the foregoing section, can be associated with self-esteem from an intrapsychic perspective.

Self-psychology (Kohut 1971, 1977) provides a framework for an examination of the development of self-esteem in the individual. I will preface my discussion of Kohut and self-psychology by defining some of the terms that may not be understandable to readers unfamiliar with his theory: self-objects are for the child the inner representations of caretakers, or parents, which he or she sees as not emotionally separate from the self and which complete the self. Nuclear self is the earliest, most essential aspect of self. As distinguished from hereditary characteristics, the nuclear self is developed in early interaction with others, primarily the caretakers.

Kohut describes the earliest development of self and self-esteem as follows:

> At the moment when the mother sees her baby for the first time and also is in contact with him (through tactile, olfactory, and proprioceptive channels as she feeds, carries, bathes him) a process that lays down a person's self has its virtual beginning. . . . I have in mind the specific interactions of the child and his self-objects [the internalized parents] through which in countless repetitions, the self- objects empathically respond to certain potentialities of the child (aspects of the grandiose self he exhibits, aspects of the idealized image he admires, different innate talents he employs to mediate creatively between ambitions and ideals), but not to others. This is the most important way in which the child's innate potentialities are selectively nourished and thwarted. The *nuclear self* is not formed via conscious encouragement and praise, but by the deeply anchored responsiveness of the self-objects, which in the last analysis, is a function of the self-objects' own nuclear selves. (1977:100)

This development takes place within a "matrix of mutual empathy." Kohut identifies empathy as the most significant element in creating and transforming the internalized images of the parents to construct a stable and cohesive nuclear self. Later in this article the parallels between this process and the psychotherapy process will be explored.

But, following the example of any minority child, what kind of empathy is possible from parents who perceive their own differences as deficiencies that are mirrored in their children? What kind of integrated self is to be found in individuals for whom caretaking has been at the hands of parents who are themselves in part self-hating, or self-devaluing in some ways because they have been consistently rejected by the larger society and by their own self-objects?

Kohut (in Goldberg 1978) indicates that within the context of normal development there is a normal level of failure of empathy. It is within that context that this article attempts to explore the narcissistic injuries experienced by rejected individuals and rejected groups. These chronic narcissistic injuries may contribute to intrapsychic structural vulnerabilities in the emerging selves of children, so that a social problem is perpetuated as a serious intrapsychic conflict. A type of narcissistic disturbance may be created thereby, which may affect many minority individuals. It is not my aim here to suggest that all minority individuals have narcissistic personality disorders. I am speaking of areas of difficulty within the large frame of a healthy ego. In fact, we might say that all individuals probably experience some degree of narcissistic difficulties since any part of the self that is different is vulnerable to rejection by self-objects, whether parents or the larger social group.

I am also attempting here to integrate Kohut's conceptualization into a descriptive-explanatory framework spanning both intrapsychic and social aspects of a minority individual's experience, Kohut (1977) himself posits a "psychological principle of complementarity" (p. 78), derived from physics, which suggests that complementary approaches are required to explain psychological phenomena. I would like to suggest here that there is a need for complementarity in the theory and practice of minority therapy, between analytic (intrapsychic, psychodynamic, and developmental psychology) and ecopsychology, which situates the individual within his or her context or environment (socioeconomic, cross-cultural, and geographical settings). In this way we might broaden Kohut's concept of caretaking parents to incorporate a social/environmental *matrix* (from the Latin *mater*, mother), a mothering environment that can be more or less empathic or rejecting.

For minority individuals, union with an omnipotent self-object may never be fully achieved because of insufficient mutual empathy within the parent-child bond, as well as between the child-parent-society bond. That is, a sense of identification with a powerful image of the parents may be weakened. For the minority person both environment and family may cause a traumatic disturbance of empathy leading to loss of self-esteem. Also, a failure in the mirroring of the child by the parents and by the larger society may lead to a limited narcissistic disturbance in an otherwise healthy personality. Kohut (1971) describes this mirroring as parental response to the child, which includes appreciation of the child and of his achievements. As a result of this failure in mirroring, the minority individual does not acquire a sense of the right to succeed (p. 108), which gives an indication that a healthy narcissism was achieved.

Kohut (1971) is explicit in indicating that parents imprint the child with their attitudes and characteristics through mirroring. But if the child's narcissistic behavior is received by the parents with consistent ambivalence, negativity, or outright rejection, because of the parents' own damaged self-image and self-esteem, it would be safe to assume that the child's attitude toward himself or herself would also be at least in part negative.

Within Kohut's developmental model, it could be argued that the earlier in the development of a minority child the parent and the social/environmental matrix, as parent, fails to a) mirror the child's characteristics and attitudes in a positive manner or b) establish an omnipotent union with the child, the more insidious and pervasive the damage to self-esteem will be. (*Omnipotent union* is understood here as a bond in which the child identifies so closely with the idealized parent that she perceives the parent's qualities as her own and thereby experiences herself as powerful.) Therefore, traits on which a differential identity will later be established, which are genetically transmitted, or physically obvious at birth, such as gender, color, or physical impairment, would be the strongest determinants of positive or negative self-esteem, depending on the attitudes of the parents and the society, as parent, toward the specific trait. Equally important to the development of the nuclear self, however, is the socioeconomic environment, the class and culture of the individual, which also influence parental attitudes toward themselves, their children, and the society.

SELF-PSYCHOLOGY AND HOMOSEXUALITY

Homosexuality is obviously mirrored neither by heterosexual parents nor by the larger society. The early development of a homosexual identity in the child cannot be ascertained within present conceptualizations of homosexuality. It would be necessary to posit that a potential toward the development of adult homosexuality derives from aspects of the nuclear self which are either supported or inhibited by the parents and the environment. Most often these potentials would *not* be supported, and this would be traumatic to the developing self.

There are two difficulties in exploring the early development of homosexual identity. First is the persistent confusion between sex role and eventual adult sexual orientation. For example, a six-year-old tomboy will not necessarily develop into an adult lesbian. Cross-dressing or cross-playing are sex-role violations, but not necessarily indications of adult homosexual orientation. This misunderstanding may preclude the empathic mirroring or parental delight in the girl's individual characteristics, including her tomboyism.

A second difficulty in exploring the early development of homosexual identity results from the fact that children are not thought of as being sexual; therefore, same-sex attachments among prepubertal children are tolerated and generally are not appreciated for their role in early development toward adult homosexuality. In addition, a distinction must be made between homosexual *behavior* and homosexual *identity*. There is no true homosexual identity in childhood, just as there is no heterosexual identity, but there are behavioral precursors of adult homosexual or heterosexual identity. Since eventual adult homosexual identity is not assumed in the child in the way that heterosexuality is, however, the behavioral precursors of homosexuality are not seen as such and remain invisible to others and to the individual. This is why, as indicated in the earlier section on coming out, the development of an adult homosexual identity often involves a rediscovering and reowning of early homosexual behavior which had remained hidden.

The result of these assumptions, which are still invested with the weight of majority opinion and moral judgment, is that homosexuality is largely seen either as a late, environmentally influenced event or as a deviation from normative development rather than as a central aspect of the early development of identity.

The denial of sexuality in children, and the denial of homosexuality as well, makes homosexuality virtually invisible in childhood. In this regard the experience of gays is different from that of other minorities. Whereas with other minorities the experience of difference may be negative and yet unavoidably present while growing up, with gays the experience of being different is not supposed to have existed in childhood. Therefore, gays may have a susceptibility to invalidation different from that of ethnic minorities, for example, because of the former's pervasive invisibility.

DIFFERENCE AS A DYNAMIC CONCEPT IN PSYCHOTHERAPY AND THE IDEALIZING TRANSFERENCE

Suggesting that parental attitudes determine a child's nuclear self and sense of identity still ignores what those attitudes may be, what determines them, and what specific impact they may have. Developmental psychology, and more specifically psychotherapeutic practice, must incorporate a more active stance toward understanding and utilizing differences among individuals and groups.

The developmental approach, with its tendency toward universalizing ("everyone is like this") and making normative a particular perspective ("everyone should be like this"), in general ignores the specific effects of difference and the quality or uniqueness of each instance. Inherent in the developmental attitude is the assumption that human nature is understandable by reducing it to simple, universal traits that can be discovered and categorized. Development thereby appears to be controllable by being kept within those categories. Within such a developmental approach, universal traits acquire quantitative and statistical weight, the weight of the majority, while difference is relegated to the periphery of the so-called normal curve.

Kohut makes a significant departure from this position by indicating that, at least within psychotherapy, idiosyncratic behavior which may lead to failures of empathy is valuable and leads to important changes in treatment. In addition, in an insightful footnote, he suggests (Kohut 1971) an analogy which is relevant here when he points to "the phenomenon of social, racial, or national prejudice in which the ingroup, the center of all perfection and power corresponds to the grandiose self, while everything imperfect is assigned to the outgroup" (p. 106).

It could be said that the scientific method is the omnipotent parental image of a grandiose psychology that assigns imperfection to everything that does not fit its a priori biases and yield to its need for control through statistical consensus, verifiability, and repeatability. Psychology as a field may have to integrate its archaic narcissism into a more mature outlook by working through difference and coming to terms with that which is outside of itself, not controllable, Other. *Difference itself must be integrated as a dynamic concept in psychological theory and psychotherapy practice.*

But how is this to be done?

One approach to this issue is to explore the assumptions underlying the concepts of transference and countertransference and to review their implications for the practice of psychotherapy. Transference in psychotherapy is an *analogy*. Through it, the client-therapist relationship is made into an *as if* relationship in which the meaning of a *real* interaction (an interaction that is not representative of anything else except itself) is transformed into a *symbolic* one. We give power to the psychotherapy interaction to represent what is outside of it. We also give power to the psychotherapist to interpret the symbolism of the interaction. Whoever controls the symbols has power.

In addition, by the client's relinquishing power to the psychotherapist as interpreter, an omnipotent union is created. Kohut sees this in young children:

> The psyche saves a part of the lost experience of global narcissistic perfection by assigning it to an archaic, rudimentary (transitional) self-object, the idealized parent imago. Since all bliss and power now reside in the idealized object, the child feels empty and powerless when he is separated from it,

and he attempts therefore to maintain a continuous union with it. (1971:37)

An analogous relationship can be created in psychotherapy which Kohut (1971) calls the *idealizing transference*. Through imitative and identificatory behavior, the goal in therapy is for the therapist's power eventually to become the client's power.

The idea that minority persons should see therapists who are members of their own minority seems to be based on an intuitive sense of how the idealizing transference works. To be able to identify with another person who is also a minority member but who is perceived as being in a position of authority is the beginning of an acknowledgment of one's own power. This power by association can also operate between a nonminority mainstream therapist and a minority client if the client can develop a sense of identification with the therapist. This, of course, requires a great deal of sensitivity on the part of the therapist to the differences between herself and the client.

This idealization must eventually be modified through "actual experience" (Kohut 1971:40–41), for example, within the child-parent relationship, through the child's recognition of the actual qualities of the parents. Through the repeated experience of disappointment at the loss of omnipotent merging with the parent the child learns both about separation and difference, as well as about love. If this process is mediated by an empathic bond, the child will be able to grieve the loss of narcissistic union and to develop a true sense of self and an experience of caring for another. Some case material may serve to illustrate this point.

CASE I

After a recent knee operation I had been unable to see clients for a few weeks. On my return to work, I had attempted to explore a lesbian (Ms. A.) client's feelings about my surgery with no great success. One day, however, she saw me on the street on crutches. During the following session she was able to tell me how upset she had been to see me looking older and uncomfortable on my crutches. It was revealed that she was afraid that she was "too much for me to deal with."

Further exploration clarified that she was afraid I would not be able to take care of her. Her feelings were a projection of her own helplessness at being unable to take care of her mother, who had suffered from a progressive illness for many years and ultimately had died of it. This client had seen me previously as the able-bodied caretaker she had lost in her mother.

Her real experience of seeing my disability and the resulting deflation of my idealized and omnipotent image permitted her to grieve the loss of her own mother and feel stronger in her ability to take care of herself and others.

In the traditional nonempathic psychotherapy relationship, transference is focused on, to the exclusion of the "real" relationship. *Actual* experience is diminished and thereby limited or negligible, and *actual* difference is ignored. The illusion of sameness, with its concomitant sense of omnipotence, is preserved. The position suggested here is that in order to integrate the experience of difference into psychotherapy as a way of developing a more cohesive self and a sense of power in the world, psychotherapy must allow for a real dialogue, as well as a symbolic one.

There can be no empathic exchange unless there is a real dialogue. Ms. A. could not fully experience empathy for me as a real person until her acceptance of my vulnerability began to dissolve the projection onto me of her need for a strong and ablebodied mother. She was then, in turn, able to accept her own vulnerability and the fact that she could not take care of others perfectly. I also had a deeper understanding and fuller empathy for her when I became more aware of my limits as a caretaker as a result of my operation. Subsequently, as the idealizing transference dissolved, Ms. A. was able to confront me with the fact that I had, in a sense, also idealized her by seeing her as less disturbed than she had really felt. As a result of my idealization I had adopted a supportive stance which limited her ability to face and accept her real feelings.

A real dialogue in psychotherapy would demand that both actual and symbolic experiences of both psychotherapist and client be integrated. The psychotherapist would then not just be the object of projections on the part of the client but would also be a real person, separate and different from the client. Conversely, the client would not just be a client who projects onto the psychotherapist but would also be a real person, larger than his role as client. The following case material serves to illustrate these points further.

CASE 2

Ms. B., a Latina lesbian in her late twenties, identified with the fact that I had professional standing and credentials. She herself was in a Ph.D. program in liberal arts. Her family came from a semirural area where they had achieved lower-middle-class status. Her father was the manager of a service station. He had a drinking problem that did not seem to affect his work.

During his drinking binges, however, he permitted himself brief affairs with women which were very hurtful to his wife and family.

Ms. B. was very attached to her family. She was the oldest of four children, two sisters and a brother. She was committed to helping them go through college as soon as she received her degree and began teaching at a university. She also wanted to be a mother herself but realized she might have to choose between helping her siblings financially and having her own child. She consciously postponed the resolution of this conflict until she completed her doctorate.

Her research was completed by the time she began treatment with me, but she was having considerable difficulty writing the dissertation. This was made even more difficult by the recent breakup of her five-year relationship with another Third World woman. Her lover had ended their relationship by having an affair with another woman.

At the time of our first interview, Ms. B. was seriously depressed. She had suicidal thoughts, had difficulty sleeping and concentrating, and had very little energy for her work. She was also very suspicious of therapy because it appeared to contradict her political views and cultural norms. She was active politically and had a well-developed political philosophy regarding the oppression of minorities.

She came to see me because she had reached a moment of panic. She was very afraid of losing control and was feeling ashamed of being "weak" because she was not able to manage her life as she had done in the past. She was also afraid of becoming dependent on therapy. In addition, in her culture one did not see a stranger to talk about one's personal problems. She felt that was part of White culture. By coming to therapy she felt she was betraying both her principles and her culture.

Ms. B. had two specific reasons for choosing to see me in particular: first, she had read my article about therapy with Latina lesbians. She said in our first interview, however, that she largely disagreed with my views although she appreciated the fact that I had written the article. Second, Ms. B. had found out that I was also a mother. With these two areas of shared values, academics and motherhood, Ms. B. was able to suspend judgment and allow herself to enter into the process of therapy that would otherwise have been alien to her experience.

After her initial confrontation with me regarding my paper, Ms. B. settled into an immediate identification with me. It was as if she had taken me into her family as a kind of surrogate mother. Within this transferred relationship Ms. B. was able to grieve the loss of her lover relationship and begin to explore the deeper issues that led to the breakup, as well as her difficulty in completing her dissertation.

Although Ms. B. was considerably less depressed after two years in therapy, she was having difficulty letting go of her former relationship. At this point in therapy an unusual turn of events took place. Ms. B.'s ex-lover became involved with another long-term client of mine, Ms. C., who was a successful business woman. Ms. C. had not revealed the full name of the woman she was seeing, nor would she have had any reason to alert me to the possible complications that might develop, since, of course, she did not know of Ms. B.'s connection with me.

Ms. B. did find out this information, however, through a friend after the affair had been going on for several months. She was angry with me for not telling her. She felt betrayed and demanded that I terminate my other client, Ms. C., or she herself would leave therapy.

I went through great pains explaining to her that, first, I had not known, and second, even if I had known I could not have revealed that information to Ms. B. without breaking confidentiality with Ms. C. Third, I could not terminate with Ms. C. before the course of her treatment was completed.

Clearly, Ms. B. was feeling jealous, but what was most difficult for her to accept was that I could see a client who was as apolitical as Ms. C. Also, Ms. B. was indignant because Ms. C., she claimed, was involved in drug dealing and, in general, seemed to have very questionable ethics.

In Ms. B.'s eyes I seemed to be guilty by association. I had either to ally myself with her or against her. It did not seem sufficient to explore with her (which she could hardly tolerate) how our current situation replayed both her experience with her ex-lover and her own mother's experience with Ms. B.'s father, being deceived and abandoned for other women. My interpretation was that she was distorting our relationship to fit her expectation that she was going to be betrayed by someone she was close to, as her own mother had been betrayed by her father.

She began to close off to me and would not accept my interpretations. With her distrust and hostility increasing, Ms. B. brought back my published paper of which she had been originally critical and proceeded to tear it apart, critically, in the session. She had also found other papers I had written and used her political analysis to destroy them in my presence.

I began to understand that she also had been experiencing an internal battle in which she directed some of that rage at herself, albeit less dramatically. I was almost certain that it was that self-hate that prevented her from writing her dissertation. I was not sure, however, how to help her understand this and break the pattern. I also was beginning to realize that I was being worn down by her hostility and feeling betrayed myself. I found myself dreading the sessions and hoping she would, in fact, bring them to an end.

A few days before one of our sessions, a close friend and colleague called me to say that another therapist, Dr. D., had called her to make inquiries about me because she had seen a new client who had been in therapy with me. This client had suggested that I had been unprofessional and broken confidentiality. My friend was understandably concerned.

I decided to call Dr. D. and clear up the accusation. Dr. D. could not discuss the case without the client's consent, but, while talking to her I realized intuitively that Ms. B. had begun to act out her betrayal by seeing another therapist without telling me and undermining my reputation with Dr. D. Dr. D. was not sure whether this client, whom she could not name, describe, or discuss, was going to return. The client had indicated that she would "think about it and call back."

My consultant was out of town and I was not totally clear how I was going to deal with this issue. I was inclined to wait until I knew more precisely how to proceed; besides, I was aware that I had angry and frightened feelings about what had happened that I needed to work through myself.

Ms. B. seemed much calmer at the beginning of our next session. She was friendlier and more cheerful. She said she was reconsidering; that maybe she had been too rigid in her position and that she wanted to continue therapy for the time being even if I were to continue to see Ms. C.

I could not contain myself. I told her with obvious anger that although I did not have any solid evidence of her seeing another therapist, it had come to my attention that a "former" client of mine had put into question my professional ethics in a therapy session with a colleague. I asked her directly whether it had been she.

Ms. B. turned red and began to shake her head. Facing this wall of denial, I suddenly had an intuition of how my own personal issues had been getting in the way. I decided to take a risk and share my insights with her.

I began by saying that I knew how she must have been feeling these past weeks (and for much of her life) because I also was feeling betrayed. I went on to tell her how as a child I had experienced family dynamics that were similar to hers and how she and I had been taking turns playing the role of the deceived and abandoned woman.

Ms. B. lowered her head and began to cry. She said she had gone to another therapist in a fit of anger, and now she was very ashamed. She acknowledged that she had been frightened when she realized how important our relationship was to her, that she had been afraid that I would choose Ms. C. over her and that she had wanted to leave me as she felt I had left her.

After this session we were able to reestablish trust and begin to work through the issues that the crisis had raised.

By breaking out of the symbolic stance, breaking out of the roles of therapist and client, and having a real interaction, empathy became possible for both client and therapist. Empathy is identification that is mediated by real feelings for a real person. In the above case the crucial empathic experience was our shared experience of betrayal.

The idealizing transference creates a pseudoempathy through identification with a figure that is in part projected. The idealizing transference can also be seen, however, as a kind of rehearsal that creates the ground for genuine caring, based on actual (not projected) awareness of one's own and other's feelings.

It should be noted that the idealizing transference between a minority client and a minority therapist may be more intense than with a nonminority therapist in regard to the trait that sets a minority person apart, for example, ethnic identity or sexual preference. This may be due to the fact that the minority therapist can potentially reflect a positive image for someone who may have been repeatedly rejected because of that specific aspect of their identity. Because of the lack in her background of people with whom she could identify, Ms. B. identified with many aspects of my life.

By contrast, each confrontation of difference between a therapist and a client is experienced as a loss especially for minority clients for whom difference is largely associated with wounding. Confronting difference can be empowering for the client, however, if he or she is then able to differentiate *and still feel cared for and valued.* The client is able to do this if the therapist can model a healthy differentiation and self-esteem.

The key is confronting difference without loss of empathy or self-esteem. I was able not to take on the client's projection, to differentiate between her projection and my reality and thereby maintain my own self-esteem. Ms. B. had identified with many aspects of my life, but these had been felt as external to her, something idealized and out of reach. Our empathic confrontation permitted her also to separate her projection from my reality as a person.

Several issues are significant in the case of Ms. B.: the importance and function of the idealizing transference in minority therapy; the role of self-revelation by the therapist and the exploration of difference in psychotherapy; and the impact of self-revelation by the psychotherapist on the transference and countertransference. These will be discussed further in the sections that follow.

The Importance and Function of the Idealizing Transference in Minority Therapy

Ms. B. chose me as a therapist both because of my identity as a lesbian Third World mother and as a professional with an advanced degree. She projected onto me the image of integration of both worlds. Through her

identification with me she could magically experience a vicarious wholeness that permitted her to begin to take greater risks in exploring her own
issues. If she had not been able to identify with me she would not have
been able to begin treatment or to continue in it. Her idealizing transference, which I did not challenge in the early part of therapy, was an essential
forerunner of the process of integrating her identity and developing her
sense of self-esteem.

SELF-REVELATION BY THE THERAPIST

Several important points should be considered here: first, why self-reveal
at all; second, when is it appropriate to self-reveal in the course of treatment; third, and most important, what are the implications of self-revelation by a therapist for the transference and countertransference?

Ms. B. had at significant moments both exhibited curiosity about our
potential differences and at the same time shied away from verifying them.
The most relevant moments when she exhibited this ambivalence were
related to my political views and political involvement, my class background, and my potential associations with non-Third World women or
with nonpolitical Third World women. She often mentioned political
events that she felt I might be interested in, but she never followed up
with inquiries as to why I was not there.

It was clear that Ms. B. was not yet ready to face our potential differences. For my part, I had some investment in being a model for this bright
young woman onto whom I projected my need for a more active political
awareness. In spite of my countertransference, specifically, my admiration
for her political analysis and concurrent feeling of intimidation by it, I
recognized that it was not appropriate for me to focus on our differences
until Ms. B. herself was ready to do so.

At the point when Ms. B. confronted me regarding Ms. C., she had
established a therapeutic alliance with me, worked through most of her
depression, and begun to feel stronger about her work. Her identity was
more integrated and she did not have to depend as much on me for a
sense of wholeness. She had, however, become rather isolated, in part
because of her unwillingness to compromise her political views but also
because of her unconscious vulnerability.

It was clear that Ms. B. was then in a much stronger position and better
able to experience our differences. At that point, however, it was easier
for her to create a situation in which I could be blamed for the crisis rather
than to look at her own inability to deal with differences in close interpersonal relationships. When I confronted her I was not certain that our

therapeutic alliance would be strong enough to contain the feelings that would ensue.

It is interesting to note that Ms. B. had attacked precisely the aspect of my life, my professional standing, that she most idealized. Her rage and subsequent acting out were a response to the threatened loss of self-object. She had incorporated me as a self-object to complete herself. I dared to be different from her projection of me, which led her to feel a temporary lack of cohesion of self to which she responded with rage.

The question as to whether a therapist should reveal personal information to a client is a complex one. I cannot claim to have a well-formulated theoretical framework within which to justify my revealing an aspect of my personal life. In retrospect, I can say that I was moved by a desire to be genuine, as well as by an unconscious understanding that Ms. B. was also capable of genuine empathy. In the light of her response, it seems that in assuming such empathy, I did in fact elicit it from her. At this point in therapy she was able both to be different from me and to experience caring for me at the same time. The essential healing aspect of the interaction was not the self-revelation itself, but rather the experience of empathy, in the present, within the context of differentiation.

At the time when I self-revealed, Ms. B. had already begun to explore our differences. It is true that this was mediated by a distorted view of me and a great deal of anger that had been transferred from her father, and more recently her lover, onto me. It also indicated, however, that she had gained enough strength and self-esteem that she could begin to challenge me.

I stepped outside of the idealized invulnerable role because that role was constricting me, just as her role was constricting Ms. B. The failure of empathy on my part was also a sign of strength: I could no longer let myself be verbally abused by her. Her projection had gone beyond the symbolic transference to a destructive acting out by impugning me to another therapist. My modeling self-valuing behavior was ultimately important for the client. I was able to defend my own wounded narcissism, unlike Ms. B.'s mother, who was unable to protect herself from Ms. B.'s father's abuse.

SELF-REVELATION, TRANSFERENCE, AND COUNTERTRANSFERENCE

Although there has been documentation to the contrary (Jourard 1964; Searles 1979), the fear persists among many psychotherapists that self-revelation on their part will largely gratify the client and destroy the transference. It is my position that transference will occur in any relationship, including therapy, whether it is promoted or not. Transference will continue to occur as long as projection occurs. The issue is how to use both the transference and countertransference reactions as tools for healing deficits in self-esteem, rather than as tools for assimilation to psychotherapy norms.

There are dangers, however, in relinquishing hiddenness and pursuing a real as well as a symbolic dialogue with a client. First, there is the danger of ignoring pathology in favor of social analysis and social activism. As explored at the beginning of the article, social analysis and hypotheses regarding the contexts within which intrapsychic conflict arises are essential to the study of individual and group differences. It was suggested that a complementary approach, combining intrapsychic and environmental factors, would be most fruitful because social structures and social issues, which affect us all, cannot by themselves account for individual pathology. The following case is illustrative of this point.

CASE 3

Ms. E., a working-class Third World lesbian with whom I shared a common language and culture, also had a borderline personality disorder. As such, part of her defense posture was to create a split between good Third World people and bad Whites, as well as between good working-class values and bad middle-class values.

Ms. E. had been raised in a family where there had been many secrets and where consequently there had been a great deal of distortion of reality and distrust. Also, the father, who had abandoned the family, was middle-class, while the mother, who was working-class, raised the children. The mother had been bitter and overworked.

In a premature attempt to be "honest" and to face our differences, I had revealed that I came from a middle-class family. In her positive transference Ms. E. could see me as an exception to her views about middle-class people. She granted me special status. But it was a specialness she conferred on me and therefore one she could take away when her negative transference held sway. At those moments she used her criticism of the middle class as a way of trying to control any behavior of mine of which she disapproved. For example, when she received a substantial raise on her job and I suggested that it would be appropriate for her to begin paying my full fee, Ms. E. resorted to accusations of my exploiting her, as all middle-class people exploited the working classes.

Self-revelation on my part fed into Ms. E.'s defense structure. It permitted her to rationalize her split rather than resolve it. There was no possibility of healing early narcissistic wounds and promoting self-esteem by identificatory maneuvers. She could neither totally identify in omnipotent union nor separate. With this client, hiddenness would have served over a long period of time to neutralize her projections and her anger.

The second danger of abandoning a neutral, hidden posture as a minority therapist is *overinvolvement,* which presents the risk of losing the boundaries of the role, becoming a real person in the client's life, and having obligations and demands to meet outside the therapy hour. Although it is also true that the distance that is commonly maintained, and sometimes to excess, between therapist and client is in large part an artifact of urban life and the demands for practicality and efficiency, in minority communities therapists often find themselves socializing with friends who are also friends of a client, or attending the same clubs or institutions as their clients. Some social involvement with clients outside the therapy hour is a fact in minority communities. This appears to promote a tendency toward merging between client and therapist and a kind of assimilation into the client's world.

I will cite an example of what can happen in the transference as a result of a social encounter between therapist and client. A curious situation was created when I agreed to participate in a benefit for a Third World lesbian mother. I was asked to read poetry in Spanish. Three clients of mine were in the audience. It was interesting to note that each one of them responded to me in a way that was characteristic of the individual transference relationship: one felt inadequate, another made remarks that indicated curiosity about my private life, and the third treated me as part of her family. Each one explored in a subsequent session how she had felt about being at a quasi-social event with me, except the one who felt inadequate. She failed to mention the event at all. When I realized that this client was not going to bring it up, I spoke about it. She said that she had felt bad because she did not feel she could ever speak in public. Further exploration revealed that she had considerable negative feelings about not being able to speak Spanish.

A real dialogue between therapist and client, one in which both reveal themselves, may also encourage more countertransference reactions than therapists usually allow. It is here that the power imbalance in psychotherapy can be most keenly exposed. The countertransference mirrors the transference in its tension between real and symbolic issues. But there is a difference. The countertransference more directly threatens the power invested in the therapist by both the therapist and the client and therefore more profoundly threatens the structure of therapy. This threat arises from the fact that a countertransference reaction may reveal that the therapist has unresolved issues as does the client. The therapist's awareness of some countertransference reactions can arouse feelings of similarity to the client, which are threatening to the therapist; if these reactions were revealed to the client, they might impinge on the idealizing transference, as in the case above.

Searles indicates that "there is some basis in reality for the patient's 'delusional transference' reactions" (1979:374). If the therapist accepts this fact, the client will have a better chance of integrating reality and diminishing projections. Searles emphasizes countertransference reactions in his work because he feels, as I do, that the personality and sense of identity of the therapist is "a most sensitive and reliably informative scientific instrument providing data as to what is transpiring, often in areas not verbally articulated by the patient, in the treatment situation" (p. 376).

The strength of the traditional taboo against dealing with the countertransference reactions directly with a client points to how much investment there is in the power structure of therapy and in the power differential of the two roles. Maintenance of the stance of the hidden therapist may ultimately not protect the client's best interest as much as it protects the therapist's claim to power and his or her investment in omnipotence and perfection.

Therapists cannot adhere rigidly to a stance of hiddenness when it is difference itself, and the sense of being seen as less than human, that cause pain. A balance must be created in therapy between the need of the client to idealize a therapist and thereby project her unresolved issues and the need to differentiate through genuine yet empathic interactions.

Minority therapists particularly, but all therapists as well, must *come out* and reveal themselves because they must model being genuine. Being genuine promotes self-esteem because it requires both acceptance of whoever we are and relating to another within the framework of acceptance of self. A benefit, as well as a risk, of having a more genuine relationship between a client and a therapist is that both persons change in such a relationship.

SUMMARY

To facilitate empowerment and self-esteem in minority clients, therapists must first give up the goal of adjustment to the ideals of the dominant group. They must begin to view mental-emotional health not only as being in harmony with prevalent values, but also at times as being at odds with them. Such change will involve adopting *a dynamic view of difference,* that is, that the process of confronting difference will result in change in both therapist and client. This view will also require an understanding of the values that psychotherapy promotes, overtly or covertly, and an acceptance that they are not absolute but rather open to many revisions.

Psychotherapy itself generally ignores difference overtly and institutionalizes it by establishing norms to which the client is expected to assimilate. One of these norms is the concept of transference and the practice by the therapist of remaining hidden as a technique to promote projection. This norm invests in the therapist the power to interpret the meaning of the therapeutic interaction, thereby disempowering the client or conferring on him or her only a vicarious power.

Assimilation into the symbolism of the transference, or being socialized into being a client, can be justified only if it is seen as an early stage in the reconstruction of the client's self-esteem. Confrontation of differences at a later stage is essential in that it begins to assume the strength of the client and validates his or her culture. At this stage, self-revelation by the therapist may be appropriate in order to initiate a real dialogue within which difference can be worked through. The exploration of the two cultures of therapist and client is a valid subject for therapy because in this process each person acquires greater strength.

In this endeavor the psychotherapist working with minority clients (and all clients are minority clients in a sense because all feel disempowered in some way as a result of their differences) must initially embrace the universe of the client. The attitude of the therapist must be analogous to that of a parent receiving the rightful narcissistic-exhibitionistic strivings of the child. This facilitates understanding of the forces and the history that have shaped the client. The therapist must find empathically in himself the same issues and the same environments with which the client struggles and must live in them with the client, re-creating a kind of omnipotent union. Within this matrix their differences can also be explored and validated.

This process of intimate exploration and rediscovery of the client's history, and rediscovery of her or his present world is itself the process of self-validation, empowerment, and creation of self-esteem. Through it the psychotherapy bond becomes a model for reuniting with others, both through acceptance and encouragement of narcissistic strivings as well as through exploration of differences. Finally, the study of this process in minority therapy can contribute to mainstream psychology and psycho-therapy in general by developing an effective model for dealing with being different and for learning to use differences for creative change.

REFERENCES

de Monteflores, C., and Schultz, S. 1978. Coming out: Similarities and differences for lesbians and gay men. *Journal of Social Issues* 34(3):59–72.

Evans, A. 1978. *Witchcraft and the Gay Counterculture.* Boston: Fag Rag Books.

Goffman, E. 1963. *Stigma: Notes on the Management of Spoiled Identity.* Englewood Cliffs, N.J.: Prentice-Hall.

Goldberg, A., ed. 1978. *The Psychology of the Self: A Casebook with the Collaboration of Heinz Kohut.* New York: International Universities Press.

Jourard, S. 1964. *The Transparent Self.* Princeton, N.J.: Van Nostrand.

Katz, J. 1976. *Gay American History.* New York: Thomas Crowell.

Kohut, H. 1971. *The Analysis of the Self.* New York: International Universities Press.

Kohut, H. 1977. *The Restoration of the Self.* New York: International Universities Press.

Searles, H. 1979. *Countertransference and Related Subjects.* New York: International Universities Press.

Whorf, B. L. 1956. An American Indian model of the universe. In J. B. Carroll, ed., *Language, Thought and Reality: Selected Writings of Benjamin Lee Whorf.* Cambridge, Mass.: MIT Press.

9

"You're a What?":
Family Member Reactions
to the Disclosure of Homosexuality

Erik F. Strommen

The present review summarizes what is known about reactions of family members to disclosure of homosexual identity, both within the family of origin and in families where the disclosing member is a spouse or parent. It is suggested that the traumatic nature of family member reaction consists of two related processes: a) the application of negative values about homosexuality to the disclosing member, and b) a perception that homosexual identity negates or violates previous family roles. Future research in this complex and understudied area could reveal much about the nature of both homosexual identity and family relationships.

Homosexuality has been a topic of psychological scrutiny since the emergence of psychology as a discipline in the late 1800s. The traditional orientation of homosexuality research has been etiological in nature, with homosexuality being viewed as either a pathological syndrome or as a set of learned pathological behaviors (Morin 1977; Turnage and Logan 1975). The removal of homosexuality from the official list of psychopathologies in 1973 (American Psychiatric Association 1980; Stoller 1973) brought on a shift in research orientation from a clinical focus to one of describing and defining the exact nature of "being homosexual." Homosexual individuals, rather than the abstract entity "homosexuality," have become the object of study. One of the most striking results of this change in perspective has been the somewhat belated discovery that gay people are members of families, not simply isolated case histories. This article reviews the available literature on gay people and their families in an attempt to summarize what is known about how the family reacts to the presence of a homosexual member and what these reactions may reveal about the nature of family relationships.

THE NATURE OF DISCLOSURE

Having to reveal or explicitly identify one's sexual preference to one's family is a familiar topic in research on homosexual identity. Contemporary Americans view homosexuality not simply as an affectional preference, but as an intrinsic social identity. As Warren (1980) put it, "Logically, homosexuality refers to a type of behavior rather than to a condition. However, homosexuals are viewed generally not just as people who do a certain type of thing, but, rather, as people who are a certain type of being" (p. 124). This "certain type of being" is defined as membership in a stigmatized minority that is the subject of severe negative sanctioning in popular social values (Plummer 1975; Warren 1980). This negative sanctioning has complex social, historical, and religious origins, and has led to the formation of a distinct satellite culture composed of self-identified gay people (Boswell 1980; Humphreys and Miller 1980; Licata and Peterson 1981). It has also led to the personal and social phenomena of having to "come out" or explicitly declare one's homosexuality as a part of one's identity, in defiance of social values (Dank 1972; Ponse 1980; Saghir and Robins 1973; Weinberg 1972).

The acquisition of a gay identity appears to be a complex, lengthy process in which the actual disclosure of one's homosexuality to others is a late event (Cass 1979, 1984). Disclosure becomes necessary because, unlike skin color or gender, which are overt physical indicators of social group membership, homosexuality is a way of feeling and acting; homosexuals are thus "invisible" both as individuals and as a group (Plummer 1975; Warren 1974; Weinberg and Williams 1974). In addition, there exists a "heterosexual assumption" that presumes membership in the heterosexual majority for all individuals, unless otherwise demonstrated (Ponse 1980). People with homosexual identities are therefore not only invisible to others, but are also actively misclassified by others as heterosexual. Homosexuals are thus required to negate explicitly this classification by disclosing their identity, in order to prevent others from developing and acting on false expectations of their behavior. Here, the term *disclosure* will be used to refer to this explicit revealing of one's sexual preference to others, particularly family members; the term *coming out* will be used only to refer to a gay person's self-realization of his or her homosexuality.

DISCLOSURE TO THE FAMILY OF ORIGIN

PARENTS

It is generally held that approximately 5 to 10 percent of the U.S. population defines itself as predominantly gay or lesbian (Bell and Weinberg 1978; Kinsey, Pomeroy, and Martin 1948; Kinsey et al. 1953). These people are obviously somebody's children, and it is not surprising that the parents of homosexuals are the relatives most often discussed in the psychological literature. This focus on parents has its origins in traditional psychoanalytic theory, which has long held that adult homosexuality has its origins in a disturbance of parent-child interactions in early childhood (Bieber 1962; Buxbaum 1959). When nonpatient samples of homosexual persons are studied, however, the results for both gay men and lesbians are consistent: homosexual adults view their parents and their upbringing as positively (or as negatively) as nonpatient heterosexual adults (Robinson et al. 1982; Shavelson et al. 1980; Siegelman 1974a, b, 1981).

Parental reaction to disclosure by a child has been studied primarily from a counseling perspective. This appears to be due to the fact that parental reaction is invariably negative, with the disclosure being perceived as a crisis by the family. Weinberg (1972) and Jones (1978) reported parental reactions as consisting of two facets. The first is the result of the parents applying their negative conceptions of homosexual identity to their child. This creates for the parent a subjective perception that the child is suddenly a stranger, "a member of another species, someone whose essential wants are unrecognizable and different" (Weinberg 1972:97). This perception apparently stems partly from the misconceptions the parent has about homosexuals (i.e., my son is a child molester, my daughter is a pervert), and partly from the fact that there is no family role for homosexuals; the child's new identity thus cuts him or her off from the family by causing the parents to apply their negative misconceptions to their child, and by negating the previous role or identity the child had as a family member (Collins and Zimmerman 1983; DeVine 1984).

The second facet of parental reaction is a direct product of the first, namely, a powerful feeling of guilt and failure. The parents believe that they have somehow caused their child to become homosexual, and are therefore responsible for their child's new, alien identity. Fairchild and Hayward (1979) provided several excellent autobiographical accounts, written by parents of gays and lesbians, which lend support to the theory that viewing the child as unfamiliar or estranged, combined with a feeling of personal responsibility for making the child this way, plunges parents into an emotional and psychological crisis.

Two studies taking a family systems perspective have attempted to identify specific patterns of reaction to a child's disclosure and have tried to isolate the variables that dictate the nature of parental response to disclosure (Collins and Zimmerman 1983; DeVine 1984). DeVine (1984) described the family system, particularly parents, as advancing through a series of states of awareness and acceptance of their child's homosexuality: a) *subliminal awareness*, where the child's gay identity is suspected due to behavioral and communicational patterns; b) *impact*, characterized by the actual discovery or disclosure, and described by the crisis atmosphere outlined above; c) *adjustment*, where the child is initially urged to change orientation or keep the homosexual identity a secret, thus maintaining respectability for the family; d) *resolution*, where the family mourns the loss of the fantasized heterosexual role for the child and dispels negative myths about homosexuality; and, finally, e) *integration*, where a new role for the child, and new behaviors for dealing with the child's gay identity, are enacted.

DeVine is careful to note that the family may stay fixed at any of these levels indefinitely, rather than necessarily achieving the (most desirable) end stage. The movement through these stages is governed by three aspects of the family as a system: the "cohesion" or closeness of family members, the "regulative structures" or rules that govern family member behavior, and the "family themes," or defining values and behaviors that dictate the family's view of themselves and their interaction with the larger community. Collins and Zimmerman (1983) made a similar point, stating that the major factors affecting reaction to a child's disclosure are the regulative structures and "family themes" of the particular family under consideration.

Certain themes are thought to be especially relevant to family reaction to disclosure. Weinberg (1972) identified two potentially conflicting "parenting themes" toward children that he viewed as influencing parental reaction to disclosure: a "love" or acceptance theme, which motivates the parent to try to accept the child's identity, and a "conventionality" theme, which urges parental rejection of the child in accord with social values. DeVine (1984) mentioned three themes that are likely to act as a source of severe conflict: a) "maintain respectability at all costs," which implies rejecting or censuring the gay family member as a way to avoid loss of status in the community; b) "as a family we can solve our own problems," which implies a lack of openness to alternative or unfamiliar values and suggests that the deviant family member is a "problem" that needs to be "fixed"; and c) "be as our religion teaches us to be," which implies rejection of the family member if homosexuality is negatively sanctioned by the family's religious values (DeVine 1984:11).

Collins and Zimmerman (1983) also reported that religion plays a large part in determining family reaction. This is certainly not surprising: it is well known that both official religious teaching and the social traditions that stem from them negatively sanction homosexual behavior in both sexes (Boswell 1980; Hiltner 1980; McNeill 1976). There is also indirect evidence to suggest that family values in regard to traditional sex roles could play a role in family reaction. Individuals possessing rigid, separate roles for the sexes are less likely to be accepting of any gay person, family member or otherwise (MacDonald 1974; MacDonald and Games 1974; Storms 1978; Weinberger and Millham 1979).

In recommending therapeutic guidelines, both DeVine (1984) and Collins and Zimmerman (1983) agreed that mourning for the lost family member, or the hoped-for role for the child, is to be encouraged. The goal is that a new role, more congruent with reality, may then be substituted for the old. The inability to adopt a new role, however, may result in the family simply casting out the child as an unacceptable family member. If the family member is an adult, or living independently of the parents, this is primarily an emotional tragedy; if the child is an adolescent, it can be much worse. Dank (1972) suggested that coming out and disclosure may be occurring at younger ages in our society, due, in part, to an increased emphasis on sexuality in general, the tolerance of homosexual behavior, and the availability of information concerning homosexuality. Whether or not this is true, there is disturbing evidence that the dramatic rise in teenage male prostitution in the United States is at least partially due to the casting out of gay adolescents by their parents (Bales 1985).

Siblings

While researchers have focused attention on the parents in the families of gay persons, there has been little discussion of the effects of disclosure on siblings. Jones (1978) suggested that sibling reactions are similar to those of parents: the sibling views the disclosing member as a stranger, assigning him or her the stigmatized role of homosexual (with all the negative values and misconceptions that entails), and no longer as a family member. There is, however, no guilt or self-blame reported on the part of siblings. The nature of sibling reaction is definitely a topic for future research, for there is evidence that siblings derive identity status as well as intimacy from one another (Schvaneveldt and Ihinger 1979). The specific variables contributing to sibling reaction, and how they are similar to and different from those affecting parental reaction, could tell us much about the nature of these family relationships. Both Jones (1978) and DeVine (1984) suggested that family members are disclosed to incrementally, one at a time, with the emotionally closest member being told first, and suggested that siblings are disclosed to in advance of parents. This, too, is a topic for future research. If siblings are the first to be disclosed to, their reactions could play a key role in determining parental reaction, either lessening or increasing its severity. To date, no research has considered sibling-parent interaction in reaction to disclosure.

GRANDPARENTS

The family of origin does not consist solely of parents and siblings. Grandparents are significant members of the family whose influence extends not only over their own children, but their grandchildren as well (Matthews and Sprey 1985; Troll 1982). Grandparents as family members have only recently been studied empirically, so it is not surprising that current research on disclosure to the family contains no references to grandparent reactions. It has been shown that different family generations differ in their opinions on family issues, but not on political ones (Douglass, Cleveland, and Maddox 1974). This finding makes it unclear to what degree grandparent reactions to homosexuality (which has both familial and political aspects) are similar to or different from parental reactions within a given family. Given the complete lack of data on grandparents to date, we simply do not know. As the U.S. population continues to age, however, grandparents will become an increasingly important segment of society and the family. Their reactions to disclosure by grandchildren is a topic that must be addressed if a complete picture of family reactions is to be assembled.

DISCLOSURE TO SPOUSES AND CHILDREN

HUSBANDS AND FATHERS

A review of the various nonpatient studies of gay men reveals that the percentage of each sample that has been or currently is married is between 14 percent and 25 percent, with 20 percent being a safe estimate. About half of these marriages produce children, meaning that approximately 10 percent of gay men are fathers as well (Harry 1983). The reasons that gay men marry are many, and include a) belief that homosexuality was only incidental to their identity at the time of marriage; b) lack of awareness of their homosexuality at the time of marriage; c) family pressure to marry; d) belief that marriage was the only way to achieve a happy adult life, regardless of sexual orientation; e) belief that marriage would help them overcome their homosexuality; f) a desire for children; and, of course, g) honest love for their spouses (Bell and Weinberg 1978; Bozett 1980; Dank 1972; Jones 1978; Nugent 1983).

For many of these men, there is no disclosure to their families, even though they may have come out to themselves and other gay persons, and are actively engaged in at least casual, anonymous sexual encounters, if not a long-term affair with another man (Bozett 1980, 1981; Humphreys 1970; Saghir and Robins 1973; Spada 1979; Voeller and Walters 1978). The reasons given for deliberate nondisclosure are both emotional and legal. Concern about the reaction of wives and children, as well as fears about job security and social status, are commonly cited.

Some research has suggested that nondisclosing married homosexual men experience their husband or father role (or both) as incompatible with their homosexual identity (Bozett 1981; Jones 1978; Ross 1971). Similar to parents and siblings, who feel alienated from the homosexual family member, these men seem to experience an alienation from themselves. They feel that their family roles cannot be reconciled with their homosexuality, and that they have two distinct, conflicting identities. There is qualitative evidence to suggest that this conflict results from having internalized the negative values of society toward homosexuality. These men see their homosexual identity as bad or undesirable, and their family identities as good, and are unable to picture the two combined. They report feeling that they are less than ideal husbands and fathers precisely because they must split their lives into two distinct parts (Bozett 1980; Humphreys 1970; Ross 1983). These men are often unhappy with their marriages as well, but report that they stay married because of concern for their children (Bozett 1980, 1981; Ross 1971; Saghir and Robins 1973).

Men who do disclose to their families present a different picture. There is often a period of casual, anonymous sexual encounters prior to disclosure, accompanied by great personal anxiety over being duplicitous with one's family; the desire to relieve this anxiety plays a role in deciding to disclose (Bozett 1980, 1981, 1982; Humphreys 1970). Surprisingly, there has been little systematic research exploring the specific reasons why some men eventually choose to disclose to their wives, and some do not. Bozett

(1982) suggested that two variables that contribute to disclosure are the husband's own self-awareness concerning his sexuality and the timing of this awareness with events in the ongoing marriage relationship. Men aware of and acting on their homosexuality prior to marriage reported a gradual distancing from their wives during the tenure of the marriage. Disclosure occurred because these men felt the need to be true to their hidden feelings.

In contrast, men who "awakened" to their homosexual feelings in the course of the marriage tended to experience "sharp conflict," a crisis brought on by their guilt over their homosexual feelings and activity. This guilt led to scapegoating of family members and breakdowns in family communication, prompting disclosure as a resolution to the family disruption. Often a change in the family structure, such as the possibility of a new child, or the children having left the home for college, precipitated this type of sharp conflict disclosure. Although several styles of adaptation to disclosure by spouses have been described, such as an asexual friendship within the marriage, or a semi-open relationship, divorce is the most common reported and expected outcome (Bozett 1981; Coleman 1985b; Collins and Zimmerman 1983; Gochros 1985; Miller 1979b; Ross 1972; Saghir and Robins 1973).

The specific reactions of wives to disclosure constitutes an understudied area. There is indirect and anecdotal evidence that the wives of disclosing gay men initially react in a manner similar to that of parents. They report feeling as if they "don't know" their husbands, and feel that they have failed as wives or somehow caused their husbands to become homosexual. Lingering hostility and bitterness is uncommon, but has been reported (Bozett 1981; Gochros 1985; Miller 1979b; Ross 1983). A difficulty with this research, however, is that little detailed work has been done directly with these women; published studies rely predominantly on the disclosing husband as a source of information about the marriage and the spouse's reaction. Yet, there have been notable exceptions.

Hatterer (1974), taking a psychoanalytic viewpoint, suggested that the long-term maintenance of a heterosexual woman/homosexual man marriage relies in part on the woman's need to maintain specific types of relationships with men. She suggested that these women "know but don't know" that the husband is gay (and therefore unable to give them a full, adult heterosexual relationship), and that these women may even gravitate to gay men in order to create and sustain the maladaptive relationship they need. Similarly, Coleman (1985b) noted that many of the wives of the gay men in his sample could be characterized as dependent on the husband, clinging to the marriage even in the face of its obvious inability to provide the type of relationship they desire.

Gochros (1985), reporting on a large sample of wives, found that disclosures were often gradual rather than abrupt, and that women's reactions depended largely on the quality of the relationship between the woman and her husband, the timing of the "official" disclosure in relation to other life stresses (such as childbirth, illness, and so on), and the woman's attitudes toward homosexuality. Once again, the wives' reactions seem reminiscent of those of parents: they report feeling shocked and stunned, and then experience a feeling of self-blame or guilt—Did I do this to myself? Have I failed as a wife? Gochros suggested that a significant aspect of the wife's reaction is the degree to which her coping mechanisms allow her to sort out the confusion, stress, and new information that accompanies the disclosure. Similar to other studies, she found that more than two-thirds of the marriages in her sample ended in divorce.

Disclosure to children represents another scantily studied topic. Bozett (1980) reported that gay fathers disclose in both direct and indirect ways. Direct disclosure is accomplished through explicit verbal admission. Indirect disclosure involves demonstrating affection for another man in the children's presence, leaving gay-oriented reading material out for children to see, or using other nonexplicit clues. Maddox (1982) and Bozett (1980) both reported that although gay fathers stated that direct disclosure was preferred, it was often motivated by external pressures, such as the need to explain parent divorce or cohabitation with a same-sex partner. This suggests that direct disclosure may be motivated as much by necessity as by a specific desire to be open and honest with the child.

Jones (1978) suggested, however, that gay fathers do choose to disclose, but prefer to wait until the child is old enough to comprehend the situation, usually in adolescence. Miller (1979a), although giving no hard numbers on how many of the forty men in his sample had disclosed to their families, reported that they felt the disclosure had brought them closer to their families by removing an unspoken obstacle in their sharing of personal feelings. This perception was shared by the majority of children interviewed as well. Bozett (1980) reported similar findings from a sample of eighteen gay fathers. Gay fathers felt that disclosure was important to their role as fathers, and that nondisclosure created a psychological distance between them and their children. Nondisclosing fathers apparently see this distance as a reasonable price to pay for avoiding the conflict and potential negative sanctioning that would accompany disclosure, especially if their wives were undisclosed to and might be told by the children (Bozett 1981; Miller 1979a).

WIVES AND MOTHERS

Lesbians in heterosexual marriages present a more complex and underresearched picture than do gay men. There appear to be fewer lesbians than gay men at all ages (Bell and Weinberg 1978; Kinsey, Pomeroy, and Martin 1948; Kinsey et al. 1953). Almost one-third of all lesbians have been married, however, with approximately half of these marriages producing children (Bell and Weinberg 1978; Saghir and Robins 1973; Schafer 1977). Thus, approximately 16 percent of lesbians are mothers. Lesbians appear to be more likely to marry, possibly as a consequence of the fact that they come out several years later, on average, than do gay men (Bell and Weinberg 1978; Saghir and Robins 1973; Schafer 1977). Because they realize their homosexuality after the popular marrying ages of twenty-one to twenty-three, they are more "at risk" for marriage than are gay men, who typically come out in their late teens (Harry 1983; Jones 1978).

Similar to gay men, lesbians marry for reasons of social conformity, family pressures, desire for a stable family life, and love for their spouses (Hanscombe and Forster 1982; Kirkpatrick, Smith, and Roy 1981; Saghir and Robins 1980). Unlike gay fathers, however, there has been little direct research on how lesbians think about their potentially conflicting identities of wife/mother and homosexual. One gets the impression that lesbians view the mother role as an aspect of their identity as a woman, and therefore do not experience the role conflict that gay men do, but there is no explicit statement to this effect (see, e.g., Hanscombe and Forster 1982).

How or why lesbians disclose (or do not disclose) to their spouses has not been studied in any detail. Similar to gay men, however, what literature does exist is based completely on the lesbian mother's description of the husband's reaction, rather than on the husband's self-reports. There is indirect evidence that husbands are often not disclosed to, and that when they are, they react in a severe and angry manner. Jones (1978) reported on a husband who was almost physically abusive to his wife in his reaction. Coleman (1985a) suggested that a wife's homosexual feelings are viewed as a kind of infidelity by the husband. Given the typical double standard that a woman's infidelity is worse than a man's, this may be one source of the husband's negative reaction.

Hanscombe and Forster (1982) and Hoeffer (1981) both reported that lesbian mothers fear custody battles with their ex-husbands, suggesting that they have not disclosed, or that if they have, enough animosity exists to result in custody litigation. Similarly, Whittlin (1983) reported that most custody cases that involve homosexual parents (usually lesbian mothers) are initiated because a custodial or visiting parent's homosexuality has been discovered by the ex-spouse. This suggests that the ex-husband's reaction is severe enough for him to seek a legal censuring of his ex-wife. Hanscombe and Forster (1982) reported that the ex-husbands of their lesbian mother sample refused to be interviewed, again suggesting continued animosity toward the lesbian mother.

As far as disclosing to children, Hanscombe and Forster (1982) and Hoeffer (1981) both reported that most lesbian mothers are open with their children about their homosexuality, but do not describe how disclosure was made or what initial effect disclosure had. Similar to the studies of children of gay fathers, however, they did report that the children of lesbians felt disclosure brought them closer to their mothers emotionally. Rand, Graham, and Rawlings (1982), in their study of mental health in single lesbian mothers, did not discuss the family's reactions to disclosure, but did report that disclosure to ex-husband, children, and employer is significantly positively correlated with the psychological well-being of the lesbian mother. This finding is congruent with the gay father literature described above, which reported that disclosing gay fathers were happier than nondisclosing fathers.

CUSTODY ISSUES

It is worthwhile to consider the scant but significant literature that has appeared on the social and legal ramifications of disclosure to one's family in the context of divorce. Parents and siblings of gay people have no direct legal stake in hiding their family member's homosexuality; the negative effects they face as relatives of a gay person are almost entirely social in nature. The disclosing gay family member, however, faces a number of both social and legal sanctions in current society, ranging from a risk of violent assault to the denial of employment and housing (Marotta 1981; Miller and Humphreys 1980). The gay or lesbian parent who discloses to a spouse faces not only these problems, but also unexpected legal difficulties in the courts over the issue of child custody (Pagelow 1980).

It has been consistently reported that if a parent's homosexuality is raised as a custody issue, it not only becomes the central issue in the custody case, but it makes a ruling in favor of the gay parent significantly less likely (Hitchens 1980; Maddox 1982; Whittlin 1983). Hitchens (1980) identified three major concerns voiced directly and indirectly by judges: a) that homosexual parents may produce homosexual children, particularly through seduction or molestation; b) that gay parents may produce gender-deviant children, such as transsexuals; and c) that children living with gay parents will suffer unusually harsh harassment by peers because they live with homosexuals. There is no evidence that the first and second concerns are justified (Golombok, Spencer, and Rutter 1983; Green 1978; Green et al. 1986; Groth and Birnbaum 1978; Hall 1978; Hoeffer 1981; Hotvedt and Mandel 1982; Kirkpatrick, Smith, and Roy 1981; Miller 1979a; Miller, Jacobsen, and Bigner 1981; Pagelow 1980; Weeks, Derdeyn, and Longman 1975). Isolated cases of the third concern, harassment by peers, have been reported (a single child in Bozett 1980, the son of a gay man; three out of thirty-seven children of both lesbians and gay men surveyed in Green 1978); no differences in popularity or friendship patterns have been found for these children, however, at least for those living with lesbian mothers (Hotvedt and Mandel 1982; Golombok, Spencer, and Rutter 1983). Apparently, both gay men and lesbians advise their children to be discreet in disclosing about their parents to others, and they themselves report discretion in their behavior around their children's friends (Golombok, Spencer, and Rutter 1983; Jones 1978; Miller 1979a).

The above studies provide evidence that the courts appear to have legally formalized the same conflict between family roles and a stigmatized homosexual identity that is present as a psychological event in the family. The courts act under many of the same false assumptions and misconceptions about homosexuality that family members do, and often deny custody to homosexual parents based on these assumptions. The courts thus perceive a homosexual identity as incompatible with family roles, particularly the parenting role. The creation of parental homosexuality as a custody issue suggests that the psychological reality of the homosexual identity/family role conflict is powerful enough to convert it into a social and legal reality as well.

CONCLUSIONS

Although our knowledge of how families respond to the disclosure of homosexual identity by a family member is at best fragmentary and incomplete, it is possible to suggest a broad model encompassing all family member reactions. In its most general form, this model has three specific components: a) the values concerning homosexuality currently held by the family members disclosed to, b) the effect these values are perceived to have on the relationship between the disclosing family member and other family members, and c) the conflict resolution mechanisms available to the family members.

Clearly, the most significant aspect of the present model is the values the family members hold concerning homosexuality. It is the implications of these values that form the basis for family member reaction. Given the popular negative sanctioning of homosexual behavior and identity, it is not surprising that family members react strongly when one of their own reveals a homosexual identity. The particular negative values held by individual family members can be expected to show some consistency, depending on which family members are being disclosed to. The members of the family of origin, parents, siblings, and most likely grandparents, can be thought to share the same values: they are united by the themes or values with which the family itself identifies. Because of these shared values, reactions could be similar within the family. The values held by spouses cannot be predicted, except to the degree that, in conformity with social values, they will tend to be negative to some degree. The values held by the children of homosexual persons represents an ambiguous topic. Young children cannot be expected to have any distinct values concerning homosexuality; school-age children and adolescents are another matter. This is definitely a topic for future research. To the degree that children internalize popular social values as they mature, we may expect that as their values become more "adult," the potential for conflict with a disclosing parent will increase.

The values held by family members, and their sources both familial and social, are significant for a model of family member reaction because it is the nature of these values that will determine how family members respond to identifying their relative as "a homosexual." This process of applying the social identity of homosexual to the disclosing member appears to involve imbuing that person with all the (negative) traits one believes apply to homosexuals in general. For the family, the most significant aspect of negative social values concerning homosexuality is the perception that homosexuals are not family members at all. This "family-lessness," when applied to a relative, appears to produce a subjective feeling of alienation from the disclosing member on the part of other family members aware of the homosexual identity. For parents, this alienation is accompanied by feelings of guilt and personal responsibility for the alienation itself. This reaction strikes the present author as only natural. Parents believe they contribute to their child's personality and achievements in most circumstances, and therefore it is not surprising that they react with feelings of failure when their child discloses a stigmatized identity that the parents themselves do not understand (and may even fear), and for which the family has no role.

The perceived incompatibility of a homosexual identity and a family role is also apparent in spousal reactions to disclosure. Although a much less studied topic, there is evidence that spouses experience the same alienation as parents, based on their own misconceptions about homosexuality, which they apply to the disclosing spouse. Similar to parents, they may also feel responsible or as if they have failed, but failed as spouses, not as parents. It should be noted that this description appears to hold for the wives of gay men; the husbands of lesbians have not been studied in sufficient detail for it to be known if they react in a similar manner. Given the apparent animosity that ex-husbands appear to have for their lesbian ex-wives, it is possible to hypothesize that they react negatively to their perceived failure as husbands, but this is only speculation. Detailed information on these men's reactions is definitely needed.

Although the children of gays and lesbians have been the subject of much legal and psychological research aimed at assessing their mental health, little is known thus far about how these children conceive of homosexual identity, what their reactions to parental disclosure are, or how their parent's homosexuality affects them. The qualitative appraisals of researchers, as well as self-reports by the children and their parents that are available, imply that disclosure improved the parent-child relationship with the disclosing adult. This is a result in striking contrast to that found for adult disclosure to adult relatives. Are children's values and role expectations more diffuse, and, as such, more open to adult homosexuality than those of adults? Or have they not yet developed a strong negative conception of homosexuals that would alienate them from their parents? The reported fact that children appreciate the need for discretion suggests they understand that others view homosexuality negatively. How these children view family roles in relation to sexual preference is definitely a topic for future work.

Perhaps the least studied and least understood feature of the present model is the role of conflict-resolution mechanisms. Whether it involves the family of origin or the marital family, disclosure is always a stressful, if not disruptive, event for family members. Because the social stereotypes for homosexuals do not include family relationships (but do include a plethora of undesirable traits), heterosexual family members find themselves alienated from the disclosing member's new identity. In short, the family members experience a conflict between their identity and role expectations for the disclosing member and the actual homosexual identity the member has adopted. The available research on the family of origin suggests the importance of regulative structures for the resolution of this conflict, and also implies that family themes dictate conflict-resolution strategies in addition to defining family member attitudes toward homosexuality. Empirical reports on the long-term outcomes of disclosure conflicts in the family of origin are lacking, however, so how specific themes are related to particular resolution strategies is not known. The literature on disclosure to spouses and children suggests a greater flexibility in resolution strategies, indicated by the broad variety of compromise living arrangements reported by these families. How these arrangements are chosen is a definite topic for future research, for it would shed much light on conflict resolution within marital families.

Finally, it is worth pausing to consider the concept of disclosure as currently formulated. The studies reviewed above all appear to regard disclosure as the deliberate revealing of one's sexual preference to others, which is assumed to be a voluntary act. This definition suggests that disclosure of sexual identity should be thought of as a particular example of the general phenomena of self-disclosure, which is the volunteering of highly personal information in the context of interpersonal relationships. Many studies in a variety of areas have suggested that self-disclosure enhances personal integrity, social interactions, and intimacy (Chelune et al. 1979; Derlega and Chaikin 1975; Jourard 1971). Corroborating evidence that self-disclosure is beneficial to psychological health can be seen in the finding that disclosure of sexual identity, at least for homosexual parents, is beneficial to their psychological well-being. Several studies report gay and lesbian parents as feeling that they "should" disclose. How and why these persons decide to disclose, or perhaps more significantly, decide not to disclose, given the potentially positive effects of self-disclosure for the individual who discloses, is a topic that must be studied in more detail. Presumably, the decision not to disclose relies, in part, on perceived family reaction, but this is not at all clear.

The decision not to disclose, or perhaps the avoidance of disclosure, raises a largely unstudied possibility: discovery rather than disclosure. Most studies do not distinguish between accidental discovery and voluntary disclosure. Is family reaction different if a family member's homosexuality is inadvertently discovered, rather than deliberately disclosed? What effect does this have on the discovered member, in contrast to the disclosing one? These questions show how much is yet to be learned about how homosexual persons deal with their families, not only in disclosure situations, but on a day-to-day basis.

A homosexual identity presents a unique situation for the family. Homosexuals are not generally viewed as having families, and are the subject of severe negative social sanctioning. When an intimate family member discloses a homosexual identity, the result is a family whose members see the disclosing member's previous role as negated. The individual family members then strive to redefine their relationship with the homosexual member, who they now treat as an embodiment of their own misconceptions about homosexuality. By studying these families, not from a clinical but from a theoretical perspective, it is possible to gain a better understanding not only of general stereotypes of homosexuality, but also of what homosexuality means to particular family roles.

ACKNOWLEDGMENTS

The author would like to thank Karen Briefer and Frederick W. Bozett for their thoughtful comments on an earlier draft of this paper.

REFERENCES

American Psychiatric Association. 1980. *Diagnostic and Statistical Manual of Mental Disorders.* 3d ed. Washington, D.C.: American Psychiatric Association.

Bales, J. 1985. Gay adolescents' pain compounded. *APA Monitor* 16(12):21.

Bell, A. P., and M. S. Weinberg. 1978. *Homosexualities: A Study of Diversity among Men and Women.* New York: Simon and Schuster.

Bieber, I. 1962. *Homosexuality.* New York: Basic Books.

Boswell, J. 1980. *Christianity, Social Tolerance, and Homosexuality.* Chicago: University of Chicago Press.

Bozett, F. W. 1980. Gay fathers: How and why they disclose their homosexuality to their children. *Family Relations* 29:173–79.

Bozett, F. W. 1981. Gay fathers: Evolution of the gay-father identity. *American Journal of Orthopsychiatry* 51:552–59.

Bozett, F. W. 1982. Heterogeneous couples in heterosexual marriages: Gay men and straight women. *Journal of Marital and Sexual Therapy* 8:81–89.

Buxbaum, E. 1959. Psychosexual development: The oral, anal, and phallic phases. In M. Levitt, ed., *Readings in Psychoanalytic Psychology,* pp. 43–55. New York: Appleton.

Cass, V. 1979. Homosexual identity formation: A theoretical model. *Journal of Homosexuality* 4:219–36.

Cass, V. 1984. Homosexual identity formation: Testing a theoretical model. *Journal of Sex Research* 20:143–67.

Chelune, G. J., R. C. Archer, J. M. Civikly, V. J. Derlega, J. A. Doster, J. Grzelak, J. R. Herron, C. L. Kleinke, J. G. Nesbitt, L. B. Rosenfeld, D. A. Taylor, and J. Waterman. 1979. *Self-Disclosure: Origins, Patterns, and Implications of Openness in Interpersonal Relationships.* San Francisco: Jossey-Bass.

Coleman, E. 1985a. Bisexual women in marriages. *Journal of Homosexuality* 11(1/2):87–99.

Coleman, E. 1985b. Integration of male bisexuality and marriage. *Journal of Homosexuality* 11(1/2):189–207.

Collins, L., and N. Zimmerman. 1983. Homosexual and bisexual issues. In J. C.

Hansen, J. D. Woody, and R. H. Woody, eds., *Sexual Issues in Family Therapy,* pp. 82–100. Rockville, Md.: Aspen Publications.

Dank, B. M. 1972. Why homosexuals marry women. *Medical Aspects of Human Sexuality* 6:14–23.

Dank, B. M. 1979. Coming out in the gay world. In M. P. Levine, ed., *Gay Men,* pp. 103–33. New York: Harper and Row.

Derlega, V., and A. Chaikin. 1975. *Sharing Intimacy: What We Reveal to Others and Why.* Englewood Cliffs, N.J.: Prentice-Hall.

DeVine, J. L. 1984. A systemic inspection of affectional preference orientation and the family of origin. *Journal of Social Work and Human Sexuality* 2:9–17.

Douglass, E., W. Cleveland, and G. Maddox. 1974. Political attitudes, age and aging: A cohort analysis of archival data. *Journal of Gerontology* 29:660–75.

Fairchild, B., and N. Hayward. 1979. *Now That You Know: What Every Parent Should Know about Homosexuality.* New York: Harvester/Harcourt Brace Jovanovich.

Gochros, J. S. 1985. Wives' reactions to learning that their husbands are bisexual. *Journal of Homosexuality* 11(1/2):101–13.

Golombok, S., A. Spencer, and M. Rutter. 1983. Children in lesbian and single-parent households: Psychosexual and psychiatric appraisal. *Journal of Child Psychology, Psychiatry, and Allied Disciplines* 24:551–72.

Green, R. 1978. Sexual identity of 37 children raised by homosexual or transsexual parents. *American Journal of Psychiatry* 135:692–97.

Green, R., J. B. Mandel, M. E. Hotvedt, J. Gray, and L. Smith. 1986. Lesbian mothers and their children: A comparison with solo heterosexual mothers and their children. *Archives of Sexual Behavior* 15:167–84.

Groth, A. N., and H. J. Birnbaum. 1978. Adult sexual orientation and attraction to underage persons. *Archives of Sexual Behavior* 7:175–81.

Hall, M. 1978. Lesbian families: Cultural and clinical issues. *Social Work* 23:380–85.

Hanscombe, G., and J. Forster. 1982. *Rocking the Cradle.* Boston: Alyson.

Harry, J. 1983. Gay male and lesbian relationships. In E. Macklin and R. Rubin, eds., *Contemporary Families and Alternative Lifestyles,* pp. 216–34. Beverly Hills, Calif.: Sage Publications.

Hatterer, M. S. 1974. The problems of women married to homosexual men. *American Journal of Psychiatry* 131:275–78.

Hiltner, S. 1980. Homosexuality and the churches. In J. Marmor, ed., *Homosexual Behavior,* pp. 219–31. New York: Basic Books.

Hitchens, D. 1980. Social attitudes, legal standards, and personal trauma in child custody cases. *Journal of Homosexuality* 5:89–95.

Hoeffer, B. 1981. Children's acquisition of sex-role behavior in lesbian-mother families. *American Journal of Orthopsychiatry* 51:552–59.

Hotvedt, M. E., and J. Mandel. 1982. Children of lesbian mothers. In J. Weinrich, B. Paul, J. C. Gonsiorek, and M. E. Hotvedt, eds., *Homosexuality: Social, Psychological, and Biological Issues,* pp. 275–85. Beverly Hills, Calif.: Sage Publications.

Humphreys, L. 1970. *Tearoom Trade.* Chicago: Aldine.

Humphreys, L., and B. Miller. 1980. Identities in the emerging gay culture. In J. Marmor, ed., *Homosexual Behavior,* pp. 142–56. New York: Basic Books.

Jones, C. 1978. *Understanding Gay Relatives and Friends.* New York: Seabury Press.

Jourard, S. 1971. *Self-Disclosure: An Experimental Analysis.* New York: Wiley.

Kirkpatrick, M., K. Smith, and R. Roy. 1981. Lesbian mothers and their children. *American Journal of Orthopsychiatry* 51:545–51.

Kinsey, A. C., W. B. Pomeroy, and C. E. Martin. 1948. *Sexual Behavior in the Human Male.* Philadelphia: W. B. Saunders.

Kinsey, A. C., W. B. Pomeroy, C. E. Martin, and P. H. Gebhard. 1953. *Sexual Behavior in the Human Female.* Philadelphia: W. B. Saunders.

Licata, S., and R. Peterson, eds. 1981. *Historical Perspectives on Homosexuality.* New York: Hawthorne Press.

MacDonald, A. 1974. The importance of sex-role to gay liberation. *Homosexual Counseling Journal* 1:169–80.

MacDonald, A., and R. Games. 1974. Some characteristics of those who hold positive and negative attitudes toward homosexuals. *Journal of Homosexuality* 1:9–27.

Maddox, B. 1982. Homosexual parents. *Psychology Today* (February):62–69.

Marotta, T. 1981. *The Politics of Homosexuality.* Boston: Houghton-Mifflin.

Matthews, S. H., and J. Sprey. 1985. Adolescents' relationship with grandparents: An empirical contribution to conceptual clarification. *Journal of Gerontology* 40:621–26.

McNeill, J. 1976. *The Church and the Homosexual.* Kansas City, Mo.: Sheed, Andrews, and McMeel.

Miller, B. 1979a. Gay fathers and their children. *The Family Coordinator* 28:544–52.

Miller, B. 1979b. Unpromised paternity: The life-styles of gay fathers. In M. Levine, ed., *Gay Men,* pp. 239–52. New York: Harper and Row.

Miller, B. 1980. Adult sexual resocialization. *Alternative Lifestyles* 1:207-32.

Miller, B., and L. Humphreys. 1980. Marginality and violence: Sexual lifestyle as a variable in victimization. *Qualitative Sociology* 3:169–85.

Miller, J., R. Jacobsen, and J. Bigner. 1981. The child's home environment for lesbian vs. heterosexual mothers: A neglected area of research. *Journal of Homosexuality* 7(1):49–56.

Morin, S. F. 1977. Heterosexual bias in psychological research on lesbianism and male homosexuality. *American Psychologist* 32:629–37.

Nugent, R. 1983. Married homosexuals. *Journal of Pastoral Care* 37:243–51.

Pagelow, M. 1980. Heterosexual and lesbian single mothers: A comparison of problems, coping, and solutions. *Journal of Homosexuality* 5:189–204.

Plummer, K. 1975. *Sexual Stigma.* London: Routledge and Kegan Paul.

Ponse, B. 1980. Lesbians and their worlds. In J. Marmor, ed., *Homosexual Behavior,* pp. 157–75. New York: Basic Books.

Rand, C., D. Graham, and E. Rawlings. 1982. Psychological health and factors the court seeks to control in lesbian mother trials. *Journal of Homosexuality* 8(1):27–40.

Robinson, B., P. Skeen, C. Hobson, and M. Herrman. 1982. Gay men's and women's perceptions of early family life and their relationships with their parents. *Family Relations* 31:79–83.

Ross, H. 1972. Odd couples: Homosexuals in heterosexual marriages. *Sexual Behavior* 2:42–50.

Ross, L. 1971. Mode of adjustment of married homosexuals. *Social Problems* 18:385–93.

Ross, M. 1983. *The Married Homosexual Man.* Boston: Routledge and Kegan Paul.

Saghir, M., and F. Robins. 1973. *Male and Female Homosexuality.* Baltimore: Williams and Wilkins.

Saghir, M., and F. Robins. 1980. Clinical aspects of female homosexuality. In J. Marmor, ed., *Homosexual Behavior,* pp. 280–95. New York: Basic Books.

Schafer, S. 1977. Sociosexual behavior in male and female homosexuals. *Archives of Sexual Behavior* 6:355–64.

Schvaneveldt, J., and M. Ihinger. 1979. Sibling relationships in the family. In W. Buff, R. Hill, F. Nye, and I. Reiss, eds., *Contemporary Theories about the Family,* vol. 1: *Research-Based Theories,* pp. 453–67. New York: Free Press.

Shavelson, E., M. Biaggio, H. Cross, and R. Lehman. 1980. Lesbian women's perception of their parent-child relationships. *Journal of Homosexuality* 5:205–15.

Siegelman, M. 1974a. Parental background of homosexual and heterosexual women. *British Journal of Psychiatry* 124:14–21.

Siegelman, M. 1974b. Parental background of male homosexuals and heterosexuals. *Archives of Sexual Behavior* 3:3–18.

Siegelman, M. 1981. Parental background of homosexual and heterosexual men: A cross-national replication. *Archives of Sexual Behavior* 10:505–13.

Spada, J. 1979. *The Spada Report.* New York: Signet.

Stroller, R. 1973. A symposium: Should homosexuality be in the APA nomenclature? *American Journal of Psychiatry* 130:1207–16.

Storms, M. 1978. Attitudes toward homosexuality and femininity in men. *Journal of Homosexuality* 3:257–66.

Troll, L. 1982. *Continuations: Adult Development and Aging.* Monterey, Calif.: Brooks/Cole.

Turnage, J., and D. Logan. 1975. Sexual "variation" without "deviation." *Homosexual Counseling Journal* 2:117–20.

Voeller, B., and J. Walters. 1978. Gay fathers. *The Family Coordinator* 27:149–57.

Warren, C. 1974. *Identity and Community in the Gay World.* New York: Wiley.

Warren, C. 1980. Homosexuality and stigma. In J. Marmor, ed., *Homosexual Behavior,* pp. 123–41. New York: Basic Books.

Weeks, R., A. Derdeyn, and M. Longman. 1975. Two cases of children of homosexuals. *Child Psychiatry and Human Development* 6:26–32.

Weinberg, G. 1972. *Society and the Healthy Homosexual.* New York: St. Martin's.

Weinberg, M. S., and C. J. Williams. 1974. *Male Homosexuals: Their Problems and Adaptations.* New York: Oxford University Press.

Weinberger, L., and J. Millham. 1979. Attitudinal homophobia and support of traditional sex roles. *Journal of Homosexuality* 4:237–46.

Whittlin, W. 1983. Homosexuality and child custody: A psychiatric viewpoint. *Conciliation Courts Reviews* 21(1):77–79.

10

Lesbian Career Development, Work Behavior, and Vocational Counseling

Kris S. Morgan and Laura S. Brown

Women's career development has recently been a popular topic in counseling psychology, for both theoretical and empirical work. This article extends that line of inquiry to address the unique career development issues of lesbians. The available literature on lesbians and work is reviewed, and parallels are drawn between the work experiences of lesbians, nonlesbian women, and other minority status groups. Three models of career development in women (Astin 1985; Farmer 1985; Gottfredson 1981) are presented, and the applicability of each theory to increasing understanding of lesbian experience is explored. Implications for vocational and work-related counseling for lesbians are suggested, and recommendations for the field are made.

Women's career development has been addressed in detail, both theoretically and empirically, in counseling psychology during the past decade (Borgen et al. 1985; Fitzgerald and Crites 1980; Osipow 1983, 1987). The unique career development issues of lesbians, however, have not been addressed. There appears to be a general consensus that understanding the career development of women requires at the least a sensitive expansion of existing male-based theories of development, if not the formulation of new theories specific to women (Fitzgerald and Crites 1980; Osipow 1983; Patterson 1973). Growing attention to the unique career development issues of African-Americans also indicates a sensitivity to diversity by the scientific community.

But the lack of attention to the career development issues of lesbians suggests that until now the assumption has been made that the experiences and needs of lesbians are subsumed under the study of the general female population. This position, common in the field of psychology of women, overlooks differences between the personal and vocational experiences of many lesbians from those of nonlesbian women (Boston Lesbian Psychologies Collective 1987), differences that influence efforts to understand the career development, vocational counseling needs, and work behavior of lesbians.

This article will review the available literature on lesbians and work, most of which is descriptive in nature, and will illustrate differences between the work experiences of lesbians, nonlesbian women, and other minority status groups. Three theoretical approaches to understanding career development in women will be briefly discussed, considering what each theory adds to the understanding of career development of lesbians. Finally, implications for vocational counseling with lesbians will be addressed. Because so little empirical data on this topic is available, our discussions will represent attempts to extrapolate and synthesize existing information, leading to new directions and questions for therapists working with this population

METHODOLOGICAL PROBLEMS AND CONSIDERATIONS

SAMPLING PROBLEMS

The parameters of the actual lesbian population in the United States are undefinable, because of the many social factors that force lesbians to hide their identities even from one another. Consequently, researchers working with this population must rely on the willingness of some lesbians to self-identify. It is thus impossible to get a truly random sample of the lesbian population. The only lesbians available for study are those who identify themselves as willing to participate in research. This problem, common to all work with sexual minorities, is a cause for concern because those subjects who willingly volunteer themselves for scientific inquiry are probably different from those who choose not to become involved in research. In the case of lesbians, it is reasonable to suggest that those lesbians who participate in studies are, as a group, more willing to disclose their sexual orientation, and possibly more comfortable with that orientation, than those lesbians who do not come forth (Bradford and Ryan 1987). As such, the data collected using lesbian samples can only be cautiously generalized to the entire lesbian population. Most attempts to study large groups within U.S. lesbian communities have also resulted in data that overrepresent the experiences of White lesbians and underrepresent those of lesbians of color. Findings detailed in this study also suffer from this problem.

A related difficulty in working with this population has to do with methods of obtaining participants. Researchers often rely on friendship networks among lesbians (the "snowballing" method of subject recruitment) to publicize studies and obtain research participants. By relying on such networks, researchers often obtain samples that are more cohesive than is the general population. An additional methodological problem relevant here is that much of the work done with this population involves self-report data, collected through surveys and interviews. Self-report data are generally unverifiable, so researchers must assume that subjects tell the truth. Clearly, this is not ideal. Until there are no risks to lesbians in being so identified, however, this state of affairs will continue to largely characterize research data on lesbians.

LESBIAN DATA SETS

This article will rely on data from the two available large nonpatient data sets of U.S. lesbian samples in making generalizations about the lesbian population. The National Lesbian Health Care Survey was an ambitious project designed to explore broad research questions; health was defined holistically, and included many dimensions of mental health (Bradford and Ryan 1987). Extensive demographic data were also gathered. Special efforts were made by the researchers to reach lesbians who were not involved in organized or visible lesbian communities, that is, those groups of lesbians (e.g., lesbians of color, rural lesbians, lesbians over fifty) who are typically hard to obtain as research participants. The 1,917 completed surveys represented lesbians from every state and geographic region of the United States. Although geographic diversity was thus achieved, the authors still found their sample to be overly homogeneous as to race (White) and class (middle) and described their subjects as significantly more educated and more likely to be employed in professional settings than was the general female (nonlesbian) population. This study provides a wealth of data about many aspects of lesbian lives. It is, to date, the most comprehensive data set available on U.S. lesbians.

Blumstein and Schwartz's (1983) study of lesbian, gay male, and heterosexual married and cohabiting couples is another source of information about the nonpatient lesbian population. This sociological interview study focused on how couples handled issues of money, work, power, and relationship maintenance. These researchers also managed to secure a large sample of lesbians from geographically diverse areas of the United States: 1,554 lesbians completed surveys, and 90 of those were interviewed in person. All of the lesbians in this study were in couple relationships, because relationship functioning was the target of this study. This data set is somewhat less comprehensive demographically than is the National Lesbian Health Care Survey, but because work was a focus of study, these data are relevant to our discussion.

LESBIAN WORK BEHAVIOR AND EXPERIENCE

Employment Patterns for Lesbians

Most lesbians work for pay outside the home. Researchers commonly report that large percentages of their lesbian samples are employed. Moses (1978) reported an employment rate of 90 percent in her sample of 92, while Tanner (1978) found that 92 percent of her sample of 24 were currently working. Blumstein and Schwartz (1983) found that 85 percent of their 1,554 lesbian respondents were employed. Jay and Young (1977) reported 70 percent employment within their sample of 962 lesbians, with an additional 20 percent engaged as students. The most current figures available are from the National Lesbian Health Care Survey; 91 percent employment was reported in that sample. Because most lesbians are not financially dependent on men, and most lesbian relationships do not assume the likelihood of financial dependency between partners (Clunis and Green 1988), working for a living is a matter of survival for lesbians that cannot be ignored. Although more than 50 percent of heterosexual women in the United States now also work outside the home for pay, the myth persists for heterosexual women that marriage and being supported by a man is an option. Lesbians, on the other hand, must assume that they will always be their own primary source of financial support.

As women, lesbians earn approximately two-thirds of what men earn; thus it would be rare that one lesbian in a couple would earn enough to support both women (and not all lesbians are in relationships). Bradford and Ryan's (1987) data indicate that as of the late 1980s, most lesbians earn substantially less for their level of education and work experience than do comparative groups of heterosexual women, all other factors held constant. Thus, this tends to be an underemployed and underpaid population, even within the norms for women's wages in the United States.

Financial Considerations for Lesbians

In addition, the egalitarian values of many lesbians encourage financial independence in partner relationships (Blumstein and Schwartz 1983;

Clunis and Green 1988). Brooks (1981) found that only 4 percent of her sample of 675 lesbians reported being supported by a partner. Lesbian couples, even long into a relationship, may have few financial resources in common, partly for fear of revealing their coupled status inadvertently. Legal barriers to recognition of lesbian relationships also make it more difficult for lesbians to subsidize a partner financially through assigning work-related benefits in ways routinely available to heterosexual working women. For example, most lesbians cannot list their partner on their employer-provided medical insurance, even if the second woman is dependent for support on the insured woman or has no health insurance of her own.

Although many nonlesbian women work to support themselves and their families, it is still usual for these women to rely—or hope to be able to someday rely—on men's wages, at least in part. Heterosexual women are still led to believe, in many cases, that they can expect financial support from a partner or ex-partner, whereas most lesbians do not share this assumption (Clunis and Green 1988).

PERSONALITY VARIABLES AFFECTING CAREER CHOICE

Lesbians and nonlesbian women may also differ on some personality characteristics or personal values that influence attitudes toward work and, subsequently, work behavior. Although there tends to be more within-group than between-group variation on most personality factors, it is possible to make some general statements about differences between lesbians and nonlesbian women. Many lesbians tend to value feminism and its ideals (Darty and Potter 1984; Morgan 1992). There is evidence that lesbians value androgyny and exhibit more gender nonconforming behaviors than do nonlesbian women (Brooks 1981), and that lesbians value independence in intimate relationships (Blumstein and Schwartz 1983; Clunis and Green 1988). Highly gender-role-stereotyped behaviors, including emotional and financial dependency in intimate relationships, are not valued and may even be stigmatized among lesbians (Blumstein and Schwartz 1983; Clunis and Green 1988), whereas similar behaviors are both common and to some degree acceptable for women in intimate heterosexual relationships (Blumstein and Schwartz 1983). From a practical standpoint, as well as an ideological one, it makes sense that lesbians as a group would tend toward less gender-role stereotypic behaviors: when women choose to live independent of men, the many household maintenance activities that have traditionally been classified as "men's work" (including the role of breadwinner) still must be done, so gender-role flexibility is a reasonable and necessary adaptive response.

Relating these values to career development, Foss and Slaney (1986) found that women who hold less traditional views about the role of women chose a significantly broader range of acceptable prospective careers for their daughters, including many more nontraditional jobs, than did women who held traditional views about gender roles. Because lesbians as a group generally have to challenge traditional gender roles while meeting the demands of day-to-day living, they may be more open to seeking nontraditional employment than are nonlesbian women. Some lesbian communities may even place higher value on lesbians performing in non-traditional job roles, leaving those lesbians who work in the pink-collar occupations feeling less valued as lesbians (Meyerding 1990). Economic reality may also influence lesbians to consider nontraditional fields from very early in their vocational development. "Men's work" continues to pay considerably more than "women's work," so opting for work in non-traditional occupations may be one way for lesbians to bridge gender-related wage gaps and mitigate the effect of living without a man's higher wages and better economic opportunity.

LESBIANS AND MINORITY GROUP STATUS

EFFECTS OF HOMOPHOBIA

Another significant difference between lesbian and nonlesbian women's work experiences is that in addition to the employment discrimination lesbians share with all women due to gender-based discrimination, lesbians face further minority status engendered by a heterosexist, homophobic society (Herek 1989; Melton 1989). The expression of hostility against lesbians and gay men is more accepted among large numbers of U.S. citizens than is bias against other groups (Herek 1989). Lesbians face at least double minority status, and more when issues such as race/ethnicity, physical disability, and age come into play. Evidence of employment dis-crimination against lesbians is mostly anecdotal at this time, coming from three main sources: courtroom testimony, personal accounts, and general psychological and sociological reports on lesbian life, which indicate that lesbians fear job discrimination (Darty and Potter 1984; Levine and Leon-ard 1984). Brooks (1981) reported that nearly two-thirds of her respon-dents were unable to state with certainty that they would not lose their jobs if their lesbianism were known. Two-thirds of Chafetz et al.'s (1974) sample reported the same fear, as did three-fifths of Levine and Leonard's

(1984) respondents. Schneider (1987) found that three-fourths of her sample believed that disclosure of their lesbian identity would cost them their jobs or income.

Notably, in one study of lesbian and gay psychologists, members of a profession considered to be quite accepting of openly lesbian and gay persons, large numbers of respondents indicated that they were reluctant to be known as gay or lesbian in their professional work settings for fear of discrimination, or that they had actually experienced negative consequences professionally when coming out (American Psychological Association 1979). APA's Division 44 (Lesbian and Gay Issues) still maintains a confidential membership status for those psychologists who fear the consequences of their sexual orientation becoming public. The available data suggest that the problem of employment discrimination against lesbians is pervasive and transsituational, even in those settings where anti-discrimination legislation presumes to protect lesbians' job status, or where the occupation is stereotyped as one that is more open and accepting. The frequent efforts made to repeal such protective legislation are also evidence of the desire on the part of many employers to be able to discriminate against sexual minority employees.

The few empirical studies that document actual or suspected incidents of employment discrimination indicate that these fears are not unfounded. Percentages reported by subjects in a variety of studies of actual or suspected experiences of job discrimination among lesbians vary from lows of 7 percent (Bell and Weinberg 1978) or 10 percent (Schneider 1987) to as high as 12 percent (Saghir and Robins 1973), 18 percent (Bradford and Ryan 1987), and 24 percent (Levine and Leonard 1984). These data clearly suggest that lesbians anticipate and face considerable levels of employment discrimination, and that such discrimination on the basis of sexual orientation continues to be, if not legal, certainly not clearly illegal in most jurisdictions. Although the evidence of employment discrimination against sexual minority persons is strong, the courts have until now been unwilling to declare gays and lesbians a "suspect class" requiring protection similar to that given people of color or older adults. This judicial silence sends the meta-message to those who wish to discriminate that they may face few consequences for their actions.

Passing and Being Out: Effects on Lesbians' Lives

The importance of the issue of managing "outness" (openness about lesbian identity) at work cannot be overstated. Both lesbian and gay politics and research on strategies for reducing homophobia indicate that the most powerful strategy for reducing societal discrimination over time is for many lesbians and gay men to be out in all spheres of life (Herek 1989). Hall (1986) reports some of the strategies lesbians use to hide their identity at work, all of which revolve around dishonesty, whether overt or by default. Hall describes the tremendous toll living a dual life exacts from lesbians who remain closeted at work, including the problem of maintaining self-esteem in the face of living a daily lie. Hall writes:

> All the forms of non-disclosure, whether the occasional substitute of "he" for "she" when describing a weekend outing with a lover or the complete fabrication of a heterosexual life, leave a lesbian in a morally untenable position. Not only is she lying . . . she is also ignoring the strong exhortations of the lesbian community to come out. (1986:73)

The psychological difficulties created by managing self-disclosure on the job are also discussed at length by Levine and Leonard (1984), Schneider (1987), and Shachar and Gilbert (1983). Eldridge and Gilbert (1990) did not find, however, that level of disclosure among their subjects affected relationship satisfaction in dual-career lesbian couples, although differences within a couple in level of disclosure were not investigated.

Lesbian couples may also face difficulties in negotiating work roles. Clunis and Green (1988:58) discuss the difficulties that can arise when one partner is more open at work than the other is:

> The more open partner may pressure her lover to be more public in order to validate the relationship, or to make a political statement to the larger world. She may not be sure whether her lover's closetedness is really necessary. Maybe it is an indication of shame about being a lesbian or about the relationship. The more closeted partner may see her caution as essential to her job, her work relationships, and her ambitions. Both partners may feel misunderstood and unsupported. When one partner is more out than the other, it is important to identify the issue as differing degrees of outness rather than differing levels of commitment to the relationship.

Because lesbian relationships are not legally recognized or socially sanctioned in this society, most coupled lesbians face further discrimination at work. Dual-career issues often go unaddressed because lesbian couples are denied access to resources available to heterosexual couples. The existence of the lesbian family unit is often denied, so lesbian partners are denied health insurance benefits for their partners or for a partner's children, who cannot legally become dependents. Because the closeted lesbian is often perceived as single and unattached by her employer, problems of job transfers or other work demands that do not consider the effect on both partners' lives are not uncommon (Hall 1986; Herek 1989). If your relationship is invisible to your employer, as is the case for so many lesbians, it may be difficult to explain the impact of its breakup on your work, or to justify your desire to have more time off if you cannot tell anyone about your need to balance this technically nonexistent relationship with work.

MINORITY GROUP MODELS OF CAREER DEVELOPMENT

This consideration of the minority status of lesbians suggests that some useful models of career development for this group might be found within the literature on career development of U.S. racial minorities. The literature on career development in African-Americans yielded the construct of "opportunity structure." Opportunity structure is each person's subjective perception of which occupational choices may be obtainable options. Such beliefs about the structure of vocational opportunity are circumscribed by societal pressures and injunctions that influence career aspirations. For example, a young African-American woman might not even consider beginning the career path to become a physician because of her belief that she would never realize that goal. Analogously, a young lesbian might rule out work with children because of the many cultural messages that it is unacceptable for lesbians to work with children in any capacity. For example, the Briggs Initiative in California in 1978 was expressly aimed at forbidding known lesbians or gay men, or anyone who was supportive of them, from teaching in the California public schools. Although the initiative eventually failed, it did not do so easily, and it was perceived as a credible effort by many voters.

It has been demonstrated that both African-American women and men and White women are not convinced that the opportunity structure is open to them. Berman and Haug (1975) examined the effect of gender and race on the discrepancy between vocational and educational goals and expectations. They found that women, both African-American and White, demonstrated the least confidence in their ability to attain their goals when compared to men of both races. Kerckhoff and Campbell (1977) studied the educational ambitions of twelfth-grade boys, comparing African-Americans to low- and high-status Whites. Their findings suggest that "one's view of the opportunity structure [fatalism] has more importance for Blacks than for Whites" (p. 710), and that perceived opportunity structure was a more powerful predictor of vocational aspiration than was socioeconomic status (SES). Turner and Turner (1975) surveyed a large student sample of females and males, both African-American and White, relating race, gender, and SES to perceived discrimination within the opportunity structure. Findings suggest that African-Americans of both genders and White women perceive the structure of opportunity as limited.

LESBIANS AS A UNIQUE MINORITY GROUP

Just as there are significant differences in the work-related experiences of lesbian and nonlesbian women, the minority status of lesbians is different from the minority status of heterosexual people of color and White non-lesbian women. First, discrimination against lesbians is both legal and socially sanctioned in this country (Herek 1989). Such discrimination is no longer legal against people of color or White women, although social norms remain more resilient to change (Falk 1989; Melton 1989). But although some locales have legislation prohibiting job and housing discrimination against lesbians and gay men, such laws remain the exception rather than the rule. Twenty-seven states still criminalize sexual behavior characteristic of same-sex relationships (Herek 1989; Schmitz 1988).

Second, lesbianism, unlike skin color or gender, can often be hidden. Part of the heterosexism of our culture is that heterosexuality is assumed, and lesbianism and lesbians are generally invisible (Brown 1989). Because a woman's lesbianism generally becomes known through her active disclosure of this information, lesbians usually have a choice about whether or not to be open at work. This choice can be a burdensome one, because the degree of outness is related to both increased job satisfaction and general mental health for lesbians, as well as to increased amounts of discrimination and hostility faced (Bradford and Ryan 1987; Schneider 1987). In one recent study examining correlates of relationship satisfaction in lesbian couples, including the variable of being out on the job, 65 percent of the 550 subjects had not come out to their employers, and 37 percent had come out to no one at work (Eldridge and Gilbert 1990).

The variable of workplace openness appears to interact with the concept of perceived opportunity structure for lesbians. Levine and Leonard (1984) found that lesbians commonly use three specific strategies to cope with job discrimination: a) self-employment; b) "job tracking," which means choosing to work in fields that accept lesbianism; and c) staying in the closet at work. For lesbians who wish to be open at work, the perceived structure of opportunity has an important impact on work behavior, prompting many to choose self-employment or to carefully consider the political/social climate of various occupations. There are, of course, other options: one is to choose to be open or selectively open at work, whatever the job, and cope with the consequences.

Schneider (1987) found that employment settings affect the degree to which lesbians are out at work. Specifically, she found that lesbians are more likely to be open about their identity when they work in small, relatively nonbureaucratized settings, in female-dominated work settings, when working with adults rather than children, and in the human service professions. Schneider also found that as income increases, lesbian self-disclosure decreases, presumably because better paid workers have more to lose by endangering their jobs, or perhaps because higher status/higher paying occupations are among the more overtly homophobic.

A third difference between lesbians and other minority status groups is the issue of identity development. People of color are usually raised with their racial/ethnic identity from birth, and gender identity is typically determined by age two. Lesbians tend to initiate the process of lesbian identity development during adolescence or even later in life. Gramick (1984), in her interviews with ninety-seven lesbians, found that the average age at which these women acknowledged their lesbianism was 21.5; she cautions, however, that the variation around this mean was great, drawing attention to the great variability by age of the inception of lesbian identity development for any particular woman. Thus, whereas people of color are aware of their ethnicity and women are aware of their femaleness throughout the process of career development, lesbians may not be aware of their lesbianism until sometime in the middle of this process, or even fter a career has been chosen and successfully embarked on for any number of years. It is not infrequent for the lesbian who comes out in later life to face a crisis simply because her career is either unsupportive of or actively hostile to her newly identified sexual orientation (Adleman 1988; Stanley and Wolfe 1989).

LESBIAN IDENTITY AND CAREER DEVELOPMENT

It is perhaps this aspect of lesbian lives—the fact that lesbian identity development is commonly a lengthy process that can begin at any time during the life span—that is the most complicating factor in trying to understand lesbian career development. If a woman acknowledges her lesbianism at an early age—before leaving high school, for example—then it is more likely that her awareness of her sexual identity will directly affect her career development than if she comes out later in life. A lesbian adolescent who wishes to be open about her sexual identity will be able to gain information about the structure of opportunity and discern which job settings are more amenable to open lesbians, although her data may be distorted by the homophobia of the setting in which she finds herself and the availability or lack thereof of lesbian role models.

Thus, a lesbian who comes out at an early age may have more of a chance to make an informed decision about how the type of career she feels drawn to may interact with her lesbianism if she is given access to undistorted information. Women who come out at a later age, by contrast, may be faced either with changing careers, or with learning to integrate their lesbianism with the career they have previously chosen, a process which itself may have the effect of slowing the coming-out process for these women.

The nonlinear nature of both the sexual identity development and career development processes leads to complex interactions. With this in mind, let us now turn our attention to three influential theoretical models of women's career development, those promulgated by Farmer (1985), Astin (1985), and Gottfredson (1981), and consider what these theories contribute to the understanding of lesbian career development. The application of these three models to the unique career development of lesbians provides a theoretical base from which to explore issues in vocational counseling for lesbians, including career choice and work satisfaction.

THREE THEORIES OF CAREER DEVELOPMENT: THEIR APPLICATIONS FOR LESBIANS

Farmer's (1985) "Model of Career and Achievement Motivation for Women and Men" is a multidimensional, developmental model focusing on background, personal, and environmental variables in career development. Background variables include gender, race, age, social status, and, it could be argued, sexual orientation. For lesbians, consideration of the last can add explanatory power to this model. Personal factors include academic ability, personality characteristics, and values. In an earlier section, some pertinent personality characteristics of lesbians, such as androgyny and the valuation of independence, were discussed. Farmer's environmental factors include opportunity structure, support for working from teachers and parents, and, for women, the value placed on women working. For lesbians, one might extrapolate that an important environmental factor might be perceived support for lesbians entering a particular field, or perceived support for lesbians qua lesbians. The role of perceived structure of opportunity on lesbian career development has also been explored above, with societal homophobia and the presence or absence of protective legislation affecting these perceptions. Thus, lesbian identity interacts visibly with each of Farmer's three factors that influence career motivation. As such, Farmer's model would strongly predict that a woman's lesbianism would influence her career development, and it offers a conceptual framework for therapists to postulate how those effects might be manifested.

Astin's (1985) "The Meaning of Work in Women's Lives: A Sociopsychological Model of Career Choice and Work Behavior," proposes that personal characteristics and social forces are the two major factors that shape work behavior. Astin outlines four major principles in her model:

> 1. Work behavior is motivated activity intended to satisfy three basic needs: survival, pleasure, and contribution. 2. Career choices are based on expectations concerning the accessibility of alternative forms of work and their relative capacity to satisfy the three basic needs. 3. Expectations are shaped in part by early socialization . . . and in part by the perceived structure of opportunity. 4. Expectations . . . can be modified by changes in the structure of opportunity, and this modification can lead to changes in career choice and in work behavior. (p. 119)

This model, emphasizing as it does both internal and external factors, is not unlike Farmer's (Osipow 1987), and it also possesses unique characteristics that seem to make it especially relevant to lesbians. Described as "sociopsychological," Astin's model explores the interactions between personal characteristics and social forces and describes how socialization influences each person's view of the opportunity structure. A feature of this model that makes it particularly appealing for application to lesbian career issues is that it provides a conceptualization of how opportunity structure changes over time as a result of social forces. This ability to account for changes in the perceived structure of opportunity has relevance to the vocational concerns of women in the process of coming out as lesbians.

As discussed earlier, a woman may engage in the coming-out process at any time during her life span, and the timing of this process will have an influence on each individual lesbian's view of the opportunity structure, her career development, and job satisfaction. Additionally, this model can account for how lesbian career pathways may be affected by changes in the social climate regarding lesbians, the inception of protective legislation in some jurisdictions, and the appearance of increasing numbers of openly lesbian role models in diverse occupations. Finally, this model offers a framework for understanding high rates of paid employment among lesbians; lesbians' expectations concerning accessibility of alternative forms of work that will meet their basic needs are different from those of heterosexual women (e.g., there is no expectation of getting married and being supported in unpaid work within the home) and would of necessity influence lesbians' work behavior.

Gottfredson's (1981) "Circumscription and Compromise: A Developmental Theory of Occupational Aspirations" describes in detail the process by which individuals narrow the field of occupational options toward making a career choice. Gottfredson outlines four developmental stages during which individuals balance internal variables, such as self-concept and personal preferences, with external factors, such as occupational images (sex type, prestige level, field) and perceptions of job accessibility. This model resembles both Farmer's and Astin's, also tending to support a conclusion that lesbian identity influences career development. One interesting feature of Gottfredson's model as applied to lesbians is the contention that, when limiting occupational options, individuals will give up their vocational interests first, their preferred status (job level) second, and will hold most tenaciously to their conceptions of the sex type of the career, that is, whether it is acceptable for males or females. Earlier, we suggested that lesbians as a group are somewhat more likely than nonlesbian women to hold feminist values, including broadened definitions of acceptable behavior for women, and valuation of traditionally male stereotyped jobs. Gottfredson's model would predict that lesbians might demonstrate different patterns of vocational decision making than heterosexual women, given lesbians' hypothesized broader definitions of what is appropriate work for women.

IMPLICATIONS FOR VOCATIONAL AND WORK-RELATED COUNSELING FOR LESBIANS

These three models, each in its own way, suggest that a woman's lesbian identity will have an effect on her process of vocational decision making. When we assume that lesbianism affects the career development and work behavior of lesbians, what are the implications for vocational counseling with this population? Vocational counseling traditionally revolves around choosing a career. For lesbian clients, a variety of factors discussed above may affect this process. Several other variables specific to the counseling process may emerge, however, when a lesbian examines vocational choice in a counseling setting.

TABLE IO.I
Guidelines for Work-Related Counseling with Lesbians

1. Recognize and work to change your own homophobic and heterexist biases.
2. Do not assume that your client is heterosexual.
3. Learn to recognize and challenge your clients' internalized homophobia and heterosexism.
4. Recognize the interactions of lesbian identity with vocational choice and work issues.
5. Attend to the influence of lesbian relationship variables on occupational choices.
6. Be aware of how a lesbian client's degree of outness affects her vocational decision making.
7. Develop an understanding of the complex effects of oppression on lesbians' psychological functioning.
8. Avoid perceiving career choices for lesbians as limited by stereotypical vocational roles.
9. Keep current with local and national legislation, both affirmation and punitive, that affects lesbian rights on the job.
10. Become knowledgeable and keep current regarding community resources for lesbians.
11. Develop an awareness of positive lesbian role models in a variety of careers.

One issue in career counseling with lesbians will always be client self-disclosure. It is possible that the lesbian client will not disclose her lesbianism to a counselor, fearing homophobic reactions or a devaluation of the trust implied by sharing that information. Therapists and counselors cannot assume that their clients are heterosexual and should not place the burden of easing self-disclosure on the shoulders of lesbian clients. Rather, therapists should indicate a priori their openness to the possibility that this client is lesbian by routinely including sexual orientation in the standard list of factors that can affect career decision making when discussing these matters with a new client.

Evidence suggests that homophobic beliefs are all too common among mental health professionals (DeCrescenzo 1985; Graham et al. 1984; Rudolph 1988). The average psychologist tends not to practice in a lesbian and gay affirmative manner consonant with the policies and ethical principles of psychology (APA Committee on Lesbian and Gay Concerns 1990). Ethical practice with lesbian clients thus requires that vocational counselors explore their own homophobic stereotypes and biases; such beliefs can be seen as an unexplored bias, either conscious or nonconscious, that will harm clients if unattended to (APA Committee on Lesbian and Gay Concerns 1990) and will result in delivery of poor quality services to all clients, lesbian and otherwise.

When vocational counseling is sought by lesbians who disclose their identity to the counselor, it is important for the counselor to be knowledgeable about how this information may interact with the client's future career. An open yet realistic view of the opportunities available for out lesbians, balancing each woman's wishes about being able to be out on the job with the realities of employment discrimination faced by lesbians, is crucial if such counseling is to be ethical and efficacious. Therapists must be careful not to steer lesbians into or away from career paths based on homophobic stereotypes, either their own or their clients. Clinicians must familiarize themselves with laws that may provide job protection or grant other civil rights to lesbians, in order to be able to discuss the options for lesbian clients in a knowledgeable way that will help the lesbian client to assess the groundedness of her concerns. A sensitivity to the complex-ities of managing lesbian identity disclosure on the job, as discussed earlier in this article, is also important. Schmitz (1988) delineates some of the job-search resources available to lesbians and their vocational counselors, including gay business networking and information on locating companies with nondiscrimination policies, using information collected by the National Gay Task Force (1981).

It may also be common for lesbians to seek help in coping with the realities of the work world, particularly in the case of those lesbians who are not affiliated with an organized lesbian community that might offer models for coping strategies. This may especially be the case when the lesbian client is new to the coming-out process. Or she may be in an environment that reduces lesbian visibility and thus access to role models because of institutionalized homophobia. Evidence suggests that lesbians have many concerns about coping with work and work-related problems. For example, when Bradford and Ryan (1987) asked their sample about their "current concerns," 57 percent of the sample cited money problems, 31 percent reported job/school worries, 18 percent named job dissatisfac-tion, and 7 percent reported worrying about not being able to find a job (percentages exceed 100 percent because subjects were free to list more than one concern). These figures clearly indicate the importance of work in lesbian lives, as well as its status as a potential source of distress.

Finally, it is vitally important that the therapist working with a lesbian client be attentive to the ways in which the client's own internalized homo-phobia may be serving as a limitation to growth. When the therapist can visualize the lesbian client as a valuable, capable human being, a lesbian client can develop new appreciation of her skills, strengths, and talents.

CONCLUSIONS AND RECOMMENDATIONS

The career development, work behavior, and vocational counseling needs of lesbians are complex phenomena, part of the larger picture of under-standing lesbian lives and realities. Sensitivity to various factors related to lesbian identity, such as gender-role socialization, minority group status, and the realities of employment discrimination is required of those who seek to understand and provide services to lesbians. As such, clinicians working in the area of career or work-related counseling with women must assume that they will be seeing lesbian clients. To provide competent, ethical services, vocational counselors must familiarize themselves with the unique realities of lesbian work and life experiences, both through further training and via the growing body of professional literature that addresses work with this population.

Socially sensitive research in this area is also needed, to explore the strengths and limitations of current theories for explaining lesbian career development. At this point, the topic of lesbians and work is largely unexplored, with opportunities for a wide range of inquiries. A number of questions require closer study, including the impact of perceived workplace homophobia on actual vocational choices of lesbians; the impact of a clear antidiscrimination stance by an employer on lesbians' vocational choices and job satisfaction; occupational stratification among lesbians; effect of cultural stereotypes about appropriate work for lesbians on lesbians' vocational aspirations; and the impact on lesbians of legislation that would either protect their job status or give them domestic-partner job benefits similar to those currently enjoyed by married heterosexuals.

Brown (1989) has suggested that lesbian and gay experiences may generate new paradigms for understanding topics previously studied from within the lens of heterosexual experience. It is possible that the development of a theory of lesbian career development, based in the experiences of the diverse population of lesbians, might shed new and different light on our paradigms for all women's career development. In order to develop such a lesbian paradigm, however, there must be a conscious attempt made to elicit information from lesbians on their career and vocational experiences.

Counseling psychology has recently devoted a great deal of attention to understanding the career development of women, but those women and their realities have been assumed by default to be heterosexual. It is now time to expand this area to address the unique needs of lesbians and thus to eliminate heterosexism in the field of career and vocational development.

ACKNOWLEDGMENTS

The first author, Kris S. Morgan, wishes to acknowledge that her work was partially funded by the Iowa Testing Program at the University of Iowa. She also extends appreciation to her advisor, Ursula Delworth, for editorial assistance and encouragement.

REFERENCES

Adleman, J. 1988. *Long Time Passing: Lives of Older Lesbians.* Boston: Alyson.

American Psychological Association. 1979. *Removing the Stigma: Final Report of the Task Force on the Status of Lesbian and Gay Male Psychologists.* Washington, D.C.: American Psychological Association.

American Psychological Association Committee on Lesbian and Gay Concerns. 1990. *Final Report of the Task Force on Bias in Psychotherapy with Lesbians and Gay Men.* Washington, D.C.: American Psychological Assocation.

Astin, H. S. 1985. The meaning of work in women's lives: A sociopsychological model of career choice and work behavior. *Counseling Psychologist* 12(4):117–28.

Bell, A. P., and M. S. Weinberg. 1978. *Homosexualities: A Study of Diversity among Men and Women.* New York: Simon and Schuster.

Berman, G. S., and M. R. Haug. 1975. Occupational and educational goals and expectations: The effects of race and sex. *Social Problems* 23:166–81.

Blumstein, P., and P. Schwartz. 1983. *American Couples: Money, Work, Sex.* New York: William Morrow.

Borgen, F. H., W. L. Layton, D. L. Veenhuizen, and D. J. Johnson. 1985. Vocational behavior and career development, 1984: A review. *Journal of Vocational Behavior* 27:218–69.

Boston Lesbian Psychologies Collective, eds. 1987. *Lesbian Psychologies: Explorations and Challenges.* Urbana: University of Illinois Press.

Bradford, J., and C. Ryan. 1987. *National Lesbian Health Care Survey: Mental Health Implications.* Richmond: Virginia Commonwealth University Research Laboratory.

Brooks, V. R. 1981. *Minority Stress and Lesbian Women.* Lexington, Mass.: D. C. Heath.

Brown, L. S. 1989. New voices, new visions: Toward a lesbian/gay paradigm for psychology. *Psychology of Women Quarterly* 13:445–58.

Chafetz, J. S., Sampson, P., Beck, P., and West, J. 1974. A study of homosexual women. *Social Work* 19:714–23.

Clunis, D. M., and Green, G. D. 1988. *Lesbian Couples.* Seattle: Seal Press.

Darty, T., and Potter, D., eds. 1984. *Women-Identified women.* Palo Alto, Calif.: Mayfield.

DeCrescenzo, T. A. 1985. Homophobia: A study of the attitudes of mental health professionals toward homosexuality. In R. Schoenberg, R. Goldberg, and D. Shore, eds. *With Compassion toward Some: Homosexuality and Social Work in America,* pp. 115–36. New York: Harrington Park.

Eldridge, N., and Gilbert, L. 1990. Correlates of relationship satisfaction in lesbian couples. *Psychology of Women Quarterly* 14:43–62.

Falk, P. J. 1989. Lesbian mothers: Psychosocial assumptions in family law. *American Psychologist* 44:941–47.

Farmer, H. S. 1985. Model of career and achievement motivation for women and men. *Journal of Counseling Psychology* 32:363–90.

Fitzgerald, L. F., and J. O. Crites. 1980. Toward a career psychology of women: What do we know? What do we need to know? *Journal of Counseling Psychology* 27:44–62.

Foss, C. J., and R. B. Slaney. 1986. Increasing nontraditional career choices in women: Relation of attitudes toward women and responses to a career intervention. *Journal of Vocational Behavior* 28:191–202.

Gottfredson, L. S. 1981. Circumscription and compromise: A developmental theory of occupational aspirations. *Journal of Counseling Psychology* 28:545–79.

Graham, D. L. R., E. I. Rawlings, H. S. Halpern, and I. Hermes. 1984. Therapists' needs for training in counseling lesbians and gay men. *Professional Psychology: Research and Practice* 15:482–96.

Gramick, J. 1984. Developing a lesbian identity. In T. Darty and S. Potter, eds., *Women-Identified Women*, pp. 31–44. Palo Alto, Calif.: Mayfield.

Hall, M. 1986. The lesbian corporate experience. *Journal of Homosexuality* 12(3/4):59–75.

Herek, G. M. 1989. Hate crimes against lesbians and gay men: Issues for research and policy. *American Psychologist* 44:948–55.

Jay, K., and A. Young, eds. 1977. *Out of the Closets: Voices of Gay Liberation.* New York: Douglas Links.

Kerckhoff, A. C., and R. T. Campbell. 1977. Race and social status differences in the explanation of educational ambition. *Social Forces* 55:701–13.

Levine, M. P., and R. Leonard. 1984. Discrimination against lesbians in the work force. *Signs: Journal of Women in Culture and Society* 9:700–10.

Melton, G. B. 1989. Public policy and private prejudice: Psychology and law on gay rights. *American Psychologist* 44:933–40.

Meyerding, J. 1990. Letter to the editor. *Lesbian Resource Center Newsletter* 15 (April):5.

Morgan, K. S. 1992. Caucasian lesbians' use of psychotherapy: A matter of attitude? *Psychology of Women Quarterly* 16:127–30.

Moses, A. E. 1978. *Identity Management in Lesbian Women.* New York: Praeger.

National Gay Task Force. 1981. *NGTF Corporate Survey.* Washington, D.C.: National Gay Task Force.

Osipow, S. H. 1983. *Theories of Career Development.* Englewood Cliffs, N.J.: Prentice-Hall.

Osipow, S. H. 1987. Counseling psychology: Theory, research, and practice in career counseling. *Annual Review of Psychology* 38:257–78.

Patterson, L. E. 1973. Girl's careers: Expressions of identity. *Vocational Guidance Quarterly* 21:268–75.

Rudolph, J. 1988. Counselors' attitudes toward homosexuality: A selective review of the literature. *Journal of Counseling and Development* 67:165–68.

Saghir, M. T., and E. Robins. 1973. *Male and Female Homosexuality: A Comprehensive Investigation.* Baltimore: Williams and Wilkins.

Schmitz, T. J. 1988. Career counseling implications with the gay and lesbian population. *Journal of Employment Counseling* 25:51–56.

Schneider, B. E. 1987. Coming out at work: Bridging the private/public gap. *Work and Occupations* 13:463–87.

Shachar, S. A., and L. A. Gilbert. 1983. Working lesbians: Role conflicts and coping strategies. *Psychology of Women Quarterly* 7:244–56.

Stanley, J. P., and S. Wolfe, eds. 1989. *The Original Coming Out Stories.* Freedom, Calif.: Crossing Press.

Tanner, D. M. 1978. *The Lesbian Couple.* Lexington, Mass.: D. C. Heath.

Turner, B. F., and C. B. Turner. 1975. Race, sex, and perception of the occupational opportunity structure among college students. *Sociological Quarterly* 16:345–60.

IV

Gender Differences in Roles and Behavior

Gender is used in our culture as a primary organizing principle for the structuring of many aspects of people's lives. Male and female gender roles, which includes being heterosexual, comprise a core part of one's identity. Lesbians and gay men appear to experience the same social pressure to conform to gender norms as do heterosexual men and women. As a result of gender socialization and status differentials, gay identity development and exploration of same-sex experiences may follow different developmental patterns in women and men: "For women, who often come out in the context of a relationship, identity and intimacy as developmental tasks may become interwoven, whereas men's socialization toward autonomy and sexual freedom may lead to the resolution of identity tasks prior to the negotiation of intimacy" (Fassinger 1991:168).

Gender differences are embedded in a cultural context of social structural and status variables (Blumstein and Schwartz 1989; Nichols 1990). Likewise, having sex with members of the same gender is defined in divergent ways across cultures, reflecting patterns of gender, kinship, and economic structure (Adam 1985; Carrier 1980). The interaction of these cultural patterns affects and reflects attitudes, ideologies, sexual division of labor, power relationships, and status differentials between genders, as well as the social organization of sexual opportunities.

Three major themes stand out for understanding gender differences in roles and behaviors as they apply to lesbians and gay men: a) how social conceptions of gender and sexual orientation are interrelated and differ across cultures; b) the impact of gender roles on gay men and lesbians; and c) the relationship among gender role norms and antigay attitudes.

In the United States in the 1990s, as in other Western cultures, "the erotic is simultaneously promoted and denied, homophobia remains the norm, the genders are segregated in many domains of social life, anti-woman practices and values are widespread" (Gagnon 1990:179). The situation differs in other cultures. The article by Blackwood reviews cross-cultural research on lesbians and reveals the important influence of differing gender systems and different levels of social stratification on patterns of lesbian experience.

In general, complex sociopolitical factors are linked with gender role and sexual orientation. This points out the importance of construing lesbian experience independently and not basing it solely on gay male models. Moreover, different gender role expectations and status differences between men and women place unequal and different constraints on women and men in sexual expression, same-sex intimacy, the meanings they attach to experiences, and gender nonconformity. Lesbians must experience their attractions in a societal context that devalues women and also devalues homosexuality. Restrictions placed on female sexuality may limit sexual expression of women's diverse potentials (Golden 1987).

A similar point can be made with regard to men and reflects also the second major theme, the impact of gender roles on gay men and lesbians. Ross (1983) examined three societies with differing degrees of gender role traditionalism and attitudes about homosexuality. He found gay men to be more "effeminate" in those societies with strict gender role segregation and antigay attitudes. In societies with more liberal attitudes and gender roles, gay men did not differ from heterosexual samples. Thus, the more male and female roles are dichotomized, the greater the tendency of cross-gender behavior among gay men. According to Ross (1987:239): "The less antihomosexual and less sex-role rigid the culture, the less homosexual men in it felt that they needed to fit into the complementary two-sex model with regard to opposite-sex characteristics."

Another example of the impact of gender roles on gay men and lesbians is that gay men are more likely than lesbians are to maintain the notion that sexual orientation is "discovered" and to define *gay* in terms of sexual arousal and sexual behavior (Hencken 1984). They generally are sexually active with male partners before labeling themselves as gay. Gay men gain sexual experiences with a variety of partners before focusing attention on one special person (Bell and Weinberg 1978). Their first committed relationships generally occur two to five years after defining themselves as gay.

These findings are consistent with data on heterosexual men who report greater interest in sexual fantasies and sexual activities that involve group sex, anonymous sex, and ready visual arousability, and who place greater value on sexual attractiveness of partners than heterosexual women (Chilman 1979; Green 1985; Hunt 1974; Phillis and Gromko 1985; Wilson 1987). Moreover, heterosexual husbands have more extramarital affairs than their wives do (Hunt 1974; Kinsey, Pomeroy, and Martin 1948; Kinsey et al. 1953). Many similarities have been found between what heterosexual and homosexual men value about intimacy, for example, an interest in sexual variety and separation of sexual behavior from love and emotional commitment (Dailey 1979).

Lesbians are more likely than gay men are to define themselves in terms of their total identity and not only their sexual behavior. They more frequently define their sexual identity in terms of affectional preferences or political choices than do gay men (Gramick 1984; Peplau and Cochran 1981; Vetere 1983). A predominant pattern for lesbians is to engage in sexual activity as a natural and logical outgrowth of a strong emotional/romantic attachment. In general, lesbians report having their first sexual experience in the context of their first relationship (Blumstein and Schwartz 1989; Ponse 1978). They tend to have few or no sexual experiences with women prior to defining themselves as lesbians. Realization of being in love with or in a relationship with a person of the same gender may serve as a catalyst for solidifying lesbian self-identification.

These findings fit with data on heterosexual women who are less likely to view sexual acts as a revelation of their true sexual self (Blumstein and Schwartz 1989) and who report sexual fantasies and sexual enjoyment in terms of interest in romantic settings and committed partners (Wilson 1987). Moreover, women, regardless of sexual orientation, value emotional expressiveness (Blumstein and Schwartz 1983; Peplau 1981) sexual exclusivity and investment in and commitment to maintain relationships (Duffy and Rusbult 1986) more highly than men.

A strong connection between gender role beliefs and antigay attitudes has been documented, reflecting a link between sexism and heterosexism. In reality, sexual orientation is not inherently related to gender role conformity or nonconformity. Gender stereotypes are, however, an important aspect of the content of antigay sterotypes. Specifically, gay men are pre-sumed to have characteristics that are culturally defined as nonmasculine, and lesbians are believed to manifest nonfeminine characteristics (Herek 1984; Kite and Deaux 1986, 1987). Moreover, gay men and lesbians who violate stereotypic expectations of gender roles by appearing effeminate or butch are more disliked than those who do not (Laner and Laner 1979; Storms 1978).

Fear of being labeled gay is a powerful socialization influence in our society which has negative consequences for both heterosexual and homo-sexual individuals. Women and men who manifest characteristics incon-sistent with those culturally prescribed for their gender, regardless of their sexual orientation, are likely to be labeled as gay (Deaux and Lewis 1984; Storms et al. 1981). For example, a woman who challenges the accepted conventions of female behavior or femininity by exhibiting autonomous behavior is frequently viewed as a lesbian.

As a result, heterosexuals often restrict their gender-role behavior for fear of being labeled homosexual and thereby stigmatized. This influence appears to be especially strong among men (Herek 1991; Pleck 1981). Attempts to avoid the stigma of being labeled gay inhibit heterosexual men's and women's ability to form close, intimate relationships with mem-bers of their own gender. As Pellegrini explained:

> Fear and distrust among women, then, is another effect of the interstruc-turing of sexism and lesbian-hating. Where woman-hating is endemic to a culture, lesbian-hating, understood as the hatred of women making their lives with other women, is sure to follow. . . . The costs to all women in energies diffused, talent and commitment wasted outright, and lives lost amid silence, denials, and invisibility are immeasurable. (1992:51)

Distrust at gender-role violation is often reflected in antigay attitudes among heterosexuals. In addition, heterosexuals with negative attitudes toward gay people are more likely to express traditional, restrictive atti-tudes about gender and family roles, and to report less approval of equality between the sexes (Herek 1984, 1988). Moreover, there are gender dif-ferences in the degree of hostility and prejudice that heterosexual people feel and express toward lesbians and gay men. It has been found that heterosexual men manifest more antigay attitudes on the average than do heterosexual women (Herek 1991; Kite 1984; Laner and Laner 1979) and that heterosexual females' attitudes toward lesbians and gay men in general do not differ in intensity, while heterosexual males hold more negative attitudes toward gay men than toward lesbians (Herek 1988; Kite 1984).

Herek's article provides an explanation for the link between antigay attitudes and male and female gender role sanctions and norms. He also points out that many males need to affirm their masculinity through the rejection of that which is defined as nonmasculine, specifically male homosexuality, but that heterosexual females have less need to reject lesbians as a part of developing their own sense of identity as women. Therefore, women may experience fewer socially defined gender pressures to feel antigay prejudice.

It should be noted that gay men and lesbians neither adhere rigidly to traditional gender roles nor consistently engage in cross-gender behavior. Rather, gay men and lesbians may be more androgynous than heterosexuals are. Specifically, lesbians not only score higher on scales of masculinity and gay men score higher on scales of femininity than heterosexual women and men, respectively, but also gay men, lesbians, and heterosexuals do not differ in self-descriptions congruent with their gender (Kurdek and Schmitt 1986; Pillard 1991). In addition, lesbian and gay communities are more accepting of behaviors that would be perceived by the larger society as violations of gender roles. As Browning, Reynolds, and Dworkin (1991) noted: "Because the boundaries of acceptable role behavior are often different within the lesbian community, lesbians may find support there for aspects of their identity as women that are not traditionally accepted by the nongay community" (p. 178).

Since traditional roles and stereotypes limit options for men and women (Garnets and Pleck 1978), gender-role flexibility among lesbians and gay men may contribute to their constructing self-images different from heterosexuals (Vargo 1987). As Morgan and Brown noted:

> From a practical standpoint as well as an ideological one, it makes sense that lesbians as a group would tend toward less gender-role stereotypic behaviors: when women choose to live independent of men, the many household maintenance activities that have traditionally been classified as "men's work" (including the role of breadwinner) still must be done, so gender-role flexibility is a reasonable and necessary adaptive response. (1991:278)

CONTEMPORARY ISSUE: HOMOPHOBIA AND ANTILESBIAN/ANTIGAY VIOLENCE

Homophobia affects heterosexuals, as well as gay men and lesbians, through its enforcement of traditional, rigid gender roles. Homophobia can be used to stigmatize, silence, and target people who are perceived as deviating from their gender role whether they are actually gay, lesbian, bisexual, or heterosexual (Blumenfeld 1992). Moreover, given how the male gender role is structured in our society, young men often use the fear of homosexuality and the expressions of hatred toward homosexuals as proof of their masculinity. As Harry explained:

> Gay-bashing serves to validate one's maleness in the areas of both violence and sexuality. It is a sexual, but not homosexual, act because it reaffirms one's commitment to sexuality exclusively in its heterosexual form. (1990:352)

The consequences of the linkage between antigay attitudes and gender-role beliefs is clearly bad for lesbians and gay men and has led to antigay and antilesbian violence. The incidence of these violent assaults has been brought to the forefront with the recent passage of the National Hate Crimes Statistics Act. The act requires the U.S. Justice Department to collect data on bias crimes, including those motivated by prejudice based on sexual orientation. This focus on antigay violence should help to document the prevalence and scope of such hate crimes nationally, and to educate law enforcement agencies about its seriousness.

Herek (1990) noted that recent evidence suggests, however, "the traditional equation of homosexuality with gender norm violation appears to be weakening" (p. 328). The loosening of this linkage would be beneficial to gay men and lesbians by reducing homophobic stereotypes. Moreover, it has direct payoff for heterosexuals as well since it would allow greater flexibility in gender roles, expanding the boundaries of acceptable behavior for heterosexual women and men. Eliminating homophobic conditioning would also help end the dehumanizing effects on heterosexuals when they demean people who are different from themselves (Blumenfeld 1992). Friedman described these possibilities in his vision for nonheterosexist male gender roles:

> Boys will respond to "girl" putdowns by saying, "Thank you. There are qualities of being female that I am proud to possess." The new males will counter sexism, heterosexism, and other forms of oppression, realizing that these hurt them by reinforcing rigid gender role stereotypes. . . .
>
> Perhaps, most important, society will expect men to be nothing less than what they have the positive potential to be. In this ideal world's romance novels, boys who become men that are sensitive, loving, gentle, and charing, will be appreciated and truly desired. (1989:9)

REFERENCES

Adam, B. D. 1985. Age, structure, and sexuality: Reflections on the anthropological evidence on homosexual relations. *Journal of Homosexuality* 11(3–4):19–33.

Bell, A. P., and M. S. Weinberg. 1978. *Homosexualities: A Study of Diversity among Men and Women.* New York: Simon and Schuster.

Blumenfeld, W. J. 1992. Introduction. In J. Blumenfeld, ed., *Homophobia: How We All Pay the Price,* pp. 1–22. Boston: Beacon.

Blumstein, P., and P. Schwartz. 1983. *American Couples: Money, Work, Sex.* New York: Morrow.

Blumstein, P., and P. Schwartz. 1989. Intimate relationships and the creation of sexuality. In B. Risman and P. Schwartz, eds., *Gender in Intimate Relationships: A Microstructural Approach,* pp. 120–29. Belmont, Calif.: Wadsworth.

Browning, C., A. L. Reynolds, and S. H. Dworkin. 1991. Affirmative psychotherapy for lesbian women. *The Counseling Psychologist* 19(2):177–96.

Carrier, J. M. 1980. Homosexual behavior in cross-cultural perspective. In J. Marmor, ed., *Homosexual Behavior: A Modern Reappraisal,* pp. 100–22. New York: Basic Books.

Chilman, C. 1979. *Adolescent Sexuality in a Changing American Society: Social and Psychological Perspectives.* Washington, D.C.: U.S. Government Printing Office.

Dailey, D. M. 1979. Adjustment of heterosexual and homosexual couples in pairing relationships: An exploratory study. *Journal of Sex Research* 15:143–57.

Deaux, K., and L. L. Lewis. 1984. Structure of gender stereotypes: Interrelationships among components and gender label. *Journal of Personality and Social Psychology* 46:991–1004.

Duffy, S. M., and C. E. Rusbult. 1986. Satisfaction and commitment in homosexual and heterosexual relationships. *Journal of Homosexuality* 12(2):1–24.

Fassinger, R. E. 1991. The hidden minority: issues and challenges in working with lesbian women and gay men. *The Counseling Psychologist* 19(2):157–76.

Friedman, J. 1989. The impact of homophobia on male sexual development. *Siecus Report* 17(5):8–9.

Gagnon, J. H. 1990. Gender preference in erotic relations: The Kinsey scale and sexual scripts. In D. P. McWhirter, S. A. Sanders, and J. M. Reinisch, eds., *Homosexuality/Heterosexuality: Concepts of Sexual Orientation,* pp.177–207. New York: Oxford University Press.

Garnets, L., and J. Pleck. 1978. Sex role identity, androgyny, and sex role transcendence: A sex role strain analysis. *Psychology of Women Quarterly* 3:270–83.

Golden, C. 1987. Diversity and variability in women's sexual identities. In Boston Lesbian Psychologies Collective, eds., *Lesbian Psychologies: Explorations and Challenges,* pp. 19–34. Urbana: University of Illinois Press.

Gramick, J. 1984. Developing a lesbian identity. In T. Darty and S. Potter, eds., *Women-Identified Women,* pp. 31–44. Palo Alto, Calif.: Mayfield.

Green, V. 1985. Experimental factors in childhood and adolescent sexual behavior: Family interactions and previous sexual experiences. *Journal of Sex Research* 21:157–82.

Harry, J. 1990. Conceptualizing anti-gay violence. *Journal of Interpersonal Violence* 5(3):350–58.

Hencken, J. 1984. Conceptualizations of homosexual behavior which preclude homosexual self-labeling. *Journal of Homosexuality* 9(4):53–63.

Herek, G. M. 1984. Attitudes towards lesbians and gay men: A factor-analytic study. *Journal of Homosexuality* 10(1–2):39–52.

Herek, G. M. 1988. Heterosexuals' attitudes toward lesbians and gay men: Correlates and gender differences. *Journal of Sex Research* 25:451–77.

Herek, G. M. 1990. The context of anti-gay violence: Notes on cultural and psychological heterosexism. *Journal of Interpersonal Violence* 5(3):316–33.

Herek, G. M. 1991. Stigma, prejudice, and violence against lesbians and gay men. In J. D. Gonsiorek and J. D. Weinrich, eds., *Homosexuality: Research Implications for Public Policy*, pp. 60–80. Newbury Park, Calif.: Sage.

Hunt, M. 1974. *Sexual Behavior in the 1970s*. Chicago: Playboy Press.

Kinsey, A. C., W. B. Pomeroy, and C. E. Martin. 1948. *Sexual Behavior in the Human Male*. Philadelphia: W. B. Saunders.

Kinsey, A. C., W. B. Pomeroy, C. E. Martin, and P. H. Gebhard. 1953. *Sexual Behavior in the Human Female*. Philadelphia: W. B. Saunders.

Kite, M. E. 1984. Sex differences in attitudes towards homosexuals: A meta-analytic review. *Journal of Homosexuality* 10(1–2):69–81.

Kite, M. E., and K. Deaux. 1986. Attitudes toward homosexuality: Assessment and behavioral consequences. *Basic and Applied Social Psychology* 7(2):137–62.

Kite, M. E., and K. Deaux. 1987. Gender belief systems: Homosexuality and the implicit inversion theory. *Psychology of Women Quarterly* 11(1):83–96.

Kurdek, L. A., and J. P. Schmitt. 1986. Interaction of sex role concept with relationship quality and relationship beliefs in married, heterosexual cohabiting, gay and lesbian relationships. *Journal of Personality and Social Psychology* 51:365–70.

Laner, M. R., and R. H. Laner. 1979. Personal style or sexual preference: Why gay men are disliked. *International Review of Modern Sociology* 9:215–28.

Morgan, K. S., and L. S. Brown. 1991. Lesbian career development, work behavior, and vocational counseling. *The Counseling Psychologist* 19(2):273–91.

Nichols, M. 1990. Lesbian relationships: Implications for the study of sexuality and gender. In D. P. McWhirter, S. A. Sanders, and J. M. Reinisch, eds., *Homosexuality/Heterosexuality: Concepts of Sexual Orientation*, pp.350–64. New York: Oxford University Press.

Pellegrini, A. 1992. S(h)ifting the terms of hetero/sexism: Gender, power, homophobias. In J. Blumenfeld, ed., *Homophobia: How We All Pay the Price*, pp. 1–22. Boston: Beacon.

Peplau, L. A. and S. D. Cochran. 1981. Value orientations in the intimate relationships of gay men. *Journal of Homosexuality* 6(3):1–19.

Pleck, J. H. 1981. *The Myth of Masculinity*. Cambridge, Mass.: MIT Press.

Phillis, D. E., and M. H. Gromko. 1985. Sex differences in sexual activity: Reality or illusion? *Journal of Sex Research* 21:437–48.

Pillard, R. C. 1991. Masculinity and femininity in homosexuality: "Inversion" revisited. In J. D. Gonsiorek and J. D. Weinrich, eds., *Homosexuality: Research Implications for Public Policy*, pp. 32–43. Newbury Park, Calif.: Sage.

Ponse, B. 1978. *Identities in the Lesbian World: The Social Construction of Self.* Boston: Allyn and Bacon.

Ross, M. W. 1983. Femininity, masculinity, and sexual orientation: Some cross-cultural comparisons. *Journal of Homosexuality* 9(1):27–36.

Ross, M. W. 1987. A theory of normal homosexuality. In L. Diamant, ed., *Male and Female Homosexuality: Psychological Approaches*, pp. 237–59. Washington, D.C.: Hemisphere.

Storms, M. D. 1978. Attitudes toward homosexuality and femininity in men. *Journal of Homosexuality* 3(3):257–63.

Storms, M. D., M. L. Stifers, S. M. Lambers, and C. A. Hill. 1981. Sexual scripts for women. *Sex Roles* 3:257–63.

Vargo, S. 1987. The effects of women's socialization on lesbian couples. In Boston Lesbian Psychologies Collective, eds., *Lesbian Psychologies: Explorations and Challenges*, pp. 161–73. Urbana: University of Illinois Press.

Vetere, V. A. 1983. The role of friendships in the development and maintenance of lesbian love relationships. *Journal of Homosexuality* 8(2):51–65.

Wilson, G. D. 1987. Male-female differences in sexual activity, enjoyment and fantasies. *Personality and Individual Differences* 8:125–27.

11

Breaking the Mirror: The Construction of Lesbianism and the Anthropological Discourse on Homosexuality

Evelyn Blackwood

This article reviews the anthropological discourse on homosexuality by examining the assumptions that have been used by anthropologists to explain homosexual behavior, and by identifying current theoretical approaches. The article questions the emphasis on male homosexual behavior as the basis for theoretical analysis, and points to the importance of including female homosexual behavior in the study of homosexuality. Cross-cultural data on lesbian behavior are presented and the influence of gender divisions and social stratification on the development of patterns of lesbian behavior are broadly explored. The article outlines suggestions for examining the cultural context of lesbian behavior, as well as the constraints exerted on women's sexual behavior in various cultures.

Recent years have seen a burgeoning of studies on homosexuality in the social sciences, much of it inspired by the feminist and gay rights movements of the 1970s. The focus of this new literature, particularly in sociology and history, concerns the historical and cultural influences on homosexual behavior. Plummer suggests that "specific ways of experiencing sexual attraction and gender behavior are bound up with specific historical and cultural milieux" (1981:12). In a similar vein, historians looking at eroticism suggest that it is "subject to the forces of culture" (D'Emilio 1983:3), and thus accessible to historical analysis. The anthropological data on cross-cultural sexual variation provide much of the groundwork for such analyses; yet, it has been one of the failings of anthropology that the field itself has developed no adequate theory regarding the cultural construction of homosexual behavior.

This article examines assumptions that have been used by anthropologists to explain homosexual behavior, and identifies the current theoretical approaches. It also questions the continued emphasis on male homosexual behavior as a general model for theoretical analysis. It will bring women's sexual behavior within the purview of the current discussion on homosexuality by separating it from the historical construction of male homosexuality and by examining the particular cultural contexts of lesbian behavior. The terms *homosexuality* and *lesbianism*, as used in this article, refer to sexual behavior between individuals of the same sex. Their use should not be construed as imposing the structure of Western sexual ideology on cross-cultural practices; in Western sexual systems, individuals who are identified by their sexual behavior form isolated subcultures. This pattern bears little resemblance to the integral nature of homosexual practices in many tribal societies.

CROSS-CULTURAL THEORIES AND STUDIES

The anthropological study of homosexuality has been limited by serious methodological and theoretical problems. As Langness has aptly stated, "it is fair to say that we have no anthropological *theory* of homosexuality" (Read 1980:vii). The reasons for this absence are numerous and have been discussed in detail by several anthropologists (Carrier 1980; Fitzgerald 1977; Read 1980; Sonenschein 1966). In particular, most anthropologists have been affected by or accepted the prejudices of Western society toward homosexual behavior, and consequently have not considered the study of homosexuality to be a legitimate pursuit. The data they have gathered are limited to brief reports of homosexual practices. According to Carrier, these reports are "complicated by the prejudice of many observers who consider the behavior unnatural, dysfunctional, or associated with mental illness" (1980:101). Discussion of the topic has, in general, been restricted to statements regarding the presence or absence of certain types of sexual acts. Such cataloging has resulted in a considerable amount of information about sexual variation, but has provided little understanding of the cultural contexts within which these behaviors occur.[1]

Certain basic assumptions have colored the brief discussion of homosexuality in the anthropological literature. The theoretical models used in the past to analyze homosexual data derived directly from Western psychological concepts of sexuality. Most anthropologists based their evaluation of homosexual practices in other cultures on the deviance model of psychology and sociology, assuming that heterosexuality represented the norm for sexual behavior, and, therefore, homosexuality was abnormal or deviant behavior. Such evaluations were often in direct contrast to the meaning or value attached to homosexual behavior in the culture studied, since many groups accepted homosexual practices within their social system. For example, Berndt labeled the male homosexual practices of Australian aborigines as "sexual abnormalities" and "perversions" (1963). Other anthropologists have shown, however, that the aboriginal practices were acceptable and institutionalized in the form of "brother-in-law" exchange among aborigines (Layard 1959; Roheim 1950; Spencer and Gillen 1927). Hill (1935) described the Navajo *nadle* (hermaphrodites) as unhappy and maladjusted individuals despite the fact that the *nadle* were (or had been) highly revered and respected by the Navajo (see Greenberg 1985 on ridiculing berdache). In a classic example of the contrast between emic and etic categories, Metraux declared that "*abnormal* sexual relationships between women (were) tolerated and *accepted*" on Easter Island (1940:108; emphasis added).

Implicit in this approach has been the belief that sexual behavior belonged to the domain of the individual (see Padgug 1979). As a private act, it has not been considered relevant to the larger functioning of the social group. For psychological anthropologists who studied sexual behavior, such behavior served as an indicator of the individual's adjustment to society. These anthropologists considered the homosexual individual to be a person unable to adjust to the prescribed gender role. As evidence, they cited the males among the Plains Indians who were thought to lack the temperament for a warrior, and so turned to the berdache role (see Benedict 1939; Mead 1935).

Another assumption in the anthropological discourse on homosexuality has been the belief in a "homosexual nature" underlying all expressions of homosexuality. This assumption was the basis of Kroeber's "homosexual niche" theory, which he used to explain the Native American berdache. He maintained that American Indian culture *accommodated* individuals who were homosexual by creating the berdache institution (Kroeber 1925, 1940). He believed that individuals took on the berdache role as the result of psychological or congenital problems, and that these individuals were found in most tribes. His ideas reflected what is currently being called "essentialism," the argument for a common transhistorical substrate of behavior or desire in all cultures.[2] In the study of homosexual behavior, this view is expressed in the perception that a certain percentage of homosexual individuals will take on the role in their culture which allows the expression of a homosexual nature, such as the Native American berdache, the Tahitian mahu, or Chukchee shaman role (see Callender and Kochems 1985 for other male roles).

Although their views were to some extent within this essentialist framework, certain anthropologists foreshadowed a later historical-cultural construction of sexuality through application of a learning theory model. Both Mead (1935) and Benedict (1934) referred to the great arc of human potential from which cultures chose particular traits. Yet, they found that this "essential" core was less and less relevant to the social design of human behavior. Benedict proposed that human behavior takes the forms that societal institutions prescribe, while Mead also argued for the malleability of humans in learning cultural forms. In considering "the homosexual," the emphasis in both their works, as noted above, was on the failure of the individual to adjust; nevertheless, it was argued that cultural factors shaped the homosexual response. Mead (1961) later pointed out that various individual personality cues combine with the cultural interpretation of sexuality to shape an individual's sex role. In contrast to the majority of anthropologists, both Mead and Benedict suggested that homosexual roles had certain valid cultural functions and were acceptable in some societies. Their suggestions opened the way for fuller analysis of the cultural context of homosexual behavior.

HISTORICAL-CULTURAL CONTEXT

Largely as a result of the feminist and gay movements of the late sixties and seventies, anthropologists began a new analysis of homosexual behavior. The feminist declaration that "the personal is political" underscored the realization, as Ross and Rapp point out, that "the seemingly most intimate details of private existence are actually structured by larger social relations" (1981:51). Further prompted by the gay movement's rejection of the Western definition of homosexuality, anthropologists realized the need to understand sexuality from a perspective which took into account the importance of both the historical period and the cultural context. They joined other social scientists in the historical constructionist approach, or more appropriately for anthropology, the historical-cultural construction of sexuality.

Recent work on the historical-cultural construction of sexuality brings definition to the cultural factors that shape sexual behavior, and, in a sense, chips away at the essentialist core by establishing the importance of external, social factors. Ross and Rapp state the following:

> Sexuality's biological base is always experienced culturally, through a translation. The bare biological facts of sexuality do not speak for themselves; they must be expressed socially. Sex feels individual, or at least private, but

those feelings always incorporate the roles, definitions, symbols and meanings of the worlds in which they are constructed. (1981:51)

Padgug has suggested the importance of the economic context in the construction of sexuality because "sexuality, class, and politics cannot easily be disengaged from one another" (1979:5). Other areas that "condition, constrain and socially define" sexuality, as suggested by Ross and Rapp are a) kinship and family systems; b) sexual regulations and definitions of communities; and c) national and "world" systems (1981:54). Patterns of homosexual behavior reflect the value system and social structure of the different societies in which they are found. The ideology regarding male and female roles, kinship and marriage regulations, and the sexual division of labor are all important in the construction of homosexual behavior. Thus, the historical-cultural factors affect and shape the expression of homosexuality.

Several recent works reflect this perspective to a greater or lesser degree. Levy (1971) suggested that the mahu of Tahiti, a traditional transvestite role for males (of which there was usually one in each village), functioned as a message to males regarding the nonmale role that they should avoid. Others include Wolf's *The Lesbian Community* (1979), on the lesbian-feminist community in San Francisco, Read's *Other Voices* (1980), on the life-style in a male homosexual tavern in the United States, Herdt's *Guardians of the Flutes* (1981) and *Ritualized Homosexuality in Melanesia* (1984), and Esther Newton's *Mother Camp: Female Impersonators in America* (1972). Carrier's (1980) cross-cultural survey established some basic correlations between sociocultural context and the expression of homosexuality. He suggested that homosexual behavior correlated with the particular cultural ideology regarding sexuality and cross-gender behavior, as well as with the availability of sexual partners.

MALE VERSUS FEMALE HOMOSEXUALITY

Until now the historical-cultural construction of homosexuality has been based predominantly on the theories of male homosexuality that have been applied to both male and female homosexual behavior or, even more abstractly, to a "transgender" homosexuality. In looking back at her classic article on the homosexual role, Mary McIntosh stated that "the assumption always is that we can use the same theories and concepts for female homosexuality and that, for simplicity, we can just talk about men and assume that it applies to women" (1981:45). Because men's and women's roles are structured differently in all cultures, however, the structure of female homosexuality must be examined as well. A one-sided discourse on homosexuality does not adequately comprehend the complex interplay of factors that shape homosexual behavior, male or female. Frequently, the construction of homosexual behavior occurs at the level of gender systems, for example, in the context of gender redefinition (cross-gender or gender-mixing roles) or gender antagonism (ritualized male homosexuality). Because of the importance of gender roles in homosexual behavior, no analysis can be complete without adequately evaluating both female and male gender roles. As Lindenbaum states, "gender is the mutual production of men and women acting in concert, whether it be in the form of cooperation or of opposition" (1984:338).

Further, the different constraints placed on women and men demand a separate analysis of lesbian behavior in order to identify the contexts of women's roles that uniquely shape its expression. Past research on homosexuality reflects the implicit assumption that lesbian behavior is the mirror image of male homosexuality. Yet, the act of having sex with a member of one's own sex may be culturally defined in rather divergent ways for women and men. The basic difference derives from the gender division which is imposed in all cultures and based on the physical differences between the two sexes. As Mead stated:

> All known human societies recognize the anatomic and functional differences between males and females in intricate and complex ways; through insistence on small nuances of behavior in posture, stance, gait, through language, ornamentation and dress, division of labor, legal social status. (1961:1451)

The different constraints imposed on men and women affect the construction of homosexual roles, behaviors, and meanings. Therefore, the factors that are significant in male homosexuality may not be significant to the construction of female homosexuality. For example, the ritual homosexuality of New Guinea men was a result of the need to separate boys from the contaminating power of their mothers and of the belief that boys did not develop strength or masculinity naturally. Adult men helped them grow through ritual insemination (see Gray 1985; also Herdt 1981, 1984). Girls, on the other hand, were believed to have an inherent femininity and reproductive competence, possessing the female essence from birth (Herdt 1981). Since it was not necessary for women to ritually implant femaleness in young girls, no ritual homosexuality analogous to male behavior existed for women. On the other hand, patterns of homosexual behavior may be similar for men and women, such as the cross-gender role among Native Americans, although still differentially affected by their separate roles and statuses. Consequently, the discourse on homosexuality must be informed by an analysis of the construction of lesbianism, which this next section will attempt to provide.

APPROACHES TO LESBIANISM

Despite the fact that no anthropological study other than Wolf's (1979) has focused on lesbianism, anthropologists and other social scientists have attempted to compare female and male homosexuality. Although their conclusions are questionable because of the lack of attention to the subject, they suggest that female homosexuality is less institutionalized, less well developed, less important, or less visible than male homosexuality (Carrier 1980; Ford and Beach 1951). The reasons given for the lack of female homosexual patterns frequently rely on the notion of biological constraints. Mead, for example, despite the prevalence of a learning theory model in most of her work, reverts to an essentialist position in her analysis of female homosexuality. She suggested that "female anatomy dictates no choices as to activity, passivity, asymmetry, or complementariness and seems to lend itself much less to institutionalization as a counter-mores activity" (1961:1471). Whitehead (1981), in considering the Native American female cross-gender role, is also inclined to place the onus on the greater constraints of female biology as compared to male biology. Such arguments do not sufficiently take into account the cultural constraints and influences on women's roles, but rather fall back on the notion of biological determinism to explain women's activities and roles. Carrier is more to the point when he suggests that the "higher status accorded men than women in most societies" may account for the lower incidence on female homosexuality (1980:103). Rather than explaining the data of lesbianism in terms of the prerequisites of physiology, patterns of lesbian behavior can be more accurately explained by the type of gender system and the autonomy of women in particular cultures.

ANTHROPOLOGICAL STUDY OF WOMEN

In looking at the anthropological data on women and lesbianism, a majority of ethnographies contain little or no data on lesbian behavior. Several factors, other than the absence of lesbianism, have contributed to this lack of information. Traditional anthropologists were concerned with the normative female role, studying women in activities that reflected the Western ideology of womanhood as supportive and nurturing of male concerns.

Ethnographers focused on the role of women in domestic activities, such as gathering, weaving, childrearing, and preparing food for their families, often to the exclusion of women's activities outside this domestic sphere. They typically assumed that within the normative female role women engaged exclusively in heterosexual behavior. Consequently, they were unable to identify nonheterosexual behavior, or if they did, they failed to understand that in many instances it was acceptable, desirable, or easily accessible to a large number of women in non-Western cultures. For example, Firth concluded that Tikopia women did not engage in lesbianism because so many male partners were available to them (1936:495). He was assuming a natural preference for heterosexuality over homosexuality.

To complicate the matter, anthropological fieldwork was done predominantly by males, talking to male informants about male activities. According to Reiter, the details of women's lives "[come] from questions asked of men about their wives, daughters, and sisters, rather than the women themselves" (1975:12). Male informants were frequently unqualified or unwilling to discuss women's business, and their hesitance or lack of knowledge was particularly critical to the process of obtaining data on lesbian behavior. Evans-Pritchard (1970) reported that Azande women kept their lesbian relations as secret as possible even from their husbands. The data he gathered from his male informants on women's homosexual relations necessarily reflected male assumptions and feelings rather than the female experience.

On the other hand, though many ethnographies contain no reports of lesbian behavior, some anthropologists have had notable success eliciting such information from female informants. For instance, Shostak's (1981) life-history of Nisa, a !Kung woman, reveals that homosexual relations among girls was an accepted adolescent phenomenon. Prior studies made no reference to lesbian behavior among the !Kung. Other data are muddled both by anthropologists' and informants' reticence on the subject. Mueller, who studied Lesotho "mummy-baby" relationships, did not obtain explicit information on the women's sexual activity because, as she admits, "I was not able to ask such personal questions, largely because of my own embarrassment" (1977:167). Gay found that mummy-baby relationships are "regarded as very personal and are only discussed reticently with a stranger whose disapproval they fear" (1985). In light of these discrepancies, references to the absence of homosexual behavior, whether female or male, may prove to be a poor basis for cross-cultural analysis.

Another problem with the anthropological data is that they have largely reflected the prevailing Western conception of lesbianism. From the late 1800s sexologists and social scientists identified masculine behavior in women as lesbianism; not surprisingly, women in "masculine" or cross-gender roles comprise nearly half of all the anthropological data on lesbianism (see Blackwood 1984a). The remainder of the data simply reports the occurrence of sexual activity among adolescent girls or adult women. Anthropologists have ignored or overlooked other types of lesbian relations. Gay (1985) candidly admitted that she was unaware of Lesotho girls' "mummy-baby" relationships, intimate girlfriend relationships, until a year after she had lived in her study area. She only then observed the relationship because her research assistant pointed it out. Thus, the anthropologist's knowledge or stereotype of Western lesbianism inhibits the collection of accurate data where relationships do not resemble the expected form.

The numerous problems with the data on lesbianism stem predominantly from the male biases and prejudices regarding lesbian behavior and women's roles. Although it is impossible to determine the universal prevalence of lesbianism, the small number of anthropological reports on the subject are more likely due to the limitation of the observers than to the condition of women's lives. Yet, even the perception that the amount of data is very small may be inaccurate. In Ford and Beach's (1951) cross-cultural survey of homosexual and lesbian behavior (the source most used in discussions of cross-cultural variation in homosexuality), seventeen out of seventy-six cultures surveyed in the Human Relations Area File reported female homosexuality. By comparison, a recent survey of lesbian behavior (Blackwood 1984a) found ninety-five cultures where lesbian and female cross-gender behavior occurred (plus several more that hinted at a possible lesbian role). Although a third of these were Native North American tribes, the amount of data nevertheless indicates the limitations of previous studies, as well as the misconceptions they have fostered regarding the prevalence of female homosexuality.

THE CONSTRUCTION OF LESBIANISM

Systems of gender, kinship, and economy (as suggested by Adam 1985) affect the construction of both female and male homosexuality. Yet, the differential experiences of gender provide the basis for divergent lesbian and male homosexual patterns. To understand the cultural factors significant to the construction of lesbian behavior, the focus in this section will be on the female role and the contexts within which lesbian behavior appears. In particular, it will outline the influence of differing gender systems and different levels of social stratification on the development of patterns of lesbian behavior.[3]

Putting aside cross-gender behavior for the moment, the construction of lesbianism, where it occurs, takes place within the sphere of female activities and networks. Women in all cultures are expected to marry and bear children; in many, they are betrothed and wed before or soon after puberty. Consequently, for the most part, lesbian behavior locates within the structure of marriage relations, but within that system a variety of sexual relations are possible.

The range of lesbian behavior that appears cross-culturally varies from formal to informal relations. These patterns may be described as follows. Informal relations among women are those that do not extend beyond the immediate social context. Examples of such would be adolescent sex play and affairs among women in harems or polygynous households. Formal lesbian relations are part of a network or social structure extending beyond the pair or immediate love relationship, and occur within such social relationships as bond friendship, sisterhoods, initiation schools, the cross-gender role, or woman-marriage. An examination of social stratification suggests that, in societies where women have control over their productive activities and status, both formal and informal relations may occur. Where women lack power, particularly in class societies, they maintain only informal lesbian ties or build institutions outside the dominant culture.

Nonclass Societies

In nonclass societies, depending on the degree of economic autonomy of women, several patterns of formal and informal lesbian relations occur. These patterns can be found in both highly stratified states, such as those of the Azande and Dahomey in Africa, and the more egalitarian !Kung of southern Africa and the Australian aborigines. The patterns in each group result from cultural factors such as kinship regulations, the marriage system, trade rights, and sexual customs. Among the Azande, the husband's kin arranged marriage by paying a brideprice to the wife's kin. The brideprice gave them the right to claim the offspring of the wife for their lineage. Wealthier men married several wives and built a dwelling in the compound for each wife. Wives were given a plot of land to cultivate, and they controlled the profits made from the produce through trade. Women married shortly after puberty, but as they fulfilled their duties as a wife, certain rights accrued to them. Consequently, despite the demands of the marriage system, some Azande women established formal lesbian relationships, often with their cowives. According to Evans-Pritchard (1970:1429), "All Azande I have known well enough to discuss this matter have asserted . . . that female homosexuality . . . was practiced in polygamous homes in the past and still [1930] is sometimes."

Azande women usually kept the sexual nature of their friendships secret from their husbands, who felt threatened by such activities yet could not forbid them. Such relationships may have been fairly common for adult women in certain other African groups where marriage was polygynous, as among the Nupe (Nadel 1942), the Haussa (Karsch-Haack 1975), and the Nyakyusa (Wilson 1963). A relationship between two Azande women could be formalized through a ritual that created a permanent bond (Evans-Pritchard 1970). This bond secured the emotional and economic support of the partner, and may have served to widen the trade network of the woman and possibly enhance her position in the community.[4] Thus, both formal and informal relationships occurred within the context of marriage among women who were in daily contact through their domestic and trade activities. It indicated that male control of female activities did not extend to interactions and concerns between females.

In other nonclass societies lesbian relations occurred in sex-segregated childhood and adolescent groups. Among the highly stratified Dahomeyans, adolescent girls prepared for marriage responsibilities by attending initiation schools, where, among other activities, they performed exercises in each other's presence to thicken their genitalia. It has been noted that they engaged in sexual activities on these occasions (Herskovits 1967). Such activity was congruent with their school training and served to heighten awareness of their erotic responses. Among the egalitarian !Kung, girls engaged in sexual play with other girls before they did so with boys (Shostak 1981). In another egalitarian group, the Australian aborigines, adolescent sex play was an acknowledged and integral part of the social system. It conformed to the kinship regulations for marriage partners (Roheim 1933), occurring among girls who were cross-cousins. Thus, an Australian girl formed lesbian relations with her female cross-cousin, whose family would later give her their son to marry, the girlfriends thereby becoming sisters-in-law.

In comparing the highly stratified social structure of Dahomey or the Azande to the more egalitarian Australian aborigines, the different constraints on lesbian behavior stand out. Herskovits (1932) stated that the adolescent period for Dahomeyan women was an acceptable time for lesbian activity. Some adult women also engaged in it, probably in the context of polygynous marriages, but this was secretly done. Azande women also maintained clandestine relationships. Roheim (1933) reported that married Australian women engaged in lesbian activities, one form of which was called *kityili-kityili*, tickling the clitoris with the finger. Although a woman's first marriage was controlled by her kin, she had the choice, following the death of her first husband, to engage in various marital and extramarital relations (Bell 1980, 1981). While Dahomeyan women were forced to conceal their lesbian activities, the lesbian relationships of the Australian women were an acknowledged part of their sexual behavior and were included in ritual activities (Kaberry 1939). Thus, different levels of social stratification and marriage systems shape different patterns of lesbian behavior in nonclass societies.

CLASS SOCIETIES

The contrast in patterns of lesbian behavior is sharper between nonclass and class societies. In those with rigid hierarchical gender systems women's sexual activities are strictly confined. Formal lesbian patterns do not exist unless they maintain a status marginal to the dominant culture. In such societies, with control of women's productive and reproductive rights vested in male kin, not only were women confined to heterosexual marriage, but also their sexual activities were restricted by law or custom to their marital partner. Islamic law called for imprisonment for homosexuality and death or divorce for a wife caught in adultery (Minai 1981). In this context, lesbian behavior, if it occurred at all, was informal and private. Clandestine relationships developed among Near Eastern women in harems and within the Muslim institution of purdah. Wives of ruling class men rarely saw their husbands and therefore sought alternative sources of relationships. Some wealthy, educated Near Eastern women could choose to remain unmarried and found great satisfaction in lesbian relationships (Abbott 1946; Bullough 1976; Walther 1981). Ultimately, the strict segregation of the sexes provided the only context for lesbian relations.

Conditions were similarly restrictive for Chinese women. The sisterhoods of Kwangtung Province provide the only available evidence of lesbian relationships in China (Sankar 1985). This institution of bond friendship necessarily arose outside the traditional marriage and kin structure. Although still guided by the cultural values of the dominant society, these women rejected the traditional gender role to form sisterhoods based on the traditions of girls' houses and celibacy vows. The availability of silk work in Kwangtung Province gave them the economic independence to refuse marriage. Some women did not engage in heterosexual relationships because of cultural sanctions imposed on those who took nonmarriage vows. Others formed lover relationships with a "sister" (Sankar 1978). Thus, in the class societies of the Near East and China the construction of lesbian relations showed two opposing trends: first, an informal pattern resulting from the restrictions of male-dominant institutions and, second, a sisterhood existing outside the social relations of the dominant culture and dependent on the success of female bonding and the tolerance of the larger society. This second type applies as well to the lesbian subculture of Western society in the last eighty years.

A formal pattern of age-graded lesbian relations appears in cultures with a dual economic system, such as Black South Africa and Carriacou in the Caribbean. In both areas males participate in a capitalist wage-labor system through migration to industrial areas, while women work the land and direct the affairs of the household. On Carriacou, husbands are separated from their wives for most of the year and at home are unable to command the exclusive attention of their wives. Older married women secure the affections and assistance of younger, often single women whom they support with income from the absentee husband (Smith 1962). This relationship provides both economic and emotional support and is a viable alternative to the domestic isolation of the women. A similar pattern exists in South Africa, the mummy-baby game. It maintains the same functions of emotional and economic support as in Carriacou, but the age range between women is smaller (Blacking 1978; Gay 1985; Mueller 1977). Despite the imposition of a capitalist wage-labor system on these groups, its effects are mitigated through female bonding in mutually beneficial relationships. In South Africa these relationships may have derived from a traditional pattern of affective relations between older and younger women (Gay 1985).

CROSS-GENDER ROLE

The cross-gender role for women constitutes another formal pattern of lesbian relations, which appears in certain classless societies and, in particular, in egalitarian societies. This role was institutionalized mainly among Western Native American tribes and integrated into the social structure of the larger society. Five Western tribes in which the cross-gender role has been observed at some length include the Mohave, Maricopa, Cocopa, Kaska, and Klamath (Blackwood 1984b). Depending on their interest and ability, some women in these tribes took on the male gender role, usually at puberty, and performed the duties associated with men, such as hunting, trapping, and, for Cocopa *warrhameh*, fighting in battle. These women were not denied the right to marry and frequently took wives with whom they established a household and raised children. The significance of the female cross-gender role lay in the ability of women to take on a male role regardless of their biology. Further, it was possible for them to cross roles without threatening the definition of the male role because men and women had equal status and occupied complementary rather than antagonistic gender roles (Blackwood 1984b).

In contrast to the flexibility of gender roles in egalitarian societies, class societies that have hierarchical gender systems define gender more rigidly. In such cultures the gender system is structured in a dichotomous fashion; neither sex participates in the behaviors nor activities of the other. In male-dominant cultures, such as Western Europe or the Near East, it is impossible for women to assume a cross-gender role because such behavior poses a threat to the gender system and the very definitions of maleness and femaleness. Those who did, such as the passing women of Western Europe, risked grave repercussions; if discovered, they faced serious punishment or even death (Crompton 1981; Faderman 1981).

CONCLUSION

The construction of lesbianism shatters some basic assumptions about women that have been propounded in the discourse on homosexuality. The perception that men maintain universal hegemony over women's sexuality is contradicted by the data on alternative sexual relationships for women. Rubin (1975) theorized that women were forced, through marriage, to be heterosexual and that this condition prevailed in all cultures. Others have subscribed to the concept of "enforced heterosexuality"; for example, Adrienne Rich has suggested that lesbianism "comprises both the breaking of a taboo and the rejection of a compulsory way of life . . . a direct or indirect attack on male right of access to women" (1980:649). In contrast to this analysis, the history of sexual relations is not one of total heterosexual dominance. The construction of sexuality in many non-class societies validated variant sexual behavior for women. Women's lives were not wholly constrained by the dictates of marriage and childbearing, nor did they live in total submission to men. Other types of sexual relations existed both before and after marriage. As the Azande example shows, various formal and informal lesbian relations coexisted with marriage, giving women several options and avenues for control of their lives and sexual activities. In many tribal societies lesbian relations were not considered deviant nor were the women "breaking taboos"; on the contrary, lesbian bonds were institutionalized and integrated into kinship and other social structures.

Social stratification and gender ideology may place serious restrictions on women's sexuality. The constraints of marriage and lack of property rights imposed on women in many societies apparently limits the development of nonmarital homosexual behavior and institutions. These constraints, however, should not be construed to be the result of the "limitations" of the female's biological sex. Enforced heterosexuality is tied to women's lack of economic power and the restriction of female activity to the domestic sphere. Further, the embeddedness of sexuality with gender roles in Western societies proscribes homosexual activity and defines women as male sex objects.

The barriers to female power and sexuality in modern society reside in the male-dominant ideologies of gender and sexuality. Nevertheless, as the Chinese sisterhoods exemplify, even within strongly patriarchal societies women are capable of forming alternative institutions that circumvent male control. Similarly, lesbians in the United States are now building their own institutions and kin structures, as well as creating sexual ideologies in opposition to the dominant society (Lockard 1985).

Patterns of lesbian behavior develop from the particular conditions of the female gender role and the types of constraints that arise from the subordinate status women occupy in many societies. These constraints establish patterns that in many cases diverge from those for male homosexual behavior and yet are not less critical to a general understanding of homosexuality. It is hoped that future research will provide a more balanced approach to the study of the construction of both female and male homosexual behavior.

ACKNOWLEDGMENTS

Many thanks go to Professors Mina Caulfield and Gilbert Herdt for their helpful comments and suggestions on this article, and to Professor John De Cecco, who originally suggested the issue of the *Journal of Homosexuality* in which this originally appeared, and for his faith in me. I also appreciate the help of professors Naomi Katz, Carolyn Clark, and Luis Kemnitzer in earlier phases of this work.

NOTES

1. Major works by nonanthropologists that make use of cross-cultural data are Bullough 1976; Burton 1956; Ellis and Symonds 1975; Ford and Beach 1951; Karsch-Haack 1975; West 1977; Westermarck 1956; also Katz's (1976) chapter on Native Americans. The first anthropological cross-cultural survey by Opler (1965) strongly reflected Western biases on homosexuality.

2. For further discussion of this theory see Weeks 1981:2–3; Whitehead 1984; Rubin 1984; De Cecco and Shively 1983/1984; and Richardson 1983/1984.

3. Gender systems can be drawn to roughly parallel levels of social stratification, that is, increased stratification, increased inequality of the sexes, though any particular society will need much greater analysis than can be provided here. The analysis here is suggestive rather than definitive.

4. Similar to men's blood-brotherhood, as described by Evans-Pritchard (1933).

REFERENCES

Abbott, N. 1946. *Two Queens of Bagdad.* Chicago: University of Chicago Press.
Adam, B. D. 1985. Age, structure, and sexuality: Reflections on the anthropological evidence on homosexual relations. *Journal of Homosexuality* 11(3/4):19–33.
Bell, D. 1980. Desert politics: Choices in the "marriage market." In M. Etienne and E. Leacock, eds., *Women and Colonization,* pp. 239–69. New York: J. J. Bergin.
Bell, D. 1981. Women's business is hard work: Central Australian aboriginal women's love rituals. *Signs: Journal of Women in Culture and Society* 7:314–37.
Benedict, R. 1934. *Patterns of Culture.* New York: Houghton-Mifflin.
Benedict, R. 1939. Sex in primitive society. *American Journal of Orthopsychiatry* 9:570–73.
Berndt, R. M., and C. H. Berndt. 1963. *Sexual Behavior in Western Arnhem Land.* New York: Johnson Reprint.
Blacking, J. 1978. Uses of the kinship idiom in friendships at some Venda and Zulu schools. In J. Argyle and E. Preston-Whyte, eds., *Social System and Tradition in Southern Africa,* pp. 101–17. Cape Town: Oxford University Press.
Blackwood, E. 1984a. Cross-cultural dimensions of lesbian relations. Master's thesis, San Francisco State University.
Blackwood, E. 1984b. Sexuality and gender in certain Native American tribes: The case of cross-gender females. *Signs: Journal of Women in Culture and Society* 10:27–42.
Bullough, V. L. 1976. *Sexual Variance in Society and History.* New York: Wiley.
Burton, R. F. 1956. Terminal essay. In D. W. Cory, ed., *Homosexuality, a Cross-Cultural Approach,* pp. 207–24. New York: Julian Press (originally published 1886).
Callender, C. and L. Kochems. 1985. Men and not-men: Male gender mixing statuses and homosexuality. *Journal of Homosexuality* 11(3/4):165–78.
Carrier, J. M. 1980. Homosexual behavior in cross-cultural perspective. In J. Marmor,

ed., *Homosexual Behavior: A Modern Reappraisal,* pp. 100–22. New York: Basic Books.

Crompton, L. 1981. The myth of lesbian impunity: Capital laws from 1270 to 1791. *Journal of Homosexuality* 6(1/2):11–25.

De Cecco, J. P., and M. G. Shively. 1984. From sexual identities to sexual relationships: A contextual shift. *Journal of Homosexuality* 9(2/3):1–26.

D'Emilio, J. 1983. *Sexual Politics, Sexual Communities: The Making of a Homosexual Minority in the U.S., 1940–1970.* Chicago: University of Chicago Press.

Ellis, H., and J. A. Symonds. 1975. *Sexual Inversion.* New York: Arno Press (reprint of *Studies in the Psychology of Sex,* vol. 1, 1897).

Evans-Pritchard, E. E. 1933. Zande blood-brotherhood. *Africa* 6:369–401.

Evans-Pritchard, E. E. 1970. Sexual inversion among the Azande. *American Anthropologist* 72:1428–34.

Faderman, L. 1981. *Surpassing the Love of Men: Romantic Friendship and Love Between Women from the Renaissance to the Present.* New York: William Morrow.

Firth, R. 1936. *We, the Tikopia.* New York: American Books.

Fitzgerald, T. K. 1977. A critique of anthropological research on homosexuality. *Journal of Homosexuality* 2:385–97.

Ford, C. S., and F. A. Beach. 1951. *Patterns of Sexual Behavior.* New York: Harper and Brothers.

Gay, J. 1985. "Mummies and babies" and friends and lovers in Lesotho. *Journal of Homosexuality* 11:(3/4):97–116.

Gray, J. P. 1985. Growing yams and men: An interpretation of Kimam male ritualized homosexual behavior. *Journal of Homosexuality* 11(3/4):55–68.

Greenberg, D. F. Why was the berdache ridiculed? *Journal of Homosexuality* 11(3/4):179–89.

Herdt, G. H. 1981. *Guardians of the Flutes: Idioms of Masculinity.* New York: McGraw-Hill.

Herdt, G. H. 1984. *Ritualized Homosexuality in Melanesia.* Berkeley: University of California Press.

Herskovits, M. J. 1932. Some aspects of Dahomeyan ethnology. *Africa* 5:266–96.

Hershkovits, M. J. 1967. *Dahomey: An Ancient West African Kingdom.* 2 vols. Evanston: Northwestern University Press.

Hill, W. W. 1935. The status of the hermaphrodite and transvestite in Navaho culture. *American Anthropologist* 37:273–79.

Kaberry, P. M. 1939. *Aboriginal Woman, Sacred and Profane.* London: George Routledge and Sons.

Karsch-Haack, F. 1975. *Das gleichgeschlechtliche leben der naturvolker* (The homosexual life of primitive peoples). New York: Arno Press (originally published 1911).

Katz, J. 1976. *Gay American History: Lesbians and Gay Men in the U.S.A.* New York: Thomas Y. Crowell.

Kroeber, A. L. 1925. *Handbook of the Indians of California.* Bulletin 78. United States Bureau of American Ethnology.

Kroeber, A. L. 1940. Psychosis or social sanction. *Character and Personality* 8:204–15.

Layard, J. 1959. Homo-eroticism in a primitive society as a function of the self. *Journal of Analytical Psychology* 4:101–15.

Levy, R. L. 1971. The community function of Tahitian male transvestitism: A hypothesis. *Anthropological Quarterly* 44:12–21.

Lindenbaum, S. 1984. Variations on a sociosexual theme in Melanesia. In G. H. Herdt, ed., *Ritualized Homosexuality in Melanesia*, pp. 337–61. Berkeley: University of California Press.

Lockard, D. 1985. The lesbian community: An anthropological approach. *Journal of Homosexuality* 11:(3/4):83–95.

McIntosh, M. 1981. The homosexual role, with postscript: The homosexual role revisited. In K. Plummer, ed., *The Making of the Modern Homosexual*, pp. 30–49. Totowa, N.J.: Barnes and Noble.

Mead, M. 1935. *Sex and Temperament in Three Primitive Societies*. 3d ed. New York: William Morrow.

Mead, M. 1961. Cultural determinants of sexual behavior. In W. C. Young, ed., *Sex and Internal Secretions*, 2 vols., pp. 1433–79. Baltimore: Williams and Wilkins.

Metraux, A. 1940. *Ethnology of Easter Island*. Honolulu: Bernice P. Bishop Museum.

Minai, N. 1981. *Women in Islam*. New York: Seaview Books.

Mueller, M. B. 1977. Women and men in rural Lesotho: The periphery of the periphery. Doctoral dissertation, Brandeis University.

Nadel, S. F. 1942. *A Black Byzantium: The Kingdom of Nupe in Nigeria*. London: Oxford University Press.

Newton, E. 1972. *Mother Camp: Female Impersonators in America*. Englewood Cliffs, N.J.: Prentice-Hall.

Opler, M. 1965. Anthropological and cross-cultural aspects of homosexuality. In J. Marmor, ed., *Sexual Inversion: The Multiple Roots of Homosexuality*, pp. 108–23. New York: Basic Books.

Padgug, R. A. 1979. Sexual matters: On conceptualizing sexuality in history. *Radical History Review* 20:3–23.

Plummer, K. 1981. *The Making of the Modern Homosexual*. Totowa, N.J.: Barnes and Noble.

Read, K. E. 1980. *Other Voices: The Style of a Male Homosexual Tavern*. Novato, Calif.: Chandler and Sharp.

Reiter, R. R. 1975. *Towards an Anthropology of Women*. New York: Monthly Review Press.

Rich, A. 1980. Compulsory heterosexuality and lesbian existence. *Signs: Journal of Women in Culture and Society* 5:631–60.

Richardson, D. 1984. The dilemma of essentiality in homosexual theory. *Journal of Homosexuality* 9(2/3):79–90.

Roheim, G. 1933. Women and their life in central Australia. *Journal of the Royal Anthropological Institute of Great Britain and Ireland* 63:207–65.

Roheim, G. 1950. *Psychoanalysis and Anthropology*. New York: International Universities Press.

Ross, E., and R. Rapp. 1981. Sex and society: A research note from social history and anthropology. *Comparative Studies in Society and History* 23:51–72.

Rubin, G. 1975. The traffic in women: Notes on the "political economy" of sex. In R. R. Reiter, ed., *Towards an Anthropology of Women*, pp. 157–210. New York: Monthly Review Press.

Rubin, G. 1984. Thinking sex: Notes for a radical theory of the politics of sexuality. In C. Vance, ed., *Pleasure and Danger: Exploring Female Sexuality*, pp. 267–319. Boston: Routledge and Kegan Paul.

Sankar, A. P. 1978. The evolution of the spinsterhood in traditional Chinese society: From village girls' houses to chai t'angs in Hong Kong. Doctoral dissertation, University of Michigan.

Sankar, A. P. 1985. Sisters and brothers, lovers and enemies: Marriage resistance in southern Kwangtung. *Journal of Homosexuality* 11:(3/4);69–81.

Shostak, M. 1981. *Nisa, the Life and Words of a !Kung Woman*. Cambridge, Mass.: Harvard University Press.

Smith, M. G. 1962. *Kinship and Community in Carriacou*. New Haven: Yale University Press.

Sonenschein, D. 1966. Homosexuality as a subject of anthropological inquiry. *Anthropological Quarterly* 39(2):73–82.

Spencer, B., and E. J. Gillen. 1927. *The Arunta*. 2 vols. London: Macmillan.

Walther, W. 1981. *Women in Islam*. Translated by C. S. V. Salt. Montclair, N.J.: Abner Schram.

Weeks, J. 1981. *Sex, Politics, and Society: The Regulation of Sexuality Since 1800*. London: Longman.

West, D. J. 1977. *Homosexuality Re-examined*. Minneapolis: University of Minnesota Press.

Westermarck, E. 1956. Homosexual love. In D. W. Cory, ed., *Homosexuality, a Cross-Cultural Approach*, pp. 101–36. New York: Julian Press.

Whitehead, H. 1981. The bow and the burden strap: A new look at institutionalized homosexuality in native North America. In S. B. Ortner and H. Whitehead, eds., *Sexual Meanings: The Cultural Construction of Gender and Sexuality*, pp. 80–115. Cambridge: Cambridge University Press.

Whitehead, H. 1984. Discussion of gender-crossing. Paper presented at the 83d Annual Meeting of the American Anthropological Association, Denver.

Wilson, M. 1963. *Good Company: A Study of Nyakyusa Age-Villages*. Boston: Beacon Press.

Wolf, D. G. 1979. *The Lesbian Community*. Berkeley: University of California Press.

12

On Heterosexual Masculinity:
Some Psychical Consequences of the
Social Construction of Gender and Sexuality

Gregory M. Herek

This article considers the proposition that to be "a man" in contemporary American society is to be homophobic—that is, to be hostile toward homosexual persons in general and gay men in particular. Starting from some empirical observations of links between homophobia and gender, I shall discuss heterosexual masculinity as a culturally constructed identity and how it has been affected by the recent emergence of gay identities. Then I shall consider how heterosexual masculine identity is constructed by individuals, and how expressing hostility toward gay people enhances such an identity. Finally, I shall propose some strategies for disentangling homophobia from heterosexual masculinity and will consider prospects for changing both.

Throughout the article I will describe explicit hostility or prejudice toward gay men and lesbian women as *homophobia*. This term usually is defined as an irrational fear or intolerance of homosexuality or homosexual persons (Herek 1984; Lehne 1976; Morin and Garfinkle 1978; Weinberg 1972). Of the many words that describe prejudice against lesbians and gay men, it is currently the most popular. It is not an ideal label, however, for many reasons. It overly psychologizes the concept of prejudice against lesbians and gay men. Although it is sometimes used to describe a cultural ideology (Morin and Garfinkle 1978), it usually is interpreted as a psychological phenomenon, focusing more on what is wrong with individuals than on social-structural problems. Homophobia, however, is manifest at both individual and societal levels. Just as the distinction between individual and institutional racism has been important to the Black movement in the United States (Carmichael and Hamilton 1968), so it is important to distinguish psychological homophobia from its institutional manifestations. Examples of institutional homophobia are laws that prohibit two consenting people of the same sex from making love in the privacy of their bedroom or that require dismissal of teachers who say that such laws should be abolished.

Another problem with this term is that its *-phobia* suffix suggests that individual prejudice is based primarily on fear and that this fear is irrational and dysfunctional. I have argued elsewhere (Herek 1984) that homophobia is tenacious partly because it is very functional for individuals who manifest it. Later I will discuss the functions homophobia serves in connection with the male sex role.

STARTING POINTS: SOME EMPIRICAL OBSERVATIONS

It is a common observation that heterosexual men are more homophobic than heterosexual women. Empirical data, however, suggest qualifications for this assertion: men are more homophobic than women in some respects but not in others. National opinion polls typically find no significant difference between males' and females' responses to questions about homosexuality (Glenn and Weaver 1979; Irwin and Thompson 1977; Levitt and Klassen 1974; Nyberg and Alston 1976–1977; Schneider and Lewis 1984). Smaller-scale experimental and questionnaire studies, in contrast, have generally found more negative attitudes among males than among females, especially with attitudes toward gay men (Herek 1986b; Kite 1984).

We can reconcile the different findings of public opinion polls and social psychological studies if we recognize each method's strengths and weaknesses. Poll data obtained from more or less representative samples allow generalization to the larger population, but they rely on only one or two items to assess attitudes concerning sexual orientation. Such single-item measures are less reliable than the multiple-item scales and behavioral measures used in more intensive psychological studies. The latter, however, are conducted with highly select samples—usually college students—and so do not produce readily generalizable results.

More important for the present context, there are differences in content. Polls focus on a single facet of attitudes, usually questions of morality or civil liberties. A frequently used item, for example, reads, "What about relations between two adults of the same sex—do you think it is always wrong, wrong only sometimes, or not wrong at all?" (Nyberg and Alston 1976–1977). Disregarding the possible bias introduced by framing the topic so negatively, such an item addresses a broad moralistic evaluation. Longer questionnaires of the sort used in laboratory studies include similar topics, but they also tap personal affective issues—personal comfort or discomfort, liking for gay persons, and general emotions associated with the topic of homosexuality. This is apparent in an item such as this: "I think male homosexuality is disgusting" (Herek 1986b). Both sets of data are revealing. Males and females probably hold roughly similar positions on general questions of morality and civil liberties, but males are more homophobic in their emotional reactions to homosexuality.

Several other empirical observations are relevant to a discussion of this gender difference in affective reactions to gay people. First, heterosexuals' negative attitudes toward lesbians and gay men are consistently correlated with traditional views of gender and family roles. This pattern undoubtedly is related to widespread stereotypes that gay people violate the demands of such roles; gay men commonly are perceived as effeminate and lesbian women as masculine (Herek 1984). Although such images are not the sole source of hostility toward gay people, they are an important contributing factor for both men and women (Laner and Laner 1979, 1980). Even controlling statistically for gender differences in sex-role attitudes (women tend to hold less traditional views than men do), this variable remains an important predictor of homophobia for heterosexuals, both female and male (Herek 1986b).

Another relevant set of empirical findings concerns the role of defensiveness in homophobia. In psychodynamic terms, defensiveness involves an unconscious distortion of reality as a strategy for avoiding recognition of some unacceptable part of the self. One mode of defense is externalization of unacceptable characteristics through projection and other strategies. This externalizing defensive style, as measured by Gleser and Ihilevich's (1969) Defense Mechanisms Inventory (DMI) may affect homophobia in heterosexual males more than in heterosexual females (Herek 1986b).

In a study of the psychological functions served by homophobia (to be discussed in detail later), I observed that attitudes toward gay people served an entirely defensive function for 20 percent of the men (n = 81) and 5 percent of the women (n = 123). This evaluation was based on content analysis of essays written by respondents to describe their attitudes toward lesbians and gay men. Persons classified as holding defensive attitudes toward gay people also showed a general tendency to externalize, as measured by the DMI. Defensive males showed the highest externalization scores of any respondents (Herek 1986a).

It is interesting that persons with defensive attitudes manifest greater conformity to what they perceived as gender-appropriate characteristics. Using a semantic differential technique with adjective pairs pretested for their relevance to gender stereotypes (e.g., hard-soft), respondents rated themselves, "men in general," and "women in general." Difference scores between ratings of self and of men and women provided a measure of self-perceptions. Defensive males perceived greater similarity between themselves and men in general and greater differences between themselves and women in general than did other males. Similarly, defensive females perceived themselves to be more like women and less like men than did other females (Herek 1986a).

This pattern suggests that the defensiveness associated with homophobia is linked to gender issues. Defensive attitudes appear to result from insecurities about personal adequacy in meeting gender-role demands. These insecurities may lead to hyperconformity to perceived standards of gender-appropriate traits (Pleck 1981). Although the sample was not systematically selected, the higher concentration of males in the defensive category suggests that such conflicts may be associated with homophobia more for heterosexual males than for females.

These findings suggest that some males' homophobia is based primarily on anxieties associated with the male role. But it would be a mistake to assume a link between homophobia and the male sex role only for overtly defensive males. Defenses are employed only when more common measures fail. The defensive males I observed probably were not qualitatively different from other homophobic males; they simply were experiencing greater difficulty maintaining a heterosexual masculine identity. Their strategy for reducing the anxiety that ensued was to exaggerate the "normal" level of homophobia associated with the male role.

This analysis points toward a hypothesis that heterosexual men have more negative reactions to gay people than do women, on the average, because such hostility is inherent in the cultural construction of heterosexual male role and identity; this is less true for heterosexual female role and identity. This process works at a social level, where heterosexual males are pressured by peers and societal standards to conform to certain behavioral patterns, and at a psychological level, where heterosexual males internalize those standards and experience anxiety that they will fail to measure up to their role. The source for this anxiety is fear of losing one's sense of self, or identity, as a heterosexual man (which is equivalent to a male's identity as a person). Conformity to social standards and defense against anxiety push heterosexual men to express homophobic attitudes and provide rewards in the form of social support and reduced anxiety, both of which increase self-esteem. In other words, heterosexual men reaffirm their male identity by attacking gay men.

THE SOCIAL CONSTRUCTION OF HETEROSEXUAL MASCULINITY

Social roles and their attendant psychological identities are not "given" by nature. Variables such as race, class, gender, and sexual orientation are human creations, based on certain observable phenomena that come to be defined in certain ways through social interaction over time. The social constructionist position holds that what most people call reality is a consensus worldview that develops through social interaction (see Berger and Luckmann 1966; Foucault 1978; Gergen 1985; Plummer 1981). In this perspective gender and sexual orientation must be understood within historical, sociological, and social psychological contexts, rather than in exclusively individualistic terms. By highlighting human plasticity, the constructionist view also allows for the possibility of change. What has been constructed can be deconstructed and reconstructed, albeit with considerable effort. Gender and sexual orientation thus should be understood as changeable ideologies rather than as biological facts.

THE CULTURAL CONSTRUCTION OF GENDER

Being a man is a crucial component of personal identity for males in our society, stemming from the early experience of gender as a self-defining characteristic. Although personal conceptions of masculine identity in contemporary America vary according to race, class, age, and other social variables (Cazenave 1984), there remains a stable common core, which I have called "heterosexual masculinity."

As an identity, heterosexual masculinity is defined both positively and negatively. Heterosexual masculinity embodies personal characteristics such as success and status, toughness and independence, aggressiveness and dominance. These are manifest by adult males through exclusively social relationships with men and primarily sexual relationships with women. Heterosexual masculinity is also defined according to what it is *not*—that is, not feminine and not homosexual. Being a man requires not being compliant, dependent, or submissive; not being effeminate (a "sissy") in physical appearance or mannerisms; not having relationships with men that are sexual or overly intimate; and not failing in sexual relationships with women (Brannon and David 1976; Pleck 1981).

In recent years writers have pointed out the maladaptive aspects of heterosexual masculinity in terms of physical health, personal happiness, and psychological adjustment (Fasteau 1974; Harrison 1978, Jourard 1971; Pleck 1981). Additionally, to the extent that heterosexual masculinity dominates politics and international relations, it may increase the likelihood of interstate warfare and thereby be maladaptive for the entire human species (Fasteau 1974). Although heterosexual masculinity may have been adequate or at least harmless in former times, historical change has rendered it today an outmoded identity seriously in need of transformation. Despite its dysfunctional aspects, it continues to meet some needs for individuals and will remain entrenched until those needs can be met in some other way.

THE CULTURAL CONSTRUCTION OF SEXUAL ORIENTATION

The historical development of our cultural ideology about sexuality is clearest in what cultural constructionists call the "making of the modern homosexual" (Plummer 1981). Over the last few centuries, the view developed that what a person *does* sexually defines who the person *is*, and negative evaluations were attached to people who did not do what they were supposed to do and who thus were not what they were supposed to be. Not being what one is supposed to be receives many labels, including criminal, wicked, and sick (see Boswell 1980; Katz 1983; Weeks 1977).

To analyze this process requires distinguishing sexual behavior from socioerotic identity. Sexual behavior is any observable action that involves sexual arousal and its continuation or satisfaction. This circular but adequate working definition emphasizes that sexual behavior is something one does. Barring some sort of injury or disability, all human beings can engage in sexual behavior, as can most other animal species. But what makes behavior sexual? What is sexually arousing? Here we can make use of Freud's (1961 [1905]) assumption that humans are born with an amorphous, unformed sexuality—we are polymorphously perverse. Our behavioral repertoire is ambisexual. Over the course of individual development, the principal source of sexual arousal becomes located in the genitals for most people, and they find that they are aroused by a relatively limited range of things in the world—typically by human beings of a particular gender with fairly specific physical and psychological qualities. In other words, people acquire preferences for certain sexual partners, acts, and situations. Obviously, people are attracted to each other for a host of reasons other than gender—for example, physical appearance, intellect, personality, sense of humor, and religious and political values. But gender is a basic consideration for most people, whether or not it is conscious.

Development of sexual behavioral preferences is common across human cultures and in other species as well. But humans differ from other species (and among cultures) in their personal and social identities based in large part on sexual preferences. In our culture, we summarize those identities with the label *sexual orientation*, defined as a pattern of sexual and affectional preferences for persons of a particular sex. In contemporary American society, those preferences and their associated identities have settled on two categories: heterosexuality and homosexuality.[1]

There is an important difference between the words *heterosexual* and *homosexual* when they are used as adjectives, describing sexual behavior of which anyone is capable, and when they are used as nouns, describing identity. As nouns *homosexual* and *heterosexual* are mutually exclusive socioerotic identities. Given this dichotomy, our society clearly approves of one identity and not the other.

The significance of this construction for human experience can better be appreciated by considering alternative forms of sexuality. In many New Guinea societies, for example, becoming a man requires incorporating the semen of other men into one's own body through homosexual acts. Once manhood is achieved, heterosexual behavior is socially prescribed (Herdt 1981, 1982; Williams 1937). In some indigenous American societies, biological males could assume women's occupations and be recognized socially as women; some men in this "berdache" role married (biological and social) males. In some tribes, a comparable role was available to biological females (Blackwood 1984; Whitehead 1981). To the extent that the concept of "sexual orientation" can be applied to such societies, it must be modified considerably.

Such cross-cultural comparisons show us that our notions of heterosexuals and homosexuals are part of a particular historically derived knowledge system. As socioerotic identities, homosexuality and heterosexuality have been created within our culture, starting from the raw material of humans' inherent ambisexuality and inevitable development of erotic and affectional preferences.

This is not to minimize the reality of homosexual or heterosexual identities or to claim that they are simply figments of our imagination that can be easily dismissed. Culturally constructed identities are not easily changed. But it is important to realize that "heterosexuals" and "homosexuals" do not exist in nature; they are constructs, ways of giving meaning to particular patterns of sexual behavior and interpersonal relationships.

Understanding the roots of institutional homophobia requires learning how our cultural sense of erotic reality developed historically—how we came to be a society of heterosexuals and homosexuals, rather than people whose sexual behavior is shaped by other influences. This historical process of defining socioerotic identities must have been very closely tied to seeing one identity as natural and preferable and seeing the other as unnatural, criminal, wicked, or sick (see Chauncey 1983; D'Emilio 1983; Katz 1983; Plummer 1981; Weeks 1977).

Through intense political struggle, lesbians and gay men have made considerable progress in shifting the realm of discourse on sexual orientation from medicine to civil liberties (e.g., see Altman 1982; D'Emilio 1983). In many cities, being a homosexual person today is more like belonging to an ethnic minority than like sharing a psychiatric diagnosis with other deviants. Being heterosexual undoubtedly has changed as well in that it has become a more salient identity. Members of dominant groups typically think of themselves not as elites but as "normal"—for example, White men think of themselves as "people" until confronted by Blacks or women (Miller 1976). As more lesbians and gay men publicly assert their identities, sexual normalcy begins to include both homo- and heteroeroticism, and more people in the dominant majority must consciously label themselves as heterosexual rather than taking it for granted.

Thus, although past American notions of masculinity have implicitly included the component of heterosexuality, that component is now more salient and often must be explicitly avowed as part of one's identity. Pressures to define (rather than assume) one's status as a heterosexual man are likely to intensify in the near future for at least two reasons. First, the epidemic of acquired immune deficiency syndrome (AIDS) is likely to lead to more overt discrimination against gay men than has been evident in the recent past. Single males, in particular, are now being confronted with publicly labeling themselves as heterosexual to avoid such stigma. Second, it appears that the mainstream American conception of masculinity is currently changing in some respects, with some men adopting superficially more flexible behavior patterns. This may be a continuation of the social shift from traditional to modern male roles (Pleck 1981), or it may reflect a new shift to a "postmodern" definition of masculinity. In either case, recent changes in the "masculine" component of heterosexual masculinity seem to be offset by fortification of the heterosexual component. Thus, the man who is "secure" in his masculinity (heterosexuality) can be gentle and can eat quiche.

These cultural and historical patterns provide an appropriate context for understanding heterosexual masculinity. They uncover its roots in social organization of interpersonal relations rather than in biological predispositions to be either heterosexual or masculine. Males in our society grow up in this context, and their identity develops through involvement with family, neighborhood, school, and society. I shall discuss this social psychological level, where cultural ideologies become a part of personal identity, in the next section.

THE PERSONAL CONSTRUCTION OF HETEROSEXUAL MASCULINITY

Personal identity (self-concept) involves what we are not at least as much as what we are (McGuire 1984). Boys may learn to be men primarily through learning not to be women, while girls can learn directly how to be women through observing readily available female role models (Lynn 1969). The negative definition of heterosexual masculinity is at least as important as its positive definition. Homophobia is thus an integral component of heterosexual masculinity, to the extent that it serves the psychological function of expressing who one is not (i.e., homosexual) and thereby affirming who one is (heterosexual). Further, homophobia reduces the likelihood that heterosexual men will interact with gay men, thereby ruling out opportunities for the attitude change that often occurs through such contact (Schneider and Lewis 1984). When such interactions occur, accidentally, heterosexual masculinity prevents individuation of the participating gay man; instead, he is treated primarily as a symbol. These assertions can be clarified best by explaining the psychological functions served by homophobia.

Heterosexual Masculinity and the Functions of Homophobia

Our sense of self is established through social interaction (Mead 1934). Expressing our opinions, beliefs, values, and attitudes toward others plays a major role in constructing our personal identities. This view derives from a particular perspective on attitudes, the functional approach, which proposes that people hold their opinions because they get some psychological benefit from doing so. In other words, attitudes and opinions serve psychological functions (Katz 1960; Smith, Bruner, and White 1956; Herek 1986c).

There are two major categories of such functions. One includes attitudes that derive their benefit directly from characteristics of the attitude object; these include heterosexual males attitudes based on utilitarian considerations of whether gay men have been (or are likely to be) a source of reward or punishment. Such considerations can be based on past interactions with individual gay men, as well as benefit or detriment from gay men as a group (e.g., a merchant who has many gay customers, a renter who must move because gentrification by gay speculators has inflated rents in his neighborhood).

A second category includes attitudes whose function is not directly related to perceived characteristics of gay men but instead results primarily through the attitude's expression. By expressing the attitude, individuals affirm their sense of self in relation to others and increase self-esteem. It is when homophobia serves an expressive function of this kind that it is integrally related to heterosexual masculinity in at least three specific ways. First, homophobia may serve a defensive-expressive function, a way of preventing anxiety that results from intrapsychic conflicts concerning one's own heterosexual masculinity. Gay men symbolize parts of the self that do not measure up to cultural standards; directing hostility at them is a way of externalizing the conflict. This is the function most likely served by homophobia for the defensive males described earlier. Second, homophobia may serve a social-expressive function. In this case, a heterosexual man expresses prejudice against gay men in order to win approval from important others and thereby increase self-esteem. Third, homophobia may serve a value-expressive function. A heterosexual man may express homophobia as part of a larger ideology that is self-defining—for example, a conservative religious ideology that prescribes strict behavioral guidelines for men and women in all facets of life.

For each of these expressive functions, homophobia helps to define what one is not and direct hostility toward that symbol. With the defensive-expressive function, homophobia serves to deny one's own homoerotic attractions and "feminine" characteristics; with the social-expressive function, it defines group boundaries (with gay men on the outside and the self on the inside); for the value-expressive function, it defines the world according to principles of good and bad, right and wrong (with oneself as good and gay men as bad).

To the extent that homophobia serves an expressive function, it is self-perpetuating. Under normal circumstances, homophobic men will not give up their prejudice as long as it continues to be functional. And their prejudice makes it unlikely that they will interact personally with gay men; rather, friendly interaction with gay men is likely to increase anxiety, incur the disapproval of friends, and call into question one's virtue. There is hope, however, for reducing homophobia and for challenging the ideology of heterosexual masculinity.

THE WAY OUT: CHANGING ATTITUDES AND IDENTITIES

Given that heterosexual masculinity and homophobia exist at both societal and individual levels, change must also come at both levels. This means changing institutions (the organization of family, work, child care, marriage), as well as people. Here, I will briefly address the latter.

The functional approach suggests some strategies for changing attitudes, all based on the assumption that we must render the current attitude dysfunctional in some way while providing benefit from the target attitude. With direct functions, this usually involves arranging pleasant interactions with the attitude target (that is, gay men). With expressive attitudes, however, this is not a simple task for reasons already mentioned. Additional steps must be taken with each of the expressive functions.

With social-expressive functions, new norms must be created. One strategy is to solicit personal statements from significant role models of heterosexual masculinity that their own attitudes toward gay men are not hostile. Another approach is to provide direct social support for men whose homophobia is being challenged; this might be most effectively achieved in the context of a therapeutic or men's group. Attacking value-expressive attitudes does not necessarily require dismantling an entire value system. Instead, it can involve making competing values salient. For example, values of justice and fair play may be raised, or values of open-mindedness or charity toward one's neighbor.

Defensive-expressive attitudes probably are the most difficult to challenge because, like any defense mechanism, they work at an unconscious level. Any attempt to make them conscious (which threatens to make conscious the repressed anxiety) is likely to be met by great resistance. To some extent, this can be used favorably by "short-circuiting" the prejudice through arousal of insight. Simply convincing a man that excessive hostility toward gay men is a sign of latent homosexuality may at least lead that man to avoid expressing his hostility. Unfortunately, it will not resolve the conflict underlying the prejudice and may, in fact, exacerbate it. One strategy might be attempting to change attitudes incrementally, starting with attitudes toward lesbians, who may be less anxiety-arousing.

My suggestions to this point have focused on changing attitudes toward gay men without changing the identity of heterosexual masculinity that underlies them. A long-term strategy for eradicating homophobia, however, must focus on heterosexual masculinity. Although a detailed consideration of how to change contemporary male roles is beyond the scope of this article, two promising avenues of inquiry deserve mention.

First, it will be useful to explore systematically how gay men deal with their own internalized homophobia in the process of coming out. As males in this culture, gay men are taught the ideal of heterosexual masculinity. When they acknowledge their own sexual preferences to themselves, however, they must discard this ideology in order to maintain their self-esteem. Although gay men often adhere to many components of the male sex role, their understanding of masculinity must somehow change in the course of accepting their homoeroticism. Research on this topic may provide insight for changing heterosexual males as well (see Nungesser 1983).

Second, this perspective will lead to a functional analysis of heterosexual masculinity. Gay men usually renounce their internalized homophobia only when its costs outweigh its benefits. Similarly, individuals will renounce heterosexual masculinity only when it becomes clearly dysfunctional to them. Although the male sex role is hazardous to the health of those who adhere to it (Harrison 1978), it also meets some basic psychological needs in much the same way that homophobic attitudes do. Approximating the ideal of heterosexual masculinity can help one's career, attract friends and admirers, increase self-esteem, and give one a sense of doing one's duty as a man. Of course, the career also may be damaging to one's physical and psychological health, the friendships may lack intimacy, the self-esteem may be based on a general inability for critical introspection and emotional expression, and doing one's duty may preclude pursuing one's own goals. Until men become aware of these costs, change is unlikely. They will become what Pleck calls "martyrs for the male role" (personal communication). And through the homophobia inherent in heterosexual masculinity, they will take many gay men and lesbians with them.

Even realizing how dysfunctional the male role can be does not make change inevitable. Men cannot change without clear alternative ways of living. Formulating such alternatives must constitute an agenda for all who hope to improve our society—gay, lesbian, and heterosexual.

NOTE

1. Although the category of bisexuality exists, its status as a true identity is suspect; regardless of its accuracy, most people seem to hold the view that one is either heterosexual or homosexual (Klein and Wolf 1985; Ruitenbeek 1973).

328   GREGORY M. HEREK

REFERENCES

Altman, D. 1982. *The Homosexualization of America, the Americanization of the Homosexual.* New York: St. Martin's.

Berger, P. L., and T. Luckmann. 1966. *The Social Construction of Reality.* Garden City, N.Y.: Doubleday.

Blackwood, E. 1984. Sexuality and gender in certain Native American tribes: The case of cross-gender females. *Signs* 10(1):27–42.

Boswell, J. 1980. *Christianity, Social Tolerance, and Homosexuality: Gay People in Western Europe from the Beginning of the Christian Era to the Fourteenth Century.* Chicago: University of Chicago Press.

Brannon, R., and D. David. 1976. The male sex role: Our culture's blueprint for manhood and what it's done for us lately. In D. Davis and R. Brannon, eds., *The Forty-Nine Percent Majority: The Male Sex Role.* Reading, Mass.: Addison-Wesley.

Carmichael, S., and C. V. Hamilton. 1968. *Black Power: The Politics of Liberation in America.* New York: Random House.

Cazenave, N. A. 1984. Race, socioeconomic status, and age: The social context of American masculinity. *Sex Roles* 11:639–56.

Chauncey, G. 1983. From sexual inversion to homosexuality: Medicine and the changing conceptualization of female deviance. *Salmagundi* 58/59:114–46.

D'Emilio, J. 1983. *Sexual Politics, Sexual Communities: The Making of a Homosexual Minority in the United States, 1940–1970.* Chicago: University of Chicago Press.

Fasteau, M. F. 1974. *The Male Machine.* New York: McGraw-Hill.

Foucault, M. 1978. *The History of Sexuality. Vol. 1: An Introduction.* New York: Pantheon.

Freud, S. 1961. Three essays on the theory of sexuality. In J. Strachey, ed. and trans., *The Standard Edition of the Complete Psychological Works of Sigmund Freud.* London: Hogarth Press (originally published 1905).

Gabay, E. D., and A. Morrison. 1985. AIDS-phobia, homophobia, and locus of control. Paper presented at the meeting of the American Psychological Association, Los Angeles, August.

Gergen, K. J. 1985. The social constructionist movement in modern psychology. *American Psychologist* 40:266–75.

Glenn, N. D., and C. N. Weaver. 1979. Attitudes toward premarital, extramarital, and homosexual relations in the U.S. in the 1970s. *Journal of Sex Research* 15:108–18.

Gleser, G. C., and D. Ihilevich. 1969. An objective instrument for measuring defense mechanisms. *Journal of Consulting and Clinical Psychology* 33:51–60.

Harrison. J. 1978. Warning: The male sex role may be hazardous to your health. *Journal of Social Issues* 34(1):65–86.

Herdt, G. 1981. *Guardians of the Flutes: Idioms of Masculinity.* New York: McGraw-Hill.

Herdt, G., ed. 1982. *Rituals of Manhood: Male Initiation in Papua, New Guinea.* Berkeley: University of California Press.

Herek, G. 1984. Beyond "homophobia": A social psychological perspective on attitudes toward lesbians and gay men. *Journal of Homosexuality* 10(1/2):1–21.

Herek, G. 1986a. Can functions be measured? A new perspective on the functional approach to attitudes. Paper submitted for editorial review.

Herek, G. 1986b. The gender gap in attitudes toward lesbians and gay men: Its measurement and meaning. Paper submitted for editorial review.

Herek, G. 1986c. The instrumentality of ideologies: Toward a neofunctional theory of attitudes and behavior. *Journal of Social Issues* 42(2):99–114.

Irwin, P., and N. L. Thompson. 1977. Acceptance of the rights of homosexuals: A social profile. *Journal of Homosexuality* 3(2):107–21.

Jourard, S. M. 1971. *The Transparent Self.* Princeton, N.J.: Van Nostrand.

Katz, D. 1960. The functional approach to the study of attitudes. *Public Opinion Quarterly* 24:163–204.

Katz, J. N. 1983. *Gay/Lesbian Almanac.* New York: Harper and Row.

Kite, M. E. 1984. Sex differences in attitudes toward homosexuals: A meta-analytic review. *Journal of Homosexuality* 10(1/2):69–81.

Klein, F., and T. J. Wolf, eds. 1985. Bisexualities: Theory and research. *Journal of Homosexuality* 11(1/2).

Laner, M. R., and R. H. Laner. 1979. Personal style or sexual preference: Why gay men are disliked. *International Review of Modern Sociology* 9:215–28.

Laner, M. R., and R. H. Laner. 1980. Sexual preference or personal style? Why lesbians are disliked. *Journal of Homosexuality* 5(4):339–56.

Lehne, G. K. 1976. Homophobia among men. In D. David and R. Brannon, eds., *The Forty-Nine Percent Majority: The Male Sex Role*, pp. 66–88. Reading, Mass.: Addison-Wesley.

Levitt, E. E., and A. D. Klassen. 1974. Public attitudes toward homosexuality: Part of the 1970 national survey by the Institute for Sex Research. *Journal of Homosexuality* 1(1):29–43.

Lynn, D. B. 1969. *Parental and Sex-Role Identification.* Berkeley, Calif.: McCutchan.

McGuire, W. J. 1984. Search for the self: Going beyond self-esteem and the reactive self. In R. A. Zucker, J. Aronoff, and A. I. Rabin, eds., *Personality and the Prediction of Behavior*, pp. 73–102. New York: Academic Press.

Mead, G. H. 1934. *Mind, Self, and Society.* Chicago: University of Chicago Press.

Miller, J. B. 1976. *Toward a New Psychology of Women.* Boston: Beacon.

Morin, S. F., and E. M. Garfinkle. 1978. Male homophobia. *Journal of Social Issues* 34(1):29–47.

Nungesser, L. 1983. *Homosexual Acts, Actors, and Identities.* New York: Praeger.

Nyberg, K. L., and J. P. Alston. 1976–1977. Analysis of public attitudes toward homosexual behavior. *Journal of Homosexuality* 2:(2):99–107.

O'Donnell, C. R., L. O'Donnell, J. H. Pleck, J. Snarey, and R. M. Rose. 1985. Psychosocial responses of hospital workers to the acquired immunodeficiency syndrome (AIDS). Paper submitted for editorial review.

Pleck, J. H. 1981. *The Myth of Masculinity.* Cambridge, Mass.: MIT Press.

Plummer, K., ed. 1981. *The Making of the Modern Homosexual.* London: Hutchinson.

Ruitenbeek, H. M. 1973. The myth of bisexuality. In H. M. Ruitenbeek, ed., *Homosexuality: A Changing Picture*, pp. 199–204. London: Souvenir Press.

Schneider, W., and I. A. Lewis. 1984. The straight story on homosexuality and gay rights. *Public Opinion* (February):16–20, 59–60.

Smith, M. B., J. S. Bruner, and R. W. White. 1956. *Opinions and Personality*. New York: Wiley.

Weeks, J. 1977. *Coming Out: Homosexual Politics in Britain, from the Nineteenth Century to the Present*. London: Quartet.

Weinberg, G. 1972. *Society and the Healthy Homosexual*. New York: St. Martin's.

Whitehead, H. 1981. The bow and the burden strap: A new look at institutionalized homosexuality in native North America. In S. B. Ortner and H. Whitehead, eds., *Sexual Meanings: The Cultural Construction of Gender and Sexuality*, pp. 80–115. Cambridge: Cambridge University Press.

Williams, F. E. 1937. *Papuans of the Trans-fly*. London: Oxford University Press.

V
Cultural Diversity Among Lesbians and Gay Men

To understand fully the experiences of lesbians and gay men, we must examine the interaction between cultural diversity and sexual orientation. Prior to acquiring a gay or lesbian identity, one has a racial or ethnic identity, which is part of the core of childhood identity. Moreover, racial and ethnic groups experience prejudice and discrimination based on their minority group status, which may place constraints on various life options. Gay men and lesbians of color are "polycultural and multiply oppressed" (Browning, Reynolds, and Dworkin 1991:181).

Recent attention has focused on cultural diversity among gay male and lesbian individuals and the important role of culture in shaping and defining the meaning of same-gender sexual and affectional behavior. Cultural values evolve over generations and are moderated by the influences of interacting cultures. Gay male and lesbian status has different meanings in various cultures (Blackwood 1985). The experiences of gay men and lesbians of color often do not parallel Anglo experience. Shared sexual orientations by themselves do not guarantee that people have a great deal in common. Thus, there is a need for a model of sexual orientation based on multiplicity, not sameness, that examines the overlapping identities and statuses of gender, race/ethnicity, and sexuality (Cohen 1991).

Several themes are relevant for understanding cultural influence on lesbian and gay male identity. One is the importance of religion within the culture and the relevance of sexuality to central beliefs in that religion. For example, Catholicism has a strong influence in many Latino cultures, providing religious salience to the view of homosexuality as a sin. The African-American community values the church as a center of the community that cultivates racial identity and group solidarity (Greene 1986; Tinney 1986). African-American gay men and lesbians, however, cannot comfortably be part of their religious community if they are out. Nonetheless, "if Black lesbians and gay men are willing to check their sexuality at the door of the church, and come bearing gifts of talent, there are relatively few problems" (Tinney 1986:73).

A second aspect focuses on gender roles, especially how the significance of clear distinctions made between male and female roles may serve to increase the difficulty for gay men and lesbians to carve out a nontraditional or androgynous role. Within Asian and Latino cultures, for example, lesbians are perceived to violate the gender role expectations for women that emphasize passivity, and reliance on and deference to men (Hildago 1984; Shon and Ja 1982).

In the first article here, Williams addresses recent changes in the "berdache" gender role among Lakota Native Americans in South Dakota. It is an excellent example of the interaction between cultural diversity and minority group status, the influences of evolving cultural values over time, and the effects of dominant cultures on minorities.

A third theme is the nature of family structure, including issues regarding the significance and influence of family, the way that families are defined, and the ways in which gender roles, sexuality, and sexual orientation are integrated into the concept of family. Ethnic communities and extended families often serve as the primary reference groups providing social networks and support for their members. The expectations of the group are often paramount over individual desires. Moreover, due to racism and the need to form group bonds against it, many gay men and lesbians of color are inextricably tied to their racial or ethnic communities (Kanuha 1990). As Moraga described:

> The family, then, becomes all the more ardently protected by oppressed peoples, and the sanctity of this institution is infused like blood into the veins of the Chicano. At all costs, la familia must be preserved. . . . So we fight back, we think our families—with our women pregnant, and our men, the indispensable heads. We believe the more severely we protect the sex roles within the family, the stronger we will be a unit in opposition to the anglo threat. (1983:110)

Coming out to the family may jeopardize both family relationships and ties with their ethnic community. It may be viewed as, in effect, putting one's allegiance to one's own ethnic group to the test. That is, a gay or lesbian identity may be perceived as a betrayal of one's own people, a loss of connection with one's own heritage, a public statement about something that reflects badly on one's culture or religion, a violation of gender-role expectations of the culture, or a sign of assimilation into White mainstream culture. As an African-American lesbian explained:

> The family is very contradictory for us. There are emotional involvements, there are ties, the roots that it represents for us all as individuals in a fundamentally racist/sexist society. That's why Black people may decide not to come out as lesbians or gay for fear of being rejected by a group of people whom you not only love but who represent a real source of security, of foundation. (Carmen et al. 1991:217)

It should be noted that the salience of racial identity within the culture, which is reflected in the family, will affect the coming-out process. In some cultures it is extremely important that one have a firm identity as a member of that group so that a violation of some aspect of the cultural norms may be experienced as affecting one's entire racial identity. An example may be found among African-Americans where lesbians and gay men receive negative sanctions for not promoting group survival of their people through propagation of the race (Icard 1986/1986).

As a consequence, relatively low rates of disclosure to families have been reported among Asian, African-American, and Latino gay men and lesbians. They often report remaining closeted and isolated with their own ethnic minority communities and within their families (Tremble, Schneider, and Appathurai 1989). Coming out may represent the risk of losing a major source of social support—one that is not easy to replace in the gay and lesbian community. For example, disclosure of sexual orientation by Asian-American gay men may be viewed as a major transgression against parental norms, especially the expectation that men carry the family name and kinship (Aoki 1983).

A fourth theme that centers on the process of reconciling one's ethnicity, gender, and sexual orientation has been referred to as forming a dual or triple identity (e.g., Latina, lesbian, and female). This process helps to frame how to manage the impact of racism, sexism, and heterosexism on identity formation. In order to integrate multiple identities, lesbians or gay men of color must establish priorities among their commitments to distinct communities: racial/ethnic, gay/lesbian, and society at large. Each of these communities has potentially conflicting value systems about homosexuality and about what they teach people to value or reject in themselves. One's minority and immigrant status often creates conflicts that, in turn, are directly relevant for understanding the meaning of gay male and lesbian identity. These conflicts may be especially acute for recent immigrants and their families. The aim for lesbian and gay men of color is to synthesize their multiple identities. A respondent in Loiacano's study (1989:23) described it this way: "Mary feels that, while her two identities were once running on parallel tracks," they are now "more like a weaving."

A fifth theme concerns the degree of the individual's interaction with and integration into the White majority culture, in particular the Anglo gay and lesbian culture and community. Lesbians and gay men of color aim to integrate potentially compartmentalized aspects of themselves. This requires an ongoing management of conflicting allegiances between those groups that represent the expression of intimacy and those that provide ethnic foundation. As Audre Lorde phrased it:

> As a Black lesbian feminist comfortable with the many different ingredients of my identity, and a woman committed to racial and sexual freedom from oppression, I find I am constantly being encouraged to pluck some one aspect of myself and present this as the meaningful whole, eclipsing or denying other aspects of myself. (1990:285)

If gay men and lesbians rely on groups and networks outside of their family and culture in which their sexual identity is more accepted, they may lose support for their racial or ethnic identity. If they stay closeted within their racial or ethnic community, however, they may not only deny that part of their identity associated with sexuality and intimate love relationships but also the potential for involvement with the broader gay and lesbian community. A gay Chinese adolescent male explained: "I am a double minority. Caucasian gays don't like gay Chinese, and the Chinese don't like gays. It would be easier to be White. It would be easier to be straight. It's hard to be both" (Tremble, Schneider, and Appathurai 1989:263). Lesbians and gay men of color may choose to identify more strongly with different groups at different times and in different situations.

Each of the articles in this part on African-American, Asian-American, and Latino gay men and lesbians highlight the interrelationships among sexual orientation, gender, race, ethnicity, and geographic location in acquiring and managing a lesbian or gay identity. The authors address the themes described above and point out the challenges and processes by which gay men and lesbians of color integrate their multiple identities.

These studies are based on small samples, however, and may not be representative of all.

CONTEMPORARY ISSUE: RACISM IN THE GAY MALE AND LESBIAN COMMUNITIES

Gay men and lesbians of color report experiences of racism within the larger gay and lesbian community (Klein 1986; Morales 1989; Tremble, Schneider, and Appathurai 1989). For example, a recent fundraising event held by a national gay and lesbian legal organization took place at the showing of a play entitled *Miss Saigon.* Members of the Asian-American gay community were outraged and felt the organization was insensitive to racist and sexist issues about the production. In addition, African-American gay men report numerous instances of being prevented from entering gay bars, clubs, and other gay social gatherings by the use of excessive identification, while White gay men are allowed entry without such scrutiny of identification. Furthermore, in a study of a lesbian community in the Southwest, the dominant group norms were derived from the Anglo members. Mexican-American lesbians tended not to interact with the White lesbians, but rather to relate primarily with each other. The Latina lesbians reported experiences of prejudice and discrimination that prevented them from feeling a part of the community (Lockard 1985).

One Native American lesbian described her experience of conflicting identity this way:

> When I went to Eureka, to my Yoruk tribe, I felt as though I was somewhat accepted but they were not always ready for me as a queer, so I had to keep that part hidden a little. It felt easier for me to live in San Francisco than at home. but when I was in San Francisco, in a lesbian group, I felt they couldn't understand the Indian part of me. They're different from what I'm used to: different values, different approaches, a different sense of humor. They didn't know about those families back home I grew up with, the disputes, the importance of questions like "How's the fishing?" There was no place where all of me was validated. (Faderman 1991:287).

Racism may take the form of being unacknowledged or unaccepted in the community or of experiencing "sexual racism" in which gender ster eotypes become linked with racial ones. "These stereotypes are masculine or feminine, and they have no bearing on the gender of the individual's biological characteristics" (Icard 1985/1986:88). For example, an Asian-American gay man may be persumed to be passive, quiet, shy, compliant, and interested in assuming a feminine role in relationships, stemming from gender and racial stereotypes.

Lesbians and gay men of color may not receive the same psychological benefits from the gay community that White gay men and lesbians receive (e.g., social support, visible role models, and simultaneous acceptance for all important aspects of one's identities) (Icard 1985/1986). Thus, their existence is denied in their own ethnic communities and also not reflected in the gay and lesbian communities (Hom 1992). These myriad forms of racism negatively affect gay men and lesbians of color. In forming a multiple identity, they face difficulties feeling a sense of belonging, fully validated, or visible. In the process of coming out to others, gay men and lesbians of color struggle about who to seek for support. In friendship and intimate relationships, they often have to negotiate across racial/ethnic lines. In seeking active involvement in the predominantly White gay and lesbian community, they have to comfort the ways that their own particular concerns may not be acknowledged or understood, or are stereotyped or used as tokens.

During the past decade, one of the major ways that gay men and lesbians of color have gained integration of their multiple identities has been to form groups and organizations specifically focused on their racial or ethnic group within the gay and lesbian community. These networks serve multiple functions. They provide a sense of community by creating new extended families that are more sensitive to their needs. They increase visibility by making their presence known in both the larger ethnic minority and gay and lesbian communities. The networks help to unify efforts toward reducing oppression in each of the communities in which they interact. Their ultimate goal is the "*right to passion* expressed in our own cultural tongues and movements" (Moraga 1983:136). In all of these ways these efforts help to integrate the various aspects of their identity.

REFERENCES

Aoki, B. 1983. Gay Asian Americans: Adapting within the family context. Paper presented at the 91st Annual Convention of the American Psychological Association, Anaheim, California, August.

Blackwood, E. 1985. Breaking the mirror: The construction of lesbianism and the anthropological discourse on homosexuality. *Journal of Homosexuality* 11(3–4):1–17.

Browning, C., A. L. Reynolds, and S. H. Dworkin. 1991. Affirmative psychotherapy for lesbian women. *The Counseling Psychologist* 19(2):177–96.

Carmen, Gail, Neena, and Tamara. 1991. Becoming visible: Black lesbian discussions. In Feminist Review, eds., *Sexuality: A Reader*, pp. 216–44. London: Virago.

Cohen, E. 1991. Who are "we"? Gay "identity" as political (e)motion (a theoretical rumination). In D. Fuss, ed., *Inside/Out: Lesbian Theories, Gay Theories*, pp. 71–92. New York: Routledge.

Faderman, L. 1991. *Odd Girls and Twilight Lovers*. New York: Columbia University Press.

Greene, B. 1986. When the therapist is white and the patient is black: Considerations for psychotherapy in the feminist heterosexual and lesbian communities. In D. Howard, ed., *The Dynamics of Feminist Therapy*, pp. 41–65. New York: Haworth.

Hildago, H. A. 1984. The Puerto Rican lesbian in the United States. In T. Darty and S. Potter, eds., *Women-Identified Women*, pp. 105–15. Palo Alto, Calif.: Mayfield.

Hom, A. Y. 1992. Family matters: A historical study of the Asian Pacific Lesbian Network. Master's thesis, University of California, Los Angeles.

Icard, L. 1985/1986. Black gay men and conflicting social identities: Sexual orientation versus racial identity. *Journal of Social Work and Human Sexuality* 4(1/2):83–92.

Kanuha, V. 1990. Compounding the triple jeopardy: Battering in lesbian of color relationships. *Women and Therapy* 9:169–84.

Klein, C. 1986. *Counseling Our Own*. Seattle: Consultant Services Northwest.

Lockard, D. 1985. The lesbian community: An anthropological approach. *Journal of Homosexuality* 11:(3–4):83–95.

Lorde, A. 1990. Age, race, class and sex: Women redefining difference. In R. Ferguson, M. Gever, T. Minh-ha, and C. West, eds., *Out There: Marginalization and Contemporary Cultures*, pp. 281–87. New York: New Museum of Contemporary Art.

Moraga, C. 1983. *Loving in the War years: Lo Que Nunca Pasó por Sus Labios*. Boston: South End.

Morales, E. S. 1989. Ethnic minority families and minority gays and lesbians. *Marriage and Family Review* 14:217–39.

Shon, S. P., and D. Y. Ja. 1982. Asian families. In M. McGoldrick, J. K. Pearse, and J. Giordano, eds., *Ethnicity and Family Therapy*, pp. 208–29. New York: Guildford Press.

Tinney, J. S. 1986. Why a black gay church? In J. Bean, ed., *In the Life: A Black Gay Anthology*, pp. 70–86. Boston:Alyson.

Tremble, B., M. Schneider, and C. Appathurai. 1989. Growing up gay or lesbian in a multicultural context. *Journal of Homosexuality* 17(1–4):253–67.

13

Persistence and Change in the Berdache Tradition Among Contemporary Lakota Indians

Walter L. Williams

This article explores the gender nonconformity role of berdache, *which ethnographers have often assumed has died out among contemporary American Indians. Ethnohistorical sources indicate intense suppression of berdaches by missionaries and government officials. The authors fieldwork in 1982 on Lakota reservations in South Dakota reveals that individuals recognized as berdaches continue to hold a social and ceremonial role. A gender-mixing status seldom talked about with outsiders (including heterosexual ethnographers) was observed. This role involves more emphasis on sexual contact with men than has been noted in recent anthropological writings.*

The *berdache* tradition in American Indian culture has been discussed since the earliest Spanish and French explorers confronted aboriginal societies. Frontiersmen and early ethnographers also described it, and a few even interviewed berdaches as late as the 1930s (Stevenson 1901–1902; Hill 1935). Nevertheless, most of the firsthand writings on the subject were based on statements by nonberdache Indians or by Whites who may have had only fleeting contact with a berdache. Some of these White observers approached the subject in a neutral manner, but the majority (including some anthropologists) expressed condemnatory attitudes reflective of Western prejudices. Most reports devoted only a paragraph or two to the berdaches, preferring to focus on less "disagreeable" topics.

Modern scholars analyzing the topic on a multitribal level have had to rely on these limited sources, as a basis for theorizing about the social function of the berdache tradition (Angelino and Shedd 1955; Blackwood 1984; Callender and Kochems 1983; Forgey 1975; Jacobs 1968; Katz 1976; Thayer 1980; Whitehead 1981). The berdaches have been presented only abstractly, rather than in a personalized way as real people, due to the deficiencies of the available data. Berdaches have not been allowed to speak for themselves. Furthermore, most anthropologists assume that the berdache tradition has died out among contemporary American Indians. As with all traditional aspects of aboriginal societies the berdache tradition has changed, but it still persists among some tribes. Changes in the tradition are the result of cultural adaptations that Indian people have made to life in a homophobic colonial environment.

One group in which the berdache tradition survives is the traditionalist Lakotas, or Sioux, in the northern plains. In their language the word for berdache is *winkte,* and refers only to biological males (Hassrick 1964; Powers 1977). According to Forgey (1975), a male on the Lower Brule reservation continued dressing in women's clothing in the 1970s, and was fully accepted as a winkte and as a respected member of the community. In 1971 the revered Lakota medicine man, Lame Deer, also reported the continued existence of winkte. In that year he held a conversation with a berdache, of whom he said, "I wasn't even sure of whether I was talking to a man or to a woman. . . . To us a man is what nature, or his dreams, make him. We accept him for what he wants to be. That's up to him. . . . There are good men among the winktes and they have been given certain powers" (Fire and Erdoes 1972:149).

Equipped with nothing more than these brief statements, I searched for information about berdaches among contemporary Lakotas. During the summer of 1982, I did fieldwork in South Dakota on the Pine Ridge and Rosebud reservations, with a brief trip to the Cheyenne River reservation. Lakota people generously took me into their households and allowed me to learn of their sacred traditions and ceremonies. Lakota berdaches spoke frankly to me of their lives and place in their tribal society.

The best way to understand winkte is to let the Lakota people speak for themselves. The people quoted here are full-blood Lakotas who have lived most of their lives on one of the Lakota reservations. They think of themselves as "traditionalists," meaning that they respect the institutionalized ways of the old people, participate in the aboriginal religious ceremonies, and reject Christianity and the competitive Protestant ethic.

Interview 1:   The informant was a sixty-year-old man who identifies as a traditionalist, takes a leadership role in community ceremonies as a drummer and chanter, and is regarded as an authority on Lakota culture. He described the winktes as follows:

> At one time the winktes were regarded as sacred people, but that has declined and today it is like "gay," like you have in California. People will

tease each other about being winkte, but you would never tease a winkte himself. The attitude of respect changed around World War II or a little after, because of social pressures, as Indians who had been educated in White schools lost respect for the traditions. But even today elderly winktes are respected as holy persons, especially by the elderly and traditional people. They are feared because of their spiritual power. They could put a curse on people who don't respect them.

Becoming a winkte comes from different things. Winktes sometimes come from families with lots of sisters and brothers. It could be how they are brought up, I don't know. Sometimes a person will change, and no longer be a winkte. So if they stay that way it is more of their own choice. It is easy to pick out a winkte. They don't marry women, but they act and talk like a woman. But they're "half and half," and will dress mostly like men. Winktes had to assume their roles because if they didn't, something bad would happen to them or their family or their tribe. But there could also be other reasons for winkte, I'm not sure.

In ceremonials, winktes would dance like a woman and wear an article or two of women's clothing, but otherwise dress as a man. This still happens today. Fifteen or twenty years ago there were still quite a number of elderly winktes on the reservation, but most of them have died since then. I saw them at the ceremonies. People take for granted that they aren't going to change him. That's his life and they accept him. . . . But the White missionaries condemned winktes, and would tell families if something bad happened it was because of the winktes. They would not even accept them into the cemetery when a winkte died, saying "their souls are lost." They ostracized winktes.

Some younger people today are called winkte, but I don't think they are really winkte because they don't have spirituality. They are just "gay"; there is a difference. Maybe they got that way from drinking or smoking. And most of them don't even know about the winkte tradition. If they did they wouldn't drink or live with each other. None of the winktes I knew were married to men. They lived alone and men would visit them. . . .

A very few winktes married women and had children, but still fulfilled the winkte role. But most were not permitted by the spirits to be married. It varies from one person to another. Winkte means "different." It is neither man nor woman, but is a third group different from men and women. That is why winktes are regarded as sacred. Only Wakan Tanka, the great spirit, can explain it, so we accept it. Winktes are gifted persons.

Interview 2: The informant was a twenty-five-year-old man who was raised by his grandfather, a prominent traditionalist medicine man. At age twelve he began to take on a medicine role, under his grandfather's direction, and learned many of the old traditions. Today people come to him for curing and to help in preparing for ceremonies. He is also a road man for the Native American Church, conducting peyote meetings.

> Winktes know medicine, but they are not medicine men. They have good powers, especially for love medicine, for curing, and for childbearing. They can tell the future.
>
> Some say winktes were born that way and you cannot change them. They had a dream, seeing women's quillwork and tools. Winktes do top quality beadwork and crafts, women's work. Most winktes did not go to war, but my grandfather told me stories about one who did. He did the cooking and took care of the camp and cured the wounds of the warriors. Winktes give secret names to people to protect them through life. Some really have strong powers, but others just wanted to be like women. They call each other "sister." Winktes had high status, and some men married a winkte as a second or third wife. If not married, the winkte had his own tipi and his men friends could visit for sex. A married man would visit a winkte for sex during the time when his wife was pregnant, or in taboo days. But this varied from band to band. My grandfather told stories that in sex the winkte usually took the passive role, but sometimes he would exchange and take the active role with his men friends.
>
> Traditionally, winktes were both joked about and respected at the same time. But when people forgot the traditional ways and the traditional medicine, by going to missionaries and boarding schools, then they began to look down on winktes and lose respect. The missionaries and government officials said winktes were no good, and they tried to get winktes to change their ways. I heard sad stories of winktes committing suicide, hanging themselves rather than change. The 1920s and 1930s were the turning point in the winkte's decline, and after that those who remained would put on men's clothing.
>
> Today people would look down on winktes and might shun them. But a few years ago one man wore eye shadow and a woman's blouse, and many accepted him but he was shunned by others. Two men might have sex today, but they'd do it in secret and if discovered would be shunned. . . . If I had lived in traditional times, I might have had a winkte for a wife, but not today. The old respect is gone.

Interview 3:   The informant was a twenty-eight-year-old woman who was raised in a traditionalist household. Although she now holds a wage job in a nearby town she continues to participate in the tribal ceremonies. She recently had gone through scarification in a Sun Dance and proudly displayed her scars.

> I grew up on the reservation, and still respect the old traditions. My uncle is now a winkte, and so was my grandfather. He died in 1980, in his seventies. He was married to my grandmother, and even had children, but

was basically homosexual though he was secretive about his male lovers. He was effeminate, quiet, easy-going, very philosophical, and very respected on the reservation. He gave people sacred names. When someone died, it was the winkte who was the first one people came to, to help out with the funeral and the ceremonies. People who don't respect their Indian traditions criticize gays, but it was part of Indian culture. It makes me mad when I hear someone insult winktes. A lot of the younger gays, though, don't fulfill their spiritual role as winktes, and that's sad, too.

Interview 4: A twenty-four year-old man does not identify as winkte, though other people think of him as winkte because of his feminine nature. He is a very gentle person who is well respected for his work with children.

The last true traditional winkte on this reservation died in the 1960s. I remember seeing him at ceremonials. You never talked disrespectfully about a winkte because it is sacred. Every true winkte has sacred powers, some more, some less. They doctored illnesses, and were wakan [sacred]. If a person took ill, a winkte could give medicine that would make a miraculous cure. One doctored my grandfather and healed his broken leg in one day. This winkte wore a woman's breastplate, shawl, and underwear, but always wore men's pants. He could do anything and everything better than a woman. He was very neat and clean, good at crocheting and cooking. Winktes were always male, never a female, but they always danced with the women, dancing at the head of the circle leading the women. They talked in a woman's dialect, but were different from both men and women.

I heard a story that if a man wanted a winkte to name his child, then he would have sex with the winkte. If a winkte names a child, then that child will take on some winkte ways. That would be good because if there was a winkte in a family, that family would feel very fortunate. Due to White influence the younger generation sometimes ridiculed winktes, but the elders respected them almost like an immortal. Today, when Indians say winkte, they mean "effeminate" or "like a woman." There are some gays on the reservation now, but "gay" and winkte are different; winkte is a gay with ceremonial sacred powers.

People have always called me winkte, in a joking or negative way, because of my effeminate mannerisms. I don't think I am spiritual enough. If I did it I would be very serious about it. But I don't want to be considered gay either, because that brings more kidding. I would be frightened to leave the reservation and my family, so I don't think I would fit into the gay life-style in the city.

Interview 5: A thirty-two-year-old man who identifies as winkte, dresses in men's clothes, but wears his hair very long like a woman. He is extremely feminine in voice and manner, and does not try to hide this but is very proud of it. He takes the traditional religion most seriously.

A winkte is two spirits, man and woman, combined into one spirit. That is me, and I get my holiness from the Sacred Pipe. From that holiness the Sioux people show respect. In the last few years, respect for winkte has increased somewhat, more than it had been, as more people return to respect for the traditions. Some mixed-blood Indians condemn "queers" but the traditional people stick up for them. Formerly, higher-class winktes had up to twelve husbands. Chief Crazy Horse had one or two winktes for wives, as well as his female wives, but this has been kept quiet because Indians don't want Whites to criticize. It's not so much that Whites influenced Indian culture, because they didn't really care very much about anything other than getting the Indians' land and wealth, but Indians just keep things like this unknown to Whites who don't understand our sacred ways.

As a winkte, I accept my feminine nature as part of my being. I dress as a man, but I feel feminine and enjoy doing women's things. I would be terribly scared to be considered as a man. It is obvious from infancy that a boy is going to be a winkte. He is a beautiful baby and the sound of his voice is effeminate; it is inborn. The mother realizes this soon, and allows the boy to do feminine things. They all end up being sexually attracted to men.

I began to be sexually active when I was eight years old, and had an affair with a forty-year-old man. Since he was good to me and for me, it was considered by my family to be o.k. and my own private business—no one else's. I still, at age thirty-two, live with my parents, and my men friends visit me at home. Straight Indian guys will go sexually with a gay here, in a way that Whites don't. A man will go out with winktes and with women, but he is not considered to be a winkte. "Homosexuals" are two he-men who live together as a couple. That is not done here; it is an effeminate and a he-man. Married men are the best. I only want to play the passive role with a he-man, though sometimes the man wants to change sex roles. I want to lie with all the men. I used to keep a list of how many men I had been with. It would be unholy for me to have sex with a woman, or with another winkte. That would be wrong, and would violate the role set for me by the Sacred Pipe. The man could be gay, but he must be masculine. . . . A man and a winkte could go through a wedding ceremony, and it would be accepted by traditional people just as a marriage between men and women. It is by the Sacred Pipe. People know that on the reservation the spirit of Big Bull is watching them, so they cannot criticize winkte. But if they were away in the city, away from the kin groups, then they might be antigay. That is a different thing.

One person I know goes in and out of a winkte role, but that is very unusual. Usually winktes hold on to their role always, for its spiritual power.

Sacred Pipe people, the traditionalists, would not object if a winkte dresses in woman's clothing in ceremonies. They would only see it as winkte getting more spiritual power. A couple of years ago I saw an eighty-year-old winkte dance in a ceremony with a woman's shawl and hairnet over his long braids, but otherwise he dressed as a man. That's the way he always dressed.

People are afraid to criticize winkte, because they fear the winkte spiritual power. To become a winkte, you have a medicine man put you on the hill for a vision quest. You can see a vision of a White Buffalo Bull Calf if you truly are a winkte by nature, or you might see another vision if Wakan Tanka wants you to.

Interview 6:   The informant is a forty-nine-year-old male who identifies as winkte. He dresses in pants, but they are women's style. His entire dress and manner suggest androgyny, with a mixture of both male and female aspects. He has always filled a winkte role and been accepted as such by his family and the reservation at large. He takes a leading role in the tribal ceremonies.

Winkte are wakan, which means that they have power as special people. Medicine men go to winkte for spiritual advice. Winktes can also be medicine men, but they're usually not because they already have the power. An example of this power is the sacred naming ceremony. It takes a winkte a full year to prepare for this. He starts with a fast and a vision quest, with sacrifices, to be fully sincere. He works with the family for the whole year, making preparations to the family and the child, and closely guiding the child for the year. A winkte can take on no more than about four children a year. Later, it is the winkte's responsibility to help look after that child. The winkte makes a medicine bag for the child, with a piece of the winkte's skin and hair, and also a holy stone, which the child will carry for protection during the rest of his life. Traditionally it was the first born and the last born that got a winkte name, but nowadays it is very rare.

People know that a person will become a winkte very early in his life. About age twelve, parents will take him to a ceremony to communicate with past winktes who had power, to verify if it is just a phase or a permanent thing for his lifetime. If the proper vision takes place, and communication with past winkte is established, then everyone accepts him as a winkte. I am now nearly fifty years old, and I have always filled a winkte role.

I was just born this way, ever since I can remember. When I was eight I saw a vision, of a person with long grey hair and with many ornaments on, standing by my bed. I asked if he was female or male, and he said "both." He said he would walk with me for the rest of my life. His spirit would always be with me. I told my grandfather, who said not to be afraid of spirits, because they have good powers. A year later, the vision appeared again, and told me he would give me great powers. He said his body was man's, but his spirit was woman's. He told me the Great Spirit made people like me to be of help to other people.

I told my grandfather the name of the spirit, and Grandfather said it was a highly respected winkte who lived long ago. He explained winkte to me and said, "It won't be easy growing up, because you will be different from others. But the spirit will help you, if you pray and do the sweat." The spirit has continued to contact me throughout my life. If I practice the winkte role seriously, then people will respect me. If someone ever makes fun of me, something bad will happen to them. Once a half-breed woman said I was a disgrace to the Indian race. I told her that a century ago, I would have been considered that much more special. She died shortly after, and I think it was because she had insulted winkte.

My spirit takes care of me. I love children, and I used to worry that I would be alone without children. The Spirit said he would provide some. Later, some kids of drunks who did not care for them, were brought to me by neighbors. The kids began spending more and more time here, so finally the parents asked me to adopt them. In all, I have raised seven orphan children.

I worked as a nurse, and a cook in an old age home. I cook for funerals and wakes too. People bring their children to me for special winkte names, and give me gifts. If I show my generosity, then others help me in return. Once I asked the spirit if my living with a man and loving him was bad. The spirit answered that it was not bad because I had a right to release my feelings and express love for another, that I was good because I was generous and provided a good home for my children. I want to be remembered most for the two values that my people hold dearest: generosity and spirituality. If you say anything about me, say those two things.

From an ethnohistoric perspective, several themes emerge from the berdache tradition among Lakotas. Despite intense pressure from White missionaries and government officials, native culture has not succumbed to attempts at cultural genocide. Winktes had to change and become secretive, but they have not vanished. They retain the respect of traditional Lakota people, though respect has declined among acculturated Indians. It is interesting that cross-dressing is not seen as that important to a continuation of berdachism. But same-sex erotic behavior does continue to have a strong association with winkte status, more so than the recent literature would suggest. This behavior, however, is seen as distinct from the Western concepts of "gay" or "homosexual," because of the strong berdache association with femininity and spirituality.

Even the descriptive variations found in these interviews are evidence of the Lakota viewpoint that individuals decide spiritual truth for themselves. Nevertheless, the general characteristics of the winktes are graphically rendered: their spiritual power, respected status, homoeroticism, the mixture of women's and men's work, their repression in the last half century, and their survival. By creative, individualized adaptation, the berdache, like American Indian culture generally, has survived.

ACKNOWLEDGMENTS

Thanks are expressed to those who helped gain contact with traditionalist Lakotas and served as valuable resource advisors: Luis Kemnitzer, Elizabeth Grobsmith, Calvin Fast Wolf, Herbert Hoover, James Young, Al White Eyes, Dale Mason, Twila Giegle, Calvin Jumping Bull, and other Lakota people who wish to remain anonymous.

REFERENCES

Angelino, H., and C. Shedd. 1955. A note on berdache. *American Anthropologist* 57:121–25.

Blackwood, E. 1984. Sexuality and gender in certain native American tribes: The case of cross-gender females. *Signs: Journal of Women in Culture and Society* 10:27–42.

Callender, C., and L. Kochems. 1983. The North American berdache. *Current Anthropology* 24:443–70.

Fire, J., and R. Erdoes. 1972. *Lame Deer, Seeker of Visions.* New York: Simon and Schuster.

Forgey, D. 1975. The institution of berdache among the North American Plains Indians. *Journal of Sex Research* 11:1–15.

Hassrick, R. 1964. *The Sioux: Life and Customs of a Warrior Society.* Norman: University of Oklahoma Press.

Hill, W. W. 1935. The status of the hermaphrodite and transvestite in Navaho culture. *American Anthropologist* 37:27–68.

Jacobs, S. 1968. Berdache: A brief review of the literature. *Colorado Anthropologist* 1:25–40.

Katz, J. 1976. *Gay American History.* New York: Thomas Crowell.

Powers, W. 1977. *Oglala Religion.* Lincoln: University of Nebraska Press.

Stevenson, M. C. 1901–1902. The Zuni Indians. *Bureau of American Ethnology Annual Report* 23:38ff.

Thayer, J. 1980. The berdache of the Northern Plains: A socioreligious perspective. *Journal of Anthropological Research* 36:287–93.

Whitehead, H. 1981. The bow and the burden strap: A new look at institutionalized homosexuality in Native North America. In S. Ortner and H. Whitehead, eds., *Sexual Meanings*, pp. 80–115. Cambridge: Cambridge University Press.

14

Issues of Identity in the Psychology of Latina Lesbians

Oliva M. Espín

Identity development for persons of ethnic or racial minority groups involves not only the acceptance of an external reality that can rarely be changed (e.g., being Black, Puerto Rican, Jewish, or Vietnamese), but also an intrapsychic "embracing" of that reality as a positive component of one's self. By definition in the context of a heterosexist, racist, and sexist society, the process of identity development for Latina lesbian women entails the embracing of "stigmatized" or "negative" identities. Coming out to self and others in the context of a sexist and heterosexist American society is compounded by coming out in the context of a heterosexist and sexist Latin culture immersed in racist society. Because as a Latina she is an ethnic minority person, she must be bicultural in American society. Because she is a lesbian, she has to be polycultural among her own people.

The dilemma for Latina lesbians is how to integrate who they are culturally, racially, and religiously with their identity as lesbians and women. The identity of each Latina lesbian develops through conscious and unconscious choices that allot relative importance to the different components of the self, and thus of her identity as woman, as lesbian, as Latina.

IDENTITY DEVELOPMENT

The term *identity* is understood here as that which each woman tells herself about who she is when she is alone with herself. The term is also understood as that which each context to which she is field sensitive calls forth in a given moment. In other words, identity is also associated with social image.

According to Erik Erikson, the crises conducive to the development of an integrated identity consist of "a state of being and becoming that can have a highly conscious (and, indeed, self-conscious) quality and yet remain, in its motivational aspects, quite conscious and beset with the dynamics of conflict." Because a "part of identity must be accounted for in that communality within which an individual finds himself" there might be "fragments that the individual had to submerge in himself as undesirable or irreconcilable or which his group has taught him to perceive as the mark of fatal 'difference' in sex role or race in class or religion.' "[1] For both lesbians and ethnic minority persons of both sexes and, indeed, for ethnic minority lesbians, the process of identity development is full of vicissitudes, and it frequently demands the submerging of different fragments of the self.

As Erikson has written, however, "certain historical periods present a singular chance for a collective renewal which opens up unlimited identities for those who, by a combination of unruliness, giftedness, and competence, represent a new leadership, a new elite, and new types . . . in a new people."[2] We seem to be living in such a period, and ethnic minority lesbians seem to be at a crucial point of this psychohistorical process.

Obviously, different individuals are at different stages of identity development, that is, at different stages of clarity about who they are, or are finding different ways of embracing the labels—imposed or chosen—by which people classify each other and themselves, including embracing those aspects of identity considered to be negative by the group or groups to which the individual belongs. The process is not necessarily linear for any given individual. In fact, identities are fluid as is the process of developing them. Donald Atkinson, George Morten, and Derald Wing Sue have evolved a model of identity development for ethnic minorities that captures the fluidity of the process and describes its phases in a clear and concise way (table 14.1).[3] Vivienne Cass has developed a similar theoretical model in reference to homosexual identity formation.[4] Both models incorporate the different possible reactions to a negative identity that ethnic minority persons and homosexuals can have at different points in life.

TABLE 14.1
Minority Identity Development Model

Stages of Minority Development Model	Attitude Toward Self	Attitude Toward Others of the Same Minority	Attitude Toward Others of a Different Minority	Attitude Toward Dominant Group
Stage 1: conformity	Self-depreciating	Group depreciating	Discriminatory	Group appreciating
Stage 2: dissonance	Conflict between self-depreciating and appreciating	Conflict between group depreciating and group appreciating	Conflict between dominant-held views of minority hierarchy and feelings of shared experience	Conflict between group appreciating and group depreciating
Stage 3: resistance and immersion	Self-appreciating	Group appreciating	Conflict between feelings of empathy for other minority experiences and feelings of culturocentrism	Group depreciating
Stage 4: introspection	Concern with basis of self-appreciation	Concern with nature of unequivocal appreciation	Concern with ethnocentric basis for judging others	Concern with the basis of group depreciation
Stage 5: synergetic articulation and awareness	Self-appreciating	Group appreciating	Group appreciating	Selective appreciating

From D. R. Atkinson, G. Morten, and D. W. Sue, *Counseling American Minorities: A Cross-Cultural Perspective*, Dubuque, Iowa: William C. Brown, 1979, 198.

In the Atkinson, Morten, and Sue model, stage one, Conformity, is characterized by a preference for dominant cultural values over one's own culture. The reference group is likely to be the dominant cultural group, and feelings of self-hatred, negative beliefs of one's own culture, and positive feelings toward the dominant culture are likely to be strong. The second stage, or Dissonance, is characterized by cultural confusion and conflict. Information and experiences begin to challenge accepted values and beliefs. Active questioning of the dominant-held values operates strongly. In stage three, Resistance and Immersion, an active rejection of the dominant society and culture and a complete endorsement of minority-held views become evident. Desires to combat oppression become the primary motivation of the person. There is an attempt to get in touch with one's history, culture, and traditions. Distrust and hatred of dominant society is strong. The reference group is one's own culture. Stage four, Introspection, is characterized by conflict at the too narrow and rigid constraints of the previous stage. Notions of loyalty and responsibility to one's own group and notions of personal autonomy come in conflict. In stage five, Synergetic Articulation and Awareness, individuals experience a sense of self-fulfillment with regard to cultural identity. Conflicts and discomfort experienced in the Introspective stage have been resolved, allowing greater individual control and flexibility. Cultural values are examined and accepted or rejected on the basis of prior experience gained in earlier stages of identity development. Desire to eliminate all forms of oppression becomes an important motivation of the individual's behavior.[5]

Vivienne Cass's model proposes six stages of development that individuals move through in order to acquire a fully integrated identity as a homosexual person. In stage one, Identity Confusion, the individual realizes that feelings, thoughts, or behavior can be defined as homosexual, and this realization presents an incongruent element into a previously stable situation in which both the individual and the environment assumed the person to be heterosexual. As a result of this incongruency the individual arrives at a self-identity potentially that of a homosexual.[6] "Where the task of stage one was to resolve the immediate personal identity crisis of 'Who am I?' the task of stage two, Identity Comparison, is to handle the social alienation that now arises." In stage three, Identity Tolerance, there is an increased level of commitment to the homosexual self-image. "At this stage, contacting homosexuals is viewed as something that has to be done in order to counter the felt isolation and alienation from others. The individual tolerates rather than accepts a homosexual identity." Stage four, Identity Acceptance, is "characterized by continued and increasing contacts with other homosexuals. These allow [the person] to feel the impact of those features of the subculture that validate and 'normalize' homosexuality as an identity and a way of life. [The individual] now accepts rather than tolerates a homosexual self-image." Entrance into stage five, Identity Pride, is characterized by the incongruencies that exist between a concept of self as totally acceptable as a homosexual and society's rejection of this concept. In order to manage this incongruency, heterosexuals and heterosexuality are devalued. A combination of anger and pride is developed, and confrontation with the environment may occur. More and more strategies previously used to conceal a homosexual identity are deliberately abandoned. Disclosure becomes a strategy for coping. Stage six, Identity Synthesis, starts "with an awareness that the 'them and us' philosophy espoused previously, in which all heterosexuals were viewed negatively and all homosexuals positively, no longer holds true. Personal and public sexual identities become synthesized into one image of self receiving considerable support from [the] environment. . . . Homosexual identity . . . instead of being seen as the identity, is now given the status of being merely one aspect of the self. This awareness completes the homosexual identity formation process."[7]

Although these two models are not identical, they describe a similar process that must be undertaken by people who must embrace negative or stigmatized identities. This process moves gradually from a rejected and denied self-image to the embracing of an identity that is finally accepted as positive. Both models describe one or several stages of intense confusion and at least one stage of complete separatism from and rejection of all representatives of the dominant society. The final stage for both models implies the acceptance of one's own identity, a committed attitude against oppression, and an ability to synthesize the best values of both perspectives and to communicate with members of the dominant group.

LATINA LESBIANS

It can be reasonably asserted that the development of identity in Latina lesbians must follow patterns similar to those described by these two models. I do not know of any studies on this topic, however. Indeed, the literature on Latina lesbians is scarce.

A professional presentation by Hortensia Amaro discussed the issue of coming out for Hispanic lesbians,[8] and some literary discussions that address the experiences of Latina lesbians have been published by Cherríe Moraga.[9] Although there might be studies in progress on this population, very few have been published. Hilda Hidalgo and Elia Hidalgo-Christensen have published two versions of a study of Puerto Rican attitudes toward lesbianism.[10] Yvonne Escaserga and her collaborators studied the attitudes of Chicana lesbians toward psychotherapy.[11] To my knowledge, no other research studies focus particularly on Latina lesbians or on the specific aspect of their identity development.

Although emotional and physical closeness among women is encouraged by Latin culture, overt acknowledgment of lesbianism is even more restricted than in mainstream American society. Hidalgo and Hidalgo-Christensen, for example, discuss the importance of *amigas intimas* (intimate female friends) for Puerto Rican women, and contrast it with the results of their research that show that most members of the Puerto Rican community strongly reject lesbianism. They found that "rejection of homosexuals appears to be the dominant attitude in the Puerto Rican community."[12] At a meeting of Hispanic women in a major U.S. city in the early 1980s, one participant expressed the opinion that "lesbianism is a sickness we get from American women and American culture." This is obviously an expression of the common belief that homosexuality is chosen behavior acquired through the bad influence of others. Socialist attitudes with respect to homosexuality are extremely traditional, as the attitudes of the Cuban and other revolutions clearly manifest. Thus, Latinos who consider themselves radical and committed to civil rights may remain extremely traditional when it comes to gay rights. In a book entitled *Pleasure and Danger: Exploring Female Sexuality*, I have discussed the impact of the prevalent Latin attitudes on Hispanic women who have a lesbian orientation.[13] These attitudes clearly add further stress to the lives of Latina lesbians who are invested in participating in the life of their communities. Although these attitudes may not seem different from those of the dominant culture, some important differences experienced by Latina lesbians are directly related to Hispanic cultural patterns. Latin families tend to treat their lesbian daughters or sisters with silent tolerance: their lesbianism will not be openly acknowledged and accepted, but they are not denied a place in the family, either. Seldom is there overt rejection of their lesbian members on the part of Hispanic families. The family may explain away the daughter's lesbianism by saying, "She is too intelligent to marry any man" or "She is too dedicated to her work to bother with dating, marriage, or motherhood." Nevertheless, because frequent contact and a strong interdependence among family members, even in adult life, are essential features of Hispanic family life, leading a double life may become more of a strain. Because of the importance placed on family and community by most Hispanics, the threat of possible rejection and stigmatization by the Latin community becomes more of a psychological burden for the Hispanic lesbian. Rejection from mainstream society does not carry the same weight. As Cherríe Moraga puts it, "That is not to say that Anglo culture does not stigmatize its women for 'gender transgression'—only that its stigmatization did not hold the personal power over me which Chicano culture did."[14]

To avoid stigmatization by the Latin community, Hispanic lesbians frequently seek other groups or networks in which their lesbian orientation will be more accepted than it is in their family and its community. As Hortensia Amaro states, however:

> Reliance on alternative support groups outside the Hispanic community would not occur without a cost. Loss of contact with the ethnic community and culture will mean lack of support for their identity as a Hispanic. On the other hand, staying within the Hispanic community and not "coming out" will represent a denial of the identity associated with sexuality and intimate love relationships.[15]

To be out of the closet only in an Anglo context deprives them of essential support from their communities and families, and, in turn, increases their invisibility in the Hispanic culture, where only the openly "butch" types are recognized as lesbian. To complicate matters even further, Latina lesbians sometimes experience discrimination or more subtle forms of racism, not only from the mainstream of American society, but also within the context of the Anglo lesbian communities in which they continue to comprise a numerical minority.

Many Latina women who are lesbians choose to remain closeted among their families, their colleagues, and society at large. Coming out may jeopardize not only the strong family ties, but also the possibility of serving the Hispanic community. This is particularly difficult because the talents of all members are such an important asset for any minority community. Because most lesbian women are single and self-supporting and unencumbered by the demands of husbands and children, it can be assumed that the professional experience and educational level of Hispanic lesbians will tend to be relatively higher than that of other Hispanic women. Because there are no statistics on Hispanic lesbians, this assertion cannot be easily proved. But if it is true, professional experience and education will frequently place Latina lesbians in positions of leadership or advocacy in their community. Their status and prestige, and thus the ability to serve their community, will be easily threatened by the possibility of being found out by the same people they are trying to serve.

CUBAN LESBIANS

Having provided some background on the development of identity in minority persons and on the experience of Latina lesbians, I will present what a group of Cuban lesbians have to say about the different components of their identity. I was prompted by a recognition of the problems encountered by Latina lesbians to study the relative importance of these identity components in a group of such women. I wanted to assess the relative degree of cultural and lesbian identity for this group. How did these women integrate the different components of the self in the process of identity formation? I decided to limit my study to Cuban women in order to reduce the number of intervening factors that may differentiate among Hispanic subgroups. Although the study focuses on Cuban women, the results serve to illustrate general principles relevant to the identity development of other Latinas and minority lesbians.

THE STUDY

I distributed a questionnaire through friendship pyramiding among Cuban lesbians in several cities in the United States and analyzed the responses primarily through the use of qualitative methods. Qualitative methodology provides a legitimate and flexible format for an exploratory study, based on a sample of convenience obtained through friendship pyramiding such as this one.[16]

I kept both the Atkinson, Morten, and Sue model of ethnic minority identity development and the Cass model of homosexual identity development as background for understanding the process of the respondents' identity formation. I made no effort, however, at coding questions on the basis of the stages described in these two models. Because there is no other study published on this specific population of lesbians, I saw value in examining how they themselves described their experience without superimposing any previously determined model of analysis.

I mailed thirty-five questionnaires: fifteen to specific individuals and twenty in small packets of five to people who had offered to contact others. Sixteen completed questionnaires were returned.[17] The respondents expressed great enthusiasm for the study, and almost all of them asked to be sent results and to be kept informed about any future studies on this matter.

It is important to acknowledge the possibility that respondents are only among those women who have sufficiently embraced the multiple components of their identity to be willing to answer and return the questionnaire. In fact, I heard through the grapevine that some of the prospective respondents felt that their lesbianism was a "trial" sent by God that they had to suffer and endure, and thus they found the questionnaire too difficult and decided not to answer it. In addition, because the questionnaire was written in English, it presupposes literacy in English on the part of prospective respondents, at least in regard to their ability to read. (Respondents were encouraged to answer in Spanish if they preferred. Although some Spanish was used, however, questionnaires were primarily answered in English.) A further consideration is that respondents were highly educated and perhaps not representative of the population of Cuban lesbians in the United States.

The questionnaire was brief. It consisted of three pages preceded by a demographic fact sheet in which such questions as occupation, place of residence, and age were asked. Because I wanted to make the questionnaire easy and to the point, some richness of data may have been lost. If the study is to be expanded in the future, in-depth interviewing should be used to follow up. The questionnaire was completely anonymous. Respondents who wanted to know the results of the study were asked to submit a request under separate letter or postcard.

Before presenting the data, I must reiterate that both sexuality and ethnicity are, in fact, fluid, lifelong processes, regardless of how "inborn," "born into," or "given at birth" they are. What I think of myself today in terms of either ethnicity or sexuality may not be what I thought yesterday or what I will think tomorrow. Because "what each woman thinks of herself" is what I define as identity for my purposes here, I have included those women who consider themselves appropriate participants of this study by responding to the questionnaire. That is why one of the respondents, a twenty-three-year-old woman born in Hialeah, Florida, a short while after her family immigrated into the United States, is included in the study. She defines herself as Cuban, so she can be considered as such for the purposes of this study.

Characteristics of the Group. The ages of the sixteen respondents range from twenty-three to forty-five with a mean of thirty-two years. Fifteen of the respondents were born in Cuba, and one was born in Florida. Eleven of the sixteen are either the oldest child or the oldest daughter in the family. Their places of residence are fairly evenly distributed across the United States. Responses came from Florida, California, the Midwest, and the Northeast.

On the basis of their parents' occupation and education in Cuba and in the United States, it can be estimated that three come from an upper-middle-class socioeconomic background, seven from a middle-class background, and six from a low-middle or working-class background. The occupations of the respondents varied, but they were all highly educated. Three of the respondents held doctorates, one was a physician, one was a lawyer, and two were law students. Five had master's degrees and five bachelor's degrees, and one was a professional writer. This high level of education may be an effect of the friendship pyramiding process of recruiting participants for the study. On the other hand, it may be that the high level of education found in this group is a confirmation of what was hypothesized earlier in this chapter concerning the level of education of Latina lesbians compared to a general population of Latinas in the United States. Fourteen of the sixteen women were raised Catholic, one was Methodist, and one Episcopalian. Only three of them practiced their religion at the time of the study. These three women were members of Dignity, a national organization of gay and lesbian Catholics.

Of the sixteen women, fifteen were involved in a committed relationship. Nine of them were in relationships with Cuban or other Hispanic women, five in relationships with Jewish women, one with an African-American woman, and one with a White Anglo woman.

The fifteen women who were born in Cuba had arrived in the United States between 1956 and 1972. Thus, their length of residence in this country ranged from seven to twenty-eight years, with a mean of eighteen years. Their age at leaving Cuba ranged from three to twenty-two. Twelve participants left Cuba between three and thirteen years of age, one left at seventeen, two at twenty, and one at twenty-two. Most of them left Cuba during their childhood years, and only three left in early adulthood.

Coming out as a lesbian occurred from twenty-one years earlier (1962) to as recently as a few months before the questionnaire was filled out. The ages of coming out ranged from sixteen to thirty-three years old. As is usual with a lesbian population, chronological age does not correlate with the number of years of being out, except for those who had been out twenty-one or eighteen years, who, obviously, were among the oldest respondents. Five of the women were out to all members of their family, including parents. Six were out to siblings or other relatives, and five were not out to anyone in their families. Most of them were out to friends, and most of them preferred to socialize with people who know they are lesbians.

Responses to the "Core" Questions. Several questions were considered to be the core questions of the study. Questions 5 and 6 asked the participants if they identified as Cuban and as lesbian, respectively. Questions 7 and 8 asked for a brief description of their process of identifying as Cuban and as lesbian. Questions 9 and 10 asked about the influence that living in the United States may have had on them as lesbians and as Cubans. Question 11 asked for the relative importance that being Cuban or being lesbian had in their lives. Question 12 asked about their decision making in choosing friends among Latin people who are not gay or among Anglo lesbians. This last question was intended to elicit reflections on the process of emotional costs involved in this decision.

Fourteen of the women, including the young woman born in Florida, identify as Cuban. The two respondents who do not identify as Cuban live in Florida. One of them is thirty-one years old. She came to this country in 1956, before the larger waves of Cuban migration, and was raised, in her own words, "as an Anglo among Anglos." The other woman who does not identify as Cuban is forty-two years old and came to Miami from Cuba in 1962, when she was twenty. She was the only woman in the group who was in a relationship with a White Anglo woman. Although she came to the United States as an adult and lives in the geographical area where the largest concentration of Cubans in the country is, she strongly rejects Cuban ways. In her words:

> It is great to be able to know and share black beans and rice and talk Spanish, but if we cannot be ourselves, we cannot share with one another if our waves do not click—to what good is Spanish if we cannot communicate? I am afraid black beans and rice are not enough. Latins are provincial, nonworldly, ignorant, superstitious, with no room for individuality, self-expression, nonprogressive, politically oppressive, bound by archaic traditions that enslave people. Come to Miami, see butch/femme still alive and well. Very disturbing. These are 17 to 25 year olds.

Among the descriptions of their process of self-definition as Cuban, two responses seem to express the general sentiment more precisely. A thirty-three-year-old woman who had lived in the United States for twenty-three years describes her process in the following way:

> As a child this self-definition was not conscious, since there was no need for awareness of ethnic identity while I lived in Cuba. Coming to the United States instantly brought to my awareness at the age of 10 what being Cuban meant in this country. I would say that the need to assert that identity was strengthened by the racism of the United States. In my teens, I passed through a period of acculturation in which to some extent I internalized society's view of ethnic groups in a very subtle way. During college, I became active in political and community activities and went through a "militant" phase in which I came to understand the nature of racism and oppression more deeply. Presently, I consider myself to have a more universal or humanistic perspective and I am able to appreciate as well as critically analyze aspects of my cultural heritage.

This woman's description of her process as an ethnic minority person clearly fits Atkinson, Morten, and Sue's model of ethnic minority identity development described earlier. When confronted with a culture different from her own, she evolved from a conformity stage as an adolescent to a more synergetic stage at this point in her life.

Another respondent, a forty-five-year-old woman, who had lived in the United States for twelve years, said the following about being Cuban in this country: "It is difficult to be cut off from the Cuban community while not feeling fully understood by Americans and sometimes even by other Latins. Being Cuban at this point in history is not easy!"

The vicissitudes of the process of self-identification as a lesbian woman are described best by the following two responses:

> First, total unawareness. Then, after sleeping with a woman, total rejection of her; as if she was an addiction. I knew this was "sick." I never went to bed with so many men in my life as I did during that period. Then, I started realizing that I was denying my own happiness. Now I am almost totally out. I feel whole.

> Although I had been intensely involved with another woman, we both denied it. When I became involved with a woman who defined herself as lesbian, I thought I was not lesbian, only "in love with her." Then, I started feeling attracted to other women, became involved in gay groups. I'm now out at work and to friends. Family is impossible, though.

The internal journeys described by these two women, as well by other respondents, fit the processes involved in developing a homosexual identity as described in Vivienne Cass's model.

It is interesting that one of the respondents does not identify as a lesbian. According to her, "No, my sexual preference does not rule my life. I like women, I love women, that is called being a lesbian, but I don't define myself as one." In spite of these words, this woman, who at forty years of age had been out for eighteen years, chose to answer the questionnaire knowing that it was about lesbians.

When asked what was more important for them, being Cuban or being lesbian, twelve women responded that both were equally important. Three women responded that being lesbian was more important and one responded that "being a Latin woman" was most important, because "being a Latin woman gives me a broader perspective culturally and politically." This person is the same one who said she did not define herself as lesbian.

When confronted with the choice of being among Latins without coming out, or living among lesbians who are not Latin or who are unfamiliar with Latin culture, eleven of the women said they had chosen or would choose the second alternative. This choice is not made without ambivalence, however. A twenty-nine-year-old woman from San Francisco explained her choice in this way: *"¡Una pregunta muy difícil!* (A very difficult question!) I have done both. I think being able to be a lesbian is too much a part of me for me to repress. I can still be Cuban if I'm around Americans."

A twenty-seven-year-old woman from Miami expressed not only the ambivalence, but also the pain and anger associated with choosing between different parts of herself:

> I guess that if the choice were absolute, I would choose living among lesbians. This answer may invalidate my answer to question 11 in which I said that being Cuban and being lesbian were both equally important for me. But I want to point out that I would be extremely unhappy if all my Latin culture were taken out of my lesbian life. I had a hard time with all the questions that made me choose between Cuban and lesbian, or at least, made me feel as if I had to choose. It made it real clear to me that I identify myself as a lesbian more intensely than as Cuban/Latin. But it is a very painful question because I feel that I am both, and I don't want to have to choose. Clearly, straight people don't even get asked this question and it is unfair that we have to discuss it, even if it is just a questionnaire.

Two of the respondents said that when confronted with the choice, they prefer to be among Latinos. The reason given by one of them for her choice was, "I feel comfortable with my people—gay or not."

Three women said that they would not choose, without explaining how they have integrated both alternatives in their lives. One woman expressed a strong rejection against the possibility of such a choice: "I would refute that choice and insist on the third alternative of not denying either aspect of myself. This is a false dichotomy as we all know, sort of like saying are you a woman or an ethnic person, such choices arise out of racism and homophobia and I refuse to even postulate such possibility for myself."

It is not clear if this woman has, in fact, answered the question in terms of her own personal choices, or if she is primarily making a statement about what she considers to be correct, or taking a political position. On the other hand, this woman was the most out person in the group. Perhaps because she was out to parents and family, as well as to all the important people in her life, she could actively act out her refusal to choose in a better way than others.

From the responses of this small group, we can conclude that it is impossible to determine that one aspect of the identity of these Cuban lesbians is more important for them than the other. The relative importance given to the different components of their identity does not appear to be related, at least in this group, to factors such as age, years of residence in the United States, place of residence, or any other factors. In fact, the two most extreme and definite positions, that of not wanting to identify as Cuban or as lesbian, are espoused by two women who are more than forty (forty-two and forty, respectively), who have been living in the United States for more than twenty years and out as lesbians for twenty or eighteen years, respectively. The woman who rejects her Cuban identity lives in Miami. The woman who rejects her lesbian identity lives in New York.

Most of the respondents, although regretting their decision, choose behaviorally to be among Anglo lesbians rather than among straight Latinos. The possibility of "passing" or not must be a factor in this decision. Obviously, they cannot hide their Hispanic identity among Anglos as they can hide their lesbian identity among Hispanics. But even when they believe that it is easier to be Cuban among lesbians than it is to be lesbian among Cubans, they do not feel fully comfortable not being both. In fact, what most of them say is that they feel more whole when they can be out both as Cubans and as lesbians. Because of the realities of racism and heterosexism that they have to confront, however, they are forced to choose for their lives those alternatives that are more tolerable or less costly to them. Some may choose to live in Miami among Cubans, even if that implies "staying in the closet." Others may choose to live in other areas of the country among Anglo lesbians, without feeling fully supported in terms of their Cuban identity.

As expressed by one of the women, however, "eating black beans and rice while speaking in Spanish with other Latina lesbians makes those beans taste like heaven!"

Implications for Psychotherapy. Some implications for the practice of psychotherapy with Latina lesbians can be derived from the discussion of the specific factors influencing the identity development of Latina lesbians and from the results of this brief study. Like all other individuals who seek psychotherapy, Latina lesbians who come to therapy do so for a variety of reasons. As with all other individuals, the formation of their identity occurs in a specific cultural, class, and historical context. For the therapist working with Latina lesbians, it is essential to understand the impact of these specific contextual variables on the individual client. But the understanding of the unique vicissitudes of identity development for Latina lesbians should be tempered by the understanding that certain processes are similar to those encountered by any lesbian woman from any cultural background who is in the process of coming out.

It is essential that the therapist understands the anger, frustration, and pain that the Latina lesbian experiences both as a lesbian and as an ethnic minority member. If the therapist is a White Anglo, it is essential that she develop awareness and understanding of how her own cultural background influences her responses to her Latina lesbian client. If the therapist has a heterosexual orientation, particularly if the therapist is also Hispanic, freedom from heterosexist biases and male-centered cultural values and from Latin stereotypes of homosexuals is essential for effective therapy. Of particular importance is the use of language in therapy when the client's associations to Spanish words that refer to her lesbian identity may all be negative.

As with all clients, it must be remembered that each woman's choices express something about who she is as an individual, as well as what her cultural values are. Lesbian choices, as any behavior that violates strict cultural norms, can present a high personal cost to any woman. In the case of Latinas, this high personal cost may additionally involve a loss of support from their ethnic group. Any encouragement of their coming out as lesbians should be done with sensitivity to the other components of their identity.

The therapist should keep in mind that there is as much danger in explaining individual differences away as culturally determined as there is in ignoring or rejecting the impact of cultural influences on each woman's choices. As always in therapy, validation of each woman's identity and of all the components of her total self is provided through the expansion of feeling states and encouragement to understand their meaning. To understand the multiplicity of tasks involved in identity development for Latina lesbians and to provide the opportunity for the accomplishment of those tasks is the first step in therapy with Latina lesbians.

ACKNOWLEDGMENTS

I wish to thank Lourdes Rodriguez-Nogues for her help with the development of the questionnaire and study and the members of my Feminist Research Methodology Group for their useful comments.

NOTES

1. Erik H. Erikson, *Life History and the Historical Moment* (New York: W. W. Norton, 1975), pp. 19–20.
2. Ibid., p. 21.

3. Donald R. Atkinson, George Morten, and Derald W. Sue, *Counseling American Minorities* (Dubuque, Ia.: William C. Brown, 1979).

4. Vivienne C. Cass, Homosexual identity formation: A theoretical model. *Journal of Homosexuality* 4 (Spring 1979):219–35.

5. Derald Wing Sue, *Counseling the Culturally Different* (New York: Wiley, 1981), 66–68.

6. Cass, "Homosexual Identity Formation," pp. 222–23.

7. Ibid., pp. 225, 229, 231, 233, 234–35.

8. Hortensia Amaro, Coming out: Hispanic lesbians, their families and communities. Paper presented at the National Coalition of Hispanic Mental Health and Human Services Organizations (COSSMHO), Austin, Texas, 1978.

9. Cherrie Moraga, *Loving in the War Years: Lo que Nunca Pasó por sus Labios* (Boston: South End Press, 1983).

10. Hilda Hidalgo and Elia Hidalgo-Christensen, The Puerto Rican lesbian and the Puerto Rican community, *Journal of Homosexuality* 2 (Winter 1976–77):109–21; Hilda Hidalgo and Elia Hidalgo-Christensen, The Puerto Rican cultural response to female homosexuality, in Edna Acosta-Belen, ed., *The Puerto Rican Woman* (New York: Praeger Publishers, 1979), pp. 110–23.

11. Yvonne D. Escaserga, E. C. Mondaca, and V. G. Torres, Attitudes of Chicana lesbians towards therapy. Master's thesis, University of Southern California, 1975.

12. Hidalgo and Hidalgo-Christensen, The Puerto Rican lesbian and the Puerto Rican community, p. 120.

13. Oliva M. Espín, Cultural and historical influences on sexuality in Hispanic/Latin women: Implications for psychotherapy, in Carole Vance, ed., *Pleasure and Danger: Exploring Female Sexuality* (London: Routledge and Kegan Paul, 1984), pp. 149–63.

14. Moraga, *Loving in the War Years*, p. 99.

15. Amaro, Coming out, p. 7.

16. See, for example, Robert Bogdan and Steven J. Taylor, *Introduction to Qualitative Research Methods* (New York: Wiley, 1975); W. J. Filstead, *Qualitative Methodology: First Hand Involvement with the Social World* (Chicago: Markham, 1970); and Barney G. Glaser and Anselm Strauss, *The Discovery of Grounded Theory: Strategies for Qualitative Research* (Chicago: Aldine, 1967).

17. Although the sample is obviously small, it is important to remember that obtaining respondents in a population surrounded by secrecy while searching for a specific ethnicity, as in this case, is not a minor task. A response rate of almost half of questionnaires sent is not considered a low response rate in itself. In addition, ten subjects or even smaller numbers are considered to be sufficient in qualitative studies when the sample is saturated (see Glaser and Strauss, *The Discovery of Grounded Theory*).

15

Gay Identity Issues Among Black Americans: Racism, Homophobia, and the Need for Validation

Darryl K. Loiacano

There is little available literature on gay and lesbian identity among Black Americans. This exploratory study involved interviewing a total of six Black American gay men and lesbian women regarding gay identity development issues. Data pertaining to the interviewees' experiences of gay identity development were obtained through a questionnaire of six open-ended questions and an interview with each participant lasting one to two hours. This article presents some of the significant challenges faced by those who were interviewed regarding their sense of self-acceptance, both as Blacks in the predominantly White gay and lesbian community and as gay men and lesbian women in the predominantly heterosexual Black community. The implications of these issues for future research and counseling intervention are discussed. In this article the term gay identity *is generally used in reference to both men and women. When women are being discussed exclusively, however, the term* lesbian identity *is used.*

In our society it is generally assumed that a child born to heterosexual parents will grow up to be heterosexual. Gay identity development can be defined as the process through which an individual progresses from an assumed state of heterosexuality to an open, affirmed state of homosexuality. This process has often been conceptualized in the form of linear stage theories (e.g., Cass 1979; Minton and McDonald 1984); Troiden 1979). Most of these stage models describe a similar progression that includes in the following order: a) a general sense of feeling different; b) an awareness of same-sex feelings; c) a point of crisis in which an individual realizes that his or her feelings can be labeled as homosexual; and d) an eventual acceptance and integration of one's gay identity. The models generally also outline a list of tasks involved in gay identity development and stress the centrality of interpersonal interactions needed to facilitate this process.

Many authors have outlined differences between men and women that are apparent in gay identity development (e.g., Faderman 1984; Groves and Ventura 1983; Schultz and de Monteflores 1978). Two of the factors thought to contribute to these differences between men and women are gender-role expectations and the influence of the feminist movement on lesbian identity development. Although gender has been considered to some extent, race has seldom been explored. A few authors have explored some of the particular challenges faced by Black Americans who are gay or lesbian (e.g., Cornwall 1979; DeMarco 1983) and have also raised theoretical questions regarding how the added pressure of racism might impact on these individuals (Icard 1986).

Writing from the perspective of a Black American lesbian, Audre Lorde (1984) has described the challenge of having several oppressed identities, of "constantly being encouraged to pluck out some one aspect of [your]self and present this as the meaningful whole, eclipsing or denying the other parts of self" (p. 120). As Lorde explains, it is healthiest for individuals to feel simultaneously accepted in all the important aspects of their identity. For Black American lesbians, it is often challenging or impossible to find a community that offers this acceptance. Lesbianism is largely considered incompatible with the role expectations of the women in the Black community. At the same time, lesbian-supportive communities and social groups often marginalize their Black American members and do not provide the level of affirmation that White American members receive.

In writing about Black gay men, Icard (1986) states that they are viewed as "inferior" members of the gay community, and thus do not receive the same degree of "psychological benefits" from the gay community that White gay men receive (p. 89). Accounts of the prejudiced treatment of Blacks in the gay community have been provided by several authors (e.g., DeMarco 1983; Icard 1986). Discrimination in admittance to bars, in advertisements, and in employment are all noted. Moreover, racial stereotyping of Black gay men and bias-related standards of beauty set forth by the gay male community also stand in the way of acceptance for Black gay men. Icard (1986:90) has made one of the most challenging and crucial observations regarding the dual oppression of Black gay men and its influence on gay identity development.

> The interpersonal relationships that gays experience are critical to the development of a positive sexual identity, particularly during what has been

described as the coming-out period. Interpersonal relationships with others who also are gay have been recognized as facilitating congruence intrapsychically as well as interpersonally. . . . For many Black gays, however, gay interpersonal relationships do not provide the kinds of positive consequences that have been defined as so important to the closure of the individual's sexual identity.

The implications of this dilemma for Black American lesbians are similar.

Johnson (1981) and Icard (1986) have underscored the importance of the Black community as a primary reference group and source of support to its members. The support that Black gay men and lesbian women receive, however, is compromised by pervasive homophobic practices and beliefs. Icard believes that many Blacks view homosexuality as a White phenomenon largely irrelevant to the interests of the Black community. It should be noted that little empirical data actually exist on the views of Black Americans on homosexuality (Johnson, 1981).

Nonetheless, choices about coming out to others, becoming involved in primary relationships, and becoming politically active in the sexual minority community may be complicated by status as a Black American. Because these tasks are all related to gay identity development, it follows that this process may be different for Black Americans and other people of color than it is for White Americans. This article presents a qualitative exploration of gay identity development issues among Black Americans through open-ended interviews with three lesbian women and three gay men who are Black Americans.

PROCEDURE

PARTICIPANTS

Because there are apparent gender differences in gay identity development (see previous discussion), both men and women were selected for this study. Three male and three female participants were located through personal contacts and through a local women's organization in a large metropolitan area. Participants were told that the study was about the coming-out experiences of Black American gay men and lesbian women. They ranged in age from twenty-five to fifty-one years, but most were between thirty and forty years old. All except one had at least a bachelor's degree, and several had received graduate-level education. All participants had a high level of awareness about social issues, and most were articulate in describing their personal experiences and perceptions of society. All except one had acquired what the author considers a positive gay identity, although a few individuals were still integrating this identity into their overall self-concepts.

INTERVIEWING PROCESS

Based on the literature on gay identity development (e.g., Cass 1979; Coleman 1981; Troiden 1979), the following open-ended questions were generated to guide each interview:

1. When were you first aware of your same-sex feelings, or the sense that your sexual identity might be different from heterosexuals? Say anything you'd like about this.
2. What was your experience of "coming out" to yourself? What made it difficult? What helped make it easier?
3. What has been your experience of "coming out" to others? Who has been supportive? Say anything else you would like about this experience.
4. What would you say were/are the major barriers to you accepting yourself as a gay man or lesbian?
5. How would you describe your relationship to the gay/lesbian community as you define this community? To the Black community as you define it? For example, how supported do you feel by these two communities as a whole?
   a. Did your "coming out" experience and identity as a gay man/lesbian woman change your sense of acceptance in the Black community? Your level of involvement in the Black community?
6. Is there any aspect of your identity that you consider central at present? If someone were to ask you who you are, and you were comfortable enough to be open with them, what would you say?

It is important to note that the author (and interviewer) in this study is a White American, because this may be an important factor in understanding and interpreting the interview data. It was reasoned that an open-ended method of interviewing would allow participants to stress what has been important to *them* regarding gay identity issues. At the same time, the questions would help gain basic demographic information and provide some minimal degree of standardization. The goal of the interviews, however, was to gain a sense of the participant's overall gay identity "story" rather than bits and pieces of standardized information.

Interviews were usually held in the participant's home or office. They lasted from one to two hours, depending on how much time it took individuals to respond to the questions. At least a day before the interview, participants received a form containing the above questions, as well as a few demographic questions regarding age, occupation, religion, and educational status. Participants were asked to fill out the form before the interview took place. One individual could not fill it out ahead of time because of a developmental disability. All but one participant agreed to have his or her interview tape recorded. Detailed notes were taken during the untaped interview. During interviews, participants responded to the questionnaire, both referring to the answers they had written down and expanding on these answers. The researcher also asked specific questions about participants' family and romantic relationships, as well as the chronological order of events they described. Later, interview tapes were transcribed and combined with the written information on the questionnaire to give a resulting profile of each participant's experience of gay identity development.

INTERVIEW THEMES

Several issues were examined on the basis of the interview data (Loiacano 1988). This article specifically focuses on gay identity issues related to the interviewees' dual identity as Black American and gay or lesbian. The identification of themes in such a qualitative interview is a subjective process. From the author's perspective, however, it seemed clear that three themes related to dual identity emerged. The interview data in these three thematic areas are summarized below.

THEME ONE: FINDING VALIDATION IN THE GAY AND LESBIAN COMMUNITY

Diane, who is thirty-one years old, stated that as she began to come out she found it difficult to fit into any particular lesbian group. She remarked that the women's community is somewhat closed to people of color and that such women are often an afterthought in planning political and social events: "Some of us [women of color] end up dropping out of planning groups or raising hell. We might want to work on the racism that's going on there, but racial issues are tough, and people don't really want to talk about them." Even when Black lesbians and other women of color were thought about, Diane felt the focus was on "reaching out" to them rather than having women of color involved in leadership roles in women's groups.

Paul, who is thirty-five, spoke angrily of the racism he had experienced in the gay community:

> I would go into a bar . . . behind young Whites who looked a hell of a lot younger than me, and they would have no problem getting in. Whereas, I would be stopped and they would ask for at least two forms of I.D. Also, just the attitudes of the bartenders. They would wait on others before they would wait on me . . . and it really saddened me because I thought because we all were gay, we all were fighting for equality. You know, we would pull together. But I found more overt racism among White gays than I did among just Whites period . . . which really upset me.

Paul was involved in bringing a lawsuit against a gay bar for discriminating against Black patrons.

Tom, who is fifty-one years old, became involved in the gay liberation movement during its beginnings in 1969. Like Paul, he expressed dismay at the racism in the gay community. He talked about watching the local gay movement gradually be taken over by White men during the early 1970s, even though it had started out as a diverse movement with members of many racial groups working together. Tom believes that he was carded more than White gay men were at bars and was assumed to be less financially successful than were White gay men. He began assuming that his presence at social occasions was less sought after than that of White gay men.

Larry, who is thirty-four years old, spoke of the stereotypes that exist in the predominantly White gay male community. He stated that there was pressure to fit one of these stereotypes, which are generally based on White male standards. He believes that being an Black American, however, made it difficult for him to conform to any particular "type." He also believes that this complicated his social and sexual exploration of the gay community. He recalls being rejected by men at dances, for example, and believes that this was partly because of his race.

THEME TWO: FINDING VALIDATION IN THE BLACK COMMUNITY

Many of the individuals interviewed discussed feeling a lack of support from the predominantly heterosexual Black community for their gay or lesbian identity. Diane talked about her hesitation to discuss her lesbian feelings while in college. The college she attended was predominantly White, and Diane relied a great deal on the Black community there for support. She considered that coming out to these individuals might jeopardize her acceptance in this group. Although Diane continued to explore her lesbian feelings internally, she also continued to date men. Several years later, as she did begin to come out to others, she feared that identification as a lesbian might pull her away from what she considered her primary reference group—Black Americans.

Another individual who was interviewed, Shirl, talked about the pressure she felt to avoid being "too out" because of the ramifications it could have for her family living in a Black community. Shirl was politically active in the gay and lesbian community at the time of her interview. She expressed anxiety about particular activities, such as being on a television program as an openly lesbian woman or being quoted in a mainstream newspaper.

Larry discussed an overall lack of support for his gay identity in the Black community in which he was raised. He spoke repeatedly of the pressure on Black men in his community to be secretive about their homosexuality. He said that the social message given to these gay men was that marriage and family always came first. Homosexual encounters were best relegated to bars and other secretive arenas, invisible to the larger community. Larry believes that there were virtually no role models for Black American gay couples in his community and little support for long-term relationships.

Mary, who is thirty-seven years old, talked about how "coming out" as a lesbian gave her new insight into the Black community. Particularly, it showed her how the community perpetuates oppression within itself, such as that against gay men and lesbians:

> I see more clearly the ways that we perpetuate horizontal violence. I see more clearly that . . . those things that we say about White folk can also be true of ourselves. And we indeed can be our greatest oppressor, which is certainly not any effort on my part to blame the victim, but just a recognition that we have probably taken too many of the attributes of the true oppressor and focused our energies . . . within, rather than clearly identifying who the oppressor is and then strategizing cohesively to address the real problem [racism].

Theme Three: The Need to Integrate Identities

A third theme that came across in the interviews was an expressed need to integrate and find simultaneous validation for one's various identities.

For the individuals interviewed these included being Black American and gay or lesbian, in addition to other identities for certain individuals. One of the major ways in which those who were interviewed seemed to gain this integration was by becoming involved in, or forming, organizations specifically for Black American gay men, lesbian women, or both.

Diane became involved in forming a local support group for Black lesbians, thinking that "they must be out there somewhere." This group helped give her a sense of belonging when this was difficult to achieve elsewhere. Paul became involved in "Black and White Men Together," an organization formed to increase dialogue between Black and White gay men. He has also been involved in "Gay AA" to address issues of alcoholism while also being supported as a gay man. Mary became involved in forming a national organization for Black American lesbians and gay men. She later became involved in a diverse religious organization from which she felt support both as a lesbian and as an Black American. Mary feels that while her two identities were once "running on parallel tracks," they are now "more like a weaving."

During his interview Larry talked emotionally about his struggle for acceptance, both as an Black American in the gay community and as a gay man in the Black community. He expressed this struggle for validation of both of his identities as a challenge to his sanity and a cause for the close scrutiny of others:

> And that is a real fear that I have . . . I fear losing sanity, and so maybe that is the reason why I scrutinize people with such care. Because I do depend upon others' perceptions of me for validation, and I have been hurt so much by that in the past . . . Because, I mean, living in an environment . . . where there's been so many things that have told me I was freaky, I was crazy, I was stupid . . . And how much I had to fight against that, and struggle . . . I had just kind of forgotten how much I fought to remain sane. I lived in a world which wanted to tell me that I wasn't. And that was a real battle.

SUMMARY AND IMPLICATIONS FOR COUNSELORS

Data from such a small sample must be perceived as exploratory and of limited generalizability. It was clear, however, that the individuals who were interviewed had significant challenges to developing and maintaining a positive gay identity. These challenges can theoretically make the development of a positive gay identity in Black Americans different from that of White Americans. Challenges arose both in the Black community and in the gay and lesbian community.

Consistent with the statements of Johnson (1981) and Icard (1986), several of the individuals who were interviewed noted the importance of the Black community as a reference group. Some feared, however, that their gay identity could compromise their acceptance in the Black community because of the homophobia there. Thus, an Black American might place less value on coming out to others than his or her White counterpart, fearing that he or she might jeopardize needed support as a racial minority. It is important to note that none of the individuals who were interviewed stated that he or she thought the Black community as a whole was less accepting of gay men and lesbian women than the White community was as a whole.

All except one of the individuals who were interviewed relayed experiences consistent with the idea put forth by Icard (1986). The benefits that Black gay men and lesbians receive from the predominantly White gay and lesbian community can be diminished by bias-related practices and beliefs related to race. The sexual and social exploration of Black American gay men and lesbian women can be limited and complicated by such beliefs and practices. Choices about dating and relationships, as well as basic self-esteem, might be affected. Overall, being out in a predominantly White gay and lesbian community may not have the same day-to-day payoffs for Black Americans that it does for White Americans. Although it is true that, historically, some of the particular accounts of racist practices related in the interviews may no longer be as relevant, all such practices are not likely to be eliminated at this time.

Finally, Black American gay men and lesbian women have the challenge of integrating at least two central identities that can be highly charged in our society—being Black and gay or lesbian. This particular challenge is likely to be similar for other people of color and is not faced by White Americans. These and other similar issues warrant further research.

Counseling professionals can enhance their work with Black American gay men and lesbian women when they are sensitive to the above issues. In counseling such clients, the following questions should be considered:

1. Does the client perceive support for his or her dual identity in the community?
2. Are there groups organized specifically for the needs of Black American gay men and lesbian women in the area, or are there groups in which racial and sexual minorities find both acceptance and validation?
3. What personal issues might the client have to confront in devel-

oping a gay identity while still affirming his or her Black identity? What messages has the client received from his or her social environment regarding the compatibility of being Black American and gay or lesbian?

4. What assumptions does the counselor (or client) have about ways of expressing one's homosexuality (e.g., the level at which one is "out") that might not be realistic for an Black American in his or her particular community?

5. Given a predominantly White community, what other Black American gay men or lesbian women can be identified as supportive and how have these individuals been received in the local gay community?

6. What are the client's preferences about seeing a counselor who is gay or lesbian, Black American, or both? As these questions imply, gay identity development never takes place in a social vacuum, and thus it is beneficial to consider the social, political, and interpersonal climate of the client.

In this study and discussion the variable of Black American identity was in effect assumed to be a constant. This, however, is never the case. Black American and other minority identity development have been conceptualized and explored by several authors (e.g., Atkinson, Morten, and Sue 1979; Cross 1971; Parkham and Helms 1981). The development of a positive gay identity among Black Americans is likely to be interrelated with the individual's stage of Black identity development. A more conclusive study would need to incorporate consideration of both of these identities into its design.

It is important to acknowledge that Black American lesbians face additional challenges as women. Their identity, as such, adds a third level of oppression that was not explored in this article but that certainly has important implications. This article also did not consider the experiences of bisexuals, transvestites, or transsexuals who are Black Americans. Many of the issues outlined above are relevant to these members of the sexual minority community as well.

The journeys shared by this study's participants were clearly ones of both pride and pain. Effective counseling intervention with these individuals can only come through further research and adequate knowledge about issues that have already been defined in the literature. This article has attempted to increase awareness of issues that may impact on the gay identity development of Black Americans. Many of these issues need further exploration and definition. The more this task is pursued, the more likely it will be that counseling professionals can help Black American gay men and lesbian women have journeys of less pain and more pride.

ACKNOWLEDGMENTS

The author thanks Dorothy Martin and the author's partner, James Croteau, for their feedback and support in preparing this article.

REFERENCES

Atkinson, D. R., G. Morten, and D. W. Sue. 1979. *Counseling American Minorities.* Dubuque, Ia.: Brown.

Cass, V. C. 1979. Homosexual identity formation: A theoretical model. *Journal of Homosexuality* 4(3):219–35.

Coleman, E. 1982. Developmental stages of the coming out process. *American Behavioral Scientist* 23(4):469–82.

Cornwall, A. 1979. Three for the price of one: Notes from a gay black feminist. In K. Jay and A. Young, eds., *Lavender Culture: The Perceptive Voices of Outspoken Lesbians and Gay Men,* pp. 466–76. New York: Jove.

Cross, W. E. 1971. The Negro-to-Black conversion experience: Towards a psychology of Black liberation. *Black World* 20(9):13–27.

DeMarco, J. 1983. Gay racism. In M. J. Smith, ed., *Black Men/White Men: A Gay Anthology,* pp. 109–18. San Francisco: Gay Sunshine Press.

Faderman, L. 1984. The "new gay" lesbians. *Journal of Homosexuality* 10(3/4):85–95.

Groves, P. A., and L. A. Ventura. 1983. The lesbian coming out process: Therapeutic considerations. *Personnel and Guidance Journal* 62(3):146–49.

Icard, L. 1986. Black gay men and conflicting social identities: Sexual orientation versus racial identity. In J. Gripton and M. Valentich, eds., Special issue of the *Journal of Social Work and Human Sexuality. Social work practice in sexual problems* 4(1/2):83–93.

Johnson, J. M. 1981. Influence of assimilation on the psychosocial adjustment of black homosexual men. Doctoral dissertation, California School of Professional Psychology, Berkeley.

Loiacano, D. K. 1988. Gay identity acquisition and the Black American experience: Journeys of pride and pain. Master's thesis, University of Pennsylvania School of Social Work, Philadelphia.

Lorde, A. 1984. *Sister Outsider.* Trumansburg, N.Y.: Crossing Press.

Minton, H. L., and G. J. McDonald. 1984. Homosexual identity formation as a developmental process. *Journal of Homosexuality* 9(2/3):91–104.

Parham, T. A., and J. E. Helms. 1981. The influences of a black student's racial identity attitudes on preference for counselor's race. *Journal of Counseling Psychology* 28:250–56.

Schultz, S. J., and C. de Monteflores. 1978. Coming out: Similarities and differences for lesbians and gay men. *Journal of Social Issues* 34(3):59–72.

Troiden, R. R. 1979. Becoming homosexual: A model of gay identity acquisition. *Psychiatry* 42:362–73.

16

Issues of Identity Development Among Asian-American Lesbians and Gay Men

Connie S. Chan

This study examined the factors that affect an Asian-American individual's choice of identification with Asian-American and lesbian or gay identity. Nineteen Asian-American lesbians and sixteen Asian-American gay men belonging to Asian-American lesbian or gay organizations answered survey questionnaires. Results indicated that most of the respondents identified more strongly with their lesbian or gay identities than with their Asian-American identities; most indicated, however, that acknowledgement of both aspects of identity was preferred. Other situational factors, including disclosure of lesbian or gay identity to family and to the Asian-American community, as well as discrimination because of sexual orientation, race, and gender, were examined in regard to identity development.

The study of identity development for ethnic minority lesbians and gay men has previously examined identity development in the context of ethnic minority and lesbian or gay identity models (Espín 1987; Wooden, Kawasaki, and Mayeda 1983).

Both studies used the theoretical Model of Homosexual Identity Formation (Cass 1979) as a model for understanding the six stages of development that an individual moves through in developing an integrated identity as a homosexual person. Cass's six stages are a) *identity confusion,* during which an individual realizes that feelings and behaviors can be defined as homosexual, creating conflict about his or her identity, which both the individual and the environment had previously defined as heterosexual; b) *identity comparison,* which occurs after the possibility of being homosexual has been acknowledged—the task of this stage is to handle the social alienation that now arises because of feeling "different" and having a sense of "not belonging" to subgroups such as peers and family; c) *identity tolerance,* during which there is an increased commitment to homosexual identity and the process of contacting other homosexuals to counter the isolation and alienation begins, but the individual tolerates rather than accepts a homosexual identity; d) *identity acceptance*, characterized by continued and increasing contacts with other homosexuals to validate and normalize homosexuality as an identity and as a way of life; e) *identity pride*, characterized by the incongruity that exists between the individual's acceptance of him- or herself as a homosexual and society's rejection of this concept, resulting in the devaluing of heterosexuals and pride in disclosure of one's identity as a homosexual; and f) *identity synthesis*, when an individual is now able to integrate his or her homosexual identity with all other aspects of self and no longer sees a clear dichotomy between the heterosexual and homosexual world.

In her study of identity development among Latina lesbian women, Espín (1987) also used the Minority Identity Development Model (Atkinson, Morten, and Sue 1979) as a model for understanding Latina identity. The five stages of this model are a) *conformity*, characterized by a preference for dominant cultural values over one's own culture; b) *dissonance*, characterized by cultural confusion and conflict, challenging accepted values and beliefs; c) *resistance and immersion*, when an individual actively rejects the dominant society and culture and endorses only minority-held views; d) *introspection*, when an individual questions the too-narrow restrictions of the previous stage and feels conflicted between loyalty to his or her own ethnic group and personal autonomy; and e) *synergetic articulation and awareness*, when individuals experience a sense of self-fulfillment with their cultural identity and accept or reject cultural values on the basis of individual merit or prior experience.

As Espín (1987:39) noted, these two models of identity development are remarkably similar in describing a process that

> must be undertaken by people who must embrace negative or stigmatized identities. This process moves gradually from a rejected and denied self-image to the embracing of an identity that is finally accepted as positive. Both models describe one or several stages of intense confusion and at least one stage of complete separatism from and rejection of the dominant society. The final stage for both models implies the acceptance of one's own identity, a committed attitude against oppression, and an ability to synthesize the best values of both perspectives and to communicate with members of the dominant groups.

Each model, however, presents a means for understanding identity development of either homosexual identity or ethnic minority identity. How does an individual who is gay or lesbian and a member of an ethnic minority group come to terms with identity issues? Two studies have examined these questions. In her study of sixteen Latina lesbians, Espín (1987) found that her respondents expressed a desire to identify as both Latina and lesbian, with varying degrees of success. She concluded that Latina lesbians face a fundamental dilemma: the conflict of the fear of stigmatization in the Hispanic community as lesbians versus the loss of support for their identity as Hispanics in the mainstream gay community. Espín concluded that although it is impossible to determine that one aspect of the identity of these Latina lesbians is more important than another, each individual makes her own choice as to those alternatives that are most tolerable, whether it is living among Cubans in Miami or among White Anglos in a lesbian or gay community.

In their study of thirteen Japanese-American gay men, Wooden, Kawasaki, and Mayeda (1983) found that the men's lack of gay political activism and their reservations about synthesizing all aspects of their identity through a more visible gay self-presentation reflected identities of identity tolerance and identity pride, the third and fourth stages in the six-stage Cass (1979) Model of Homosexual Identity Formation. Only half their respondents were open with their families about their gay identity. Wooden et al. suggested that their respondents' reservations about being more visibly and actively gay may be partially explained by their fears of nonacceptance in the Japanese-American community.

Although Wooden, Kawasaki, and Mayeda's study did not focus primarily on cultural issues, it is likely that conflicting cultural values may help to explain some of the respondents' reluctance to identify themselves as openly gay. In Asian cultures being gay is frequently viewed as a rejection of the most important of roles for women and men—that of being a wife and mother for women and that of a father carrying on the family line through procreation of heirs for men. The family is valued as the primary social unit throughout a person's life, and the most important obligation, especially as a son, is the continuation of the family through marriage and the bearing of children. If a daughter or son is lesbian or gay, the implication is that not only is the child rejecting the traditional role of a wife-mother or son-father, but also that the parents have failed in their role and that the child is rejecting the importance of family and Asian culture.

Because identification as lesbian or gay may be perceived as a rejection of Asian cultural values, Asian-American lesbians and gay men can be considered to have conflicting dual identities. On the one hand, to be lesbian or gay is to reject traditional family roles and cultural values; to identify as being Asian American may, however, require negating one's lesbian or gay identity, at least within the family. How do individuals who identify as being both lesbian-gay and Asian-American develop their dual identities? Does an individual usually identify more strongly with either a lesbian-gay or ethnic-minority identity?

What are some of the factors that might help in understanding the issues of development of a dual identity? This study examined the following factors and looked at their effects on the concept of ethnic minority and lesbian or gay identity among Asian-American lesbians and gay men:

1. activism and participation in the Asian-American and lesbian-gay communities;
2. choice of community (Asian-American versus lesbian or gay) in which individuals felt more comfortable;
3. self-definition of identity;
4. disclosure or nondisclosure of lesbian or gay identity to their families;
5. Asian cultural factors in acceptance of lesbianism or gayness;
6. perceptions of lesbian and gay Asian-Americans by the lesbian-gay community, the Asian-American community, and the mainstream American society; and
7. perceptions of discrimination because they are lesbian or gay or Asian-American or because they are both lesbian-gay and Asian-American.

METHOD

PARTICIPANTS

The participants were nineteen women and sixteen men between the ages of twenty-one and thirty-six who identified themselves as being both lesbian-gay and Asian-American. The term *Asian-American* was not defined in the questionnaire but included all persons of Asian descent in the study. Of the respondents, 90 percent were of Chinese, Korean, or Japanese ancestry, with the remaining 10 percent from Filipino, Bangladesh, and Indian backgrounds.

Sixty questionnaires were distributed at two events: a retreat of an organization called Asian Lesbians of the East Coast and at a film showing sponsored by the Alliance for Massachusetts Asian Lesbians and Gay Men. Nineteen women and sixteen men completed questionnaires that were returned by mail within one month to make up the present sample of thirty-five questionnaires.

MEASURES

The four-page questionnaire consisted of thirty-five items, including five demographic information questions and several questions related to the issues of community affiliation, "coming out," identity, and discrimination. Most of the questions were open-ended, with six questions offering multiple-choice answers, such as "In which community do you feel more comfortable? Asian-American, Lesbian or Gay, Neither." The questionnaire was developed after a pretrial sampling of seven lesbian or gay Asian-Americans and feedback from several ethnic minority, lesbian, and gay researchers to whom the preliminary questionnaire was presented. The questionnaire was completely anonymous.

RESULTS AND DISCUSSION

Given the small sample and the exploratory nature of this study, the results of this survey were analyzed through the use of qualitative methods (Bogdan and Taylor 1975). Except where it is specifically noted that the answers to a question were different for lesbians than for gay men in the sample, the answers were not differentiated by gender.

CHARACTERISTICS OF THE GROUP

Eight of the thirty-five respondents were first-generation Asian-Americans (they were born in Asia), nineteen were second-generation, and the remaining eight were third-, fourth-, or fifth-generation Asian-Americans. Their educational background was high, with more than 90 percent having attended college. Most of the respondents were working in professional occupations or attending graduate school. All respondents were currently living on the East Coast.

Table 16.1 is a summary and compilation of the questionnaire results, which are discussed below.

SOCIAL AND POLITICAL ACTIVITY

Because this survey questionnaire was distributed at two Asian lesbian-gay events, the sample group was expected to reflect an interest in both Asian and lesbian-gay activities. Surprisingly, most of the respondents indicated that they did not attend social or political events in the Asian-American community but did attend similar events in the lesbian-gay community. Many in this group responded that the only Asian-American events they

TABLE 16.1
Results of Questionnaire

1. Participation in social or political events in the following communities:

Asian-American only	0
Lesbian/gay only	26
Both lesbian/gay and Asian-American	9

2. In which community do you feel more comfortable?

Lesbian/gay	20
Asian-American	10
Neither or both	5

3. What do you consider to be your identity?

Asian-American lesbian woman or gay man	20
Lesbian or gay Asian-American	9
Neither or both	7

4. Disclosure of lesbian/gay identity to family:

Yes	27
No	8

Disclosure of lesbian/gay identity to parents:

Yes	9
No	26

Disclosure of lesbian/gay identity to friends:

Yes	34
No	1

5. Easier or harder to come out to other Asian-Americans?

Easier	4
Harder	27
No difference	4

6. Feel acknowledged and accepted in lesbian/gay community?

Yes	4
No	30
Unsure	1

7. Experienced discrimination because of being Asian?

Women	17 (of 19)
Men	3 (of 16)

Experienced discrimination because of being lesbian/gay?

Women	5
Men	12

Experienced more discrimination because of being both Asian and lesbian/gay?

Women	17
Men	12

attended were lesbian-gay Asian events but said they would participate in lesbian-gay events that were not Asian oriented.

CHOICE OF COMMUNITY

When asked, "In which community do you feel more comfortable (Asian-American or lesbian-gay) and why?" the respondents who chose the lesbian-gay community gave the following reasons:

- "The Asian community feels too conservative to me."
- "I have more in common with gay men than with straight Asians."
- "I 'came out' first as a lesbian, before coming to terms with my identity as a Filipina American."

Those who felt more comfortable in the Asian-American community explained:

- "I relate to myself as an Asian person first."
- "My culture and beliefs are so Asian."
- "The gay community is so White and sometimes racist. I feel more comfortable with Asians and people of color."
- "Because Asians are more easily identified, I can't always tell if someone is gay."

The respondents who refused to choose one community over another, stated "neither." One lesbian asserted, "I do not want to choose. I am a part of both communities, but the one I identify with best is the Asian-American lesbian community."

Choice of Identity—Terms and Identification

To determine whether individuals differentiate between feeling a part of a community and acknowledging their own personal identity, respondents were asked which terms they used to identify themselves and with which part of their identity (Asian-American or lesbian-gay) they more strongly identified. Results indicated that the two concepts (community identification and personal identification) are similar for the respondents.

The respondents who used the terms *Asian-American lesbian* or *Asian-American gay man* to identify themselves answered that they identified more strongly with the lesbian or gay part of their identity:

- "I choose gay, because I feel that my sexual orientation transcends my Asian-American identity. I also feel that I can have a greater impact in changing attitudes in the gay population. "
- "I say lesbian; I have greater numbers of friends who are lesbians than are Asian, and I feel closer to them."
- "I more strongly identify with the lesbian and gay identity because I was politicized by my lesbianism and feminism."

In contrast, the respondents who said that they identified themselves by the terms *gay Asian-American* or *lesbian Asian-American* and reported that they identified more strongly as Asian-American made statements such as the following:

- "I identify as Asian-American because similar backgrounds and experiences are stronger bonds for me than sexual identity."
- "My Asianness, because that is what I am, first and foremost."
- "Asian-American, because I can't deal with the White-dominated lesbian and gay scene. I guess I'm more race conscious than sexual-orientation conscious."

This question was designed to force the respondent to choose one aspect of identity over another, but seven respondents refused to choose. They reflect the reality that most Asian lesbians and gay men feel most complete when they can be accepted as being both lesbian-gay and Asian-American, as the following comments indicate:

- "I identify as being both. I cannot separate the two parts of who I am."
- "While the Asian-American community supports my Asian identity, the gay community only supports my being a gay man; as a result I find it difficult to identify with either."
- "The only identification I can feel comfortable with is one that acknowledges both my lesbian and my Asian-American identities."

These results suggest that when a choice of identification is required more respondents identified themselves as lesbian or gay than as Asian-American but that others refused to choose because it would mean denying an important part of their identity. It is likely that each person determines for herself or himself, depending on the stage of identity development she or he is in, whether it is more comfortable to be Asian among lesbians and gay men or lesbian-gay around Asians or whether both are intolerable and she or he must be acknowledged as both Asian and as lesbian or gay by everyone. Because identity development is a fluid, ever-changing process, an individual may choose to identify and ally more closely with being lesbian or gay or Asian-American at different times depending on need and situational factors.

DISCLOSURE OF LESBIAN OR GAY IDENTITY

Another factor examined was whether or not respondents had disclosed their lesbian or gay identity to their families. Results indicated that most respondents have come out to someone in their family. A sibling, usually a sister, was overwhelmingly the first person in the family to whom this group had come out. Although 77 percent (twenty-seven) have come out to a family member, however, only nine respondents (26 percent of the entire sample) have come out to their parents. When one takes into account that 6.2 is the mean number of years this group has been out, the percentage of respondents who have come out to their parents seems low. In addition, almost all respondents reported that they were out to most of their friends. It seems, then, that there are specific cultural values defining the traditional roles that help to explain the reluctance of Asian-American lesbians and gay men to come out to their parents and families.

ASIAN CULTURAL FACTORS

In addition to traditional family expectations, overt acknowledgment of homosexuality may be even more restricted by Asian-American cultural norms than it is in mainstream American society. When respondents were asked to describe the Asian-American perception of lesbian and gay Asian-Americans, more than half responded that there was a denial of the existence of Asian-American lesbians and gay men. This supports the idea that homosexuality is commonly perceived by ethnic minority groups as a "White, Western phenomenon. " These results are similar to those noted by Espín (1987), who found that Latina lesbians were reluctant to be out in the Latino community, and noted, "Because of the importance placed upon family and community by most Hispanics, the threat of possible rejection and stigmatization by the Latin community becomes more of a psychological burden for the Hispanic lesbian . . . rejection from mainstream society does not carry the same weight" (p. 40).

Assuming a similar importance of family and community relationships in Asian cultures, it is likely that Asian-American lesbians and gay men have not come out to their parents because of the overwhelming fear of rejection and stigmatization. As one respondent reported, "I wish I could tell my parents—they are the only ones who do not know about my gay identity, but I am sure that they would reject me. There is no frame of reference to understand homosexuality in Asian-American culture."

In addition, it seems that some Asian-American lesbians and gay men choose to remain closeted not only among their families but in the Asian-American community as well. To measure this, I used the question, "Do you find it easier or harder to 'come out' to other Asian-Americans?" Those respondents who thought it was harder commented that this was so because homosexuality is such a taboo in Asian cultures and that they felt neither acknowledged nor accepted by other Asian-Americans. In contrast, the small number who thought "coming out" to Asian-Americans was easier indicated that they felt this way because they felt other Asian-Americans would understand what being part of a minority group was like and would feel sympathetic. As might be expected, these four respondents identified more strongly with being Asian-American than with being lesbian or gay.

PERCEPTIONS OF LESBIAN OR GAY ASIAN-AMERICANS BY OTHERS

Given the difficulty associated with coming out to other Asian-Americans by the majority of respondents, it is likely that lesbian and gay Asian-Americans seek out other communities in which their gayness would be more accepted than within their families or ethnic communities. But results also indicated a perception by respondents that the lesbian and gay community does not acknowledge their existence either. A large majority of the respondents reported that they felt stereotyped or unacknowledged by the lesbian and gay community. As one respondent reported, "It is a problem to find my support only within the lesbian community, because I feel that I am either seen as 'exotic' and stereotyped, or unaccepted because I am Asian and not like the majority of White lesbians." Again, these results suggest that Asian-American lesbians and gay men, like other ethnic minority lesbians and gay men, find themselves in the position of not feeling totally comfortable in either community, because part of their identity is not being acknowledged. Results of this study suggest that Asian-American lesbians and gay men find their support and affiliation with the Asian-American or lesbian-gay communities (or both) depending on which aspect of their identities they are focusing on, as well as which situational factors are involved.

DISCRIMINATION BECAUSE OF RACE OR SEXUAL ORIENTATION

Another factor examined in this study was whether or not respondents had been discriminated against because of their race, their sexual orientation, or both. These questions were the only ones in which gender was found to be a differentiating factor. The majority of men reported that they felt more frequently discriminated against because they were gay than because they were Asian. In contrast, the majority of women felt that they had experienced more discrimination because they were Asian than because they were lesbians. Both lesbians and gay men felt that they experienced more discrimination overall because of being both Asian and lesbian or gay, what Wooden, Kawasaki, and Mayeda (1983) termed a double minority status.

These results may be explained in two ways: first, by the theory that gay men and lesbians, regardless of race, may experience different kinds of discrimination. The gay men in this study may have reported greater discrimination for their sexual orientation than for their Asianness because male homosexuality is less accepted than is lesbianism by society. That these gay men are also Asian in race may be less important than their sexual orientation in experiencing discrimination.

The reverse may be true for Asian lesbians, however. Gender discrimination may play a larger role than sexual orientation. The "passive but exotic" sexual stereotypes of Asian women may be so dominant that all Asian women, regardless of sexual orientation, feel discriminated against because of their race and sex. Moreover, the stereotype may be so strong that the possibility that an Asian woman could be a lesbian may not even enter into the picture. As a result, lesbian Asian-Americans perceive greater discrimination because of being Asian women than because of their sexual orientation. Like their Asian gay male counterparts, however, the women in this study did report that they have experienced greater discrimination overall because of their double minority status as both Asian and lesbian and, perhaps, triple minority status as Asian, lesbian, and a woman.

CONCLUSION

The results of this exploratory study indicate that the self-identification of lesbian and gay Asian-Americans is reflected in several factors: choice of community identification, choice of terms (*Asian-American lesbian* or *gay man* versus *lesbian* or *gay Asian-American*), situational factors such as whether they had disclosed their lesbian or gay identity to their families and the Asian-American community, and their own perceptions of how they are perceived by the lesbian-gay community. Results also indicate that the majority of respondents identified more strongly with their lesbian or gay identity than with their Asian-American identity, although several respondents insisted on acknowledging both aspects of their identity as Asian-Americans and as lesbians or gay men.

In terms of the Model of Homosexual Identity Formation (Cass 1979), most of the respondents in this study reflected identities of Stage 4 (identity acceptance) and Stage 5 (identity pride), because they generally accept and are openly proud of their lesbian or gay identities (with some exceptions of nondisclosure to parents). In terms of the ethnic Minority Identity

Development Model (Atkinson, Morten, and Sue 1979), most of the respondents reflected strong Asian-American identification and are in Stage 4 (introspection) and Stage 5 (synergetic articulation and awareness).

Because all the respondents were solicited from Asian-American lesbian and gay organizations and thus may identify more strongly with being Asian-American than with being lesbian or gay, these results may not be generalizable to a larger Asian lesbian and gay population. Further studies might include a more random sampling of lesbian and gay Asian-Americans, as well as use of quantitative analysis methods, more comprehensive interviews with a larger sample, or both.

Finally, some implications for understanding identity development can be derived from the results of this study. The results suggest that the extent to which an individual identifies as Asian-American or as lesbian or gay can depend on several factors, including the perceptions of homophobia in the Asian-American community, perceptions of racism in the lesbian-gay community, disclosure or nondisclosure of homosexuality to family and community, and affiliation with the Asian-American and lesbian-gay communities. Identity development is an ever-changing process, and individuals may base their identification with one identity or community on their changing needs for support, as well as on desires to share cultural factors. Some of these needs are met better by other lesbians or gay men, some by other Asian-Americans, some only by other lesbian or gay Asian-Americans. Ideally, it seems that individuals who have double and triple minority status feel most complete when they can acknowledge and be accepted for each of their identities as lesbian or gay, as Asian-American, and as women or men.

REFERENCES

Atkinson, D. R., G. Morten, and D. W. Sue. 1979. *Counseling American Minorities.* Dubuque, Ia.: Brown.

Bogdan, R., and S. J. Taylor. 1975. *Introduction to Qualitative Research Methods.* New York: Wiley.

Cass, V. C. 1979. Homosexuality identity formation: A theoretical model. *Journal of Homosexuality* 4:219–35.

Espín, O. M. 1987. Issues of identity in the psychology of Latina lesbians. In Boston Lesbian Psychologies Collective, eds., *Lesbian Psychologies,* pp. 35–51. Urbana: University of Illinois Press.

Wooden, W. S., H. Kawasaki, and R. Mayeda. 1983. Lifestyles and identity maintenance among gay Japanese-American males. *Alternative Lifestyles* 5:236–43.

VI
Relationships and Parenthood

This part examines the impact of sexual orientation on two central aspects of human development—relationships and parenting. Same-gender relationships develop within a culture that provides virtually no societal legitimization nor institutional support and actively endorses heterosexual bias toward gay male and lesbian relationships. Not only are lesbian and gay male couples generally denied the community recognition, legal protection, and economic benefits accorded to married heterosexual partners, but also there is no legal status of lesbian and gay male relationships, except in the very few (and very recent) instances in which domestic partnerships can be registered with public authorities. If they are parents, lesbians and gay men may lose custody of their children as a result of heterosexist assumptions embedded in family law. In addition, most institutional policies (e.g., insurance regulations, inheritance laws, and hospital visitation rules) do not acknowledge lesbian and gay male relationships. Moreover, same-gender relationships are confronted with negative social sanctioning from family members and do not have socially prescribed roles and behaviors that typically define and structure heterosexual relationships.

Since society does not provide explicit or clear models of interaction, lesbian and gay male partners rely more on innovative processes for creating their own idiosyncratic rules, expectations, and goals in their relationships, instead of adopting or conforming to preexisting culturally defined guidelines for relationships (Peplau and Cochran 1990). This trial-and-success approach to relationships may provide gay men and lesbians an opportunity for greater creativity in structuring their relationships than is true for heterosexuals. Therefore, it is important to define same-gender relationships without using heterosexuality as the model or standard.

Several common issues have been identified that characterize long-term lesbian and gay partnerships. These include: a) external pressures caused by social prejudice, lack of social validation, and social stigma; b) effects of previous gender role socialization, including expectations about gender roles, especially with regard to issues of autonomy and intimacy; c) differences between the two partners in acceptance of gay identity, stage of coming out, degree of outness, and political activism; d) maintaining friendships that do not conflict with the lover relationship; and e) managing the interdependence of each partner's commitment to work and the relationship.

Peplau's article summarizes research that has focused on the characteristics of sexual and romantic relationships that occur between same-gender partners. This research has refuted stereotypes about gay male and lesbian relationships. Moreover, the same-gender and cross-gender comparisons have provided an opportunity to examine the relative impact of sexual orientation and gender on the factors that characterize intimate relationships regardless of sexual orientation.

New models and theories based on the experiences and patterns in lesbian and gay relationships may contribute to more general analyses of close relationships (Brown 1989). Future research, however, needs to focus on diversity within gay male and lesbian relationships by examining variables such as age, cohort, class, ethnicity, openness about sexual orientation, and the relationship of each partner to the gay and lesbian community.

The second aspect of human development to be addressed in this part is parenting. Lesbians and gay men frequently are parents. Since women more often receive custody of children after a divorce, however, gay men are less likely than lesbians to live with their children. In addition, gay men and lesbians today are choosing to become parents through alternative insemination, foster parenting, and adoption.

Three issues have received considerable attention regarding lesbian and gay male parents. First, research has focused on the question of whether lesbians and gay men are suitable parents, primarily because of custody and adoption issues. Second, research has focused on the stereotypic negative effects of lesbian or gay male parents on children. Third, some research has examined the effects on the child of the presumed social stigma of having a gay male or lesbian parent. These studies are concisely summarized in the articles by Falk and Bozett presented in this part.

In general, the findings have supported the conclusions that lesbian mothers and gay fathers are likely to be good parents, to have no ill effects on their children because of their sexual orientation, and that children can cope with this family arrangement satisfactorily (Bozett 1987, 1988; Green et al. 1986; Miller 1979, 1987). Lesbians and gay men also have the potential to be positive role models of nontraditional gender roles, interpersonal relationships, and individual diversity (Riddle 1978).

There appears to be growing awareness of parenthood in the lesbian and gay male community. Gay male couples who are denied foster children, lesbians choosing to have children, and issues about visitation rights if a couple breaks up are issues that are widely discussed in the popular media. Still, there is an important need for more practical attention to the concerns of lesbian and gay parents.

Overall, research has emphasized the similarity of gay male and lesbian parents to heterosexual parents. As a result, many interesting dimensions of the uniqueness of lesbian and gay parenting have not been explored. Additional research is important because of the growing number of lesbians and gay men who are choosing to parent, and because of continuing concerns of parents regarding custody issues.

Among the topics deserving research are the following: a) coparents: what characteristics make lesbian or gay male parenting unique; positive effects of lesbian and gay parenting such as the child's increased gender role flexibility and appreciation of diversity; the roles of coparents, biological versus nonbiological coparent, and the effects of the legal status of each of the coparents vis-à-vis the child; b) children: impact on children growing up in families where their biological father is not known to them, for example, because of alternative insemination; strategies used to teach children skills to counter homophobia and the stigma that may be associated with having an atypical family; effects of having coparents who share equal power; effects on second-generation gay males and lesbians of having a gay or lesbian parent; the issue of whether male and female children are reared differently by male or female same-gender parents; unique issues that become relevant when the child becomes adolescent; and c) families of origin: issues regarding grandparents and strategies used to counter the homophobic stigma they may experience. Several of these issues are not unique to lesbian and gay male families; thus, studies with well-designed comparison groups may be especially important.

CONTEMPORARY ISSUE: LEGAL RECOGNITION AND SPOUSE/FAMILY BENEFITS

Current concerns for many same-gender couples and their children center around the ongoing struggle for legal definitions for unmarried domestic partners, legal recognition of same-gender relationships, and ceremonies and rituals affirming gay male and lesbian partnerships. For example, in San Francisco, lesbian and gay men can register as domestic partners at the County Clerk's office in a process analogous to obtaining a marriage license. Also, the 1990 census included for the first time a category for unmarried partners, defined as "two unrelated adults in a close, personal relationship" (Beyette 1990:E1). In 1989 New York's highest court ruled that a gay couple was legally a family under New York City's rent control laws. A few unions and employers, including the American Psychological Association, the *Village Voice*, and Ben and Jerry's Homemade, offer health insurance to the domestic partners of their employees or members (*New York Times*, September 1990). Recently, medical, dental, and bereavement benefits were provided by the Lotus Development Corporation to gay and lesbian couples but not to unmarried heterosexual couples because it was argued that the unmarried heterosexuals could get married if they chose to do so, while lesbians and gay men cannot: "In giving homosexual employees a contract to sign to attest to their long-term commitments, 'we are providing a parallel process to getting married' " (*New York Times*, September 1991:12).

The issues, however, are not clear-cut. Debates are taking place within the gay male and lesbian community regarding legal recognition of same-gender marriages and the practice of marriagelike ceremonies. Some view these efforts as a form of capitulation to heterosexist norms that would render invisible the unique qualities of lesbian and gay male relationships. Furthermore, some view marriage as participation in an oppressive, patriarchal tradition. Others, in contrast, perceive legal recognition as the next step toward validation of gay and lesbian relationships and believe that affirming such partnerships will provide community and public support for gay male and lesbian couples and their children.

REFERENCES

Beyette, B. 1990. Tallying new famly ties. *Los Angeles Times* (March 23):E1–E2.

Brown, L. S. 1989. New voices, new visions: Toward a lesbian/gay paradigm for psychology. *Psychology of Women Quarterly* 13(4):445–58.

Bozett, F. W. 1987. Children of gay fathers. In F. W. Bozett, ed., *Gay and Lesbian Parents*, pp. 39–57. New York: Praeger.

Bozett, F. W. 1988. Social control of identity by children of gay fathers. *Western Journal of Nursing Research* 10:550–65.

The courts are again asked to redefine family. 1990. *New York Times* (September 23).

Green, R., J. B. Mandel, M. E. Hotvedt, J. Gray, and L. Smith. 1986. Lesbian mothers and their children: A comparison with solo parent heterosexual mothers and their children. *Archives of Sexual Behavior* 15:167–84.

Lotus offers benefits for homosexual pairs. *New York Times* (September 7):12.

Miller, B. 1979. Gay fathers and their children. *Family Coordinator* 28:544–52.

Miller, B. 1987. Counseling gay husbands and fathers. In F. W. Bozett, ed., *Gay and Lesbian Parents*, pp. 175–87. New York: Praeger.

Peplau, L. A., and S. D. Cochran. 1990. A relationship perspective on homosexuality. In D. P. McWhirter, S. A. Sanders, and J. M. Reinisch, eds., *Homosexuality/Heterosexuality: The Kinsey Scale and Current Research*, pp. 321–49. New York: Oxford University Press.

Riddle, D. I. 1978. Relating to children: Gay as role models. *Journal of Social Issues* 34(3):38–58.

17

Lesbian and Gay Relationships

Letitia Anne Peplau

Public awareness of lesbian and gay couples is growing; attention to homosexuality in the popular media is increasing. Social scientists have also begun to describe and analyze the nature of gay and lesbian relationships. The new scholarship on homosexual relationships is important both to the scientific community and to the general public.

For the emerging science of close relationships (Kelley et al. 1983), research on homosexual couples broadens the existing knowledge base by increasing the diversity of types of relationships studied to include same-sex partnerships. In the past, virtually all research on adult love relationships has focused on heterosexual dating and marriage. New studies of homosexual couples expand the range and generality of scientific knowledge about intimate relationships.

For the growing research literature on homosexuality, studies of gay and lesbian relationships also represent a new direction. Until recently, scholarship on homosexuality focused primarily on questions of pathology, individual psychological adjustment, and etiology. For example, a recent annotated bibliography included close to 5,000 citations from the social sciences, humanities, and popular press (Dynes 1987). Only 36 of these entries were classified as dealing with gay or lesbian "couples." In contrast, there were 207 entries on psychiatry, psychotherapy, "cures," and related topics, and another 155 entries on the experiences of lesbians and gay men in prison or with the police.

For the general public, accurate information about gay and lesbian relationships is also useful. Scientific research can replace biased stereotypes with factual descriptions of the nature and diversity of homosexual couples. Research can also inform the discussion of new legal and public policy issues that arise as gay men and lesbians become a more visible and vocal part of society. This point is illustrated in the following case descriptions, based on recent legal cases.

CASE 1: EMOTIONAL PAIN AND SUFFERING

A man in a long-term gay relationship was killed by a reckless driver. The surviving partner sued the driver for damages resulting from the grief and psychological distress of losing a spouse-equivalent. The driver's lawyer countered that gay men's relationships bear little resemblance to marriage, and that it would be ridiculous to provide such payment. This case hinges on fundamental questions about the nature of gay men's relationships. How similar are long-term gay partnerships to heterosexual marriage? What is the intensity of love and attachment experienced in enduring gay relationships, and what is the depth of grief that accompanies bereavement?

CASE 2: A LESBIAN MOTHER

A young woman married her college sweetheart, had two daughters, divorced her husband, and retained custody of the children. Some time later, she began a lesbian relationship and set up a joint household with her female partner. At this point, her former husband sued to gain custody of the children, claiming that the mother was an "unfit" parent. It was proposed that she might retain custody if she promised to end her lesbian relationship. At issue here are basic questions about the ability of a lesbian mother to provide a healthy family life, the role models provided by partners in a lesbian relationship, and the impact of a lesbian couple on children in the household.

CASE 3: THE CRIME-OF-PASSION DEFENSE

During a heated argument, a young man bludgeoned his lover to death with a fire iron. The defense acknowledged that the man had committed the murder, but pleaded that the act was committed in a moment of passion—a defense that could potentially lead to a lesser charge than premeditated homicide. The defendant's case rested on showing that gay relationships are as emotionally intense as heterosexual ones, perhaps even more so. The lawyer argued that a threat to a relationship could send a gay man "over the edge" psychologically. In addition, since both partners were recent immigrants from a culture that is highly intolerant of homosexuality, the defense attorney argued that his client was denied the kinds of social support that might have enabled him to cope more effectively with the crisis in his relationship. The case raises questions about the nature of love, passion, and jealousy in gay relationships, and the social support experienced by homosexuals.

Although existing research does not definitively resolve the questions raised by these cases, it does provide beginning answers. This article reviews social science research on gay and lesbian relationships. It begins by summarizing major research findings relevant to four common stereotypes about gay and lesbian relationships in America. Then, theoretical issues raised by the study of lesbian and gay couples are considered. The article concludes with a discussion of the variation and diversity that exists among same-sex relationships.

It is important to emphasize at the outset that most of the available studies of homosexual relationships are based on samples of younger, urban, primarily White individuals. Occasionally, studies have involved fairly large samples (e.g., Blumstein and Schwartz 1983) or have included ethnic samples (e.g., Bell and Weinberg 1978 surveyed both Black and White respondents), but none has been completely representative of either lesbians or gay men. So it is essential to acknowledge this limitation in our newly accumulating body of research.

DEBUNKING STEREOTYPES ABOUT LESBIAN AND GAY RELATIONSHIPS

Empirical social science research on gay and lesbian relationships dates mainly from the mid-1970s. To date, the work has been largely descriptive-seeking to test the accuracy of prevailing social stereotypes about gay and lesbian relationships and to provide more reliable information. (For other reviews, see De Cecco 1988; Harry 1983; Larson 1982; Peplau and Amaro 1982; Peplau and Cochran 1990; Peplau and Gordon 1983; Risman and Schwartz 1988.)

Myth 1: Homosexuals don't want enduring relationships—and can't achieve them anyway.

Homosexuals are often depicted in the media as unhappy individuals who are unsuccessful in developing enduring same-sex ties. Drifting from one sexual liaison to another, they end up old and alone. Existing data sharply counter this stereotype.

Studies of homosexuals' attitudes about relationships find that most lesbians and gay men say they very much want to have enduring close relationships (e.g., Bell and Weinberg 1978). Other studies have investigated the extent to which lesbians and gay men are successful in establishing intimate relationships. In surveys of gay men, between 40 percent and 60 percent of the men questioned were currently involved in a steady relationship (e.g., Bell and Weinberg 1978; Harry 1983; Jay and Young 1977; Peplau and Cochran 1981; Spada 1979). These figures may actually *under*represent the true frequency of enduring relationships because men in long-term relationships tend to be somewhat older and less likely to go to bars—both factors that would reduce the chances of these men being included in current studies (Harry 1983). In studies of lesbians, between 45 percent and 80 percent of women surveyed were currently in a steady relationship (e.g., Bell and Weinberg 1978; Jay and Young 1977; Peplau et al. 1978; Raphael and Robinson 1980; Schafer 1977). In most studies, the proportion of lesbians in an ongoing relationship was close to 75 percent.

These estimates are not completely representative of all lesbians and gay men in the United States. They do indicate, however, that a large proportion of homosexuals have stable close relationships. Research also suggests that a slightly higher proportion of lesbians than gay men may be in steady relationships.

Given that substantial proportions of lesbians and gay men are involved in intimate relationships, a next question concerns the longevity of these partnerships. Lacking marriage records and representative samples, it is hard to make judgments about how long "typical" homosexual relationships last. Most studies have been of younger adults, whose relationships have lasted for a few years, as would be true for heterosexuals in their twenties. The few studies that have included older gay men and lesbians have found that relationships lasting twenty years or more are not uncommon (e.g., McWhirter and Mattison 1984; Raphael and Robinson 1980; Silverstein 1981).

In a short longitudinal study, Blumstein and Schwartz (1983) followed a large sample of lesbian, gay male, cohabiting heterosexual, and married couples over an eighteen-month period. At the time of initial testing, lesbians, gay men, and heterosexuals were about equal in predicting that their current relationship would continue, although both lesbians and gay men speculated that gay men usually have less stable relationships than lesbians. At the eighteen-month follow-up, most couples were still together. Breakups were rare among couples who had already been together for more than ten years: 6 percent for lesbians, 4 percent for gay men, 4 percent for married couples. (None of the heterosexual cohabiting couples had been together for more than ten years.) Among couples who had been together for two years or less, the breakup rate was also fairly low—less than one relationship in five ended during the eighteen-month period. Minor differences were found in rates of breakup among the different types of couples: 22 percent for lesbian couples, 16 percent for gay male couples, 17 percent for cohabiting couples, and 4 percent for married couples. Although these group differences are quite small, they do run counter to the suggestion that lesbians are more likely to have enduring partnerships. More important, however, is the general pattern of relationship continuity found for all groups.

The basic point to draw from these studies is that gay and lesbian relationships are very much a reality in contemporary life.

Myth 2: Gay relationships are unhappy, abnormal, dysfunctional, and deviant.

It is often believed that gay and lesbian relationships are inferior to those of heterosexuals. For example, a study of heterosexual college students found that they expected gay and lesbian relationships to be less satisfying, more prone to discord, and "less in love" than heterosexual relationships (Testa, Kinder, and Ironson 1987). To investigate this stereotype scientifically, researchers have assessed the psychological adjustment of homosexual dyads, and have often used a research strategy of comparing the relationship functioning of matched samples of homosexual and heterosexual couples. The central question has been how well gay and lesbian relationships fare on standard measures of relationship satisfaction, dyadic adjustment, or love.

Illustrative of this research is a study that Susan Cochran and I conducted (Peplau and Cochran 1980). We selected matched samples of fifty lesbians, fifty gay men, fifty heterosexual women, and fifty heterosexual men—all currently involved in "romantic/sexual relationships." Participants were matched on age, education, ethnicity, and length of relationship, and all completed a detailed questionnaire about their current relationship.

Among this sample of young adults, about 60 percent said they were "in love with their partner; most of the rest indicated they were "uncertain." On Rubin's standardized Love and Liking Scales, lesbians and gay men generally reported very positive feelings for their partners. Lesbians and gay men also rated their current relationships as highly satisfying and very close. No significant differences were found among lesbians, gay men, and heterosexuals on any of these measures of relationship satisfaction.

We also asked lesbians, gay men, and heterosexuals to describe in their own words the "best things" and "worst things" about their relationships. Responses included such comments as these: "The best thing is having someone to be with when you wake up," or "We like each other. We both seem to be getting what we want and need. We have wonderful sex together." Worst things included "My partner is too dependent emotionally," or "Her aunt lives with us!" Systematic content analyses (Cochran 1978) found no significant differences in the responses of lesbians, gay men, and heterosexuals—all of whom reported a similar range of joys and problems. To search for more subtle differences among groups that may not have been captured by the coding scheme, the "best things" and "worst things" statements were typed on cards in a standard format, with information about gender and sexual orientation removed. Panels of judges were asked to sort the cards, separating men and women, or separating heterosexuals and homosexuals. The judges were not able to identify correctly the responses of lesbians, gay men, or heterosexual women and men. (Indeed, judges may have been misled by their own preconceptions; they tended, for instance, to assume incorrectly that statements involving jealousy were more likely to be made by homosexuals than by heterosexuals.)

Other studies have portrayed similar findings, and have extended the range of relationship measures used. In general, most gay men and lesbians perceive their relationships as satisfying. Homosexual and heterosexual couples who are matched on age and other relevant background characteristics do not usually differ in levels of love and satisfaction, nor in their scores on standardized measures such as the Locke-Wallace Scale or Spanier's Dyadic Adjustment Scale (see Cardell, Finn, and Marecek 1981; Dailey 1979; Duffy and Rusbult 1986; Kurdek and Schmitt 1986b, c, 1987a; Peplau, Cochran, and Mays 1986; Peplau, Padesky, and Hamilton 1982).

None of this is to say that all gay and lesbian couples are happy and problem-free. Rather the point is that homosexual couples are not necessarily any more prone to relationship dissatisfactions and difficulties than are heterosexuals. Although the likelihood of relationship problems may be similar regardless of sexual orientation, however, there may nonetheless be differences in the types of problems most commonly faced by gay, lesbian, and heterosexual couples. For example, therapists have suggested that issues of dependency and individuation may be especially salient in lesbian relationships (e.g., Roth 1985; Sang 1985; Smalley 1987). Recently, psychotherapists have begun to develop new programs of couples counseling geared specifically for gay or lesbian couples (e.g., Berzon

1988; Boston Lesbian Psychologies Collective 1987; Gonsiorek 1985; Stein and Cohen 1986).

In summary, research findings indicate that it is no longer useful or appropriate to describe homosexual relationships in the value-laden language of "abnormal relationships" or "deviance." There is growing recognition of the wide diversity of "families" today—single-parent families, "recombinant families" incorporating children from two previous marriages, and so on. Lesbian and gay partnerships should be included among this diverse array of family types.

There is also increasing evidence from historians (e.g., Boswell 1980) and anthropologists (e.g., Herdt 1981) that our own culture's negative evaluation of homosexual couples has not been shared universally. In other times and places, human culture has recognized and approved of gay partnerships. Interesting, too, are recent efforts by sociobiologists to consider ways in which homosexual relationships might be functional rather than dysfunctional for individuals, in the sense of enhancing their reproductive success and causing their genes to influence the direction of evolutionary change. A detailed discussion of this perspective is presented by Weinrich (1987).

Myth 3: "Husband" and "wife" roles are universal in intimate relationships.

C. A. Tripp notes that "when people who are not familiar with homosexual relationships try to picture one, they almost invariably resort to a heterosexual frame of reference, raising questions about which partner is "the man" and which "the woman" (1975:152). This issue has generated a good deal of empirical research (see reviews by Harry 1983; Peplau and Gordon 1983; Risman and Schwartz 1988).

Historical accounts of gay life in the United States suggest that masculine-feminine roles have sometimes been important. For example, Wolf described lesbian experiences in the 1950s in these terms:

> The old gay world divided up into "butch" and "femmes." . . . Butches were tough, presented themselves as being as masculine as possible . . . and they assumed the traditional male role of taking care of their partners, even fighting over them if necessary . . . Femmes, by contrast, were protected, ladylike. . . . They cooked, cleaned house, and took care of their "butch." (1979:40)

More recently, there has been a sharp decline in the occurrence of gender-linked roles in gay and lesbian relationships. Some have attributed this change to the effects of the feminist and gay rights movements and to the general loosening of traditional gender norms in American society (Marecek, Finn, and Cardell 1982; Risman and Schwartz 1988; Ross 1983).

Today, however, research shows that most lesbians and gay men actively reject traditional husband-wife or masculine-feminine roles as a model for enduring relationships (see Blumstein and Schwartz 1983; Harry 1983, 1984; Jay and Young 1977; Lynch and Reilly 1986; Marecek, Finn, and Cardell 1982; McWhirter and Mattison 1984; Peplau and Amaro 1982; Saghir and Robins 1973). Currently, most lesbians and gay men are in "dual-worker" relationships, so that neither partner is the exclusive "breadwinner" and each partner has some measure of economic independence. Further, examination of the division of household tasks, sexual behavior, and decision making in homosexual couples finds that clear-cut and consistent husband-wife roles are uncommon. In many relationships there is some specialization of activities, with one partner doing more of some jobs and less of others. But it is rare for one partner to perform most of the "feminine" activities and the other to perform most of the "masculine" tasks. That is, the partner who usually does the cooking does not necessarily also perform other feminine tasks, such as shopping or cleaning. Specialization seems to be based on more individualistic factors, such as skills or interests.

Nonetheless, a small minority of lesbians and gay men do incorporate elements of husband-wife roles into their relationships. This may affect the division of labor, the dominance structure, sexual interactions, the way partners dress, and other aspects of their relationship. In some cases, these role patterns seemed to be linked to temporary situations, such as one partner's unemployment or illness. For other couples, however, masculine-feminine roles may provide a model of choice.

Given that traditional husband-wife roles are not the template for most contemporary homosexual couples, researchers have sought to identify other models or relationship patterns. One model might be based on differences in age, with an older partner acting, in part, as a mentor or leader. In his studies of gay male relationships, Harry (1982, 1984) found that the age-difference pattern characterized only a minority of gay male couples. When it did occur, the actual differences in age tended to be relatively small, perhaps five to ten years. Harry also found that in these couples, the older partner often had more power in decision making. McWhirter and Mattison (1984) also observed age differences among some of the male couples they studied, and reported that age differences of five years or more were characteristic of couples who had been together for thirty years or more.

Finally, another pattern is based on friendship or peer relations, with partners being similar in age and emphasizing companionship, sharing, and equality in the relationship (e.g., Harry 1982, 1983; Peplau et al. 1978; Peplau and Cochran 1981). A friendship script typically fosters equality in relationships. In contrast to marriage, the norms for friendship assume that partners are relatively equal in status and power. Friends also tend to be similar in interests, resources, and skills. Available evidence suggests that most American lesbians and gay men have a relationship script that most closely approximates best friendship.

In summary, contemporary homosexual relationships follow a variety of patterns or models. Most common are relationships patterned after friendship. Among both lesbians and gay men, a minority of couples may incorporate elements of traditional masculine-feminine roles into their relationships. For others, age differences may be central to role patterns. We currently know little about the causal factors responsible for these different patterns. That many lesbians and gay men are able to create satisfying love relationships that are not based on complementary, gender-linked role differentiation challenges the popular view that such masculine-feminine differences are essential to adult love relationships.

Myth 4: Gays and lesbians have impoverished social support networks.

Although there is growing public awareness of the existence of gay and lesbian communities, stereotypes continue to depict homosexuals as socially isolated and lacking in social support. It is certainly true that in a homophobic society, gays and lesbians may suffer from social alienation and estrangement. We should not minimize the psychological stress that results from social rejection and stigma. What is noteworthy, however, is the extent to which contemporary lesbians and gay men seem able to overcome these obstacles and to create satisfying social networks. This is especially important because of growing evidence that emotional support, guidance, assistance, and other forms of social support contribute to mental and physical health.

Illustrative of research on social support is a comparative study of lesbian and heterosexual women conducted by Aura (1985). She compared the social support experiences of fifty lesbians and fifty heterosexual women. All women were currently in a primary relationship and were matched for age, education, and length of their relationship. None had children in their household. Women filled out detailed questionnaires about many specific types of social support. Results showed that both groups of women held similar values about the importance of social support. In addition, women reported receiving similar total amounts of support from their personal relationships. Lesbians and heterosexuals, however, often received support from different sources. In particular, many lesbians depended somewhat less on relatives and more on their partner or friends than did heterosexuals. For example, lesbians and heterosexuals reported receiving similar amounts of material assistance, such as help in moving or getting a ride to the airport, but lesbians relied more on friends and heterosexuals relied more on family.

Research by Lewin investigated the social support experiences of lesbian and heterosexual divorced mothers raising children (Lewin 1981; Lewin and Lyons 1982). Lewin found that both lesbian and heterosexual mothers were equally likely to turn to their parents or other family members for support. About 84 percent of the lesbian mothers said that most or all of their relatives were aware of their homosexuality. Although this initially created stress for many lesbians and their families, over time the families seemed to come to terms with the situation. One woman who had been estranged from her family reported that she now sees her mother daily because her son stays with his grandmother after school. For both lesbian and heterosexual mothers, kinship ties were often of central importance for child care and "to offer a sense of stability, an opportunity to continue family tradition, and emotional comfort" (in Lewin and Lyons 1982:262). Results suggest that the presence of children may increase the similarity in social support experiences of lesbian and heterosexual women.

Kurdek (1988) studied social support among gay men and lesbians in couples. When asked who provided social support, virtually everyone listed not only their partner but also other friends. In addition, 81 percent of the gay men and 86 percent of the lesbians cited a family member as a source of support—most often their mother or a sister. Using the standardized Social Support Questionnaire developed by Sarason and his associates (1983), Kurdek found no differences between gay men and lesbians in the source of support or in satisfaction with support. Overall levels of support received by gays and lesbians were similar to and slightly higher than those reported by Sarason for a college student sample (see also D'Augelli 1987; D'Augelli and Hart 1987; Kurdek and Schmitt 1987b).

In summary, despite potential obstacles to the establishment of meaningful social relations, many lesbians and gay men are able to create supportive social networks.

THEORETICAL ISSUES IN THE STUDY OF GAY AND LESBIAN RELATIONSHIPS

To date, much of the work on gay and lesbian relationships has been descriptive, designed to fill gaps in the existing data base. But newer research has had a stronger theoretical or conceptual focus. Three approaches can be distinguished: a) work that seeks to test the general applicability of relationship theories initially developed with heterosexuals; b) work that uses comparative studies of gay, lesbian, and heterosexual relationships to test ideas about the impact of gender on interaction; and c) work that seeks to create new theories about same-sex relationships.

The General Applicability of Theory: Social Exchange Theory

Most social science concepts, models, and theories of relationships have been based explicitly or implicitly on heterosexual experiences. Efforts to investigate the applicability of such theories to new populations of lesbians and gay men are important to the development of a science of relationships. Evidence that existing theories can usefully be applied to homosexual relationships would also have practical significance, suggesting that work on same-sex couples can build on the existing literature rather than start anew.

Social exchange theory (Burgess and Huston 1979; Kelley and Thibaut 1978) has been one of the most influential theoretical perspectives on relationships. Several studies have now tested predictions derived from exchange theory among lesbian-and gay male couples. In general, research has confirmed the generalizability of exchange theory to this new population and has shown the usefulness of exchange concepts in understanding relationship processes.

For example, Mayta Caldwell and I (1984) investigated the balance of power in lesbian relationships. In our sample of young adults, 61 percent of lesbians said that their current relationship was equal in power. We explored two factors that might tip the balance of power away from equality. First, we considered the "principle of least interest"—the prediction that when one person is more dependent, involved, or interested in continuing a relationship, that person is at a power disadvantage. We found strong support for this prediction.

We also investigated the impact of personal resources on power. The prediction here is that when a person has substantially more resources than the partner, he or she will have a power advantage. In our sample, differences in both income and education were significantly related to imbalances of power, with greater power accruing to the lesbian partner who was relatively better educated or earned more money. Studies of gay male relationships by Harry (1984) have also shown that a power advantage can accrue to the partner who has a higher income and who is older.

Work by Blumstein and Schwartz (1983), however, raises the possibility that the importance of specific resources, such as money, may differ across groups. In their large-scale study, Blumstein and Schwartz found that money was related to power in heterosexual relationships and was "an extremely important force" in determining dominance in gay male relationships. But for lesbians, income was unrelated to power. This is a good illustration of the notion that personal resources are not universal, but rather depend on the values of the partners in a relationship.

Another way in which research has drawn on exchange principles concerns commitment in gay and lesbian relationships. The question here is whether the forces affecting commitment might be different in homosexual versus heterosexual relationships. As Levinger (1979) and others have pointed out, commitment and permanence in a relationship are affected by two separate types of factors. The first concerns the strength of the positive attractions that make us want to stay in a relationship. Although stereotypes depict gays and lesbians as having weaker attractions to their partners than do heterosexuals, we have already seen that research does not support this view. In general, homosexuals do not appear to differ from heterosexuals in the level of satisfaction and love they feel for their primary partner.

The second factor maintaining the stability of relationships are barriers that make the ending of the relationship costly, in either psychological or material terms. For heterosexuals, marriage usually creates many barriers to dissolution, including the cost of divorce, the wife's financial dependence on her husband, joint investments in property, concerns about children, and so on. Such factors may encourage married couples to "work" to improve a declining relationship, rather than end it. In contrast, gay and lesbian couples may be less likely to experience comparable barriers to the ending of a relationship—they cannot marry legally, their relatives may prefer that they end their relationship, they are less likely to have children in common, and so on. Another barrier to ending a relationship might be the lack of alternative partners or resources. To the extent that a current partner is the "best available," we are less likely to leave.

This exchange theory analysis suggests that for all types of relationships, the level of commitment should be related to attractions, barriers, and alternatives. Because of differences in the social context of homosexual and heterosexual relationships, lesbian and gay male couples may tend to have fewer barriers than heterosexuals. As a result, possible differences in commitment between heterosexual and homosexual couples may result from barriers to dissolution rather than from attractions to the partner.

Empirical research has investigated these predictions. Kurdek and Schmitt (1986c) compared self-reported attractions, barriers, and alternatives in gay, lesbian, heterosexual cohabiting, and married couples. They found no differences across the groups in attractions. All groups were equally likely to report feelings of love and satisfaction. Barriers—assessed by statements such as "many things would prevent me from leaving my partner even if I were unhappy"—did differ. Married couples reported significantly more barriers than either gays or lesbians reported, and cohabiting heterosexual couples reported the fewest barriers of all. In answering questions about available alternatives to the current relationship, lesbians and married couples reported the fewest alternatives; gay men and heterosexual cohabitors reported the most alternatives. For all groups, love for the partner was significantly related to perceiving many barriers to leaving, few alternatives, and many attractions. In summary, differences between gay, lesbian, and heterosexual couples were found in the barriers they perceived to ending a relationship, not in the quality of the relationship itself. Kurdek and Schmitt did not relate these factors to commitment.

Rusbult (1988) investigated the dynamics of commitment more directly, testing what she calls an "investment model" of commitment based on social exchange principles. After initial tests of her model with heterosexuals, Duffy and Rusbult (1986) conducted a comparative study of homosexual and heterosexual relationships to test the generalizability of her findings. This research found that lesbians, gay men, and heterosexuals all generally described their relationships in quite similar ways. All groups reported strong attraction to their partner (that is, high rewards and low costs from the relationship and high satisfaction), moderately high investments in the relationship, and moderately poor alternatives. All types of couples also reported strong commitment. Consistent with exchange theory principles, commitment was predicted by satisfaction, investments, and alternatives for lesbians, gay men, and heterosexuals.

These studies found somewhat different patterns of results, with Kurdek and Schmitt reporting that sexual orientation was related to differences in barriers and alternatives, and Duffy and Rusbult finding no effects of sexual orientation. Further research will be needed to explore these issues more fully. Nonetheless, available evidence does clearly suggest the usefulness of applying principles from social exchange theory to homosexual relationships. This is an important demonstration of the generalizability of the theory. Equally important, it suggests that those interested in understanding the dynamics of gay and lesbian relationships can at least sometimes take existing theory as a starting point.

THE IMPACT OF GENDER ON RELATIONSHIPS: CONTRASTING GENDER VERSUS POWER INTERPRETATIONS

Comparative studies of same-sex and cross-sex couples provide a new approach to investigating how gender affects close relationships. For example, by comparing how women behave with male versus female partners, we can begin to disentangle the effects on social interaction of an individual's own sex and the sex of their partner. This comparative research strategy is not identical to an experiment in which participants are randomly assigned to interact with a male or female partner. In real life, individuals are obviously not randomly assigned to have heterosexual or homosexual relationships. Nonetheless, strategically planned comparisons can be informative. This point is illustrated by studies investigating gender versus power interpretations of social interaction patterns.

It has been observed that when trying to influence a partner, women and men tend to use somewhat different tactics. Women may be more likely to use tears and less likely to use logical arguments. Why? One interpretation views this sex difference as resulting from differential gender socialization—women have learned to express emotion, men to use logic. But a second interpretation is also plausible: in male-female relationships, men often have the upper hand in power. Influence tactics may stem from the partner's relative dominance in the relationship, not from male-female differences in dispositions to use particular influence tactics. Several studies have used comparisons of gay, lesbian, and heterosexual relationships to investigate these compelling interpretations.

In a study of influence strategies in intimate relationships, Toni Falbo and I (1980) compared the tactics that lesbians, gay men, and heterosexuals reported using to influence a romantic partner. We also asked questions about the balance of power in the relationship. Our results led to two major conclusions. First, gender affected power tactics, but only among heterosexuals. Whereas heterosexual women were more likely to withdraw or express negative emotions, heterosexual men were more likely to use bargaining or reasoning. But this sex difference did not emerge in comparisons of lesbians and gay men influencing their same-sex partner. Second, consistent with the dominance interpretation, regardless of gender or sexual orientation, individuals who perceived themselves as relatively more powerful in the relationship tended to use persuasion and bargaining. In contrast, partners low in power tended to use withdrawal and emotion.

Howard, Blumstein, and Schwartz (1986) also compared influence tactics in the intimate relationships of homosexuals and heterosexuals. They found that dependent (lower-power) partners in all three types of couples used different influence tactics than did the more powerful. Regardless of sexual orientation, a partner with relatively less power tended to use "weak" strategies, such as supplication and manipulation. Those in positions of strength were more likely to use autocratic and bullying tactics, both "strong strategies." Further, individuals with male partners (i.e., heterosexual women and homosexual men) were more likely to use supplication and manipulation. Similarly, Kollock, Blumstein, and Schwartz (1985) found that signs of conversational dominance, such as interrupting a partner in the middle of a conversation, were linked to the balance of power. Although interruption has sometimes been viewed as a "male" behavior, it was, in fact, more often engaged in by the more powerful person in the relationship, regardless of gender. Taken together, the results of these studies provide considerable support for the dominance interpretation of sex differences in male-female interaction.

These studies demonstrate the potential benefits of using strategic comparisons of same-sex and cross-sex couples to help understand the causes of sex differences in personal relationships. (For an illustration of using comparisons of homosexual and heterosexual couples to test social versus evolutionary theories of partner selection, see Howard, Blumstein, and Schwartz 1987.)

New Theories: Stage Models of the Development of Gay Relationships

There have been several attempts to create models of stages in the development of relationships among gay men (e.g., Harry and Lovely 1979; McWhirter and Mattison 1984) and lesbians (e.g., Clunis and Green 1988). These models have typically been empirically based efforts to generate theory from clinical observations or from research studies of same-sex couples. The goal has been to capture patterns unique to gay or lesbian relationships.

For example, an early model of gay male relationships was proposed by Harry and Lovely (1979), well before the current AIDS epidemic. Observing that sexual exclusivity was uncommon in the relationships of gay men, Harry and Lovely proposed a two-stage model of gay male relationship development. Initially, they hypothesized, there is a relatively brief "honeymoon" phase of sexual monogamy. Over time, there is a transformation of relationships from sexually closed to open ones" (pp. 193–94). Indeed, they suggested that sexual openness may be necessary for the survival of gay relationships over time.

In 1980 David Blasband and I tested this two-stage model with a sample of forty gay male couples (Blasband and Peplau 1985). Our data provided little support for the generality of this model. Of the forty couples, only 20 percent indicated that their relationship was initially closed and later became sexually open. The rest reported other patterns. Roughly 20 percent indicated that their relationship had always been sexually open, 30 percent said it had always been closed, and the rest followed other patterns. Two couples said that they had once had a sexually open relationship but decided to become closed because of problems they were experiencing.

We were not surprised to find such a wide variety of patterns. As research on heterosexual courtship and couple development has shown (Levinger 1983), it is exceedingly difficult to find universal, invariant stages in the development of relationships. Efforts to identify fixed and invariant stages are probably only successful when cultural scripts are rigid and widely accepted. Left to their own devices, humans are more creative in the range of relationship patterns they construct.

More recently, detailed stage models of gay and lesbian relationships have been presented. Based on a study of 156 male couples, McWhirter and Mattison (1984) proposed a six-stage model of development. Their stages, roughly linked to the length of the relationship, are blending, nesting, maintaining, building, releasing, and renewing. Partly building on the McWhirter and Mattison work, Clunis and Green (1988) proposed a six-stage model for the development of lesbian relationships including these stages: prerelationship, romance, conflict, acceptance, commitment, and collaboration. These stage theorists have acknowledged variation among couples. As Clunis and Green comment, "Not every couple starts with the first stage. Some couples never go through all the stages, and certainly not in the order they are presented" (p. 10). Similarly, McWhirter and Mattison caution that "characteristics from one stage also are present in other stages, and they overlap. Remember, too, that not all male couples fit this model" (p. 16). These stage models represent innovative attempts to characterize the unique relationship progression of contemporary gay and lesbian relationships. Further research will be needed to assess how well these models apply to other samples of lesbian and gay male couples (e.g., Kurdek and Schmitt 1986a).

In summary, a good deal has been learned about gay and lesbian couples during the past decade. The field has begun to move beyond basic descriptive studies in the direction of theory development and testing. The use of strategic comparisons of same-sex and cross-sex dyads appears to be a useful way to shed light on the impact of sexual orientation and gender on couples. New concepts and models based on lesbian and gay experiences need to be tested and refined, and their possible contribution to more general analyses of human relationships should be explored.

DIVERSITY AMONG GAY AND LESBIAN RELATIONSHIPS

Having debunked old stereotypes about homosexual relationships, we must continue to avoid the tendency to characterize the "typical lesbian couple" or the "typical gay male relationship." There are enormous variations among lesbian couples, as there are among gay male couples. To understand this diversity, two goals are important: first, we need to describe major ways in which homosexual couples differ from one another, for instance in dominance, or patterns of communication, or modes of conflict resolution, or degree of commitment (cf. Bell and Weinberg 1978). Second, we need to identify factors that produce these variations or, more technically, to identify the causal conditions affecting interaction patterns.

VARIATION BASED ON GENDER

A major source of variation in same-sex relationships appears to be gender. In the 1950s and 1960s, discussions of homosexuality often assumed that there were many commonalities among the experiences of gay men and lesbians—based on their "deviant" status or "abnormal" sexual orientation. Empirical research has seriously challenged this notion. Gagnon and Simon (1973) first articulated the opposite view, that it is one's socialization as male or female that most profoundly structures one's life experiences. Gagnon and Simon contended that the "female homosexual follows conventional feminine patterns in developing her commitment to sexuality and in conducting not only her sexual career but her nonsexual career as well" (p. 180). Focusing on sexuality, they suggested that lesbian sexuality would tend "to resemble closely" that of heterosexual women, and to differ radically from the sexual activity patterns of both heterosexual men and gay men. Current research clearly supports this assertion.

Although gender differences are evident in many aspects of gay and lesbian relationships, they are perhaps seen most easily in the area of sexuality (cf. Schafer 1977). Results of comparative studies of lesbians, gay male, and heterosexual relationships—including our own work at UCLA and the large-scale study of Blumstein and Schwartz (1983)—converge on three trends.

First, in all three types of relationships, *sexual frequency* declines with the duration of the relationship. In relationships of comparable duration, the frequency of sex with the primary partner is greatest among gay men, intermediate among heterosexuals, and lowest among lesbians.

Second, *sexual exclusivity versus openness* is an issue for all couples. In general, heterosexuals and lesbians are more supportive of sexual monogamy in relationships than are gay men. Their behavior corresponds. Sexual exclusivity in relationships is least common among gay men at all stages in their relationship. For example, Blumstein and Schwartz reported that among couples together for two to ten years or more, 79 percent of gay men have had sex with another partner in the previous year, compared with only 11 percent of husbands and 9 percent of wives. For lesbians, the comparable figure was 19 percent.

Third, levels of *sexual satisfaction* are similar across lesbian, gay male, and heterosexual couples, suggesting that couples in each group find their sexual relations equally gratifying on average (e.g., Masters and Johnson 1979).

The gender differences in these data are large and support the view that men want sex more often than women do and that men more highly value sexual novelty. Heterosexual relationships are, on some measure, a compromise between the preferences of the man and the woman (cf. Symons 1979). In contrast, same-sex partnerships are more extreme—men with male partners have sex more often and are less inclined toward sexual exclusivity. Women with female partners have sex least often, and differ sharply from gay men in their rates of nonmonogamy. Further explorations of the way in which gender affects the relationship experiences of gay and lesbian couples would be useful. (These generalizations are based on research conducted before the AIDS crisis. It remains to be seen how AIDS may alter patterns of sexual behavior.)

VARIATION BASED ON PERSONAL VALUES

Another source of differences among same-sex couples concerns the personal values about intimacy that individuals bring to their relationship. We have begun to explore individual differences in values about the nature of love relationships (Peplau et al. 1978; Peplau and Cochran 1980, 1981). Consistent with discussions in the relationship literature, we have found two basic value dimensions for relationships. These dimensions have sometimes been called intimacy and independence, attachment and autonomy, or closeness and separation. We have conceptualized these distinctions as value orientations and have developed two independent scales, one to assess each orientation.

We have called the first of these orientations *dyadic attachment*. It concerns the value placed on having an emotionally close and relatively secure love relationship. As one gay man described what he wants in a love relationship: "The most important thing . . . is the knowledge that someone loves and needs me. . . . It would be a stabilizing force in my life, and give me a sense of security" (cited in Spada 1979:198). On our measure, a person who scores high on attachment strongly values permanence, security, shared activities, sexual exclusivity, and "togetherness."

The second theme we have called *personal autonomy*, and it concerns the boundaries that exist between an individual and his or her partner. While some individuals wish to immerse themselves entirely in a relationship to the exclusion of outside interests and activities, others prefer to maintain personal independence. On our measure, a person who scores high on personal autonomy emphasizes the importance of having separate interests and friendships apart from a primary relationship and preserving independence within the relationship by dividing finances equally and making decisions in an egalitarian manner.

Our research has shown that these same two value themes are relevant to the experiences of lesbians, gay men, and heterosexuals. In all samples, the two measures are independent—not polar opposites. Some individuals may want to combine a high degree of togetherness with a high level of independence, others prefer a high degree of togetherness and low independence, and so on. These relationship values are predictive of variations among relationships in such factors as love and satisfaction, perceived commitment, types of problems experienced, and sexual behavior, although these linkages are not always very strong.

An important direction for future research will be to identify other sources of diversity among lesbian and gay male relationships. Other factors worth exploring include the impact of age (or cohort), ethnicity (e.g., Peplau, Cochran, and Mays 1980), length of a relationship, or degree of integration in a lesbian or gay community. Ultimately, we will want to develop a fuller picture of how interaction in gay and lesbian couples is affected by characteristics of the individual partners, by features of the dyad itself, and by social and cultural conditions.

CONCLUSION

This article has reviewed a growing body of scientific research on gay and lesbian relationships. Research has shown that most lesbians and gay men want intimate relationships and are successful in creating them. Homosexual partnerships appear no more vulnerable to problems and dissatisfactions than their heterosexual counterparts, although the specific problems encountered may differ for same-sex and cross-sex couples. Characterizations of gay and lesbian relationships as "abnormal" or "dysfunctional" are not justifiable. Another myth that has been disconfirmed is the belief that most homosexual couples adopt "husband" and "wife" roles. Finally, new work has found that gay men and lesbians do not typically have impoverished social support networks. It is important that mental health practitioners, educators, and the general public become more informed about the realities of same-sex relationships, so that misconception can be replaced with up-to-date scientific knowledge.

Scholars are increasingly emphasizing the rich diversity that exists among gay and lesbian couples. Much needed research remains to be done to describe the varieties of same-sex partnerships, and to understand how such factors as ethnicity, social class, openness about one's sexual orientation, and participation in gay or lesbian communities influence the experiences of lesbian and gay male couples. The debunking of derogatory social stereotypes about homosexual relationships should also clear the way for an open discussion of the special problems that do affect contemporary gay and lesbian couples. The enormous impact of the AIDS epidemic on homosexual relationships is just beginning to receive the attention it deserves (e.g., Carl 1986; Risman and Schwartz 1988). New research investigating the effects on relationships of alcohol abuse (e.g., Weinberg 1986) and physical violence (Leeder 1988; Renzetti 1988; Waterman, Dawson, and Bologna 1989) is also important, and illustrates some of the many useful new directions for future research.

Studies of lesbian and gay couples can contribute to the emerging science of close relationships. The applicability of general theories, such as social exchange theory, to homosexual couples has now been demonstrated in several studies, and further research of this sort would be useful. This work suggests the possibility of developing general theories capable of explaining a wide variety of relationship types. Studies of same-sex partnerships can also provide a new perspective on the impact of gender on close relationships. Comparisons of same-sex and cross-sex couples provide a new research strategy for testing competing interpretations of sex differences in interaction. New theories based on the distinctive experiences of gay and lesbian couples are an important new direction for future work.

ACKNOWLEDGMENTS

The author gratefully acknowledges the valuable assistance of Amanda Munoz and Steven L. Gordon in the preparation of this article.

REFERENCES

Aura, J. 1985. Women's social support: A comparison of lesbians and heterosexuals. Doctoral dissertation, University of California, Los Angeles.

Bell, A. P., and M. A. Weinberg. 1978. *Homosexualities: A Study of Diversity Among Men and Women.* New York: Simon and Schuster.

Berzon, B. 1988. *Permanent Partners: Building Gay and Lesbian Relationships that Last.* New York: Dutton.

Blasband, D., and L. A. Peplau. 1985. Sexual exclusivity versus openness in gay male couples. *Archives of Sexual Behavior* 14(5):395–412.

Blumstein, P., and P. Schwartz. 1983. *American Couples: Money, Work, Sex.* New York: Morrow.

Boston Lesbian Psychologies Collective, eds. 1987. *Lesbian Psychologies: Explorations and Challenges.* Urbana: University of Illinois Press.

Boswell, J. 1980. *Christianity, Social Tolerance, and Homosexuality.* Chicago: University of Chicago Press.

Burgess, R. L., and T. L. Huston, eds. 1979. *Social Exchange in Developing Relationships.* . New York: Academic Press.

Caldwell, M. A., and L. A. Peplau. 1984. The balance of power in lesbian relationships. *Sex Roles* 10:587–600.

Cardell, M., S. Finn, and J. Marecek. 1981. Sex-role identity, sex-role behavior, and satisfaction in heterosexual, lesbian, and gay male couples. *Psychology of Women Quarterly* 5(3):488–94.

Carl, D. 1986. Acquired immune deficiency syndrome: A preliminary examination of the effects on gay couples and coupling. *Journal of Marital and Family Therapy* 12(3):241–47.

Clunis, D. M., and G. D. Green. 1988. *Lesbian Couples.* Seattle: Seal Press.

Cochran, S. D. 1978. Romantic relationships: For better or for worse. Paper presented at the Western Psychological Association meeting, San Francisco, April.

Dailey, D. M. 1979. Adjustment of heterosexual and homosexual couples in pairing relationships: An exploratory study. *Journal of Sex Research* 15(2):143–57.

D'Augelli, A. R. 1987. Social support patterns of lesbian women in a rural helping network. *Journal of Rural Community Psychology* 8(1):12–21.

D'Augelli, A. R., and M. M. Hart. 1987. Gay women, men, and families in rural settings: Toward the development of helping communities. *American Journal of Community Psychology* 15(1):79–93.

DeCecco, J. P., ed. 1988. *Gay Relationships.* Binghamton, N.Y.: Haworth Press.

Duffy, S. M., and C. E. Rusbult. 1986. Satisfaction and commitment in homosexual and heterosexual relationships. *Journal of Homosexuality* 12(2):1–24.

Dynes, W. R. 1987. *Homosexuality: A Research Guide.* New York: Garland.

Falbo, T., and L. A. Peplau. 1980. Power strategies in intimate relationships. *Journal of Personality and Social Psychology* 38(4):618–28.

Gagnon, J. H., and W. Simon. 1973. A conformity greater than deviance: The lesbian. In *Sexual Conduct,* pp. 176–216. Chicago: Aldine.

Gonsiorek, J. C., ed. 1985. *A Guide to Psychotherapy with Gay and Lesbian Clients.* New York: Harrington Park Press.

Harry, J. 1982. Decision making and age differences among gay male couples. *Journal of Homosexuality* 8(2):9–22.

Harry, J. 1983. Gay male and lesbian relationships. In E. Macklin and R. Rubin, eds., *Contemporary Families and Alternative Lifestyles: Handbook on Research and Theory,* pp. 216–34. Beverly Hills, Calif.: Sage.

Harry, J. 1984. *Gay Couples.* New York: Praeger.

Harry, J., and R. Lovely. 1979. Gay marriages and communities of sexual orientation. *Alternative Lifestyles* 2(2):177–200.

Herdt, G. H. 1981. *Guardians of the Flutes: Idioms of Masculinity.* New York: McGraw-Hill.

Howard, J. A., P. Blumstein, and P. Schwartz. 1986. Sex, power, and influence tactics in intimate relationships. *Journal of Personality and Social Psychology* 51(1):102–9.

Howard, J. A., P. Blumstein, and P. Schwartz. 1987. Social or evolutionary theories? Some observations on preferences in human mate selection. *Journal of Personality and Social Psychology* 53(1):194–200.

Jay, K., and A. Young. 1977. *The Gay Report: Lesbians and Gay Men Speak Out about Sexual Experiences and Lifestyles.* New York: Summit Books.

Jones, R. W., and J. E. Bates. 1978. Satisfaction in male homosexual couples. *Journal of Homosexuality* 3(3):217–24.

Kelley, H. H., E. Berscheid, A. Christensen, J. H. Harvey, T. L. Huston, G. Levinger, E. McClintock, L. A. Peplau, and D. R. Peterson. 1983. *Close Relationships.* New York: W. H. Freeman.

Kelley, H. H., and J. W. Thibaut. 1978. *Interpersonal Relations: A Theory of Interdependence.* New York: Wiley-Interscience.

Kollock, P., P. Blumstein, and P. Schwartz. 1986. Sex and power in interaction: Conversational privileges and duties. *American Sociological Review* 50:34–46.

Kurdek, L. A. 1988. Perceived social support in gays and lesbians in cohabiting relationships. *Journal of Personality and Social Psychology* 54(3):504–9.

Kurdek, L. A., and J. P. Schmitt. 1986a. Early development of relationship quality in heterosexual cohabiting, gay, and lesbian couples. *Developmental Psychology* 22:305–9.

Kurdek, L. A., and J. P. Schmitt. 1986b. Relationship quality of gay men in closed or open relationships. *Journal of Homosexuality* 12(2):85–99.

Kurdek, L. A., and J. P. Schmitt. 1986c. Relationship quality of partners in heterosexual married, hetersexual cohabiting, and gay and lesbian relationships. *Journal of Personality and Social Psychology* 51:711–20.

Kurdek, L. A., and J. P. Schmitt. 1987a. Partner homogamy in married, heterosexual cohabiting, gay, and lesbian couples. *Journal of Sex Research* 23:212–32.

Kurdek, L. A., and J. P. Schmitt. 1987b. Perceived emotional support from family and friends in members of gay, lesbian, and heterosexual cohabiting couples. *Journal of Homosexuality* 14:57–68.

Larson, P. C. 1982. Gay male relationships. In W. Paul, J. D. Weinrich, J. C. Gonsiorek, and M. E. Hotvedt, eds., *Homosexuality: Social, Psychological, and Biological Issues*, pp. 219–32. Beverly Hills, Calif.: Sage.

Leeder, E. 1988. Enmeshed in pain: Counseling the lesbian battering couple. *Women and Therapy* 7(1):81–99.

Levinger, G. 1979. A social psychological perspective on marital dissolution. In G. Levinger and O. C. Moles, eds., *Divorce and Separation*, pp. 37–63. New York: Basic Books.

Levinger, G. 1983. Development and change. In H. H. Kelley, E. Berscheid, A. Christensen, J. H. Harvey, T. L. Huston, G. Levinger, E. McClintock, L. A. Peplau, and D. R. Peterson, *Close Relationships*, pp. 315–59. New York: W. H. Freeman.

Lewin, E. 1981. Lesbianism and motherhood: Implication for child custody. *Human Organization* 40(1):6–14.

Lewin, E., and T. A. Lyons. 1982. Everything in its place: The coexistence of lesbianism and motherhood. In W. Paul, J. D. Weinrich, J. C. Gonsiorek, and M. E. Hotvedt, eds., *Homosexuality: Social, Psychology, and Biological Issues*, pp. 249–74. Beverly Hills, Calif.: Sage.

Lynch, J. M., and M. E. Reilly. 1986. Role relationships: Lesbian perspectives. *Journal of Homosexuality* 12(2):53–69.

McWhirter, D. P., and A. M. Mattison. 1984. *The Male Couple*. Englewood Cliffs, N.J.: Prentice-Hall.

Marecek, J., S. E. Finn, and M. Cardell. 1982. Gender roles in the relationships of lesbians and gay men. *Journal of Homosexuality* 8(2):45–50.

Peplau, L. A., and H. Amaro. 1982. Understanding lesbian relationships. In W. Paul, J. D. Weinrich, J. C. Gonsiorek, and M. E. Hotvedt, eds., *Homosexuality: Social, Psychological, and Biological Issues*, pp. 233–48. Beverly Hills, Calif.: Sage.

Peplau, L. A., and S. D. Cochran. 1980. Sex differences in values concerning love relationships. Paper presented at the annual meeting of the American Psychological Association, Montreal, September.

Peplau, L. A., and S. D. Cochran. Forthcoming. A relationship perspective on homosexuality. In D. P. McWhirter, S. A. Sanders, and J. M. Reinisch, eds., *Homosexuality/Heterosexuality: The Kinsey Scale and Current Research*. New York: Oxford University Press.

Peplau, L. A., S. D. Cochran, and V. M. Mays. 1986. Satisfaction in the intimate relationships of Black lesbians. Paper presented at the annual meeting of the American Psychological Association, Washington, D.C., August.

Peplau, L. A., S. Cochran, K. Rook, and C. Padesky. 1978. Women in love: Attachment and autonomy in lesbian relationships. *Journal of Social Issues* 34(3):7–27.

Peplau, L. A., and S. L. Gordon. 1983. The intimate relationships of lesbians and gay men. In E. R. Allgeier and N. B. McCormick, eds., *The Changing Boundaries: Gender Roles and Sexual Behavior*, pp. 226–44. Palo Alto, Calif.: Mayfield.

Peplau, L. A., C. Padesky, and M. Hamilton. 1982. Satisfaction in lesbian relationships. *Journal of Homosexuality* 8:23–35.

Raphael, S. M., and M. K. Robinson. 1980. The older lesbian: Love relationships and friendship patterns. *Alternative Lifestyles* 3(2):207–30.

Renzetti, C. M. 1988. Violence in lesbian relationships. *Journal of Interpersonal Violence* 3(4):381–99.

Risman, B., and P. Schwartz. 1988. Sociological research on male and female homosexuality. *Annual Review of Sociology* 14:125–47.

Ross, M. W. 1983. Femininity, masculinity, and sexual orientation: Some cross-cultural comparisons. *Journal of Homosexuality* 9(1):27–36.

Roth, S. 1985. Psychotherapy issues with lesbian couples. *Journal of Marital and Family Therapy* 11:273–86.

Rusbult, C. E. 1988. Commitment in close relationships: The investment model. In L. A. Peplau, D. O. Sears, S. E. Taylor, and J. L. Freedman, eds., *Readings in Social Psychology*, 2d ed., pp. 147–57. Englewood Cliffs, N.J.: Prentice-Hall.

Saghir, M. T., and E. Robins. 1973. *Male and Female Homosexuality: A Comprehensive Investigation.* Baltimore: Williams and Wilkins.

Sang, B. 1985. Lesbian relationships: A struggle toward partner equality. In T. Darty and S. Potter, eds., *Women-Identified Women*, pp. 51–66. Palo Alto, Calif.: Mayfield.

Sarason, I. G., H. M. Levine, R. B. Basham, and B. R. Sarason. 1983. Assessing social support: The Social Support Questionnaire. *Journal of Personality and Social Psychology* 44:127–39.

Schafer, S. 1977. Sociosexual behavior in male and female homosexuals: A study in sex differences. *Archives of Sexual Behavior* 6(5):355–64.

Silverstein, C. 1981. *Man to Man: Gay Couples in America.* New York: William Morrow.

Smalley, C. 1987. Dependency issues in lesbian relationships. *Journal of Homosexuality* 14(1–2):125–35.

Spada, J. 1979. *The Spada Report: The Newest Survey of Gay Male Sexuality.* New York: Signet.

Stein, T. S., and C. J. Cohen, eds. 1986. *Contemporary Perspectives on Psychotherapy with Lesbians and Gay Men.* New York: Plenum.

Symons, D. 1979. *The Evolution of Human Sexuality.* New York: Oxford University Press.

Testa, R. J., B. N. Kinder, and G. Ironson. 1987. *Journal of Sex Research* 23:163–72.

Tripp, C. A. 1975. *The Homosexual Matrix.* New York: Signet.

Waterman, C. K., L. J. Dawson, and M. J. Bologna. 1989. Sexual coercion in gay male and lesbian relationships: Predictors and implications for support services. *Journal of Sex Research* 26(1):118–24.

Weinberg, T. S. 1986. Love relationships and drinking among gay men. *Journal of Drug Issues* 16(4):637–48.

Weinrich, J. D. 1987. *Sexual Landscapes.* New York: Scribner's.

Wolf, D. G. 1979. *The Lesbian Community.* Berkeley: University of California Press.

18

Lesbian Mothers:
Psychosocial Assumptions in Family Law

Patricia J. Falk

Discrimination persists in courts' consideration of lesbian mothers' petitions for custody of their children. Courts often have assumed that lesbian women are emotionally unstable or unable to assume a maternal role. They also often have assumed that their children are likely to be emotionally harmed, subject to molestation, impaired in gender role development, or themselves homosexual. None of these assumptions is supported by extant research and theory.

The phrase "lesbian mother" is often viewed as a contradiction in terms (Hitchens 1979–1980; Hitchens and Price 1979).[1] "Until recently the existence of lesbian mothers was almost unrecognized in American society, for most people believe that homosexuality is inconsistent with the ability or desire to procreate" (Riley 1975:799). In the last ten years, however, there has been a dawning appreciation in both the legal and social scientific communities that lesbianism and motherhood are not mutually exclusive categories. According to Basile (1974), "lesbian mothers have always raised children in our society, but this fact has only recently come to the attention of our courts" (p. 3). Basile was referring to the legal system, but this statement has equal applicability to society in general and the social sciences in particular. Lesbian women can become mothers in a number of ways, including adoption, artificial insemination by a known or unknown donor (AID), heterosexual intercourse during marriage, or heterosexual intercourse for the sole purpose of procreation.

Given the nascent recognition of lesbian motherhood, it is not surprising that an accurate appraisal of the number of women who fall into this category is unavailable. The estimates of lesbian mothers who reside with their children are substantial: from 1.5 million (Davies 1979) to 5 million (Rivera 1979).

LEGAL ASSUMPTIONS

In recent years there has been a significant increase in the number of reported cases involving the custody rights of lesbian mothers in divorce or child protection proceedings and in the related scholarly discussion in both law and social science. Many cases involving the rights of lesbian mothers previously have been unpublished. Even when they were reported, courts often eliminated or truncated their discussions concerning the mother's sexual orientation (Basile 1974; Rivera 1979). Thus. one reason for the "increase" of these cases may simply be that the topic is more discussable and therefore that more cases are being reported. Also, with the growth of the gay rights movement, more lesbian women are willing to admit their sexual orientation and fight in court for the custody of their children (Hitchens 1979–1980).

Nonetheless, lesbian mothers, especially those who "admit" their sexual orientation, still have a difficult time obtaining custody of their children (Browne and Giampetro 1985). Commentators (e.g., Davies 1979; Moses and Hawkins 1982; Rand, Graham, and Rawlings 1982) have estimated that a lesbian mother's likelihood of success is no more than 50 percent. Although the general prospects are not encouraging, there appears to be a trend in the direction of granting custody to lesbian mothers (Kraft 1983).

In most jurisdictions, the legal criterion employed in child custody cases is the so-called best interests of the child. This standard is ambiguous and highly subjective, and legal decision makers, therefore, wield a considerable degree of discretion. Some states have attempted to articulate, through legislation, factors bearing on this standard, including parental fitness; grounds for divorce; age, health, and sex of the child; quality of the home environment; mental and physical health of the parents; and preferences of the child and parents (Basile 1974). In this connection, it is important to note that the issue of the morality of homosexuality also appears in many court opinions (Basile 1974; Harris 1977), but because this is not an empirical assumption, it will not be directly addressed in the following discussion.

The major problem encountered by lesbian mothers in child custody cases appears to be the attention paid by legal decision makers to the issue of homosexuality, to the exclusion of their consideration of other factors commonly associated with a determination of the child's best interests (*Harvard Civil Rights and Civil Liberties Law Review* 1984; Hitchens and Price 1979). Once the issue of parental homosexuality is raised, other factors and issues become secondary (Hitchens 1979–1980). Also, courts tend to fashion their decisions based more on their attitudes or stereotypes about gay individuals than the facts in any particular case (*Harvard Civil Rights and Civili Liberties Law Review* 1984; Hitchens and Price 1979).

Legal decision makers often focus on the mother's homosexuality without even attempting to establish a causal relation between the mother's sexual orientation and the child's welfare. Not only should this nexus be made, but it should be substantiated by more than mere supposition (Kraft 1983). When the courts do attempt to articulate a relation between a mother's sexual orientation and her child's development, however, they often rely on general assumptions and not on expert testimony or empirical research findings.

Before examining these assumptions, two caveats are in order. First, I will focus only on the most common and salient psychosocial assumptions. The second caveat is that courts often do not articulate, with any degree of specificity, their assumptions regarding the impact on a child of being raised by a homosexual parent. Instead, the courts couch their decisions in general language about the "harm" of the custody arrangement or environment (*Irish v. Irish* 1981). Thus, the following assumptions are overtly present only when the court seeks to specify the nature of the harm resulting from a lesbian mother's retaining custody of her children. There are two major categories of developmental empirical assumptions that appear in lesbian mother/child custody cases: a) those concerning the lesbian mother and her life-style, and b) those concerning the effect of the lesbian mother and her life-style on the development of the child.

Courts make two general assumptions about lesbian mothers themselves. First, courts often express the belief that all homosexual individuals, including lesbian mothers, are mentally ill (Davies 1979; Mucklow and Phelan 1979; Rand, Graham, and Rawlings 1982; Riley 1975) and therefore supposedly incapable of being good parents. In *Thigpen v. Carpenter* (1987), for example, the court highlighted an expert witness's testimony that the mother had been found to be "emotionally stable," thus implying that this issue is one to be resolved in a case involving a lesbian mother.

Second, it is commonly assumed that lesbian women are less maternal than their heterosexual counterparts and thus are poor mothers (Miller, Jacobsen, and Bigner 1981; Moses and Hawkins 1982; Mucklow and

Phelan 1979). The court in *DiStefano v. DiStefano* (1978) (see also *Bark v. Bark* 1985; *Hall v. Hall* 1980) pointed out that the mother had failed to keep her lesbian relationship separate from her role as a mother and that this failure had a detrimental effect on her children. The underlying assumption was that lesbian women are less maternal because, it is asserted, their chief priority is their relationship with another adult, rather than their children.

Assumptions about the parent-child interaction tend to be more specific than those about lesbian mothers per se. This second set can be further subdivided into two categories: a) those dealing with the child's general health and welfare, and b) those dealing with the child's gender or sexual development. One common assumption falling into the first category is that children raised by lesbian mothers are more likely to develop psychological or mental problems (Golombok, Spencer, and Rutter 1983; see, e.g., *Doe v. Doe* 1981; *In re Jane B.* 1976; *In re Mara* 1956; *S.E.G. v. R.A.G.* 1987).

Courts often assume that these children are more likely to be sexually molested by the custodial parent, her partner, or her acquaintances (Davies 1979; Hall 1978; Harris 1977; Kraft 1983; Miller, Jacobsen, and Bigner 1981; Moses and Hawkins 1982). One example of a court's assumption that a child with a lesbian mother (or gay father) is more likely to be sexually molested was presented by *J.L.P. (H.) v. D.L.P.* (1982). In that case, a gay father had presented expert testimony that child molestation was more common in the heterosexual population than among gay persons. The court was extremely skeptical of all the evidence, but was particularly critical of testimony on the molestation issue: "Every trial judge, or for that matter, every appellate judge, knows that molestation of minor boys by adult males is not as uncommon as the psychological experts' testimony indicated" (*J.L.P. [H.] v. D.J.P.* 1982:869).

With regard to the gender or sexual development of a child of a lesbian mother, courts have made two assumptions. First, judges have stated their belief that the gender role development of the child will be significantly impaired. For example, in *N.K.M. v. L.E.M.* (1980), the court denied a lesbian mother custody of her daughter and supported its decision, in part, by stating that it was concerned that the child would experience sexual disorientation as a result of living with the mother. The same issue arose in *Spence v. Durham* (1973), in which the court expressed fear about the danger that the mother would "instill tendencies toward 'sexual aberrations' in the girls" (p. 551).

The second assumption with respect to gender or sexual development, and perhaps the most uniformly cited assumption, is that the child will be more likely to become homosexual than a child raised by heterosexual parents (for reviews, see Basile 1974; Campbell 1978; Davies 1979; Golombok, Spencer, and Rutter 1983; Green 1978, 1982; Hall 1978; Harris 1977; Hitchens 1979–1980; Hitchens and Price 1979; Kraft 1983; Kirkpatrick, Smith, and Roy 1981; Moses and Hawkins 1982; Riley 1975; Weeks, Derdeyn, and Langmon 1975). Riley (1975) pointed out that this assumption is based on the questionable value judgment that having a child become homosexual is a negative consequence. In this connection, the opinion in *N.K.M. v. L.E.M.* (1980) is also instructive: "Allowing that homosexuality is a permissible life style—an 'alternate life style,' as it is termed these days—if voluntarily chosen, yet who would place a child in a milieu where she may be inclined toward it?" (p. 186). It is noteworthy that several courts either have rejected this assumption outright (see, e.g., *Bezio v. Patenaude* 1980) or have stated that they were unable to determine the accuracy of this assumption (see, e.g., *Jacobson v. Jacobson* 1981). One of the best examples of the former approach is the majority opinion in *Conkel v. Conkel* (1987): "The court takes judicial notice that there is no consensus on what causes homosexuality, but there is substantial consensus among experts that being raised by a homosexual parent does not increase the likelihood that a child will become homosexual" (p. 986).

One final assumption that does not fit neatly into either of the previous categories, but appears to be based on the broader impact of having a lesbian mother, is that children of such mothers are going to be traumatized or stigmatized by society or their peers (Basile 1974; Campbell 1978; Hall 1978; Hitchens 1979–1980; Hitchens and Price 1979; Kraft 1983; Moses and Hawkins 1982). The "stigma" assumption is remarkably common in legal opinions involving lesbian mothers. In *S.E.G. v. R.A.G.* (1987), the court wrote, "We wish to protect the children from peer pressure, teasing, and possible ostracizing they may encounter as a result of the 'alternate life style' their mother has chosen" (p. 166). Similarly, the court in *Thigpen v. Carpenter* (1987) commented that "homosexuality is generally socially unacceptable, and the children would be exposed to ridicule and teasing by other children" (p. 514). The courts in *N.K.M. v. L.E.M.* (1980) and *Jacobson v. Jacobson* (1981) also indicated their concern with possible stigma. In addition to these opinions, at least three cases relied on an article by Lewis (1980), which is discussed in the next section, to support the assumption that discrimination against gay parents may cause the child to be isolated from his or her peers (*Constant A. v. Paul C.A.* 1985; *Dailey v. Dailey* 1981; *S. v. S* 1980). But compare the opinions in *M.A.B. v. R.B.* (1986), *M.P. v. S.P.* (1979), *S.N.E. v. R.L.B.* (1985), and *Doe v. Doe* (1981) in which the courts eschewed the effect of stigma.

SOCIAL SCIENCE RESEARCH

MENTAL HEALTH OF LESBIAN WOMEN

The best studied of the assumptions used to deny lesbian mothers custody is the notion that lesbians are apt to be mentally ill. Harris (1977) summarized the present "state of the art" as follows: "Numerous studies geared specifically to testing the 'lesbian' psyche have found lesbians to have the same or lower incidence of psychiatric disorder than matched heterosexual controls" (p. 85). Armon (1960) found no differences in psychological adjustment between homosexual and heterosexual women. Thompson, McCandles, and Strickland (1971) discovered that gay women are more self-confident, independent, composed, and self-sufficient than their heterosexual counterparts (Harris 1977; Rand, Graham, and Rawlings 1982; Riley 1975) and that lesbian women do not differ in important ways from heterosexuals on measures of defensiveness, personal adjustment, and self-evaluation (Harris 1977). Siegelman (1972) found that lesbian women score higher on tender-mindedness and score lower on depression, submission, and anxiety than heterosexual women.

Rand, Graham, and Rawlings (1982) studied twenty-five lesbian mothers, using interviews, subscales of the California Psychological Inventory (Gough 1957) and the Affectometer (Kamman et al. 1978), and they found that the lesbian mothers were at least as psychologically healthy as the larger standardized sample. Rand, Graham, and Rawlings (1982) also found correlations between psychological health and expression of lesbianism, lending partial support to their hypothesis that mothers who expressed their lesbianism would be psychologically healthier than those who did not.

In comparing lesbian and heterosexual mothers and their children, Green et al. (1986) found that lesbian mothers scored higher on self-confidence, dominance, and exhibition on the Adjective Checklist (Gough and Heilbrun 1965) than their heterosexual counterparts, whereas heterosexual mothers scored higher on abasement and deference. There were no significant differences between the two groups on the Bem Sex-Role Inventory (Bem 1974) and various attitude scales.

Thus, the current research tends to negate the assumption that lesbian women are commonly mentally ill. Furthermore, if courts are truly concerned with the psychological welfare of lesbian mothers, then they should be cognizant of the potentially damaging consequences of placing restrictions on their associational and expressive rights in light of Rand, Graham, and Rawlings's (1982) findings.

Parenting Ability of Lesbian Mothers

Mucklow and Phelan (1979) studied the self-concepts and maternal attitudes of lesbian and heterosexual mothers and found no significant differences between the groups. Although cautious about the generalizability of their findings, Mucklow and Phelan (1979) suggested that lesbian and heterosexual mothers may be more alike than different in their maternal attitudes and self-concepts.

Miller, Jacobsen, and Bigner (1981) found that lesbian mothers were more child-oriented, as opposed to task- or adult-oriented, than their heterosexual counterparts and that lesbian mothers tended to assume a principal role in child-care responsibility. Miller, Jacobsen, and Bigner (1981) concluded that their study tended to negate the stereotype that heterosexual mothers are more child-oriented than lesbian ones.

Kirkpatrick, Smith, and Roy (1981) assessed twenty children and their lesbian mothers and twenty children and their single, heterosexual mothers on a number of measures. Although the main focus of this research was on the children and their development, the authors did interview both sets of mothers and found them to be similar in their maternal interests, life-styles, and child-rearing practices.

Finally, Moses and Hawkins (1982), writing about an unpublished study by Riddle, suggested that homosexual individuals make as good parents as heterosexuals and that they must be highly motivated. Riddle commented, "Sexual orientation has little to do with whether or not one wants to be a parent, but it has a lot to do with motivation because of the high costs of being a gay parent at this time" (quoted in Moses and Hawkins 1982:200).[2]

In summary, the research on the maternal attitudes and caregiving behaviors of lesbian mothers indicates either that there are no substantial differences between this group and their heterosexual counterparts or that lesbian mothers may actually be more child-oriented than heterosexual mothers. Thus, no research to date has substantiated courts' assumptions that lesbian women make poor mothers or that a gay sexual orientation weakens or undermines a woman's parenting ability.

MENTAL HEALTH OF CHILDREN RAISED BY LESBIAN MOTHERS

The only systematic empirical study of the mental or psychological health of children reared by lesbian mothers was conducted by Golombok, Spencer, and Rutter (1983), who compared twenty-seven lesbian and twenty-seven heterosexual families. Using various questionnaires to assess the children's emotions, behavior, and relationships, the researchers found no significant differences in psychological health between the two groups of children. Additionally, Golombok, Spencer, and Rutter used interviews with the mothers to determine the presence of psychiatric problems in their children, but found that only a small minority of the children had significant psychiatric problems. Notably, the proportion was substantially greater in the heterosexual single-parent group than in the lesbian group. More children in the heterosexual group had been referred for psychiatric care than in the homosexual group. Golombok, Spencer, and Roy concluded that the majority of comparisons "failed to show any differences between the groups of children in their rates of difficulties with emotions, relationships, or behaviour" (p. 510).

Although Golombok, Spencer, and Rutter's (1983) work is the only extant systematic study in this area, some clinical reports are also available. Lewis (1980) interviewed twenty-one children from eight families with lesbian mothers and found that families with teenagers appeared to have the most adjustment problems. In a few of these families, children exhibited gross maladaptive behavior at the time of the mother's disclosure of her lesbianism. The youngest child in the family seemed least able to deal with his or her ambivalence toward the mother. Lewis also found that the children believed that the breakup of their parents' marriage was more traumatic than learning of their mother's sexual orientation. According to Lewis, it was virtually impossible to segregate the impact of the mother's homosexuality from the effect of the parents' divorce.

Reporting on two cases of children of gay parents, Weeks, Derdeyn, and Langmon (1975) found some evidence of sexual and emotional difficulties but cautioned that it was difficult to distinguish specific problem areas that were directly related to parental homosexuality. In particular, Weeks and colleagues noted that the children in their study had problems common to children of divorced parents.

Summarizing these tentative results, no evidence exists for a direct relationship between a mother's sexual orientation and the mental health of her offspring. Other factors, such as marital discord and divorce, appear to be more highly correlated with a child's psychological adjustment than does the mother's sexual orientation.

Sexual Molestation of Children
Raised by Lesbian Mothers

Given the difficulty of gathering accurate information on the incidence of sexual molestation, it is hardly surprising to discover a dearth of data on its rate of occurrence in lesbian versus heterosexual households. Several authors have attempted to rebut the assumption of increased incidence of child molestation in lesbian mother households by pointing out that sexual molestation in the United States is "essentially a heterosexual male act" (Riley 1975:862). Similarly, Hall (1978) wrote, "This fear persists in spite of the high incidence of heterosexual assaults involving underage females and the absence in court records of any such incidents between lesbians and minor female children" (p. 383). Finally, Riley (1975:858, n. 370) provided this quote from a letter by psychologist John Money to the defendant in one lesbian mother child custody case:

> In the worst cases of the battered-child syndrome I have encountered the criminal neglect, assault and injury of the child has been perpetrated by a heterosexual mother and/or father. By contrast, some of the most tender devotion and care of sick and ailing children I have seen has been performed by a mother or father with an active homosexual history.

Briefly, then, there is no evidence either that homosexual parents are more likely to seduce or allow their children to be seduced than their heterosexual counterparts or that lesbian mothers or their acquaintances molest children more often than do heterosexual individuals. Research on the point is scant, however.

Gender Role Development of Children
Raised by Lesbian Mothers

Unlike some of the assumptions discussed above, there have been several empirical studies of the effects of lesbian mothers on their children's gender role development. In a comparison of lesbian and heterosexual families using a number of measures, including structured interviews and questionnaires, Golombok, Spencer, and Rutter (1983) found no evidence of inappropriate gender identity in any of the children and showed that the sexes were clearly differentiated on sex-typed behavior scales. There were no differences between children reared in lesbian households and those in heterosexual households with respect to gender identity, sex role behavior, or sexual orientation. The authors noted, however, that almost all the children with lesbian mothers had been in heterosexual households for at least two years and that this history may have been significant because gender identity and sex role behavior may be established early in preschool days. Thus, these researchers concluded that their findings may not be generalizable to lesbian families in which the mother adopted or conceived by artificial insemination by a known or unknown donor (AID) and in which, therefore, no man was present.

Green et al. (1986), in their study of households with lesbian and heterosexual mothers, found no significant differences between the two groups of children on various personality measures. When the mothers were questioned about "cross-dressing" in their children, there were no differences between the boys, but daughters of lesbian women tended to cross-dress more frequently.

Hoeffer (1981) studied forty matched lesbian and heterosexual mothers and their children. She discovered no significant differences between the two groups of children on measures of gender role behavior, including choice of toys. Lesbian mothers preferred a more nearly equal mixture of sex-typed masculine and feminine toys than did the heterosexual mothers, although both groups were more likely to encourage play with neutral toys than sex-typed ones. Hoeffer noted that the mothers' influence on their children's gender role behavior was limited to the extent that they were involved in their children's play activities and that the children's choices were influenced by models other than their mothers, notably peers.

Kirkpatrick, Smith, and Roy (1981) found no significant differences in gender role development between the children raised by lesbian mothers and those raised by unmarried heterosexual mothers. One interesting finding of this study was that children giving answers suggestive of gender problems were more likely to share a history of some physical difficulty in early life than to have in common mothers with a particular sexual orientation.

Kweskin and Cook (1982) compared lesbian and heterosexual women on their self-described gender role behaviors and their ratings of ideal gender role behavior in children and found that there was a significant relationship between the two measures, such that the mother's own classifications were better indicators of the ideal child's ratings than was the mother's sexual orientation or the child's gender. In this sense, the authors suggested that sexual orientation may not be a meaningful research variable.

Finally, in an unpublished study reported in Moses and Hawkins (1982:185) and Nungesser (1980), Ostrow (1977) found that the sexual preference of the parent had no direct effect on the children's play choices.

The results do indicate that regardless of the parents' sexuality, some of the play choices conformed to traditional patterns of sex-typing and some did not. . . . These findings are not surprising since a majority of the parents are committed to nonsexist child-rearing. The children are still influenced to a great degree, however, by television, peers, teachers, and relatives. This would explain their conformity to societal standards of behavior considered appropriate for boys and girls.

Thus, taking even the most conservative view of this relatively well-developed area of research, it is apparent that lesbian mothers do not exert a detrimental influence on their children's gender role development. As Ostrow and others noted, this finding is understandable given the diversity of influences on a child, only one of which is his or her mother.

Sexual Orientation of Children Raised by Lesbian Mothers

One of the most widely used assumptions in child custody cases involving a lesbian mother is that children brought up by a homosexual parent will also become gay, what Riley (1975) has called the "universal latency fear." It is hardly surprising that this assumption is so common considering the homophobic attitudes that many legal decision makers exhibit toward lesbian mothers (Goldyn 1981). Judges often consider the possibility of a child's becoming homosexual to be one of the most undesirable and perhaps even "tragic" outcomes of awarding custody to lesbian mothers.

Surprisingly, little research has been done in this area. Perhaps the best-known study was conducted by Green (1978), who interviewed children being raised by lesbian and by transsexual parents to determine their sexual identity. For the younger children, Green used toy and game preference, peer group composition, clothing preference, roles in fantasy games, vocational aspiration, and the Draw-a-Person Test. The adolescents' sexual identity was assessed by obtaining information on the child's romantic crushes, erotic fantasies, and interpersonal sexual behavior. Green found that psychosexual development appeared to be typical or normal in thirty-six of the thirty-seven studied children. In explaining this result, Green pointed out that children do not live in a universe composed entirely of the home environment but are also influenced by television, reading, school, and nonschool recreation with peers and their families. Green tentatively concluded that children raised by transsexual or homosexual parents do not differ appreciably from children raised in heterosexual families in terms of sexual identity.

In a later article, Green (1982) reported on the results of interviews with twenty-one children who had been raised in households with lesbian mothers for about three-and-a-half years. Of the older children, five reported sexual experiences, and all were heterosexual. Green also found that none of the children was experiencing sexual identity conflict.

Golombok, Spencer, and Rutter (1983) found, vis-à-vis the sexual orientation of the prepubertal children in their sample, that there were no significant differences between the children of heterosexual women and those of lesbian women in patterns of childhood friendships. All the children tended to have predominantly same-sex friends. These authors also investigated the sexual orientation of pubertal and postpubertal adolescents in lesbian households and heterosexual mother households by asking them about romantic crushes and friendships. They found that there was no difference between the two groups of children in terms of sexual orientation and that the patterns were typical for the age groups.

In short, research on the sexual orientation of children of lesbian mothers does not confirm the "contagion" assumption inherent in so many court decisions. This finding is consistent with the research literature on the etiology of homosexuality; researchers have been unable to identify one family pattern associated with the development of a homosexual orientation.

SOCIAL STIGMA

Unlike the six assumptions examined so far, the assumption that children reared in lesbian households will be harmed by the stigma associated with homosexuality is not based on the quality of the mother's parenting ability or the parent-child interaction but instead derives from an external societal source. Because stigma is a societal byproduct, it is not in the mother's or child's ability to change. Nonetheless, courts have frequently based denial of custody on the possibility of stigma, even when they have recognized that a lesbian mother can hardly be expected to eliminate societal homophobia singlehandedly (Kraft 1983).

Some commentators (e.g., Basile 1974) have argued that the use of the stigma assumption in child custody cases involving a lesbian mother is a denial of equal protection, because courts have refused to consider the impact of stigma in interracial custody disputes, and lesbian mothers merit the same consideration. As Moses and Hawkins noted:

> We must certainly expect that the children of gay parents will have to cope with prejudice, misunderstanding, and possibly even negative peer reac-

tions. But then, so may the children of Black parents, poor Appalachian parents, divorced parents, and parents with physical impairments such as blindness, deafness, or paraplegia. The fact that a child's parents are different from the majority of White middle-class unimpaired parents is not usually considered an appropriate reason for removing a child from the home. We see no reason why sexual preference should be any different in this respect, unless it can be shown that there is some clear and consistent impairment because of this. (1982:200)

Assuming for argument that the stigma assumption does have relevance, or legal merit, in child custody cases involving a lesbian mother, it is unfortunate that little research has been undertaken on this issue. In Lewis's (1980) interviews with children of lesbian mothers, she found that the younger children focused on the need for secrecy, felt a sense of separation or "differentness" from their peers, and feared being ostracized by them. Lewis, however, also found:

Almost without exception, the children were proud of their mother for challenging society's rules and for standing up for what she believed. Problems between the mother and children seemed secondary to the children's respect for the difficult steps she had taken. (1980:203)

Using interviews of both children and mothers in lesbian and heterosexual households, Green et al. (1986) found that there were no differences between the two groups of children in terms of peer group relationships, popularity, and social adjustment.

Nungesser (1980), reporting on the results of Bryant's (1975) unpublished study of lesbian mothers, stated that the majority of the children were not conscious of society's negative attitude toward their mothers. Those who were aware tended to resemble the children in Lewis's (1980) study:

In some cases, children are embarrassed for their friends or the general public to know their mother is a lesbian, but the majority of children combine any embarrassment or initial uncomfortableness with an understanding that society has created the prejudice; that it is society, and not their mothers that should re-examine its position. (Bryant 1975:73A [in Nungesser 1980:184])

A few authors have approached the question of stigma from a more theoretical perspective. Some have maintained that the possible stigma associated with being reared in a lesbian household may have its compensations. Kraft (1983) noted that in one court's view, "a child who struggles with societal disapproval may be better equipped in adulthood to form independent moral convictions" (p. 184). Miller, Jacobsen, and Bigner (1981) suggested that lesbian mothers may compensate for the potential stigma their children may suffer by being more child-oriented than are single heterosexual mothers. Thus, stigmatization may be offset in some cases by lesbian mothers who recognize its occurrence and make efforts to counteract its influence. Riley (1975) attempted to deflate the importance of the stigma assumption by pointing out that lesbian women's index of recognition is low and therefore the stigma problem may never surface in any particular case. Regardless, when courts focus on the supposed stigma encountered by children of lesbian women, they merely perpetuate the very stigma that they find detrimental (Kraft 1983).

In summary, although some evidence suggests that children of lesbian mothers may be affected by social stigma, the available research and theory also indicate that legal decision makers may be overemphasizing the severity, and even perpetuating the effect, of this stigma.

CONCLUSION

Given the scarcity of research on lesbian mothers and their children and the methodological problems inherent in such work, conclusions are necessarily tentative. Nonetheless, it is important to note that no research has identified significant differences between lesbian mothers and their heterosexual counterparts or the children raised by these groups. Researchers have been unable to establish empirically that detriment results to children from being raised by lesbian mothers.

There continues to be an urgent need for further research in this area. Such research would permit legal decision makers to make better or more informed choices with regard to awarding custody. The major implication for legal decision makers appears to be that many of the assumptions on which they have traditionally based their opinions cannot be supported by the extant empirical and theoretical literature. Debunking these myths may leave judges in an uncomfortable posture. The majority of researchers recommend that legal decision makers should focus less or not at all on the sexual orientation of a potential custodian and more on the quality of the relationship between the parent and the child (Golombok, Spencer, and Rutter 1983; Green 1982; Lewis 1980; Rivera 1979). Basile (1974) commented, "The best interests of the child lay with a loving parent, not with a heterosexual parent or a homosexual parent" (p. 18).

ACKNOWLEDGMENT

The author wishes to thank Gary Melton for his editorial assistance.

NOTES

1. The following analysis will focus primarily on lesbian mothers and not the larger homosexual parent population. This decision was made for two reasons. First, the majority of child custody cases that are reported involve lesbian mothers rather than gay men. The majority of cases involving gay men concern visitation rights and raise related but different issues (Hitchens 1979–1980). Second, although some recent research has focused on gay fathers (Bozett 1981; Robinson and Skeen 1982; Skeen and Robinson 1984), the general dearth of empirical and theoretical literature on this group made inquiry in this area quite difficult.

2. Riddle, as discussed in Moses and Hawkins (1982), also pointed out that the cities of Chicago, New York, and San Francisco have employed gay homes as foster homes for several years without deleterious consequences.

REFERENCES

Armon, V. 1960. Some personality factors in overt female homosexuality. *Journal of Projective Techniques* 26:292–309.

Bark v. Bark, 479 So.2d 42 (Ala. Civ. App. 1985).

Basile, R. A. 1974. Lesbian mothers I. *Women's Law Reporter* 2(2):3–18.

Bem, S. 1974. The measurement of psychological androgyny. *Journal of Consulting and Clinical Psychology* 42:155–62.

Bezio v. Patenaude, 381 Mass. 563, 410 N.E.2d 1207 (1980).

Bozett, F. W. 1981. Gay fathers: Evolution of the gay-father identity. *American Journal of Orthopsychiatry* 51:552–59.

Browne, M. N., and A. Giampetro. 1985. The contribution of social science data to the adjudication of child custody disputes. *Capital University Law Review* 15:43–58.

Bryant, B. S. 1975. Lesbian mothers. Master's thesis, California State University, Sacramento.

Burdens on gay litigants and bias in the court system: Homosexual panic, child custody, and anonymous parties [Note]. 1984. *Harvard Civil Rights and Civil Liberties Law Review* 19:497–559.

Campbell, R. W. 1978. Child custody when one parent is a homosexual. *Judges' Journal* 7:38–41, 51–52.

Conkel v. Conkel, 31 Ohio App. 3d 169, 509 N.E.2d 983 (1987).

Constant A. v. Paul C. A., 334 Pa. Super. 49, 496 A.2d 1 (1985).

Dailey v. Dailey, 635 S.W.2d 391 (Tenn. App. 1981).

Davies, R. C. 1979. Representing the lesbian mother. *Family Advocate* 1(3):21–23, 36.

DiStefano v. DiStefano, 60 A.D.2d 976, 401 N.Y.S.2d 636 (1978).

Doe v. Doe, 222 Va. 736, 284 S.E.2d 799 (1981).

Goldyn, L. 1981. Gratuitous language in appellate cases involving gay people: "Queer baiting" from the bench. *Political Behavior* 3:31–48.

Golombok, S., A. Spencer, and M. Rutter. 1983. Children in lesbian and single-parent households: Psychosexual and psychiatric appraisal. *Journal of Child Psychology and Psychiatry* 24:551–72.

Gough, H. G. 1957. *California Psychological Inventory*. Palo Alto, Calif.: Consulting Psychologists Press.

Gough, H. G., and A. Heilbrun. 1965. *The Adjective Checklist*. Palo Alto, Calif.: Consulting Psychologists Press.

Green, R. 1978. Sexual identity of 37 children raised by homosexual and transsexual parents. *American Journal of Psychiatry* 135:692–97.

Green, R. 1982. The best interests of the child with a lesbian mother. *Bulletin of the American Academy of Psychiatry and the Law* 10:715.

Green, R., J. B. Mandel, M. E. Hotvedt, J. Gray, and L. Smith. 1986. Lesbian mothers and their children: A comparison with solo parent heterosexual mothers and their children. *Archives of Sexual Behavior* 15:167–84.

Hall v. Hall, 95 Mich. App. 614,291 N.W.2d 143 (1980).

Hall, M. 1978. Lesbian families: Cultural and clinical issues. *Social Work* 23:380–85.

Harris, B. S. 1977. Lesbian mother child custody: Legal and psychiatric aspects. *Bulletin of the American Academy of Psychiatry and the Law* 5:75–89.

Hitchens, D. 1979–1980. Social attitudes, legal standards and personal trauma in child custody cases. *Journal of Homosexuality* 5(1/2):89–95.

Hitchens, D., and B. Price. 1979. Trial strategy in lesbian mother custody cases: The use of expert testimony. *Golden Gate University Law Review*, 451–479.

Hoeffer, B. 1981. Children's acquisition of sex-role behavior in lesbian-mother families. *American Journal of Orthopsychiatry* 51:536–44.

In re Jane B., 85 Misc. 2d 515, 380 N.Y.S.2d 848 (N.Y. Sup. Ct. 1976).

In re Mara, 3 Misc. 2d 174, 150 N.Y.S.2d 524 (N.Y. Fam. Ct. 1956).

Irish v. Irish, 102 Mich. App. 75, 300 N.W.2d 739 (1980).

J.L.P. (H.) v. D.L.P., 643 S.W.2d 865 (Mo. App. 1982).

Jacobson v. Jacobson, 314 N.W.2d 78 (N.D. 1981).

Kamman, R., D. Christie, R. Irwin, and G. Dixon. 1978. *The Affectometer: An Inventory of Subjective Well-Being*. Punedin, New Zealand: University of Ontago.

Kirkpatrick, M., C. Smith, and R. Roy. 1981. Lesbian mothers and their children: A comparative survey. *American Journal of Orthopsychiatry* 51:545–51.

Kraft, P. 1983. Recent developments: Lesbian child custody. *Harvard Women's Law Journal* 6:183–92.

Kweskin, S. L., and A. S. Cook. 1982. Heterosexual and homosexual mothers' self-described sex-role behavior and ideal sex-role behavior in children. *Sex Roles* 8:967–75.

Lewis, K. G. 1980. Children of lesbians: Their point of view. *Social Work* 25:198–203.

M.A.B. v. R.B., 134 Misc. 2d 317, 510 N.Y.S.2d 960 (N.Y. Sup. Ct. 1986).

M.P. v. S.P., 169 N.J. Super. 425, 404 A.2d 1256 (1979).

Miller, J. A., R. B. Jacobsen, and J. J. Bigner. 1981. The child's home environment for lesbian v. heterosexual mothers: A neglected area of research. *Journal of Homosexuality* 7(1):49–56.

Moses, A. E., and R. O. Hawkins, Jr. 1982. *Counseling Lesbian Women and Gay Men: A Life-Issues Approach.* St. Louis: C. V. Mosby.

Mucklow, B. M., and G. K. Phelan. 1979. Lesbian and traditional mothers' responses to adult response to child behavior and self-concept. *Psychological Reports* 44:880–82.

N.K.M. v. L.E.M., 606 S.W.2d 179 (Mo. App. 1980).

Nungesser, L. G. 1980. Theoretical bases for research on the acquisition of social sex-roles by children of lesbian mothers. *Journal of Homosexuality* 5(3):177–87.

Ostrow, D. 1977. Gay and straight parents: What about the children? Bachelor's thesis, Hampshire College, Amherst, Mass.

Rand, C., D. L. R. Graham, and E. I. Rawlings. 1982. Psychological health and factors the court seeks to control in lesbian mother custody trials. *Journal of Homosexuality* 8(1):27–39.

Riley, M. 1975. The avowed lesbian mother and her right to child custody: A constitutional challenge that can no longer be denied. *San Diego Law Review* 12:799–864.

Rivera, R. R. 1979. Our straight-laced judges: The legal position of homosexual persons in the United States. *Hastings Law Journal* 30:799–955.

Robinson, B. E., and P. Skeen. 1982. Sex-role orientation of gay fathers versus gay nonfathers. *Perceptual and Motor Skills* 55:1055–59.

S. v. S., 608 S.W.2d 64 (Ky. App. 1980), *cert. denied,* 451 U.S. 911, *reh'g denied,* 452 U.S. 910 (1982).

S.E.G. v. R.A.G., 735 S.W.2d 164 (Mo. Ap. 1987).

Siegelman, M. 1972. Adjustment of homosexual and heterosexual women. *American Journal of Psychiatry* 120:477–81.

Skeen, P., and B. E. Robinson. 1984. Family backgrounds of gay fathers: A descriptive study. *Psychological Reports* 54:999–1005.

S.N.E. v. R.L.B., 699 P.2d 875 (Alaska 1985).

Spence v. Durham, 16 N.C. App. 372, 191 S.E.2d 908 (1972), *rev'd,* 283 N.C. 671, 198 S.E.2d 537 (1973), *cert. denied,* 415 U.S. 918 (1974).

Thigpen v. Carpenter, 21 Ark. App. 194, 730 S.W.2d 510 (1987).

Thompson, N., B. McCandless, and B. Strickland. 1971. Personal adjustment of male and female homosexuals and heterosexuals. *Journal of Abnormal Psychology* 78:237–40.

Weeks, R. B., A. P. Derdeyn, and M. Langmon. 1975. Two cases of children of homosexuals. *Child Psychiatry and Human Development* 6:26–32.

19

Gay Fathers:
A Review of the Literature

Frederick W. Bozett

This article reviews the research literature on gay fathers, and includes brief historical perspectives and statistical data. The major portion of the article compares studies of gay fathers with other groups, such as lesbian mothers and nongay fathers. Because the literature is sparse, and the research has severe limitations such as small sample size, few definitive statements about these men can be made with certainty. Even so, tentative generalizations are proposed. The article concludes with suggestions for future research.

The study of both homosexuality and fatherhood has increased dramatically in the recent past. As the viability of gay life-styles has become more widely accepted, many divorced men and women with and without children have entered the gay community rather than the world of the formerly married (Hunt and Hunt 1977). There has also been a heightened interest in the expressive function of men, with the role of father garnering the most attention (Benson 1968; Hanson and Bozett 1985; Lamb 1981; Lynn 1974, 1979; Pederson 1980). The study of gay men who are also fathers is a logical outgrowth of the studies of homosexuality and fatherhood. The purpose of this article is to review the research that has been reported on gay fathers. Limitations of the studies will be mentioned, and directions for further research will be provided.

GAY FATHERS: HISTORICAL AND
STATISTICAL PERSPECTIVES

Although the term *gay father* may seem antithetical, it is likely that gay men have married and fathered children since ancient times. Psychoanalytic, pathologically oriented reports of married gay men appeared in the

1950s and 1960s (Allen 1957; Bieber et al. 1962; Bieber 1969; Imielinski 1969). Anecdotal, more accepting reports began to emerge in the 1970s (Brown 1976; Clark 1977; Mager 1975; Shilts 1975). The first sociological study, and one of major importance, was reported by Miller (1978, 1979b). Since then, several additional studies have added to the knowledge base on gay fathers.

Although accurate statistics on most aspects of homosexuality are impossible to obtain, estimates of the number of gay fathers can be made. It is generally accepted that 10 percent of the United States population is homosexual (Churchill 1971; Kingdon 1979; Kinsey, Pomeroy, and Martin 1948). Based on a total population of 230 million in 1983 (U.S. Bureau of the Census), that means there are about 23 million gays in the United States. Also, about 20 percent, or 4.6 million of the gay male population has been married at least once (Bell and Weinberg 1978; Jay and Young 1979; Spada 1979). Furthermore, it is estimated that 25 percent to 50 percent, or from 1. 1 to 2.3 million gay men, are natural fathers (Bell and Weinberg 1978; Miller 1979a). The actual number of gay fathers is likely higher than these figures suggest because they do not take into account gay men who have married more than once, who have adopted children, or who are unwed. The number of children of gay fathers is unknown, but combined estimates of the children of gay men and lesbians range from 6 million (Schulenburg 1985) to 14 million (Peterson 1984).

REVIEW OF THE RESEARCH

Although the study of fathers/fatherhood/fathering has increased in the recent past, the research literature on gay fathers remains sparse. The purpose of the following section is to synopsize the research to date. It would be ideal if the studies could be synthesized with an emphasis on their common themes or variables. Because the few studies available are divergent in their purpose, sampling, and methodologies, however, this is impossible. Thus, a logical grouping of the studies is made according to whether or not comparison groups were employed. This, then, is the organization that will be followed in this review.

RESEARCH IN WHICH GAY FATHERS WERE THE SOLE FOCUS OF STUDY: NO COMPARISON GROUP

Two major studies (Bozett 1979, 1980, 1981a, b, 1984, 1985, 1986, 1987, 1988; Miller 1978, 1979a, b, 1983, 1986) and one less major report constitute the research in this category. The research by both Bozett and

Miller were qualitative sociological studies. Data were collected by tape recorded interviews lasting from two to five hours each. Sample size ranged from eighteen to fifty. Both researchers claimed to have achieved saturation of the categories generated from the interviews, implying that sample sizes were adequate because additional interviews would not have generated new data. According to Glaser and Strauss (1967), interviews that exceed twenty-five respondents provide only variation on themes that have already been discovered. The method Bozett used was grounded theory (Glazer and Strauss 1967), which is an inductive, hypothesis-seeking strategy that has as its purpose to generate and suggest, but not test, properties and hypotheses about a general phenomenon. Miller used life history depth interviews utilizing phase analysis (Lofland 1971) within the social construction of reality framework (Berger and Luckmann 1966). Both researchers were interested in discovering how men who are both gay and husband/father resolve these apparently conflicting and contradictory statuses or identities.

Bozett derived the theory of "integrative sanctioning" to explain the career of the gay father. By participating over time in both the father world and the gay world, the gay father progresses from being attached primarily to the heterosexual world to a primary connection with the gay world. This progression is achieved by means of disclosing his gay identity to nongays and his father identity to gays and receiving mostly positive sanctions, which have an integrative effect. Others' approbations of both identities are introjected into the self as positive, which have the effect of certifying and confirming the two identities of gay and father as compatible and acceptable. Bozett's research was process-oriented. It described the gay fathers' objective, public career from before and during marriage, achieving fatherhood, through separation and (usually) divorce to the development of a gay life-style.

Paralleling the objective, public career path, the more subjective private career of identity redefinition from heterosexuality to homosexuality is emphasized. Included is an exploration of disclosures and sanctions of the gay identity to various categories of nongays, such as wife and children. Equally important is the disclosure of the father identity to gays and their sanctioning, and how the effects of nongays' and gays' responses (sanctions) lead the father to achieve integration. Integration is defined as a state in which the gay and father identities are congruent, and are appropriately overtly manifested; both identities are accepted by both the father himself and others in his proximate social world as nondichotomous. Integration is complete, partial, or absent depending on whether the father accepts his homosexuality, to whom he discloses it, and how central each identity is to him.

Miller organized his data along a four-point continuum to show the typical steps in gay fathers' normal careers: covert behavior, marginal involvement, transformed participation, and open endorsement. The continuum is an ideal-type model, an abstraction of the phenomenon created by emphasizing only the key characteristics in the sequential development of gay fathers' status passage.

Respondents at the covert behavior point on the continuum engage in furtive sex with other men, but tend to think of this action as nothing more than a genital urge. These men have unstable self-concepts, one day thinking they are homosexual and another day thinking they are not. They operate on the periphery of the gay world trying to compartmentalize gay activities from their family life. During marital coitus, they often fantasize about male erotica. They want to view their marriages as "duties" and do not perceive viable alternative life-styles. Children are another important reason why these men remain married.

Respondents at the marginal involvement point on the continuum engage in same-sex sexual behavior, and their self-identity, but not their public identity, is homosexual. Compared with men earlier on the continuum, marginally involved respondents have an expanded repertoire of gay sexual outlets. Because they are known about by some suspecting audiences, these men often resemble, as one man said, "a crazy quilt of contradictions." Playing the role of the eccentric, engaging in word games of mixed messages, provides a smokescreen for their emotional whereabouts from both gays and nongays. These men are ideologically ambivalent about the gay world, sometimes viewing it as exotic and other times discounting it entirely. Similarly, they have ambivalent commitment to their marriages, occasionally entertaining ideas of divorce. They stay married fearing permanent separation from their children, wanting to avoid stigma, perceiving a lack of viable alternative life-styles, and unwilling to endure the decreased standard of living necessitated by divorce.

Respondents at the transformed participation point on the continuum engage in homosexual behavior and have self-identities, and to a limited extent, public identities that reflect acceptance of the validity of their behavior. These men have disclosed to their (ex)wives and parents, but not to their children or employers. Their gay involvement is social and emotional, as well as sexual. This acculturation into the gay world involves four areas of concern: a) disadvantages of advanced age or late arrival on the scene, or both; b) the necessity of learning new gay social definitions and skills; c) the need to reconcile prior fantasies to the realities of the gay world; and d) balancing and compartmentalizing their gay and father roles.

Respondents at the open endorsement point on the continuum not only engage in homosexual behavior and have public and self-identities reflective of the behavior, but also openly champion the gay community. Initially, there is a political and social tendency toward gay separatism, but, over time, the respondents integrate their gay and nongay worlds; homosexuality is blended into their everyday lives. Many of these men have custody of their children, who know their father is gay. Their non-work activities often revolve around their lover, the children, and a network of friends and organizations, rather than gay commercial establishments.

Miller identified several caveats regarding the moral career continuum. For example, the continuum should not be construed as verifying transient states into types. Additionally, movement out of marriage into an openly gay identity is not unilateral. There are many negotiations back and forth, in and out of the closet. "Doing" and "being" gay involve complex processes with numerous gradations resulting in the blurring of lines between continuum points. There is not a finite number of stages, not every gay father becomes publicly gay, and not everyone passes through every step. Consequently, it is more accurate to talk about career paths, or sets of careers, rather than a single path. Additionally, it is important to stress that few respondents move easily or accidentally from step to step in this career sequence. Rather, each level is achieved by a painful searching process, negotiating with both the self and the larger world.

From his data, Miller drew these conclusions:

1. The event most responsible for initiating movement along the continuum and reconstructing gay fathers' perceptions of the gay community is the experience of falling in love with another man.
2. Factors hindering movement along the continuum include an inability to perceive the gay world as a viable alternative, as well as perceived lack of support from other gays, economic difficulty, family pressure, poor health, wives' dependence, homophobia in respondents or community, and religious/moral scruples.
3. Highly compartmentalized life-styles, gay celibacy, or deceit sometimes repress open marital conflict, but unresolved tension characterizes gay fathers' marriages. In contrast, men who leave their spouses and enter the gay world report gay relationships to be more harmonious than marital relationships.

4. Respondents report gayness to be compatible with fathering and that the salience of fathering increases once having left their marriages.

5. Men who come out perceive less discrimination from family, friends, and coworkers than those who are closeted anticipate. Wives tend to be upset by their husbands' revelations; the respondents are typically surprised by the positive reactions of their children and their parents.

6. Daughters tend to be more accepting than sons, although most children feel their fathers' honesty brings them closer together.

7. There were few reported instances of neighborhood homophobia directed against gay fathers' children, possibly because the children tried to disclose only to people they knew would react favorably.

8. There was no indication that the children of gay fathers are disproportionately homosexual themselves although, of the children who turned out to be gay, there were more lesbian daughters than gay sons.

9. In spite of the increased public stigma, gay fathers achieved a sense of psychological well-being as their stigmatized careers progressed. This is largely due to their becoming integrated within a supportive gay community that helps reduce cognitive dissonance and neutralizes stigma. Well-being is seen in gay fathers being less anxious, depressed, and guilty about their sexuality, in a reduction of stress-related conditions (ulcers, substance abuse, and sleeping and eating disorders), in a stabilization of their self-concept, and in increased congruence between their public and self-identities. In sum, the research of Bozett and Miller are complementary and help to explain the evolution of the gay father identity, or what Miller (1978) referred to as adult sexual resocialization.

The third and last research study discussed in this section is by Skeen and Robinson (1984), who described the family backgrounds of gay fathers. They conducted a nationwide study by questionnaire of subjects from the Catholic gay fellowship Dignity. From their total sample of 285 respondents (a 55 percent response rate), thirty subjects had fathered one or more children. The principal section of the questionnaire measured respondents' perceptions of mothers' and fathers' acceptance of their homosexuality, description of relationships with parents, parents' expectations, and family atmosphere during childhood. The authors reported that the profile of early family backgrounds of the gay fathers in their study was generally positive. Most subjects were reared in intact homes where heterosexual relationships were role modeled, and unusual amounts of marital discord were not common. Maternal and paternal relationships were described more as adequate and positive than inadequate and negative, although relationships with mothers were perceived to be slightly better than with fathers. Most subjects believed that their parents perceived them as worthy individuals, although fathers somewhat less so than mothers. The respondents valued stability of family relationships, even though all were divorced from their wives in favor of homosexual relationships. Both their children and lovers were valued and were listed as important to their lives.

STUDIES OF GAY FATHERS IN RELATION TO A COMPARISON GROUP

Gay Fathers and Lesbian Mothers Compared. Two studies (Turner, Scadden, and Harris 1985; Wyers 1984) are in this category (see table 19.1).[1] The purpose of these studies was to identify similarities and differences between the marital and parental behaviors of lesbian mothers and gay fathers as spouses and parents. Both studies utilized face-to-face structured interviews; the Wyers study employed a pretested questionnaire. The respondents in the study by Turner, Scadden, and Harris numbered ten gay fathers and eleven lesbian mothers, and, in the Wyers study, thirty-two men and thirty-four women. All respondents in both studies were Caucasian except for three Black lesbians. Mean ages of fathers was 37 and 40.1, and for mothers was 35 and 35.5. In the Turner, Scadden, and Harris study, the average income for fathers was $24,500, and for mothers $13,500. In the Wyers report it was $29,962 for fathers, and $13,602 for mothers. Also, the men had more education than the women had.

Wyers (1984) reported that ten (31.3 percent) of the men and twenty-five (73.5 percent) of the women in his study were unaware of their homosexuality when they married. This is an interesting finding because most men come out at eighteen years of age (Dank 1971; Harry and Devall 1978; Saghir and Robins 1973), and lesbians do so in their early twenties (Schafer 1977; Saghir and Robins 1973). In both studies, the majority of respondents had been married only once; four women and two men had married more than one time. Length of marriage for the fathers was three to twenty-two years, and for mothers from one to twenty-two years. The

TABLE 19.1

A Comparison of Selected Variables from the Turner, Scadden, and Harris (1985) and Wyers (1984) Studies

Variables	Study	Gay Fathers	Lesbian Mothers
Number	Turner et al.	10	11
	Wyers	32	34
Mean age	T	37	35
	W	40.1	35.5
Mean income	T	$24,500	$13,500
	W	$25,962.50	$13,602.56
Length of marriage, years	T	4–15	1–22
	W	3–22 (mean = 11)	1–17 (mean = 8.6)
Total number of children	T	17 (11–Male) (6–Female)	20 (8–Male) (12–Female)
	W	NR*	NR*
Age of children	T	4–14	7–22
	W	(Mean = 15.1)	(Mean = 14.38)
Live with children	T	NR*	NR*
	W	3 (1 = part-time)	24 (2 = part-time)
Live with lovers	T	9	4
	W	15	12
Children do *not* know parent is G/L	T	2	0
	W	3 (3 = not sure)	2
Mean age of children at discovery of parents' homosexuality	T	NR*	NR*
	W	11.1	8.1

*NR = not reported

men tended to rate their marriages as more satisfactory than did the women. The total number of children for fathers in the Turner, Scadden, and Harris (1985) study was seventeen (eleven males, six females), ranging in age from four to fourteen. Mean age of children of fathers in the Wyers study was 15.1 (total number, sex, or age of children were not reported). Lesbian mothers in the Turner, Scadden, and Harris study had a total of twenty children (eight males, twelve females), ranging in age from seven to twenty-two years. Wyers reported the mean age of lesbian mothers' children as 14.38. In the Wyers study, only one child lived with its father, several children lived with both parents, but most lived with their mothers. Also, mothers commonly had custody. Living arrangements of children were not specified in the Turner, Scadden, and Harris study, although it was reported that "all except one gay/lesbian parent had custody of, shared custody of, or [had] regular contact with their children" (p. 9). Nine out of ten and fifteen out of thirty-two gay fathers were living with lovers, whereas four out of eleven and twelve out of thirty-four lesbian mothers had lovers. More gay fathers than lesbian mothers reported having good relationships with their ex-spouses. Also, Turner, Scadden, and Harris reported that the majority of live-in lovers, both gay and lesbian, acted in the stepparent role.

Turner, Scadden, and Harris (1985) asked questions regarding children's sex-role development. Half of the fathers and somewhat more than half of the mothers did not encourage sex-typed toys for their children; the others indicated some encouragement. Most of the parents made efforts to provide an opposite sex-role mode, with fathers making more of an effort than mothers. Nearly all the subjects in the Turner, Scadden, and Harris study reported that their children seemed to be developing "normal" sex-role identification, and the parents perceived them to be similar to other children of their age and sex. Sex-role development was not addressed in the Wyers study.

All the children of lesbian mothers in the Turner, Scadden, and Harris (1985) study knew of the mother's sexual orientation, whereas Wyers (1984) reported that one did not know, and one probably knew but it had not been discussed. Two fathers' children in the Turner, Scadden, and Harris study did not know about the father's homosexuality, whereas in the Wyers study eleven of the fathers reported that their children did not know, and six fathers were uncertain or sure that all their children did not know. Reasons the fathers gave for not coming out to their children were fear that it would damage the children, fear of rejection, fear that the children would not understand, the thought that it would be too upsetting, or that it was not their business, and fear of peer rejection, as well as other miscellaneous reasons. Most children of lesbian mothers found out directly from the mother herself. The children of gay fathers may have found out from the father, but were more likely than the children of lesbians to have found out from their mother. In some instances, both spouses told the children, children overheard their parents discussing it, or they figured it out for themselves.

Overall, parents reported that their children's initial reaction to knowledge of their homosexuality had been positive or constituted few if any problems. The range of reactions was from positive with no problems, to mild reactions, to anger and confusion. Some parents reported that they were uncertain of the initial impact. Also, more untoward reactions were reported by gay fathers than by lesbian mothers. Overall, current impact was rated as positive for children of both gay fathers and lesbian mothers.

The average age of children finding out about their mother's homosexuality was 8, and for fathers it was 11.1 (Wyers 1984). Children who were told at an earlier age were reported to have had fewer difficulties than those who found out when they were older (Turner, Scadden, and Harris 1985).

Wyers (1984) reported that 58.8 percent of the children of lesbian mothers and 21.1 percent of the children of gay fathers experience relationship problems with other people because of their knowledge of their parents' homosexuality, although most of the problems are not considered to be serious. Wyers also reported that it was significantly more difficult for gay fathers than for lesbian mothers to acknowledge their homosexuality. Both the men and women stated that having children made the coming out process more difficult. Lesbians most feared losing custody, whereas gay fathers' greatest fear was damaging their children. In Wyers' study, all spouses except two of the men's and five of the women's knew. It is also interesting that, in the Wyers study, less than half the lesbian mothers and gay fathers indicated support by their families after they learned of the respondents' homosexuality. Lesbians tended to turn to friends for support, whereas it was more common for gay fathers to seek professional assistance. Turner, Scadden, and Harris (1985) made the following generalizations from their study: a) parents' homosexuality seems to create few long-term problems for children, who seem to accept it better than parents anticipate; b) most subjects report positive relationships with their children; c) parents' sexual orientation is of little importance in the overall parent/child relationship; and d) lesbian/gay parents try harder to create stable home lives and positive relationships with their children than one would expect from traditional heterosexual parents.

Gay Fathers, Heterosexual Fathers, Lesbian Mothers, Heterosexual Mothers Compared. One study (Harris and Turner 1985–1986) compared all four groups. The sample size, however, is exceedingly small for meaningful comparisons to be made: ten gay fathers, two heterosexual single fathers, thirteen lesbian mothers, and fourteen heterosexual single mothers. Data were obtained from mailed questionnaires. Ages of the gay/lesbian (G/L) parents ranged from twenty-nine to fifty-three years (median = 39), whereas the heterosexual (H) parents ranged from nineteen to forty-seven years (median = 25). The majority were Caucasian, highly educated, and were employed mostly in professional positions. The three major religions (Catholicism, Protestantism, Judaism) were represented, with 30 percent of the sample claiming no religion. Four persons had never married. Several subjects had married from two to five times. Median length of marriage was six years. Number of children ranged from one to seven, with their ages ranging from five to thirty-one.

The authors reported that few differences were found between the G/L and H parents, with the major differences reflecting their sex or residence, not their sexual orientation. Except for the H parents' tendency to make a greater effort to provide an opposite sex-role model for their children, no significant differences were found in the relationship of the G/L and H parents with their children. Differences found between G/L parents were that the gay fathers had higher incomes and were more likely to live with lovers or male friends. Also, they felt more satisfaction with their first child, had fewer disagreements with their partner over discipline, and were more likely to encourage play with sex-typed toys. Lesbian mothers, however, were more likely to realize benefits of their homosexuality for their children in the areas of accepting their own sexuality, increasing their empathy and tolerance for others, and exposing themselves to new points of view. It is noteworthy that no G/L subject reported that a spouse or child demonstrated a positive response to the discovery that the parent was gay. This is contrary to Bozett (1980, 1981b), who found that several spouses and children reacted positively. Similar to most parents, G/L subjects admitted to having some difficulties in child rearing and getting along with their children. The authors summarized their findings by stating that being gay is compatible with effective parenting, and that the parents' sexual orientation is not the major issue in these parents' relationships with their children.

Gay Fathers and Gay Nonfathers Compared. Two brief studies compared gay fathers and gay nonfathers, Robinson and Skeen (1982) and Skeen and Robinson (1985). Both derived their sample from the same members of Dignity as previously described. The study by Robinson and Skeen (1982) compared the two groups on sex-role orientation, as measured by the Bem Sex Role Inventory (1974). Categorical scoring was applied to the responses, and comparisons were made to ascertain if there were any relationships between masculinity and fatherhood. The findings indicate that there were none. Gay men who father children were no more masculine than gay men who do not father children. A diverse pattern of sex-role orientation was found in which the subjects scored equally often in the androgynous, masculine, feminine, and undifferentiated categories. Interestingly, gay fathers scored more nonandrogynous (masculine, feminine, undifferentiated). Also, fewer fathers scored masculine than in any other category. This study, the researchers concluded, supports other research that indicates that sexual behavior and sex-role orientation are unrelated phenomena, and develop out of separate experiences.

The other study by Skeen and Robinson (1985) compared gay and nongay fathers' relationships with their parents. Data from the same sample of respondents from Dignity were used. Included in the questionnaire were items that dealt with marital status and children, and the relationship with each parent. No differences were found between the two groups' perceptions of their early family life and relationships with their fathers and mothers. Both groups were reared in intact homes without much marital discord, and they perceived their family of orientation as pleasant. Both groups did perceive their mothers as more accepting, yet their perceptions of their fathers were also primarily positive. The authors concluded that this study supports other research that questions the Freudian-based concept of a direct causal link between early family relationship patterns and sexual orientation.

Gay Fathers and Heterosexual Fathers Compared. Scallen (1981) assessed the relationship between sexual orientation and fathers' child rearing attitudes and behaviors. Self-assessments of both sets of fathers in the performance of the paternal role were also explored. The sample consisted of twenty homosexual and twenty heterosexual fathers, and a control group of twenty fathers. The fathers were comparable on demographics of age, education, income, and employment. Data were obtained from responses to the Eversoll Father Role Opinionnaire, the Kinsey Scale, the Father/Son/Daughter Practice Report, and a demographic questionnaire. There were no significant differences between the two groups on the paternal problem-solving dimensions, on the degree of emphasis placed on recreation, or on the subjects' self-reports pertaining to the encouragement of autonomy. The findings suggest, however, that sexual orientation does have a relationship to espoused paternal attitudes. Gay fathers were found to be more endorsing of paternal nurturance, less endorsing of economic provision, and somewhat less traditional in their overall paternal attitudes than were heterosexual fathers. Gay fathers also appeared to have a substantial psychological investment in the paternal role. Moreover, they demonstrated a significantly more positive self-assessment of their performance in the paternal role than did the heterosexual fathers. Lastly, the data indicate that most subjects in all groups appeared to endorse an active, caretaking stance regarding the paternal role, which, according to Scallen, tends to substantiate the trend toward increasing paternal role expectations.

STUDIES IN WHICH GAY FATHERS WERE PART OF A LARGER STUDY (NOT THE FOCAL CONCERN)

There are three additional studies, one of which consisted of a large sample from the San Francisco Bay Area (Bell and Weinberg 1978), and two (Jay and Young 1977; Spada 1979) that derived data from international samples (mostly from the United States). The Bell and Weinberg (1978) study employed structured face-to-face interviews of 979 respondents, whereas the other two studies used mailed questionnaires with samples that ranged from over a thousand (Spada 1979) to more than four thousand (Jay and Young 1977). These studies provided important evidence toward the understanding of homosexuality, and also helped corroborate findings from previous studies. In addition, they helped verify qualitative data. Some of the major statistical findings from these studies are presented in table 19.2, with emphasis on gay men who married and had children. These data are presented without further discussion.

LIMITATIONS OF THE RESEARCH

Most studies of gay fathers are based on nonrandom small sample sizes, with subjects who are Caucasian, middle- to upper-middle-class, well educated with occupations commensurate with their education, who come mostly from urban centers, and who are relatively accepting of their homosexuality. There is severely limited knowledge of gay fathers who vary from these demographics. Moreover, the validity and reliability of the instruments used in the studies reported are not always addressed. Although the qualitative studies of Bozett and Miller are complementary, their replication with samples with different demographics and from more diverse settings are needed in order to develop a substantive theoretical construct in which practitioners and researchers can have confidence.

GENERALIZATIONS

From this review of the literature, and keeping in mind the limitations just discussed, the following tentative generalizations can be proposed:

1. A significant number of gay men are fathers who usually marry only once.
2. Gay fathers describe their family backgrounds as generally positive.
3. There is no difference between gay and nongay fathers' relationship with their parents.

TABLE 19.2

A Comparison of Selected Variables from the Bell and Weinberg (1978), Jay and Young (1977), and Spada (1979) Studies

Studies	Homosexualities (Bell and Weinberg)		The Gay Report (Jay and Young)	The Spada Report (Spada)
VARIABLES				
Subjects	979		5,291	1,038
Sample source	San Francisco Bay Area		International	International
Methodology	Structured Interview		Mailed Questionnaire	Mailed Questionnaire
Age	25–46		14–78	16–77
	Average Age:			
	Caucasian: 36.97			
	Black: 27.20			
Number of male subjects	686		4,329	1,038
Race	Caucasian: 575		Caucasian: 91%	Caucasian: 858
	Black: 111	Men	All others represented	All others represented
	686			
Percent of married: Past or present	Caucasian: 20%		19%	17%
	Black: 13%			
Married more than once	Caucasian: 15%		NR*	NR*
	Black: 0%			
Marital satisfaction	Majority: Moderately happy to very happy.		NR*	Majority: Not happy
Homosexuality involved in reason for divorce	Caucasian Black		Separated Yes: 78%	NR*
	Yes: 54% 23%		Divorced Yes: 45%	
	No: 46% 77%			

	Caucasian	Black	
Number of children in first marriage	N: 116	N: 14	NR*
	%	%	
None	50	29	
One	25	50	
Two	15	21	
Three	5	0	
Four or more	5	0	
Number of children (natural, adopted, step) over 12 who know or suspect father is gay	Caucasian N: 46	Black N: 2	NR*
	%	%	
None	61	100	
One	24	0	
Two	15	0	
Three or more	0	0	
How children over 12 found out father is gay	Caucasian N: 14	Black N: 0	NR*
	%	%	
Father told	36	0	
Spouse told	29	0	
Told by others	7	0	
Guessed/Surmised	29	0	

TABLE 19.2
Continued

Studies	Homosexualities (Bell and Weinberg)		The Gay Report (Jay and Young)	The Spada Report (Spada)
VARIABLES				
Children's overall reaction			NR*	NR*
	Caucasian N: 17	Black N: 0		
	%	%		
No reaction	71	0		
Tolerant/understanding	29	0		
Negative reaction	0	0		
Worry, fear for my welfare	0	0		
Indifference	0	0		
Some other reaction	0	0		
Effect of children knowing on relationship			NR*	NR*
	Caucasian N = 17	Black N = 0		
	%	%		
No effect	76	0		
Strengthened relationship	12	0		
Weakened relationship	6	0		
Destroyed relationship	0	0		
Other changes in relationship	6	0		

*NR = Not Reported

4. Gay men who father children are no more masculine than gay men who do not father children.

5. Reasons for gay fathers' remaining married are a) lack of a perceived viable alternative, b) commitment to their children, and c) knowledge that divorce would lower their standard of living.

6. Some gay fathers may be relatively content in their marriages, but most are not.

7. Gayness and traditional marital relationships are often discordant compared to relationships established when gay fathers move into the gay world.

8. Two factors that govern the style of gay fathers' sexual expression are a) whether they live with or without their wife, and b) the father's degree of occupational autonomy.

9. Awareness of one's homosexuality occurs later in gay men who marry than it does for the gay male population in general.

10. Gay fathers appear to proceed through a relatively predictable process from unacceptance of their homosexuality with little knowledge of the gay world, to acceptance with an increased congruence between their public and self-identities.

11. In spite of increased public stigma, gay fathers achieve a sense of psychological well-being as their stigmatized careers progress.

12. Gay fathers have more difficulty acknowledging their homosexuality than do lesbian mothers.

13. Having children at home makes coming out more difficult for gay fathers.

14. Gay fathers have more difficulty disclosing their gay identity to their children than do lesbian mothers. Moreover, the problem may be more pronounced among Black men.

15. Most children's reactions to their gay fathers' disclosure is reported by the fathers as "none" or "tolerant and understanding." Nevertheless, more untoward reactions from children are reported by gay fathers than by lesbian mothers.

16. Gay fathers, more than lesbian mothers, report that their children have difficulties with peers because of the parent's homosexuality.

17. Children who are told at an earlier age are reported to have fewer difficulties managing the knowledge of their fathers' homosexuality.

18. Being gay is compatible with effective parenting.

19. The father's homosexuality seems to create few long-term problems for their children, who appear to accept it better than fathers anticipate.

20. Gay fathers usually do not have physical custody of their children.

21. Gay fathers who do not have physical custody of their children tend to maintain consistent contact with them.

22. Most gay fathers report positive relationships with their children.

23. The father's sexual orientation is of little importance in the overall father/child relationship.

24. Gay fathers try harder to create stable home lives and positive relationships with their children than one would expect from traditional heterosexual parents.

25. Gay fathers make efforts to provide opposite sex role models for their children.

26. In comparison to heterosexual fathers, it appears that sexual orientation is related to espoused paternal attitudes: a) gay fathers are more endorsing of paternal nurturance, b) gay fathers are somewhat less traditional in their overall paternal attitudes, c) gay fathers have a substantial investment in the paternal role, and d) gay fathers assess themselves more positively in their performance of the paternal role.

DIRECTIONS FOR FUTURE RESEARCH

Specific recommendations for research studies will not be listed here because the author has recently done so elsewhere (Bozett 1985, 1987). The suggestions here address several general challenges that must be accepted if substantive progress in this important area of research is to be made.

First, it is imperative that entire gay father family units be studied. These families take a variety of forms, from single custodial to step- or multifamily households. The patterns of interactions of family members with one another, the family dynamics, the relationship of the family to supra- and infrastructures, and the process and progress of the family life-cycle over time needs investigation to achieve an understanding of gay fathers and their families, and to determine the effect being reared in such a family has on children's development.

The approach to the study of the gay father and the gay father family must derive from a theoretical framework that is sufficiently inclusive to allow for wide variations of gay fathering styles. Sexual orientation per se does not dictate specific fathering behaviors. Moreover, it is not likely that being gay will guarantee nurturing, sensitive, father/child relationships, as the research to date suggests. Future studies must either generate theory, or be based on theory that is sufficiently encompassing to explain and, more important, predict positive and negative gay father family outcomes. Certainly, not all gay fathers, like not all nongay fathers, are suited to the paternal role. Nor is it likely that all gay fathers carry it out successfully.

Only through ongoing study of gay father family units in their multiple forms, and in their extremes from positive to negative, will an assertion that gay fathering is viable, positive, or even desirable become convincing.

CONCLUSION

In sum, there are only a handful of studies on gay fathers. These studies are highly diverse and provide only a glimpse into this substantive area of study. It is a good beginning. Much theorizing and research is still needed, however, for there to be a comprehensive and objective understanding of the phenomenon of gay fathers.

NOTE

1. More data are presented in these research studies than are reported here. The data included in this article are those which the author believes to be most germain to this review.

REFERENCES

Allen, C. 1957. When homosexuals marry. *Sexology* (February):416–20.
Bell, A. P., and M. S. Weinberg. 1978. *Homosexualities: A Study of Diversity Among Men and Women.* New York: Simon and Schuster.
Benson, L. 1968. *Fatherhood: A Sociological Perspective.* New York: Random House.
Bem, S. L. 1974. The measurement of psychological androgyny. *Journal of Consulting and Clinical Psychology* 42:155–62.
Berger, P., and T. Luckmann. 1966. *The Social Construction of Reality: A Treatise in the Sociology of Knowledge.* New York: Doubleday.
Bieber, I. 1969. The married homosexual male. *Medical Aspects of Human Sexuality* 3:76–84.
Bieber, I., H. Dain, P. Dince, M. Dreillich, H. Grand, R. Gundlach, M. Kremer, A.

Rilkin, C. Wilber, and T. Bieber. 1962. *Homosexuality: A Psycho-analytic Study.* New York: Basic Books.

Bozett, F. W. 1979. Gay fathers: The convergence of a dichotomized identity through integrative sanctioning. Doctoral dissertation, University of California, San Francisco. *Dissertation Abstracts International* 40:2608B–9B.

Bozett, F. W. 1980. Gay fathers: How and why they disclose their homosexuality to their children. *Family Relations* 29:173–79.

Bozett, F. W. 1981a. Gay fathers: Evolution of the gay-father identity. *American Journal of Orthopsychiatry* 51:552–59.

Bozett, F. W. 1981b. Gay fathers: Identity conflict resolution through integrative sanctioning. *Alternative Lifestyles* 4:90–107.

Bozett, F. W. 1984. Parenting concerns of gay fathers. *Topics in Clinical Nursing* 6:60–71.

Bozett, F. W. 1985. Gay men as fathers. In S. M. H. Hanson and F. W. Bozett, eds., *Dimensions of Fatherhood,* pp. 327–52. Beverly Hills, Calif.: Sage Publications.

Bozett, F. W. 1986. Identity management: Social control of identity by children of gay fathers when they know their father is a homosexual. Paper presented at the Seventh Biennial Eastern Nursing Research Conference, New Haven, Connecticut, April.

Bozett, F. W. 1987. Gay fathers. In F. W. Bozett, ed., *Gay and Lesbian Parents,* pp. 3–22. New York: Praeger.

Bozett, F. W. 1988. Gay fatherhood. In P. Bronstein and C. P. Cowan, eds., *Fatherhood Today: Men's Changing Role in the Family,* pp. 214–35. New York: Wiley.

Brown, H. 1976. Married homosexuals. In H. Brown, ed., *Familiar Faces, Hidden Lives,* pp. 108–30. New York: Harcourt Brace Jovanovich.

Churchill, W. 1971. *Homosexual Behavior Among Males: A Cross-Cultural and Cross-Species Investigation.* Englewood Cliffs, N.J.: Prentice-Hall.

Clark, D. 1987. *The New Loving Someone Gay.* Berkeley, Calif.: Celestial Arts.

Dank, B. 1971. Coming out in the gay world. *Psychiatry* 34:180–97.

Festinger, L. 1957. *A Theory of Cognitive Dissonance.* Evanston, Ill.: Row Peterson.

Glaser, B., and A. Strauss. 1967. *The Discovery of Grounded Theory.* Chicago: Aldine.

Hanson, S. M. H., and F. W. Bozett. 1985. *Dimensions of Fatherhood.* Beverly Hills, Calif.: Sage.

Harris, M. B., and P. H. Turner. 1985–1986. Gay and lesbian parents. *Journal of Homosexuality* 12(2):101–13.

Harry, J., and W. Devall. 1978. *The Social Organization of Gay Males.* New York: Praeger.

Hunt, M., and B. Hunt. 1977. *The Divorce Experience.* New York: McGraw-Hill.

Imielinski, K. 1969. Homosexuality in males with particular reference to marriage. *Psychotherapy and Psychosomatics* 17:126–32.

Jay, K., and A. Young. 1979. *The Gay Report.* New York: Summit.

Kingdon, M. A. 1979. Lesbians. *The Counseling Psychologist* 8:44–45.

Kinsey, A. C., W. B. Pomeroy, and C. E. Martin. 1948. *Sexual Behavior in the Human Male.* Philadelphia: W. B. Saunders.

Lamb, M. E., ed. 1981. *The Role of the Father in Child Development.* New York: Wiley.

Lofland, J. 1971. *Analyzing Social Settings.* Belmont, Calif.: Wadsworth.

Lynn, D. 1974. *The Father: His Role in Child Development.* Monterey, Calif.: Brooks/ Cole.

Lynn, D. 1979. *Daughters and Parents: Past, Present, and Future.* Monterey, Calif.: Brooks/Cole.

Mager, D. 1975. Faggot father. In K. Jay and A. Young, eds., *After You're Out,* pp. 128–34. New York: Gage.

Miller, B. 1978. Adult sexual resocialization: Adjustments toward a stigmatized identity. *Alternative Lifestyles* 1:207–34.

Miller, B. 1979a. Gay fathers and their children. *The Family Coordinator* 28:544–52.

Miller, B. 1979b. Unpromised paternity: The lifestyles of gay fathers. In M. Levine, ed., *Gay Men: The Sociology of Male Homosexuality,* pp. 239–52. New York: Harper and Row.

Miller, B. 1983. Identity conflict and resolution: A social psychological model of gay family men's adaptations. Doctoral dissertation, University of Alberta, Edmonton.

Miller, B. 1986. Identity resocialization in moral careers of gay husbands and fathers. In A. Davis, ed., *Papers in honor of Gordon Hirabayashi,* pp. 197–216. Edmonton, Canada: University of Alberta Press.

Pederson, F. A., ed. 1980. *The Father-Infant Relationship.* New York: Praeger.

Peterson, N. 1984. Coming to terms with gay parents. *USA Today* (April 30):30.

Robinson, B., and P. Skeen. 1982. Sex-role orientation of gay fathers versus gay nonfathers. *Perceptual and Motor Skills* 55:1055–59.

Saghir, M., and E. Robins. 1973. *Male and Female Homosexuality.* Baltimore: Williams and Wilkins.

Scallen, R. M. 1981. An investigation of paternal attitudes and behaviors in homosexual and heterosexual fathers. Doctoral dissertation, California School of Professional Psychology, Los Angeles. *Dissertation Abstracts International* 42:3809B.

Schafer, S. 1977. Sociosexual behavior in male and female homosexuals. *Archives of Sexual Behavior* 6:355–64.

Schulenburg, J. 1985. *Gay Parenting.* New York: Doubleday.

Shilts, R. 1975. Gay people make babies too. *The Advocate* (October 22):25.

Skeen, P., and B. Robinson. 1984. Family backgrounds of gay fathers: A descriptive study. *Psychological Reports* 54:99–105.

Skeen, P., and B. Robinson. 1985. Gay fathers' and gay non-fathers' relationship with their parents. *Journal of Sex Research* 21:1–6.

Spada, J. 1979. *The Spada Report.* New York: New American Library.

Turner, P. H., L. Scadden, and M. B. Harris. 1985. Parenting in gay and lesbian families. Paper presented at the First Annual Future of Parenting Symposium, Chicago, March.

U.S. Bureau of the Census. 1983. *Statistical Abstracts of the United States.* 104th ed. Washington, D.C.: U.S. Government Printing Office.

Wyers, N. L. 1984. *Lesbian and Gay Spouses and Parents: Homosexuality in the Family.* Portland, Ore.: School of Social Work, Portland State University.

VII

Adolescence, Midlife, and Aging

An important topic was not included in our introductory overview article in this book because of time limitations on the original lecture. The topic is life span perspectives on lesbian and gay male development—from the first awareness of same-gender sexual and affectional feelings through adolescence, adulthood, and old age. Although we cannot adequately summarize this large topic here, it may be useful to provide a brief review and a greater number of relevant references than we have provided in the other introductions that were more adequately covered in the overview article.

At the outset it is important to caution the reader new to developmental psychology that this field emphasizes the commonalities and descriptive themes of the human life span (Kimmel 1990). It cannot prescribe normal development, nor can it encompass all of the diversity that naturally exists. Ethnic, racial, and gender variation may be understated, for example. The discussions earlier in this book on gender and cultural diversity apply here, even if they are not stated explicitly. If one does not fit the pattern, it is the pattern that needs to be stretched to fit the individual variation. A major contribution of gay and lesbian psychology has been to challenge and to stretch the models of developmental psychology.

Many adult lesbians and gay men report that they had sexual feelings and experiences during late childhood and early adolescence that provided their first cues about their sexual orientation. These early same-gender erotic feelings, even more than actual homosexual experiences, were found in a large retrospective study to be critical in establishing later adult homosexuality; this finding, however, is more often true for males than for females (Bell, Weinberg, and Hammersmith 1981). Thus, about the time some adolescents are beginning to date and explore heterosexual feelings and behaviors, others are sensing that they are different, that they are attracted to same-gender friends, or are experiencing crushes on persons of the same gender. Martin (1982) described the variety of ways some gay male adolescents attempt to hide their feelings, often resulting in isolation, elaborate patterns of deception, avoidance of gay-related behaviors, and fear of accidental discovery. Schneider (1989) discussed parallel experiences for lesbians.

A number of these adolescents may also be stigmatized by behavior, mannerisms, or preferences that others interpret as lesbian or gay. Occasionally, some precocious adolescents identify as gay or lesbian and this fact may become known, or may be openly acknowledged. The resulting stigma can lead to antigay/lesbian violence (Hunter 1990), severe pressure in school (Hunter and Schaecher 1987), and the need for special educational resources (Ashkinazy 1984; Rofes 1989). Often they experience considerable harassment from peers and seldom have family support (Gibson 1989).

A range of services specifically directed to lesbian and gay youth are needed (Slater 1988). Appropriate services include peer-based support groups, drug- and alcohol-free meeting space, and education about AIDS prevention. Homeless lesbian and gay teenagers, many who have run away from abusive homes to urban areas, are among the most highly at-risk populations of young people today. Several model programs now exist including the Hetrick-Martin Institute for the Protection of Lesbian and Gay Youth in New York City, which operates the Harvey Milk Alternative School for lesbian and gay male students, and Project 10 in Los Angeles (Rofes 1989).

One theme that has received considerable attention in the psychological literature is adolescents coping with the knowledge of being lesbian or gay (Herdt 1989). The focus has often been on providing guidance and useful background information to counselors, therapists, and physicians (Paroski 1987; Remafedi 1985, 1987; Slater 1988; Sobocinski 1990). Malyon (1981) pointed out three general styles lesbian or gay male adolescents use to deal with their sexual and affectional feelings. Some *repress* them out of awareness, but often they emerge later, sometimes with harmful consequences. A second style is consciously to *suppress* or hide the feelings; this response, however, may interfere with the development of a sense of identity that includes one's sexuality. Others disclose their sexual orientation, which may result in confrontations that may be painful or lead to family rejection. Often a family will refer their adolescent for therapy when sexual feelings are emerging that disturb heterosexual expectations or conflict with stereotypes of normal adolescent sexuality. Family relations are usually difficult for lesbian and gay adolescents, and the coming-out process is risky (Borhek 1988; Savin-Williams 1989a, b). The article by Gonsiorek in this part discusses a wide range of issues that lesbian and gay adolescents often face.

Another theme currently receiving attention is suicide among adolescents in general, and among lesbian and gay adolescents in particular. Even though suicide rates are actually much higher among older White men than among adolescents, and racial differences are marked, the suicide rate among adolescents is alarming (Kimmel and Weiner 1985). Although a great deal of attention has been given to possible causes of suicide among adolescents, rarely has sexual orientation been seriously considered. Gibson (1989), in a federal report on youth suicide, noted that problems in self-acceptance, abuse and rejection from family members and from peers, isolation, problems in relationships, substance abuse, depression, school failure, and being forced out of the home prematurely present risk factors for suicide that are greater for gay, lesbian, bisexual, and transsexual youth than for other adolescents. His review of the data suggested that suicide is the leading cause of death for this group. Similarly, Harry (1989) concluded that lesbians and gay men are more likely to commit suicide than are heterosexuals, but that much better data are needed on this complex topic. The article by Remafedi, Farrow, and Deisher reprinted here is a good step toward a better understanding of this tragic aspect of lesbian and gay adolescence in our heterosexist society.

Midlife and aging among lesbians and gay men has also begun to emerge from the shadows of heterosexist views of normal human development. This dimension of development is especially important because few lesbian and gay adolescents have family role models for their future life course. In the past, negative stereotypes of lonely, depressed, ostracized old dykes and queens leading lives of quiet desperation were common, and added to the burden of fear and stigma younger lesbians and gay men had to face. Today, we are viewing the elder generation as pioneers, as well as survivors, who can provide a link with the history of lesbians and gay men. One book on older gay men quoted a respondent born in 1926:

> I've been gay longer than it's been popular. I was gay when you had to wear red socks to be identified as gay. I walked into a bar in Chicago and had the place go absolutely dead on me because I wasn't dressed for that city. They thought I was vice. The piano player, Joy, recognized me from Hawaii and California and began playing "California Here I Come." I went to talk to her and that cleared the air. But I didn't make out that night even though I was a new face in town. Talk about harassment! They backed a paddy wagon up to the back door of one of those bars and emptied everyone right into the wagon. In those days we used to get a lot of heat and there was no such thing as entrapment. They'd just come in and bust everyone there. And get away with it! (Vacha 1985:69)

One important finding from the emerging field of lesbian and gay gerontology is that the population is very diverse (Adelman 1990; Friend 1989; Quam and Whitford 1992). For example, many older lesbians and gay men have lived openly, often as a same-gender couple, for many years. Others have spent the majority of their adult years hiding their homosexuality, sometimes in a heterosexual marriage. Many have children and grandchildren. All of the samples studied have been troubled by lack of generalizability because the population is hidden and difficult to identify, but we can be confident that the actual population is even more diverse than these samples indicate. A second major finding is that same-gender sexual orientation does not cause maladjustment with aging. Even the stigma of an unpopular sexual orientation does not appear to have much negative effect on most older lesbians and gays—perhaps because they have learned to live with it well enough to grow old. Third, a substantial proportion of those studied appear to be aging with levels of satisfaction, including sexuality, comparable to other people. Fourth, there are special concerns that affect older lesbians and gay men, but by and large the major issues are similar to other older people: health, social support, financial security, a sense of independence, and the freedom to live one's life as one chooses. Finally, there may be advantages to aging as a gay man or lesbian, including the possibility of creating one's family and social roles to suit one's individual needs. A woman interviewed in a study of older lesbians described her life in ways that illustrate many of these points:

> Just because I'm old and sick and eighty-five doesn't mean I didn't have quite a gay life. You see I've loved a lot of women and a lot of women have loved me. In fact, if I weren't sick that would still be the case.

But let me tell you about my life right now. My health is very poor. I no longer have a physical feeling for anyone. And I should have it because it makes you forget yourself. I miss it. . . .

The most important thing in my life now is to get my health back. After all I have my sister Rebeccah that I have to take care of. She was a genius but now she has lost her memory. Sometimes she's lucid. She's in a home. I sent the home two checks today. I'm responsible for her care. . . .

My family is very important to me, but I'm not very important to my family. It's not because I'm gay; it's because they have children and they're preoccupied with them.

I need somebody most every day of the week. I have some people from GLOE [Gay and Lesbian Outreach to Elders], and a woman from Catholic Charities comes in once a week for $5.50 an hour. She does a good job. She cleans the house. . . .

I have friends who come by and cook me dinner every now and then and I have friends who take me to my doctors appointments. These are new and younger gay friends.

At one point, I thought gay people were no good. But now all these gay people are helping me. It's not my family that is taking care of me; it's my gay friends. They have been wonderful to me. . . .

I took a bath all by myself today. I'm weak but I can still bathe by myself. You want to know about old age; that's old age. (Adelman 1986:207–9)

A variety of social service agencies and social organizations have emerged for older lesbians and gay men, including SAGE in New York City, GLOE in San Francisco, and Project Rainbow in Los Angeles. These groups offer social activities, assistance with health and legal problems, bereavement counseling, and a variety of specialized interest groups (Dunker 1987; Kimmel 1979; Raphael and Meyer 1988; Schwartz 1984). The development of these organizations has represented an important component of the empowerment of the lesbian and gay community. Not only do these services meet important needs of vulnerable members of the community, but also they provide an intergenerational resource for the successful aging of persons of all ages.

The two articles reprinted here represent different facets of research on the broad topic of adult development and aging. The selection by Sang is a previously unpublished report of her study on midlife issues for lesbians. It uses a unique research methodology and explores a topic that has been overlooked until recently. Other studies and personal descriptions of lesbian midlife experiences have been published in Sang, Warshow, and Smith (1991). Studies of midlife issues for gay men have also been published in a volume edited by Lee (1990). The second article by Kimmel was a pioneering description of gay adult development based on his early exploratory study of older gay men and provides a broad theoretical perspective on the field. Other research on this emerging topic is listed in a bibliography published by the National Association of Lesbian and Gay Gerontology (see resource list below).

CONTEMPORARY ISSUE: HIV/AIDS

The impact of acquired immune deficiency syndrome (AIDS) on adolescents is a high priority for public health today. Young people often feel they are immune from dangers, so they are more likely to take risks. Also young people tend to be more sexually active, and may be uninformed about AIDS prevention because of social taboos about sexuality education. Calderone (1985), for example, noted that in comparison with Australia, England, and Sweden, North American children "have the least, and the longest delayed sex education . . . and the Swedes the earliest and widest provision" (p. 703). The need for comprehensive sexuality education is clear. Friedman provided a graphic example of one type of such public education:

> The image is clear in my mind: a large billboard featuring a jean-clad, shirtless, 16-year-old boy encouraging males to practice masturbating with a condom in place. A vision of the future? No. Surprisingly, I saw these posters in train stations in Sweden two years ago. The image remains vividly in my mind as a symbol of ideal sexual development for boys. The poster— in its entirety—affirmed being a male. It affirmed being sexual, with masturbation as an acceptable expression of sexual behavior. And, it affirmed being responsible. (1989:8)

With regard to AIDS and aging, we may optimistically assume that medical advances will allow persons infected with HIV/AIDS to live for extended periods of time. The physical and psychosocial effects of growing older with the disease, however, are unknown. Therefore, a critical issue for research is on the impact of AIDS on older gay men and lesbians (Allers 1990). Likewise, SAGE in New York City has expanded its services to include programs for persons with HIV/AIDS, including support groups for seniors with AIDS and for their care partners, friendly visitors, and specialized training for hospital and nursing home staff.

Lesbians, while much less frequently infected with HIV/AIDS than gay men, have carried a major burden of coordinating and providing services to people infected with the virus, so their community has also been deeply affected.

A remark attributed to Margaret Mead noted that communities may be defined by the fact that they care for their vulnerable members. Since the mid-1970s, the lesbian and gay male communities have established services to care for their most vulnerable members: adolescents, persons with AIDS, and elders. In many ways, the building of a community has taken place within our lifetime. Now we can be empowered by it and nurture its growth for the future.

RESOURCES

GLOE (Gay and Lesbian Outreach to Elders), c/o Operation Concern, San Francisco.

Hetrick-Martin Institute, 401 West Street, New York, NY 10014 (formerly Institute for the Protection of Gay and Lesbian Youth); (212) 633–8920.

National Association of Gay and Lesbian Gerontology (NALGG), 1853 Market St., San Francisco, CA 94103; Bibliography, $10.

SAGE (Senior Action in a Gay Environment), 208 West 13th St. New York, NY 10011; (212) 741-2247.

Project Rainbow: Society for Senior Gay and Lesbian Citizens in Los Angeles, 255 South Hill St., Room 410, Los Angeles, CA 90012; (213) 621-3180.

Project 10, Fairfax High School, 7850 Melrose Ave., Los Angeles, CA 90046; (213) 651-5200.

REFERENCES

Adelman, M., ed. 1986. *Long Time Passing: Lives of Older Lesbians.* Boston: Alyson.

Adelman, M. 1990. Stigma, gay lifestyles, and adjustment to aging: A study of later-life gay men and lesbians. *Journal of Homosexuality* 20(3/4):7–32.

Allers, C. T. 1990. AIDS and the older adult. *The Gerontologist* 30:405–7.

Ashkinazy, S. 1984. Working with gay and lesbian youth. *Practice Digest* 7(1):21–23.

Bell, A. P., M. S. Weinberg, and S. K. Hammersmith. 1981. *Sexual Preference: Its Development in Men and Women.* Bloomington: Indiana University Press.

Borhek, M. V. 1988. Helping gay and lesbian adolescents and their families: A mother's perspective. *Journal of Adolescent Health Care* 9:123–28.

Calderone, M. S. 1985. Adolescent sexuality: Elements and genesis. *Pediatrics* 74 (Supplement):699–703.

Dunker, B. 1987. Aging lesbians: observations and speculations. In Boston Lesbian Psychologies Collective, ed., *Lesbian Psychologies*, pp. 72–82. Urbana: University of Illinois Press.

Friedman, J. 1989. The impact of homophobia on male sexual development. *Siecus Report* 17(5):8–9.

Friend, R. A. 1989. Older lesbian and gay people: Responding to homophobia. *Marriage and Family Review* 14(3/4):241–63.

Gibson, P. 1989. Gay male and lesbian youth suicide. *Report of the Secretary's Task Force on Youth Suicide*, pp. 3-110–3-142. Publication no. (ADM) 89–1623. Washington, D.C.: U.S. Department of Health and Human Services.

Harry, J. 1989. Sexual identity issues. *Report of the Secretary's Task Force on Youth Suicide*, pp. 2-131–2-142. Publication no. (ADM) 89–1623. Washington, D.C.: U.S. Department of Health and Human Services).

Herdt, G. 1989. Introduction: Gay and lesbian youth, emergent identities, and cultural scenes at home and abroad. *Journal of Homosexuality* 17(1/2):1–42.

Hunter, J. 1990. Violence against lesbian and gay male youths. *Journal of Interpersonal Violence* 5:295–300.

Hunter, J., and R. Schaecher. 1987. Stresses on lesbian and gay adolescents in schools. *Social Work in Education* 20:180–90.

Kimmel, D. C. 1979. Adjustments to aging among gay men. In B. Berzon and R. Leighton, eds., *Positively Gay*, pp. 146–58. Millbrae, Calif.: Celestial Arts.

Kimmel, D. C. 1990. *Adulthood and Aging: An Interdisciplinary, Developmental View.* 3d ed. New York: Wiley.

Kimmel, D. C., and I. B. Weiner. 1985. *Adolescence: A Developmental Transition.* Hillsdale, N.J.: Erlbaum.

Lee, J. A., ed. 1991. Gay midlife and maturity. *Journal of Homosexuality* 20(3/4).

Malyon, A. K. 1981. The homosexual adolescent: Developmental issues and social bias. *Child Welfare* 60:321–30.

Martin, A. D. 1982. Learning to hide: The socialization of the gay adolescent. *Adolescent Psychiatry*, 10:52–65.

Paroski, P. A., Jr. 1987. Health care delivery and the concerns of gay and lesbian adolescents. *Journal of Adolescent Health Care* 8:188–92.

Quam, J. K., and G. S. Whitford. 1992. Adaptation and age-related expectations of older gay and lesbian adults. *The Gerontologist* 32:367–74.

Raphael, S., and M. Meyer. 1988. The old lesbian: Some observations ten years later. In M. Shernoff and W. A. Scott, eds., *Sourcebook on Lesbian/Gay Health Care*, pp. 68–72. Washington, D.C.: National Lesbian and Gay Health Foundation.

Remafedi, G. J. 1985. Adolescent homosexuality: Issues for pediatricians. *Clinical Pediatrics* 24:481–85.

Remafedi, G. 1987. Male homosexuality: The adolescent's perspective. *Pediatrics* 79:326–30.

Rofes, E. 1989. Opening up the classroom closet: Responding to the educational needs of gay and lesbian youth. *Harvard Educational Review* 59:444–53.

Sang, B., J. Warshow, and A. J. Smith, eds. 1991. *Lesbians at Midlife: The Creative Transition.* San Francisco: Spinsters.

Savin-Williams, R. C. 1989a. Coming out to parents and self-esteem among gay and lesbian youths. *Journal of Homosexuality* 18(1/2):1–35.

Savin-Williams, R. C. 1989b. Parental influences on the self-esteem of gay and lesbian youths: A reflected appraisals model. *Journal of Homosexuality* 17(1/2):93–109.

Schneider, M. 1989. Sappho was a right-on adolescent: Growing up lesbian. *Journal of Homosexuality* 17(1/2):111–30.

Schwartz, M. 1984. Senior Action in a Gay Environment: SAGE. *Practice Digest* 7(1):17–20.

Slater, B. R. 1988. Essential issues in working with lesbian and gay male youths. *Professional Psychology: Research and Practice* 19:226–35.

Sobocinski, M. R. 1990. Ethical principles in the counseling of gay and lesbian adolescents: Issues of autonomy, competence, and confidentiality. *Professional Psychology: Research and Practice* 21:240–47.

Vacha, K. 1985. *Quiet Fire: Memoirs of Older Gay Men.* Trumansburg, N.Y.: Crossing Press.

20

Mental Health Issues of Gay and Lesbian Adolescents

John C. Gonsiorek

The mental health concerns of gay and lesbian adolescents are best under-stood within the context of cultural limitations, including a problematic conceptualization of adolescence, homophobia, and erotophobia. Within this framework, background information about homosexuality is presented; and the special social pressures and psychological problems of gay and les-bian youth are discussed, with particular attention paid to internalized homophobia, developmental issues, and the "coming-out" process. Differ-ences between gay and lesbian mental health issues are highlighted. Finally, practical suggestions regarding treatment planning are provided.

Considerable controversy and confusion surround homosexuality in ado-lescence. This paper attempts to reduce confusion by illuminating the controversies, providing basic information on the social and psychological challenges facing gay and lesbian adolescents, and outlining strategies for managing their mental health concerns.

Confusion about gay and lesbian adolescents is rooted in a number of historic and cultural issues, including a problematic conceptualization of adolescence, homophobia, and general erotophobia. These factors act in concert with prejudice and other irrational reactions to create apprehen-sion and misunderstanding.

Although gay and lesbian adolescents are a heterogeneous group, there are patterns to the social pressures they encounter and to their psycholog-ical coping strategies, giving some unity to their psychosocial experiences. These experiences do not constitute a separate psychology of gay and lesbian adolescence; rather, they are a series of developmental events and psychological responses that occur in addition to, and are interwoven with, the standard social and psychological challenges facing any adolescent.

This discussion will emphasize *preventative* mental health strategies and utilization of community resources, in keeping with the basic principle that homosexuality is a nonpathologic variant in the continuum of sexual orientation. The majority of gay and lesbian adolescents, given the opportunity to develop within a supportive and informed environment, present no more serious mental health problems than the general adolescent population. Thus, the focus of mental health treatment for gay and lesbian adolescents should be on those individuals who have psychological concerns superimposed on their *struggles* with sexual orientation and on those adolescents who have been particularly traumatized by their experiences as sexual minority members.

BARRIERS TO UNDERSTANDING HOMOSEXUALITY IN ADOLESCENCE

The Problematic Conceptualization of Adolescence

The concept of "adolescence" is relatively new. Throughout most of human history, persons were considered fully adult at a time in life that is now labeled adolescence. This was true in our own society until the industrial revolution and remains true in many Third World countries today. Previously, individuals made a swift transition from childhood to adulthood, bypassing what is now considered to be a developmentally separate and unique time in life (Aries 1962). Moreover, there is a modern trend to prolong the duration of adolescence, particularly among upper socioeconomic strata. Adolescence no longer ends at age eighteen, the traditional legal beginning of adulthood, but extends through the college-age years. Even the legal benchmark of adulthood is drifting upward in years, as indicated by changes in the minimum drinking age. Ironically, the development and expansion of adolescence runs contrary to a trend toward earlier sexual maturation. Consequently, the biologic hallmark of adulthood has steadily diverged from the cultural concept of adulthood.

The modern concept of adolescence is a sociological and anthropological phenomenon that is accompanied by powerful psychological events. Individuals in the adolescent age range are commonly depicted as immature and incapable of adult decision making. Adolescents themselves may accept this view. Our institutions expect and tolerate immature behavior from them. The end result is the construction of a psychosocial reality of adolescence that is not easily discarded and that heavily influences understanding of adolescent sexuality.

In our culture, sexual expression is reserved for adults and, specifically, heterosexual, married adults. Our culture's assumptions do not include sexual expression as an adolescent prerogative. In fact, youthful sexual expression has been construed as an institutional problem requiring a response from parents, schools, clergy, physicians, mental health professionals, and the court system. It is to be understood, categorized, legislated, pathologized, cured, and ultimately suppressed. This view is widely held despite the fact that, throughout human history, individuals were fully sexual, adult, and reproducing at ages that are now viewed as too immature to permit sexual expression. This tense and incongruent state of affairs has led some commentators to refer to our culture's treatment of adolescents as a type of "colonization" (Mendel 1971). The incongruities between the biologic, cultural, and psychosocial realities of adolescence contribute to the general confusion about adolescent sexuality.

Homophobia

Our culture is hostile to homosexuality and expresses this overtly and covertly. All individuals are socialized to varying degrees to be negatively predisposed toward homosexuality. The spectrum of negative biases range from denial that homosexuals exist to indictments of homosexuality as diseased or criminal. The reader is referred to several excellent resources for an in-depth discussion of prejudice (Allport 1954) and its specific applications to homosexuality (Martin 1982; Gonsiorek 1982).

Homophobia refers to an irrational and distorted view of homosexuality or homosexual persons. Among heterosexual persons, homophobia is most commonly manifested as prejudice or general discomfort with homosexuality. The intensity of these feelings is modulated by a number of factors, including personal history, contact with homosexual individuals, and individual psychological makeup. For example, there appears to be an inverse relationship between levels of homophobia and interaction with gay and lesbian individuals (Staats 1978). Among homosexual individuals, the effects of homophobia are more complex and will be described later under the rubric of "internalized homophobia," that is, negative attitudes toward homosexuality that are incorporated into self-image, creating various psychological distortions and reactions (Malyon 1982). Within the context of the present discussion, the importance of homophobia is its contribution to the general discomfort that emerges when the issue of adolescent homosexuality is raised. It is particularly important for health professionals to be aware of these feelings when working with gay and lesbian patients (Gonsiorek 1980).

EROTOPHOBIA

Our culture is obsessed with sex, yet phobic and deeply distrustful of sexuality. Considerable attention is focused on sexual behavior, rather than the integration of intimacy and sexuality. Foucault (1978) suggested that our society entertains a great deal of discourse about sexuality, with little resolution or psychological integration of its personal meaning. This vacillation between obsession and phobia further complicates our understanding of adolescent homosexuality.

BASIC INFORMATION ABOUT HOMOSEXUALITY

The following principles have emerged from the literature on homosexuality over the past two decades and underlie the subsequent discussion of the psychosocial concerns of gay and lesbian youth.

1. There is no intrinsic relationship between sexual orientation and psychopathology (Gonsiorek 1982; Meredith and Riester 1980). Homosexual individuals present a full spectrum of psychological adjustment, from the well adjusted to the severely disturbed. Although sexual orientation per se is unrelated to psychological adjustment, it should be recognized that the effects of homophobia and prejudice have adversely affected many gay and lesbian individuals.
2. Approximately 5–10 percent of the population is predominantly homosexual. The estimate for males approaches the higher figure, and for females, the lower.
3. Attempts to change sexual orientation are beset with ethical problems (Davison 1982), are generally unsuccessful over time (Coleman 1982), and often contribute to negative self-esteem and mental health problems (Hammersmith and Williams 1973; Gonsiorek 1984). The more recent works purporting to change sexual orientation are as problematic and unconvincing as earlier studies. They range from the pseudoscientific (Pattison and Pattison 1980), to the overtly hostile (Socarides 1978), to the scientifically flawed and deceptive (Masters and Johnson 1979), despite the fact that the research and clinical problems involved are well illuminated (Gonsiorek 1981, 1982; Martin 1984).

SOCIAL PROBLEMS OF GAY AND LESBIAN ADOLESCENTS

Although it is difficult to distinguish external stressors from the psychological events they mobilize, it is important to note that many of the problems that are experienced by gay and lesbian youth appear to be psychological or intrapsychic in nature, but actually stem from external stress and lack of support. Verbal and physical abuse from peers is one of the most obvious stressors. During adolescence, individuals are more polarized in their sex roles than at any other time in their lives. Males experience intense peer pressure to be "tough" and "macho," and females to be passive and compliant. Although social sex roles are not intrinsically related to sexual orientation, the distinction is poorly understood by most adolescents, as well as by most adults. Adolescents are frequently intolerant of differentness in others and may castigate or ostracize peers, particularly if the perceived differentness is in the arena of sexuality or sex roles. Rejection by peers need not be experienced directly in order to be felt keenly. Many gay and lesbian youth observe the treatment of peers and clearly understand what could happen to them if they appear to be, or are known to be, different. Conflict with family members regarding sexual orientation is another major external stressor for the adolescent. Many adolescents who disclose their sexual orientation to their family are rejected, mistreated, or become the focus of the family's dysfunction. Further information regarding gay and lesbian adolescents in the context of their families is available in a number of excellent books (Borhek 1979, 1983; Fairchild and Hayward 1979; Silverstein 1977) and through a support group, Parents and Friends of Lesbians and Gays, which has local chapters in many cities.

Compounding the problems of rejection by peers and family is a lack of institutional support. Treatment facilities that otherwise deal effectively with disturbed or acting-out adolescents may be overwhelmed by a comparatively well-adjusted, well-behaved gay or lesbian teenager. This is particularly true if he or she is nonwhite, lower class, or gender atypical. Often the sexual orientation of the client, rather than the more salient issues, becomes the focus of treatment. Staff members may tolerate or even support expressions of prejudice from other adolescents in the milieu. And even the well-intentioned and nonjudgmental staff may simply lack information regarding resources and treatment options for gay and lesbian adolescents.

Ironically, gay and lesbian adolescents have been relatively unsupported even by adult homosexual communities. Because of the lingering myth that associates homosexuality and pedophilia, many homosexual adults have feared that reaching out to young people would end in accusations of sexual abuse. Unfortunately, these fears may be realistic and justified, given the current levels of prejudice and misinformation. Isolated from well-functioning gay and lesbian adult role models by lack of access and fears of reprisal, young gay men and lesbians frequently resort to bars or public meeting places where they are apt to meet persons who are intoxicated, marginally functional, and emotionally or sexually exploitative.

In recent years, adult gay and lesbian communities and other interested parties have taken the first steps toward creating services for youth. The Harvey Milk School in New York City and its parent organization, The Institute for the Protection of Lesbian and Gay Youth, are excellent examples of progress. In addition to spearheading the development of a high school for lesbian and gay youth, the organization has provided a variety of other services in the New York City metropolitan area. The Minnesota Task Force for Gay and Lesbian Youth sponsors support groups and social gatherings for young people, locates knowledgeable and sympathetic social services and health care, and is developing other programs. Such organizations regularly face pressure and criticism, however, both from wary members of the homosexual communities and conservative elements within the larger society.

PSYCHOLOGICAL PROBLEMS OF GAY AND LESBIAN YOUTH

INTERNALIZED HOMOPHOBIA

One of the greatest impediments to the mental health of gay and lesbian individuals is "internalized homophobia." The following is a brief synopsis of the concept, which has been discussed at length elsewhere (Malyon 1982). Gay and lesbian persons, like heterosexuals, are raised with culturally sanctioned antihomosexual biases. These biases mobilize other psychological processes that extend beyond the development of prejudice. Children who will eventually be bisexual or homosexual often develop an awareness of being different at an early point in their lives. They may not understand the sexual nature or the precise meaning of their differentness, but they quickly learn that it is negatively regarded. As these young people develop and mature, they reach a fuller understanding of the nature of their differentness and the negative societal reaction to it. These negative feelings may actually be incorporated into self-image, resulting in varying degrees of internalized homophobia. Negative feelings about a part of one's self (i.e., sexual orientation) may be overgeneralized to encompass the entire self. Symptoms may range from a tendency toward self-doubt in the face of prejudice to unmistakable, overt self-hatred.

Internalized homophobia has various expressions. The overt type presents in persons who consciously accuse themselves of being evil, second class, or inferior because of their homosexuality. They may abuse substances or engage in other self-destructive or abusive behaviors. Because overt homophobia is so psychologically painful and destabilizing, it is less prevalent than covert forms. Few persons can tolerate conscious self-deprecation. Covert forms of internalized homophobia are the most common. Affected individuals appear to accept themselves, yet sabotage their own efforts in a variety of subtle ways. For example, homophobic gay and lesbian individuals may abandon career or educational goals with the excuse that external bigotry will keep them from their objectives. Internalized homophobia may take the form of tolerating discriminatory or abusive treatment from others. When gay and lesbian persons are met with bigotry and oppression, they are forced to make a choice. Neutrality is not among their options. To say no, either behaviorally or symbolically, is self-affirming; to tolerate second-class status is, in effect, to affirm a view of one's self as inferior.

Covert forms of internalized homophobia may be exceedingly subtle. For example, a gay or lesbian individual may pursue a course of action, such as a premature or poorly planned disclosure of sexual orientation to others, that is doomed to failure and then use the failure for purposes of self-criticism. The challenge for gay and lesbian individuals is to develop a sophisticated decision-making process about disclosure, responding to prejudice and ostracism, and other potentially threatening situations. When is it important to take a stand? When is it too risky? What are the consequences of action or inaction? How should a response be paced and timed? In other words, gay and lesbian persons must develop the skills to perform a complex "cost-benefit analysis" when faced with external bigotry and oppression. They can err by not standing up for themselves and thereby undermine their sense of self-worth; or they can err by allowing themselves to be provoked into rash or impulsive behavior, with the same negative consequences. In general, understanding and modifying the subtle manifestations of internalized homophobia are important steps in achieving mental health.

Covert internalized homophobia also operates on a community level. For example, some gays and lesbians hold themselves to a higher than normal standard of conduct and, as a result, may be unusually negative and critical toward others who do not meet their unrealistic expectations. This contributes to infighting within gay and lesbian communities and to an inclination to enforce morally absolute standards of conduct and political belief. Community debates about political questions, bisexuality, sexual values, and ethics frequently take on a morally absolute tone. Beyond finding viable and ethical solutions to problems, there is a preoccupation with achieving a "perfect" response to each question at hand. The covert message here is: "If we find the correct answer to the question, *then* perhaps we will be good enough."

Finally, one of the most sensitive indicators of internalized homophobia is the way in which an individual views other members of his or her own community. The client's excessive criticism of other gay and lesbian persons may signify his or her own discomfort. Health professionals treating gay and lesbian youth should help them begin the process of undoing internalized homophobia before patterns of self-defeating behaviors are ingrained. Support groups are particularly helpful in this regard. Many gay and lesbian adolescents can identify and reverse poor self-esteem and self-defeating behaviors, unless shame, guilt, and denial are already well entrenched.

DEVELOPMENTAL EXPERIENCES PARTICULAR TO GAY AND LESBIAN ADOLESCENTS

It is common for gay and lesbian teenagers to withdraw from typical adolescent social experiences. For some, socializing with either gender may be emotionally difficult. Interactions with persons of the same gender may arouse strong sexual or emotional feelings. Interacting with the opposite gender may be a painful reminder of absent heterosexual interest and differentness from peers. Consequently, gay and lesbian youth may avoid the normal interpersonal experimentation that is so much a part of adolescence. Observing this phenomenon, a popular comedian, Lily Tomlin, has observed, "In the 1950s, no one was gay; people were just shy." The suppression and repression of same-sex desires and interests is often accomplished at the expense of normal adolescent interpersonal skill development.

Adolescents may also employ a variety of psychological defenses to avoid confronting their homosexual interest. Denial, one of the most common defenses, sometimes generalizes far beyond sexual arenas. As sexual drive increases during adolescence, great intrapsychic energy is required to maintain denial. The net effect of this escalating emotional blockade is that some adolescents reach adulthood as strangers to their own inner emotional life and have developed habits of constricting any strong feelings. Other clients resort to reaction formation. One adult described his experience of adolescence as "the best little boy in the world" syndrome. He coped with feelings of inferiority by pleasing others, a futile attempt to prove to himself that he was lovable. This strategy often leads to loss of identity, self-neglect, disregard for personal needs, and destructive habits of overprotecting others. Yet other adolescents retreat to areas that are relatively conflict-free, such as academics, special interests, or hobbies. This avoidance may be destructive by compromising interpersonal social skills development.

For some teenagers for whom defenses fail, the recognition of homosexual feelings may emerge in a self-destructive way. Although the relationship between suicide and conflict regarding sexual identity is poorly understood and inadequately investigated, preliminary data and impressions from clinicians suggest that suicide attempts may be much more common among gay and lesbian adolescents than in the general population (Kruks 1986). Most major studies of adolescent suicide have avoided questions about the victim's sexual orientation. This remains an important area of inquiry, possibly neglected because of the pernicious effects of homophobia.

THE COMING-OUT PROCESS

During adolescence or early adulthood, most gays and lesbians experience a "coming-out" process that has been discussed by various authors (Troiden 1979; Cass 1979; Hencken and O'Dowd 1977). Most theories describe an initial period of denial that is followed by crisis, during which defenses against same-sex feelings can no longer be maintained. Subsequently, a period of emotional and behavioral experimentation with homosexuality ensues. Dissolution of a first relationship may lead to another period of crisis, during which the individual reexperiences negative feelings about being gay or lesbian. Expectations, issues of identity, and internalized homophobia are reexamined. Finally, most of the coming-out models describe a final stage of integration and identity formation during which the individual accepts being gay or lesbian and integrates this identity into his or her life and personality. Although the process is frequently described in discrete stages, it is generally unpredictable and confusing, with many stops and starts. In particular, denial weaves in and out, periodically halting progress. The process may be peppered by crisis provoked by self-defeating or self-punishing behaviors. For example, although persons in the initial stages of coming out are well advised to develop a support network as a first priority, many become involved in brief and tumultuous romantic involvements and subsequently experience considerable anxiety and self-recrimination. Other individuals reveal their sexual orientation to others impulsively and without adequate forethought and preparation. They may be unprepared for the negative responses that leave them distrustful and isolated. Even with the best preparation, however, unpredictable reactions in others may occur, causing significant distress.

The coming-out process represents a shift in the person's core sexual identity and may be accompanied by dramatic levels of emotional distress. Adolescent males, in particular, may display virtually any psychiatric symptom, especially if they are without support or without adequate information about sexuality. In general, the best predictor of the client's prognosis is his or her premorbid level of function rather than the presenting symptomatology. Despite the temporary severity of emotional dysfunction, most gay and lesbian clients weather the coming-out crisis and emerge several years later with reduced symptomatology and improved functioning.

The psychiatric symptoms that are sometimes seen during the coming-out process are, at least in part, attributable to an unfortunate coincidence of events. Few individuals choose to come out for reasons of personal growth or self-actualization. Most come out because they feel compelled to do so. Often, homosexual feelings have abruptly emerged and broken through denial or other defenses. The disruption may be precipitated by a real or perceived relationship or infatuation with someone of the same gender. Poor social skills, as previously discussed, may leave the client ill equipped to manage the complicated series of interpersonal events. Patterns of denial, emotional constriction, and lack of introspection compound the problem. Finally, at this time in life, few persons have a support system within the gay and lesbian community; most are acquainted only with individuals who are homophobic or poorly informed. Remafedi (1987) has described varieties of psychological problems in gay male adolescents.

DIFFERENCES BETWEEN LESBIAN
AND GAY INDIVIDUALS

Lesbian and gay identity development differ from each other in a number of ways that are especially prominent during adolescence and the coming-out period. The coming-out process for males appears more abrupt and more likely to be associated with psychiatric symptoms, whereas the process for women often appears characterized by greater fluidity and ambiguity. Differences in the tempo of identity development are influenced by patterns of sexual socialization. Because women are allowed a broader range of behavioral and emotional interactions with other women, many lesbian teenagers experience their emerging sexual and emotional intimacy as mere friendship. Because men are confined to more narrow patterns of expression, longing for emotional and physical contact with other males is apt to be perceived as clearly homosexual. Consistent with traditional sex-role socialization, males are more prone to sexual acting out during the coming-out process, and women are more likely to respond with reflection and self-absorption. Of course, these generalizations are more or less true of any single individual, depending on the flexibility of his or her sexual role and other aspects of personality structure.

Stereotypic sex-role behaviors may persist as the young person begins intimate relationships. Men are apt to sexualize their relationships, to be competitive, autonomous, and independent, rather than intimate. Women, on the other hand, are socialized to develop and express intimacy, but they may be less skilled in maintaining autonomy and individuality. Based on these stereotypes, problems in gay male relationships can be expected early on, as the two men struggle to develop a sense of being a couple and to contain their tendency toward competition and independence. There may be a tendency for sexual aspects of the relationship to predominate and for disagreement about sexual expression to be perceived as a threat to self-esteem. If the men can develop a greater capacity for intimacy and mutual cooperation, however, problems with autonomy and competitiveness tend to diminish with time. According to this model, a different pattern of strengths and weaknesses would be anticipated for lesbian relationships. A sense of being coupled often emerges quickly and with considerable vigor. At later stages in the relationship, problems may develop if autonomy and individuality do not counterbalance the forces toward merger and dependency. The constraints of sex-role socialization are not unique to gay and lesbian relationships. They may be intense and quickly apparent, however, because the partners in the relationship are of the same gender. Helping gay and lesbian adolescents understand the influences of their sex-role socialization tends to be helpful in reducing the likelihood of later relationship problems.

TREATMENT OF THE GAY
AND LESBIAN ADOLESCENT

A number of resources detail psychotherapeutic management of gay and lesbian adolescent clients (Malyon 1981, 1982; Roesler and Deisher 1972; Daher 1977). A few common pitfalls of clinical management are outlined below.

Health practitioners frequently err by minimizing the adolescent client's homosexual desires and interests. A teenager who expresses such feelings is overcoming considerable peer and cultural pressure to remain hidden. Whether the client is heterosexual, homosexual, or bisexual, dismissing his or her concerns is intimidating and overwhelming, and may actually intensify anxiety.

Some health professionals fear that discussing same-sex concerns will "create" homosexuality. In reality, sexual orientation appears to be established relatively early in childhood, and there is little evidence that it is plastic or changeable. Clinical experience suggests that professionals cannot alter an adolescent's sexual orientation, but can merely obscure it by cooperating in avoidance, denial, and shame.

Another typical error is to push the adolescent toward a premature resolution of sexual identity. Even in the best of circumstances, understanding and accepting one's sexual orientation and identity is an ongoing process that spans a number of years. Persons who are bisexual or who have been sexually abused may require even more time. Health professionals who focus on the quality of the adolescent's interpersonal relationships, general coping skills, and a gradual exploration of sexuality are likely to be more effective and genuinely helpful than those who insist on a particular time frame or sexual orientation as the outcome of treatment. Young persons struggling with sexual identity benefit from sound and complete information about human sexuality and from clear and consistent messages that sexual orientation does not determine the value of a person, mental health status, or the quality of life. The optimal treatment milieu provides ample time to resolve sexual-identity concerns and encourages self-acceptance, knowledge, and reasonable experimentation. In this environment, most adolescents will resolve sexual-identity confusion. When resolution does not occur, problems such as sexual abuse, emotional deprivation, family dysfunction, prolonged external stress and prejudice, and other psychosocial issues should be suspected. In particular, chronic confusion about sexual identity can be one of the sequelae of sexual abuse.

SERVICES NEEDED BY GAY AND LESBIAN ADOLESCENTS

SUPPORT GROUPS

In general, support groups are the most valuable resources for gay and lesbian adolescents. They provide an opportunity for developing social skills, discussing the meaning of sexuality and sexual identity, finding support and understanding from peers, sharing information, and socializing. Unlike group therapy, support groups generally do not focus on in-depth exploration of psychological issues. The optimal group has male and female adult facilitators who can moderate activities and direct adolescents to appropriate medical, mental health, substance abuse, or other services, as needed. Participation in the support group may preclude the need to obtain other individual mental health services. Mental health professionals frequently err by addressing social problems with the tools that they know best, that is, mental health services. The danger of this approach is to focus on psychopathology and to avoid the more central social and developmental issues. Some gay and lesbian adolescents will require psychotherapy, but it should not be considered the first and foremost response to the troubled teenager. In the absence of obvious, severe individual psychopathology, a practical approach is to refer the client to a support group while a thorough mental health evaluation is being conducted. More often than not, improvement will ensue, and the need for mental health services will diminish.

FAMILY SUPPORT

Organizations such as Parents and Friends of Lesbians and Gays can be invaluable in reducing the isolation and discomfort of families with homosexual children through organizational resources, support, and information. More dysfunctional families may require mental health services, but, again, most families need information and support rather than therapy.

HEALTH CARE AND SOCIAL SERVICES

Those gay and lesbian adolescents who do require health care, mental health and substance-abuse treatment, or various social services often need help in identifying providers who are informed and sensitive. In communities where quality services for gays and lesbians do not exist, they can be successfully developed within existing agencies by knowledgeable and sensitive health professionals, youth workers, or lay advocates. Institutions can improve their care of gays and lesbians through in-service training, discussions among personnel regarding attitudes toward homosexuality, and appropriate use of consultants. It is this author's belief that general competence, specific knowledge of gay and lesbian issues, sensitivity, and freedom from bias are the qualities desired in someone who provides health care and social services to gay and lesbian youth. Sexual orientation of the provider is of much less importance and does not predict the above qualities. Gonsiorek (1980:302–5) has described the provider-client relationship in detail.

ROLE MODELS

A healthy socialization process involves positive role models. Ideally, the socialization experience for gay and lesbian adolescents will include learning from competent gay and lesbian adults. Observing how successful adults develop productive and ethical life-styles, resolve problems of identity disclosure, obtain support, manage a career, and build relationships can be extremely valuable for teenagers. Formal structures for providing role models are emerging in a few gay and lesbian communities across the country.

ADVOCACY AND EDUCATION

Some of the approaches to the problems of gay and lesbian youth are neither personal nor professional, but actually political, social, or educational in nature. Improvements in health and social services require political advocacy. Health care professionals play an important role in educating colleagues in institutions by setting a standard and model for competent, nonprejudiced, and professional services. Reading materials for gay and lesbian adolescents (Hanckel and Cunningham 1979; Stanley and Wolfe 1980; Berzon and Leighton 1979) are an important source of accurate and complete information about sexuality.

AIDS EDUCATION

Gay male adolescents should be particularly targeted for AIDS risk-reduction efforts. Because many of these young men have not yet developed well-entrenched patterns of sexual behavior, they may be most amenable to learning responsible and safe sexual expression. The educational message should be clear, frank, and positive. The Hetrick-Martin Institute (formerly the Institute For the Protection of Gay and Lesbian Youth) in New York City has developed materials for youth AIDS education. Many local AIDS organizations around the country are also developing such materials.

SUMMARY

Understanding the mental health concerns of gay and lesbian adolescents begins with a recognition of the historic and cultural factors that negatively influence attitudes toward adolescent sexual expression and homosexuality. Although psychopathology is not intrinsically associated with a homosexual identity, lack of family and community support and intense social pressures may precipitate a youth's emotional distress and psychological dysfunction. His or her coping strategies may be further compromised by internalized homophobia, poor social skills, and the constraints of sex-role stereotypes. Although psychotherapy is warranted in particular cases, most gay and lesbian teenagers derive the greatest benefit from participating in support groups, locating appropriate adult role models, and obtaining sensitive educational information and supportive care. The most powerful treatment for the emotional concerns of gay and lesbian youth is to normalize their experiences as adolescents.

REFERENCES

Allport, G. W. 1962. *The Nature of Prejudice.* Reading, Mass.: Addison-Wesley.
Ariès, P. 1962. *Centuries of Childhood. A Social History of Family Life.* New York: Random House.
Berzon, B., and R. Leighton, eds. 1979. *Positively Gay.* Millbrae, Calif.: Celestial Arts.
Borhek, M. 1979. *My Son Eric.* New York: Pilgrim Press.
Borhek, M. 1983. *Coming Out to Parents: A Two-Way Survival Guide for Gay/Lesbian Persons and Their Parents.* New York: Pilgrim Press.
Cass, V. 1979. Homosexual identity formation: A theoretical model. *Journal of Homosexuality* 4:219–35.

Coleman, E. 1982. Changing approaches to the treatment of homosexuality. *American Behavioral Scientist* 25:397–406.

Daher, D. 1977. Sexual identity confusion in late adolescence: Therapy and values. *Psychotherapy: Theory Research and Practice* 14:12–17.

Davison, G. 1982. Politics, ethics and therapy for homosexuality. *American Behavioral Scientist* 25:423–34.

Fairchild, B., and N. Hayward. 1979. *Now That You Know: What Every Parent Should Know about Homosexuality.* New York: Harcourt Brace Jovanovich.

Foucault, M. 1978. *The History of Sexuality.* Vol. 1. New York: Random House.

Gonsiorek, J. 1980. What health care professionals need to know about gay men and lesbians. In M. Jospe, J. Niberding, and B. Cohen, eds., *Psychological Factors in Health Care*, pp. 297–311. Lexington, Mass.: Heath.

Gonsiorek, J. 1981. Book review of W. H. Masters and V. E. Johnson, *Homosexuality in Perspective. Journal of Homosexuality* 6:81–88.

Gonsiorek, J. 1982a. Introduction (to Mental Health Section). In W. Paul, J. Weinrich, J. Gonsiorek, and M. Hotvedt, eds., *Homosexuality: Social, Psychological and Biological Issues*, pp. 57–70. Beverly Hills, Calif.: Sage.

Gonsiorek, J. 1982b. Results of psychological testing on homosexual populations. *American Behavioral Scientist* 25:385–96.

Gonsiorek, J. 1982c. Social psychological concepts and the understanding of homosexuality. *American Behavioral Scientist* 25:483–92.

Gonsiorek, J. 1984. Psychotherapeutic issues with gay and lesbian clients. In P. A. Keller and L. G. Ritt, *Innovations in Clinical Practice: A Source Book*, vol. 3, pp. 69–84. Sarasota, Fla.: Professional Resource Exchange.

Hammersmith, M., and C. Williams. 1973. Homosexual identity: Commitment, adjustment and significant others. *Sociometry* 36:56–79.

Hanckel, F., and J. A. Cunningham. 1979. *A Way of Love, a Way of Life: A Young Person's Introduction to What It Means to Be Gay.* New York: Lothrop Lee and Shepard.

Hencken, J., and W. O'Dowd. 1977. Coming out as an aspect of identity formation. *Gay Academic Union* 1:18–22.

Kruks, G. 1986. Personal communication.

Malyon, A. 1981. The homosexual adolescent: Developmental issues and social bias. *Child Welfare* 60:321–30.

Malyon, A. 1982. Psychotherapeutic implications of internalized homophobia in gay men. In J. Gonsiorek, ed., *Homosexuality and Psychotherapy: A Practitioners Handbook of Affirmative Models*, pp. 59–70. New York: Haworth Press.

Martin, A. D. 1982. Learning to hide: The socialization of the gay adolescent. *Adolescent Psychiatry* 10:52–65.

Martin, A. D. 1984. The emperor's new clothes: Modem attempts to change sexual orientation. In E. Hetrick and T. S. Stein, eds., *Innovations in Psychotherapy with Homosexuals*, pp. 23–58. Washington, D.C.: American Psychiatric Press.

Masters, W. H., and V. E. Johnson. 1979. *Homosexuality in Perspective.* Boston: Little, Brown.

Mendel, G. 1971. *Pour décoloniser l'enfant: Sociopsychanalyse de l'autorité.* Paris: Payot.

Meredith, R. L., and R. W. Riester. 1980. Psychotherapy, responsibility and homosexuality: Clinical examination of socially deviant behavior. *Professional Psychology Research and Practice* 11:174–93.

Pattison, E. M., and M. L. Pattison. 1980. Ex gays: Religiously mediated change in homosexuals. *American Journal of Psychiatry* 137:1553–62.

Remafedi, G. 1987. Adolescent homosexuality: Psychosocial and medical implications. *Pediatrics* 79:331–37.

Roesler, T., and R. Deisher. 1972. Youthful male homosexuality. *Journal of the American Medical Association* 219:1018–23.

Silverstein, C. 1977. *A Family Matter: Parents' Guide to Homosexuality.* New York: McGraw-Hill.

Socarides, C. 1978. *Homosexuality.* New York: Jason Aronson.

Staats, G. 1978. Stereotype content and social distance: Changing views of homosexuality. *Journal of Homosexuality* 4:15–27.

Stanley, J., and S. Wolfe. 1980. *The Coming Out Stories.* Watertown, Mass.: Persephone Press.

Troiden, R. 1979. Becoming homosexual: A model of gay identity acquisition. *Psychiatry* 42:362–73.

21

Risk Factors for Attempted Suicide in Gay and Bisexual Youth

Gary Remafedi, James A. Farrow, and Robert W. Deisher

Studies of human sexuality have noted high rates of suicidality among homosexual youth, but the problem has not been systematically examined. This work was undertaken to identify risk factors for suicide attempts among bisexual and homosexual male youth. Subjects were 137 gay and bisexual males, fourteen through twenty-one years of age, from the upper Midwest and Pacific Northwest. Forty-one subjects (41/137) reported a suicide attempt; almost half of these described multiple attempts. Twenty-one percent of all attempts resulted in medical or psychiatric admissions. Compared to nonattempters, attempters had more feminine gender roles and adopted a bisexual or homosexual identity at younger ages. Attempters were more likely than peers to report sexual abuse, drug abuse, and arrests for misconduct. The findings parallel previous studies' results and also introduce novel suicide risk factors related to gender nonconformity and sexual milestones.

According to most recent statistics, more than five thousand adolescents and young adults (aged fifteen to twenty-four) in the United States take their own lives each year (National Center for Health Statistics 1986). During the past twenty-five years, suicide rates for young men quadrupled, and self-inflicted death became the second leading cause of adolescent mortality. These disturbing trends have led to an ongoing search for epidemiological, psychological, and sociological risk factors. Despite considerable progress and new information, the unifying characteristics of young victims are still incompletely understood (Hoberman 1989).

The impact of sexual identity on suicide risk is a relatively uncharted area of research. To date, most surveys of suicide attempters and psychological autopsies of victims have not examined sexual dimensions beyond gender (Remafedi 1988). Surveys of homosexual populations, however, have raised questions about suicide risk in relation to sexual orientation. An unusual prevalence of suicide attempts and ideation among homosexual persons has surfaced repeatedly as an incidental finding in studies of human sexuality (Jay and Young 1979; Bell and Weinberg 1978; Saghir and Robins 1973; Roesler and Deisher 1972; Remafedi 1987a).

Forty percent of five thousand homosexual men and women who were surveyed by Jay and Young (1979) seriously considered or attempted suicide. Bell and Weinberg (1978) found that a thousand Black and White homosexual men were, respectively, twelve and three times more likely than heterosexual men to report suicidal ideation or attempts. The homosexual men were more likely to have made attempts during adolescence than adulthood. Saghir and Robins (1973) reported that all suicide attempts in a cohort of homosexual adults occurred during adolescence, often in association with a history of childhood gender atypical behavior or emotional disturbance. In two different studies of homosexual and bisexual adolescents (Roesler and Deisher 1972; Remafedi 1987a), one-third of boys reported attempts, and repeat attempts were common.

Two-thirds of randomly sampled U.S. psychiatrists (Kourany 1987) believed that the self-injurious acts of homosexual adolescents were more serious and lethal than those of their heterosexual peers. The recent *Report of the Secretary's Task Force on Youth Suicide* (U.S. Department of Health and Human Services 1989) projected that gay adolescents were two to three times more likely than peers to attempt suicide, accounting for as many as 30 percent of completed youth suicides each year. Theoretical risk factors include "coming out" at a young age, gender atypicality, low self-esteem, substance abuse, running away, involvement in prostitution, and other psychosocial morbidities. Such predictors have not been studied empirically, however. This work was undertaken to identify risk factors for suicide attempts among gay and bisexual youth, with a broader goal to advancing understanding of self-inflicted deaths among adolescents.

SUBJECTS

Subjects were 137 males, between fourteen and twenty-one years of age, who identified themselves as gay (88 percent) or bisexual (12 percent). They were recruited during a one-year period (1988) through advertisements in gay publications (30 percent) and bars (5 percent), social support groups for gay and lesbian youth (20 percent) and university students (15 percent), a youth drop-in center (19 percent), and referral from peers (11

TABLE 21.1
Demographic Characteristics (Means and Percent Frequency
Distribution [%F]) of Suicide Attempters and Nonattempters

Variable	Attempters (n = 41)	Nonattempters (n = 96)
Mean age, y (SD)	19.25 (1.63)	19.83 (1.63)
Mean grade level (SD)	11.58 (1.86)	12.42 (1.98)
Race, %F		
White	76	85
Black, Native American, Hispanic, Asian	24	15
Residence, %F		
Urban	66	71
Suburban/rural	34	29
Interview location, %F		
Minneapolis	59	74
Seattle	42	26
Primary financial support, %F		
Employment (self)	43	55
Parents	35	34
Other	22	11
Religion, %F		
Catholic	20	24
Protestant	24	35
Other*	29	24
None	27	17

*Includes non-Christian faiths or religiosity, without specific affiliation.

percent). None was referred from mental heath treatment facilities. Interviews took place in Minneapolis or Seattle. The project was advertised as a study of health issues for gay and bisexual male youth, twenty-one years of age or younger.

Participants resided in the states of Minnesota (67 percent), Washington (31 percent), South Dakota (1 percent), or Wisconsin (1 percent). The ethnic/racial composition of the group was 82 percent White, 13 percent African-American, 4 percent Hispanic, and 1 percent Asian. Other demographic characteristics are summarized in table 21.1. Thirty percent of participants (41/137) reported at least one suicide attempt.

METHODS

All participants completed a structured interview regarding demography, education, home environment, sexuality, and psychosocial history (adapted from a previous study of adolescent homosexuality; Remafedi

1987b). Suicide attempts were defined as deliberate acts intended to cause death. Suicide attempts were assessed in interviews, using Weisman and Worden's Risk Rescue Rating Scale (1972). When subjects reported multiple attempts, only the latest three were used.

According to Weisman and Worden (1972), the overall seriousness of a suicide attempt is "a balance of calculated factors related to the degree of irreversible damage and the resources that facilitate or hinder rescue." Weisman and Worden's method rates attempts by degrees of risk and rescuability and provides a composite ratio of risk and rescue factors. "Risk points" correspond to the method of injury, subsequent physical impairment, and the type of medical care administered. "Rescue points" are determined by the victim's location, request for help, the rescuer's identity, and the duration of time until discovery. The total risk and rescue points are converted to respective scores, which correspond to intervals on Likert-type scales ranging from "least" to "most" risky or rescuable. When the victims sought help for themselves, their attempts automatically receive a "most rescuable" score. The composite risk-rescue ratio is computed by dividing the risk score by the sum of risk and rescue factors.

All participants also completed (in interviews) the Scale for Suicide Ideation (Beck, Kovacs, and Weissman 1979), which measures current suicidal intent by scaling various dimensions of self-destructive thoughts and wishes. Four other written instruments were administered. The Bem Sex Role Inventory (Bem 1974) was used to rate masculinity and femininity and to classify sex-role as feminine, masculine, androgynous (i.e., high masculine/high feminine), or undifferentiated (i.e., low masculine/low feminine). Current levels of depression and hopelessness were respectively measured with the Beck Depression Inventory (Beck et al. 1961) and the Hopelessness Scale (Beck et al. 1974). Finally, personal attitudes toward homosexuality were rated by the Modified Attitudes Toward Homosexuality Scale (Price 1982).

Subjects gave verbal and written consent to study procedures. Participation was voluntary and confidential. Completion of procedures required approximately 1.5 hours. Subjects were reimbursed for participation and were given a list of resources for social support and mental health and medical care. Those who indicated active suicidal intent or other acute problems were immediately referred for care, according to a protocol approved by the University of Minnesota Human Subjects Committee. Study procedures were administered by a physician (Minneapolis) and a nurse (Seattle).

STATISTICAL ANALYSIS

Response frequencies and means were computed for the suicide attempter and the nonattempter comparison groups. Independent samples χ^2 and t tests were used to compare responses from the two groups. To limit the chance occurrence of significant findings, a .01 level of statistical significance was chosen for univariate analyses. Multiple logistic regression analysis was used to identify variables that were independently predictive of suicide attempts at a .05 level of significance.

RESULTS

DESCRIPTION OF SUICIDE ATTEMPTS

Thirty percent of subjects (41/137) reported at least one suicide attempt, and almost half the attempters (18/41) reported more than one attempt. A total of sixty-eight suicide attempts were described and rated by Weisman and Worden's method. The mean age at the time of suicide attempts was 15.5 years. Ingestion of prescription or nonprescription drugs and self-laceration accounted for 80 percent of attempts. The remainder involved hangings, carbon monoxide poisonings, jumping, firearms, and automotive crashes. Twenty-one percent of the suicide attempts (14/68) resulted in a medical or psychiatric hospitalization. Almost three out of four attempts (50/68) did not receive any medical attention. These included some attempts with high potential lethality, including two intentional car accidents, two carbon monoxide asphyxiations, and ingestions of large quantities of antidepressants, acetaminophen, aspirin, or intravenous heroin.

In 44 percent of cases, subjects attributed suicide attempts to "family problems," including conflict with family members and parents' marital discord, divorce, or alcoholism. One-third of attempts were related to personal or interpersonal turmoil regarding homosexuality. Almost one-third of subjects made their first suicide attempt in the same year they identified themselves as bisexual or homosexual. Overall, three-fourths of all first attempts temporally followed self-labeling. Other common precipitants were depression (30 percent), conflict with peers (22 percent), problems in a romantic relationship (19 percent), and dysphoria associated with personal substance abuse (15 percent). In one case, a suicide attempt followed notification of a partner's human immunodeficiency virus seropositivity.

TABLE 21.2
Number (and Percent Frequency Distribution) of Suicide
Attempts (n = 45), Classified by Likelihood of Risk and Rescue

| Likelihood | Risk of Morbidity/Mortality | | |
of Rescue	Low	Moderate	High
Least	1 (2)	0	0
Moderate	5 (11)	20 (45)	1 (2)
Most	10 (22)	8 (18)	0

Fifty-four percent of all suicide attempts (37/68) received risk scores in the "moderate to high" lethality range. The remaining attempts were of the "low risk" type. In one-third of all cases (23/68), recovery was unassisted, and rescue scores could not be assigned by Weisman and Worden's criteria. These ranged from trivial injuries not needing treatment to severe insults with fortuitous recoveries. A rescue was initiated by the victim (24 percent) or by another person (76 percent) in the remaining forty-five cases. Fifty-eight percent (26/45) of these cases received scores in the "moderate to least" rescuable range. In other words, the predicted likelihood of rescue was moderate to low, despite the actual occurrence of an intervention.

Table 21.2 depicts the distribution of risk and rescue scores for the forty-five attempts for which both scores were available. Almost half of them (45 percent) were associated with moderate risk and moderate likelihood of rescue. Composite risk-rescue scores also were computed for these attempts. Thirty-six percent (18/45) received scores at or above Weisman and Worden's empirically derived mean (40) for adult attempters hospitalized in medical or psychiatric units.

UNIVARIATE ANALYSES

The following is a summary of the similarities and differences among the comparison groups. Further detail is provided in table 21.3. There were no statistically significant differences ($P < .01$) between attempters and nonattempters with regard to age, educational level, race, religion, residence, or source of financial support. The majority of all participants (107/137, 78 percent) had received some type of professional mental health care. Mean scores for current depression, hopelessness, and suicide intent (as measured by the respective instruments), however, were uniformly low for attempters and nonattempters. Also, no statistically signif-

TABLE 21.3

Psychosocial Characteristics (Mean and Percent Frequency Distribution [%F])
of Suicide Attempters and Nonattempters

Variables	Attempters (n = 41)	Nonattempters (n = 96)	df	P Value*
Sexual milestones: mean ages, y (SD)				
Earliest bi/homosexual attraction	9.27 (2.89)	10.66 (3.84)	130	.050
Bi/homosexual self-labeling	13.74 (3.22)	15.44 (2.61)	132	.002
First homosexual experience	14.38 (2.48)	16.13 (2.54)	129	.000
First heterosexual experience	14.61 (2.56)	16.10 (1.87)	57	.030
Coming out to others	15.62 (2.92)	16.95 (2.22)	128	.005
Psychosocial stressors, %F				
Parents' martial status				
Unmarried	7	6		
Divorced	61	42	3	.08
Married	27	50		
Mother knows son's sexuality	87	81	1	.44
Supportive maternal response	32	38	4	.62
Father knows son's sexuality	65	56	1	.45
Supportive paternal response	23	15	4	.58
Friendship loss	42	28	1	.18
Peer suicide	39	27	1	.24
Discrimination	61	46	1	.15
Violence	39	38	1	1.00
Sexual abuse	61	29	1	.0008
Psychosocial problems, %F				
Running away	49	36	1	.25
Arrest	51	28	1	.01
Prostitution	29	17	1	.20
Ethanol ever use	78	83	1	.62
Illicit drug use	85	63	1	.01
Personal mental health, %F				
Any mental health services	88	74	1	.12
Chemical dependency treatment	22	6	1	.01
No current suicide intent (item from Scale for Suicide Ideation)	68	84	1	.06
No suicide plan (item from Scale for Suicide Ideation)	93	98	1	.32
Family mental health,† %F				
Depression	43	40	1	.92
Attempted/complete suicide	38	22	1	.12
Psychiatric hospitalization	44	45	1	.12

continued

TABLE 21.3 *continued*

Variables	Attempters (n = 41)	Nonattempters (n = 96)	df	P Value*
Psychometric indices: mean scores (SD)				
Beck Depression Inventory	10.78 (8.60)	7.68 (7.20)	135	.03
Scale for Suicide Ideation	6.90 (6.40)	4.61 (4.50)	135	.04
Hopelessness Scale	4.37 (0.50)	2.90 (0.40)	135	.10
Attitudes toward homosexuality	56.24 (14.5)	56.35 (0.19)	133	.97
Bem-masculinity raw score	4.75 (0.66)	5.04 (0.79)	135	.04
Bem-femininity raw score	5.08 (0.66)	4.91 (0.61)	135	.15
Bem classification, %F				
Masculine	7.3	26.0		
Feminine	36.6	17.7		
Androgynous	26.8	32.3	3	.01
Undifferentiated	29.3	24.0		

*P values correspond to χ^2 tests for nominal variables and t tests for continuous variables.
†Includes first- to-third-degree relatives.

icant ($P < .01$) differences were noted in the reported occurrence of depression, attempted or completed suicide, and psychiatric hospitalization among family members. Approximately one-third of subjects in both groups were acquainted with a peer who had committed suicide.

Differences in gender role and sexual orientation development were prominent. Based on the Bem classification, attempters were more likely than nonattempters to be feminine or undifferentiated, and less likely to be masculine or androgynous ($P = .01$). Compared to nonattempters, attempters described themselves as bisexual or homosexual ($P = .002$) and shared this with other persons ($P = .005$) at younger ages. They also engaged in homosexual ($P = .0001$) and heterosexual activity ($P = .03$) to the point of orgasm at younger ages than their peers, although differences in the mean ages of first heterosexual activity were not statistically significant. As indicated by table 21.3, bisexual or homosexual self-identification generally preceded first sexual experiences with either gender.

Suicide attempters were more likely than nonattempters ($P = .0008$) to report sexual abuse, broadly defined as being forced, pressured, or tricked to have sex. Detailed descriptions of incidents were not obtained. Twenty-nine percent of attempters and 17 percent of nonattempters accepted money for sex on at least one occasion. Both groups reported similar personal attitudes toward homosexuality, reactions from parents and friends, and experiences with discrimination and violence.

Compared to peers, a larger proportion of attempters reported illicit drug use (85 percent versus 63 percent, $P = .01$) and arrest for criminal activities (51 percent versus 28 percent, $P = .01$). Twenty-two percent of attempters (vs 6 percent of nonattempters, $P = .01$) had undergone chemical dependency treatment. Theft (40 percent) and possession of illicit substances (20 percent) accounted for the majority of reported arrests. The remaining violations included assault, vandalism, disorderly conduct, disturbing the peace, trespassing, prostitution, and other sex offenses.

Multivariate Analyses

The univariate analyses revealed a total of nine variables that were associated with suicide attempts at the .01 level of statistical significance. Multiple logistic regression analysis was undertaken to identify which were predictive of attempts, when controlling for the other variables. Of the nine variables, five were entered into the analysis based on their conceptual inclusivity and completeness of ascertainment in this study. From the four items related to sexual milestones, age at the time of bisexual or homosexual self-labeling was selected. From the two items regarding substance abuse, ever having used illegal drugs was chosen. Finally, feminine gender role, criminal apprehension, and sexual abuse were included. All five variables were obtained in 96 percent (132/137) of cases.

Based on the multiple logistic regression analysis, ever having used illicit drugs, feminine gender role, and age at the time of bisexual or homosexual self-labeling were independently associated with suicide attempts at the .05 level of statistical significance (table 21.4). Feminine gender roles and illicit drug use each were associated with greater than a threefold risk of attempted suicide. According to the model, the likelihood of an attempt diminished with advancing age at the time of bisexual or homosexual self-labeling. With each year's delay in self-identification, the odds of a suicide attempt declined by more than 80 percent.

TABLE 21.4
Summary Table: Regression Analysis of Suicide Attempts

Variable	Odds Ratio	95% Confidence Interval	Regression Coefficient	SE	P Value
Constant	—	—	0.24	1.24	—
Label age	0.82	0.69–0.96	−0.21	0.08	0.01
Drug use	3.63	1.07–12.24	1.29	0.61	0.03
Feminine	3.03	1.10–8.31	1.11	0.50	0.03
Sex abuse	2.23	0.90–5.53	0.81	0.45	0.08
Arrest	1.87	0.74–4.67	0.62	0.46	0.06

DISCUSSION

Approximately one-third of gay and bisexual youth in this study reported at least one intentional self-destructive act, and almost half of them repeatedly attempted suicide. The gravity of some attempts is reflected in the rate of subsequent hospitalization (21 percent), the lethality of methods (54 percent, moderate to high risk), and the victims' inaccessibility to rescue (62 percent, moderate to least rescuable). The findings support psychiatrists' concerns about the severity of suicide attempts among homosexual youth (Kourany 1987).

In this sample, bisexuality or homosexuality per se was not associated with self-destructive acts. Most of the subjects did not attempt or plan suicide. From the perspective of many attempters, however, sexual concerns were circumstantially or temporally related to self-harm. One-third of all suicide attempts were attributed to personal or interpersonal turmoil about homosexuality. One-third of first attempts occurred in the same year that subjects identified their bisexuality or homosexuality, and most other attempts happened soon thereafter. The apparent connection between sexual milestones and attempts may be a clue to the appropriate timing of suicide-prevention efforts.

Based on the univariate analyses, suicide attempts were not explained by experiences with discrimination, violence, loss of friendship, or current personal attitudes toward homosexuality. Unlike other reports (Rotheram 1987), this study did not find a significant association between attempts and running away from home. Gender nonconformity and precocious psychosexual development were, however, predictive of self-harm. Compared to peers, suicide attempters recognized homosexual attractions and told other persons at younger ages. First sexual experiences with males and females also occurred at younger ages among suicide attempters than among their peers. For each year's delay in bisexual or homosexual self-labeling, the odds of a suicide attempt diminished by 80 percent. These findings support a previously observed, inverse relationship between psychosocial problems and the age of acquiring a homosexual identity (Remafedi 1987a). Compared to older persons, early and middle adolescents may be generally less able to cope with the isolation and stigma of a homosexual identity.

A feminine or undifferentiated gender role may accentuate a gay adolescent's sense of differentness and further exacerbate problems (Martin 1982). Severely gender-atypical male children have been observed to experience a "pervasive psychological disturbance" (Coates and Person 1985) and an "abnormal amount of depression and social conflict resulting from peer rejection, isolation, and ridicule of their feminine behavior" (Rosen, Rekers, and Friar 1977). In general, masculine and androgynous boys and girls alike have better self-esteem (Lamke 1982) and lower rates of substance use and psychological distress (Horwitz and White 1987) than feminine or undifferentiated youth. Among male and female college students, masculinity and androgyny are associated with positive adjustment to stress (Roos and Cohen 1987) and minimal fearfulness (Dillon, Wolf, and Katz 1985).

The univariate analyses also revealed an association between sexual abuse and suicide attempts. When controlling for other variables in the multiple regression analysis, however, sexual abuse was not a statistically significant predictor. The contribution of sexual abuse to suicide risk may have been subsumed by other variables, such as drug use or gender atypicality. For example, gender-atypical boys may be vulnerable to sexual assault, as well as suicide. Alternatively, abused boys may develop substance abuse problems that heighten suicide risk. Also noteworthy, sexual abuse did not appear to have a major impact on sexual identity, because bisexual or homosexual identification usually preceded sexual experiences.

The attempters in this study resembled actual suicide victims in regard to high levels of family dysfunction (Thompson 1987; Shaffer 1974; Hoberman and Garfinkel 1988; Peck 1984), personal substance abuse (Hoberman and Garfinkel 1988; Peck 1984; Brent et al. 1988; Poteet 1987; Shaffer 1988; Slap et al. 1989; Rich et al. 1986), and other antisocial behaviors (Shaffer 1974, 1988; Shaffi et al. 1985). Family problems were the most frequently cited reason for attempts. Eighty-five percent of attempters reported illicit drug use, and 22 percent had undergone chemical dependency treatment. More than half (21/41) of the attempters had been arrested for misconduct. Like other boys who eventually complete suicide (Thompson 1987; Shaffi et al. 1985; Cosand, Bourque, and Krauss 1982), many subjects made multiple unsuccessful attempts. In general, many of the psychosocial problems associated with gay suicide attempts (e.g., family discord, substance abuse, and conflict with the law) are familiar correlates of completed youth suicide. Such problems often complicate "coming out" at an early age (Remafedi 1987a) and may further contribute to the high rate of suicide in this group.

In contrast to some psychological autopsies of young victims (Thompson 1987; Poteet 1987; Shaffi et al. 1985), this study found low levels of active depression, hopelessness, and suicidal intent among attempters. Moreover, the attempters and nonattempters had similar family histories of depression, suicide, and psychiatric hospitalization. Although chronic or heritable forms of depression did not account for suicide attempts in this group, the results must be interpreted cautiously. Acute depression and hopelessness at the time of the attempt may have since lifted with treatment or the passage of time, and subjects may not have been well informed of family mental histories.

The circumstances, prevalence, and severity of suicide attempts in this cohort may not reflect the general population of homosexually oriented boys and girls. Because of the social stigma of homosexuality, a probability sampling of homosexual youth was unfeasible. An effort was made, however, to enhance the generalizability of the findings by recruiting subjects from diverse settings and geographical areas. Gay-identified adolescents are a subset of all youth who will eventually disclose a homosexual orientation (Remafedi 1990). As our own findings suggest, the experiences of openly gay and bisexual youth may be quite different from those of other boys who are confused, hiding, or delayed in identifying sexual feelings. Likewise, the risks for suicide among lesbian girls may be quite different from those among boys because of the gender, gender role, sexual identity development, and cultural differences.

Acknowledging these limitations, the unusual prevalence of serious suicide attempts remains a consistent and disturbing finding in the existing reports of young homosexual males. The rate of completed suicide among homosexual attempters is unknown, as is the relative contribution of homosexual adolescents to total youth suicides. These issues merit further investigation to illuminate the epidemiology of adolescent suicide, the direction of suicide prevention programs, and the care of individual clients. We hope that this study's findings will lead to other investigations of sexuality and suicide among representative samples of youth in schools or other community settings. Ultimately, the study of suicide among gay and bisexual youth may shed new light on the unifying characteristics of adolescent victims, unraveling the common threads of risk that transcend the issue of sexual orientation.

ACKNOWLEDGMENTS

Statistical consultation was provided by Kinley Larntz, Professor of Statistics. Special thanks to Robert Blum, Kevin Cwayna, Barry Garfinkel, Mary Story, Kenneth Winters, and John Yoakam, for their consultation, and to Dean McWilliams, Joy Love, and W. S. Foster for their technical assistance.

REFERENCES

Beck, A. T., C. H. Ward, M. Mendelson et al. 1961. An inventory for measuring depression. *Archives of General Psychiatry* 4:561–71.

Beck, A. T., A. Weissman, D. Lester et al. 1974. The measurement of pessimism: the hopelessness scale. *Journal of Consulting and Clinical Psychology* 42:861–65.

Beck, A. T., M. Kovacs, and A. Weissman. 1979. Assessment of suicidal intention: the scale for suicide ideation. *Journal of Consulting and Clinical Psychology* 47:343–52.

Bell, A., and M. Weinberg. 1978. *Homosexualities: A Study of Diversity Among Men and Women.* New York: Simon and Schuster.

Bem, S. 1974. The measurement of psychological androgyny. *Journal of Consulting and Clinical Psychology* 42:155–62.

Brent, D. A., J. A. Perper, C. E. Goldstein et al. Risk factors for adolescent suicide. 1988. *Archives of General Psychiatry* 45:581–88.

Coates, S., and E. S. Person. 1985. Extreme boyhood femininity: Isolated behavior or pervasive disorder. *Journal of the American Academy of Child Psychiatry* 24:702–9.

Cosand, B. J., M. L. Bourque, and J. F. Krauss. 1950. Suicide among adolescents in Sacramento County, California, 1950–1979. *Adolescence* 17:917–30.

Dillon, K. M., E. Wolf, and H. Katz. 1985. Sex roles, gender, and fear. *Journal of Psychology* 119:355–59.

Hoberman, H. M. 1989. Completed suicide in children and adolescents: A review. *Residential Treatment for Children and Youth* 7:61–88.

Hoberman, H. M., and B. D. Garfinkel. 1988. Completed suicide in children and adolescents. *Journal of the American Academy of Child and Adolescent Psychiatry* 27:689–95.

Horwitz, A. V., and H. R. White. 1987. Gender role orientations and styles of pathology among adolescents. *Journal of Health and Social Behavior* 28:158–70.

Jay, K., and A. Young, eds. 1979. *The Gay Report: Lesbians and Gay Men Speak Out About Their Sexual Experiences and Lifestyles.* New York: Simon and Schuster.

Kourany, R. F. 1987. Suicide among homosexual adolescents. *Journal of Homosexuality* 13(4):111–17.

Lamke, L. K. 1982. The impact of sex-role orientation on self-esteem in early adolescence. *Child Development* 53:1530–35.

Martin, A. D. 1982. Learning to hide: the socialization of the gay adolescent. *Adolescent Psychiatry* 10:52–65.

National Center for Health Statistics. 1986. *Vital Statistics of the United States.* Vol. 2: *Mortality, Part A.* Hyattsville, Md.: NCHS.

Peck, M. 1984. Suicide in late adolescence and young adulthood. In C. L. Hatton and S. M. Velenti, eds., *Suicide: Assessment and Intervention,* pp. 220–30. Norwalk, Conn.: Appleton-Century-Crofts.

Poteet, D. J. 1987. Adolescent suicide: A review of 87 cases of completed suicide in Shelby County, Tennessee. *American Journal of Forensic Medicine and Pathology* 8:12–17.

Price, J. H. 1982. High school students' attitudes toward homosexuality. *Journal of School Health* 52:469–74.

Remafedi, G. 1987a. Adolescent homosexuality: Psychosocial and medical implications. *Pediatrics* 79:331–37.

Remafedi, G. 1987b. Male homosexuality: The adolescent's perspective. *Pediatrics* 79:326–30.

Remafedi, G. 1988. Adolescent homosexuality: A challenge to contemporary society. *Journal of the American Medical Association* 258:222–25.

Remafedi, G. 1990. Adolescent homosexuality. *Medical Clinics of North America* 74:1169–79.

Rich, C. L., R. C. Fowler, D. Young, and M. Blenkush. 1986. San Diego suicide study: Comparison of gay to straight males. *Suicide and Life-Threatening Behavior* 16:448–57.

Roesler, T., and R. W. Deisher. 1972. Youthful male homosexuality. *Journal of the American Medical Association* 219:1018–23.

Roos, P. E., and L. H. Cohen. 1987. Sex roles and social support as moderators of life stress adjustment. *Journal of Personality and Social Psychology* 3:576–85.

Rosen, A. C., G. A. Rekers, and L. R. Friar. 1977. Theoretical and diagnostic issues in child gender disturbances. *Journal of Sex Research* 13:89–103.

Rotheram, M. J. 1987. Evaluation of imminent danger for suicide among youth. *American Journal of Orthopsychiatry* 57:102–10.

Saghir, M. T., and E. Robins. 1973. *Male and Female Homosexuality: A Comprehensive Investigation.* Baltimore: Williams and Wilkins.

Shaffer, D. 1974. Suicide in childhood and early adolescence. *Journal of Child Psychology and Psychiatry* 15:275–91.

Shaffer, D. 1988. The epidemiology of teen suicide: An examination of risk factors. *Journal of Clinical Psychiatry* 49:36–41.

Shaffi, N., S. Carrigan, J. R. Whittinghill, and A. Derric. 1985. Psychology autopsy of completed suicide in children and adolescents. *American Journal of Psychiatry* 142:1061–64.

Slap, G. B., D. F. Vorters, S. Chaudhuri, and R. M. Centor. 1989. Risk factors for attempted suicide during adolescence. *Pediatrics* 84:762–72.

Thompson, T. R. 1987. Childhood and adolescent suicide in Manitoba: A demographic study. *Canadian Journal of Psychiatry* 32:264–69.

U.S. Department of Health and Human Services. 1989. *Report of the Secretary's Task Force on Youth Suicide.* Vol. 3: *Prevention and Interventions in Youth Suicide.* Rockville, Md.: DHHS.

Weisman, A. D., and J. W. Worden. 1972. Risk-rescue rating in suicide assessment. *Archives of General Psychiatry* 26:553–60.

22

Existential Issues of
Midlife Lesbians

Barbara E. Sang

I usually like to read the psychological literature that is relevant to my own life. Naturally, at middle age, I was curious to know if other women's experience was similar to my own. As I read accounts of midlife and attended conferences on the subject, I found that some of the issues that were important to me were missing: because middle age has been examined almost exclusively from a heterosexual and male perspective, this might explain why the findings did not always fit my own experience and those of other middle-aged lesbians I knew. As Fertitta (1987) points out, models of adult aging and development have been based on the nuclear family, and therefore we have little knowledge about the development of individuals who do not marry, child-free women, lesbians; gay men and ethnic minorities.

Current research on middle-aged women suggests that this is a time when women are searching for their own identity, separate from children and husbands (Rubin 1979). Rubin's study of 160 middle-aged women from all walks of life showed them to be searching for a sense of self. The midlife transitions for these women was a time often filled with turmoil and self-doubt as old roles were being shed and the shape of new ones were not apparent. Because of a lifetime of putting other people's needs before their own, these women have abandoned important parts of themselves.

In another study on middle-aged women it was found that the higher the husband's occupational status, the more likely was a woman to place the role of wife first, even if she worked (Lopata and Barnewolt 1984).

Junge and Maya (1985) found their highly educated sample of upper-middle-class women in their forties to be struggling with a clash between their traditional upbringing and the emerging options of the women's movement. Although more than half their sample worked, at least part-time, they still partially retained their identity as "home makers" and felt guilty and conflicted when away from the home.

Most lesbians have rejected the traditional female role, not only by relating sexually to women but by being economically independent of men (Love 1975). Furthermore, many lesbians are childless. Such mid- life issues as holding a job for the first time, being on one's own out in the world, and finding her identity separate from her mate are not likely to be relevant to most lesbians.

Since lesbian women have not necessarily gone through the traditional stages of female development, I wanted to know what their experiences and concerns would be at midlife. I wondered to what extent lesbians have been freer to develop their own unique potential as female individuals as a result of their nonconformity to social roles. I also wanted to know who was out there? What are we like at midlife? What is new to *us* at this time of life? What gives our life meaning? My main concern was to describe as many lesbian women I could find between the ages of forty and fifty-five. At this point in time I felt it would be best to focus my research on ourselves rather than comparing lesbians to heterosexual women and men. I also tried my best not to look at midlife lesbians from a heterosexual midlife perspective, but it is possible I was influenced by it nevertheless.

This research will be concerned mainly with existential issues because such issues are more likely to come up at midlife. What I mean by existential is the searching for something that goes beyond everyday survival; it involves a quest for deeper levels of life's meaning and the formulation of one's philosophy of life. Spiritual and more cosmic concerns may come to the forefront. The existential position emphasizes a conflict that flows from the individual's confrontation with the givens of existence: death, freedom, isolation, and meaninglessness (Yalom 1980).

RECRUITING MIDLIFE LESBIANS FOR THE STUDY

Based on my own experiences as a middle-aged lesbian and those of my middle-aged lesbian friends, I began to get a sense of the questions I wanted to ask other midlife lesbian women. My first step was to organize and to participate in several midlife lesbian discussion groups. Feedback from these groups enabled me to develop a preliminary questionnaire, which was filled out by twenty-one midlife lesbians (Sang 1987). This open-ended essay questionnaire was expanded subsequently to include several additional questions and demographic information (Sang 1991). The following are examples of some of the questions asked: "How do you feel about being middle aged?"; "Are there any issues (thoughts, feelings, conflicts, fears, problems, aspirations, and so forth) that are *new* to you as a middle-aged person?"; "What gives your life meaning?" The number of questions was limited to fourteen in order to allow the subjects to focus more intensely on a few select areas. This research was not intended to include all aspects of the midlife lesbian experience and therefore many interesting and important questions were not addressed.

I intentionally biased my results by including my proposal and rationale for the study with the questionnaire. In a sense, I was inviting lesbian women to collaborate with me rather than simply being "subjects" in the traditional sense. This approach to research is becoming increasingly more characteristic of studies being conducted in the lesbian community (Krieger 1985; Hunnisett 1986; Sang 1989). Although names were optional, many respondents gave their full name. Each woman put considerable effort into telling her story, and her own unique personality and struggle toward growth came through clearly. The degree to which the women shared intimate and personal details about themselves surprised me and further suggested that this approach to research was conducive to openness.

Description of the Midlife Lesbian Respondents

A total of 110 self-identified lesbians between the ages of forty and fifty-nine completed a midlife lesbian questionnaire. I recruited these women through lesbian friendship networks, newsletters, conferences, professional organizations, and older women's magazines, such as *Broomstick* and *Hot Flash*. The grassroots newsletter *Lesbian Connection* proved to be the best source of participants. Although considerable effort was made to include minority women, only 5 percent of this sample were minorities.

The average age of the 110 participants in this study was forty-seven years old. The respondents were from twenty-four different states, including Hawaii, and from Canada, Holland, and Israel. The states with the highest percentage of respondents were New York (13 percent) and California (11 percent). Other popular states were Arizona (8 percent), Massachusetts (6 percent), Georgia (5 percent), and Maryland (5 percent). A little more than half (57 percent) of the lesbian women had been married heterosexually at some point in their lives.

Forty-four percent of this sample have had one or more children. The majority of women who "came out" as lesbians in midlife had children (75 percent). At the time of the study, 67 percent of the women were in a lesbian relationship of varying duration and the other 33 percent were single. The lesbians in this study were a highly educated group of women, perhaps even more educated than other lesbian populations that have been studied. A large number hold doctorates (24 percent) or had training beyond the bachelor's degree (BA+, MA, MSW = 45 percent). The remaining lesbians hold bachelor degrees (12 percent), had some college (12 percent), or received a high school diploma (6 percent).

The majority (78 percent) of midlife lesbians in this sample were professionals. The others were in business or held working-class jobs. About half (52 percent) held careers or did work that can be considered nontraditional for women, for example, psychologist, dean, professor, financial analyst, and truck driver. Virtually all lesbians in this sample were self-supporting. The average age they became self-supporting was twenty-six years. Women who identified themselves as lesbians in their teens and twenties became self-supporting around twenty-three years of age.

In addition to being mostly White, highly educated, and middle-class, this sample is not representative in another respect: 34 percent are mental health professionals. It also takes considerable time and effort to fill out a questionnaire of this nature. Considering these biases, the findings may not necessarily apply to all middle-aged lesbians of today.

The midlife lesbian respondents could be divided into three groups based on the age they considered themselves to be "lesbian": the teens and twenties (39 percent), the thirties (29 percent) and midlife (25 percent). (The coming-out age of 7 percent of the sample is unknown.) Several interesting differences were found between these three groups, which will be reported where relevant.

Some Additional Characteristics of the Midlife Lesbian Sample: Sexuality and Menopause

Half (50 percent) of the midlife respondents reported that their sex life was more open and exciting than in the past. Better sex was attributed to being able to be more open and vulnerable, to enhanced communication, and to less pressure to have an orgasm; touching, loving, and sharing have become more important. Several women (9 percent) were experiencing "sexual problems" because of a partner's illness or lack of interest in sex. Approximately one quarter (26 percent) of this midlife lesbian sample reported being celibate.

The specific question on the menopause was introduced later in the study, and therefore only seventy-five women received this question instead of 110. Twenty percent of the lesbians in this smaller sample were in the menopause (no period for at least one year). An additional 15 percent have had hysterectomies. Irregular periods (24 percent), hot flashes (23 percent) and depression and irritability (3 percent) were also reported. Several women were receiving hormone replacement therapy (11 percent). Only a small number of lesbians reported physical pain or discomfort as a result of the changes taking place in their bodies (3 percent).

For the most part, midlife was found to be a highly satisfying, productive, and creative time for the majority of lesbians in this study. This is not to deny that midlife, just as any other time in life, can be a difficult period for some women. A few women in this study were dealing with serious physical illness or loss of a partner or a job.

Several major themes emerged for this midlife sample that will be elaborated on in the following sections.

THE FREEDOM OF MIDDLE AGE

GREATER SELF-CONFIDENCE AND SELF-Acceptance

The majority of midlife lesbians reported feeling more fulfilled, more self-confident and self-accepting, and more comfortable with who they are. Practically all the lesbians in this study liked themselves better at this age (93 percent) and felt midlife to be the best period of their life (76 percent). Some of the reasons for liking themselves better were that they were "more mellow," "better grounded," "less defensive," "kinder, softer, wiser," "more balanced," and had "greater self-knowledge and acceptance of their faults."

How does she feel about being middle aged? One lesbian responded: "Happy! I feel very contented—am healthy and have let go of many 'shoulds.' I live in the present and am beginning to pursue new interests as well as deepen old avocations." Another subject said:

> One, if not *the* greatest blessing about being middle-aged dykes is that while heterosexual women are frantically chasing the rainbow of "lost youth" and are frightened by their loss of "beauty" and "sex appeal"—we old dykes are daily growing more comfortable and *accepting* of our aging faces and bodies and are therefore able to see beneath the superficial to the glowing beauty of a mellow soul.

MORE SELF-DIRECTED

Another important feeling that accompanies the self acceptance of middle age is related to the freedom one experiences in not caring what other people think. The following are some typical responses: "I no longer feel the necessity of apologizing for who I am"; "I am much more free to do what I want to do—need no permission"; "I don't have to prove myself anymore"; "I seem to have less bravado and more feeling of real stature and accomplishment."

A lesbian from the Midwest writes: "Middle age brings with it the right to generalize from one's own experience—you've got enough life under your belt by then—one hopes! I have confidence that I know what I'm talking about now. Theories don't interest me." Another lesbian had this to say: "I quite like it; each year seems to get better despite some of the seemingly endless struggles. Generally, I feel better about myself and my life than I ever have . . . more focused yet more diverse in my interests and activities."

Thus, middle age for lesbians is a time to be oneself; one is more authentic as a person—less concerned with pleasing others and fitting into a prescribed mold. Many respondents felt that because of their lesbianism, they spent a lifetime fighting to be themselves rather than conforming to societal expectations of women at the time. As a result, in middle age they find themselves quite skilled at being able to stand up for what they believe and to be who they feel they are. In other words, in fighting their oppression as lesbians they have developed a stronger sense of self. These findings are consistent with Neugarten's (1968) study on middle age in which, for both men and women, this is a period of maximum capacity; there is a substantial repertoire of strategies for dealing with life.

A TIME TO PLAY AND HAVE FUN

The lesbians in this study have been career or work oriented most of their adult lives. A major theme that emerged for this group is a desire to have more fun and to be less achievement oriented. Many lesbians reported not wanting to push or strive anymore the way they did in their twenties and thirties. Several women have retired or have shortened their work hours to accommodate other needs, such as creative expression or intimacy. As one lesbian put it, "A lot more play and a lot less caring—don't have to be serious and work all the time—relate more to people—not be so work-oriented." Another lesbian said, "I feel less and less achievement-oriented in my career, more to do my best and get the work done."

And still another lesbian writes, "Although my production is still rather high I have the feeling that I care less about public prestige." A few women report consciously having to make time in their busy schedules for fun and enjoyment: "I think I would try to be less compulsive, less a perfectionist and play more. I am so serious about my work that I often overdo. I still need to learn how to relax and have fun and that it is okay to do so."

The less-pressured orientation toward work and achievement in this lesbian sample is similar to what Christine Downing (1987), Jungian writer and professor of religious studies, finds to be one of the important lessons she has learned in her "passage through the menopause." She writes, "I had lived much of my adult life in the heroic mode questing, accomplishing, competing . . . it was time to wrestle with that hero and free myself from bondage to that mode." Downing speculates that for women who have lived in a more traditionally feminine mode before menopause, middle age may be a time to acknowledge and integrate their heroic capacities.

For many lesbians in this study, work itself at this point in their lives has become easier, less stressful, and consequently more enjoyable and satisfying. They have a new sense of freedom; lesbians describe themselves as more open, playful, and spontaneous. These are the qualities that have been found to be characteristic of the creative attitude (Lieberman 1977; Maslow 1977). According to Ashley Montagu (1983), we were never intended to "grow up" into the kinds of adults most of us have become. Growing means retaining the valuable traits of childhood, such as curiosity, playfulness, flexibility, and humor. Middle age, therefore, for the lesbian sample appears to be a time of heightened creative expression. Paradoxically, what seems to be happening is that as these women are "pushing" less, they are better able to be more creative, whether it be in their careers or outside interests. (Several women in this study have made significant contributions to society during this period through teaching, writing, political activity, and art.) Brooks-Gunn and Kirsch (1984) also report that midlife may be a time of great growth, expansion, and satisfaction.

A TIME FOR CHANGE, REFOCUSING, AND INTEGRATION

Although I am aware that the term "midlife crisis" comes from a heterosexual model of the aging process, I included a question on it to see whether it had any relevance to lesbians. Approximately half (46 percent) of the midlife lesbian respondents indicated that they had or were going through what could be called a "midlife crisis." Such a "crisis" took the form of an illness, loss of a relationship, or an awareness of one's limitations. A forty-five-year-old woman says, "I passed a serious crisis at forty to forty-two—had to let go of all hopes and dreams and finally accept myself as an average person regarding set values and goals." The loss of possibilities and options is felt to be part of this crisis. A "crisis" usually forces the individual to reevaluate her needs and priorities and, in the process, may facilitate growth and development. A lesbian who recovered from a life-threatening illness became more aware of what she needed to take care of herself and what gave her pleasure. She made several basic changes in her life, one of which was a move from an urban to a rural setting. A lesbian woman who left a nineteen-year-old relationship felt that for the first time she had lost her sense of self.

A significant crisis reported for middle-aged males was the inadequacy of their achievements (Baruch and Brooks-Gunn 1984; Levinson 1978). Only one or two women in this study, in contrast, expressed anguish over not having achieved enough. It seems that lesbians derive satisfaction from many areas of their lives, and therefore the work arena is not their sole focus. The majority of lesbians in this sample (87 percent) reported being satisfied with their work.

Those respondents who did not experience an actual midlife crisis reported that at midlife they made a conscious decision to reshape their lives or do something different. A woman who freelanced for fifteen years wanted the security of a regular job; a woman who worked in a constraining academic environment most of her work life opted for the freedom of independent practice. Lesbians who had been exceptionally active politically became less so now, whereas those who had not been political became involved for the first time. A woman who had been a serious athlete all her life was learning to deal with lessened endurance.

One lesbian, reflecting on whether or not she had a midlife crisis, had this to say:

> Hard to say. I did a major reevaluation of my life as I turned thirty-five. As I approached forty I decided to shake things up—very deliberately (quit work—moved across the country—moved in with my lover—played out a lifelong dream of full-time writing). But I have felt (and placed myself) in major transitions a *lot*. I question things a lot—maybe I never really had a midlife crisis.

A significant change reported by several women was the awareness for the first time of feelings toward other women. Several women who had buried their lesbian feelings at an earlier age were more accepting of them at midlife. One woman reported that coming out in middle age contributed to the positive way she felt about herself. She said, "I feel close to being whole—like a major piece of the puzzle of my life fell into place." A few of the women who are just coming out reported feeling sexual for the first time.

Self-discovery in middle age may also take the form of a change in inner awareness or increased knowledge about the self. One lesbian writes: "This feels to be the most expansive and deepening time of my life. I grow daily more profoundly aware of myself—particularly lately of the 'shadow side'—and grow more loving and appreciative of *all* the ways I am inside myself and the world."

Another midlife change for this group of lesbians was more emphasis on the spiritual realm. Middle age was also a time to reconnect with former interests and aspects of the self. A school teacher envisioned herself moving to the country, leading a spiritual life, learning a new musical instrument, and reading all the books she never had time for. A woman who has not written poetry since adolescence felt the need to resume this form of self-expression at age forty-nine.

"Letting go" or knowing when you have outgrown something was another important theme for the lesbians in this sample. This can include relationships that are not working, habits, or "life dreams" (Nichols 1986). It can also include a different way of relating to the world. Having spent most of her life being "strong, independent, and reasoned after the male model of wholeness," one subject reported this change in herself: "Middle age is a time to reclaim and reinvent the female principle—to be 'power-filled' as opposed to 'powerful'—to be in touch with one's vulnerability and to allow things to flow rather than manage it."

Middle age can be a time to try new things; but it can also be a time to return to old things in a new way. A respondent who majored in English but who went into a different field had just begun to write in her current profession. She experienced a new sense of vitality and adventure in being able to combine both interests. She had found something meaningful in her life that gave her a sense of direction and importance.

Based on my own experience and that of a few friends and clients, it seemed to me that a part of the integration process that takes place in middle age has to do with reestablishing connections with interests and parts of the self that existed during the adolescent period. This is a time when many paths and options are open, particularly for women who have rejected traditional roles. Tapping into this period can be a source of renewal and vitality. In contrast to the women in other midlife studies who had no dreams in adolescence other than getting husbands (Junge and Maya 1985; Roberts and Newton 1987; Rubin 1979), adolescence appears to be a rather complex period for lesbians. A little more than half (62 percent) the midlife lesbians in this study reported career expectations as adolescents. Also, about half the group described themselves as non-traditional adolescents for that time period, that is, they were bookish, rebellious, and athletic. Women who identified themselves as lesbians in their teens and twenties were more likely to have had career expectations (79 percent) and to have been nontraditional adolescents (60 percent) as compared to women who identified as lesbians in their thirties and in midlife (Sang 1990).

Several frequently reported life issues that were *new* to middle-aged lesbians were maintaining good health (33 percent), financial security and retirement (28 percent), creative expression (11 percent), and care of aging parents (5 percent). Several women reported weight gain to be a midlife issue (16 percent), but it was not clear whether such weight gain was a normal part of the aging process (Thiriet and Kepes 1987) or of sufficient magnitude as to be a health threat.

THE AWARENESS OF TIME

The awareness of one's time running out is reported to be a characteristic of middle age and is also a major issue for the women in this study. Time at midlife is experienced as passing more quickly; there is not enough time to do all the things one would like. It becomes necessary to be clear about priorities and limits. Many lesbian women stressed the desire to use their time wisely and not get caught up in meaningless activity. Several women reported always putting off to some future date the very things that were important and decided at middle age not to do this anymore. A lesbian woman who earned her living working in an office took a risk and quit her job to be a full-time painter. Another woman who wanted to try her hand at sculpture but never found the time built this activity into her schedule.

Middle age can also be a time in which one lives more in the moment and enjoys the simple things in life—a flower or the smell of good food. It is a time to be in touch with one's "core being."

What Gives Life Meaning

Midlife lesbians derived meaning and satisfaction from intimate relationships (47 percent), friendships (38 percent), and work (37 percent). Other sources of meaning were spirituality (20 percent), children (13 percent), hobbies and interests (10 percent), and personal growth and development (9 percent). Many women also expressed their own personal sources of meaning, such as "making a difference in the world" or "being your own person."

Most studies on midlife women found these women to place greater importance on relationships and caring for others (Gilligan 1982; Peck 1986; Roberts and Newton 1987; Rubin 1979), whereas midlife men were more concerned with work accomplishments (Levinson 1978; Valiant 1977). At midlife, traditional women are first getting in touch with work and independent interests while the midlife task for men is to get more in touch with feelings and intimacy. For lesbian women in this study, work and relationships have been an important source of meaning in the past and continue to be at midlife. In her sample of sixty-eight midlife lesbians from the West Coast, Fertitta (1987) also found lesbians to give career *and* love relationships high priority. Careers had greater saliency for lesbians than for her control group of midlife heterosexual women who were never married and were childless. It is noteworthy that in the present study, women who identified themselves as lesbians in midlife also appeared to be more similar to traditional women: intimate relationships were more meaningful to them (61 percent) than work (21 percent). Because these women just came out, the excitement, newness, and novelty of relating to women may account for the importance placed on relationships as compared to work. Women who came out at midlife are just as likely to have professional careers (82 percent) as women who came out in their teens and twenties (86 percent) and to be just as satisfied with their work.

In response to the question, "What gives your life meaning or satisfaction," one midlife lesbian replied as follows: "Good work—being useful—producing good things, e.g., good poems—a sense of growing, learning. A strong connection to others: conversation, working together, sex, giggling, beauty." Another replied, "People and a significant other and a sense of doing something that is worthwhile and maybe even important. I also need nature—to be near the water with some regularity, to be outside, to appreciate the beauty of nature."

In addition to relationships and work, the lives of lesbians in this study were significantly enriched by a wide range of interests, such as artistic expression, reading, political participation, sports and the out-of-doors, gardening, gourmet cooking, meditation, yoga, travel, theater, and so forth. Each midlife lesbian had, on average, ten interests or hobbies. Interests play an important part in defining individual identity and in giving meaning to a person's life (Storr 1988). Finding time for interests was a continual struggle for many of the midlife lesbians because their lives were so full.

A striving for balance and wholeness was a major theme for midlife lesbians in this study. Finding a balance between work life and home life was made difficult by the fact that many lesbian women held responsible jobs with long hours. One respondent turned down a prestigious position with a higher salary so she could have more time to devote to her relationships and outside interests.

One lesbian woman wrote: 'My philosophy revolves around the concept of *balance* between inner and outer focus, work and play, and so forth. It also includes the notion of integrating aspects of self previously compartmentalized. I think positive action comes from integration and balance for myself."

That most lesbians in this study were concerned with creating a balanced life for themselves can be seen clearly in their descriptions of what they considered to be a "good day." A "good day" consisted of some combination of work, an intimate relationship, interactions with friends and family, physical activity, contact with the outdoors, creative expression, involvement with community, and a nice meal. The following is a typical example of the midlife lesbian's idea of a "good day":

> Wake up early, about 6:15, coffee and fruit, get any household chores over, take a walk if weather is good, go back to bed and have a sexual hour with my lover, get up with her and shower or bathe, read a book at the table while she eats a bowl of cereal. Both of us go to work or study or do whatever work we have, then get together again around 4 PM, take a nap, spend an evening alone or with friends, go to sleep about 11 PM.

Although many of the lesbian respondents expressed an interest in giving even more time to others and to their community, they also reported wanting to take better care of themselves; more time to be alone and the need for exercise and proper nutrition. Of equal concern to these women is the quality of their lives; considerable emphasis is place on personal growth and development through a process of change and self-awareness.

THE LIFE PHILOSOPHIES OF MIDLIFE LESBIAN WOMEN

One of the more interesting findings in my pilot study on midlife lesbians (Sang 1987) was that, based on forty or more years of experience, each woman appeared to have developed her own life philosophy. It was not simply work, interests, or relationships that gave these lesbians' lives meaning and direction; rather, it was the philosophical framework in which these activities were embedded.

For many of the women, their life philosophy was a part of a spiritual quest. One example of an individual subject's life philosophy, which was expressed spontaneously, is as follows: "My own personal and spiritual growth and unfolding brings me my greatest delight and is really at the center of all I do in the world. My life and my work are one and both are my spiritual journey."

Sheinkin and Golden (1985) point out that the existential questions and issues that surface at middle age need to be incorporated into some kind of personal philosophy to give life meaning and value.

In the present study the respondents were specifically asked, "What is your life philosophy? Describe it as best as you can." As expected, each lesbian woman had her own unique philosophy or worldview that guided her life. I found that these life philosophies seemed to fall into five distinct categories, which are as follows:

1. *Love, care, and respect for others* (63 percent):* This category includes making a difference in people's lives, accepting people for themselves, and developing and maintaining friendships. *Example:* "To respect my feelings and those of others. To be kind to others and see the wonder that connects one human being to another."

2. *Concern about society, community, and the environment* (56 percent): Included in this category are life philosophies which express connections with the universe, respect for the planet, being political, promoting peace, justice, and equality. *Example:* "I believe I should live easy on the earth, live harmoniously with the earth and all creatures and help when the opportunity arises in my path."

3. *Self-development and living life to its fullest* (55 percent): The following themes apply to this category: making the most of each day, being in the moment, being true to oneself, living the best one can, and participating in the fullness of life. *Example:* "I will seek to live life fully with zest and sensitivity and compassion for others. I will, now more than ever, concentrate on giving something back."

---

*A particular individual's life philosophy could fall into more than one category. Percentages are based on the total number of concepts expressed.

4. *Health, happiness, and the enjoyment of life* (28 percent): Themes expressed in this category are the achievement of joy and pleasure, appreciation of life and what it has to offer, and humor. *Example:* "Smile each day. Laugh often. Don't forget to take time to play and time to be alone. Hug a tree, stand in the rain."

5. *Choosing our destiny* (25 percent): We are basically in control of what happens to us. We take responsibility for our lives. *Example:* "My time on earth in my current form is intended to help one learn and grow on a spiritual level. That I do have a part in creating my reality and I'm not a victim."

The life philosophies of lesbians in this study clearly reflect a concern with nurturing or caring, whether that caring is for the self, for others, for the community, or for the planet. Each lesbian wants to take in, enjoy, and develop herself and, at the same time, give back to others and the environment. This reciprocal relationship between the personal, the political, the spiritual, and the environment was expressed by each woman in her own unique way. The sense of balance that many lesbians were trying to create for themselves at midlife also involved the giving to the self and the giving to others and to nature. Such concern with caring could in part be attributed to the fact that so many of the lesbians in this sample are in the helping professions. It can also be attributed to the fact that women are socialized to value nurturing and caring (Gilligan 1982; Miller 1976).

SUMMARY AND CONCLUDING REMARKS

Not much is known about women's developmental issues at mid- life, particularly women who have utilized their potential. Existing models of adult development have not taken into account women who, from an early age, did not conform to the traditional female role. This sample of midlife lesbians tended to be a highly educated, professional group of women who have been self-supporting most of their adult lives. A little more than half are childless. Most have developed many outside interests.

The study's findings suggest that lesbian women have different developmental issues at midlife than those reported for both males and traditional females. One of the major midlife issues that emerged for lesbians in this study was the need to *balance* the diverse aspects of their lives, that is, work, relationships, interests, community, and spirituality. Unlike traditional women and men who were first getting in touch with a part of themselves that had been excluded until midlife, for example, the career realm or intimacy, lesbians have been developing in both these areas over a lifetime. These results suggest that lesbians do not fit entirely into existing male or female theories of midlife. The lives of midlife lesbians in this sample appear to be more diverse and complex than those reported for other midlife adults. Middle-age lesbians seem to have more roles and aspects of the self to integrate.

Although lesbians share some of the same midlife characteristics as other adults of this period, such as a time for change or increased freedom, the nature of the issues within each of these categories may be different. For example, increased freedom for the traditional woman has to do with fewer responsibilities to children and husband, and, for the first time in her life, thinking about her own needs and interests. In contrast, increased freedom for lesbians has to do with the confidence to take more risks and to not care what others think.

Generativity, the need to pass on one's knowledge and skills to a future generation, is a characteristic often associated with middle age (Erikson 1959). Only a few lesbians in this study mentioned it, but, then again, I did not specifically ask about it. Based on each woman's questionnaire as a whole, I had the sense that for this group of lesbians generativity is a lifelong process and not one that is limited to midlife. At midlife lesbian women in this sample were at their peak. This is a highly creative time for these women because of experience, increased spontaneity, and the integration that is taking place. Thus, what lesbians give of themselves at midlife may be qualitatively different from what they were able to give at other stages of their lives. The concept of generativity as we know it may be based on a heterosexual male perspective, that is, the need for the individual to make his own "personal contribution." Lesbians in this study seemed more concerned with helping to build a better world; there appeared to be less emphasis on making one's mark. Clearly, more exploration is needed in this area.

Even within this sample of 110 mostly professional, White, middle-class lesbian women, there were considerable differences in life patterns and midlife issues. Some women came out later in life, others had children, some were coping with illness, while still others were concerned with retirement. These findings further suggest that existing models of adult development need to be modified to include individuals with different life experiences. As social times change, so will the nature of midlife issues for lesbians.

The middle-age lesbians in this study are a group of self-actualized women who hope to continue growing and developing. There is considerable optimism about the future based on the confidence that comes with having coped effectively with one's past. As one respondent put it, "I have no idea of what will unfold for me but I have an abiding trust based on my experience so far that my life will always delight me and bring me richness of all sorts."

ACKNOWLEDGMENTS

I would like to express my appreciation to all the women who took the time to participate in this study. I also wish to thank my friend and colleague Robyn Posin for her theoretical/conceptual input into this article.

REFERENCES

Baruch, G., and J. Brooks-Gunn. 1984. The study of women in midlife. In G. Baruch and J. Brooks-Gunn, eds., *Women in Midlife*. New York: Plenum Press.

Brooks-Gunn, J., and B. Kirsch. 1984. Life events and the boundaries of midlife for women. In G. Baruch and J. Brooks-Gunn, eds., *Women in Midlife*. New York: Plenum Press.

Downing, C. 1987. *Journey Through Menopause—A Personal Rite of Passage*. New York: Crossroad.

Erikson, E. 1959. Growth and crises of the healthy personality. *Psychological Issues* 1:50–100.

Fertitta, S. 1987. Newer-married women in the middle years: A comparison of lesbians and heterosexuals. Paper presented at the Annual Convention of the American Psychological Association New York, August.

Gilligan, C. 1982. *In a Different Voice*. Cambridge, Mass.: Harvard University Press.

Hunnisett, R. 1986. Developing phenomenological methods for researching lesbian existence. *Canadian Journal of Counseling* 20:255–68.

Junge, M., and V. Maya. 1985. Women in their forties: a group portrait and implications for psychotherapy. *Women and Therapy* 4:3–19.

Krieger, S. 1985. Beyond "subjectivity": The use of the self in social science. *Qualitative Sociology* 8:309–24.

Levinson, D. 1978. *The Seasons of a Man's Life*. New York: Ballantine.

Lieberman, N. 1977. *Playfulness: Its Relationship to Imagination and Creativity*. New York: Academic Press.

Lopata, H., and D. Barnewolt. 1984. The middle years: changes and variations in social-role commitments. In G. Baruch and J. Brooks-Gunn, eds., *Women in Midlife*. New York: Plenum Press.

Love, B. 1975. A case for lesbians as *role* models for healthy adult women. Paper presented at the Annual Convention of the American Psychological Association, Chicago.

Maslow, A. 1977. The creative attitude. In W. Anderson, ed., *Therapy and the Arts.* New York: Harper Colophon.

Miller, J. 1976. *Toward a New Psychology of Women.* Boston: Beacon Press.

Montagu, A. 1983. *Growing Young.* New York: McGraw-Hill.

Neugarten, B. 1968. The awareness of middle age. In B. Neugarten, ed., *Middle Age and Aging.* Chicago: University of Chicago Press.

Nichols, M. 1986. *Turning Forty in the 80s: Personal Crisis, Time for Change.* New York: W. W. Norton.

Peck, T. 1986. Women's self-definition in adulthood: From a different model? *Psychology of Women Quarterly* 10:274–84.

Roberts, P., and P. Newton. 1987. Levinsonian studies of women's adult development. *Psychology and Aging* 2:154–63.

Rubin, L. 1979. *Women of a Certain Age: The Midlife Search.* New York: Harper and Row.

Sang, B. 1978. Some existential issues of middle-age lesbians. Paper presented at the meeting of the American Psychological Association, Atlanta, August.

Sang, B. 1989. New directions in lesbian research, theory and education. *Journal of Counseling and Development* 68:92–96.

Sang, B. 1990. Reflections of midlife lesbians on their adolescence. In E. Rosenthal, ed., *Women, Aging and Ageism.* New York: Haworth Press.

Sang, B. 1991. Moving towards balance and integration. In B. Sang, J. Warshaw, and A. Smith, eds., *Lesbians at Midlife: The Creative Transition,* pp. 206–14. San Francisco: Spinsters.

Sheinkin, L., and G. Golden. 1985. Therapy with women in the later stages of life: A symbolic quest. *Women and Therapy* 4:83–93.

Storr, A. 1988. *Solitude. A Return to the Self.* New York: Free Press.

Thiriet, M., and S. Kepes. 1987. *Women at Fifty.* New York: Schocken.

Vaillant, G. 1977. *Adaptation to Life.* New York: Little, Brown.

Yalom, I. 1980. *Existential Psychotherapy.* New York: Basic Books.

23

Adult Development and Aging:
A Gay Perspective

Douglas C. Kimmel

To provide a model for understanding gay adult development and aging, Levinson's developmental periods are applied to the existing data on older gays. In addition, an historical lifeline for a hypothetical gay person born in 1910 is presented to illustrate the relationship between developmental data and historical events. The lack of data on older lesbians and non-advantaged males is noted. Stereotypes of lonely, depressed, sexually frustrated aging gay men are clearly not valid for the majority of respondents studied. Older gays do have particular needs, however, such as support during bereavement, assistance if physically disabled, and a reduction in stigmatization.

During the 1970s adult development began to attract considerable attention in social science research and the media (e.g., Gould 1972; Levinson 1978; Sheehy 1976; Vaillant 1977). Nearly all the respondents in these studies, however, are—or are assumed to be—heterosexual. The only overtly gay person studied, Alan Poe, a respondent in the thirty-year longitudinal investigation by Vaillant (1977), raised so many questions about the nature of normality in adult development that a separate chapter in that work was devoted to these issues. In the chapter, Vaillant described Poe's critique of the study:

> "I've got a bone to pick with you guys; I am a homosexual." Then, he tossed a Grant Study reprint at me. He pointed out where in my summary of the Study I had discussed delinquency, alcoholism, psychosis, and homosexuality as equivalent, albeit rare, defects among the Grant Study men. . . . I realized that Alan Poe was a Study member to whom I needed to listen. (1977:352–53)

Poe recognized that he was gay only after his third marriage ended in divorce and he had his second homosexual affair at age fifty. He also was a poet, a pacifist, and an extremely hard worker whose appearance resembled "a gruff, tough tugboat captain." At one point he pointed out to Vaillant: "This science of the total man is crucial now; it can't have blind spots" (p. 355).

Thirty years ago, or even five years ago, respondents might not indicate nor probably be asked their sexual orientation. So we are left with the impression that nearly all adult development is heterosexual. Today we know better than to assume that Alan Poe was the only homosexual in those studies; perhaps a few of the apparent heterosexuals also had homosexual affairs in addition to their marriages (for example, Levinson's [1978] report briefly notes that five of his forty respondents discussed homosexual experiences). But the myth that homosexuality is an extraordinary phenomenon has tended to preclude the study of ordinary homosexuals as ordinary adults, whose development during adulthood is probably far more similar to than different from that of ordinary heterosexuals.

What happens to gay people when they grow older? This question may haunt a young gay person who does not have easy access to gay parent or grandparent figures to serve as role models. Since the development of a positive identity involves a sense of the future course of that identity, the lack of information about gay adult development has allowed the stigma of homosexuality to intertwine with the stereotypes about aging in our society. Thus, highly negative views of gay aging have been produced, leading to even greater difficulty in the development of a positive gay identity among young homosexuals. Fears about aging as a gay person have been used to dissuade young people from accepting their homosexuality, further hindering self-acceptance. Likewise, older gay persons may believe their eventual development is reflected in such a pathetic figure as the one created by Thomas Mann in his *Death in Venice* (1925 [1913]) since, it is assumed, homosexuality is essentially a tragic life-style.

The importance of an examination of the process of adult development among homosexuals is not limited to its significance for gay men and lesbians, however. Since gay people comprise about 10 percent of the population, this group represents a significant facet of all adult age groups—for example, the number of persons over age sixty-five who would be expected to be homosexual is twice the number of persons over sixty-five living in nursing homes or other institutions. An examination of gay adult development may raise new issues and question old assumptions that will expand the understanding of adulthood for all men and women. In addition, the gay life-style may provide both unique supports and special challenges in comparison with heterosexual life-styles.

There has been almost no research on the patterns of adult development and aging among homosexual men and women.* Only five empirical studies dealing with aging homosexuals have been reported since 1967 (Francher and Henkin 1973; Kelly 1974; Kimmel 1977, 1979; Minnigerode 1975; Weinberg 1969; Weinberg and Williams 1974). Moreover, the eight reports based on these five empirical studies have examined only male respondents. In addition, because the gay population is largely invisible, these studies have been unable to obtain representative samples; all are skewed toward White, well-educated respondents of relatively high socioeconomic status, although each has attempted to obtain a reasonable nonclinical sampling of adult gay men.

This article will attempt to sketch some of the most apparent characteristics of gay adult development. To do this in the absence of solid data is risky and speculative. The article will suggest far more research questions than it attempts to answer; if it stimulates study of adult development in general or gay adult development in particular, its main intent will be fulfilled.

Much of the information on which this discussion is based is drawn from an exploratory study of fourteen gay men over the age of fifty-five in New York City (Kimmel 1977, 1979); all of the respondents were White, and nearly all were well educated and middle class. The limitations of these data are obvious. The article also reflects conversations with therapists about their older gay clients/patients (Kimmel 1977), readings other than those cited above that deal with gay development (e.g., Brown 1976; Tripp 1975), and countless conversations with gay men and women of various ages. The absence of empirical data on lesbian development (or female development, in general) is reflected in this article. It is hoped that this will not provide so much of a male bias as to make the presentation irrelevant for women, since greater research on lesbian development should be a first priority in this almost uncharted area.

PATTERNS OF DEVELOPMENT AMONG HOMOSEXUAL PERSONS

Sexual orientation is far more complex than a dichotomy between exclusive heterosexuality and exclusive homosexuality. The Kinsey studies (Kinsey, Pomeroy, and Martin 1948; Kinsey et al. 1953) made it clear that

---

*Note that this article was originally published in 1978. For more recent studies, see the references in the introduction to part 7.

there is a continuum between these two extremes. A person who is pre-dominately heterosexual may engage in homosexual activities; a person who is predominately homosexual may marry and produce offspring; a person who is celibate may be either homosexual, heterosexual, or some-where between these two extremes in sexual orientation or affectional preference.

The importance given to same-sex sexual play during childhood may be affected by the person's sexual orientation. One of my respondents vividly remembered sex play during childhood sixty years earlier and noted that all his playmates were probably grandfathers now, and certainly were not homosexual. Another felt a keen attraction for other boys, although he did not recognize the sexual interest at that time. Another sought out an older boy for sex at the age of four. Six of the fourteen respondents felt they were gay during childhood, though this may be an attempt to explain their later identity. Most of the rest "knew" they were gay early in adolescence.

When, during adolescence, sexual maturation brings greater erotic awareness, it would seem that individuals begin to recognize their sexual orientation, sense their differentness if they are predominantly or exclu-sively gay, and begin to integrate the psychosocial meaning of their ori-entation into the rest of their lives and growing sense of self. A recent study of gay male and lesbian members of the American Psychological Association (APA) (Riddle and Morin 1977) found the ages of thirteen or fourteen to be the average age at which they became aware of homo-sexual feelings (table 23.1). Since females typically mature about two years earlier than males do, the gay males either tend to be "early maturers" as Tripp (1975) suggested or there is more of a gap between puberty and

TABLE 23.1
Average Reported Ages of Selected Events in the Lives of Lesbian and Gay Male Psychologists

	Lesbians	Gay Males
Aware of homosexual feelings	14	13
First same-sex sexual experience	20	15
Understood the term *homosexual*	16	17
First homosexual relationship	23	22
Considered self homosexual	23	21
Disclosed identity to parent	30	28
Disclosed identity professionally	32	31
(N)	(63)	(138)

NOTE. Adapted from Riddle and Morin (1977).

awareness of homosexual feelings for these women than for these men. There is a five-year difference between these men and women in the age of first same-sex sexual experience, constituting a delay of two years from awareness to first experience for males and a delay of six years for females. These data probably reflect the greater social pressure on males to engage in sex and greater pressure on females not to act on sexual impulses.

The next developmental period—late adolescence and early adult-hood—may be especially significant for lesbians and gay men. While it might be assumed that heterosexual adolescents feel little conflict between their psychosocial identity in a heterosexually oriented world and their attraction toward members of the opposite sex, lesbian and gay male ado-lescents may experience a profound conflict in these areas. This is not to imply that heterosexual adolescents may not feel guilt or conflicts about their sexuality; homosexuals, however, are likely to feel guilt, anxiety, or conflicts about their sexual orientation in addition to whatever reactions they may have to their sexuality per se. This conflict is reflected in the data in table 23.1. For example, gay males did not define themselves as homosexual until age twenty-one, on the average; for the lesbian respon-dents, it was age twenty-three. Certainly, the vast majority of heterosexuals do not deliberate their sexual orientation for a decade or more after puberty. Also, lesbians did not disclose their sexual orientation to their parents until age thirty (age twenty-eight for gay males)—far beyond the point that parents of heterosexual children "learn" of their child's heter-osexuality.

It is possible that this crisis early in the gay person's adult life—one that can involve extensive family disruption, intense feelings, and some-times alienation from the family—may be one of the most significant a gay person will face. Once resolved, it may provide a perspective on major life crises and a sense of crisis competence that buffers the person against later crises. It and other adolescent and young adult experiences of "gay oppression" may also, on the other hand, leave a residue of anger and a sense of vulnerability not uncommon among minority group members.

Since lesbians and gay males have in common with other lesbians and gay males only their sexual orientation, there is a wide diversity of life-styles and patterns of occupation, marital status, feelings about parent-hood, socioeconomic status, ethnic background, religion, and politics dur-ing adulthood. (In this sense, gay persons considered as a "group" are most akin to the elderly as a "group," the latter having only their age in common.) There are at least six social-sexual patterns that gay persons may follow for varying lengths of time during adulthood: a) heterosexual marriage with or without periodic homosexual relations, following or followed by a gay life-style; b) celibacy with a homosexual affectional orientation; c) raising children, including adopted children; d) long-term gay friend/lover relationship(s); e) gay life-style with no long-term sexual relationships; and f) bisexual life-style without marriage.

In my study of fourteen gay men between the ages of fifty-five and eighty-one, all these patterns except the last one were mentioned; each of the combinations within the first pattern was reported. Specifically, three of the men had a consistent pattern of long-term relationships: one had been with his lover for thirty years, another had a lover of forty years who died and he had had a new lover for five years, and the third had a lover for twenty-five years who died and he had been with his current lover for thirteen years. Another respondent was living in a nonsexual relationship with a man who had been his lover many years earlier.

The remaining ten respondents were currently living alone. Four of these had previously been married (heterosexually) and two of them had children, while one was a grandfather. Three of the marriages ended by divorce or separation. The fourth man had had several homosexual affairs early in life, but unlike some of the other married men reported that he lived an entirely heterosexual life during his two marriages; both marriages were ended by the death of his wife, when he then reentered the gay world.

The other six men had lived alone all their adult lives and reported occasional homosexual affairs that had been of short duration. One of these men had been entirely celibate until he had his first sexual experience with another person at the age of fifty-six. Another adopted a heterosexual son earlier in life and is now a grandfather, maintaining close relations with his son's family. One respondent summarized the evolution of his life-styles in these words:

> I was aware of [homosexuality] in me when I was about fourteen or fifteen years old, but I didn't know what to do about it. There was nobody to go to to get educated. I just sort of suffered along not knowing what to do. . . . I finally came to terms with myself when I was about twenty-six. . . . I finally made myself admit that I was homosexual and that it was silly to pretend otherwise. And that gave me such a lift, such a feeling of confidence in myself, I guess, that there was something in life for me to enjoy beside the routine things. . . . About this time [1934, age twenty-six] was the first fairly long love affair that I had. . . . I shared my life with this fellow—he was younger than I was—for about eight years. Then after he graduated from college and had been working a year or two, he got an offer for a

good job out on the West Coast and that ended that. It was after that that I got married [at thirty-six]. Probably it was a feeling of a need for somebody else because I did miss him so much. One of the reasons I got married was that I wanted children. And I did care for my wife. I was married for eighteen years, divorced in 1962 [at age fifty-four]. I had fallen in love three times with a man during those years I was married. I did nothing about it in the sense of trying to have a sexual relation. My wife may have sensed something during one or another of those times. But it was not something she held up against me and she didn't bring it into the divorce proceedings or anything like that.

Other studies of gay men during adulthood report fairly consistent findings. For example, Weinberg and Williams (1974) reported that older respondents (over the age of forty-five) attended homosexual clubs and bars less frequently, were more likely to be living alone, and reported less frequent sex compared to younger respondents. There was no evidence, however, of other characteristics stereotypically associated with aging homosexual men:

> We find no age-related differences in self-acceptance, anxiety, depression, or loneliness. In fact, our data suggest that in some respects our older homosexuals have greater well-being than our younger homosexuals. Older respondents worry less about exposure of their homosexuality, have more stable self-concepts, and are less effeminate. (Weinberg and Williams 1974:217)

Respondents in my study generally support these observations, with the exception that, while indicating that sex may be less frequent than it was when they were young, all felt that it remained important in their lives, and half felt that it was more satisfying now than when they were younger. One sixty-three-year-old respondent commented "Less accent on the genitals, more on the total person now."

Although patterns of adult development among lesbians have not been examined, it can be assumed that there are both important differences and significant similarities between the patterns for gay men, nongay men, lesbians, and nongay women. One interesting facet of these differences may be that gay men, in my experience, seldom feel that their sexual orientation involved a choice; more often, the choice for men has been whether or not to marry and have children. Among lesbians there seems to be more of a sense of choosing homosexuality, often after considerable experience with heterosexuality. This observation may be consistent with the Kinsey et al. (1953) finding that women's sexuality peaks at a much later age than is the case for men. Also, in the Riddle and Morin (1977) study of psychologists, lesbians were more likely to be or have been heterosexually married than were gay men (41 percent to 18 percent). Another possible difference is the often-stated observation that lesbians are more likely to be in a long-term relationship. Again, such a hypothesis was supported by the Riddle and Morin data: 56 percent of the lesbian respondents, compared to 36 percent of the gay males, were living with a same-sex lover.

Aging appears to bring somewhat less dramatic changes for gay men and women than is the case for heterosexuals. Francher and Henkin (1973) noted that, developmentally, the major life crisis for their respondents occurred not with aging, but earlier in life when they had to adjust to their sexual orientation. This crisis usually resulted in some degree of isolation from the family structure. They suggest that this leads to the homosexual community functioning as a quasi-family. One implication of this is that self-selected friendship networks may be at least as supportive as children or other relatives, if they have been selected with those qualities in mind (Kimmel 1977). Francher and Henkin also suggest that the dominant early-life crisis for gay men may affect their pattern of aging because they are less involved in the developmental changes and crises within families that typically affect the patterns of aging for heterosexual men.

The respondents in my study also pointed out the advantages and problems of gay aging. Among the problems were the hostility (both overt and subtle) they had experienced, the importance of youthful attractiveness in the gay world, loneliness around family-centered holidays, and the tendency to withdraw into a relatively closed circle of friends that does not automatically provide social contact with young people, as families typically do. A particularly poignant problem was associated with the death of a long-term lover. Among the advantages were a continuity of life, conscious preparation for self-reliance during the later years, experience in all the relevant skills for maintaining oneself and one's home, and the importance of a self-created friendship network and social supports.

Kelly (1977) also discussed the problems faced by older gays, including the typical aging problems of the loss or death of friends, fear of physical illness requiring institutionalization, and the stigmatization of old age. In addition, he pointed out the discrimination related to their sexual orientation, including legal discrimination when a long-term lover dies, and hostility toward homosexuals demonstrated by even "the liberal elements of current society." Kelly concludes:

Although the research findings reported in this article are based on a non-probability sample of one community, there seems to be no further rationale for the application of certain "blanket" stereotypes about aging gay men, as these men, at least, are living proof that such assertions are not always accurate. There is little evidence in this study to suggest that being gay causes problems in old age, but there is a great deal of evidence to suggest that societal stigma cause [sic] problems for aging gays. Only when society becomes aware of and accepts this important distinction can full acceptance and equality for older gay people become a real possibility. (1977:331–32)

Since much of the literature in gerontology has suggested that kinship supports are the basic source of aid in old age, perhaps the most significant issue faced by older gays—and, in fact, by all old people—is expressed by one of the respondents in my study:

> I wonder whether there'll be anybody to take care of me. My sister is ten years younger than I am. But she is rather ill herself. And if she goes before me, who is going to take care of me? My friend [lover of five years] said he will, so he intends to be around until the end, you see. But I'm making provision. . . . Hopefully I'll have enough money at the end for him or whoever does the job that I'll be taken care of.

ADULT DEVELOPMENTAL PERIODS

Although Levinson's (1978) forty respondents were all married, his study of adult development from adolescence to midlife among men in four different occupations provides a description of the developmental periods experienced by men (mostly middle class and college educated) born in the United States in the 1930s and 1940s. The question is to what degree the fairly consistent developmental patterns Levinson observed occur among gay men and women.

In Levinson's scheme, the period of "Childhood and Adolescence" extends up to about age seventeen. Using the data on psychologists (table 23.1), it is interesting to note that the adolescent developments for gay men and lesbians in this scheme included becoming aware of homosexual feelings (age thirteen to fourteen), first same-sex sexual experience for men (age fifteen), and understanding the term *homosexual* (age sixteen to seventeen).

According to Levinson, "Early Adult Transition," from age seventeen to twenty-two, marks the boundary between adolescence and adulthood. Its tasks are to move from the preadult to the adult world, to form an initial adult identity, and to make and explore initial choices for adult lifestyles. For many persons these are the college undergraduate years. The developments during this period for gay psychologists were having one's first same-sex sexual experience (for lesbians: age twenty) and considering oneself "homosexual" (for gay men: age twenty-one).

The next period, "Entering the Adult World," age twenty-two to twenty-eight, involves making and testing a number of initial choices about occupation, love relationships, peer relationships, values, and life-style. The man (and perhaps woman, although Levinson studied only men) is faced with the issue of exploring the possibilities of adulthood while also creating a relatively stable life structure. The psychologists in the APA study reported establishing their first homosexual relationship during this period. Probably intent on finishing graduate school during this period, these professional people tended to hide their sexual orientation until professional credentials were earned.

The "Age Thirty Transition," lasting from about the age of twenty-eight to thirty-three, is described thus by Levinson:

> This transition . . . provides an opportunity to work on the flaws and lim-itations of the first adult life structure, and to create the basis for a more satisfactory structure with which to complete the era of early adulthood. At about 28 the provisional quality of the twenties is ending and life is becoming more serious, more "for real." A voice within the self says: "If I am to change my life—if there are things in it I want to modify or exclude, or things missing I want to add—I must now make a start, for soon it will be too late." (1978:58)

The developmental events of coming out seem to reflect this period clearly. Riddle and Morin's respondents reported acquiring a positive gay identity and disclosing that identity to friends and parents between the ages of twenty-eight and thirty. Disclosing one's identity professionally occurred at thirty-one or thirty-two.

These periods conclude the "novice phase" of early adulthood in Lev-inson's scheme. There follows a period of "Settling Down" (ages thirty-three to forty), for which the two central tasks are establishing a niche and "making it" through a project or a personal enterprise. For the men Lev-inson studied, this involved climbing the ladder of status within their fields. As a relatively stable period, this is the first of a series of alternating stages of stability and transition, each lasting about five years, for example, the "Midlife Transition" (age forty to forty-five) and the "Age Fifty Tran-sition" (age fifty to fifty-five).

How well does this scheme fit gay adult development? Given the obvious fact that the data from which the developmental progression is drawn are culture-bound and linked to a particular period in history, it seems plausible that it may apply to both gay and nongay men (and maybe women) who are part of that culture and historical period. For example, the fourteen gay men I studied show interesting manifestations of this developmental scheme.

All three men with long-term lovers were involved in these relationships during the "Settling Down" period, although two began earlier (at ages eighteen and twenty-six). Also during this period, one had his first gay sex at age thirty-three, while the celibate man realized he was gay at thirty-four. One respondent married at thirty-six, and another had his first serious gay affair at thirty-five.

Some respondents had significant "Midlife Transition" periods. One divorced at thirty-nine and drank heavily until he joined Alcoholics Anonymous at forty-six. Another, who had married at twenty-five, met his long-term gay "friend" at forty. Another had his first lengthy affair at forty for six years. And one respondent met his present roommate (who was then his lover) at age forty-four.

The "Age Fifty Transition" seemed especially significant for many of the respondents. One reported that he "accepted his homosexuality much more" at age fifty-two. Another told his boss that he was gay at fifty-four. A respondent whose lover died when he was forty-eight met a new long-term lover when he was fifty. Another man divorced his wife at fifty-four and attempted suicide. The long-term celibate had his first sex at fifty-six. A married man became open about his homosexuality and moved to New York City when he was fifty-four.

Finally, Levinson's "Late Adult Transition" (age sixty to sixty-five) period also seemed to be significant for some. One had a "nervous breakdown" at age sixty. Another (who attempted suicide earlier) became much more "personally liberated" at sixty-four. The celibate man had his first "close sexual relationship" at age fifty-nine. Another man "came out" (in his words) at sixty-six. And another man whose lover died when he was fifty-eight met a new apparently long-term lover at age sixty.

Clearly, whether adult development among gay men and women fits the pattern Levinson described, these gay men indicate that developmental changes continued for them. The pattern of changes suggests that the developmental progression Levinson proposed deserves a careful analysis based on more complete data.

INDIVIDUAL DEVELOPMENT
AND HISTORICAL TIME

In examining adult development, it is especially important to consider the interaction of the individual's development with the historical situation during which the developmental events took place (Kimmel 1974). The illustrative chart of historical events, including milestones of gay adult development, shown in table 23.2 represents the historical period and life-cycle events of a person who became sixty-five in 1975. We can see clearly that a young person dealing with being gay in the 1970s has an entirely different set of historical-cultural conditions to ease the development of a positive gay identity from that of a person who grew up in the early 1900s. Two of the respondents in my study made this point very clearly:

> *First Respondent:* It was like living in the underground because the only people who were evident that were gay were actors, interior decorators, hair dressers; they, of course, were the flamboyant type. . . . But for a white-collar or blue-collar worker to be gay would be very degrading. A normal homosexual in those days would be considered somebody who did evil

TABLE 23.2
Historical and Life-cycle Events for a Gay Person Born in 1910

Year	Age	Historical Event	Life-cycle Event
1914	4	World War I begins in Europe	Walking, talking, playing with others
1916	6	Wilson elected president	Enters first grade
1922	12	Heterosexual "sexual revolution" underway	Puberty; aware of homosexual feelings
1927	17	Lindbergh flies the Atlantic	First same-sex sexual experience
1929	19	Stock market crash; start of the Great Depression	Begins work or college
1932	22	Roosevelt elected president	First homosexual relationship
1941	31	United States enters World War II	Adult life-styles: single, long-term relationship, or marriage (heterosexual)
1950	40	Korean War; McCarthy investigations	Midlife transition
1960	50	"Space Age"; Kennedy elected president	Age 50 transition
1965	55	Women's movement; reexamination of gender roles begins	Culmination of middle adulthood
1970	60	Gay liberation movement	Late adult transition
1975	65	Post-Watergate "morality"; Ford has assumed the presidency	Retirement (?)

NOTE. Early life-cycle events based on Riddle and Morin's (1977) sample of gay psychologists; stages from Levinson (1978).

things in an alleyway. So everyone, when they came out, went into the closet, as the expression goes. . . . Of course, my lover and I didn't meet in a gay bar. There were no bars then. It was Prohibition. . . . [Gay people] would meet at bath houses on the beach and railway terminals, places where people could congregate and not be noticed; or motion picture theaters or just eye contact on the street.

Second Respondent: I went to high school in the 1920s and that was a pretty lively time, too. There were all kinds of social revolutions going on around the world and one of them was sexual. People were being a lot more frank and honest about sex than they had been previously. But it was mainly heterosexual relationships that were being much more free. I didn't come across anybody I was sure was gay.

As my respondents recall it, gay bars began to appear during and after World War II. But this period was followed by one of intense fear, especially in the Washington, D.C., area, generated by the McCarthy investigations into both Communists and homosexuals. My one respondent who lived in Washington escaped this fear because he was living an exclusively heterosexual life at the time, but others became even more circumspect. Some of my respondents remained in long-term gay relationships; although, in at least one case, they lived separately—as did Howard Brown and his friend/lover (Brown 1976).

To understand the nature of gay adult development, we must consider the effect of such historical factors. For example, that older gay men tend to go to bars less often than younger gay men may in part reflect the greater importance of private circles of friends during their earlier gay life—a pattern that has continued, despite the increased openness of the gay bar as a social center for younger gay men. Likewise, the marked decrease in men sharing a long-term relationship after the age of fifty may mean not that these older men have lost such a relationship, but that their age-cohort was less likely to have formed such relationships because of the cultural pressures of their historical period.

CENTRAL RESEARCH ISSUES

The two most obvious research needs in the study of adult development in general, and gay adult development in particular, are studies on women and studies of persons who are not well educated, economically successful, and White. Cross-cultural and multiethnic studies would be especially helpful.

In filling the gaps in our knowledge, the issue of obtaining a meaningful sample is likely to remain particularly troublesome. For obvious reasons the homosexual population is a largely invisible one that cannot be described demographically. Studies of gay aging are plagued by problems associated with self-selected volunteer respondents, the difficulty of obtaining respondents that represent the range of variation within the gay population, and the inevitable question of the similarity of the respondents to the heterosexual majority. Thus, researchers need to develop innovative procedures to obtain the sample that is most appropriate for the particular goals of the study (see Warren 1977).

It may be useful to define the research goal in terms of sample design. This could involve the use of either of two related strategies. One could focus on the comparability of samples within the gay population, neither of which need be representative of any specific group, for example, aging gay men and women with and without long-term lovers who are otherwise similar in education, social class, retirement status, and so on. A second approach would entail the systematic inclusion of a range of variation along a single dimension, such as income, living arrangement, ethnic background, or marital status, with other relevant variables held constant—as in a study of aging gay women with long-term lovers who vary widely in income.

Another important research issue in studies of gay adult development involves the cross-sectional (by age) nature of these studies, which confounds the age of the respondents with the historical period in which they grew up. As is the case for all gerontological research, it is important to examine the effects of historical factors on adult development before assuming that differences between age groups represent developmental factors. Because openness about homosexuality has increased dramatically within the last decade, studies of gay development might examine pre- and postliberation differences separately from age differences. For example, long-term relationships formed after 1969 may differ from those formed earlier, and this difference may interact with the age of the persons in the relationship, as well as with the length of the relationship.

As noted, longitudinal or at least follow-up studies of patterns of gay development are needed. Although longitudinal research, too, has methodological difficulties (e.g., selective drop-outs), all respondents can be compared with themselves at earlier points and the effects of historical factors, such as gay liberation, can be noted, even as they confound the developmental data. Since young gay people have little opportunity to observe the course of homosexual development, such research may be especially educational for the gay community. Ideally, both cross-sectional and longitudinal studies of gay human development may be combined to reveal the range of life-styles at various points in historical time and the long-term evolution of these life-styles over the life span of successive generations of gay people.

SPECIAL NEEDS OF OLDER GAY ADULTS

There is a need for increased advocacy of the special concerns of vulnerable members of the gay community. In an important sense, a community may be defined by its function of caring for its vulnerable members. For the gay community, these would especially include adolescent and elderly or infirm gay persons; gay persons with disabilities; gay parents; minority gays; and gay persons living in poverty. Greater community support needs to be provided for these groups of gay persons, possibly through community centers or special programs designed to provide special gay services in conjunction with existing programs in the wider community.

The group that is the concern of this article—older gay men and lesbians—is likely to be especially well hidden within the larger community because of the social stigma of homosexuality during the greatest part of their lives that forced many to remain firmly "in the closet." Nearly all the respondents in my study experienced either overt or subtle oppression as gay persons, for example, fear of arrest, actual arrest, loss of inheritance from a lover, or separation from a lover due to health. In one case, a respondent lost his lover to the lover's siblings when the lover became too ill to be cared for at home; the respondent could not ask for time off from work to care for his long-term friend because he could not disclose the relationship to his employer. As a result, when the lover died, the respondent had to visit the mortuary after the family had left and did not attend the funeral, despite a relationship of forty years.

At least three major concerns are of special importance for elderly gay persons: bereavement, physical disability, and stigmatization (both in general and by the gay community).

When a long-term relationship is ended by death of one partner, there is seldom any opportunity for counseling or support. As with heterosexual widows, there are a number of important needs during this period (see Caine 1974). Legal and inheritance problems are often especially significant, both in planning one's estate and in the surviving lover's actual inheritance of the intended property. Competent legal counsel is particularly important for gay persons since almost all state laws are written for heterosexual families. Additional problems include the frequent exclusion of all except blood relatives from intensive care units, attitudes of physicians and hospital staff toward the gay lover, difficulties of expressing affection in hospital or nursing home settings, and the too frequent exclusion of the lover and other gay friends from funeral planning and participation.

Chronic physical disability may also raise many of the same issues in terms of hospitals, nursing homes, and health care professionals who may not understand or respect gay relationships or friendships. Assuming that similar proportions of gay persons are in nursing homes or other chronic care facilities as in the general community, about 10 percent of nursing home residents may be assumed to be homosexual. Yet, no provision is made for these persons. Nursing homes often do not recognize the sexual/affectional needs of their heterosexual residents, let alone the needs of homosexual persons. Even nursing homes that allow private conjugal visits would not be likely to allow this for a homosexual couple. Moreover, it is often possible for a relative of the resident to prevent visits by a homosexual friend or lover. Fortunately, there are plans among gay persons in at least one U.S. city to create a gay retirement community that may alleviate some of these problems. But greater education and raising the level of consciousness among the health care profession is clearly required.

Stigmatization of gay persons because of their unpopular sexual orientation occurs throughout the life span. In the older years, however, it may be combined with the stigma of old age in our youth-oriented society. Although it is unclear whether this stigma is as great among lesbians as among gay men, the importance of a youthful appearance and one's status as a "sex object" can stigmatize older gay men—both in the eyes of younger gay men and in the older man's own eyes. This is compounded by the "dirty old man" stereotype that tends to be attached to older men who are sexually active and is further reinforced by the myth that homosexuals are tragic figures whose life inevitably ends badly. Not only does this stigmatization tend to reduce the feelings of self-worth among older gay men who grew up during a period of intense antigay stigmatization, but also it tends to segregate the gay male world into the young and the old so that effective links across these gay generations are less frequent than in the heterosexual world. Thus, gay people need to examine their own attitudes about aging and to find ways to reduce the stigmatization of the more senior members by their own community.

While it would be expected that some older gays currently benefit from many of the services provided by existing agencies to the general elderly population, older gays who are homebound or infirm because of physical illness or disability may desire gay-oriented nonprofessional services, such as friendly visitors, telephone reassurance, escort services (to doctors or on errands), and aid with grocery shopping. A friendly visitor could provide an important link to the gay community for an elderly person who could not attend a gay social center or church group, purchase or read gay-oriented newspapers, or correspond with gay friends because of visual, hearing, or mobility impairments. These services could be provided by volunteers from the gay community if the elderly person could call on a program or center for senior gays. A "hot line" could also provide referrals to gay legal services, gay physicians who accept Medicare and Medicaid, and to other services that are available for gay as well as nongay persons in the community.

Creating such a program of services should involve a needs assessment of the elderly gay community. The difficulty in conducting such research is apparent, however, since persons with the greatest needs are also least likely to volunteer or even to be aware of such studies or programs. Innovative approaches to these problem areas are required.

CONCLUSIONS

Four conclusions seem apparent from the present state of knowledge about gay adult development. The first, and most obvious, is that relatively little is known about the process of life span development among gay persons; this gap in knowledge is especially acute for lesbians and for gay men who are not relatively well educated, economically well off, and White. While research is only beginning to explore the adult years of development in general, it is important that studies of gay men and lesbians be included in future studies of this important topic and also that more research be generated on gay development during childhood, adolescence, and in old age. Second, although there is evidence that older gay men differ from younger gay men, it is not at all clear whether these differences result from aging per se, or from the different historical periods in which the individual had to deal with all that being a homosexual in our society entails. Third, the stereotypes of the lonely, depressed, sexually frustrated aging gay man are not valid for the majority of relatively elite male respondents studied to date; although nothing is known about aging lesbians, the same conclusion is probably valid. Fourth, there are unique concerns that are significant for older gay men and lesbians; their nature and extent is not yet accurately known, but further innovative research may provide some realistic assessment of these special needs.

REFERENCES

Brown, H. 1976. *Familiar Faces, Hidden Lives: The Story of Homosexual Men in America Today.* New York: Harcourt Brace Jovanovich.

Caine, L. 1974. *Crazy Lady.* New York: William Morrow.

Francher, J. S., and J. Henkin. 1973. The menopausal queen: Adjustment to aging and the male homosexual. *American Journal of Orthopsychiatry* 43:670–74.

Gould, R. L. 1972. The phases of adult life: A study in developmental psychology. *American Journal of Psychiatry* 127:521–31.

Kelly, J. 1974. Brothers and brothers: The gay man's adaptation to aging. Doctoral dissertation, Brandeis University.

Kelly, J. 1977. The aging male homosexual: Myth and reality. *The Gerontologist* 17:328–32.

Kimmel, D. C. 1974. *Adulthood and Aging: An Interdisciplinary, Developmental View.* New York: Wiley.

Kimmel, D. C. 1977a. Patterns of aging among gay men. *Christopher Street* (November):28–31.

Kimmel, D. C. 1977b. Psychotherapy and the older gay man. *Psychotherapy: Theory, Research and Practice* 14:386–93.

Kimmel, D. C. 1979. Life-history interviews of aging gay men. *International Journal of Aging and Human Development* 10:239–48.

Kinsey, A. C., W. B. Pomeroy, and C. E. Martin. 1948. *Sexual Behavior in the Human Male.* Philadelphia: Saunders.

Kinsey, A. C., W. B. Pomeroy, C. E. Martin, and P. H. Gebhard. 1953. *Sexual Behavior in the Human Female.* Philadelphia: Saunders.

Levinson, D. J., et al. 1978. *The Seasons of a Man's Life.* New York: Knopf.

Mann, T. *Death in Venice and Other Stories.* 1925 [1913]. Translated by K. Burke. New York: Knopf.

Minnigerode, F. A. 1975. Towards an adult developmental psychology of male homosexuality. Paper presented at the meeting of the Western Psychological Association, April.

Riddle D., and S. Morin. 1977. Removing the stigma: Data from individuals. *APA Monitor* (November):16, 28.

Sheehy, G. 1976. *Passages: Predictable Crises of Adult Life.* New York: Dutton.

Tripp, C. A. 1975. *The Homosexual Matrix.* New York: McGraw-Hill.

Vaillant, G. E. 1977. *Adaptation to Life.* Boston: Little, Brown.

Warren, C. A. B. 1977. Fieldwork in the gay world: Issues in phenomenological research. *Journal of Social Issues* 33(4):93–107.

Weinberg, M. S. 1969. The aging male homosexual. *Medical Aspects of Human Sexuality* (December):66–67, 71–72.

Weinberg, M. S., and C. J. Williams. 1974. *Male Homosexuals: Their Problems and Adaptations.* New York: Oxford University Press.

VIII
Health

Only a few years ago little attention was given to specialized health concerns of lesbians and gay men. For men, venereal diseases such as gonorrhea, syphilis, and nonspecific urethritis were typical gay-related diseases (Rowan and Gillette 1978). Lesbians were relatively free of venereal diseases in comparison with heterosexual women (Robertson and Schachter 1981). Only a small number of physicians were openly gay or lesbian, and most lesbians and gays did not disclose their sexual orientation to their physician; very few physicians specialized in gay medicine (Calazza 1984).

A lesbian and gay male health movement began to emerge during the 1970s. The Gay Nurses' Alliance was the first professional health-related organization; groups also formed in public health, medicine, psychology, psychiatry, and social work. In 1976 the National Gay and Lesbian Health Coalition was founded and held its first conference in 1978 (Garnets and D'Augelli in press). At the beginning of the 1980s, research was focusing on developing a vaccine against viral hepatitis, then epidemic among gay men. In 1981, however, the disease that came to be known as acquired immune deficiency syndrome (AIDS) was identified.

History will tell the story of the development of the epidemic and its eventual resolution through a vaccine or an effective treatment, but the role of gay men has been clear for some time. Through tragic loss of life, large numbers of gay men brought the disease to the attention of medical researchers. Like the proverbial canary in a coal mine that revealed the presence of deadly gas so that the miners could escape, gay men sounded the alarm about AIDS. When the end of the AIDS epidemic finally comes, it may be hoped that the potential worldwide devastation will be reduced by medical research set in motion by the untimely death of gay men.

In the early days of the first alarm, the gay male and lesbian community had already become organized to achieve important goals, such as removing homosexuality from the list of mental disorders used by the mental health establishment, and had created structures that could be mobilized for the new challenge of AIDS. One such structure was the American Psychological Association (APA) Committee on Lesbian and Gay Concerns, which mobilized APA's organizational structure to provide leadership, lobbying, and expertise to begin the fight against AIDS. It was soon recognized that psychology must be at the forefront of the prevention effort, since the transmission routes of the disease through blood and semen quickly become known, and therefore the disease could be avoided by changing behavior.

Morin's article, in a 1988 issue of the *American Psychologist* devoted to AIDS, reprinted here, summarized the central role played by psychology. Tragically, that article still reflects in large measure the current situation. Prevention remains the only alternative; fear and discrimination persist; useless legislation requiring mandatory testing continues to be proposed and passed; and the extent of the epidemic grows and grows. Herek's (1990) provocative discussion of the similarities between AIDS and earlier epidemics in terms of stigma has summarized these points succinctly.

It is important to note that AIDS is not a disease of gay men. Women and men are at risk of infection through intravenous drug use, sexual relations, and contaminated medical equipment or supplies (especially in Third World countries where inadequate supplies force their reuse); children are at risk at childbirth to a mother infected with HIV/AIDS, and possibly by breast feeding from an infected mother. In the United States, a large number of women and children with AIDS are African-American or Hispanic. A disproportionate number of African-American and Hispanic men, as compared to White men, are diagnosed with AIDS. For many people of color, access to health care is inadequate. Clearly, the new face of AIDS is of people of color (Lester and Saxxon 1988).

Other ethnic or racial minorities also have unique issues with regard to HIV/AIDS infection. For example, Aoki and Ja (1987) pointed out the reluctance of Asians to rely on persons outside the family (except doctors) for care, but also families are often reluctant to provide care because of cultural values and stigmas associated with AIDS.

Lesbian health care was generally overlooked until the 1983–1988 survey conducted by the National Lesbian and Gay Health Foundation. That study suggested that many health concerns were associated with the discrimination and stress that resulted from being a member of stigmatized minorities as lesbians and as women. A concise summary of their findings is reprinted here. The data they reported on older lesbians are found in Bradford and Ryan (1991). The most striking finding in the latter report is that access to health care is limited by economic factors, with 27 percent lacking health insurance. They conclude that report with this poignant comment:

> Our review of the data from midlife lesbians results in a picture both heartening and disturbing. A very large majority of the women in our sample are in good or excellent overall health, socially, mentally and physically. But this health has been hard-won and accomplished with the support and help of counselors and other gay people, rather than through the social institutions which provide safety and structure for heterosexual individuals and couples. (Bradford and Ryan 1991:163)

Alcoholism has long been seen as a major health problem in the lesbian and gay male community, and several studies in the 1970s found that 29–35 percent of lesbians and gay men were alcohol dependent (Zigrang 1982). Many of these reports, however, were based on potentially biased samples, including patrons of gay/lesbian bars. A more recent study by McKirnan and Peterson (1989a) used a large community sample (n = 3,400) to provide an analysis of the patterns of alcohol and drug use, comparing gay men and lesbians with data from the general population. They found that a greater proportion of lesbians and gay men used alcohol, marijuana, or cocaine, and also reported higher rates of alcohol problems, as compared to the general population. Contrary to previous reports, however, lesbians and gay men did not show higher rates of heavy alcohol use compared to the general population; the difference was that a smaller number reported abstaining, while a larger number reported moderate use among the gay and lesbian sample. Moreover, the lesbian and gay male sample did not show the gender and age patterns typically found in the general population. That is, instead of using less, gay women were similar to gay men in their use of alcohol and drugs, and use did not decline with age as much in the lesbian and gay male sample. Each factor contributed to greater overall substance use by gays and lesbians than is reported in the general population. These findings also suggested that the effects of gender and age role norms do not operate for lesbians and gay men in the same ways that they function in the general population.

The reasons gay men and lesbians are more likely to use alcohol and drugs, and are at higher risk for alcohol problems, are complex (McKirnan and Peterson 1988, 1989b). Among the likely reasons are stress resulting from social oppression and discrimination, guilt from internalized homophobia, loneliness associated with social isolation, and pressure from others to fulfill family roles that are not appropriate without heterosexual marriage. In addition, for many, bars play a prominent role in lesbian and gay social life. Also, gay and lesbian role models when one is coming out may teach alcohol use. Moreover, some people use alcohol or drugs to overcome inhibitions about engaging in same-gender dating and sexual behavior.

Clearly, the use and abuse of alcohol and other forms of chemical dependency are major health concerns for some lesbians and gay men. There are many effects of alcohol use. Persons at risk for AIDS are less likely to practice safer sex after drinking; one is more likely to be involved in an accident, to be arrested, or to use poor judgment; long-term health effects of alcohol abuse are well known. It is likely that substance use also plays an important role in physical abuse of gay and lesbian partners, which is finally beginning to receive attention (Schilit, Lie, and Montagne 1990).

The discussion reprinted here by Ratner on substance abuse treatment succinctly summarizes a variety of issues relevant for gay men and lesbians, critiques traditional programs, and points out the need for specialized services.

Another health issue of considerable importance is antilesbian and anti-gay violence. As noted in the part on adolescence, many young gay males are abused by their families for being feminine or because their sexual orientation is revealed (Harry 1989). Some may be driven even to suicide. The article by Garnets, Herek, and Levy reprinted here summarizes the mental health consequences of hate crimes on the survivor and suggests treatment concerns for the survivor, significant others, and the broader gay and lesbian community.

CONTEMPORARY ISSUE: EFFECT OF SOCIAL OPPRESSION ON HEALTH

How can gay men and lesbians, as stigmatized minorities, cope with oppression without also harming their own physical and mental health? Clearly, if one recognizes the link between social oppression and physical health, then our psychological perspective must attend to a broad range of social and personal health issues. For example, stress from fear of anti-lesbian or antigay violence, discrimination, and heterosexist bias is likely to be associated with anxiety, depression, and substance abuse. Some older lesbians and gays may be hassled, ignored, denied relevant privileges (such as conjugal visits from a spouse in a nursing home), or have their care taken over by their biological families against their wishes. Disabled gays and lesbians face greater stigma, and their sexuality may often be ignored. Homophobia, now compounded by AIDS-related stigma, may compromise health care and mental health care. Lesbians and gay men of color, those with low income, and adolescents who have left home often lack health insurance and access to the full range of health care.

Despite being vulnerable to these forms of oppression, gays and lesbians have demonstrated resiliency. Through the support of a variety of resources, including the lesbian and gay community, most have turned many crises into competent adaptations. Nonetheless, civil rights protections, reduced heterosexist discrimination, full access to health care, and an end to homophobia and to antigay and antilesbian violence would be good medicine for everyone, including lesbians and gay men.

REFERENCES

Aoki, B. K., and D. Y. Ja. 1987. AIDS and Asian Americans: Psychosocial issues. Paper presented at the meeting of the American Psychological Association, New York, August.

Bradford, J., and C. Ryan. 1991. Who we are: Health concerns of middle-aged lesbians. In B. Sang, J. Warshow, and A. J. Smith, eds., *Lesbians at Midlife: The Creative Transition*, pp. 147–63. San Francisco: Spinsters.

Calazza, S. 1984. Medical practice with gay men in 1984. In F. Schwaber and M. Shernoff, eds., *Sourcebook on Lesbian/Gay Healthcare*, 97–99. New York: National Gay Health Education Foundation.

Garnets, L. D., and A. R. D'Augelli. In press. Empowering lesbian and gay communities: A call for collaboration with community psychology. *American Journal of Community Psychology*.

Harry, J. 1989. Parental physical abuse and sexual orientation in males. *Archives of Sexual Behavior* 18:251–61.

Herek, G. M. 1990. Illness, stigma, and AIDS. In G. R. VandenBos and P. T. Costa, eds., *Psychological Aspects of Serious Illness*, pp. 107–50. Washington, D.C.: American Psychological Association.

Lester, C., and L. L. Saxxon. 1988. AIDS in the Black community: The plague, the politics, the people. *Death Studies* 12:563–71.

McKirnan, D. J., and P. L. Peterson. 1988. Stress, expectancies, and vulnerability to substance abuse: A test of a model among homosexual men. *Journal of Abnormal Psychology* 97:461–66.

McKirnan, D. J., and P. L. Peterson. 1989a. Alcohol and drug use among homosexual men and women: Epidemiology and population characteristics. *Addictive Behaviors* 14:545–53.

McKirnan, D. J., and P. L. Peterson. 1989b. Psychosocial and cultural factors in alcohol and drug abuse: An analysis of a homosexual community. *Addictive Behaviors* 14:555–63.

Robertson, P., and J. Schachter. 1981. Failure to identify venereal disease in a lesbian population. *Sexually Transmitted Diseases* 8 (April–June):75–76.

Rowan, V. L., and P. J. Gillette. 1978. *The Gay Health Guide.* Boston: Little, Brown.

Schilit, R., G-Y. Lie, and M. Montagne. 1990. Substance use as a correlate of violence in intimate lesbian relationships. *Journal of Homosexuality* 19(3):51–65.

Zigrang, T. A. 1982. Who should be doing what about the gay alcoholic? *Journal of Homosexuality* 7(4):27–35.

24

The National Lesbian Health Care Survey: An Overview

Caitlin Ryan and Judith Bradford

Although more research has been conducted over the last decade on and by lesbians, most has involved samples of convenience, focusing on "psychological" variables. This work has generally been carried out by lesbian graduate students or practitioners utilizing their own client base or patient population. Descriptive studies have been small in scale and have explored lesbianism as a life-style or have focused on the relationships of lesbian couples. No previous research has been large enough in scale or comprehensive enough in scope to permit development of a broad definition of lesbian "health" that includes the diversity of lesbian experience. Since funding for lesbian research has been either nonexistent or inadequately available to undertake a national study, this survey represents the first attempt at gathering a sample sufficiently large and diverse enough to provide some speculative data describing lesbian health care needs and concerns. As such, it is an historic work that could not have been carried out without the participation of hundreds of lesbians and some of their gay male colleagues and friends throughout the United States.

This article describes the results of a large-scale, comprehensive study of lesbian health, the National Lesbian Health Care Survey, which was conducted under the coordination of Caitlin Ryan and Judy Bradford through the National Lesbian and Gay Health Foundation (NLGHF) from 1983 to 1988. The purpose of the survey has been to expand knowledge about the health care needs and concerns of women. A preliminary report, prepared for the National Institute of Mental Health, focused on the mental health aspects of lesbians' lives (Bradford and Ryan 1987). A complete report that includes all aspects of general health and mental health was published by NLGHF in July 1988. A chapter about respondents forty to sixty years old was recently published (Bradford and Ryan 1991). Initial funding for the survey was provided by the Ms. Foundation for Women with a $10,000 grant in 1984. Additional awards of $7,500 from the Chicago Resource Center and $1,000 from the Sophia Fund, along with contributions from individual lesbians of several hundred dollars, carried the project through the development and data-gathering phases.

Stimulated by the need for normative data about the health of lesbians, members of the board of the NLGHF formulated plans for the lesbian health care survey in 1982. During the next two years funding sources were sought, and a core research team made up of NLGHF board members and a research consultant, Dorothy Parkel of Atlanta, worked together to develop the questionnaire and sampling methodology.

Research involved the process of creating community awareness of lesbian health concerns as much as gathering the actual data from participants. The story of the National Lesbian Health Care Survey is as vital to our sense of who we are as lesbians as it is to the actual process of undertaking the study. A book describing the rich and powerful experience of participants and the researchers' struggle to complete the project is planned.

It is perhaps a metaphor for the barriers in undertaking lesbian research to report the difficulties in inputting the survey data, once actual data were obtained. Four data keypunch firms were hired and, with the exception of the last one, each reneged on their work, eventually refusing to complete the questionnaires and returning them to the Survey Research Lab, unentered. The last company stated that their keypunchers had walked off the job because they were afraid of getting AIDS from handling the questionnaires.

METHODOLOGY

QUESTIONNAIRE

Approximately one hundred individuals participated in developing the questionnaire either directly or by providing feedback. After three different versions were pretested in various locations throughout the United States in 1984, the final instrument, consisting of 104 items, was completed in the fall of 1984. Health was defined in holistic terms and incorporated the following aspects of lesbians lives:

- Community and social life
- General health and health care
- Gynecological health and health care
- Mental health and health care
- Substance abuse and eating disorders
- Physical and sexual abuse and help-seeking behaviors
- Discrimination
- Self-care
- "Outness"

Demographic questions were designed to reflect the uniqueness of lesbian life-styles through the participation of lesbians representing diverse racial, ethnic, and regional backgrounds.

Initially, the questionnaires were to be targeted to ten major cities in which strong distribution networks had been identified; news of the study, however, resulted in increased offers to help distribute them in other parts of the country. Thus, questionnaires were distributed as widely as possible. This was accomplished by mailing more than two thousand letters to lesbian and gay health organizations and practitioners; in addition, the study was publicized by the American Psychological Association, the National Organization for Women, the National Association of Social Workers, the National Coalition of Black Gays and Lesbians, the Council on Social Work Education, and the American Public Health Association.

Eventually, questionnaires reached all fifty states and U.S. territories as the original distributors developed dispersion networks in their communities and enlisted the aid of friends and acquaintances as second- and third-level distributors. Special efforts were made to reach as diverse a sample as possible. This included outreach to lesbians in the military, lesbians who were living in shelters, prisons, and on reservations, as well as lesbians of diverse ethnic, racial, and age groups. To reach lesbians who were not affiliated with a lesbian and gay community, advertisements were placed in gay newsletters, other publications, and in women's centers and bookstores. Of the more than four thousand 4,000 questionnaires distributed, approximately half (1,925) were completed and returned.

DATA MANAGEMENT AND ANALYSIS

Lack of sufficient funding delayed analysis of the data until 1986, when the Project Coordinator requested support from the National Institute of Mental Health to fund the analysis. Questionnaires were sent to the Survey Research Laboratory at Virginia Commonwealth University in Richmond. A code book was prepared and all questionnaires were coded by graduate assistants during December 1986 and January 1987.

FINDINGS

DEMOGRAPHIC CHARACTERISTICS

As indicated in table 24.1, the respondents were demographically less diverse than American women as a whole, although the sample did include some representatives from subgroups of all categories of American women. For example, more than four-fifths (81 percent) were between the ages of twenty-five and forty-four (age range, seventeen to eighty years); only 28 percent of American women are in this age group. They also were better educated—most (97 percent) were high school graduates, whereas about 70 percent of American women in general have graduated from high school. Furthermore, 85 percent of the respondents (versus 33 percent of all American women) had attended college, and almost 70 percent had graduated (versus 18 percent of American women as a whole).

Not surprisingly, this higher level of education was reflected in the respondents' occupations, which were classified according to the U.S. Census Bureau's occupational codes. Approximately three-fourths (73 percent) were professionals, managers, or administrators or officials; only one-fourth of American women are in these occupational categories. Despite their high educational level, however, 88 percent of the sample earned less than $30,000 annually.

Three-fourths of the respondents said they had a primary relationship or were "somewhat involved" with a woman. In 1984, 62 percent of American women were legally married to a man—a percentage similar to that of lesbians who said they had a primary relationship with a woman (60 percent). Only a few respondents (3 percent) were married to or living with a man. In discussing the number of persons in their household, respondents did not differ greatly from women in general (two-person households were more common among the respondents, whereas a larger percentage of the general female population tended to have households of four or more people).

TABLE 24.1
*Demographic Characteristics of the Sample Compared to the
Adult Female Population in the United States (in percentages)*

Characteristic	Sample (N = 1,917) Unweighted	Weighted	Adult Female Population 1980[a]
AGE			
17–24	8.8	8.9	12.5
25–34	48.0	48.4	16.6
35–44	32.2	32.5	12.0
45–54	7.0	7.1	9.7
55 or older	3.1	3.1	23.4
EDUCATION			
Did not graduate from high school	2.4	2.5	29.1
High school graduate	9.5	9.5	37.9
Vocational training	2.5	2.5	—
Some college	16.3	16.4	15.3
College graduate	26.0	26.2	—
Advanced studies	11.6	11.6	17.7
Advanced degree	31.2	31.3	—
TYPE OF WORK			
Professional	39.5	53.3	25.2
Manager/official	14.8	19.9	—
Clerical	6.9	9.3	42.5
Service worker	5.2	7.0	16.8
Craftsperson	3.8	5.1	2.3
Operative/unskilled worker	2.9	4.1	9.7
Private household worker	0.8	1.1	2.1
Farmer	0.1	0.1	—
WORK STATUS			
Employed full-time	66.6	—	—
Employed part-time	18.5	—	—
Student	21.6	—	—
Unemployed	9.0	—	—
PERSONAL INCOME			
$9,999 or less	27.6	27.9	—
$10,000–19,999	35.8	36.2	—
$20,000–29,999	23.5	23.8	—
$30,000–39,000	7.9	8.0	—
$40,000–49,999	4.1	4.2	—
MARITAL STATUS			
Married	—	—	61.9
Never married	—	—	17.6
Divorced	—	—	—
Separated	—	—	8.0
Widowed	—	—	12.5
RELATIONSHIP STATUS			
Primary relationship is with a woman	59.9	—	—
Single and somewhat involved with a woman	17.5	—	—
Single and not involved	19.1	—	—
Living with a male lover	0.4	—	—
Legally married to a man	2.2	—	—

continued

TABLE 24.1   *continued*

| Characteristic | Sample (N = 1,917) | | Adult Female Population 1980[a] |
	Unweighted	Weighted	
NUMBER OF PEOPLE IN THE HOUSEHOLD			
One	20.9	22.7	23.2
Two	45.7	49.7	31.7
Three	13.0	14.1	17.5
Four to five	8.7	9.4	22.7
Six or more	3.7	4.0	4.9
RACE/ETHNICITY			
White (non-Hispanic)	88.2	88.5	83.1
Black (non-Hispanic)	5.6	5.6	11.7
Hispanic	4.2	4.2	6.4
Asian/Pacific Islander	0.8	0.8	1.2
Aleut/Eskimo/American Indian	0.6	0.6	0.6
Other	0.3	0.3	3.0
RELIGIOUS AffILIATION			
None	64.5	66.2	—
Protestant	11.2	11.5	—
Catholic	7.8	8.0	—
Gay church	2.4	2.5	—
Quaker	0.5	0.5	—
Christian Science	0.2	0.2	—
Mennonite	0.2	0.2	—
Mormon	0.2	0.2	
Other Christian	0.6	0.6	
Jewish	7.3	7.4	
Unitarian	1.0	1.0	
Pagan, witch	0.8	0.8	—
Buddhist	0.5	0.5	—
Unity	0.3	0.3	—
Islamic	0.2	0.2	—

[a] *1984 Statistical Abstracts of the United States* (104th ed.), U.S. Department of Commerce, Washington, D.C., 1984.

In most cases, the racial distribution of the sample was similar to that of American women in general, with almost 12 percent of the sample representing lesbians of color. African-Americans were underrepresented among minorities.

Although religious information was unavailable for the adult female population as a whole, one can assume that the percentage of American women with religious affiliations is significantly higher than was true of the respondents. Like the population as a whole, most respondents (86 percent) had been raised as Protestants, Catholics, or Jews. At the time of the survey, however, less than one-third (27 percent) were currently affiliated with one of these religions. Two-thirds (66 percent) said they were not currently affiliated with any religion. Note that among the remaining respondents, some had joined the Quaker or Unity church or a gay church,

TABLE 24.2

Region	Birthplace	Current residence (in percentages)
North East	31	25
North Central	28	21
South	26	28
Mountain	5	7
Pacific	10	19

each of which are known to be supportive of gay people and to recognize gay relationships.

Finally, the percentages of respondents who were born and currently live in various regions of the United States are shown in table 24.2 (less than 1 percent were born or currently lived in Puerto Rico or another U.S. territory).

Note that substantial proportions of those born in the Northeast or North Central regions no longer lived there. Nearly twice as many lived in the Pacific region as had been born in these states. Only 10 percent of the women still lived in the town or city of their birth. More than half the sample (52 percent) lived in major metropolitan areas at the time of the survey. Only 11 percent lived in towns, with 1 percent living in rural areas. At the time of the survey, thirty respondents were living in prison (n = 9), in a shelter (n = 19), or on an Indian reservation (n = 2).

PHYSICAL HEALTH

GENERAL HEALTH PROBLEMS

The most frequently reported health problem for all age groups was overweight—32 percent of all respondents reported this, from a low of 27 percent among those seventeen to twenty-four years old, to a high of 35 percent of those between the ages of thirty-five and forty-four. Other health problems experienced by at least one in five respondents included allergies, back problems, ulcers, and stomach trouble. Heart problems were reported by 2 percent, high blood pressure by 4 percent, and diabetes by 1 percent. No respondents reported current infection with hepatitis A or B.

Respondents were much more likely to be receiving treatment for some conditions than for others. All individuals with heart trouble, for example, were receiving care. Less than half of those with weight problems were being treated, however. All age groups reported that their first choice for receiving care was from a private practitioner. Second and third choices included community clinics, women's health centers, emergency rooms, and HMOs.

Consistent with these preferences, 66 percent reported their usual place of care to be a private office, 16 percent a community clinic, and 12 percent a women's health center. For three-fourths, a medical doctor was the usual care provider. Almost one in five were usually seen by a chiropractor and 13 percent by a nurse.

Ten percent did not have a usual provider and 6 percent said they saw no one when they needed assistance with a health problem. The most common reason for not receiving care was lack of financial resources, reported by 16 percent. Other reasons reported by significant numbers included being embarrassed or afraid, lack of trust in providers, having bad experiences in the past, and having family and friends who could provide care.

The most common problem experienced with providers was their assumption of the individual's heterosexuality—this happened to 27 percent of respondents. Other past and present problems with providers included language barriers, lack of trust in the staff, difficulty in talking with the provider, not sharing information with the patient, and giving the patient wrong information. Seventeen percent would not reveal their lesbian identity to health care workers. Only 33 percent felt that the health care they received was very good.

OBSTETRICS AND GYNECOLOGICAL PROBLEMS

Among twelve common gynecological problems listed in the questionnaire, the most frequent problem respondents had experienced in the past was severe menstrual cramps (38 percent), followed by heavy menstrual bleeding, irregular periods, an unusual discharge between periods, premenstrual syndrome (PMS), and breast lumps or growths (less than 11 percent in each case). Like the female population in general, older women were more likely to report breast lumps and heavy menstrual bleeding, whereas younger women were more likely to report severe cramps, irregular periods, unusual discharges, and PMS.

At the time of the survey, severe menstrual cramps were again listed as the main complaint—24 percent of the women said they were currently suffering from the problem. Eighteen percent said they suffered from PMS; less than 13 percent of the women listed any of the other gynecological complaints.

The most likely sources of treatment were private physicians (51 percent) and women's health centers or community clinics (23 percent).

Older women were more likely to see a private physician, whereas younger women tended to be treated at a health center or clinic.

The distressing information revealed by the survey was that almost one-fourth (2.3 percent) of the respondents were either treating themselves for a current gynecological problem or getting no treatment at all (14 percent and 9 percent, respectively). This behavior was most notable among respondents with less education. The largest percentage of these women said they had not sought treatment because they could take care of the problem themselves. Some said, however, that they could not afford to seek treatment; were uncomfortable, embarrassed, or afraid of getting treatment; did not trust the health care staff at places they knew; or have had negative experiences at these places.

Almost 30 percent of the respondents had been pregnant. It is interesting to note that women with the least education *and* the most education were most likely to have been pregnant. Only 16 percent had actually given birth to a child. Women who did not become pregnant listed eleven categories of reasons, including fear, sterility, career needs, finances, lack of a partner, and no desire for men. Nevertheless, 44 percent indicated that they would consider adoption and one-third agreed that donor insemination with a known donor was a viable option.

Concern About Sexually Transmitted Diseases

Participants were asked four questions about sexually transmitted diseases (STDs): Do you worry about getting sexually transmitted diseases? Does the fear of disease keep you from performing certain sex acts? How has AIDS (acquired immune deficiency syndrome) affected your life? Where would you turn most often for information about sexually transmitted diseases? Less than 25 percent of the women said they worried about getting STDs, and the majority of these were younger women. Proportionately, Blacks were twice as likely to fear these diseases.

Less than 15 percent of the sample said that fear of STDs kept them from engaging in some (unspecified) sexual acts. Again, younger women and Blacks were more likely than other respondents to change their sexual behavior because of such fears.

AIDS

When asked how AIDS had affected their lives, six out of ten lesbians reported the following: worry about gay male friends; becoming more aware of the issue; concern for those affected; getting involved with AIDS; feeling frightened, angry, sad; and understanding the political implications. Only one out of ten lesbians were concerned about contagion; service workers were most likely to say they were concerned about becoming infected. It is important to note that the data were gathered in 1984 and early 1985, almost eight years ago. It is the perception of the researchers that these responses would be different at this time.

One lesbian in the sample had AIDS. Her risk factor was secondary hemophilia. Her lover also completed the questionnaire. Both reported feeling isolated and cut off from the lesbian community in the midwestern city where they lived.

MENTAL HEALTH

The survey findings indicated utilization of professional counseling services by nearly three-quarters of the respondents.

Depression, Anxiety, and Fear. More than a third (37 percent) of the respondents said they had experienced a long depression and sadness in the past, and 11 percent were experiencing these feelings at the time of the survey. Women in the seventeen to twenty-four and thirty-five to forty-four age groups were more likely than others to report current depression, and women who worked as operatives (skilled and unskilled laborers) were noticeably more likely to report depression than were other occupational groups. Twenty-one percent of the sample reported having had suicidal thoughts "sometimes" or "often," and 18 percent (almost one out of five) had actually attempted suicide, usually with drugs.

Nearly one in five (19 percent) had suffered constant anxiety and fear and 12 percent another type of mental health problem at some point in the past; 7 percent and 8 percent, respectively, were currently experiencing such problems. Women in the youngest age bracket, women without a high school education, low-income women, and service workers were most likely to report current problems involving anxiety and fear.

Sources of Worry. The most common cause of worry among respondents of all ages, races, and income levels was money, followed by problems with their lover and job worries. In response to a question asking if they had been too nervous to cope with ordinary responsibilities within the past year, more than half (56 percent) of the respondents said they felt that way "sometimes" or "often." Generally, respondents with higher levels of education and higher income levels were more likely to have reported this feeling. White women also were more likely to have experienced this feeling than were Blacks or Hispanics.

Eating Disorders. Almost two-thirds of the respondents (65 percent) said they overate "sometimes" or "often"; about one-fourth (26 percent) reported that they underate "sometimes" or "often." Symptoms of bulimia were rare: only 2 percent of the women said they sometimes overate then vomited, and less than 1 percent said they did so often. Women in the higher income brackets were less likely than other groups to overeat. Not surprisingly, lower income was associated with undereating.

USE OF TOBACCO, ALCOHOL, AND OTHER SUBSTANCES

Forty-one percent of the survey respondents said they smoked cigarettes: 30 percent smoked them regularly and 11 percent did so occasionally. Among these smokers, approximately half said they were worried about their smoking.

More than eight in ten (83 percent) of the respondents said they consumed alcohol at least once a month. Thirty-one percent said they drank regularly—25 percent said "more than once a week" and 6 percent said "every day" (daily drinking was most common among women in the $40,000 or higher income bracket).

Almost half the sample (47 percent) reported using marijuana at least occasionally. Younger lesbians and Blacks were more likely to use this drug than were other respondents. Twenty percent had tried cocaine— these respondents were more likely to be Black, Hispanic, and young. Only 1 percent reported regular use. Few of the women used tranquilizers, and only a few said they ever used heroin or uppers.

PHYSICAL ABUSE, SEXUAL ATTACK, AND INCEST

More than one-third of the sample (37 percent) reported having been severely beaten or physically abused at some point in their lives. Six percent had been physically abused both in childhood and adulthood. Most of those abused in childhood were abused by a male relative. Among those abused as adults, more than half (53 percent) had been abused by a lover and about one-fourth (27 percent) by their husbands. White women were less likely to have been abused.

One-fifth (21 percent) of the sample had been raped or sexually attacked as children, and 15 percent had been sexually abused as adults. A few (4 percent) had been abused during both childhood and adulthood. Most of the abusers were men. Only one-third of these sexually abused women had sought help. Although the rate of sexual abuse in adulthood was similar among Whites, Blacks, and Hispanics, one-third of all Black women, one-fourth of the Hispanic women, and one-fifth of the White women had been abused as children.

Among the respondents who had reported experiencing incest with at least one relative during childhood (19 percent), the most common perpetrator was a brother, followed by a father or an uncle. White women were least likely to have had an incestuous relationship in childhood: 16 percent versus 31 percent for Blacks and 29 percent for Hispanics.

"OUTNESS"

According to research on the psychological benefits of coming out (see, for example, Brooks 1981; Lewis 1984) and on the dynamics involved (Ryan 1982; Sanders and Brink 1982), the benefits of coming out ("outness") include health-facilitating effects and an opportunity for personal integration. It also poses difficult challenges, however. Brooks (1981), Gartrell (1983), and Gebhard (1971) have documented the discrimination experienced by lesbians who have deliberately come out or have been discovered accidentally.

Respondents most likely to be out in all areas of their lives were twenty-five to thirty-four years old, had vocational training, were craftswomen or laborers, or were White. Although 88 percent of the women were open about their lesbianism with all gay people they knew, 19 percent had never told any of their family members and 29 percent had not told their coworkers that they were lesbians. In other words, the dominant pattern seemed to be compartmentalizing aspects of their lesbian identity. Although being out apparently made it easier to obtain needed help and support, it also increased the likelihood of discrimination.

DISCRIMINATION

The majority of women in the sample had experienced some form of discrimination for being lesbian. For example, more than half (52 percent) had been verbally attacked, 15 percent had lost their jobs or had been discharged from the armed services, and 8 percent had been physically attacked. Almost one in ten respondents (8 percent) believed that their sexual orientation had negatively affected the quality of health care they had received.

SOURCES OF HELP

Seventy-three percent of the respondents either were receiving counseling at the time of the survey or had received it in the past, from professionals such as doctors, therapists, and social workers. Thirty-six percent had received counseling through nonprofessional sources of help, such as peer support groups and healing circles. Most respondents preferred to see a private counselor; 63 percent had done so. The factors that affected the likelihood of seeking mental health counseling included age, education, income, religious affiliation, and race. Respondents were more concerned about the counselor's gender than his or her sexual orientation or ethnicity. Eighty-nine percent preferred to see a woman; only 10 percent said the counselor's gender did not matter. Thirty-three percent said the counselor's sexual orientation did not matter, whereas 66 percent preferred to see a lesbian or gay therapist.

Feeling sad or depressed was the most common reason for seeking mental health counseling—half the sample had received counseling for these reasons. In addition, 44 percent had sought counseling for problems with personal relationships. Twenty-one percent of the sample had sought help with problems specifically related to their sexual orientation. Sixteen percent of the respondents had sought help for their drinking or use of other drugs.

Twenty-one percent of the respondents who had not received counseling said they had thought about it. Their reasons for not actually obtaining counseling included not knowing where to go, not having enough money, and fear of coming out.

SELF-CARE

Over two-fifths (44 percent) of the respondents believed they could handle their own mental health problems if their problems were not too serious. Only 6 percent, however, felt they could treat themselves if the problems became serious. One-fourth of the women felt they could handle problems with alcohol or other drugs if the problems were not too serious. Better-educated women, women with higher incomes, and non-Black women were more likely to seek help for serious mental health problems.

COMMUNITY AND SOCIAL LIFE

The large majority of respondents who are young, live in urban areas, and are employed as professionals or managers have access to a variety of activities for women and for lesbians only. Mental health implications for lesbians who are not in these demographic categories, however, warrant concern.

According to responses to questions about their community and social lives, respondents were socially involved primarily with other lesbians, friends from their racial or ethnic background, or with gay and straight men, rather than with the general community. For example, 38 percent of the respondents participated in lesbian/gay rights groups and 30 percent participated in women's rights groups, whereas only 16 percent belonged to a religious organization and only 11 percent belonged to a neighborhood association.

Approximately 75 percent lived in communities where lesbian activities were available. The most common activities were lesbian/gay rights groups; women's support groups; social groups; women's rights groups; union, trade, or professional groups; and health centers or clubs. Most respondents participated in such activities at least several times a year (younger women were likely to attend these events more often).

As mentioned in the Demographic section, three-fourths of the respondents either had a primary relationship or were involved with a lover. In this group, half were living with their lover and one-fourth were living alone.

Most of the respondents' female friends were lesbians (64 percent). Approximately one-third had equal numbers of gay and straight women friends. Seventy-eight percent of respondents said they had close male friends. Male friends were more evenly balanced between gay and straight than were female friends, although most reported having fewer male friends than female friends. Finally, 61 percent of the sample tended to choose friends from their own ethnic group.

CONCLUSION

As the survey indicates, lesbians not only experience the difficulties faced by American women as a whole but also the problems of being lesbian in a heterosexual society. Lesbians who are members of a racial or ethnic minority experience a third set of difficulties. The survey documented inequities in service delivery for lesbians living outside of urban areas and for low-income and young lesbians. It also documented a surprisingly high use of mental health services—about 75 percent of the sample had received counseling at some point. This, however, may be seen as a strength, in terms of actively seeking out resources to help them adapt to a "hostile" environment.

Survey findings suggested several areas that involve the mental health of American women as a whole and require further mental health research:

- The effects of low pay on women of high academic achievement.
- The needs of older women, especially those living alone.

- The prevalence of physical and sexual abuse among women.
- The relationship between substance abuse and depression and suicide.
- The effect of traditional and nontraditional occupations on social connectedness and mental health.

The study also indicated several questions specifically related to the mental health of lesbians that need further investigation:

- How are lesbians affected by dual discrimination on the basis of their gender and their sexual orientation (and the effects of triple discrimination in the case of racial and ethnic minorities)?
- What is the impact of coming out or remaining in the closet on mental health?
- What strengths do most lesbians have that enable them to survive in a nonsupportive environment?
- How has the AIDS epidemic affected lesbians who either have contracted the disease or are discriminated against by the general public because of incorrect perceptions about who is at risk?

With regard to health services overall, unless service providers are able to view lesbianism as an acceptable life-style and not as a symptom of mental illness or deviance, they risk delivering services that will be harmful rather than helpful or will prevent lesbians from accessing them.

REFERENCES

Bradford, J., and C. Ryan. 1987. *National Lesbian Health Care Survey: Mental Health Implications.* Washington, D.C.: National Lesbian and Gay Health Foundation.

Bradford, J., and C. Ryan. 1991. Who we are: Health concerns of middle-aged lesbians. In B. Sang, J. Warshow, and A. J. Smith, eds., *Lesbians at Midlife: The Creative Transition,* pp. 147–63. San Francisco: Spinsters.

Brooks, V. R. 1981. *Minority Stress and Lesbian Women.* Lexington, Mass.: D. C. Heath.

Gartrell, N. 1983. Gay Patients in the Medical Setting. In C. C. Nadelson and D. B. Marcotto, eds., *Treatment Interventions in Human Sexuality.* New York: Plenum Press.

Gebhard, P. 1971. Incidence of Overt Homosexuality in the U.S. and Western Europe. *Homosexuality. Final Report and Background Paper* (DHEW Publication HMS 72–9116). Rockville, Md.: National Institute of Mental Health Task Force).

Lewis, L. A. 1984. The coming-out process for lesbians: Integrating a stable identity."
    Social Work 29:464–69.
Ryan, C. C. 1982. Coming out among professional women: A survey of attitudes and
    practices in a southern city. Master's thesis, Smith College School of Social Work.
Sanders, J. M., and P. J. Brink. 1982. Los Angeles lesbians: A survey. Unpublished
    research report.

25

AIDS: The Challenge to Psychology

Stephen F. Morin

Psychologists are in a strategic position to be of assistance in responding to the AIDS crisis. Preventing the spread of the AIDS virus is a major public health goal; psychologists as specialists in behavioral change have played a major role in planning successful prevention campaigns. Psychologists as health care providers have given needed emphasis to psychosocial issues in designing and implementing appropriate models of AIDS patient care. The greatest challenge to psychology, however, will come in attempting to alleviate the social, cultural, economic, and political reactions that will follow in the wake of the growing number of AIDS cases.

On Friday, June 5, 1981, the Centers for Disease Control (CDC) reported the first case of what would later be known as acquired immune deficiency syndrome (AIDS) (CDC 1981). By 1982 CDC recognized a major new epidemic emerging. The epidemiological data available in 1983 pointed to viral transmission through sexual contact and shared needle use. Since then, the role of psychology and the social sciences has been clear. AIDS is a behaviorally transmitted disease.

Scientific and medical breakthroughs over the years have allowed us to better understand the nature and magnitude of this epidemic. The identification of what would later be known as the human immunodeficiency virus (HIV), as announced in April 1984, has allowed a much fuller understanding of the virology and epidemiology of the epidemic. With each new breakthrough, the worldwide magnitude of this epidemic is more fully appreciated.

To understand what we are facing, it may be useful to think of three separate epidemics, each distinctly linked to the others (Mann 1988). First, an epidemic of HIV infection (the virus causing AIDS) began silently in the mid-1970s and progressed unnoticed until 1981. The second epidemic involved the diseases characterized by the case surveillance definition of AIDS. The number of people disposed with such diseases has grown rapidly, as has the number of resulting deaths. The third epidemic, which has received far less attention, involves the social, cultural, economic, and political reaction to the HIV and AIDS epidemics. This third epidemic of reaction, which is just beginning, is as much a part of the pathology of AIDS as the virus itself. Each of the three epidemics represents a different challenge to psychology. This article attempts to assess psychology's response so far and to suggest what needs to be done in the future.

BREAKING THE CHAIN OF TRANSMISSION

In the absence of a vaccine or cure, the only way to stem the HIV epidemic is by breaking the chain of viral transmission. Because the virus is transmitted by behaviors, prevention efforts must focus on encouraging behavioral change that would reduce transmission of the virus through sexual contact or shared use of needles.

Psychologists have long been involved in efforts to influence various health-related behaviors, such as encouraging people to stop smoking, to change their diet to reduce cardiovascular risk, and to wear seat belts (Institute of Medicine/National Academy of Sciences [IOM/NAS] 1986). Psychologists have also been directly involved in attempts to control transmission of sexually transmitted diseases and reduce intravenous drug abuse. Psychology's role in this effort cannot be underestimated.

Beginning as early as 1983, psychologists were involved in the planning and design of an extensive prevention campaign in San Francisco targeted at reducing the sexual transmission of the AIDS virus among gay and bisexual men. The campaign was based on theoretical models and research data drawn from other areas of health psychology that logically provided a starting point for this effort (McKusick, Conant, and Coates 1985). Activities included media efforts, all of which were shaped after extensive marketing research that included focus groups. Town meetings, workshops, seminars, and phone information referral services were used to inform the community. Individual health education and counseling were made available at alternative test sites for anonymous AIDS antibody testing. To aid those identifying themselves as having problems, the city hired trained mental health professionals to lead groups that focused on stress reduction, safer sexual practices, and development of better coping skills for AIDS-related bereavement. In addition, more than seven thousand gay and bisexual men attended one-session meetings sponsored by a local community-based organization that engaged in structured discussions of how each of them might personally participate in ending the AIDS epidemic (Communications Technologies 1987). Representatives from the gay community were routinely included in all aspects of designing the campaign.

As a result of this extensive and sophisticated prevention campaign, San Francisco has reported few new HIV infections among gay and bisexual men over the last two years (Winkelstein et al. 1987). Studies of sexual behavior indicate that gay and bisexual men in San Francisco are far less likely to engage in sexual activity that may transmit HIV than men in other parts of the country (Coates, Stall, and Hoff 1988). The San Francisco prevention model is now being replicated in many cities across the country. This success gives public health officials new hope that prevention efforts designed to facilitate behavioral change can control the spread of HIV.

It is said that knowledge is our best weapon against AIDS. Giving information about how HIV is transmitted, however, appears to be a necessary but not sufficient condition to facilitate behavioral change. This is consistent with findings in other areas in which there are behavioral risk factors for disease (Leventhal and Cleary 1980). Therefore, prevention campaigns based almost exclusively on giving information are not likely to be successful. In the evolution of the San Francisco prevention model, the use of theoretical models and behavioral research findings placed greater attention on prevention services to help people change behavior and on community-level interventions to change group norms. Thus, the involvement of behavioral principles helped to organize the prevention campaign and to suggest options that might not otherwise have been considered or given priority.

An accurate assessment of individual risks is essential to facilitating behavioral change. The practical importance of accurate information is that it allows individuals to assess their own personal risk. This, in turn, allows those with high-risk behaviors the opportunity to label such activity as problematic (Catania, Kegeles, and Coates 1988). Once high-risk behaviors are identified as a problem, the individual will typically change through self-initiated actions or through seeking assistance from others. Assistance can be informal as in seeking help from friends or it can be structured as in seeking a medical or psychological intervention. Self-help approaches have also evolved to assist people in reducing or eliminating high-risk sexual behavior.

It is important to note that "threat" is not always accurately perceived. This is particularly true among specific groups, such as adolescents and ethnic minorities who may underestimate personal risk. A technical ability to reach groups at increased risk with credible messages that will facilitate the individual's labeling high-risk behaviors as problematic is essential to the success of targeted prevention campaigns. Likewise, threat is often overestimated among those without behavioral risk factors. Accurate information can reduce unwarranted anxiety in such cases.

Building peer and community support for reducing the risk of spreading HIV is critically important. The successful San Francisco model of AIDS risk reduction has relied heavily on shifting community norms so that low-risk activities are a community expectation. Community-based prevention programs have involved groups targeted for the prevention message in implementing the behavioral change program. Thus, the gay community has become a part of the prevention planning, which, in turn, has increased the likelihood that the program will be successful. Other groups potentially at risk, such as ethnic minorities and adolescents, must also be involved in planning prevention campaigns targeted to each group.

Although a great deal of quality social science research on AIDS prevention has begun, the unmet need in this area is remarkable. The planning, conduct, and evaluation of targeted prevention programs for specific groups needs to be well documented so that other programs can benefit from what is learned. Behavioral research needs to be set as a high priority within the Alcohol, Drug Abuse, and Mental Health Administration (ADAMHA) and most particularly within the National Institute of Mental Health (NIMH). Psychologists and other social scientists with expertise in the prevention area need to be redirected toward AIDS prevention efforts. New scholars need to be attracted to and specifically trained for careers in behavioral prevention, with heavy emphasis on AIDS prevention. The formation of a panel to address behavioral issues and AIDS by the National Academy of Sciences and the focus on AIDS prevention at the 1988 Vermont Conference on Primary Prevention are recent efforts that must be commended. Unfortunately, much of the prevention activities in the United States and across the world are conducted with minimal input from behavioral scientists. Programs are often limited to giving AIDS information. Little attention or emphasis is directed toward what we have already learned are essential components of behavioral change programs. Psychologists must be proactive in advocating for more sophisticated prevention programs. Technical assistance on how best to facilitate behavioral change should be made available to all those conducting local targeted prevention campaigns.

RESPONDING TO THOSE IN NEED

The major task for organized health and social services is to respond to those who become sick as a result of HIV infection. It will continue to be a particular responsibility for all those involved in health care delivery. The Centers for Disease Control estimate that as many as 1.4 million Americans are currently infected with HIV; the World Health Organization estimates that more than 5 million people throughout the world are infected. Although initially it was thought that only a small portion of those infected would go on to develop AIDS and die as a result of the infection, more recent CDC estimates indicate that as many as 99 percent of those infected will go on to develop AIDS (Lui, Darrow, and Rutherford 1988). The nations of the world are not currently prepared to address the health care delivery needs of the more than 1 million people who, in the absence of major medical breakthroughs, will become sick with AIDS in the next five years.

Evaluation research is an essential component of health care planning. Sophisticated evaluations are needed for AIDS-related health care delivery models. Thus far, experience suggests that home and community-based services are more clinically appropriate and more cost-effective than inpatient services. Models also need to be developed for the coordination of social services, including disability benefits, housing, practical support, and nutritional programs.

Specialized services will be needed for those with multiple diagnoses. Outpatient substance abuse treatment and outpatient mental health treatment must be integrated into service models for intravenous drug users and people with AIDS who also have significant mental disorders. Programs must be designed that will be appropriate for the cultural and linguistic background of those in need of the services. Specialized foster home placement programs need to be coordinated for pediatric AIDS cases. Psychological expertise is essential in coordinating these services so that they become more efficient and give increased emphasis to psychosocial issues.

Psychologists as health care providers have a special role in managing care of individuals with chronic and debilitating illnesses. Psychological assistance is often appropriate in inpatient management, as well as in the planning of transition from the hospital to the home or alternative placements. Psychological interventions assist patients in tolerating medical procedures and in complying with medication regimes. Psychosocial support can build the patient's motivation to cooperate and to strive for recovery from serious bouts of illness or prepare the individual to die with dignity.

AIDS mental health issues have often received less attention due to the magnitude of the medical crisis. Emotional reactions to an AIDS diagnosis are typically in keeping with the fatal prognosis associated with such a diagnosis (Morin and Batchelor 1984). Specialized mental health services have been developed for people with AIDS, people with AIDS-related complex (ARC), people with HIV infections who are not yet ill, and significant others of each group, including family members (Morin, Charles, and Malyon 1984). Each of these groups has unique needs, and specific training is required to address these needs (McKusick 1986).

This epidemic will continue to create educational and training needs for psychologists and other mental health providers. The epidemic has also precipitated a need for volunteers. The bulk of services for people with AIDS is provided by emotional support volunteers. Those with special training in mental health are also needed to serve in an adjunct capacity to these volunteer programs. The volunteer corps of mental health providers that have developed in many parts of the country must be expanded to meet a growing need.

The HIV epidemic has produced new ethical dilemmas for some mental health providers. Most notably, the duty to protect others from HIV infection has emerged as an issue of considerable concern for those working directly with people with HIV infection, particularly if such individuals continue to be sexually active without adequately informing potential partners. Few guidelines are currently available in state statutes or in training for professional providers on how to handle this situation. The desire to maintain confidentiality so as to enhance the therapeutic relationship must be balanced against the need to protect others from potential infection. At a minimum, reducing the risk of transmission to a sexual partner must be integrated into individual treatment plans for those who have HIV and who continue high-risk activity. In a rare case involving a truly recalcitrant patient, it may be necessary to breach confidentiality in order to seek assistance from a local health department whose job includes controlling communicable and sexually transmitted diseases. Such an approach is far more appropriate than having an individual mental health provider attempt to undertake case interviews, contact tracing, and contact notification. Consensus on how to handle these unusual but important cases needs to be developed within the professional community of health and mental health providers.

Extensive psychological expertise is needed in dealing with problems associated with recalcitrant patients. Extensive expertise is also needed in planning for the clinical management of patients with AIDS-related dementia. Although severe forms of AIDS-related dementia are rare, their clinical management is particularly difficult. Unusual cases will continue to attract a disproportionate amount of attention. The needs for the foreseeable future, however, will be for basic health and mental health services. Attention must be focused on improving the quality and appropriateness of these basic services.

SOCIAL, ECONOMIC, AND POLITICAL REACTIONS

The AIDS epidemic will be the greatest test for the American people since the Vietnam War. Indeed, by early 1989 the death toll from AIDS will have exceeded that from the Vietnam conflict. Although fear is a natural reaction to an epidemic, the level of fear among those without behavioral risk factors has been irrational and excessive. This fear can be expected to continue. Information can be of assistance in reducing the level of fear but is unlikely to eliminate it. Unfortunately, fear is often converted into actions with devastating consequences.

The Commission on the HIV Epidemic, appointed by President Reagan, has identified discrimination against people with AIDS and people with HIV infections as a major deterrent to an adequate public health response (Presidential Commission on the HIV Epidemic 1988). Those who fear discrimination in employment, housing, or access to governmental services are not likely to come forward to participate in public health programs.

Discrimination is only part of the problem. Stigma associated with AIDS has led to people being shunned socially and suffering significant psychological damage even though they maintain employment and housing. Stigma and discrimination are problems not only for people with AIDS and those with HIV infections but also for those who are perceived to be potential "AIDS carriers," whether they are or not. AIDS has disproportionately affected groups, such as gay men and intravenous drug users, who are already subjected to substantial stigma. Violence directed toward those infected with the virus or perceived to be at increased risk for infection has also been widely reported. Little attention has been paid to national, state, or local programs specifically designed to reduce stigma and decrease the frequency of incidents of discrimination and violence.

The economic impact of AIDS will be profound. The lifetime cost of medical care per AIDS patient is currently about $80,000, a figure similar to the cost of treating other serious illnesses (Bloom and Carliner 1988). The direct medical cost of the 270,000 cases projected between 1981 and 1991 would be about $22 billion. These costs will generate public policy concerns about who will pay and how much should be allocated to any one disease (Sisk 1987). The AIDS epidemic will serve to highlight an already strained system of financing health care in the United States. The implications for the Third World, where in many countries the cost of one HIV antibody test exceeds the average expenditure per person for health care, will be far more devastating. Direct medical costs alone, however, do not accurately assess the economic impact of the AIDS epidemic. Medical costs are only about one-fifth of the total cost to society when loss of productivity is included due to the fact that AIDS primarily afflicts working-aged adults. Thus, others estimate that the total cost of AIDS in the United States during 1991 alone will be $66.5 billion (Scitovsky and Rice 1987).

Social and economic reactions to AIDS have led to political pressure to enact drastic public policy measures that are unwarranted based on current scientific and medical evidence. In 1988 a total of 147 AIDS bills were pending in the California legislature. Similar interest has emerged in other states across the country. With a few notable exceptions, those who set public policy at the state and federal level have avoided adopting measures that do not follow the recommended guidelines of public health, scientific, and medical groups. Yet, the political pressure for quick and decisive action for problems that require long-term and well-planned programming is likely to build. This increased political pressure will test the will of those who make public policy.

Mandatory testing is perhaps one of the better examples of how public policy can be driven by public fears. Those who support such a policy of mandatory testing appear to be motivated by a desire for personal security, which they perceive as resulting from separating the infected from the uninfected. Public health officials from across the country have expressed little support for mandatory testing. Likewise, routine screening of blood during hospital admissions or for people applying for marriage licenses has been rejected because of the high cost and lack of significant public health benefit. At the same time, public health officials have voiced support for offering voluntary HIV antibody testing to all those seeking family planning assistance or prenatal care, as well as for those presenting themselves for treatment for sexually transmitted diseases or drug abuse.

Psychologists have been central to efforts to shift emphasis from testing to counseling as a means of promoting behavioral change. A consensus among health professionals has emerged that testing should only be conducted as part of more extensive prevention education and counseling programs. Although education involves providing individuals with information about HIV transmission and risk reduction, counseling involves individualized assessment of risk behaviors, facilitation of behavioral change, and resolution of psychological problems that might arise during the process. A coalition of professional associations has formed to advocate for adequate funding for quality prevention education and counseling to accompany HIV testing programs. Because the goal is to influence voluntary behaviors, it is important that such programs themselves be completely voluntary. Confidentiality and antidiscrimination protections are also important in order to encourage people to feel free to come forward for such services.

It would be unwise to assume that public policy will be set on the basis of credible scientific data or made on the basis of recommendations from medical, professional, or public health authorities. The attitudes and desires of the general public will eventually guide governmental responses to AIDS. Therefore, the public at large must be brought into activities that respond constructively to the AIDS crisis. People want to do something about AIDS. Planning is needed on how to capture this sentiment in ways that will minimize negative social reactions and help advance an effective national and international response to the HIV and AIDS epidemics.

Although enormous progress has been made in facilitating behavioral changes to lessen the spread of HIV, and planning has begun to address the medical and psychological needs of those who have become sick or who will become sick in the near future, planning has barely begun to deal with the possible social reactions to an epidemic of this size. As the number of AIDS cases grows and the seriousness of the epidemic becomes clearer to all, reducing the social, political, and economic consequences of this epidemic will emerge as the principal challenge to psychology and social science in the years to come. In responding to each area of need, psychology has a unique opportunity to make a difference.

REFERENCES

Bloom, D., and G. Carliner. 1988. The economic impact of AIDS in the United States. *Science* 239:604–9.
Catania, J. A., S. M. Kegeles, and T. J. Coates. 1988. Towards an understanding of

risk behavior. The CAPS AIDS Risk-Reduction Model (ARRM). Unpublished manuscript, University of California, Center for AIDS Prevention Studies, San Francisco.

Centers for Disease Control. 1981. Pneumocystis pneumonia—Los Angeles. *Morbidity and Mortality Weekly Report* (June 5):250–52.

Coates, T. J., R. D. Stall, and C. C. Hoff. 1988. *Changes in Sexual Behavior of Gay and Bisexual Men Since the Beginning of the AIDS Epidemic.* Washington, D.C.: U.S. Congress, Office of Technology Assessment.

Communications Technologies. 1987. A report on designing an effective AIDS prevention campaign strategy for San Francisco: Results from the fourth probability sample of an urban gay male community. Unpublished manuscript. (Available from Communications Technologies, Inc., 260 California St., San Francisco, CA 94111.)

Institute of Medicine/National Academy of Sciences. 1986. *Confronting AIDS. Directions for Public Health, Health Care and Research.* Washington, D.C.: National Academy Press.

Leventhal, H., and P. D. Cleary. 1980. The smoking problem: A review of the research and theory in behavioral risk notification. *Psychological Bulletin* 88:370–405.

Lui, K., W. Darrow, and G. W. Rutherford. 1988. A model-based estimate of the mean incubation period for AIDS in homosexual men. *Science* 240:1333–35.

Mann, J. 1988. Global AIDS: Epidemiology, impact, projections and the global strategy. Invited address to the International Meeting of Health Ministers, London, England, January.

McKusick, L., ed. 1986. *What to Do About AIDS: Physicians and Mental Health Professionals Discuss the Issues.* Los Angeles: University of California Press.

McKusick, L., M. Conant, and T. J. Coates. 1985. The AIDS epidemic. A model for developing intervention strategies for reducing high-risk behavior in gay men. *Sexually Transmitted Diseases* 12:229–34.

Morin, S. F., and W. Batchelor. 1984. Responding to the psychological crisis of AIDS. *Public Health Reports* 99:4–9.

Morin, S. F., K. A. Charles, and A. K. Malyon. 1984. The psychological impact of AIDS on gay men. *American Psychologist* 39:1288–93.

Presidential Commission on the Human Immunodeficiency Virus Epidemic. 1988. *Report of the Presidential Commission an the HIV Epidemic* (1988 0–214–701:QL3). Washington, D.C.: U.S. Government Printing Office.

Scitovsky A., and D. Rice. 1987. Estimates of the direct and indirect costs of acquired immunodeficiency syndrome in the United States, 1985, 1986, and 1990. *Public Health Reports* 102:5–17.

Sisk, J. 1987. The cost of AIDS: A review of the estimates. *Health Affairs* (Summer):5–21.

Winkelstein, W., M. Samuel, N. Padian, J. A. Wiley, W. Lang, R. E. An, and J. Levy. 1987. Reduction in human immunodeficiency virus transmission among homosexual/bisexual men: 1982–1986. *American Journal of Public Health* 76:685–89.

26

Treatment Issues for Chemically Dependent Lesbians and Gay Men

Ellen F. Ratner

Statistics on the prevalence of chemical dependency among the estimated twenty to thirty million gay men and lesbians is sketchy at best, and only in recent years have researchers begun to explore the extent of the problem in the lesbian and gay community. As Mosbacher (1988:47) points out in her review of the literature on alcohol and substance abuse among lesbians (a statement that also applies to gay men): "The extent of . . . [the problem] has never been reliably documented. The few available studies are limited by small sample size, lack of controls, nonrandom samples or inconsistent definitions of homosexuality." The problem is compounded by the fact that many lesbians and gay men are unwilling to answer questions about either their sexual orientation or their abuse of alcohol or other substances (Ratner 1988). Furthermore, the definition of terms such as *alcoholism* will vary, depending on the individual (Nardi 1982).

REVIEW OF THE LITERATURE ON PREVALENCE

Although information about the prevalence of substance abuse among gay and lesbian Americans is imprecise, a review of the existing literature on the problem in the gay and lesbian community provides some indication of the scope of the problem. The first study appeared in 1973, when Saghie and Robins reported that 35 percent of lesbians and 30 percent of gay men drank excessively. In the heterosexual population, the figures were 5 percent and 20 percent for women and men, respectively. Later studies conducted in the 1970s produced figures of 31 percent among gay men and women living in Los Angeles (Fifield, DeCrescenzo, and Lathan 1975) and 29 percent among gay men living in the Kansas City area (Lohrenz et al. 1978).

In the 1980s several important studies on the prevalence of chemical dependency were conducted: the *One in Ten* study (1983) on alcoholism among lesbians and gay men in Alaska, and Morales and Graves' study (1984) on abuse of alcohol and other drugs among 453 lesbians and gay men in San Francisco. In the Alaskan study, 35 percent of the respondents reported that they had encountered the following problems because of alcohol: drunk-driving charges, physical health problems, and blackouts. On the basis of their study, Morales and Graves estimated that 20 percent of lesbians and gay men in San Francisco were substance abusers. When intravenous drug users were included, approximately 46 percent of lesbians and 32 percent of gay men were or had been substance abusers.

In 1984–85 Bradford and Ryan (1987) conducted a nationwide survey of lesbians sponsored by the National Lesbian and Gay Health Foundation and found that 6 percent of the respondents drank alcohol daily, 25 percent drank it at least once a week, and 14 percent were worried about their drinking. (The percentage of women who consumed alcohol daily increased significantly among respondents forty-five years of age and older.) Stall and Wiley (1988) recently reported alarming differences in the rates of drug use among gay and heterosexual men. Gay men not only used drugs more often but used a greater variety of drugs than did heterosexual men.

FACTORS CONTRIBUTING TO SUBSTANCE ABUSE

Despite the different geographic areas and sampling methods used in the studies, it is clear that gay men and lesbians have more problems related to substance abuse than do heterosexuals (McKirnan and Peterson 1989). Explanations for the phenomenon include internalization of society's homophobia, nonacceptance of self, fear of coming out (Finnegan and McNally 1987; Kus 1985; Levin 1987; McKirnan and Peterson 1988).

For example, McKirnan and Peterson (1988) have speculated that the higher incidence of problem drinking among lesbians and gay men— especially those who are over thirty years of age—may be related to the society's expectations concerning role changes (marriage, children, a mortgage) that occur among heterosexual adults—role changes that may serve to restrict excessive drinking in the majority of the general population. Among older lesbians in particular, the coming out process may have been especially stressful.

Smith (1979, 1982) suggested that the unique stresses confronting gay men and lesbians may account for the fact that substance abuse is more prevalent in the gay and lesbian community than in the general population. The strain of leading a double life, low self-esteem related to discrimination in the general society and in the workplace, family rejection and lack of understanding, lack of social supports, particularly for older gay men or lesbians, the stress of coming out, and fear of AIDS are all factors that can lead to substance abuse.

Mental health issues also compound the problems of many lesbians and gay men. For example, more than half the women in Bradford and Ryan's survey (1987) said they had been too nervous to cope with ordinary responsibilities in the previous year, and 18 percent had attempted suicide. Three-fourths had sought counseling, and an additional 21 percent had considered it but did not know where to go or did not have the money. On the basis of their data, Bradford and Ryan concluded that for women who lack societal support, the act of seeking counseling is a choice for health and a positive coping mechanism.

For obvious reasons, AIDS has vastly increased the stress experienced by gay men, who worry not only about their own health but the health of their friends and lovers as well. Not so obvious, however, is the stress that the disease poses for lesbians, many of whom rely on a social network made up of gay men, as well as lesbians, and thus experience the losses related to AIDS.

Because alcohol may suppress the immune system, the possible relationship between drinking and AIDS has received great attention in the gay community (*Alcohol, Drugs and AIDS*, undated). A study conducted in San Francisco (Stall et al. 1986) found that approximately two-thirds of the respondents did not practice safer sex after drinking. Although no reliable studies have been done that link chemical dependency with AIDS, anecdotal reports suggest that people who use alcohol and drugs excessively may be at increased risk for HIV infection. Thus, the risk of infection is an important factor to address during treatment.

Needless to say, treatment of any chemically dependent individual requires more than the admonition "Don't drink" and "Go to AA meetings." As Mosbacher points out, however, "health professionals treating . . . alcohol and substance abusers are often handicapped by a scarcity of accurate information on the topic" (p. 47). The following list indicates some of the unique problems and experiences that gay and lesbian clients face:

- Families are likely to have difficulty acknowledging and accepting not only homosexuality but addiction as well.
- Specifically designed community treatment resources may be unavailable, and in groups such as AA, which may be oriented toward heterosexuals, members may not be accepting.
- Clients who have hidden their sexual orientation from the general society fear employment, career, and other problems that are likely to result if they come out.
- Treatment personnel may not understand the special problems experienced by gay men and lesbians and discourage them from talking about such problems.
- Clients must learn to engage in sexual activities while sober and practice safer sex, too.
- Religious guilt may increase during sobriety.
- Role models for successful interpersonal relationships may be lacking.
- Substance abuse, coupled with a history of sexual or physical abuse, creates a greater problem than does either type of abuse alone.
- Victims of antigay violence or harassment may have greater difficulties with sobriety.

As a result, traditional treatment methods often fail. For example, 53 percent of the clients who enter Pride Institute in Minneapolis—the only inpatient treatment center for chemically dependent gay men and lesbians—say that they have been inpatients at least once before. Many of them say that they never talked about issues related to their sexual orientation. Thus, to treat chemically dependent gay clients successfully, the therapist must appreciate these unique problems. The following section addresses some aspects of treatment that grow out of the factors just discussed.

ASSESSMENT NEEDS DURING TREATMENT

Although many treatment programs have staff who are sensitive to the needs of gay clients, and some offer support groups for gay men and lesbians, they must incorporate specific treatment strategies for this population. As mentioned earlier, because most gay men and lesbians have grown up in the face of discrimination and because many of them have internalized society's views, they are at risk for becoming chemically dependent. Thus, to treat the client successfully, the therapist must assess a wide variety of factors, including a) homophobia, b) the coming-out experience, c) social network, d) spirituality and religion, e) relationship with the family of origin, and f) history of relationships and sexual behavior.

HOMOPHOBIA

In the early stages of the recovery process, the client's homophobia should be assessed because it may have contributed to his or her dependence on alcohol or other drugs. In addition, internalized homophobia often is a theme in all areas of the client's life. Their social, work, and family relations may be colored by internalized homophobia. A complete assessment, with an instrument such as the Ryan Homophobia Assessment (Ryan 1982), and a history of the client's coming-out experience is important in the initial assessment.

In group psychotherapy, the therapist can ask clients what terms they heard while growing up; what role models they had, if any; what movies they saw; what experiences they had; and how they themselves viewed gay men and lesbians. Stereotyped behaviors on the part of gay men and lesbians observed by a client during adolescence and his or her reactions to those behaviors should be explored. Because the client may have started using drugs during adolescence and may not have worked out these issues, they must be addressed before the individual can be treated successfully.

Some gay men and lesbians are so dominated by internalized homophobia that they are incapable of engaging in sex while sober. The sexual act, the most obvious indicator of sexual orientation, is the point at which they must confront their own sexuality. Smith (1979) described a complex group of sexual conflicts that included compartmentalization of different personality states in which the "executive" self denies responsibility for the sexual self and abdicates control of the sexual self to a chemical. Thus, blackouts may seem beneficial because they blot out an act viewed as shameful and embarrassing. Smith also pointed out that the reduced sexual desire and functioning related to alcoholism may be a barrier to sober sex.

Finally, the therapist must deal specifically with the client's internalized notions of what being gay means and the derogatory terms heard during adolescence. In addition, because violence against gay people is common (8–10 percent of lesbians and 20 percent of gay men have had such experiences; see Ryan and Bradford 1986), the implications of these experiences must be fully explored.

COMING-OUT EXPERIENCE

In their book *Dual Identities,* Dana Finnigan and Emily McNally (1987) described the stages involved in coming out and how those experiences affect chemically dependent behavior. For example, a person may be in one stage of denial about his or her chemical dependency and in another stage about being gay. Thus, to be effective, the therapist must assess both stages of denial. The clinician must be wary of clients who enter treatment claiming to be comfortable with their sexual orientation and therefore insist that talking about life-style issues is unnecessary.

It is important to remember that coming out is a process and that problems involved in the process may be associated with excessive bouts of drinking or drug taking, particularly if the individual has been unable to discuss feelings about the process or is trapped in the stage of nonacceptance of self. Finally, as Gonsiorek (1982:15) pointed out, the coming-out process can be highly stressful for the person who has been functioning well in heterosexual society.

SOCIAL NETWORK

An examination of the social network also can help a client understand how much energy has been devoted to being with others who are addicted to alcohol or other drugs. The Attneave Family Network Map (Attneave 1977) can be helpful in this process. A social network can often involve as many as a hundred people, including coworkers, family members, friends, former friends, and others. An important aspect of therapy is helping clients to recognize that making positive changes in their social network does not mean developing an entirely new life.

Many substance abusers, no matter what their sexual orientation, isolate themselves in some way—either by associating primarily with other substance abusers or by avoiding people altogether. This behavior can be addressed by interventions such as training in socialization techniques, bond-building, and maintaining friendships. The results of such interventions can be dramatic. For example, the client's first meaningful encounters with other members of the gay and lesbian community while not under the influence of drugs can affect their future sobriety. Making the client aware that a gay and lesbian community is available can be accomplished by making the client aware of gay or lesbian newspapers, involving the client in community events where drugs are unavailable, and processing these events afterward. Processing these experiences during treatment is critically important because clients may remain isolated if they continue to feel different. If they view participants in such events as being "too gay" or as exhibiting too much stereotypical behavior, their painful but familiar isolation may be reinforced.

SPIRITUALITY AND RELIGION

Gay men and lesbians have traditionally been excluded from worship by the Jewish and Christian religions. They have been told they are sinful, that it is their duty to get married and raise a family, that God views them as being different from heterosexual people. Thus, the client's religious guilt may increase during the recovery process as memory returns.

Biblical concerns, excommunication, and perceived or real judgmental behavior by religious organizations must be addressed. Past behavior not condoned by religious groups may have increased the client's drinking or drug taking.

Religious education and indoctrination during adolescence can have a crucial effect on substance abuse and addiction. Providing the client with written reference materials and referrals to people who understand the biblical arguments about homosexuality can markedly reduce religion-based guilt and shame, especially if a recovering client attempts to conform to what he or she perceives as society's normative views and values.

RELATIONSHIP WITH THE FAMILY OF ORIGIN

In most instances, the families of gay men and lesbians cannot accept the gay family member without some initial ambivalence and distancing. When the gay family member also is an alcoholic or a drug addict, the family's ability to accept becomes even more difficult. Secretiveness and fragmentation of one's identity can be a major factor in keeping chemically dependent people chemically dependent. Because knowing oneself requires an understanding of repetitive patterns—patterns that often have been present in families for generations—a genogram (a three-generation map of family history) can help the client recognize these patterns. During the early stages of recovery, the client should examine the family genogram for the following:

- patterns of substance abuse or other addictive behavior;
- family members who had a difficult life-style, yet were successful in some way;
- family patterns of conducting intimate relationships;
- events such as illness, births, and marriages that may provide insight into the family's adaptive patterns; and
- alliances, feuds, long-standing examples of distancing among family members.

Such an exploration may represent the first time the chemically dependent client has understood the family pattern or has felt connected with the family of origin.

HISTORY OF RELATIONSHIPS AND SEXUAL BEHAVIOR

Because a positive sexual identification can be a cornerstone of sobriety, an assessment of sexual history is critically important. For example, the therapist should obtain information about the client's relationships with people of both sexes, sexual fears, and patterns of sexual behavior. In addition, the client's family life is crucial because fantasies often reveal concerns and guilt over imagined rather than sexual acts.

SEXUAL IDENTITY

Because of society's stereotypes, many lesbians and gay men are confused about gender and who one chooses to love, that is, who they are. Questions about gender identification and roles, such as "butch" or "femme," can be explored with clients in the early stages of sobriety, particularly if the therapist is nonjudgmental. Sobriety also can give clients the freedom to examine and reduce rigid role constraints of all types.

SEXUAL COMPULSIVENESS

The relationship between chemical dependency and sexual compulsiveness has been the subject of much discussion. As Carnes (1985) pointed out, the pathological pattern of compulsive sex can be observed among both gay and heterosexual people. People who are compulsive about drugs tend to exhibit compulsive behavior in other areas of their lives, including the sexual area. Those who exhibit compulsive sexual behavior have unrealistic ideas about the nature of relationships and how they are formed or sustained. In addition, the guilt and shame associated with promiscuous behavior are likely to lead to the use of alcohol or other drugs as a means of escape.

CURRENT INTIMATE RELATIONSHIPS

If the client is involved in an intimate relationship, the therapist must assess the nature of that relationship. For example, is codependency a factor in the relationship? (For a thorough discussion of the problem of codependency, see Finnegan and McNally 1988.) How will the couple handle holidays, particularly in relation to drinking? Has the client's partner come out, or is he or she still struggling with the issue? Are there any conflicting patterns in the partner's family genogram? Has the partner exhibited jealousy because the client attends twelve-step meetings? Answering these and other questions is critical to successful treatment.

AIDS-RELATED BEHAVIOR

An important component of treatment for gay men who are not practicing safer sex, whether HIV-positive or not (and for lesbians who are at risk for HIV infection) is the "behavior buddy"—a treatment technique the author developed for use in treatment settings. With a behavior buddy, the client can talk about sexual behaviors, anticipated behaviors, the possibilities of acting out old behaviors, and so on. Behavior buddies are recommended for recovering individuals who understand the twelve-step process, the relationship between sexual behavior and AIDS and HIV infection, and the reasons for guilt about past sexual behavior.

NEED FOR SPONSORSHIP

All chemically dependent individuals who are recovering need a sponsor. When the recovering person is a gay man or a lesbian, the important questions are whether to choose a gay or heterosexual sponsor and whether to choose a member of the same or opposite sex. Clients must understand that the important point is not to select a sponsor to whom they could possibly be sexually attracted. Some clients avoid this possibility by choosing a gay sponsor of the opposite sex. Others choose two sponsors: one gay, the other heterosexual.

PARTICIPATION BY THE FAMILY OF ORIGIN IN TREATMENT

Enlisting the participation of the family of origin in therapy during the early stages of the client's recovery can be extremely helpful. Often, it is the first time that honest communication has occurred in the family. When families meet with other families in which a member is recovering, they have opportunities to change their attitudes about both homosexuality and chemical dependency. During family treatment, the therapist should address the following: family patterns of alcohol and drug use, the family's reactions to the gay family member, the openness of family communication, the degrees of agreement among family members about how forthright the client should be about his or her sexual orientation and chemical dependency, and how long the lack of communication about the client's situation has continued.

Communication between family and client can be enhanced if family members attend Alcoholics Anonymous or Narcotics Anonymous meetings with the client and undertake the Alanon or Naranon program for themselves. In addition, the therapist should arrange a follow-up appointment for the family three to six months after the client's initial interview.

The goals of the family treatment are to a) identify family members and significant others who are co-alcoholics and refer them for treatment, if appropriate; b) educate family members about alcoholism as a familial disease; c) identify family problems that could offset the client's recovery; d) introduce the principles of the twelve-step recovery system; and e) help family members and others to confront their feelings about the client's sexual orientation.

CONCLUSION

The points made here and in the other chapters of this book make it clear that lesbians and gay men have unique experiences and needs. As a result, therapists who treat gay substance abusers must have a firm grasp of both the issues involved in chemical dependency and of the significant problems that confront gay men and lesbians. All of these complex factors have an impact on recovery.

REFERENCES

Alcohol, Drugs, and AIDS: What's the Connection? Undated. San Francisco: San Francisco AIDS Foundation, AIDS/Substance Abuse Task Force.

Attneave, C. 1977. *Attneave Family Network Map.* Boston: Boston Family Institute.

Bradford, J., and C. Ryan. 1987. *Mental Health Implications: National Lesbian Health Care Survey.* Washington, D.C.: National Lesbian and Gay Health Foundation.

Brandsma, M. M., and E. M. Pattison. 1982. Homosexuality and alcoholism. In E. M. Pattison and E. Kaufman, eds., *Encyclopedic Handbook of Alcoholism,* pp. 736–41. New York: Gardner Press.

Carnes, P. 1985. *Out of the Shadows: Understanding Sexual Addiction.* Minneapolis, Minn.: CompCare.

Evans, S., and S. Schaefer. 1980. Why women's sexuality is important to address in chemical dependency treatment programs. *Treatment and Rehabilitation* (September):37–40.

Fifield, L., T. A. DeCrescenzo, and J. D. Lathan. 1975. *On My Way to Nowhere: Alienated, Isolated, Drunk: An Analysis of Gay Alcohol Abuse and an Evaluation of Alcoholism Rehabilitation Services for the Los Angeles Gay Community.* Los Angeles: Gay Community Services Center and Office of Alcohol Abuse and Alcoholism, Los Angeles County.

Finnegan, D., and E. McNally. 1987. *Dual Identities.* Center City, Minn.: Hazelden.

Finnegan, D. C., and E. B. McNally. 1988. The lonely journey: Lesbians and gay men who are codependent. In M. Shernoff and W. A. Scott, eds., *The Sourcebook on Lesbian and Gay Healthcare*, pp. 173–79. Washington, D.C.: National Lesbian and Gay Health Foundation.

Gonsiorek, J. C. 1982. The use of diagnostic concepts in working with gay and lesbian populations. *Journal of Homosexuality* 7(1):9–20.

Kus, R. 1985. Gay alcoholism and non-acceptance of self: The critical link. Paper presented at the Conference of Nursing Research, Honolulu.

Levin, J. 1987. Homophobia in lesbian, chemically dependent inpatients. A study in progress presented at the meeting of the American Association of Physicians for Human Rights, August.

Lewis, C. E., M. T. Saghir, and E. Robins. 1982. Drinking patterns in homosexual and heterosexual women. *Journal of Clinical Psychiatry* 43:277–79.

Lohrenz, L. J., J. C. Connelly, L. Coyne, and K. E. Spare. 1978. Alcohol problems in several midwestern homosexual communities. *Journal of Studies on Alcohol* 39:1959–63.

McKirnan, D. J., and P. L. Peterson. 1988. Stress, expectancies, and vulnerability to substance abuse: A test of a model among homosexual men. *Journal of Abnormal Psychology* 97:461–66.

McKirnan, D. J., and P. L. Peterson. 1989. Alcohol and drug use among homosexual men and women. *Addictive Behaviors* 14:545–53.

Marschall, R. 1980. Homosexual alcoholic group therapy: A specialized treatment. Paper presented at the meeting of the National Council on Alcoholism, Seattle, May.

Morales, E. S., and M. A. Graves. 1983. *Substance Abuse: Patterns and Barriers to Treatment for Gay Men and Lesbians in San Francisco.* San Francisco: Department of Public Health.

Mosbacher, D. 1988. Lesbian alcohol and substance abuse. *Psychiatric Annals* 18(1):47, 49–50.

Nardi, P. M. 1982. Alcoholism and homosexuality: A theoretical perspective. *Journal of Homosexuality* 7(4):9–25.

One in Ten: A Profile of Alaska's Lesbian and Gay Community (A Preliminary Report of Findings). 1986. Anchorage, Alaska: Identity.

National Gay and Lesbian Task Force. 1986. *Anti-Gay Violence: Victimization and Defamation.* Washington, D.C.: National Gay and Lesbian Task Force.

Ratner, E. F. 1988. A model for the treatment of lesbian and gay alcohol abusers. *Alcoholism Treatment Quarterly.*

Ryan, C. 1982. *The Ryan Homophobia Assessment.* Northampton, Mass.: Smith College School of Social Work.

Saghir, M., and E. Robins. 1973. *Male and Female Homosexuality.* Baltimore: Williams and Wilkins.

Smith, T. M. 1979. *Specific Approaches and Techniques in the Treatment of Gay Male Alcohol Abusers.* San Francisco: Alcoholism Evaluation and Treatment Center.

Smith, T. M. 1982. Specific approaches and techniques in the treatment of gay male alcohol abusers. *Journal of Homosexuality* 7(4):53–69.

Stall, R., and J. Wiley. 1988. A comparison of alcohol and drug use patterns of homosexual and heterosexual men. *Drug and Alcohol Dependence* 22:63–73.

Stall, R., L. McKusick, J. Wiley, T. J. Coates, and E. G. Ostrow. 1986. Alcohol and drug use during sexual activity and compliance with safe sex guidelines for AIDS: The AIDS Biobehavioral Research Project. *Health Education Quarterly* 13:359–71.

Zigrang, T. A. 1980. Who should be doing what about the gay alcoholic? *Journal of Homosexuality* 7(4):27–35.

27

Violence and Victimization of Lesbians and Gay Men: Mental Health Consequences

Linda Garnets, Gregory M. Herek, and Barrie Levy

This article describes some of the major psychosocial challenges faced by lesbian and gay male survivors of hate crimes, their significant others, and the gay community as a whole. When an individual is attacked because she or he is perceived to be gay, the negative mental health consequences of victimization converge with those resulting from societal heterosexism to create a unique set of problems. Such victimization represents a crisis for the individual, creating opportunities for growth as well as risks for impairment. The principal risk associated with antigay victimization is that the survivor's homosexuality becomes directly linked to her or his newly heightened sense of vulnerability. The problems faced by lesbian and gay male victims of sexual assault and the psychological impact of verbal abuse also are discussed. Suggestions are offered to assist practitioners in helping the survivors of antigay hate crimes.

Like other survivors of the violence that pervades American society, lesbian and gay male crime victims must confront the difficulties created by victimization. And, as members of a stigmatized group, lesbians and gay men face numerous psychological challenges as a consequence of society's hostility toward them. When individual victimization and societal prejudice converge in antigay hate crimes, lesbian and gay male survivors face additional, unique challenges. Those challenges are the principal focus of this article.

Owing to the widespread prevalence of antigay prejudice in the United States (Herek 1990; Herek 1991) and the large number of lesbian and gay male victims of hate crimes in this country (Berrill 1990; Herek 1989), American gay people as a group might be expected to manifest significantly higher levels of psychological distress and impairment than heterosexuals.

Yet, this is not the case; the lesbian and gay male community does not differ significantly in mental health from the heterosexual population (Gonsiorek 1982; Gonsiorek and Weinrich 1991). Obviously antigay victimization does not inevitably lead to psychological dysfunction.

This article treats antigay victimization as creating a crisis for the survivor, with opportunities for subsequent growth as well as risks for impairment (e.g., Caplan 1964). This conceptualization does not deny or minimize the negative consequences of victimization, both physical and psychological, immediate and long-term. But neither does it relegate lesbian and gay male targets of hate crimes to passivity. Instead, it should encourage researchers and mental health practitioners to view the survivors of antigay victimization as active, problem-solving individuals who are potentially capable of coping with the aftermath of the attack and using the experience as an opportunity for growth.

THE PSYCHOLOGICAL AFTERMATH OF VICTIMIZATION

In addition to dealing with the physical consequences of injury and the practical aftermath of having one's possessions stolen or damaged, crime victims often experience a variety of psychological symptoms. Common behavioral and somatic reactions to victimization include sleep disturbances and nightmares, headaches, diarrhea, uncontrollable crying, agitation and restlessness, increased use of drugs, and deterioration in personal relationships (e.g., Frieze, Hymer, and Greenberg 1984; Janoff-Bulman and Frieze 1983a). Victimization creates psychological distress for several reasons. First, it dramatically interferes with everyday processes of denial through which people are able to feel secure and invulnerable, that "it can't happen to me" (Janoff-Bulman and Frieze 1983b). The world suddenly seems less predictable; people seem more malevolent. Because their victimization did not result from accidental or natural forces but was intentionally perpetrated against them, survivors are likely to feel a reduction in their previous level of basic trust (Bard and Sangrey 1979).

Second, the experience of victimization interferes with perceptions of the world as an orderly and meaningful place. Survivors often try to restore some sense of meaning and predictability by asking "Why me?" and many respond to the question with self-blame. This is not necessarily maladaptive. Blaming specific behaviors related to the victimization (*behavioral self-blame*) may constitute an effective coping strategy because it helps survivors feel a sense of control over their own lives and provides strategies for avoiding revictimization (Janoff-Bulman 1979, 1982). In contrast, blaming one's victimization on perceived character flaws (*characterological self-blame*) is associated with low self-esteem, depression, and feelings of helplessness (Janoff-Bulman 1979). Although behavioral self-blame may sometimes be adaptive, observers may react more negatively to victims who blame themselves than to victims who attribute their circumstances to chance factors (Coates, Wortman, and Abbey 1979), thereby exacerbating survivors' psychological distress.

A third reason why victimization creates psychological distress is that it often leads people to question their own worth. Survivors may devalue themselves because they perceive that they have been violated and because they experience a loss of autonomy, first at the hands of the perpetrator and subsequently as they must rely on others to help them recover from the victimization (Bard and Sangrey 1979). Survivors also may internalize the social stigma associated with being a victim. Others often react negatively to them, seeing them as weak or inferior, of having failed in the basic task of protecting themselves, of somehow deserving their fate (e.g., Coates, Wortman, and Abbey 1979). Such social reactions may lead survivors to feel ashamed or embarrassed at their perceived "failure."

Severe psychological responses to victimization may be of short or prolonged duration, and may be immediate in their onset or delayed by years after the victimization. Severe reactions are diagnosed as *post-traumatic stress disorder*, or PTSD (American Psychiatric Association 1987; Frederick 1987), indicated by the persistence of three types of symptoms for at least one month consequent to victimization: a) persistent reexperiencing of the victimization (e.g., via memories, intrusive thoughts, dreams, or intense distress from activities or events triggering recollection of the event); b) persistent avoidance of trauma-associated stimuli or a numbing of general responsiveness (e.g., diminished interest in significant activities, feelings of detachment from others, restricted affect, sense of a foreshortened future); and c) persistent symptoms of increased arousal (e.g., sleep disturbances, exaggerated startle response, difficulty concentrating).

The crisis following victimization is likely to create different challenges as time passes (e.g., Tsegaye-Spates 1985). Bard and Sangrey (1979), for example, highlighted three important stages: a) an *impact* phase, when victims typically feel vulnerable, confused, helpless, and dependent on others for even the simplest decisions; b) a *recoil* phase, characterized by mood swings and a "waxing and waning" of fear, rage, revenge fantasies, and displacement of anger (often onto loved ones); and c) a *reorganization* phase, when survivors assimilate their painful experience, put it into perspective, and get on with their lives. Most victims successfully negotiate these stages of recovery, although not necessarily in a linear sequence and often only after a period of several years (Sales, Baum, and Shore 1984). The victimization is not likely ever to be entirely forgotten, however; the self can no longer be regarded as invulnerable. Survivors must nevertheless reestablish a perception of the world as not entirely threatening, as a meaningful place in which most events make sense. Additionally, they must regain self-perceptions as worthy, strong, and autonomous (Janoff-Bulman and Frieze 1983b).

PSYCHOLOGICAL CONSEQUENCES OF HETEROSEXIST STIGMA

In addition to the victimization for which all Americans are at risk, lesbians and gay men are targeted for attack specifically because of their sexual orientation (Berrill 1990) The psychological consequences of antigay hate crimes must be examined against the background of cultural heterosexism. Heterosexism is an ideological system that denies, denigrates, and stigmatizes any nonheterosexual form of behavior, identity, relationship, or community (Herek 1990). American culture is pervaded by a heterosexist ideology that simultaneously makes lesbians and gay men invisible and legitimizes hostility, discrimination, and even violence against them (Herek 1990). Heterosexist stigma also creates two interrelated challenges that lesbians and gay men must confront in the course of their psychosocial development: overcoming internalized homophobia and coming out.

Because most children internalize society's ideology of sex and gender at an early age, gay women and men usually experience some degree of negative feeling toward themselves when they first recognize their own homosexuality in adolescence or adulthood. This sense of *internalized homophobia* often creates a "basic mistrust for one's sexual and interpersonal identity" (Stein and Cohen 1984:61) and interferes with the process of identity formation (Malyon 1982). Coming out[1] becomes a process of reclaiming disowned or devalued parts of the self, and developing an identity into which one's sexuality is well integrated (Malyon 1982; Stein and Cohen 1984).

In the course of coming out, most lesbians and gay men successfully overcome the threats to psychological well-being posed by heterosexism. Psychological adjustment appears to be highest among men and women who are committed to their gay identity and do not attempt to hide their homosexuality from others (Bell and Weinberg 1978; Hammersmith and

Weinberg 1973). As with other stigmatized minorities, gay men and lesbians probably maintain self-esteem most effectively when they identify with and are integrated into the larger gay community (Crocker and Major 1989). Conversely, people with a homosexual orientation who have not yet come out, who feel compelled to suppress their homoerotic urges, who wish that they could become heterosexual, or who are isolated from the gay community may experience significant psychological distress, including impairment of self-esteem (Bell and Weinberg 1978; Hammersmith and Weinberg 1973; Malyon 1982; Weinberg and Williams 1974; see also Hodges and Hutter 1979). Chronically hiding one's sexual orientation can create a painful discrepancy between public and private identities (Humphreys 1972; see also Goffman 1963), feelings of inauthenticity, and social isolation (Goffman 1963; Jones et al. 1984).[2]

VICTIMIZATION OF LESBIANS AND GAY MEN

CONSEQUENCES FOR THE VICTIM

When people are attacked because they are perceived to be gay, the consequences of victimization converge with those of societal heterosexism to create a unique set of challenges for the survivor. Perhaps most important is that the victim's homosexuality becomes directly linked to the heightened sense of vulnerability that normally follows victimization. One's homosexual orientation consequently may be experienced as a source of pain and punishment rather than intimacy, love, and community. Internalized homophobia may reappear or be intensified. Attempts to make sense of the attack, coupled with the common need to perceive the world as a just place, may lead to feelings that one has been justifiably punished for being gay (Bard and Sangrey 1979; Lerner 1970). Such characterological self-blame can lead to feelings of depression and helplessness (Janoff-Bulman 1979), even in individuals who are comfortable with their sexual orientation.

The aftermath of victimization probably is affected by the survivor's stage in the coming-out process (e.g., Cass 1979; Troiden 1988). Those who have come out have already faced a major threat to their self-esteem and have emerged intact and possibly stronger for the experience. Additionally, lesbians and gay men in the course of coming out may develop coping skills (i.e., a "crisis competence"; Kimmel 1978) that they subsequently can use when new life crises occur. Coming out does not "prepare" gay men and women for subsequent victimization, but it does provide them with tools that they can use in coping: supportive social networks, community resources, and nonheterosexist interpretations of the victimization experience. Lesbian and gay male survivors who are in the later stages of coming out prior to their assault have the benefit of being able to balance their victimization experience against many other positive experiences associated with being gay.

Women and men who are still in the early stages of coming out, in contrast, are unlikely to have the requisite social support and strongly developed gay identity that can increase their psychological resilience and coping skills (Miranda and Storms 1989). Like closeted gay men with AIDS, closeted survivors of victimization face the prospect of a double disclosure—that they are gay and that they were victimized or have AIDS—with increased risks for stigmatization (e.g., Herek and Glunt 1988). If the survivor's homosexuality becomes known, heterosexual family members or friends may blame the victimization on it. Lacking a more positive interpretation and feeling especially vulnerable to others' influence, the survivor may well accept this characterological attribution (e.g., Bard and Sangrey 1979) and its attendant feelings of helplessness, depression, and low self-esteem. If closeted survivors can avoid public disclosure of their sexual orientation in such a potentially hostile setting as a police station, they are likely not to report the victimization. They may even minimize or deny its impact to themselves, a tactic that can intensify and delay the resolution of psychological and physical problems (Anderson 1982; Koss and Burkhart 1989; Myers 1989).

SEXUAL ASSAULT

Antigay sexual assault may give rise to unique problems in addition to the reactions described above. Lesbians may be directly targeted for sexual assault by antigay attackers, or raped "opportunistically" (i.e., when the perpetrator of another crime inadvertently discovers that his victim is a lesbian).[3] Rapists often verbalize the view that lesbians are "open targets" and deserve punishment because they are not under the protection of a man. Because many lesbians are not accustomed to feeling dependent on or vulnerable around men, a sexual attack motivated by male rage at their life-style constitutes a major assault on their general sense of safety, independence, and well-being. Any physiological response by the victim during the assault or the decision not to resist can raise doubts later regarding her complicity or her sexuality. Such doubts may be exacerbated by reactions from significant others when she describes details of or feelings about the victimization experience.

In addition to the humiliation and degradation that are common components of all sexual victimization, antilesbian rape may also include attempts by the perpetrator to degrade lesbian sexuality. For example, a lesbian couple sought counseling from one of the authors (Levy) after they were forced at gunpoint to engage in sexual behaviors together, then raped. When behaviors that formerly were expressions of love become associated with humiliation, violence, and victimization, lesbian partners can experience serious difficulty redefining their sexuality positively.

Male-male sexual assault is largely an invisible problem in contemporary American society, often assumed to occur only in prisons and similar settings. The few reports that have been published, however, indicate that it is a serious problem outside of institutions (Anderson 1982; Kaufman et al. 1980; Myers 1989). As with rape of females by males, male-male rape is a crime of violence—often antigay violence—rather than a crime of sexuality (Anderson 1982; Groth and Burgess 1980; Kaufman et al. 1980). Contrary to the popular stereotype, the perpetrators of male rape often identify themselves as heterosexual (Groth and Burgess 1980). Whereas the feminist movement has made important gains in sensitizing law enforcement personnel, caregivers, and society at large to the problems faced by female rape survivors, male rape survivors remain hidden and isolated. Although victims of male-male rape can be either heterosexual or gay, we focus here on the special mental health consequences for gay men.

Male gender-role socialization creates distinct problems for gay male rape survivors. Because most men have internalized the societal belief that sexual assault of men is beyond the realm of possibility, the male victim's sudden confrontation with "his own vulnerability, helplessness, and dependence on the mercy of others" can be devastating (Anderson 1982:150). Men may have trouble accepting their rape experience as real, not only because it happened to them, but because it happened at all. This may interfere with their subsequent recovery. If internalized homophobia resurfaces or is intensified, gay male survivors may interpret the rape as punishment for their sexual orientation, with all of the attendant problems detailed above. If a man did not resist, he may later blame himself and wonder whether he somehow was complicitous in the rape. Self-doubts are especially likely to follow when the assailant successfully forces the victim to ejaculate in the course of the assault (Groth and

Burgess 1980). The victim may retrospectively confuse ejaculation with orgasm, and may interpret his own physiological response as a sign of personal consent to the rape. Paralleling the experience of some lesbian rape victims, gay men may experience their sexual assault as an attempt to degrade gay male sexuality, which may later give rise to fearful or aversive feelings associated with their normal sexual behavior.

Words Can Never Hurt Me?
Consequences of Verbal Victimization

Most discussions of antigay hate crimes focus on physical and sexual assaults. Yet verbal harassment and intimidation are the most common forms of victimization of lesbians and gay men; most survey respondents report that they have been the target of antigay verbal abuse (Berrill 1990). Although researchers, practitioners, and policymakers alike may be tempted to recall the children's chant that "Sticks and stones may break my bones," the potentially damaging effects of "mere" words should not be minimized.

Most people in American society find epithets such as *nigger* and *kike* to be offensive precisely because they convey raw hatred and prejudice. Such words have been used historically by oppressors to remind the oppressed of their subordinate status (Unger 1979). Similar levels of hatred arc conveyed by words such as *faggot, dyke,* and *queer,* and the threats of violence (implicit and explicit) that accompany them. Such antigay verbal abuse constitutes a symbolic form of violence and a routine reminder of the ever-present threat of physical assault. Its "cost" to the perpetrator in time, energy, and risk is minimal, yet it reinforces the target's sense of being an outsider in American society, a member of a disliked and devalued minority, and a socially acceptable target for violence.

Like hate-motivated physical violence, antigay verbal assault challenges the victim's routine sense of security and invulnerability, making the world seem more malevolent and less predictable. The psychological effects of verbal abuse may be as severe as those following physical assaults, and possibly more insidious because victims of verbal abuse may find its "psychic scars" more difficult to identify than physical wounds. It affects how one feels about oneself with no physical injury to which to attribute the feelings. Two of us (Garnets and Levy) have observed that victims often minimize the impact of a hate-motivated verbal attack and subsequently do not understand the reason for their feelings of fear or self-hatred.

Because verbal abuse may be experienced as a near-encounter with violence, it can seriously restrict day-to-day behaviors of lesbians and gay men. Most gay respondents to victimization surveys indicate that their public behavior is affected by their fear of physical attack (Berrill 1990). Verbal harassment and intimidation reinforce this climate of fear. Not knowing whether a specific instance of verbal harassment is likely to culminate in physical violence, many gay women and men probably follow the adaptive strategy of avoiding possible occasions of verbal abuse just as they avoid potential assault situations. Consequently, their day-to-day behaviors are restricted and they lose considerable control over their lives. Victims who are more closeted may experience heterosexist verbal abuse as an involuntary public disclosure of their sexual orientation. They may respond by withdrawing even further into the closet.

CONSEQUENCES OF VICTIMIZATION FOR OTHERS

In the aftermath of antigay violence, victims turn to significant others for social support. A lover, family, and friends can greatly enhance a survivor's coping resources (Bard and Sangrey 1979). Yet, these others also must deal with the victimization experience. In cases of murder, they must cope with physical loss of the victim. With other crimes, they must deal with the survivor's immediate reactions (including her or his displaced feelings of anger). They must make sense of the event for themselves and deal with their own self-blame. Same-sex partners are at special risk for secondary victimization (Berrill and Herek 1990) as they assist the survivor in seeking services. They may be denied access to hospital visitation, for example, because they are not considered "immediate family." They are likely not to be eligible for or recognized by social workers or victim assistance agencies. Indeed, much of the postattack experience may serve to remind a gay couple that the larger society is hostile to them as gay people.

In addition to the victim's significant others, the entire gay community is victimized by antigay assaults. Hate crimes create a climate of fear that pressures lesbians and gay men to hide their sexual orientation. Needing to reduce their own feelings of vulnerability, some members of the community are likely to blame the victims of violence, often focusing on "obvious" behavior, gestures, or clothing. Such victim-blaming reinforces key aspects of the cultural ideology of heterosexism, such as the prescription that men and women should conform to highly restrictive norms of gender-appropriate behavior[4] and the belief that being gay is wrong and deserves punishment (Herek 1990). Victim-blaming also may discourage observers from taking precautions for reducing their risk of victimization—both personal precautions, such as taking a self-defense class, and community precautions, such as organizing neighborhood street patrols.

SUGGESTIONS FOR MENTAL HEALTH PRACTITIONERS

As a crisis, antigay victimization creates opportunities for growth, both at the individual and community levels. Survivors who cope successfully may infuse their lives with greater meaning or purpose than before and enjoy a strengthened sense of self-worth. They may take control of parts of their lives that they previously had not been able to manage while at the same time accepting that some events are beyond their control (Burt and Katz 1987). They may redefine previous setbacks they experienced as the result of prejudice rather than personal failings, thereby increasing their self-esteem (e.g., Crocker and Major 1989). Previously complacent survivors may become outraged by the injustice of their victimization and may become politically militant (e.g., Birt and Dion 1987), with a subsequent increase in feelings of self-efficacy and empowerment. Violence may shock community members into taking collective action that channels their feelings of helplessness and anger (for an example, see Wertheimer 1990). Perhaps the most famous example of a positive community response to victimization was the 1969 "Stonewall Rebellion," which followed a police raid on a Greenwich Village gay bar and marked the beginning of the modern movement for gay rights (e.g., D'Emilio 1983).

Mental health practitioners can help gay male and lesbian victims of hate crimes maximize the positive aspects of their response. Before working with lesbian or gay male victims, however, professional caregivers must be aware of their own heterosexist biases and assumptions, and should be familiar with current and accurate information about gay male and lesbian identity, community, and mental health concerns. Among the basic assumptions to be avoided are that a homosexual identity or life-style is negative and unhealthy; that all clients are heterosexual unless they identify themselves as gay; and that biological family members necessarily constitute a client's significant others. In reality, homosexuality is not correlated with psychopathology; many crime victims are gay but do not choose to come out; and gay clients may define their family in terms of a same-sex lover and gay friends (Cohen and Stein 1986; Gonsiorek and Weinrich 1991; Morin and Charles 1983). Professionals should carefully respect confidentiality concerning clients' sexual orientation. In most jurisdictions, gay people whose sexual orientation becomes known to others can lose their jobs or apartments, lose custody of their children, and even be liable to criminal prosecution (Berrill and Herek 1990). Professionals who fail to understand these potentially negative consequences can themselves become secondary victimizers (e.g., by inadvertently revealing a client's sexual orientation to law enforcement personnel).

Practitioners should be aware of the different needs and experiences of gay men and lesbians from different sectors of the gay community. Although space limitations do not permit its consideration here, the mental health consequences of antigay victimization are likely to vary according to the survivor's race, age, and social class, among other variables.

For heuristic purposes, mental health interventions with gay male and lesbian survivors can be conceptualized according to the *impact, recoil,* and *recovery* phases described by Bard and Sangrey (1979). Crisis interventions are necessary in the *impact* phase, when the first concern is whether the victim is safe from further attacks and whether she or he requires immediate medical care. The focus of the crisis intervention is assessing the meaning that the victim is deriving from her or his experience, feelings about the self, and the degree to which the victimization is equated with being gay or lesbian. Additionally, the mental health professional should assess internal and external coping resources: a) learned coping skills; b) support networks, such as a lover, family, or friends who can assist the victim in meeting immediate needs; and c) existing or potential involvement in gay and lesbian community networks. Previously effective coping skills usually are not adequate to deal with the shock and fear of this stage of the reaction to physical or sexual violence. Assessment will suggest to victim and practitioner alike ways to build on previous coping resources or the need to develop new ones.

In the *recoil* phase, mental health professionals can help greatly by allowing survivors to ventilate the horror and terror that the victimization evokes. By listening empathically, the professional can give the survivor who is feeling alienated and isolated a sense of connection to another person. The therapeutic goal at this stage is to support victims as they regain their self-confidence and sense of competence and wholeness, and while their feelings of guilt, shame, helplessness, and embarrassment diminish.

REDUCING NEGATIVE AFFECT

Survivors should be encouraged to feel and express anger toward the assailant(s), especially survivors who are blaming themselves or are depressed (Bard and Sangrey 1979; Bohn 1984). Anger can be constructively directed, for example, by encouraging involvement in activist groups organized against antigay violence or in self-defense classes. Intervening to prevent self-blaming and guilt feelings involves helping the survivor to review decisions made before, during, and after the assault. In order to combat the distorted retrospective perceptions that lead to self-blame, survivors need to remember that their decisions were based on their perceptions and knowledge *at the time of the attack*, in a life-threatening situation. The aim is for survivors to see that they responded as best they could under the circumstances (Levy and Brown 1984).

Victims who manifest the symptoms of post-traumatic stress disorder may benefit from recently developed strategies that aim to reexpose the survivor to the memory of the traumatic event. These strategies include systematic desensitization, flooding or implosive therapy, and stress inoculation. Reexposure is accompanied by techniques of cognitive restructuring of false assumptions about oneself and the world (e.g., self-blame and the view of the world as malevolent; Fairbank, Gross, and Keane 1983; Frank et al. 1988; Steketee and Foa 1987). The cognition that "bad things happen because I am gay" can be reformulated to "bad things happen."

Gay male and lesbian survivors of hate violence often have to cope with negative feelings specifically about their sexual identity. If victimization has forced premature disclosure of the survivor's gay identity, it may have amplified the feelings of vulnerability, alienation, and exposure that often are part of the coming-out process. These feelings must be explored with the aim of separating the victimization experience from the coming-out experience. In addition, the survivor must be helped to feel the positive effects of disclosing her or his identity that also are part of coming out. When survivors who are in the later stages of coming out question their homosexuality as a result of the assault, the practitioner should review the bases for the client's coming-out decisions of the past, with the aim of reestablishing her or his positive identity as a lesbian or gay man.

FACILITATING POSITIVE AFFECT

Self-confidence can be mended through consciousness raising, which can help survivors to locate their victimization in a social context. Understanding that the crime was based on global hatred that has its roots in a heterosexist society can relieve the survivor's feelings of being personally targeted and blameful. As Bohn (1984) noted, groupwork may be especially valuable for gay survivors because it permits identification with other lesbian and gay male victims and helps them to realize that they are not alone. Gay survivors in groups can share their reactions to victimization, express their anger, and develop analyses of their victimization that bond them to the larger gay community and its support systems.

Survivors inevitably are faced with the question of whether to report their victimization. At some point in the recovery process, this decision must be explored. In addition to its importance for the criminal justice system, reporting the incident has several potential benefits for the survivor. It can offer a constructive channel for anger, increase feelings of efficacy, and provide the satisfaction of helping to protect other members of the community from the sort of victimization one has experienced. At the same time, survivors should not be led to believe that reporting the crime necessarily will lead to arrest and prosecution of the attackers; indeed, such a result is unlikely in many cases (e.g., Bard and Sangrey 1979). The practitioner assists the survivor in weighing the benefits and risks in reporting, and ensures that the survivor makes her or his own decision. Because reporting also may lead to secondary victimization by insensitive or prejudiced criminal justice personnel (Berrill and Herek 1990), an increase in the survivor's sense of powerlessness can be prevented if the practitioner helps the survivor to become adequately prepared and to develop a good support system.

Working through these many issues and feelings eventually permits the survivor to integrate the experience of victimization into her or his larger worldview and to get on with life. This *reorganization* process may require considerable time to complete, especially if a victim denies or represses awareness of the victimization for months or even years after it occurs (Koss and Burkhart 1989; Myers 1989). Greater involvement with the gay community is likely to be particularly helpful in achieving reorganization.

INTERVENTIONS AFTER SEXUAL ASSAULT

Survivors of antigay sexual assault need to separate the victimization from their experience of sexuality and intimacy, and develop positive feelings about sexual expression that are not intruded on by images of the assault. Gay male survivors are at special risk for phobic or aversive feelings toward male sexuality because their normal sexual behavior will superficially resemble the sexual assault (if for no other reason than that both involve another male). Lesbian survivors also may experience fear reactions and flashbacks to the assault triggered by normal sexual contact. Practitioners must support survivors (and their partners) to allow healing time for the fear to diminish. Survivors should be encouraged to initiate sexual contact in stages and to determine their own readiness for gradually increasing sexual involvement. The aim is to regain a sense of being in charge of one's own body, in contrast to the powerlessness and fear experienced during the assault.

Practitioners should be aware of the heterosexist bias that sexual assault survivors may experience if they come in contact with the criminal justice or medical systems. For example, police may not believe that male-male rape occurs, may be hostile, or may assume that, because he is gay, the victim deserved or brought on the attack (Anderson 1982). Physicians and emergency room staff may assume that a lesbian rape victim is heterosexual, and consequently display insensitivity in asking questions about previous sexual experience, contraception, and significant others (Orzek 1988). Practitioners play an important role by advocating for survivors, helping them to advocate more effectively for themselves, and educating other professionals about sensitive responses to gay male and lesbian clients.

INTERVENTIONS WITH SIGNIFICANT OTHERS

Lovers, family, and friends also must deal with the losses and hardships imposed by the victimization, make sense of it, and regain a perception of the world as a stable and predictable place. Sometimes a lover or best friend will also have been victimized in the attack. In such cases where the victims cannot provide each other with primary support as they ordinarily would, both survivors may need assistance in expanding their support networks.

Mental health professionals must respond to the needs of significant others while at the same time helping them to respond, in turn, to the victim's needs. Professionals may need to educate the significant others about the dynamics of violence, defuse their fears, and encourage their support for the primary victim. Significant others might benefit from exposure to educational materials (printed, audio, video) about homosexuality, victimization, and hate crimes. When internalized homophobia among significant others (gay and lesbian, as well as heterosexual) makes it difficult for them to be supportive, professionals should assist the survivor in handling others' negative or nonsupportive reactions (e.g., through role playing).

CONCLUSION

The trauma associated with antigay victimization may become linked to survivors' homosexuality. Although this often results in intensification of psychological problems associated with being gay or lesbian, it also may lead to further consolidation of the survivor's gay or lesbian identity and involvement with her or his community. Mental health practitioners can play an important role by assisting lesbian and gay male survivors, their significant others, and their communities in successfully reconstructing survivors' lives, and mobilizing confrontation of hate crimes as a community problem. Researchers have an important role to play in filling gaps in information about the mental health consequences of antigay hate crimes, and the effectiveness of individual and community-based intervention strategies. Most important, mental health practitioners and researchers should work with the lesbian and gay community to develop public awareness and comprehensive programs to prevent hate-motivated violence.

NOTES

1. "Coming out" (or "coming out of the closet") refers to the sequence of events through which individuals recognize their own homosexual orientation and disclose it to others. Conversely, being "in the closet" or "closeted" refers to passing as heterosexual (e.g., Dynes 1985). Coming out is a continuous process: after coming out to oneself, one is continually meeting new people to whom one's sexual orientation must be disclosed. Consequently, different gay people are out to varying degrees.

2. Attempting to pass as heterosexual may increase some individuals' risk for victimization. Men who are hiding their homosexuality may be more prone to victimization when they seek sexual partners outside the relative safety of the gay community (e.g., Harry 1982; Miller and Humphreys 1980; for an autobiographical account, see Bauman 1980). Additionally, because of the stigma attached to homosexuality and because discrimination against lesbians and gay men remains legal in most jurisdictions (see Herek 1990) closeted lesbians and gay men alike can be blackmailed with threatened involuntary revelation of their sexual orientation to family, employers, or others (Bell and Weinberg 1978; Harry 1982; Rofes 1983).

3. Currently, operational definitions of hate crimes exclude male-female sexual assault unless the perpetrator can be shown to have attacked some aspect of the victim's identity other than her gender (e.g., her race, religion, or sexual orientation). Because space limitations prevent us from considering this definitional issue in detail, we focus here on the mental health consequences of male-female sexual assaults in which the victim is a lesbian and is targeted because of her sexual orientation (for more general discussions of the aftermath of sexual assault see, e.g., Brownmiller 1975; Burgess 1985; Ledray 1986).

4. Heterosexuals, too, are victimized by antigay hate crimes (Berrill 1990). The threat of victimization probably also causes many heterosexuals to conform to gender roles and to restrict their expressions of (nonsexual) physical affection for members of their own sex (e.g., Herek 1986).

REFERENCES

American Psychiatric Association. 1987. *Diagnostic and Statistical Manual of Mental Disorders.* 3d rev. ed. Washington, D.C.: American Psychiatric Association.

Anderson, C. L. 1982. Males as sexual assault victims: Multiple levels of trauma. *Journal of Homosexuality* 7(2/3):145–62.

Bard, M., and D. Sangrey. 1979. *The Crime Victim's Book.* New York: Basic Books.

Bauman, R. 1986. *The Gentleman from Maryland: The Conscience of a Gay Conservative.* New York: Arbor House.

Bell, A. P., and M. S. Weinberg. 1979. *Homosexualities: A Study of Diversity Among Men and Women.* New York: Simon and Schuster.

Berrill, K. T. 1990. Anti-gay violence and victimization in the United States. *Journal of Interpersonal Violence* 5:274–94.

Berrill, K. T., and G. M. Herek. 1990. Primary and secondary victimization in anti-gay hate crimes: Official response and public policy. *Journal of Interpersonal Violence* 5:401–13.

Birt, C. M., and K. L. Dion. 1987. Relative deprivation theory and responses to discrimination in a gay male and lesbian sample. *British Journal of Social Psychology* 26:139–45.

Bohn, T. 1984. Homophobic violence: Implications for social work practice. In R. Schoenberg and R. S. Goldberg, eds., *With Compassion Toward Some: Homosexuality and Social Work in America.* New York: Harrington Park Press.

Brownmiller, S. 1975. *Against Our Will: Men, Women, and Rape.* New York: Simon and Schuster.

Burgess, A. W., ed. 1985. *Rape and Sexual Assault: A Research Handbook.* New York: Garland.

Burt, M. R., and B. L. Katz. 1987. Dimensions of recovery from rape: Focus on growth outcomes. *Journal of Interpersonal Violence* 2:57–81.

Caplan, G. 1964. *Principles of Preventative Psychiatry.* New York: Basic Books.

Cass, V. 1979. Homosexual identity formation: A theoretical model. *Journal of Homosexuality* 4:219–35.

Coates, D., C. B. Wortman, and A. Abbey. 1979. Reactions to victims. In I. H. Frieze, D. Bar-Tal, and J. S. Carroll, eds., *New Approaches to Social Problems,* pp. 21–52. San Francisco: Jossey-Bass.

Cohen, C., and T. Stein. 1986. *Psychotherapy with Lesbians and Gay Men.* New York: Plenum.

Crocker, J., and B. Major. 1989. Social stigma and self-esteem: The self-protective properties of stigma. *Psychological Review* 96:608–30.

D'Emilio, J. 1983. *Sexual Politics, Sexual Communities: The Making of a Homosexual Minority in the United States, 1940–1970.* Chicago: University of Chicago Press.

Dynes, W. 1985. *Homolexis: A Historical and Cultural Lexicon of Homosexuality.* New York: Gay Academic Union.

Fairbank, J. A., R. Gross, and T. M. Keane. 1983. Treatment of posttraumatic stress disorder. *Behavior Modification* 7:557–67.

Frank, E., B. Anderson, B. D. Stewart, C. Danou, C. Hughes, and D. West. 1988.

Efficacy of cognitive behavior therapy and systematic desensitization in the treatment of rape trauma. *Behavior Therapy* 19:403–20.

Frederick, C. J. 1987. Psychic trauma in victims of crime and terrorism. In G. VandenBos and B. Bryant, eds., *Cataclysms, Crises, and Catastrophes: Psychology in Action*, pp. 59–108. Washington, D.C. : American Psychological Association.

Frieze, I. H., S. Hymer, and M. S. Greenberg. 1984. Describing the victims of crime and violence. In A. Kahn, ed., *Victims of Crime and Violence: Final Report of the APA Task Force on the Victims of Crime and Violence*, pp. 19–78. Washington, D.C.: American Psychological Association.

Goffman, E. 1963. *Stigma: Notes on the Management of Spoiled Identity.* Englewood Cliffs, N.J.: Prentice-Hall.

Gonsiorek, J. C. 1982. Results of psychological testing on homosexual populations. *American Behavioral Scientist* 25:385–96.

Gonsiorek, J. C., and J. D. Weinrich. 1991. *Homosexuality: Social Psychological, and Biological Issues.* 2d ed. Newbury Park, Calif.: Sage.

Groth, A. N., and A. W. Burgess. 1980. Male rape: Offenders and victims. *American Journal of Psychiatry* 137(7):806–10.

Hammersmith, S. K., and M. S. Weinberg. 1973. Homosexual identity: Commitment, adjustment, and significant others. *Sociometry* 36(1):56–79.

Harry, J. 1982. Derivative deviance: The cases of extortion, fag-bashing, and shakedown of gay men. *Criminology* 19(4):546–64.

Herek, G. M. 1986. On heterosexual masculinity: Some psychical consequences of the social construction of gender and sexuality. *American Behavioral Scientist* 29(5):563–77.

Herek, G. M. 1989. Hate crimes against lesbians and gay men: Issues for research and policy. *American Psychologist* 44:948–55.

Herek, G. M. 1990. The context of anti-gay violence: Notes on cultural and psychological heterosexism. *Journal of Interpersonal Violence* 5:316–33.

Herek, G. M. 1991. Stigma, prejudice, and violence against lesbian and gay men. In J. Gonsiorek and J. Weinrich, eds., *Homosexuality: Social, Psychological, and Biological Issues,* 2d ed. Newbury Park, Calif.: Sage.

Herek, G. M., and E. K. Glunt. 1988. An epidemic of stigma: Public reactions to AIDS. *American Psychologist* 43:886–91.

Hodges, A., and D. Hutter. 1979. *With Downcast Gays: Aspects of Homosexual Self-Oppression.* 2d ed. Toronto: Pink Triangle Press.

Humphreys, L. 1972. *Out of the Closets. The Sociology of Homosexual Liberation.* Englewood Cliffs, N.J.: Prentice-Hall.

Janoff-Bulman, R. 1979. Characterological versus behavioral self-blame: Inquiries into depression and rape. *Journal of Personality and Social Psychology* 37:1798–1809.

Janoff-Bulman, R. 1982. Esteem and control bases of blame: Adaptive- strategies for victims versus observers. *Journal of Personality* 50:180–92.

Janoff-Bulman, R., and I. H. Frieze, eds. 1983a. Reactions to victimization [special issue]. *Journal of Social Issues* 39(2).

Janoff-Bulman, R., and I. H. Frieze. 1983b. A theoretical perspective for understanding reactions to victimization. *Journal of Social Issues* 39(2):1–17.

Jones, E. E., A. Farina, A. H. Hastorf, H. Markus, D. T. Miller, and R. A. Scott. 1984. *Social Stigma: The Psychology of Marked Relationships.* New York: Freeman.

Kaufman, A., P. DiVasto, R. Jackson, D. Voorhees, and J. Christy. 1980. Male rape victims: Noninstitutionalized assault. *American Journal of Psychiatry* 137(2):221–23.

Kimmel, D. C. 1978. Adult development and aging: A gay perspective. *Journal of Social Issues* 34(3):113–30.

Koss, M. P., and B. R. Burkhart. 1989. A conceptual analysis of rape victimization: Long-term effects and implications for treatment. *Psychology of Women Quarterly* 13:27–40.

Ledray, L. E. 1986. *Recovering from Rape.* New York: Holt, Rinehart, and Winston.

Lerner, M. J. 1970. The desire for justice in reactions to victims. In J. M. Macaulay and L. Berkowitz, eds. *Altruism and Helping Behavior,* pp. 205–29. New York: Academic Press.

Levy, B., and V. Brown. 1984. Strategies for crisis intervention with victims of violence. In S. Saunders, A. Anderson, C. Hart, and G. Rubenstein, eds., *Violent Individuals and Families: A Handbook for Practitioners,* pp. 57–68. Springfield, Ill.: Charles C. Thomas.

Malyon, A. K. 1982. Psychotherapeutic implications of internalized homophobia in gay men. *Journal of Homosexuality* 7(2/3):59–69.

Miller, B., and L. Humphreys. 1980. Lifestyles and violence: Homosexual victims of assault and murder. *Qualitative Sociology* 3(3):169–85.

Miranda, J., and M. Storms. 1989. Psychological adjustment of lesbians and gay men. *Journal of Counseling and Development* 68:41–45.

Morin, S., and K. Charles. 1983. Heterosexual bias in psychotherapy. In J. Murray and P. R. Abramson, eds., *Bias in Psychotherapy,* pp. 309–38. New York: Praeger.

Myers, M. F. 1989. Men sexually assaulted as adults and sexually abused as boys. *Archives of Sexual Behavior* 18:203–15.

Orzek, A. M. 1988. The lesbian victim of sexual assault: Special considerations for the mental health professional. *Women and Therapy* 8(1/2):107–17.

Rofes, E. E. 1983. *"I Thought People Like That Killed Themselves": Lesbians, Gay Men and Suicide.* San Francisco: Grey Fox Press.

Sales, E., Baum, M., and B. Shore. 1984. Victim readjustment following assault. *Journal of Social Issues* 40(1):117–36.

Stein, T. S., and C. J. Cohen. 1984. Psychotherapy with gay men and lesbians: An examination of homophobia, coming out, and identity. In E. S. Hetrick and T. S. Stein, eds., *Innovations in Psychotherapy with Homosexuals,* pp. 60–73. Washington, D.C.: American Psychiatric Press.

Steketee, M. S., and E. B. Foa. 1987. Rape victims: Post-traumatic stress responses and their treatment. *Journal of Anxiety Disorders* 1:69–86.

Troiden, R. 1988. *Gay and Lesbian Identity: A Sociological Analysis.* New York: General Hall.

Tsegaye-Spates, C. R. 1985. The mental health needs of victims: An introduction to the literature. In A. W. Burgess, ed., *Rape and Sexual Assault: A Research Handbook,* pp.35–45. New York: Garland.

Unger, R. 1979. *Female and Male: Psychological Perspectives.* New York: Harper and Row.

Weinberg, M. S., and C. J. Williams. 1974. *Male Homosexuals: Their Problems and Adaptations.* New York: Oxford University Press.

Wertheimer, D. M. 1990. Treatment and service interventions for lesbian and gay male crime victims. *Journal of Interpersonal Violence* 5:384–400.

Conclusion: Implications for Practice, Research, and Public Policy

What is the appropriate response to the rage one feels about antigay violence, blatant discrimination, deep-seated prejudices that are unfair, unjust, and unfounded—to the homophobia and heterosexism that is endemic in our society?

Too often the response has been for lesbians and gay men to internalize the stigma, rage, and despair. For much of modern European history, same-gender sexual and affectional orientation has been an individual condition, variously labeled as a sin, a sickness, or a mental illness. With the beginning of the contemporary gay movement in 1969, a paradigm shift occurred that has altered the view of homosexuality from an individual condition to a collective identity (Hay 1990).

This book documents the success of this collective movement within American psychology during the past two decades. In her presidential address to the Society for the Psychological Study of Lesbian and Gay Issues—a Division of the American Psychological Association (APA)—Laura Brown described the implication of this paradigm shift. She suggested that there is a lesbian and gay male perspective that "may create different ways of knowing and understanding oneself and one's reality"

(Brown 1989:449). A key element is the potential for "normative creativity" that results from the relative absence of social norms and expectations for lesbians and gay men. In addition, the ability to move in and out of the stigmatized status, and the marginal nature of the lesbian and gay male status, provide the potential to perceive and to conceptualize social and interpersonal reality in new and creative ways. Thus, lesbian and gay psychology is on the cutting edge of psychology as it begins to focus on the study of human diversity (cf. Goodchilds 1991).

Three important examples of this new paradigm of lesbian and gay psychology represent the three areas of psychology we have emphasized throughout this book: practice, research, and public policy. The first focuses on issues in psychotherapy with lesbians and gay men (Garnets et al. 1991). It concludes a six-year project begun by the APA's Committee on Lesbian and Gay Concerns in 1984 to document specific instances of bias in psychotherapy against lesbians and gay men, and specific examples of more appropriate practice. The energy involved in conducting this survey, analyzing the data, and having it published in *American Psychologist* is an example of the positive use of the rage and horror toward psychotherapy that has stigmatized, traumatized, and attempted to change gay men and lesbians into heterosexuals. Moreover, this report represents a culmination of a fifteen-year effort to remove the stigma of mental illness from homosexuality through the development of a lesbian- and gay-affirmative model of psychotherapy. It is also an example of the new paradigm of psychology that is better because it includes and is sensitive to all aspects of human diversity.

A second example focuses on research and represents the culmination of another long-term project. In 1977 Morin documented the extent of heterosexual bias in psychological research up to that time. He noted, for example, that the search for the cause, cure, and diagnostic cues for homosexuality were dominant themes; research that did not look on homosexuality as an abnormality, or worse, was only then beginning to emerge. The anger and frustration about such obviously inaccurate and biased research led to the formation in 1985 of a task force sponsored by the APA Board of Scientific Affairs and the Board of Social and Ethical Responsibility in Psychology to develop guidelines for avoiding heterosexist bias in psychological research. The report of this task force also reflects the new paradigm in psychology (Herek et al. 1991). It pointed out the fallacy of assuming that everyone is heterosexual, or that all important research questions should be defined from the point of view of heterosexuals. Instead, it argued that "overcoming these biases . . . will lead to more ethical science, as we learn how better to respect the dignity and worth of individuals, to strive for the preservation of fundamental human rights, and to protect the welfare of our research participants" (p. 963).

A third important article concerns psychology and the law on lesbian and gay male civil rights (Bersoff and Ogden 1991). It is a good example of the ways in which psychology can be translated to affect public policy; unfortunately, so far the results of significant court cases have been mixed. Nonetheless, the arguments raised by psychology with regard to laws that criminalize same-gender sexual behavior or certain types of sexual behavior (e.g., "deviate sexual intercourse" or "sodomy") have had some positive effect, and have been reflected in some majority as well as minority opinions. It is probable that similar issues will again come before the courts and that the APA will continue to file amicus briefs in support of the rights of lesbians and gay men.

The use of psychology to influence public policy also reflects the new paradigm: being lesbian or gay is not a personal problem (or mental illness), but a minority-group identity. Thus, prejudice against gays and lesbians should be seen as analogous to racial or religious prejudice. Likewise, legal discrimination against homosexuals should be viewed as violations of civil rights and privacy issues.

Let us conclude with a broad perspective on what this new paradigm about lesbians and gay men can contribute to our diverse society. Discrimination, prejudice, homophobia, and heterosexist bias affect not only lesbians and gay men but all of society as well. There is a cost to society of a military policy that excludes gays and lesbians and involves secrecy, deceit, and hypocrisy, resulting in the loss of some of the best personnel. There is a cost to society in rigid adherence to traditional gender roles, enforced by homophobia and antigay/lesbian violence, threats, and reciprocal fear and distrust. There is a cost to society as well for the antisexual ideology that paints condoms, sex education, surveys of sexual behavior, and same-gender sexual relations with a broad brush of condemnation while at the same time the media glorify erotic imagery, suggestive heterosexual television and movie themes (even involving unmarried teenagers), and violence of all kinds. We suggest that the emerging lesbian- and gay-affirmative paradigm in psychology can help our society evaluate the costs and destructive impact of these outdated and wrong-headed views. On one hand, it can suggest different models for examining such important issues as violence, sexuality, restrictive gender roles, and AIDS prevention. On the other hand, it can reduce the constraints imposed by homophobia and heterosexist bias on the general population. The resulting freedom may also affect sexism and racism, as we acknowledge our multicultural diversity and relish the richness it provides.

Finally, it is provocative to apply this new paradigm to the inevitable threat to human survival from worldwide overpopulation. It has been suggested that disease, war, or famine are the only solutions that nature can impose. We would suggest another option: same-gender sexual attraction. This alternative clearly does not rule out propagation at adequate levels but it will limit it effectively and humanely, without disease, famine, or war. Therefore, the long-term survival of our species may depend on a dramatic increase in the number of individuals whose lovemap inclines them to a same-gender orientation.

There is obviously a need for a continuing dialogue on a wide range of lesbian and gay and bisexual political, legal, emotional, sexual, and relational issues. The recent emergence of courses in gender studies and in lesbian and gay studies at many universities is an important indication of this need. The growing number of books and bookstores devoted exclusively to gay and lesbian topics is also an important sign of a burgeoning interest in these issues. Organizations such as the Society for the Psychological Study of Lesbian and Gay Issues provide resources for such dialogue and study.

Practitioners in mental health and related fields also should be reminded of the importance of current changes and emerging research that affect psychological issues of major concern to bisexuals, lesbians, and gay men. Obviously, these concerns are not limited to one class discussion, or to a specific client, but have implications for one's approach to human diversity in all of its aspects, as well as to human sexuality in all of its richness and complexity.

REFERENCES

Bersoff, D. N., and D. W. Ogden. 1991. APA amicus curiae briefs: Furthering lesbian and gay male civil rights. *American Psychologist* 46:950–56.

Brown, L. S. 1989. New voices, new visions: Toward a lesbian/gay paradigm for psychology. *Psychology of Women Quarterly* 13:445–58.

Garnets, L., K. A. Hancock, S. D. Cochran, J. Goodchilds, and L. A. Peplau. 1991. Issues in psychotherapy with lesbians and gay men: A survey of psychologists. *American Psychologist* 46:964–72.

Goodchilds, J. D., ed. 1991. *Psychological Perspectives on Human Diversity in America.* Washington, D.C.: American Psychological Association.

Hay, H. 1990. Identifying as gay—there's the key. *Gay Community News* (April 22–28):5.

Herek, G. M., D. C. Kimmel, H. Amaro, and G. B. Melton. 1991. Avoiding heterosexist bias in psychological research. *American Psychologist* 46:957–63.

Melton, G. B. 1989. Public policy and private prejudice: Psychology and law on gay rights. *American Psychologist* 44:933–40.

Morin, S. F. 1977. Heterosexual bias in psychological research on lesbianism and male homosexuality. *American Psychologist* 32:629–37.

Glossary

alternative insemination: Introduction of sperm into the vagina without sexual intercourse for the purpose of producing a child. Sometimes called artificial insemination.

androgynous: Blending of both masculine and feminine characteristics in an individual's personality.

butch: Dress, mannerisms, and behavior of a woman or man that fits the stereotype of masculinity.

cohort: In developmental psychology, a group of people born at about the same time. As members of one cohort move through the life span together, they experience similar historical influences that differ from those experienced by members of other cohorts.

cross-gender: Behavior, mannerisms, or dress of an individual that is more typical for a person of the other gender, such as a man who dresses as a woman.

cultural diversity: Variation among individuals within nations and between cultures, including variations in sexual orientation.

deconstruct: In social science theory, to pull apart the various levels of meaning that have been associated with concepts, such as gender or sex.

dominant culture: The cultural group that controls the major aspects of social power, values, and norms within a society.

dual (triple) identity: Two or more distinct characteristics of individuals that compound their status as a cultural minority, such as a woman who is a member of an ethnic or racial minority. In some cases, central characteristics associated with the distinct identities may conflict and the individual attempts to keep them separate, such as Latina and lesbian or African-American and gay.

essentialism: In social science theory, the view that a characteristic of an individual is the result of the individual's uniqueness, such as genetic heritage, individual experience, or basic make-up. The opposite view is that of *social constructionism.*

ethnicity: Racial, cultural, national, or religious group or family background.

gender: Female or male. Unlike *sex,* this term does not also refer to sexual behavior and is therefore less ambiguous.

gender identity: The individual's basic conviction of being male or female; it is part of one's self-identification.

gender nonconformity: Behavior, dress, or mannerisms that do not conform to the stereotypes associated with an individual's gender.

gender role: Characteristics and social expectations that are culturally associated with being male or female.

gender role traditionalism: Beliefs and values consistent with traditional conceptions of males and females as opposite sexes, such as their respective roles in conception and parenting of children.

hate crimes: Criminal behavior directed at an individual because of her or his perceived group identification, such as Japanese, lesbian, or female.

heterosexist bias: The assumption that everyone is, or should be, heterosexual. Also, the application of heterosexual assumptions to persons who are not heterosexual, such as the idea that all women are going to marry someday.

identity development: A gradual process of integrating one's diverse sense of self into a relatively firm belief in the continuity of oneself over time and across the various social aspects of one's life.

identity disclosure: Revealing to others one's sexual orientation, as a crucial aspect of one's identity.

lesbian-feminist movement: A perspective that emerged in the 1970s linking lesbian and feminist issues within the context of the oppressed social position of women.

lesbian/gay-affirmative approach: In psychology or psychotherapy, the view that lesbian and gay male identity, culture, and history is as valid as any other. Also, affirmation of the positive potential of an individual's lesbian or gay male identity and behavior.

life span development: In psychology, the view that individual lives can be usefully understood from the perspective of their unique course from conception through death, including childhood, adolescence, adulthood, and old age.

lovemap: A concept proposed by John Money that represents an individual's unique depiction of the ideal lover, love affair, and sexual or erotic activity.

male-dominated: Situations in which men have markedly greater power, rights, and privileges than do women.

minority group status: Within a society, the relatively lesser power and prestige held by some groups (as compared to the dominant group) when defined by characteristics such as their culture, ethnic background, race, or sexual orientation.

new gay lesbians: Term coined by Lillian Faderman to contrast lesbians who come out in the context of the feminist movement with those lesbians who came out prior to the emergence of the feminist movement.

normative characteristic: Behavioral, physical, or social attribute that is regarded as typical or expected according to the values of one's cultural group or society.

outing: Revealing in a public manner that an individual is lesbian or gay without her or his consent.

paradigm: A model or pattern that is widely accepted as an explanation of some aspects of perceived reality; a *paradigm shift* is a reinterpretation of an accepted paradigm, or the substitution of a new paradigm for a previously accepted interpretation or way of perceiving reality.

patriarchal oppression: The systematic domination of women by men in a given society or culture leading to women's disadvantaged social, political, and economic status.

patriarchy: Domination or rule by males, especially older males, or the reckoning of lineage through male heirs only.

social category: A grouping of individuals based on some trait or behavior that is socially defined as a relevant way to categorize individuals; examples include "intelligent," "jock," or "single."

social constructionism: In sociology, the view that reality is created by social processes so that, for example, sexual orientation exists as a relevant category of human behavior because it was defined as such by social forces in one's environment. It is often contrasted with *essentialism.*

social scripts: In psychology, the idea that one's behavior is structured and defined by social definitions of appropriate and expected behavior; examples include dating or sexual interactions.

social stratification: In sociology, the idea that many societies have strata of differing status, prestige, and power; it is often measured by income, education, or occupation.

social structure: The way in which a society is organized and power, prestige, and status are distributed among the citizens.

stage theory: In psychology, the view that one develops from one level to another through a discrete series of steps or stages.

status differential: The difference between one's social prestige and that of another.

status variables: Characteristics that are taken into account when defining or measuring one's social status; examples include level of education, type of occupation, age, and social background of one's family.

stigmatized status: The perception by oneself or by others that one is damaged in some socially relevant way. For example, one's skin may be too dark or too light, one might be physically impaired, or one might not conform to stereotypes about the behavior appropriate for one's gender.

Acknowledgments

Introduction: Lesbian and Gay Male Dimensions in the Psychological Study of Human Diversity

L. D. Garnets and D. C. Kimmel, Lesbian and gay male dimensions in the psychological study of human diversity, in J. Goodchilds, ed., *Psychological Perspectives on Human Diversity in America*, pp. 143–92 (Washington, D.C.: American Psychological Association). Copyright 1991 by the American Psychological Association. Reprinted by permission.

Part 1: The Meaning of Sexual Orientation

J. D'Emilio, Gay politics and community in San Francisco since World War II. *Socialist Review* 55 (January 1981):77–104. Revised and reprinted in M. M. Vicinus and G. Chauncey, Jr., eds., *Hidden from History: Reclaiming the Gay and Lesbian Past*, pp. 456–73 (New York: New American Library, 1989). Copyright 1981. Reprinted with permission of J. D'Emilio and *Socialist Review*.

M. G. Shively and J. P. De Cecco, Components of sexual identity, *Journal of Homosexuality* 3(1):41–48. Copyright 1977. Reprinted by permission of The Haworth Press, Inc.

G. M. Herek, The context of antigay violence: Notes on cultural and psychological heterosexism, *Journal of Interpersonal Violence* 5:316–33. Copyright 1990. Reprinted by permission of Sage Publications, Inc.

Part 2: Origins of Sexual Orientation

D. Richardson, Recent challenges to traditional assumptions about homosexuality: Some implications for practice, *Journal of Homosexuality* 13(4):1–12. Copyright 1987. Reprinted by permission of The Haworth Press, Inc.

J. Money, Sin, sickness, or status? Homosexual gender identity and psychoneuroendocrinology, *American Psychologist* 42:384–99. Copyright 1987 by the American Psychological Association. Reprinted by permission.

P. W. Blumstein and P. Schwartz, Bisexuality: Some social psychological issues, *Journal of Social Issues* 33(2):30–45. Copyright 1977. Reprinted by permission of the Society for the Psychological Study of Social Issues.

Part 3: Identity Development and Stigma Management

R. R. Troiden, The formation of homosexual identities, *Journal of Homosexuality* 17(1/2):43–73. Copyright 1989. Reprinted by permission of The Haworth Press, Inc.

C. de Monteflores, Notes on the management of difference, in T. Stein and C. Cohen, eds., *Contemporary Perspectives on Psychotherapy with Lesbians and Gay Men*, pp. 73–101 (New York: Plenum). Copyright 1986. Reprinted by permission of Plenum Publishing Corporation.

E. F. Strommen, "You're a what?": Family member reactions to the disclosure of homosexuality, *Journal of Homosexuality* 18(1/2):37–58. Copyright 1989. Reprinted by permission of The Haworth Press, Inc.

K. S. Morgan and L. S. Brown, Lesbian career development, work behavior, and vocational counseling, *Counseling Psychologist* 19:273–91. Copyright 1991 by Division 17 of the American Psychological Association. Reprinted by permission of Sage Publications, Inc.

Part 4: Gender Differences in Roles and Behavior

E. Blackwood, Breaking the mirror: The construction of lesbianism and the anthropological discourse on homosexuality, *Journal of Homosexuality* 11(3/4):1–17. Copyright 1986. Reprinted by permission of The Haworth Press, Inc.

G. M. Herek, On heterosexual masculinity: Some psychical consequences of the social construction of gender and sexuality, *American Behavioral Scientist* 29:563–77. Copyright 1986. Reprinted by permission of Sage Publications, Inc.

Part 5: Cultural Diversity Among Lesbians and Gay Men

W. L. Williams, Persistence and change in the Berdache tradition among contemporary Lakota Indians, *Journal of Homosexuality* 11(3/4):191–200. Copyright 1986. Reprinted by permission of The Haworth Press, Inc.

O. M. Espín, Issues of identity in the psychology of Latina lesbians, in Boston Lesbian Psychologies Collective, eds., *Lesbian Psychologies: Explorations and Challenges*, pp. 33–55 (Urbana: University of Illinois Press). Copyright 1987. Reprinted by permission of the University of Illinois Press.

D. K. Loiacano, Gay identity issues among Black Americans: Racism, homophobia, and the need for validation, *Journal of Counseling and Development* 68(1):21–25. Copyright 1989 by AACD. Reprinted with permission.

C. S. Chan, Issues of identity development among Asian-American lesbians and gay men, *Journal of Counseling and Development* 68(1):16–20. Copyright 1989 by AACD. Reprinted with permission.

Part 6: Relationships and Parenthood

L. A. Peplau, Lesbian and gay relationships, in J. C. Gonsiorek and J. D. Weinrich, eds., *Homosexuality: Research Implications for Public Policy*, pp. 177–96 (Newbury Park, Calif.: Sage). Copyright 1991. Reprinted by permission of Sage Publications, Inc.

P. J. Falk, Lesbian mothers: Psychosocial assumptions in family law, *American Psychologist* 44:941–47. Copyright 1989 by the American Psychological Association. Reprinted by permission.

F. W. Bozett, Gay fathers: A review of the literature, *Journal of Homosexuality* 18(1/2):137–62. Copyright 1989. Reprinted by permission of The Haworth Press, Inc.

Part 7: Adolescence, Midlife, and Aging

J. C. Gonsiorek, Mental health issues of gay and lesbian adolescents, *Journal of Adolescent Health Care* 9:114–22. Copyright 1988 by the Society for Adolescent Medicine. Reprinted by permission of Elsevier Science Publishing Co., Inc.

G. Remafedi, J. A. Farrow, and R. W. Deisher, Risk factors for attempted suicide in gay and bisexual youth, *Pediatrics* 87:869–75. Copyright 1991. Reprinted by permission of *Pediatrics*.

B. E. Sang, Existential issues of midlife lesbians. Reprinted by permission of Barbara E. Sang. Copyright 1993 by Columbia University Press.

D. C. Kimmel, Adult development and aging: A gay perspective, *Journal of Social Issues* 34(3):113–30. Copyright 1978. Reprinted by permission of the Society for the Psychological Study of Social Issues.

Part 8: Health

C. Ryan and J. Bradford, The national lesbian health care survey: An overview, in M. Shernoff and W. A. Scott, eds., *The Sourcebook on Lesbian/Gay Healthcare*, pp. 30–40 (Washington, D.C.: National Lesbian and Gay Health Foundation). Copyright 1988. Reprinted by permission of the authors.

S. F. Morin, AIDS: The challenge to psychology, *American Psychologist* 43:838–42. Copyright 1988 by the American Psychological Association. Reprinted by permission.

E. F. Ratner, 1988. Treatment issues for chemically dependent lesbians and gay men. In M. Shernoff and W. A. Scott, eds., *The Sourcebook on Lesbian/Gay Healthcare*, pp. 162–68 (Washington, D.C.: National Lesbian and Gay Health Foundation). Copyright 1988. Reprinted by permission of the author.

L. Garnets, G. M. Herek, and B. Levy, Violence and victimization of lesbians and gay men: Mental health consequences, *Journal of Interpersonal Violence* 5:366–83. Copyright 1990. Reprinted by permission of Sage Publications, Inc.

Index

Mr. Bill Kaminski
12 Siesta Ct
Bloomington, IL 61704

Designer: Susan Clark

Text: Garamond

Compositor: Impressions, a division of Edwards Brothers

Printer: Edwards Brothers

Binder: Edwards Brothers